Financial Accounting

Financial Accounting

JAMES J. BENJAMIN
Texas A&M University

ARTHUR J. FRANCIA
University of Houston

ROBERT H. STRAWSER
Texas A&M University

 1975

BUSINESS PUBLICATIONS, INC.   Dallas, Texas   75231

Irwin-Dorsey International   London, England   WC2H 9NJ
Irwin-Dorsey Limited   Georgetown, Ontario   L7G 4B3

First Printing, April 1975
Second Printing, January 1977

ISBN 0-256-01727-1
Library of Congress Catalog Card No. 74–24460
Printed in the United States of America

Preface

THIS TEXTBOOK introduces the student to all aspects of financial accounting from the basic concept of the transaction, through financial statements, into the interpretation of these statements. It is intended for use in the beginning or introduction to financial accounting course for business and non-business majors. The text includes a balanced presentation of the procedures, techniques and fundamental principles underlying financial accounting and reporting. Up-to-date pronouncements of the accounting profession are considered throughout the text and integrated in a clear illustrative manner, not just quoted verbatim. A clear and concise introduction to the accounting process is developed in the early chapters of the text as a basis for special consideration given in later chapters to contemporary topics such as price-level adjustments, business combinations, and income tax considerations. The text is intended to present a balanced perspective of accounting practice and theory. The approach used is straightforward; completeness of coverage is achieved using simple but accurate terms and examples. It is a teachable text geared to student understanding of the basic concepts and practices—not a reference manual.

The first chapter introduces the functions of accounting and a brief discussion of basic financial accounting concepts. The basic accounting process is presented and illustrated in the next three chapters. The transactions of a single company for the initial month of its operations are used in illustrating transaction analyses and, then, the entire accounting process. The authors have found that this repetition greatly enhances student understanding of the basic concepts. Chapter 5 follows with a discussion of the accounting problems of service, retailing, and manufacturing companies. Chapter 6 considers accounting systems and internal control, tying this material into the basic accounting process.

The next section of the text deals with accounting for current and long-term assets. Chapter 7 discusses cash and temporary investments, Chapter 8 receivables, Chapter 9 inventories and Chapter 10 long-term assets. Chapter 11 considers problems in accounting for partnerships and Chapters 12 through 14 deal with accounting for stockholders' equity and liabilities. A discussion of present value with an application to financial accounting is included in an appendix to the liabilities chapter.

The remaining chapters discuss contemporary relevant financial accounting topics. Chapter 15 deals with accounting for long-term investments and consolidated financial statements. The consolidated income statement is presented in an appendix to Chapter 15, covering such topics as profit on intercompany sales and accounting for minority interests. Chapter 16 is concerned with financial statement analysis, Chapter 17 considers the statement of changes in financial position, Chapter 18 deals with price-level adjusted financial statements, and income tax considerations is the subject of Chapter 19. The text is written, and appendixes are included, in a manner so that the order of presentation may be altered and/or individual topics may be covered or omitted at the discretion of the instructor without any loss in continuity.

The important concepts of each chapter are covered by discussion questions and exercises. These materials are useful for both classroom discussion or outside assignment. Ample problems, including alternate sets of A and B problems covering comparable material to provide maximum flexibility, are included. The problems are written so that they are interesting and a learning tool for the student, not overburdening or tricky.

Acknowledgments

We are indebted to many students and colleagues for their help, comments, and constructive criticisms which assisted in making this text a reality. Our special thanks go to John E. Pearson, Kenneth S. Most, and Larry Gene Pointer of the College of Business Administration of Texas A&M University, John J. Willingham of the University of Houston, and Ossian MacKenzie and G. Kenneth Nelson of the College of Business of the Pennsylvania State University for providing us with encouragement in our efforts and with environments in which this book could be created. Vincent C. Brenner of the Louisiana State University, Ronald M. Copeland of the University of South Carolina, Paul E. Dascher of Drexel University, Larry N. Killough of the Virginia Polytechnic Institute and State University, Philip W. Ljungdahl of Texas A&M University, and Ronald J.

Patten of the University of Connecticut provided us with help and encouragement in writing this text. Walter Kingsberry, Cindy Ludwig, Kathy Smith, Lynn Dolbey, Michael Griswald, Larry Klein, Cheryl Low, and James Shoemaker were among the many student assistants who worked with us in this project. Of course, the authors are responsible for any shortcomings of this text.

March 1975   James J. Benjamin
                                             Arthur J. Francia
                                             Robert H. Strawser

Contents

1

Accounting:
An Introduction

ACCOUNTING has been described as ". . . the art of recording, classifying, and summarizing in a significant manner and in terms of money, transactions and events which are, in part at least, of a financial character, and interpreting the results thereof."[1] This definition emphasizes the ". . . creative skill and ability with which the accountant applies his knowledge to a given problem."[2] Another view of the function of accounting, very similar to that reported above, is that "the primary function of accounting is to accumulate and communicate information essential to an understanding of the activities of an enterprise, whether large or small, corporate or non-corporate, profit or non-profit, public or private."[3] The importance of this second definition is the direct relevance of accounting to many and varied types of undertakings, both private and public, and profit and not-for-profit.

Implicit in any definition of accounting is the importance of the accountant's role in the reporting function. In fact, the primary role of the accountant is reporting and communicating information which will aid various users in the financial community in making economic decisions. These users of accounting information include current and potential owners, managers, creditors, and others. In the past, when businesses were less

---

[1] American Institute of Certified Public Accountants, *Accounting Terminology Bulletin No. 1—Review and Resume* (New York: AICPA), p. 9.

[2] Ibid.

[3] *Accounting and Reporting Standards for Corporate Financial Statements* (Columbus, Ohio: American Accounting Association, 1957), p. 1.

1

complex than they are today, there were usually only a very limited number of users of accounting information. For example, at the turn of the century most businesses in the United States were managed and operated by their owners. Since these owners were intimately involved in the day-to-day operations of their businesses there was little or no need for accounting reports. The owner or decision-maker already had firsthand knowledge of the information he required in order to operate the business effectively. Today, however, the situation is quite different. Many organizations have increased in both size and complexity. In many instances, the ownership and the management of a business have been separated. Firms are frequently managed by professional managers for their absentee owners who exercise a minimal amount of formal control over the operations of the business except in the most general sense. These owners often have virtually no involvement in the day-to-day activities of the business. Even professional managers (at all but the most basic levels of authority in the firm) have little *firsthand* involvement in the most fundamental of these activities. There decisions are, more often than not, made on the basis of reports and summaries which are prepared by their subordinates. Although the above discussion might overstate the case just a bit (the corner pizza parlor may still be owner-operated, but then again, it could well be a franchise operation), the basic point is that most decisions are made on the basis of summary-type reports rather than firsthand information.

What then is the role of accounting and the accountant in this process? One observation that has been made is that the task of the accountant is to observe, interpret, summarize, and communicate information in a form which will enable the user of the data to evaluate, control, plan, and even predict performance. It is essential to note the importance of the term "user" in this context. A user could be a manager involved in the evaluation and direction of the continuing operations of the business; a present or a potential stockholder (owner) seeking information for an impending investment decision; a bank officer in the process of reviewing a loan application; a supplier making a decision with regard to a credit application; a federal, state, or local revenue officer evaluating the propriety of a tax return; or even a citizen attempting to assess the performance of some governmental unit. In each of the circumstances mentioned above, and in countless other situations as well, user needs are met, at least in part, by a report prepared by an accountant.

ACCOUNTING AS A PROCESS OF COMMUNICATION[4]

Accounting may be regarded as a process of communication in a very real sense. Events occur on a continuing basis which affect the operations

---

[4] This discussion is based on Norton M. Bedford and Vahe Baladouni, "A Communication Theory Approach to Accountancy," *The Accounting Review,* October 1962, pp. 650–59.

of an organization. The accountant acts as an observer-reporter, observing events or transactions as they take place, evaluating the significance of these events to the users (and potential users) of his report, and recording, classifying, and summarizing the events in an accounting report which is then transmitted to a user. The user receives the report, analyzes its content, and utilizes the information contained therein in making economic decisions. Of course, these decisions made by the user cause new events to take place setting the chain in process again through another cycle.

Two factors are of major importance in this process of communication by accountants—fidelity and significance. Fidelity is the correspondence between what is understood by the user of accounting statements and what the accountant intended to express in his report. The accountant preparing the report and the person using it must have a mutual understanding and agreement as to certain basic points regarding its preparation and content. In other words, the accountant must know the user's needs and perceptions.

Significance, on the other hand, refers to the relationship between the events which take place and the accounting report which attempts to summarize these events. It is the degree of relevance and adequacy which the accounting report has in relation to the events which occur. The basic consideration in this instance is that the report should, to the degree possible and/or practicable, include and describe all of the significant events which did, in fact, take place. In the ideal situation, a user would make the same decision based on his analysis of a report that he would have made using firsthand information obtained on a personal basis.

FINANCIAL ACCOUNTING AND MANAGERIAL ACCOUNTING

Although there is considerable overlap between the two, accounting may be thought of as consisting of two basic segments, financial accounting and managerial accounting. The basic difference between these two segments or divisions of accounting lies in their orientation. Financial accounting is primarily concerned with users who are *external* to the firm and managerial accounting is concerned with *internal* users. Financial accounting attempts to provide external user groups such as current or potential owners, creditors, government agencies, and other interested parties with information concerning the status of the firm and the results of its operations. The objective of financial accounting is to provide these users with the information they require for making decisions. Managerial accounting attempts to provide the information which is necessary for internal decision making to those who are charged with this responsibility within the firm.

This text is primarily concerned with financial accounting, but of necessity (and by design), it also touches on numerous areas which deal with managerial accounting as well. For example, the determination of the cost of the products which are produced by a manufacturing firm may be regarded as a problem that lies within the domain of managerial accounting but it is also a concern of financial accounting, since determining the cost of inventory is an important consideration for financial reporting purposes.

FINANCIAL STATEMENTS

Financial statements are the reports in which the accountant summarizes and communicates basic financial data. The purpose of financial statements is to provide the information which is required in the decision making process. The basic financial statements which are included in typical accounting reports issued to external users are: the balance sheet, the income statement, the statement of capital, and the statement of changes in financial position. Each of these statements is considered and described in detail in separate chapters later in this text, but we will introduce them in general terms at this point.

Balance Sheet. The balance sheet or statement of financial position is the accounting statement that provides information regarding the *financial position* of the firm at a particular *point in time.* The balance sheet is described in detail in Chapter 2 of this text.

The Income Statement. The income statement or operating statement provides data as to the *results of operations* of the firm for a specific *period of time,* usually a year. The income statement is also discussed in Chapter 2.

The Statement of Capital. The statement of capital reports the details of the equity of the owners in the business. The capital of a business is equal to the direct investments made by the owners plus the earnings of the business and less any withdrawals made by owners. In the case of a business organized as a corporation, this statement is referred to as the statement of retained earnings. The statement of capital is described in Chapter 2 and the statement of retained earnings is discussed in Chapter 13.

The Statement of Changes in Financial Position. This statement indicates the sources from which the firm obtained its resources and the uses which were made of these resources during an accounting period. In the past, this statement was referred to as a statement of sources and uses of funds. It describes how the financial resources of the firm have changed during the accounting period. The statement of changes in financial position is described in Chapter 17.

These brief comments, which will be elaborated upon in detail in subsequent sections of this text, provide the reader with a thumbnail sketch of the basic financial statements which appear in a typical annual report of a business, a major end product of the accountant's work. We will now introduce certain of the basic accounting concepts which underlie the preparation of financial statements by the accountant.

BASIC ACCOUNTING PRINCIPLES AND UNDERLYING CONCEPTS

The concepts underlying the practice of accounting are referred to as "generally accepted principles of accounting." It is important to note that these "principles" are general rules or guides to action which have evolved over time and have gained acceptance by the consensus of the accounting profession and the financial community. Underlying these principles are several basic concepts which will be briefly described in the paragraphs that follow. These concepts will also be discussed in detail and elaborated upon throughout the remainder of the text.

Entity Concept. The entity concept is the basis for the distinction which is made by the accountant between a business and its owner(s). In accounting, an organization, often referred to as an entity, is treated as a unit which is separate and distinct from its ownership and is accounted for as such. The affairs and transactions of the owners of a business are not combined or commingled with those of their firms. This is true irrespective of the form of organization used by the business. The entity concept is a distinction which is made in accounting even though it may not be true in a legal sense.

Going-Concern Concept. The going-concern concept is the basic assumption made by the accountant that an entity will continue its operations for an indefinite future period of time. For purposes of accounting, it is assumed that a business has a perpetual life span, that is, it will continue to operate indefinitely. This concept is used in accounting unless there is compulsive evidence to the contrary—for example, if a firm is in the process of bankruptcy proceedings.

Monetary Concept. The monetary concept is the assumption made by the accountant that the transactions and events which occur in a business may be recorded in terms of money. As the definition of accounting indicates, accounting is ". . . the art of recording, classifying, and summarizing in a significant manner and *in terms of money* . . ."[5] The monetary concept is closely related to the concepts of both historical cost and stable dollar, which are described below.

Historical Cost. As indicated above, the historical cost concept is closely related to both the monetary concept and the going-concern concept. It is the assumption that the original cost of a resource, and not its current market value or replacement cost, is the basis normally used in

---

[5] American Institute of Certified Public Accountants (emphasis added).

accounting for the resources of an entity. This assumption has been justified by accountants on the grounds of its objectivity. Its proponents argue that historical cost is a fact, whereas, in many instances, market values or replacement costs may be somewhat subjective. Historical cost has also been justified on the basis of the going-concern concept—since an entity is assumed to have an indefinite life and since many (if not most) of its resources are acquired for use rather than for resale, there is little need to consider the amount which might be realized if these resources were sold.

Stable Dollar. The stable dollar assumption is closely related to both the monetary concept and the historical cost concept described above. It assumes that all dollars are of equal worth or value, that is, of the same purchasing power. Thus, the relevant transactions of an entity are recorded and its accounting reports are prepared assuming a stable unit of measure. Under the stable dollar concept, a dollar spent in 1930 is assumed to be equal to a dollar spent in 1965, which is equal to a dollar spent in 1975, etc. In other words, any changes which may occur in the purchasing power of the dollar caused by either inflation or deflation are ignored.

Consistency. As previously indicated, accounting principles do not comprise a detailed set of rules and procedures that apply to each and every situation. Rather, they are more in the nature of general guidelines. This is why the accountant may record a particular transaction in alternative ways. Also, different firms may use different accounting methods. For this reason the concept of consistency is required. Briefly stated, the consistency concept requires that once a firm adopts a particular accounting method for its use in recording a certain type of transaction, it should continue to use that method for all future transactions of the same category. Note that this concept applies only to the accounting methods used by a particular firm. It does not apply to the methods used by different firms, even though these firms may be engaged in the same line of business or industry. Consistency, for example, would require that Coca Cola, Inc., use the same accounting methods in its reports from one year to the next so that the users of its financial statements are able to make comparisons of the financial position of the company and the results of its operations between and among years. It would not require, however, that Coca Cola and Pepsico, Inc., use the same accounting methods, even though these *firms* may be somewhat similar in many respects. The financial statements of Coca Cola and Pepsico may or may not be readily comparable, depending on the accounting methods selected by each of the firms.

Matching Concept. A major objective of the business is, of course, to earn income. Income may be defined as the excess of revenues over expenses. Revenues are the proceeds received or to be received from the sale of goods or services by a business. Expenses are the costs incurred in the process of generating revenues. The matching concept is related to the measurement of the earnings or income of a firm. It provides that the revenues which are realized and recognized during a particular period should be matched against the expenses incurred in earning that revenue. Revenue is recorded as it is earned, not necessarily as cash is received. For example, assume that an accountant prepares a tax return for a client during the month of March, bills the client for this service in April, and is paid in May. The revenue earned by the accountant from the preparation of this tax return would be considered as income for the month of March, since that is when the accountant had performed the work which entitled him to his fee. Likewise, expenses are recorded as they are incurred, not necessarily as they are paid. Examining the above example from the viewpoint of the client, the cost of having the tax return prepared by the accountant would be an expense. This expense would be recorded at the point in time it was incurred, in March, rather than when it was actually paid (in May).

Materiality. The materiality concept indicates that the accountant should be primarily concerned with those transactions which are of real significance or concern to the users of his report. For example, assume that a firm acquires a pencil sharpener at a cost of $5. It is expected that this sharpener will be used by the business over a five-year period before it will have to be replaced. In theory, since this pencil sharpener will be of benefit to the firm during each of the five years it is used, a portion of its cost should be considered as an expense of each of these years. In practice, however, this would be neither realistic nor practical. The benefits which might be obtained by allocating the cost of the pencil sharpener over the five-year period would simply not be worth the cost that it would involve. This example is, of course, a clear-cut case. A precise definition of what is or is not material is often elusive in particular circumstances. A general understanding of the basic concept of materiality may be obtained from the following example. Assume that a transaction occurs. It is recorded in Accounting Report #1 in a manner that is *theoretically correct.* In alternative Accounting Report #2, it is recorded in a way that is *expedient,* but not necessarily correct in terms of theory. If a user of an accounting report would make the same decision irrespective of whether he based his decision on Accounting Report #1 (theoretically correct) or Accounting Report #2 (expedient, but not necessarily theoretically correct) the item obviously does not affect the decision and is therefore immaterial or insignificant in amount. On the other hand, if the user would make a different decision on the basis of Accounting Report #1 than he might make using Accounting Report #2, the item would be considered material since it affected the decision made by the user. Clearly then, decisions as to whether a particular item is or is not material must be made by the accountant and depend on the exercise of his professional judgment.

INFLUENCES ON ACCOUNTING PRINCIPLES

As previously indicated, accounting principles derive their authority from their general acceptance and use by the accounting profession and the financial community. Some of the more important influences on accounting are described in the paragraphs which follow.

American Institute of Certified Public Accountants. The AICPA is the primary professional association of certified public accountants (CPAs) in the United States today. For a number of years this organization has been actively involved in research which is intended to improve accounting practices and procedures. It is responsible for the preparation of the uniform CPA examination that is used in all states and which must be successfully completed in order for an individual to become a certified public accountant. The AICPA is the accounting equivalent of the American Bar Association (for attorneys) and the American Medical Association (for physicians).

Financial Accounting Standards Board. This organization came into existence in July of 1973 as the successor to the Accounting Principles Board of the AICPA. It is an independent board whose membership consists of distinguished accountants experienced in industry, government, education, and public accounting. Like its predecessor, the Accounting Principles Board, the FASB sponsors research in accounting matters and issues formal opinions as to the proper accounting treatment and financial statement presentation of particular items. These statements become, by definition, generally accepted accounting principles.

Securities and Exchange Commission. This government agency is responsible for regulating the financial reporting of firms that offer securities for sale to the public through national (and interstate) securities exchanges, such as the New York Stock Exchange and the American Stock Exchange. The SEC has worked closely with the accounting profession in establishing and improving accounting practices, particularly in the area of financial reporting.

Internal Revenue Service. Although in most cases the IRS influences accounting in an indirect rather than a direct manner, the income tax code and regulations do affect accounting procedures and methods. The effects of income taxes on accounting information will be discussed in detail in Chapter 19 of this text.

National Association of Accountants. The NAA is the professional association of accountants employed in industry, and as such, is normally concerned with matters which are primarily related to managerial accounting. Like the AICPA, it sponsors research in accounting and issues periodic reports to its membership.

Cost Accounting Standards Board. This is the managerial accounting equivalent of the FASB. It is charged with establishing uniform cost accounting standards for defense contractors who are awarded government contracts. The CASB was established in 1971 and the costs of research and investigation into defense contract problems are paid by the U.S. Government. Reports of the Board are presented to the Congress of the United States.

American Accounting Association. The AAA is primarily concerned with matters relating to accounting education and a portion of its membership consists of accounting faculty of colleges and universities. Like the other professional organizations mentioned above, it sponsors research in accounting and related matters and issues reports from time to time.

The reader should note that the brief descriptions included above are intended to provide a general indication of the major thrust and composition of the organizations described. In many cases, there is considerable overlap in the objectives and even the membership of these groups. All of these organizations share the common objective of seeking to improve accounting practice and financial reporting on both a national and multinational basis.

OPPORTUNITIES IN ACCOUNTING

The accounting profession in the United States has achieved a professional status that is comparable to that of both the legal and medical professions. Certified public accountants (CPAs) are accountants who have completed educational requirements specified by the state in which they are licensed and who have successfully completed the uniform CPA examination. Accountants are employed in a wide variety of positions; any organization, regardless of its purpose, that requires information to be recorded, processed, and communicated usually needs the services of an accountant.

CPAs, in large and small public accounting firms, render a wide variety of services to their clients on a professional basis, much as do attorneys. The services offered by CPA firms include: auditing—the conducting of examinations and rendering of professional opinions as to the fairness of the financial statements of organizations; taxes—tax planning and preparation of local, state, and federal tax returns; SEC work—assisting organizations in filings with the Securities and Exchange Commission; and management services—assisting in the design and installation of accounting systems and, in general, services of an advisory nature that do not fall under any one of the other categories mentioned above.

Many accountants are employed by industry and other profit and not-for-profit organizations. These accountants work in maintaining and improving the information systems of their organizations and are engaged in a wide variety of other tasks and duties.

Accountants also find employment in local, state, and federal government, ranging from small local municipal agencies to large federal organizations such as the Internal Revenue Service, Securities and Exchange Commission, and the General Accounting Office. It may interest the reader that special agents of the Federal Bureau of Investigation must be either trained attorneys or accountants.

At the turn of the present century there were fewer than 250 certified public accountants in the United States. Today there are more than 100,000 CPAs, and the accounting profession continues to grow at an astonishing rate. One author noted that the growth rate for CPAs was about 6 percent per year—four times that of the U.S. population as a whole—and made the tongue-in-cheek comment that if this growth rate continued, by the year 2080 every man, woman, and child in the U.S. would be a CPA![6] An indication that this growth is likely to continue is the increasing demand for accounting graduates which indicates that 16,000 new accountants will be needed in 1976 in public accounting alone (compared to fewer than 9,000 in 1971).[7] This demand is also reflected in the average starting salaries paid to accounting graduates in public accounting, which increased from an average of $6,600 in 1964 to $10,500 in 1972.[8] Along these same lines it is interesting to note that presidents of large U.S. corporations more often have a background in accounting than in any other single functional area. Clearly, there is a future in accounting.

APPENDIX TO CHAPTER 1

As this chapter indicated, the task of the accountant is to prepare accounting reports which transmit meaningful data to decision makers. To accomplish this purpose, the accountant must ascertain the information required by users. The needs of the users must be the guiding principle for the accountant in the preparation of his reports.

The reading which follows elaborates on the role of accounting as a communicating device. This article compares certain accounting and information system concepts with analogous concepts in professional football. Basically, the problems of data accumulation and reporting in business and professional football are very similar.

---

[6] Howard F. Stettler, "CPAs/Auditing/2000+," *The Journal of Accountancy,* May 1968, p. 56.

[7] Eric N. Melgren, *The Supply of Accounting Graduates and the Demand for Public Accounting Recruits,* New York: American Institute of Certified Public Accountants.

[8] American Institute of Certified Public Accountants, *What's It Like to Be An Accountant?,* New York: AICPA, 1972.

PROFESSIONAL FOOTBALL AND INFORMATION SYSTEMS*

The Concept Is Based On The Fact That Football Possesses A Great Number Of Easily Identifiable Characteristics, All Of Which Are Directly Related To The Decision-Making Process Of The Game

By Frank Ryan, Arthur J. Francia, and Robert H. Strawser

During a National Football League game between the New York Jets and the Cleveland Browns, in the second quarter the Browns needed seven yards on third down. Wide receiver Gary Collins raced down the right sideline, trying to elude the two Jet defenders who were double-covering him, when suddenly his teammate, tight end Milt Morin, curled over the middle to take the pass and make the first down with several yards to spare. After the play had ended, it was obvious to nearly everyone watching that Collins was in fact a decoy and Morin had been the intended receiver all along.

A thorough analysis of the Browns' tendencies by the Jets could possibly have nullified the completion. The Browns at the time were primarily a pattern team, executing most of their pass plays according to predetermined plans, which incorporated their field position, the down, the yardage needed to gain a first down, the game situation, and anticipated defense. If the Jets had sufficiently familiarized themselves with the Browns' *modus operandi,* they would have known that the Browns, who led by a touchdown at the time, rarely use the long pass on third down, instead relying on short passes to the backs and to the tight end. With this knowledge, the Jets could have played percentage ball by assigning a single man to cover Collins, thus freeing the other defensive back to assist in the coverage on Morin.

This situation illustrates a fact of modern football life. The sport is structured in such a way that careful acquisition and evaluation of the observable details associated with each play can lead to meaningful trends analysis. In fact, most coaches, on all levels of the sport, compile some statistics or frequency counts which convey information on their opponents as well as themselves. Unfortunately, to accomplish this task manually in a thorough and complete manner is time consuming to the extent of being impossible in the practical world of winning football.

The application of data processing to professional sports is developing quite rapidly.[1] In football, computer technology finds an opportunity to provide a practical and valuable assist to the coaching method in the area of strategy preparation. While it is standard operating procedure to review

---

* *Management Accounting,* March 1973.

[1] For a review of several computer applications in athletics, see J. Gerry Purdy, "Sports and EDP . . . It's a New Ball Game," *Datamation,* June 1, 1971.

the films of previous games and to chart tendencies in a variety of situations, data processing methods can nevertheless lead to inadequate and even misleading information. The purpose of this article is to compare certain accounting and information systems concepts with analogous concepts in professional football. The authors feel that fundamentally the basic problems of data accumulation and retrieval in business and professional football are very similar.

The Reporting Function

The Committee on Accounting Concepts and Standards of the American Accounting Association commented on the function of accounting as follows:

> The primary function of accounting is to accumulate and communicate information essential to an understanding of the activities of an enterprise, whether large or small, corporate or non-corporate, profit or non-profit, public or private.[2]

The research staff of the National Association of Accountants, in "The Field of Management Accounting," stated that:

> Accounting is . . . one of the so-called staff functions of management in which certain members of the management group apply specialized knowledge, skills, and techniques to assist and guide decision making and control. It is the management accountant's responsibility to design the company's financial information system, to administer its operation, and to communicate the results in a form usable by management. Communication includes interpretation in order that everyone concerned may grasp the significance of the data reported.[3]

Implicit in these statements is the importance of the accountant's reporting function. The task of the accountant is to observe, interpret, summarize, and communicate data in a form which will enable the user of the data to evaluate, control, plan, and even predict performance.

Exhibit 1 presents a "matrix of communication"[4] developed on the premise that accounting is a function of communication processes. Although this model was originally developed as a description of the financial reporting process, it is applicable to the management accounting process and the game of football as well. In its original form, the model stresses the importance of the accountant's reporting function. It is the task of the accountant to prepare accounting reports which will transmit meaningful

---

[2] *Accounting and Reporting Standards for Corporate Financial Statements,* American Accounting Association, Columbus, Ohio, 1957.

[3] "The Field of Management Accounting," *NAA Bulletin,* Section 3, June 1963, p. 10. Prepared by the research staff of NAA for the guidance of members of the committees on Research Planning and Accounting Development.

[4] Norton M. Bedford and Vahe Baladouni, "A Communication Theory Approach to Accountancy," *The Accounting Review,* October 1962, p. 653.

Exhibit 1
The Matrix of Communication

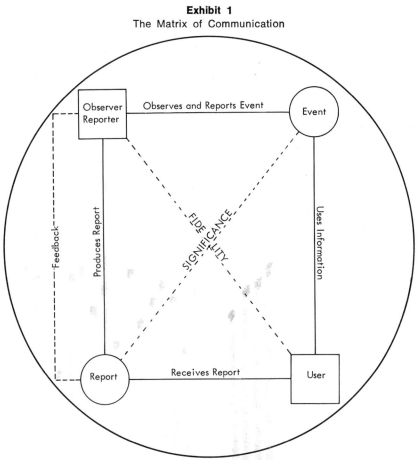

This Exhibit was adapted, with permission, from Norton M. Bedford and Vahe Baladouni, "A Communication Theory Approach to Accountancy," *The Accounting Review*, October 1962, p. 653.

data to decision makers. To accomplish this purpose, the accountant must first ascertain the type of data required by the users of the reports. The needs of these users must be the guiding principle for the accountant in the preparation of his report.

These same concepts are also applicable to professional football. The scout observing a future opponent gathers information which can be used to prepare meaningful reports. These reports transmit informative data to the coaching staff, who use them in planning for the next game. In order to accomplish this purpose, the scout must also first ascertain, in some detail, the information needs of the coaching staff. As in the case with accounting statements, the needs of users must be the guiding principle in the preparation of the report. The parallel relationship of the information needs in a business situation and in professional football are presented in outline form in Exhibit 2.

Exhibit 2

Parallel Relationship of Information Needs

Matrix Component	Business	Football
1. The matrix of communication situation (indicated by the large circle) . . .	This represents the composition and workings of the economic system (both within and without the firm) in which the communication situation of accountancy takes place.	This represents the composition and workings of football in which the communication of information takes place.
2. The four basic elements of the communication situation		
a. The event circle . . .	This circle represents the world of economic events of a business enterprise.	This circle represents a football game (or games).
b. The observer-reporter square . . .	This square represents the accountant. The accountant is to be thought of as comprising the entire accounting staff of the firm as well as the firm's external auditors.	This square represents the scout. The scout is to be thought of as representing the entire coaching staff of a team.
c. The report circle . . .	This circle represents the accounting reports and financial statements of a firm.	This circle represents the scouting reports of a team.
d. The user square . . .	This square represents the user of accounting statements both internal and external.	This square represents the user of the scouting reports, the coaching staff.
3. The direction of information flow . . .	The direction of information flow is indicated by the arrows along the horizontal and vertical lines (counter-clockwise).	The direction on information flow is indicated by the arrows along the horizontal and vertical lines (counter-clockwise).
4. The relationships among the elements		
a. Event to Observer-Reporter. . .	This is the relationship between the accountant (Observer-Reporter) and the world of economic events (Event) of a business enterprise.	This is the relationship between the scout (Observer-Reporter) and the football game (or games) (Event).

b. Observer-Reporter to Report	This is the relationship between the accountant (Observer-Reporter) and the accounting statements (Report).	This is the relationship between the scout (Observer-Reporter) and the scouting report (Report).
c. Report to User	This is the relationship between the user of accounting statements (User) and the accounting statements (Report).	This is the relationship between the user of the scouting report (User) and the scouting report (Report).
d. User to Event	This is the relationship between the user of accounting statements (User) and the world of socio-economic events (Event) of the related business enterprise.	This is the relationship between the user of the scouting report (User) and the subsequent football game (or games) (Event).
5. Fidelity	This is the correspondence between what is understood by the user of accounting statements (User) with what the message(s) is (are), or is (are) intended to be, expressed by the accountant (Observer-Reporter).	This is the correspondence between what is understood by the coaching staff (User) with what the message(s) is (are) or is (are) intended to be, expressed by the scout (Observer-Reporter).
6. Significance	This is the degree of relevance and adequacy which accounting statements (Report) have in relation to the world of economic events (Event) they represent.	This is the degree of relevance and adequacy which the scouting reports (Report) have in relation to the football game (or games) (Event) they represent.
7. Feedback	The accountant (Observer-Reporter) can accomplish feedback and correction by interpreting to himself the accounting statements (Report) he has encoded but not yet released.	The scout (Observer-Reporter) can accomplish feedback and correction by interpreting to himself the scouting report (Report) he has encoded but not yet released.

Columns one and two of this Exhibit were adapted, with permission, from Norton M. Bedford and Vahe Baladouni, "A Communication Theory Approach to Accountancy," *The Accounting Review*, October 1962, p. 654.

The PROBE Concept

To meet the information needs of football coaches, PROBE was conceived as a means of utilizing the computer to process and evaluate football data.[5] It is a generalized report generating system for application in football strategy analysis. This concept is based on the fact that football possesses a great number of easily identifiable characteristics, such as down, distance, field position, relative score, offensive formations, defenses, weather, personnel, etc., all of which are directly related to the decision-making processes of the game. These factors must be evaluated relative to one another in order that new information results.

The system is effected as a multistep operation. First, the coaching staff must define in a precise and consistent fashion the complete terminology that it requires to describe the football events that confront the coaches. Terminology varies from team to team and in fact the basic structure of football ideas change from coach to coach. For the main part these terminology schemes are incomplete, serving only to describe what the coach's own team does, not in general what the opponents do. It is not an easy task to establish a precise terminology base which is rich enough to describe all football maneuvers, and which is simple to use in practice.

An input form is prepared which includes all of the basic play terminology required to describe the football factors being analyzed. The design of this input document is critical because of the timing problem involved. Obviously, the more information desired, the more time is required to encode the data. Since the time of the coach or scout encoding the information is limited, it is essential that the input document allow him to gather all of the information needed in the minimum time possible.

The basis of football analysis is the study of game films in which each play is recorded in detail on a separate input form. A professional game will normally include anywhere from 100 to 150 plays, offensive and defensive combined. Films are viewed by a coach (or coaches) and each play is analyzed and recorded. Items which might be included among the encoded information are the following:

1. The number of the play (all plays in the game are numbered sequentially)
2. The down
3. The yardage necessary for a first down
4. The field position
5. The type of formation
6. The type of play
7. Fakes

---

[5] The system was developed by Frank Ryan Computer Services in conjunction with the Chi Corporation of Cleveland, Ohio.

8.   Backfield action
9.   Blocking action
10. Patterns run by receivers
11. The configuration of the defensive line
12. The shifting patterns of the defense
13. The operational defensive actions that are repeated
14. The nature of the pass coverage
15. The result of the play
16. Weather
17. Personnel

The information recorded on each input sheet can be transformed in a variety of ways to machine readable form, thus creating a football data base. Each week data is added to the information bank, updating the data base.

At this point it should be noted that the scouting function is often also performed "live." Usually a coach will send one of his assistants to scout a game which involves a future opponent. While this phase of scouting lacks much of the precision found in extracting data from films, it frequently provides an important supplement to the analysis of game films. For example, it provides information on weather, tempo, mood, sideline signals, etc. It should be noted that while "live" scouting depends on the intuitive grasp or feel of the scout, for many years it was the only method teams had of scouting an opponent.

The overall purpose is, of course, to obtain as much information as is possible concerning the specific strengths and weaknesses of an opponent. While each play in a football season is an event that will never specifically recur, the strengths and weaknesses of a team do recur in well defined statistical patterns which are particularly susceptible to trend analysis. Simply put, most football teams normally follow similar patterns of play when confronted with similar situations, modified by predetermined strategies. Thus, for planning purposes in football it is important that detailed information concerning both your opponent and your own team be known to management, i.e., the coaches.

The information desired by the coach should, of course, determine the manner in which the data will be manipulated and also the format of the subsequent report generation. The analysis technique developed must be flexible enough to allow the report to provide answers to the "usual" football analysis questions with minimal effort. It should also be flexible enough to retrieve "unusual" information on command as it is required. Just as is the case in a business situation, the report should fit the needs of the user, rather than fitting the user to the report.

There is the need for a general purpose "standard" report which shows the overall tendencies, e.g., running game, passing game, and use of personnel. This general report should be sophisticated enough to indicate a profile of the team's operational decisions and tendencies. This type of information depends on the reliability of the football data base. As an example of the type of information that may be learned, the analysis of several games of one team revealed that whenever it encountered a third down situation with the ball between its own fifteen and twenty yard lines on the right side of the field it ran its fullback on a draw play. If this information were available to its opponent, the linebackers could "key" on the fullback in this (and perhaps similar) situations to stop the play before it got started.

In addition to the standardized type of report described above, special reports may be requested according to the relevant needs of the moment. For example, if a coach wished to know by field position, down, and the distance for a first down, where the San Francisco Forty-Niners most frequently throw the screen pass, PROBE could provide the answer in a matter of seconds.

A critical aspect of the report generation phase is the determination of the optimal manner of presenting the information to the user. One coach may prefer graphical description of the data while another may prefer a detailed listing of successive events that occurred (such as all third down plays, in sequence, run from the left hash mark).

An ideal data bank would be one which includes all aspects of a game, both offensively and defensively, and which could be accumulated with appropriate weighting factors for data acquired in nonstandard situations. Weighting is necessary because a team may appear to have a strong passing attack when playing another team which has a weak pass defense or which has injured players. Another team may appear to be a blitzing team only because its opponent is particularly vulnerable to blitzing. The number of combinations of apparent strengths and weaknesses is large if a specific team is considered in the perspective of its play against other teams. All of these factors should be taken into consideration if accurate analysis is desired. Weighting would be an attempt to provide a standardization of all data accumulated on a specific team against all of its opponents.

Of course, the raw data without weighting would also be available for those coaches who desire it. It does provide a measure of reliable "gross" information. Any football information system should have the capacity to permit the retrieval of the tendencies of a team in a particular situation and to calculate the probability of success or failure based upon previous attempts in the same or similar situations. External factors such as weather, injuries, and other exogenous playing conditions must also be considered. This type of information requires the continuous analysis of games in order to maintain an information bank which is always current.

As an alternative to using a "query" system which can be specialized from team to team and from report to report, a team might rely on the same "standard" set of reports for analyzing every opponent. If this alternative is chosen, a great deal of care must be exercised because the same reports will be produced each week without regard to the nature of the opponent of the team being scouted or to the specific requirements of the coach. For example, standard reports might be used to describe a team's offensive tendencies without taking into account the defenses upon which the offensive tendencies were shaped. In effect, little emphasis would be placed on different circumstances with misleading information as a possible result. This danger may be compounded if a coach is influenced by the results of a specific report one week because of the favorable results obtained from its use. The use of this report may well yield marginal or even poor results in the future, however, because the future analysis would be based on different criteria.

Conclusion

Just as the impact of the computer has been felt by almost every business in the last two decades, the application of data processing to professional sports has developed quite rapidly in recent years. The computer has been used in professional football in processing scouting reports for individual players (for the pro draft of college players) and for teams (strategy analysis as described above). As is the case in most business-oriented decision situations, the present philosophy of planning in professional football is one of user-preparation of statistics (that is, preparation by the coaches themselves) and subjective decisions which are sometimes based on minimal information. In most business firms, managers have increased their demands for data from the company's information system. More detailed reports are often requested at more frequent time intervals. A parallel situation exists in football: it appears that there is in general a definite need for a more sophisticated football data bank and professionally prepared reports for the use of coaches in their decisions. Just as the manager relies on the information system to collect and process data for decision making (his major function), the football coach would be free to coach without spending time collecting data and preparing reports with a data bank which has been transcribed by an assistant. This would eliminate a substantial part of the timing problem in getting information to the players just as it enables the manager to make his decisions on a timely basis.

KEY DEFINITIONS

American Accounting Association The American Accounting Association (AAA) is an accounting organization which is primarily concerned with accounting education and research. Its membership consists of accounting faculty of colleges and universities as well as practicing accountants.

American Institute of Certified Public Accountants The American Institute of Certified Public Accountants (AICPA) is the professional association of Certified Public Accountants (CPAs) in the United States. It is involved in research intended to improve accounting practices and procedures.

Balance sheet The balance sheet or statement of financial position is a general purpose financial report which presents the financial position of the firm as of a particular point in time.

Consistency concept This concept requires that once a firm adopts a particular accounting method for its use in recording a certain type of transaction, it should continue to use that method for all future transactions of the same category.

Cost Accounting Standards Board The CASB is the managerial accounting equivalent of the FASB. It is charged with establishing uniform cost accounting standards for defense contractors who are awarded government contracts.

Entity concept This concept is the basis for the distinction which is made between the entity and its owners. The entity is treated as a unit separate and distinct from its ownership and is accounted for as such.

Expenses Expenses are the costs which are incurred in the process of generating revenues.

Fidelity of accounting information Fidelity of accounting information is the correspondence between the information the accountant wishes to convey and the user's perception of the meaning of the information the accountant reports. The accountant and the user must have a mutual understanding as to certain basic concepts in order for the communication to be valid.

Financial Accounting Standards Board The Financial Accounting Standards Board is an independent board which conducts research and issues opinions as to the correct treatment and presentation of financial information. Its membership includes accountants from industry, government, education, and public accounting. It is the successor to the Accounting Principles Board of the AICPA.

Going-concern concept This concept is the assumption made by the accountant that the business will operate indefinitely unless there is evidence to the contrary.

Historical cost concept. The historical cost concept is the assumption that the original acquisition cost of a resource, not its current market value nor replacement cost, is the basis to be used in accounting for the resources of an entity.

Income statement The income statement is a summary of the operations of a firm. It reports the income (or loss) of the company during a specified period of time.

Internal Revenue Service The Internal Revenue Service (IRS) is a government agency which is charged with the collection of taxes. The income tax code and regulations often affect the procedures and methods of accounting.

Matching concept The matching concept requires the accountant to match the revenues earned during the accounting period with the expenses which were incurred to generate these revenues during this period.

Materiality concept This concept indicates that the accountant should be primarily concerned with those transactions which are of real significance to the users of his report. No specific value can be assigned to any transaction to determine materiality, but if the information would affect a financial statement user's decisions, then it is material.

Monetary concept This is the assumption made by the accountant that all transactions of the business can be recorded in terms of dollars.

National Association of Accountants The National Association of Accountants (NAA) is a professional association of industrial accountants which is concerned primarily with managerial accounting.

Revenues Revenues are the proceeds received or to be received from the sale of goods or services by a business.

Securities and Exchange Commission The Securities and Exchange Commission (SEC) is a government regulatory agency which reviews the financial reporting practices of companies that offer securities for public sale through any national or interstate stock exchange. It works closely with the accounting profession to improve financial accounting practices.

Significance of accounting information Significance of accounting information is the relationship between the actual transactions of the company and the reports which summarize them. The accounting statements should disclose the events which occurred in a manner such that the user would reach the same decision based on the report that he would have made with firsthand information.

Stable dollar assumption This concept assumes that any fluctuation in the purchasing power of the dollar is not significant. For this reason, changes in the purchasing power of the dollar are not recognized in the accounts.

Statement of capital The statement of capital summarizes investments made by the owners, additions to capital from earnings, and withdrawals made by owners during the accounting period.

Statement of changes in financial position This statement indicates the sources from which the resources of a company were obtained and the uses which were made of these resources during an accounting period. It shows how the company's financial position has changed.

Users of accounting information A user of accounting information is anyone who will read and analyze the financial statements in order to use the information contained therein to meet his own needs.

QUESTIONS

1. What is the purpose of accounting?
2. Is accounting useful for both profit and not-for-profit businesses? Explain.
3. Has the need for accounting (and accountants) increased in the United States since the turn of the century? Explain.
4. Who are some of the users of financial statements? Do their needs differ? Why?
5. Explain the similarities and differences between managerial accounting and financial accounting.

6. What are the basic financial statements issued by the typical business? (Briefly describe each statement.)

7. Why is the entity concept necessary in accounting?

8. Discuss the relationship between the monetary concept, the historical cost concept, and the stable dollar assumption. Are these assumptions realistic?

9. Why have accountants adopted the consistency concept?

10. How can the accountant determine whether a particular item is material in amount?

11. What is the role of the Financial Accounting Standards Board in accounting?

12. Financial statements are prepared in accordance with "generally accepted accounting principles." What are "generally accepted accounting principles" and how are they determined?

13. If you were uncertain as to whether a particular procedure was in accordance with "generally accepted accounting principles" where would you go to find out?

14. What is meant by the term "certified public accountant"? How does one become a CPA?

Financial Statements

FINANCIAL statements are the end product of the accountant's work. The basic objective of the financial statements of a business is to provide the information which is required by various users for making economic decisions. As was indicated in Chapter 1, the basic accounting statements which are included in the accounting reports normally issued to users are the balance sheet, the income statement, the statement of capital, and the statement of changes in financial position. We will discuss the balance sheet, income statement, and statement of capital in this chapter. The statement of changes in financial position will be considered in Chapter 17.

THE BALANCE SHEET

The balance sheet or statement of financial position is the accounting statement which provides information regarding the financial position of the firm at a particular point in time. It includes information as to the assets, liabilities, and equities of the business as of a given date.

Assets are the economic resources of the business. An asset is an economic right or a resource that will be of either present or future benefit to the firm. In general, assets are things of value that are owned by the business. The assets of a business may take various forms. For example, assets include: cash, merchandise held for sale to customers, land, buildings, and equipment. In other words, assets are the resources which are used by the business in its continuing operations.

At any point in time the total of the assets of a business are, by definition, equal to the total of the sources of these assets. A business obtains its assets from two basic sources: its owners and its creditors. Creditors lend resources to the firm. These debts, referred to as liabilities, must be repaid at some specified future date. Owners invest their personal resources in the firm. These investments and any profits retained in the business are referred to as owners' equity. Thus, the sources of a firm's assets are its liabilities and owners' equity.

The relationship among the assets, liabilities, and owners' equity of a business may be summarized by the accounting equation: Assets = Liabilities + Owners' Equity (A = L + OE). The concept expressed in this simple equation underlies the recording process of accounting and also serves as the basis of one of the principal financial statements, the balance sheet. In other words, the balance sheet includes a listing of the assets owned by the firm and the sources from which these assets were obtained, liabilities and owners' equity.

$$\frac{\text{Assets}}{\text{A}} = \frac{\text{Sources}}{\text{L} + \text{OE}}$$

The balance sheet or statement of financial position is a statement which reports the financial position of the firm at a particular point in time. The balance sheet discloses the three major categories included in the above equation: assets, liabilities, and owners' equity.

The accounting equation also indicates that the owners' equity is equal to the interest of the owners in the net assets (assets — liabilities) of the business. That is, by transposition, the accounting equation may be restated as follows:

$$A - L = OE$$

Transaction Analysis

A transaction is an event which takes place during the life of a business. In order to illustrate the process of recording transactions and the effect this has on the financial position of a business, we will review the transactions of a small service organization, Kilmer Contractors, during May 1976, the initial month of its operations.

May 1.   Bill Kilmer organized Kilmer Contractors and invested cash of $10,000 in the business.

This increase in the asset cash and the corresponding increase in the investment by the owner, referred to as capital, would be reflected in the balance sheet as follows:

	ASSETS	=	LIABILITIES	+ OWNER'S EQUITY
	Cash	=		*Capital*
May 1	$10,000	=		$10,000

This transaction is an investment of funds in a business by its owner. The asset cash was received by the firm and the owner's equity, or capital was increased. Note that the basic accounting equation balances.

May 2.   The company purchased painting supplies, paying the $3,000 purchase price in cash.

The increase in supplies and the offsetting decrease in the cash of the business would be reflected in the balance sheet as follows:

	ASSETS		=	LIABILITIES	+ OWNER'S EQUITY
	Cash	*+ Supplies =*			*Capital*
Balance	$10,000		=		$10,000
May 2	(3,000)	$3,000			
	$ 7,000 +	$3,000 =			$10,000

This transaction represents an exchange of one asset for another. The asset supplies was increased while the asset cash was decreased. Capital was not affected. The equation is still in balance.

May 5.   Kilmer Contractors borrowed $2,000 from the Virginia National Bank.

This increase in both assets (cash) and liabilities (notes payable) would affect the balance sheet as follows:

	ASSETS		=	LIABILITIES	+ OWNER'S EQUITY
	Cash	*+ Supplies =*	*Note Payable*	*+*	*Capital*
Balance	$7,000 +	$3,000 =			$10,000
May 5	2,000		$2,000		
	$9,000 +	$3,000 =	$2,000	+	$10,000

This transaction is the receipt of an asset, cash, in exchange for a liability, the promise to pay a creditor at some future time. It reflects the promise of the business to repay $2,000 at a future date in order to have cash on hand and available for use at this time. Again, capital is not affected; what has occurred is an exchange of a promise to pay, the liability, notes payable, for the asset cash. The basic accounting equation remains in balance.

May 10.   Kilmer signed a contract whereby he agreed to paint two houses sometime during the next few weeks. The customer paid the fee of $1,100 per house in advance.

This increase in cash and the corresponding increase in liabilities, unearned fees, would be reflected by the business as follows:

	ASSETS		=	LIABILITIES			+ OWNER'S EQUITY
	Cash	*+ Supplies =*	*Note Payable +*	*Unearned Fees*	*+*		*Capital*
Balance	$ 9,000 +	$3,000 =	$2,000		+		$10,000
May 10	2,200			$2,200			
	$11,200 +	$3,000 =	$2,000 +	$2,200	+		$10,000

The company has agreed to paint two houses at a future date and has received its fee now, before it has done the work. The receipt of the $2,200 increases cash and the liability, unearned fees, by the same amount. Unearned fees is not a liability in the sense that the company will be required to repay the money. Rather, it represents an obligation on the part of Kilmer Contractors to perform a service at some future date. Capital is not affected by this transaction, and the accounting equation, $A = L + OE$, remains in balance.

May 12. Bill Kilmer, the owner, withdrew $1,000 from the business for his personal use.

This decrease in cash and the corresponding decrease in the owner's capital balance would be reflected in the balance sheet as follows:

	ASSETS			=	LIABILITIES			+	OWNER'S EQUITY
	Cash	+	*Supplies*	=	*Note Payable*	+	*Unearned Fees*	+	*Capital*
Balance	$11,200	+	$3,000	=	$2,000	+	$2,200	+	$10,000
May 12	(1,000)								(1,000)
	$10,200	+	$3,000	=	$2,000	+	$2,200	+	$ 9,000

This transaction represents a withdrawal of a portion of the owner's investment from the business. Cash and capital were both decreased by $1,000. The accounting equation is still in balance.

May 15. Kilmer Contractors repaid $500 of the $2,000 it borrowed from the Virginia National Bank.

This decrease in both cash and liabilities would affect the balance sheet as follows:

	ASSETS			=	LIABILITIES			+	OWNER'S EQUITY
	Cash	+	*Supplies*	=	*Note Payable*	+	*Unearned Fees*	+	*Capital*
Balance	$10,200	+	$3,000	=	$2,000	+	$2,200	+	$9,000
May 15	(500)				(500)				
	$ 9,700	+	$3,000	=	$1,500	+	$2,200	+	$9,000

This transaction is a reduction of both liabilities and assets. The business repaid $500 of the $2,000 it owed to the bank. Both cash and the note payable decreased by this amount. Capital is not affected and the accounting equation remains in balance.

The transactions of Kilmer Contractors for the first fifteen days of May are summarized in Illustration 2–1.

At this point in time, we will prepare a balance sheet for Kilmer Contractors. This balance sheet appears in Illustration 2–2.

The balance sheet example for Kilmer Contractors was overly simplified for purposes of illustration. Illustration 2–3 presents the actual balance sheet at the end of 1972 and 1973 for Anheuser-Busch, Inc. and includes

Illustration 2–1

KILMER CONTRACTORS
Total Transactions, May 1 to May 15, 1976

	ASSETS		=	LIABILITIES		+	OWNER'S EQUITY
	Cash	+ Supplies	= Note Payable	+ Unearned Fees	+		Capital
May 1	$10,000						$10,000
May 2	(3,000)	$3,000					
May 5	2,000		$2,000				
May 10	2,200			$2,200			
May 12	(1,000)						(1,000)
May 15	(500)		(500)				
	$ 9,700 +	$3,000 =	$1,500	+ $2,200	+		$ 9,000

Illustration 2–2

KILMER CONTRACTORS
Balance Sheet
May 15, 1976

ASSETS		LIABILITIES + OWNER'S EQUITY	
Cash	$ 9,700	Note Payable	$ 1,500
Supplies	3,000	Unearned Fees.	2,200
		Capital	9,000
	$12,700		$12,700

far more additional account titles and classifications. The reader should note that these classifications are not arbitrary distinctions made by the accountants who prepared the balance sheet. They represent generally followed classifications which are intended to assist the user of the balance sheet in analyzing and interpreting it for his use.

BALANCE SHEET CLASSIFICATIONS

The various classifications included in the balance sheet are intended to assist the user of the statement in acquiring as much information as possible concerning the business. It might appear that if a firm desired to provide the user of its statements with the maximum information possible, it could supply him with a listing of all transactions which took place during the period so that the user could perform his own analysis. However, large firms routinely enter into hundreds of thousands or even millions of transactions during any given period. It is therefore highly unlikely that any user would have either sufficient time, the inclination, or the ability to analyze this type of listing. To simplify the analysis of financial statements, firms group similar items in order to reduce the number of classifications which appear on the balance sheet. For example, a chain store may own many buildings of different sizes, at various locations and

Illustration 2–3

consolidated

balance

sheet

ASSETS	December 31, 1973	December 31, 1972
	(In Thousands)	
Current Assets:		
Cash (including certificates of deposit of $30,179,000 in 1973 and $28,116,000 in 1972)	$ 38,227	$ 41,369
Marketable securities (short-term), at cost which approximates market	21,851	27,448
Accounts and notes receivable, less allowance for doubtful accounts of $881,000 in 1973 and $845,000 in 1972	48,004	38,098
Inventories, at lower of cost or market (Note 2)—		
Finished goods	5,528	5,218
Work in process	19,290	16,878
Raw materials and supplies	42,887	36,966
Total current assets	175,787	165,977
Investments and Other Assets:		
Investments in and advances to unconsolidated subsidiaries (Note 1)	26,864	21,151
Investment properties	8,675	8,639
Deferred charges and other non-current assets	12,668	10,722
	48,207	40,512
Plant and Equipment, at cost:		
Land	21,491	19,649
Buildings	312,530	285,068
Machinery and equipment	473,128	432,486
Construction in progress	78,082	65,591
Other real estate	2,445	2,571
	887,676	805,365
Less accumulated depreciation	346,440	313,694
	541,236	491,671
	$765,230	$698,160

serving different functions, but instead of listing these assets separately, all buildings will normally be grouped and presented as a single amount on the balance sheet.

Assets

When assets are acquired by a business they are recorded at the cost of acquisition or original purchase price. This is true even if the business

Illustration 2–3 (continued)

ANHEUSER-BUSCH, INCORPORATED, AND SUBSIDIARIES

LIABILITIES and SHAREHOLDERS EQUITY	December 31, 1973	December 31, 1972	
	(In Thousands)		
Current Liabilities:			
Accounts payable	$ 59,707	$ 33,975	The accompanying statement should be read in conjunction with the Notes To Consolidated Financial Statements
Accrued salaries and wages	13,032	8,903	
Accrued taxes, other than income taxes	18,867	24,712	
Estimated federal and state income taxes	3,038	7,034	
Other current liabilities	4,882	6,623	
Total current liabilities	99,526	81,247	
Long-Term Debt (Note 9):			
4¼% notes payable maturing 1975	128	416	
3⅜% debentures maturing 1975 to 1977, less $2,956,000 in treasury in 1973 and $4,422,000 in 1972	1,499	1,523	
4½% debentures maturing 1975 to 1989, less $7,592,000 in treasury in 1973 and $8,610,000 in 1972	21,008	21,890	
5.45% debentures maturing 1975 to 1991, less $7,770,000 in treasury in 1973 and $7,700,000 in 1972	28,430	30,700	
6% debentures maturing 1976 to 1992, less $4,951,000 in treasury in 1973 and $5,422,000 in 1972	42,349	44,578	
	93,414	99,107	
Accumulated Deferred Income Taxes	54,281	41,456	
Accumulated Deferred Investment Tax Credit Being Amortized	17,225	14,370	
Shareholders Equity (Notes 3 and 4):			
Common stock, $1 par value, authorized 60,000,000 shares; issued 45,608,283 shares	45,608	45,601	
Capital in excess of par value (principally arising from stock dividends)	57,957	57,700	
Retained earnings	400,431	361,891	
	503,996	465,192	
Less cost of 540,388 shares of treasury stock	3,212	3,212	
	500,784	461,980	
	$765,230	$698,160	

has paid only a portion of the initial cost in cash at the time of acquisition and owes the remaining balance to the seller of the asset.

Assets will vary somewhat in their characteristics such as their useful life in relationship to the business' operating cycle, physical attributes, and frequency of use. Accountants attempt to describe certain of the relevant characteristics of assets on the balance sheet by the use of general classifications such as current assets, long-term (or fixed) assets, and other assets. Within these broad categories there are also several sub-classifications. The usual ordering of assets on the balance sheet is in terms of liquidity—the order in which the assets would normally be converted into cash or used up.

Current Assets. Generally, current assets include cash and other assets which are expected to be converted into cash, sold, or used in operations or production during the current accounting period. The accounting period is usually considered to be one year for most businesses. The general subclassifications of current assets normally found in the balance sheet include cash, marketable securities, accounts receivable, inventories, and prepaid expenses. These individual asset categories are briefly described below.

Cash. Cash includes all cash which is immediately available for use in the business including cash on hand, in cash registers, and in checking accounts. Cash is discussed in detail in Chapter 7.

Marketable Securities. Marketable securities are temporary investments in stocks, bonds, and other securities which are readily salable and which management intends to hold only for a relatively short period of time. Marketable securities are discussed in Chapter 7.

Receivables. The accounts receivable balance represents the amount which is owed to the business by its customers. If a business has a significant amount of receivables from sources other than its normal trade customers, the receivables from customers are normally classified as trade accounts receivable and the amounts owed by others are classified as other accounts receivable.

A balance sheet may also include notes receivable. Notes receivable are the receivables (from customers or others) for which the business has received written documentation of the creditors' intent to pay. Both accounts receivable and notes receivable are discussed in Chapter 8.

Inventories. Inventories represent the cost of goods or materials which are held for sale to customers in the ordinary course of business, in the process of production for such sale, or to be used in the production of goods or services to be available for sale at some future date. Inventories are described in Chapter 9.

Prepaid Expenses. Prepaid expenses represent expenditures which were made in either the current or a prior period and which will provide benefits to the firm at some future time. For example, a fire insurance policy which protects the assets of a firm for a three-year period may be purchased during the current year. Although the policy was paid for and a portion of the protection used during the current year, the firm benefits from the insurance protection in future years as well. Therefore, the portion of the cost of the policy which is applicable to future years would be considered a prepaid expense at the end of the current year.

Fixed Assets. Fixed or long-term assets are those assets which are acquired for use in the business rather than for resale to customers. They are assets from which the business expects to receive benefits over a number of future accounting periods. Since fixed assets are used in the operations of the firm, and benefits are derived from this use or availability, the cost of these assets is considered an expense of those periods which benefit from their use.

The actual classifications which may be included in the balance sheet under the fixed asset caption will, of course, vary depending upon the type of business and the nature of its operations. The accounting for fixed assets is described in Chapter 10.

Other Assets. The classification, other assets, includes those assets which are not appropriately classified under either the current or the fixed asset categories described above. This classification may include both tangible and intangible assets. Tangible assets are those that have *physical* substance, such as land held for investment purposes. Intangibles are assets *without* physical substance, such as patents, copyrights, goodwill, etc. This distinction will be discussed in detail in Chapter 10.

Liabilities

Liabilities are debts. They represent claims of creditors against the assets of the business. Creditors have a prior legal claim over the owners of the business. In the event a business is liquidated, creditors will be paid the amounts owed them before any payments are made to owners. Creditors are, of course, concerned with the ability of the business to repay its debts. In certain instances, creditors may earn interest on the amount due them. Normally, a liability has a maturity or due date at which time it must be satisfied.

Liabilities, just as assets, fall into several descriptive categories. The two basic classifications which are usually employed in the balance sheet are current liabilities and long-term liabilities. Both of these general classes may also have sub-classifications.

Current Liabilities. Current liabilities include those obligations for which settlement is expected to require the use of current assets or the origination of other current liabilities. Examples of current liabilities include accounts payable, notes payable, taxes payable, and unearned revenues. These are described in the following paragraphs.

Accounts Payable. Accounts payable are claims of vendors who sell goods and services to the company on a credit basis. Accounts payable are usually not evidenced by a formal, written document such as is the case with a note.

Notes Payable. Notes payable normally arise from borrowing or, on occasion, from purchases, and are evidenced by a written document. Notes payable may or may not be interest bearing. Notes usually have a fixed or determinable due date.

Taxes Payable. This liability includes any local, state, and federal taxes which are owed by the business at the end of the accounting period but are payable in the next period.

Unearned Revenues. Unearned revenues are amounts collected from customers for goods which have not been shipped or services which have not yet been performed.

Long-Term Liabilities. Long-term liabilities generally represent claims which will be paid or satisfied in a future accounting period (or periods). Examples of long-term liabilities are bonds payable and mortgages payable.

Owners' Equity

Owners' equity represents the claims of the owners against the net assets of the firm. Owners normally assume risks which are greater than those of creditors since the return on investment to the owners is usually undefined. In the event of bankruptcy, claims of creditors take priority over those of owners and must be satisfied first. After all creditors have been paid, any assets that remain will then be available to the owners of the firm.

Accounting for owners' equity is influenced by the legal status of the company—the form of its organization. The legal forms of business recognized and used most extensively in the United States are the sole proprietorship, the partnership, and the corporation. There are certain legal differences associated with these types of organizations which will be considered in Chapters 11 and 12. Basically, the owners' equity of a business is normally divided into two major classifications based on the source of the equity: direct investments made by the owner and profits retained in the business. Owners' equity accounts will be discussed in detail in later chapters.

THE INCOME STATEMENT

The income statement or operating statement provides data concerning the results of operations of the firm for a specific period of time, usually a year. The results of the operations of a business are determined by its revenues, expenses, and the resulting net income. Revenues are the gross increases in assets or gross decreases in liabilities which are recognized and result from the sale of either goods or services. Expenses are gross decreases in assets or gross increases in liabilities that occur as a result of the operations of a business. Net income is the excess of revenues over the related expenses for an accounting period. The revenues, expenses, and the resulting net income for a period are presented in the firm's income statement.

The usual accounting concept of income is based on determining, as objectively as possible, the income earned during a particular accounting period by deducting the expenses which were incurred from the revenues earned. Revenues are the proceeds received from the sale of goods and the rendering of services. Expenses are the costs which are incurred in the process of generating revenues. The accounting concept of income assumes that various rules and principles will be followed. These principles require the accountant to exercise his professional judgment in their application since the accounting concept of income measurement stresses the fair determination of income. The reader should note that fair presentation of income does not mean precise presentation. Accounting is an estimating process that requires the accountant to view transactions as objectively as possible in determining both the financial position of a firm and its income for the period.

Since the income statement presents the results of operations for an accounting period, information included in this statement is usually considered to be among the most important data provided by the accountant. This is because profitability is a major concern of those interested in the economic activities of an enterprise.

Transaction Analysis. In the first section of this chapter, the operations of Kilmer Contractors for the first fifteen days of May, 1976, were analyzed. None of the transactions which occurred during this period were relevant to the income statement since they affected neither the revenues earned nor the expenses incurred. We will now follow the activities of the company for the remainder of May to see how revenue and expense transactions affect *both* the income statement and the balance sheet. Recall that the balance sheet of Kilmer Contractors as of May 15, 1976, was as follows:

Illustration 2–4
KILMER CONTRACTORS
Balance Sheet
May 15, 1976

ASSETS		LIABILITIES AND OWNER'S EQUITY	
Cash	$ 9,700	Note Payable	$ 1,500
		Unearned Fees.	2,200
Supplies	3,000	Capital	9,000
	$12,700		$12,700

This balance sheet is the starting point for the continuation of our example. Before proceeding, however, certain fundamental relationships should be reexamined. Recall that all assets are obtained from two basic sources, creditors and owners. At this point, we are concerned with the latter, the assets contributed by owners.

Owners may contribute assets either: (1) directly, that is, by investment; or (2) indirectly, by allowing the *income* earned by the firm to remain with the business and not withdrawing it for their personal use. In other words, just as a direct investment made by the owner increases his equity, the income earned by the firm also increases both the assets and the owners' equity of the firm. Since income is the excess of revenues over expenses $(R - E)$, the basic accounting equation expressed earlier in the chapter may be expanded and restated for purposes of illustration as follows:

Assets = Liabilities + Owners' Equity + Revenue − Expense

$$A = L + OE + R - E$$

Keep in mind that this restatement is made for purposes of illustration only and does not really change either the substance or the meaning of the equation itself. It merely emphasizes the fact that one way in which the owners' equity of a business may be increased is by income—that is, revenues less expenses. Nothing else is changed. Now let us return to the Kilmer Contractors example.

May 17. Kilmer Contractors painted its first house and billed and collected cash of $700 from the customer.

This transaction was a sale of services for cash. It would affect Kilmer Contractors as follows:

	ASSETS			=	LIABILITIES			+ OWNER'S EQUITY	
					Notes		*Unearned*		*Revenue*
	Cash	+ *Supplies*	=		*Payable*	+	*Fees*	+ *Capital*	+ *(Expense)*
Balance	$ 9,700	+ $3,000	=		$1,500	+	$2,200	+ $9,000	
May 17	700								$700
	$10,400	+ $3,000	=		$1,500	+	$2,200	+ $9,000	+ $700

This transaction reflects the fact that the firm has begun to earn revenue. Cash was received and the owner's equity of the business was increased by the amount of the revenue earned, $700. The basic accounting equation is still in balance.

May 19. Kilmer Contractors painted a second house and billed (but did not collect) its fee of $900.

This transaction was a sale of services to a customer on a credit basis. It would affect the business as indicated below:

	ASSETS				=	LIABILITIES			+ OWNER'S EQUITY	
		Accounts				*Notes*		*Unearned*		*Revenue*
	Cash	+ *Receivable*	+ *Supplies*	=		*Payable*	+	*Fees*	+ *Capital*	+ *(Expense)*
Balance	$10,400		+ $3,000	=		$1,500	+	$2,200	+ $9,000	+ $ 700
May 19		$900								900
	$10,400	+ $900	+ $3,000	=		$1,500	+	$2,200	+ $9,000	+ $1,600

Again, this transaction records the revenue earned by the firm in painting a customer's house. Unlike the previous transaction, however, cash was not received. The customer was billed for the service and will pay Kilmer Contractors at some future date. Accounts receivable have increased and owner's equity (revenue) has increased by $900, the fee which was charged for painting the house. This transaction illustrates the very important point that revenue is recorded as it is earned, not necessarily as cash is received. This concept reflects the *accrual* basis of accounting.

May 25.   Kilmer paid his employees salaries of $400.

This transaction was the payment of an expense in cash. It would affect Kilmer Contractors as follows:

	ASSETS			=	LIABILITIES		+	OWNER'S EQUITY	
	Cash	+ *Accounts Receivable*	+ *Supplies*	= *Notes Payable*	+	*Unearned Fees*	+ *Capital*	+	*Revenue (Expense)*
Balance May 25	$10,400 +	$900	+ $3,000	= $1,500	+	$2,200	+ $9,000	+	$1,600
	(400)								(400)
	$10,000 +	$900	+ $3,000	= $1,500	+	$2,200	+ $9,000	+	$1,200

Expenses of $400 were incurred and paid in cash. This transaction reduces both cash and owner's equity. The reduction in owner's equity is due to the fact that an expense has been incurred, thereby reducing income. (Remember that revenues less expenses equals income.) The accounting equation is still in balance.

May 31.   Kilmer Contractors painted one of the two houses contracted for on May 10.

By painting one of the two houses, Kilmer Contractors has partially satisfied a non-cash liability by the rendering of services and therefore earned income. This transaction would be reflected as follows:

	ASSETS			=	LIABILITIES		+	OWNER'S EQUITY	
	Cash	+ *Accounts Receivable*	+ *Supplies*	= *Notes Payable*	+	*Unearned Fees*	+ *Capital*	+	*Revenue (Expense)*
Balance May 31	$10,000 +	$900	+ $3,000	= $1,500	+	$2,200	+ $9,000	+	$1,200
						(1,100)			1,100
	$10,000 +	$900	+ $3,000	= $1,500	+	$1,100	+ $9,000	+	$2,300

On May 10, Kilmer signed a contract to paint two houses and received his fee of $1,100 per house in advance. No income was earned at the point the cash was received because no work had been done at that time. Kilmer Contractors had an obligation to paint the two houses at some future date. This was a liability to perform services, which was previously recorded as unearned fees. Now one of the two houses contracted for has been painted and that portion of the income has been earned. The liability, unearned fees, has been reduced by $1,100 and the income for the current period has been increased by the same amount. These facts require that the statements be adjusted in order to reflect the current status of the contract. Again, this transaction emphasizes the point that income is recorded as it is earned, *not* as cash is received. The accounting equation remains in balance.

May 31. The unused painting supplies on hand at this date had an original cost of $2,000.

The facts of this transaction indicate that an expense has been incurred and should be recorded. It will affect Kilmer Contractors as indicated below:

	ASSETS			=	LIABILITIES		+ OWNER'S EQUITY	
	Cash	*Accounts* + *Receivable*	+ *Supplies* =		*Notes* *Payable* +	*Unearned* *Fees*	+ *Capital* +	*Revenue* *(Expenses)*
Balance May 31	$10,000 +	$900	+ $3,000 = (1,000)		$1,500 +	$1,100	+ $9,000 +	$2,300 (1,000)
	$10,000 +	$900	+ $2,000 =		$1,500 +	$1,100	+ $9,000 +	$1,300

During the month of May, Kilmer Contractors used supplies that had an original cost of $1,000. This amount was determined by subtracting the $2,000 cost of the supplies which were on hand at May 31 from the $3,000 total cost of supplies available for use (that is, the supplies on hand at the beginning of the month plus the supplies purchased during the month). As in the previous May 31 transaction, an adjustment is required. The asset, supplies, was decreased by $1,000 (the cost of the supplies used) from $3,000 (the total supplies available for use during the month of May) to $2,000 (the cost of supplies on hand at May 31). This transaction reflects the fact that expenses, like revenues, are recorded as they are incurred or used rather than when cash is disbursed. The accounting equation remains in balance.

All of the transactions of Kilmer Contractors for the month of May are summarized in Illustration 2–5 as follows:

Illustration 2–5

KILMER CONTRACTORS
All Transactions for the Month of May

	ASSETS			=	LIABILITIES		+ OWNER'S EQUITY	
	Cash	*Accounts* + *Receivable*	+ *Supplies* =		*Notes* *Payable* +	*Unearned* *Fees*	+ *Capital*	*Revenue* + *(Expense)*
May 1	$10,000						$10,000	
May 2	(3,000)		$3,000					
May 5	2,000				$2,000			
May 10	2,200					$2,200		
May 12	(1,000)						(1,000)	
May 15	(500)				(500)			
	$ 9,700 +	$ 0	+ $3,000 =		$1,500 +	$2,200	+ $ 9,000 +	$ 0
May 17	700							700
May 19		900						900
May 25	(400)							(400)
May 31						(1,100)		1,100
May 31			(1,000)					(1,000)
	$10,000 +	$900	+ $2,000 =		$1,500 +	$1,100	+ $ 9,000 +	$1,300

We are now in a position to prepare a balance sheet and an income statement for Kilmer Contractors. The balance sheet would be as follows:

Illustration 2–6

KILMER CONTRACTORS
Balance Sheet
May 31, 1976

ASSETS		LIABILITIES AND OWNER'S EQUITY	
Cash	$10,000	Notes Payable	$ 1,500
Accounts Receivable	900	Unearned Fees	1,100
Supplies	2,000	Capital	10,300
	$12,900		$12,900

The income statement for the month of May would appear as follows:

Illustration 2–7

KILMER CONTRACTORS
Income Statement
For the Month Ended May 31, 1976

Revenue		$2,700
Less: Expenses		
Supplies Used	$1,000	
Salaries	400	
Total Expenses		1,400
Income		$1,300

The revenues reported in the income statement include $700 earned by painting the house on May 17, $900 earned on May 19 by painting a second house, and $1,100 earned by painting one of the two houses contracted for on May 10 ($700 + $900 + $1,100 = $2,700). The expenses of $1,400 include the salaries of $400 paid to Kilmer Contractors' employees on May 25 and the cost of the painting supplies used during the month of May. The cost of the supplies used was determined by subtracting the cost of the supplies on hand at May 31, $2,000, from the $3,000 cost of the supplies which were available for use during the month ($3,000 − $2,000 = $1,000). Again, note that revenues are recorded as they are earned and expenses are recorded as they are incurred, not necessarily as cash is either paid or received. As previously indicated, this practice is referred to as the accrual basis of income.

The income for the month is the difference between the total revenues earned ($2,700) and the total of the expenses ($1,400) which were incurred in order to generate these revenues ($2,700 − $1,400 = $1,300). At the end of the period, this income is added to the owner's capital account.

INCOME STATEMENT CLASSIFICATIONS

As was the case with the balance sheet, classifications which appear in the income statement are intended to be descriptive, functional categories of revenues and expenses. There are many different formats employed for income statements. Variations among industries are substantial and, to compound this problem, variations among firms in the same industry can also be significant. Consequently, the classifications which are used in the income statement will be discussed in detail in later chapters of this text.

At this point it might be helpful to examine the changes between the balance sheet of May 15 and that of May 31 in order to fully understand the relationship between the income statement and the balance sheet. Balance sheets at May 15 and May 31 are reported in a comparative format in Illustration 2–8.

Illustration 2–8
KILMER CONTRACTORS
Comparative Balance Sheets

ASSETS	May 15	May 31	Change
Cash	$ 9,700	$10,000	$ 300
Accounts Receivable	0	900	900
Supplies	3,000	2,000	(1,000)
	$12,700	$12,900	$ 200

LIABILITIES AND OWNER'S EQUITY			
Notes Payable	$ 1,500	$ 1,500	$ 0
Unearned Fees	2,200	1,100	(1,100)
Capital	9,000	10,300	1,300
	$12,700	$12,900	$ 200

Each change in Illustration 2–8 can be explained by the transactions that affected the particular asset, liability, or the owner's equity. (These were summarized in Illustration 2–5.)

The change in owner's equity is particularly important because it represents the net increase or decrease in the owner's investment in the firm. This change can be explained by the transactions which occurred on May 17, 19, 25, and the two adjustments which were made on May 31. These same transactions are the ones which appear in a summarized form in the income statement. In other words, the change in capital which took place during the period May 15 to 31 is due to the earnings of the company. These changes in owner's equity are included in a statement of capital (referred to as a statement of retained earnings for a corporation). The statement of capital reports the details of the equity of the owners in the business. Capital is equal to the direct investments made by the owners plus the earnings of the business and less any withdrawals made by owners. Note that the statement of capital for Kilmer Contractors, which covers the entire month of May, includes the investment made by Kilmer on May 1 and the withdrawal made on May 15. In other words, it summarizes all of the transactions which affected owner's equity during the month of May.

A statement of capital for Kilmer Contractors is presented in Illustration 2–9:

Illustration 2–9

KILMER CONTRACTORS
Statement of Capital
For the Month Ending May 31, 1976

Capital at May 1, 1976.		$ 0
Add:		
Investment	$10,000	
Income for May.	1,300	11,300
Deduct:		
Withdrawal.		(1,000)
Capital at May 31, 1976		$10,300

As indicated above, this statement of capital indicates how and why the owner's equity of Kilmer Contractors changed during the month of May.

The balance sheet, income statement, and statement of capital presented above were deliberately kept brief and simple for purposes of illustration. They do, however, illustrate the basic principles and procedures which are followed in the preparation of financial statements. A combined income statement and statement of retained earnings for Anheuser-Busch, Inc., for 1973 is presented in Illustration 2–10.

AN OVERVIEW

The purpose of this chapter was to introduce the basic financial statements used by a business; these are the end product of the accountant's work. The objective of financial statements is to provide data which are useful to various users in making economic decisions.

The chapter introduced the reasons that asset, liability, and owners' equity balances change from one accounting period to another, and the general categories included in balance sheets or statements of financial position.

The sources of the assets of a business are creditors and owners. Since the total of the assets must equal the total of the sources of these assets, liabilities plus owners' equity are equal to the assets of a business. The general categories included in the balance sheet (assets, liabilities, and

Illustration 2–10

	1973	1972
	(In Thousands)	
Sales	**$1,442,720**	$1,273,093
Less federal and state beer taxes	**333,013**	295,593
	1,109,707	977,500
Costs and Expenses (Notes 5 and 6):		
Cost of products sold	**875,361**	724,718
Marketing, administrative and general expenses	**112,928**	108,008
	988,289	832,726
	121,418	144,774
Other Income and Expenses:		
Interest income	**4,818**	3,299
Interest expense	**(5,288)**	(6,041)
Purchase discounts, other income and expenses, net . . .	**5,287**	4,855
Income before Income Taxes and Extraordinary Item	**126,235**	146,887
Provision for Income Taxes (Note 8):		
Current	**44,978**	62,305
Deferred	**15,680**	8,182
	60,658	70,487
Income before Extraordinary Item	**65,577**	76,400
Extraordinary Item — Loss on discontinued Houston Busch Gardens operation, net of income tax benefit of $4,006,000 (Note 7)	**—**	4,093
Net Income	**65,577**	72,307
Retained Earnings at Beginning of Year	**361,891**	315,693
	427,468	388,000
Cash Dividends, $.60 per share in 1973 and $.58 per share in 1972	**27,037**	26,109
Retained Earnings at End of Year	**$ 400,431**	$ 361,891
Income Per Share of Common Stock:		
Income before extraordinary item	**$1.46**	$1.70
Extraordinary item	**—**	.09
Net income	**$1.46**	$1.61

consolidated statement of income and retained earnings

The accompanying statements should be read in conjunction with the Notes To Consolidated Financial Statements

owners' equity) are further classified into meaningful descriptive categories in order to provide the user with additional detailed information concerning the financial position of the firm.

The transactions which occur during an accounting period will change the amounts from one balance sheet to the next. Any firm's balance sheet may be thought of as a photograph of its financial position at a specific point in time.

This chapter also introduced the income statement and the general categories or classifications included in the income statement.

The income statement discloses the income earned by the company during a period and how it was earned. Only those transactions that have an impact on revenues or expenses will be included in the income statement. These same transactions will also have an impact on owners' equity. This impact is explained in the statement of capital.

KEY DEFINITIONS

Accounting equation or dual-aspect concept   The accounting equation may be expressed as follows: assets = sources of assets or assets = liabilities + owners' equities.

Accounting cycle   The length of the accounting or operating cycle of any company is the period of time required for the company to acquire the basic resources to produce, manufacture goods, receive purchase orders, ship goods, and collect cash from the sale. This cycle depends on many factors and could vary from a short period of time for a company in the grocery industry to a long period of time for a company in the liquor industry.

Accounting period   The accounting period is the longer of one year or one accounting cycle.

Accounts payable   Accounts payable represent amounts the company owes to its creditors for purchases of goods or services in the ordinary course of business.

Accounts receivable   Accounts receivable represent the amounts owed by customers to the company for goods or services which were sold in the ordinary course of business.

Assets   An asset is something of value owned by the business.

Cash   Cash is any medium of exchange which is readily accepted and used for transactions. Besides currency or demand deposits, cash usually includes certain negotiable instruments, such as customer's checks.

Current assets   Current assets include cash and other assets which are expected to be converted into cash, sold, or used in operations or production during the current accounting period.

Current liabilities   Current liabilities include those obligations for which settlement is expected to require the use of current assets or the creation of other current liabilities.

Fixed assets   Fixed or long-term assets are those assets which are acquired for use in the continuing operations of a business over a number of accounting periods rather than for resale to customers.

Intangibles   Intangibles are assets without physical substance, such as patents.

Inventory   Inventories include materials which are used in production, goods which are in the process of production, and finished products held for sale to customers.

Liabilities   Liabilities represent claims of creditors against the assets of a business.

Liquidity   Liquidity normally refers to the order in which assets would be converted into cash or used up.

Long-term liabilities   Long-term liabilities generally represent claims which will be paid or satisfied in a future accounting period.

Marketable securities   Marketable securities are temporary investments in stocks, bonds, and other securities which are readily salable and which management intends to sell within a relatively short period of time.

Net income   Net income is the excess of revenues earned over the related expenses incurred for an accounting period.

Notes payable   Notes payable normally arise from borrowing and are evidenced by a written document or formal promise to pay.

Owners' equity   Owners' equity, also referred to as net worth or capital, represents claims against the assets by the owners of the business. The total owners' equity represents the amount that the owners have invested in the business including any income which may have been retained in the business since its inception.

Owners' withdrawals   Owners' withdrawals are the removal from the business of cash or other assets by the owners of that business.

Prepaid expenses   Prepaid expenses represent expenditures which were made in either the current or a prior period and which will provide benefits to the firm at some future time.

Tangible assets   Tangible assets are those assets that have physical substance.

Transactions   Transactions are events which occur during the life of a business.

Unearned revenues   Unearned revenues are amounts collected from customers for goods which have not been shipped or services which have not yet been performed.

QUESTIONS

1. What are the main sources of assets for a company? Why does each source provide assets?

2. A = L + OE expresses what accounting concept? Explain the concept.

3. What is a transaction?

4. What is an asset? Distinguish between current and long-term assets.

5. What is a liability? Distinguish between current and long-term liabilities.

6. Explain the difference between liabilities and owners' equity.

7. What does the balance in the capital account represent?

8. What are some advantages of preparing a balance sheet?

9. What periods of time are covered by the income statement, the statement of capital, and the balance sheet? How is this recorded in the headings of the statements?

10. What is the relationship between the balance sheet and the income statement at the end of the accounting period?

EXERCISES

2–1   Using these abbreviations, classify each of the following account titles as to what section of the balance sheet they would appear in.

CA –Current Assets
FA –Fixed Assets
OA –Other Assets
CL –Current Liabilities
LTL–Long-Term Liabilities
OE –Owners' Equity

CA Cash
OE Capital
CL-LTL Note Payable
CA FA Prepaid Insurance
CA Accounts Receivable
FA Plant & Equipment
CA FA Investments
OA Patents

CL Taxes Payable
CA Inventory
CL Wages Payable
CL Accounts Payable
CA Marketable Securities
FA Land
OA Goodwill
CL Interest Payable

2–2   Fill in the missing amounts:

	Company	
	Allen	Barr
Assets–January 1, 1975	$120	$ (d) *150*
Liabilities–January 1, 1975	80	55
Owners' Equity–January 1, 1975.	(a) *40*	95
Assets–December 31, 1975	130	(e) *190*
Liabilities–December 31, 1975	(b) *94*	70
Owners' Equity–December 31, 1975.	(c) *36*	120
Revenues in 1975	15	(f) *49*
Expenses in 1975	19	24

OE = 40 + 15 − 19 = 36 = B
A change in O.E.

2–3   Give an example of a transaction which will:

a.   Increase an asset and increase owners' equity.   *Owner adding money*
b.   Increase an asset and increase a liability.   *Credit Purchase*
c.   Increase one asset and decrease another asset.   *Cash Purchase*
d.   Decrease an asset and decrease owners' equity.   *Owner with drawl (Salary)*
e.   Decrease an asset and decrease a liability.   *Paying of A/P with cash*

2–4   Given the following information, answer the questions below:

Revenue, 1975 . . . . $24,000
Liabilities–December 31, 1975   25,000
Investments by owner, 1975.   4,000
Withdrawals, 1975   12,000
Owners' Equity–January 1, 1975.   27,000
Owners' Equity–December 31, 1975.   35,000

a.   What are the Total Assets on December 31, 1975?   *60,000*
b.   What is Net Income for the year?   *16,000*
c.   What is Total Expense for 1975?   *8,000*

2–5 Fill in the missing figures in the information below:

	1975	1976	1977
Assets–January 1	$100,000	$120,000	$ f _147,000_
Liabilities–January 1	60,000	c _67,000_	72,000
Owners' Equity–January 1	a _40,000_	d _58,000_	75,000
Withdrawals	20,000	15,000	17,000
Investments by owners	18,000	16,000	—
Owners' Equity–December 31	b _58,000_	e _75,00_	57,000
Income	$ 20,000	$ 16,000	g _—1,000_

2–6   For each transaction listed below, indicate the effect on the total assets, total liabilities, and owners' equity of the business. Identify the effect of each transaction by using a (+) for an increase, a (−) for a decrease, and a (0) for no effect.

		Assets	Liabilities	Owners' Equity
a.	The owner invested cash in the business	(+)	(0)	(+)
b.	Purchased a building for cash	(0)	(0)	(0)
c.	Borrowed cash from the bank.	(+)	(+)	(0)
d.	Purchased equipment on credit	(+)	(+)	(0)
e.	Provided a service and collected cash.	(+)	(0)	(+)
f.	Paid wages in cash to employees	(−)	(0)	(−)
g.	Paid a bank loan	(−)	(−)	(0)

PROBLEMS

Series A

2A–1   Certain transactions of the Ricketts Company for September 1975 are shown below in equation form. Give a short explanation of the probable nature of each transaction.

			ASSETS			=	LIABIL-ITIES	+	OWNERS' EQUITY
	Cash	+ Accounts Receivable	+ Supplies	+	Equip-ment	=	Accounts Payable	+	Capital
Beginning Balance	$10,000 +	$5,000	+ $3,000	+	$12,000 =		$10,000	+	$20,000
(a)					+8,000		+8,000		
(b)	+1,000								+1,000
(c)	–3,000						–3,000		
(d)	+2,000	–2,000							
(e)	–4,000		+4,000						
(f)	–3,000								–3,000
Ending Balance	$ 3,000 +	$3,000	+ $7,000	+	$20,000 =		$15,000	+	$18,000

2A–2 Certain transactions of the Kreuger Company for the month of October are shown below in equation form. Provide a description of the probable nature of each transaction.

	ASSETS				=	LIABILITIES		+	OWNERS' EQUITY	
	Cash	+	Accounts Receivable	+ Supplies +	Equip- ment	=	Accounts Payable	+	Wages Payable	+ Capital	+	Revenue (Expense)
Beginning Balance	$ 8,000 +	$ 9,000	+ $3,000 + $ 8,000	=	$7,000	+ $1,000	+ $20,000 +	0
(a)		+6,000						+6,000
(b)	−2,000						−2,000	
(c)			+2,000		+2,000			
(d)	−5,000			+5,000				
(e)	+10,000	−10,000						
(f)	−4,000				−4,000			
(g)			−3,000					−3,000
(h)						+2,000		−2,000
Ending Balance	$ 7,000 +	$ 5,000	+ $2,000 + $13,000	=	$5,000	+ $3,000	+ $18,000 +	$1,000

2A–3 Dave Karwin opened a roofing business on June 1 and during the month of June completed the following transactions.

June 1 Dave Karwin formed the Karwin Roofing Service with an initial investment of $15,000.

3 The Company purchased roofing shingles, paying the $4,000 purchase price in cash.

7 Karwin received $3,500 as advance payment on a contract to roof two houses during the month of July.

12 Karwin Roofing Service borrowed $3,000 from the Sharpstown State Bank.

15 Dave Karwin withdrew $2,500 from the business for personal use.

30 Karwin Roofing Service made its first payment of $1,000 on the $3,000 loan from Sharpstown State Bank.

Indicate the effects of the transactions on the equation provided below.

ASSETS	=	LIABILITIES	+ OWNER'S EQUITY
Roofing Cash + Supplies	=	Notes Unearned Payable + Fees	Karwin, + Capital

2A–4 The following transactions occurred during the initial month of operations of Kingsbery Automotive Service.

> The owner contributed $15,000 cash.
> Auto parts purchased on account, $5,000.
> Paid rent for the first month, $2,500.
> Repaired cars for a $2,200 fee and billed the customers.
> Auto parts used, $1,150.
> Collected $850 on customers' accounts.
> Paid $1,000 to creditors.

a.   Indicate the effects of these transactions on the equation provided below.

ASSETS			= LIABILITIES +	OWNER'S EQUITY	
	Auto	Accounts	Accounts	Kingsbery,	Revenue
Cash +	Parts +	Receivable =	Payable	+ Capital	+ (Expense)

b.   Prepare a balance sheet and an income statement at the end of the month.

2A–5   Sam Jones opened an auto repair business on January 1, 1975. At the end of 1975, Jones Auto Repair had the following balances of assets, liabilities, and owner's equity:

$A = L + OE.$

Accounts Payable.	$ 5,000
Accounts Receivable	20,000
Building	30,000
Capital	?
Cash	10,000
Land	12,000
Notes Payable	12,000
Prepaid Insurance	5,000
Supplies	8,000
Unearned Fees.	16,000
Wages Payable	2,000

Prepare a balance sheet at December 31, 1975.

2A–6   Below is a balance sheet for Rich Exterminator Company at October 31, 1975.

RICH EXTERMINATOR COMPANY
Balance Sheet
October 31, 1975

ASSETS		LIABILITIES AND OWNERS' EQUITY	
Cash	$7,500	Note Payable	$2,200
Supplies	2,000	Unearned Fees.	300
	$9,500	Capital	7,000
			$9,500

The unearned fees are the result of receiving in advance a $100 fee for each of three jobs to be performed in the future.

During the month of November, the following transactions occurred.

Nov.   2   Rich Company exterminated a house and billed and collected $100 cash from the customer.

7   Rich Company exterminated a house and billed but did not collect its fee of $150.

11   Rich paid his employees salaries of $200.

17   Rich Company exterminated two of the three houses contracted for in October.

30   The unused supplies on hand at this date had an original cost of $1,500.

a.   Prepare an income statement for Rich Exterminator Company for the month of November.

b.   Prepare a balance sheet at November 30, 1975.

Series B

2B–1   Selected transactions of the Burns Company for January are listed below in equation form. Give a brief explanation of the nature of each transaction.

		ASSETS					LIABIL- ITIES		OWNERS' EQUITY
Cash	+	Accounts Receivable +	Equip- ment	+ Building +	Land	=	Accounts Payable	+	Capital
Beginning Balance									
$20,000 +		$10,000 +	-0-	+ $30,000 +	$10,000	=	$20,000	+	$50,000
(a) +5,000						=			+5,000
(b)			$+6,000			=	+6,000		
(c) -5,000					+5,000	=			
(d) +3,000		-3,000				=			
(e) -4,000						=	-4,000		
(f) -1,000						=			-1,000
Ending Balance									
$18,000 +		$ 7,000 +	$ 6,000 +	$30,000 +	$15,000	=	$22,000	+	$54,000

2B–2   The effects on the accounting equation of The Hartford Company are shown on page 48. Write a short explanation of the probable nature of each of the transactions.

2B–3   Bill Smith opened a shoe repair shop on September 1. During the initial month of operations, the shop completed the following transactions:

Sept.   1   Smith invested $20,000 in the business.

　　　　3   The company purchased supplies for $2,000 cash.

　　　　6   The company borrowed $5,000 from the bank.

　　　15   The business purchased $1,000 of equipment on credit.

　　　20   The company made a payment of $1,000 on the bank loan.

　　　25   Smith withdrew $1,000 cash from the business.

Indicate the effects of each transaction on the equation provided below.

	ASSETS		= LIABILITIES	+ OWNER'S EQUITY
Cash +	Supplies +	Equipment	= Notes Payable +	Capital

2B-2 (continued)

| | ASSETS | | | | | LIABILITIES | | | OWNERS' EQUITY | |
	Cash	Accounts Receivable	Land	Supplies	Prepaid Insurance	Accounts Payable	Unearned Fees	Wages Payable	Capital	Revenue (Expense)
Beginning Balance	$4,320	$9,370	$19,780	$470	$1,400	$5,460	$1,500	$1,320	$27,060	-0-
(a)					-400					$ -400
(b)				-290						-290
(c)							-300			+300
(d)								+1,200		-1,200
(e)	+4,000	-4,000								
(f)	-3,000					-3,000				
(g)	+2,000									+2,000
Ending Balance	$7,320	$5,370	$19,780	$180	$1,000	$2,460	$1,200	$2,520	$27,060	$ 410

2B–4 John King began operating a tax return preparation service on January
1. During the month of January, the transactions on page 49 were
completed:

Jan. 2 The owner invested $10,000 cash in the business.
   4 The business acquired $3,000 of supplies on account.
   5 Rent of $500 was paid for an office building.
  11 Prepared tax returns on credit for a $3,000 fee.
  15 Salaries of $1,000 were paid to employees.
  25 Collected $1,500 on customer accounts.
  30 Cash of $1,000 was paid to creditors.
  31 Supplies of $1,000 were used.

a. Show the effects of these transactions on the equation provided
below.

ASSETS			= LIABILITIES	+ OWNER'S EQUITY	
		Accounts	*Accounts*		*Revenue*
Cash +	*Supplies* +	*Receivable* =	*Payable*	+ *Capital* +	*(Expense)*

b. Prepare an income statement for the month of January.
c. Prepare a balance sheet as of January 31.

2B–5 The following information was taken from the records of J. S. Wylie and
Company as of July 31, 1975. Prepare the balance sheet at that date.

Wages payable.	$ 5,000
Cash	2,345
Land	30,000
Prepaid rent	300
Accounts payable.	1,470
Capital	?
Inventory.	5,990
Equipment.	15,200
Buildings.	33,450
Accounts receivable.	1,350
Patents (just purchased)	7,000
Mortgage payable (due January 31, 1984).	40,000
Marketable securities	1,035
Estimated taxes payable	3,000
Unearned revenue.	750

2B–6 The August 1, 1975 balance sheet for Dickson Building Company is
presented on the following page.

DICKSON BUILDING COMPANY
Balance Sheet
August 1, 1975

Cash	$ 9,500	Accounts payable	$ 7,250
Accounts receivable.	3,070	Unearned revenue.	150
Supplies	6,500	Wages payable	3,110
Prepaid insurance	500	Notes payable	8,000
Interest receivable.	30	Owners' equity	20,325
Equipment.	19,235		$38,835
	$38,835		

During August, the following transactions occurred.

Aug. 1 Purchased $5,000 of supplies on account.

4 Received revenues of $8,150 cash. Supplies used were $4,270.

7 Received $1,250 on customers' accounts.

9 Received $30 interest.

15 Paid wages of $3,110 in August but still owe $2,750 in wages as of the end of the month.

18 Paid $2,500 to creditors.

31 Accrued interest expense on notes payable of $20 (interest payable).

31 Recognized insurance expense of $100.

31 Owners withdrew $3,500 in cash.

Required:

a. Prepare a balance sheet at August 31, 1975.

b. Prepare the income statement for the month of August.

3

The Recording Process

BECAUSE THE number of transactions which occur in even a small business causing its assets, liabilities, equities, revenues, and expenses to increase and decrease occur much too frequently to prepare a new set of financial statements each time a transaction takes place, an alternative method of recording information must be employed. The description of this recording process, which is basic to every accounting system, is the subject matter of this chapter. The accounting system described, referred to as the "double-entry" system, is applicable to all situations in which financial information must be collected and processed. In small firms the system may be maintained by hand, just as described in this chapter, while in larger organizations it will usually be implemented using mechanical or electronic data processing equipment. In any situation, however, the basic principles involved are the same.

THE ACCOUNT

For purposes of reporting and analysis, the transactions of an entity are summarized or grouped in individual accounts. An account is simply a place or means of summarizing all of the transactions that affect a particular asset, liability, equity, revenue, or expense item. The accounting system of a firm includes an individual account for each type or classification of individual asset, liability, owners' equity, revenue, and expense. The increase or decrease in each of these items will be recorded in its own account using "debits" and "credits." At this point we cannot overemphasize the fact that the words "debit" and "credit" are simply terms used to identify *left* and *right* sides of an account, respectively, and have absolutely no other meaning in their accounting usage. (The reader who accepts this statement as a fact and keeps it in mind will save himself untold grief and will greatly enhance his understanding of the recording process.) For purposes of discussion, a typical account may be illustrated as follows:

(Account Title)

| (debit side) | (credit side) |

This form of presentation is often referred to as a "T-account."

It was indicated earlier that the "double-entry" method is used in accounting in order to record transactions. To understand the double-entry method a simple rule must be kept in mind: for every transaction recorded, the total dollar amount of the debits must be equal to the total dollar amount of the credits. Since we already know that assets must be equal to liabilities plus owners' equity, the following rules of "debit" and "credit" may be established and used in recording the transactions of an entity:

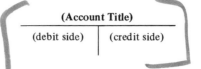

Assets		=	Liabilities		+	Owners' Equity	
debit (+)	credit (−)		debit (−)	credit (+)		debit (−)	credit (+)

Because of the equation:

$$\text{ASSETS} = \text{LIABILITIES} + \text{OWNERS' EQUITY}$$

and the rule:

$$\text{TOTAL DEBITS} = \text{TOTAL CREDITS}$$

the procedures (or rules) for recording increases and decreases in the accounts logically follow:

To increase an ASSET, debit the account.
To decrease an ASSET, credit the account.

To increase a LIABILITY or OWNERS' EQUITY, credit the account.
To decrease a LIABILITY or OWNERS' EQUITY, debit the account.

Since revenues and expenses increase and decrease owners' equity respectively, the rules of debit and credit for owners' equity apply to revenue and expense accounts. Because revenues increase owners' equity, the rule for recording increases or decreases in this account is the same as that for owners' equity:

To increase REVENUE, credit the account.
To decrease REVENUE, debit the account.

On the other hand, since expenses decrease owners' equity, the rule for recording expenses is opposite of that for owners' equity:

To increase an EXPENSE, debit the account.
To decrease an EXPENSE, credit the account.

In order to illustrate the operation of these rules, assume that a firm obtains a $2,000 cash loan from its bank. This transaction would increase the firm's cash, an asset, by $2,000 and also increase its loans payable, a liability, by the same amount. In order to record this transaction, the firm would debit (increase) its cash account for $2,000 and, at the same time, credit (increase) its loans payable account for $2,000. This transaction would be summarized in the accounts of the firm as follows:

	Cash		Loans Payable
2,000			2,000

Note that the total of the debits (in this instance a debit to the cash account of $2,000) is equal to the total of the credits (a credit to the liability account, loans payable for the same amount). In addition, the accounting equation, $A = L + OE$ remains in balance since the assets and liabilities were both increased by $2,000 (owners' equity was not affected).

When the firm repays its loan to the bank, the payment of $2,000 would decrease the firm's asset, cash, by $2,000 and decrease its liability, loans payable, by the same amount. This transaction would be recorded in the accounts by a debit (decrease) to loans payable of $2,000 and a credit (decrease) to cash of $2,000. The effects of the two transactions, the loan and its repayment, are recorded in the accounts as follows:

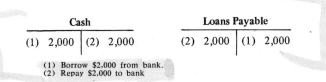

	Cash			Loans Payable	
(1) 2,000	(2) 2,000		(2) 2,000	(1) 2,000	

(1) Borrow $2,000 from bank.
(2) Repay $2,000 to bank

Again the total debits are equal to the total credits and the accounting equation remains in balance.

It is often useful to consider, analyze, and record the transactions of a business as they occur. The simplest example of this process is the use of the general journal entry, which could be used to record the two transactions explained above as follows:

	Debit	Credit
Cash	2,000	
Loans Payable		2,000
Loans Payable	2,000	
Cash		2,000

A general journal entry, usually referred to as a journal entry, is a simple means of recording the transactions of a firm in terms of debits and credits. As illustrated above, the format for each journal entry is to write the title of the account to be debited and the amount of the debit on the first line, then indent and write the title of the account to be credited and the amount of the credit on the second line. This is simply a matter of convention.

For purposes of illustration, transactions will be recorded initially in general journal form and then transferred to the individual "T-accounts" (as illustrated in the foregoing). This latter process is referred to as "posting," transferring information from the general journal to the ledger (the book of entry which contains all the accounts of the firm). The same data which were used in Chapter 2 in order to illustrate the preparation of financial statements for Kilmer Contractors will be employed again in this example.

AN ILLUSTRATION

In order to illustrate the recording process described above, we will again follow the activities of Kilmer Contractors, the small painting contractor described in Chapter 2, through May, the initial month of its operations. In this process we will review the procedures which are involved in:

1. The preparation of general journal entries.
2. Posting these general journal entries to the ledger.
3. The preparation of a trial balance before adjustment.
4. The preparation of adjusting journal entries.
5. Posting these adjusting entries to the ledger.
6. The preparation of the adjusted trial balance.
7. The preparation of closing entries.
8. Posting these closing entries to the ledger.
9. The preparation of the after-closing trial balance.
10. The preparation of the financial statements.

General Journal Entries

The transactions of Kilmer Contractors which occurred during the month of May 1976, would be recorded as follows:

May 1.   Bill Kilmer organized Kilmer Contractors and invested cash of $10,000 in the business.

This transaction is an investment of funds in a business by its owner. Cash held by the firm and the owner's equity account, capital, were both increased. It would be recorded as follows:

Cash 10,000
    Bill Kilmer, Capital.   10,000

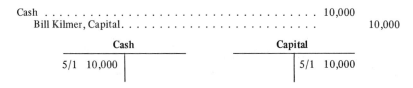

As indicated above, the increase in the asset cash would be recorded by a debit to the cash account and the corresponding increase in the investment by the owner would be recorded by a credit to the capital account. This entry illustrates the rule that increases in assets are recorded by debits and increases in equities are recorded by credits. Note that the basic accounting equation, $A = L + OE$, is in balance and the total debits are equal to the total credits. This will hold true for each of the transactions of the business as they are recorded.

May 2.   The Company purchased painting supplies, paying the $3,000 purchase price in cash.

This transaction represents an exchange of one asset for another. The asset supplies was increased while the asset cash was decreased. It would be recorded as follows:

Supplies 3,000
    Cash   3,000

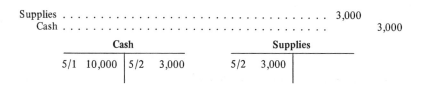

The increase in the asset supplies would be recorded by a debit to the supplies account while the cash outlay would be recorded by a credit to the cash account. This entry follows the rule that increases in assets are recorded by debits while decreases in assets are recorded by credits.

May 5.   Kilmer Contractors borrowed $2,000 from the Virginia National Bank.

This transaction is the receipt of an asset, cash, in exchange for a liability, the promise to pay a creditor at some future date. It reflects the promise of the business to repay $2,000 at a future date in order to have cash on hand and available for use at this time. It would be recorded by the following entry:

Cash 2,000
      Note Payable   2,000

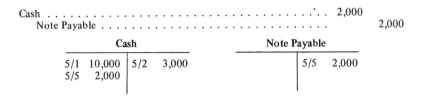

The increase in the asset cash is recorded by a debit to the cash account and the increase in the liability note payable is recorded by a credit to the note payable account. This transaction illustrates the rule that increases in assets are recorded by debits and increases in liabilities are recorded by credits.

May 10. Kilmer signed a contract whereby he agreed to paint two houses sometime during the next few weeks. The customer paid Kilmer the fee of $1,100 per house in advance.

The company has agreed to paint two houses at a future date and has received its fee now, before it has done the work. The receipt of the $2,200 increases cash and the liability, unearned fees, by the same amount. Unearned fees are not a liability in the sense that the company will be required to repay the money. Rather, this account represents an obligation on the part of Kilmer Contractors to render a service at some future date. This transaction would be recorded by the following entry:

Cash 2,200
      Unearned Fees   2,200

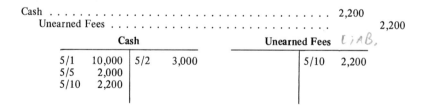

The increase in the asset cash would be recorded by a debit to the cash account while the increase in the liability unearned fees would be recorded by a credit to the unearned fees account. Again, this entry illustrates the rule that increases in assets are recorded by debits and increases in liabilities are recorded by credits.

May 12. Bill Kilmer, the owner, withdrew $1,000 from the business for his own personal use.

This transaction is a withdrawal of a portion of the owner's investment from the business. Cash and capital were both decreased by $1,000. It would be recorded as follows:

Withdrawals 1,000
    Cash   1,000

Cash				Withdrawals		
5/1	10,000	5/2	3,000	5/12	1,000	
5/5	2,000	5/12	1,000			
5/10	2,200					

The withdrawal of $1,000 in cash from the business by the owner would be recorded by a debit to the withdrawals account and a credit to the cash account. This entry illustrates the rule that decreases in equity accounts are recorded by debits and decreases in asset accounts are recorded by credits.

May 15. **Kilmer Contractors repaid $500 of the $2,000 it borrowed from the Virginia National Bank.**

This transaction is a reduction of both liabilities and assets. The business repaid $500 of the $2,000 it owed to the bank. Both cash and the note payable decreased by this amount. The following entry would be made:

Note Payable 500
    Cash   500

Cash				Note Payable		
5/1	10,000	5/2	3,000	5/15	500	5/5	2,000
5/5	2,000	5/12	1,000			
5/10	2,200	5/15	500			

The repayment of $500 to the bank would be recorded by a debit to the liability account note payable and a credit to the asset account cash. This entry illustrates the rule that decreases in liabilities are recorded by debits while decreases in assets are recorded by credits.

May 17. **Kilmer Contractors painted its first house and billed and collected a fee of $700 from the customer.**

This transaction indicates that the firm has begun to earn revenue. It is a sale of services for cash. Cash was received and the owner's equity of the business was increased by the amount of the revenue earned. It would be recorded by the following entry:

Cash 700
    Painting Fees   700

Cash				Painting Fees O.e. Acct.	
5/1	10,000	5/2	3,000	5/17	700
5/5	2,000	5/12	1,000		
5/10	2,200	5/15	500		
5/17	700				

The sale of services for cash would be recorded by a debit to the cash account and a credit to the revenue account painting fees. This entry illustrates the rule that increases in assets are recorded by debits and increases in revenues are recorded by credits.

May 19.   Kilmer Contractors painted a second house and billed (but did not collect) its fee of $900.

Again, this transaction records the revenue earned by the firm in painting a customer's house. Unlike the previous transaction, however, cash was not received. The customer was billed for the service rendered and will pay Kilmer Contractors at some future date. Accounts receivable have increased and owner's equity (revenue) has increased by $900, the fee charged for painting the house. This transaction illustrates the very important point that revenue is recorded as it is earned, not necessarily as cash is received. This concept reflects the *accrual* basis of accounting. The transaction would be recorded by the following entry:

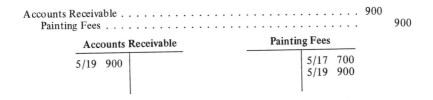

```
Accounts Receivable . . . . . . . . . . . . . . . . . . . . . . . . . .   900
    Painting Fees . . . . . . . . . . . . . . . . . . . . . . . . . .          900
```

Accounts Receivable		Painting Fees	
5/19 900			5/17 700
			5/19 900

This sale of services to a customer on a credit basis would be recorded by a debit to the asset accounts receivable and a credit to the revenue account, painting fees. Again, this transaction illustrates the rule that increases in assets are recorded by debits and increases in revenues are recorded by credits.

May 25.   Kilmer paid salaries of $400 to his employees.

Expenses of $400 were incurred and paid in cash. This transaction reduces both the cash balance and owner's equity. The reduction in owner's equity is due to the fact that an expense has been incurred, thereby reducing income. (Remember that revenues less expenses equals income.) The transaction would be recorded by the following entry:

```
Salaries . . . . . . . . . . . . . . . . . . . . . . . . . . . . . . . .   400
    Cash . . . . . . . . . . . . . . . . . . . . . . . . . . . . . . .           400
```

Cash				Salaries *ae, Acct,*	
5/1	10,000	5/2	3,000	5/25 400	
5/5	2,000	5/12	1,000		
5/10	2,200	5/15	500		
5/17	700	5/25	400		

The payment of salaries to employees would be recorded by a debit to the expense account, salaries, and a credit to the asset account, cash. This entry illustrates the rule that increases in expenses are recorded by debits and decreases in assets are recorded by credits.

Posting

The second step in the recording process would be to post each of the journal entries to the appropriate ledger accounts. Posting is the process of transferring the individual debits and credits of each entry to the appropriate account or accounts in the ledger. This step enables the accountant to summarize and group the transactions which occurred according to the individual accounts which they affect. For each transaction, the debit amount in the journal entry is posted by entering it on the debit side of the appropriate ledger account and each credit amount in the entry is posted by entering it on the credit side of the appropriate ledger account. This process was illustrated in the previous section on general journal entries. Recall that the initial transaction of Kilmer Contractors was as follows:

May 1.   Bill Kilmer organized Kilmer Contractors and invested cash of $10,000 in the business.

This transaction was recorded by the following general journal entry:

```
Cash  . . . . . . . . . . . . . . . . . . . . . . . . . . . . . . . . . . . . . . . . .  10,000
      Bill Kilmer, Capital. . . . . . . . . . . . . . . . . . . . . . . . . . . . .          10,000
```

It would be posted to the ledger as follows:

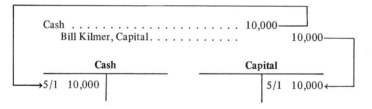

The debit to cash of $10,000 in the journal entry is posted to the debit side of the cash account in the general ledger and the credit to capital of $10,000 is posted to the credit side of the capital account in the general ledger. The date in the ledger accounts provides a reference back to the original source of the posting, the general journal. Usually, a page reference will also be provided by each entry in the journal and each account in the general ledger in order to facilitate the cross-referencing of transactions.

Each of the transactions of the Kilmer Company would be posted in this manner. In our example, the transactions journalized in the previous section are posted to the "T" accounts included in Illustration 3–1. The dates of the transactions appear by each amount and are included for reference purposes.

Illustration 3–1

Cash				Accounts Receivable			Supplies		
5/1	10,000	5/2	3,000	5/19	900		5/2	3,000	
5/5	2,000	5/12	1,000						
5/10	2,200	5/15	500						
5/17	700	5/25	400		900			3,000	
	10,000								

Note Payable				Unearned Fees			Capital		
5/15	500	5/5	2,000		5/10	2,200		5/1	10,000
			1,500			2,200			10,000

Withdrawals			Painting Fees		
5/12	1,000			5/17	700
				5/19	900
	1,000				1,600

Salaries		
5/25	400	
	400	

Trial Balance

After all of the transactions which were initially recorded in the general journal have been posted to the general ledger, the next step in the accounting process would be to prepare a trial balance. A trial balance is simply a listing of all of the accounts included in the general ledger along with the balance, debit or credit, of each account. The purpose of a trial balance is simply to prove the equality of the debits and credits and to "catch" or detect any obvious errors which may have occurred in either the recording or the posting process. The reader should note, however, that even if the total of the debits in the trial balance is equal to the total of the credits, this only proves that the accounts are "in balance"; it does not indicate that errors have not been made. (For example, a posting could have been made to the wrong account.)

The trial balance of Kilmer Contractors at May 31, 1976, before adjustments would be as follows:

Illustration 3–2
KILMER CONTRACTORS
Trial Balance Before Adjustment
May 31, 1976

tr.iAl BAlANcE

	Debit	Credit
Cash	$10,000	
Accounts receivable	900	
Supplies	3,000	
Note payable		$ 1,500
Unearned fees		2,200
Capital		10,000
Withdrawals	1,000	
Painting fees		1,600
Salaries	400	
Total	$15,300	$15,300

Adjusting Entries

As previously indicated, the accrual basis of accounting requires that revenues be recorded as they are earned and expenses be recorded as they are incurred. This procedure is followed without regard to either the receipt or disbursement of cash. At the end of any period, then, there will usually be transactions which are still in the process of completion or which have occurred but have not yet been recorded. These transactions require adjusting entries. In the case of Kilmer Contractors, adjustments are required for: (1) the revenue which was earned by painting one of the two houses contracted for on May 10, and (2) the painting supplies which were used during the month of May. These adjustments, referred to as adjusting entries, would be recorded in the accounts by the general journal entries presented below.

May 31. Kilmer Contractors painted one of the two houses contracted for on May 10.

This adjustment records the partial satisfaction of a non-cash liability by the rendering of services (that is, painting one of the two houses) and the earning of income. It would be recorded by the following journal entry:

Unearned Fees. 1,100
    Painting Fees 1,100

Unearned Fees		Painting Fees	
5/31 1,100	5/10 2,200	5/17	700
		5/19	900
		5/31	1,100

Recall that on May 10 Kilmer signed a contract whereby he agreed to paint two houses at a future date and received his fee of $1,100 per house in advance. No income was earned at the point the contract was signed and the cash received because no work had been done at that time. Kilmer Contractors had an obligation to paint the two houses at a future date. This was a liability to perform services, which was reflected as unearned fees. Now, at the end of May, one of the two houses contracted for has been painted and that portion of the income has been earned. The liability, unearned fees, has been reduced by $1,100 and the income for May has been increased by the same amount. These facts require that the financial statements be adjusted in order to reflect the current status of the contract. Again, this transaction emphasizes the fact that income is recorded as it is earned, *not* as cash is received.

The decrease of $1,100 in the liability, unearned fees, would be recorded by a debit to the unearned fees account and the increase in the revenue, painting fees, would be recorded by a credit to the painting fees account. This adjusting entry illustrates the rule that decreases in liabilities are recorded by debits and increases in revenues are recorded by credits.

May 31.   The unused painting supplies on hand at this date had an original cost of $2,000.

The facts of this transaction indicate that an expense has been incurred during the month which has not yet been recorded in the accounts. The following adjusting entry would be required at May 31:

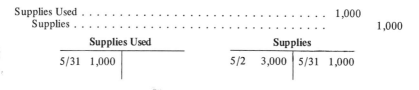

Supplies Used 1,000
  Supplies   1,000

Supplies Used		Supplies	
5/31 1,000		5/2 3,000	5/31 1,000

During May, Kilmer Contractors used supplies that had an original cost of $1,000. This amount was determined by subtracting the $2,000 cost of the supplies which were still on hand at May 31 from the $3,000 total cost of supplies that were available for use (that is, the supplies on hand at the beginning of the month plus the supplies purchased during the month). As in the previous May 31 transaction, an adjusting entry was required. The asset, supplies, was decreased by $1,000 (the cost of the supplies used), from $3,000 (the total supplies available for use during the month of May) to $2,000 (the cost of supplies still on hand at May 31). This transaction reflects the fact that expenses are recorded when incurred or used rather than when cash is disbursed.

The increase in the supplies used expense would be recorded by a debit to the supplies used account. The decrease in the asset, supplies, would be recorded by a credit to the supplies account. This adjusting entry illustrates the rule that increases in expenses are recorded by debits and decreases in assets are recorded by credits.

After these two journal entries have been made, all of the transactions of Kilmer Contractors which occurred during the month of May have been recorded in the accounts.

Posting the Adjusting Entries

The adjusting entries would then be posted to the ledger in the same manner as were the regular journal entries. This has been done in Illustration 3–3 below. Again, the dates of the transactions are included for the use of the reader for purposes of reference. (Note that the two adjusting entries are dated May 31.)

Illustration 3–3

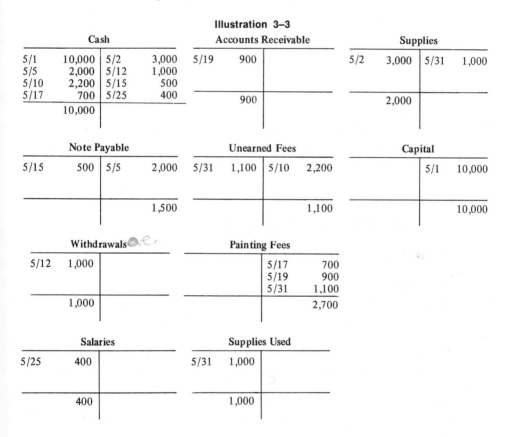

Cash			
5/1	10,000	5/2	3,000
5/5	2,000	5/12	1,000
5/10	2,200	5/15	500
5/17	700	5/25	400
	10,000		

Accounts Receivable			
5/19	900		
	900		

Supplies			
5/2	3,000	5/31	1,000
	2,000		

Note Payable			
5/15	500	5/5	2,000
			1,500

Unearned Fees			
5/31	1,100	5/10	2,200
			1,100

Capital			
		5/1	10,000
			10,000

Withdrawals			
5/12	1,000		
	1,000		

Painting Fees			
		5/17	700
		5/19	900
		5/31	1,100
			2,700

Salaries			
5/25	400		
	400		

Supplies Used			
5/31	1,000		
	1,000		

Trial Balance After Adjustment

The next step in the recording process would be the preparation of a trial balance *after* adjustment. This trial balance is simply the trial balance which was prepared after the adjusting entries were made and posted to the general ledger. The trial balance after adjustment for Kilmer Contractors is presented in Illustration 3–4 below.

Illustration 3–4
KILMER CONTRACTORS
Trial Balance After Adjustment
May 31, 1976

	Debit	Credit
Cash	$10,000	
Accounts receivable	900	
Supplies	2,000	
Note payable		$ 1,500
Unearned fees		1,100
Capital		10,000
Withdrawals	1,000	
Painting fees		2,700
Salaries	400	
Supplies used	1,000	
Totals	$15,300	$15,300

Again, the only difference between the trial balance above and the trial balance before adjustment presented in Illustration 3–2 is the inclusion of the effect of the adjusting entries which were made.

Closing Entries

The purpose of closing entries is to close out the temporary accounts (revenues, expenses, and withdrawals) into the owner's equity (capital) account. This process is facilitated by the introduction of a temporary account created solely for the closing process. This account is known as the *income summary account* and is used to collect or summarize all of the revenues and expenses of the firm in a single account which is then, in turn, closed to the capital account (or the retained earnings account for a corporation).

The purpose of the closing process is to systematically reduce all of the balances in the temporary accounts to a zero balance at the end of the accounting period. This means that at the beginning of the next period all revenues, expenses, and drawing accounts will have a zero balance so that these accounts can again be used in order to record the results of operations of that period.

The closing process is accomplished by the preparation of journal entries known as closing entries. These entries are recorded in the general journal and posted to the ledger in the same manner as all other transactions are processed.

We will now illustrate the closing process for Kilmer Contractors. The journal entries which are required to close out the revenue and expense accounts would be made at the end of the month of May, the accounting period used in this illustration. Referring back to the trial balance after adjustment for Kilmer Contractors (Illustration 3–4) the temporary accounts were as follows:

	Balance	
	Debit	*Credit*
Withdrawals	$1,000	
Painting fees		$2,700
Salaries	400	
Supplies used	1,000	

The entry to close out the revenue account would be:

May 31. Painting Fees 2,700
              Income Summary.   2,700

Painting Fees				Income Summary		
		5/17	700		5/31	2,700
		5/19	900			
		5/31	1,100			
5/31	2,700		2,700			
			0			

Revenue accounts have credit balances. Therefore, the entry which is required in order to close out the balance in a revenue account consists of a debit to the revenue account for the total revenue for the period and a credit to the income summary account for the same amount. This entry closes out (i.e.—brings the account balance to zero) and revenue account and transfers the total for the period to the credit side of the income summary account.

In our illustration, the painting fees account is now closed and has a zero balance, and the $2,700 revenue from painting fees has been transferred to the credit side of the income summary account.

The two expense accounts would be closed out by the following entry:

May 31. Income Summary 1,400
              Salaries.   400
              Supplies Used   1,000

Salaries				Supplies Used				Income Summary			
5/25	400			5/31	1,000			5/31	1,400	5/31	2,700
	400	5/31	400		1,000	5/31	1,000				
	0				0						

Expense accounts have debit balances. Therefore, the entry which is required in order to close out the balance in an expense account credits the account for the total expense for the period and debits the income summary account for this amount. This closing entry reduces the expense account balance to zero and transfers the expense for the period to the debit side of the income summary account.

In our example, both the salaries and the supplies used expense accounts are now closed out and the total of these two accounts ($400 + $1,000) which is the total expense for the period has been transferred to the debit side of the income summary account.

The balance in the income summary account ($2,700 − $1,400 = $1,300) is then transferred to Kilmer's capital account by the following closing entry:

May 31. Income Summary. 1,300
            Capital.   1,300

Income Summary				Capital		
5/31	1,400	5/31	2,700		5/1	10,000
5/31	1,300		1,300		5/31	1,300
			0			

As indicated above, all revenue and expense accounts are closed to the income summary account. Therefore, the credit side of the income summary account will include the total revenue for the period while the debit side of the account will include the total expenses. The account balance will be the income or loss of the business for the period. If the total of the credits (revenues) in the income summary account exceeds the total of the debits (expenses), revenues are greater than expenses and the difference is the income for the period. On the other hand, if the total of the credits (revenues) is less than the total of the debits (expenses), expenses exceed revenues and the difference is the loss for the period. In either case the balance in the income summary account after all of the revenue and expense accounts have been closed is transferred to the capital account.

In the Kilmer Contractors example the balance in the income summary account, a credit of $1,300 (revenues of $2,700 less expenses of $1,400), was closed out and the income for the period was transferred to the capital account.

As a final step in the closing process the balance in any drawing or withdrawals account is closed out to owner's equity. In the Kilmer Contractors illustration this step would be to close the balance in the withdrawals account directly to capital.

Withdrawals made by the owner do not pass through the income summary

May 31.   Capital   1,000
           Withdrawals   1,000

Withdrawals				Capital		
5/12	1,000			5/31	1,000	5/1	10,000
	1,000	5/31	1,000			5/31	1,300
	0						

account since they are not an expense of the period and therefore do not enter into the determination of income. Withdrawal or drawing accounts have debit balances. Therefore, the closing entry which is required to close withdrawals credits the withdrawal account and debits the capital account for the drawings made by the owner during the period.

In the Kilmer Contractors example, the withdrawals of $1,000 are closed out and transferred to the capital account as a reduction of the end-of-period capital balance.

The closing process can be depicted graphically as follows:

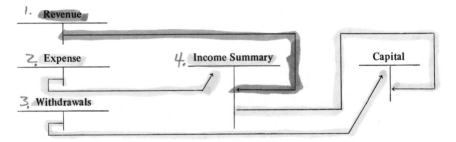

In terms of the specific accounts which were used in the Kilmer Contractors illustration, the closing process is shown in Illustration 3–5, after all of the closing entries are posted to the accounts.

After-Closing Trial Balance

After all of the temporary accounts have been closed out, a trial balance, referred to as an after-closing trial balance, may be prepared as a test of the equality of the total debits and credits. The after-closing trial balance of Kilmer Contractors is presented in Illustration 3–6 on page 68. Since all of the temporary accounts have been closed out, the after-closing trial balance includes only the permanent or balance sheet accounts.

FINANCIAL STATEMENTS

After all of the adjusting and closing entries have been prepared and made and the posting process has been completed, the general ledger ac-

Illustration 3–5

Painting Fees	
(c) 2,700	2,700
	0

2, Salaries			4, Income Summary	
400	(c) 400		(c) 1,400	(c) 2,700
			(c) 1,300	
0				0

2, Supplies Used			5, Capital	
1,000	(c) 1,000		(c) 1,000	10,000
				(c) 1,300
0				10,300

3. Withdrawals	
1,000	(c) 1,000
0	

(c) designates closing entry.

After Closing Expence + Income Accts

Illustration 3–6

KILMER CONTRACTORS
After-Closing Trial Balance
May 31, 1976

Trial Balance

	Debits	Credits
Cash	$10,000	
Accounts receivable.	900	
Supplies	2,000	
Note payable		$ 1,500
Unearned fees		1,100
Capital		10,300
	$12,900	$12,900

count balances will be up to date as of the end of the period. The information regarding the assets, liabilities, capital, revenues, and expenses included in the general ledger will be used as a basis for preparing the financial statements. Asset, liability, and capital balances as of the end of the period will be taken from the general ledger accounts and used to prepare the balance sheet or statement of financial position. As previously indicated, the after-closing trial balance may be used to check the accuracy of the balance sheet since it includes all permanent accounts which appear in the balance sheet.

The revenues and expenses for the period will also be taken from the general ledger and used to prepare the income statement. The trial balance before adjustment and the detailed amounts which are included in the income summary account may be used as a check on the accuracy of the income statement since both of these sources include the details of the revenues and expenses for the period.

The statement of capital will also be prepared using the capital account from the general ledger as a source. The financial statements for Kilmer Contractors for the month of May are included in Illustrations 3–7, 3–8, and 3–9.

$A = L + O.E.$

Illustration 3–7

KILMER CONTRACTORS
Balance Sheet
May 31, 1976

ASSETS		LIABILITIES AND OWNER'S EQUITY	
Cash	$10,000	Note Payable	$ 1,500
Accounts Receivable	900	Unearned Fees	1,100
Supplies	2,000	Capital	10,300
	$12,900		$12,900

$P = Income$

$Rev. - EXP.$

Illustration 3–8

KILMER CONTRACTORS
Income Statement
For the Month Ending May 31, 1976

Revenue from painting services		$2,700
Supplies Used	$1,000	
Salaries	400	
Total Expenses		1,400
Income		$1,300

At this time, several points should be noted by the reader in review. First, the general journal entries were prepared as the transactions occurred. These entries represent a chronological record of the transactions

Illustration 3–9

KILMER CONTRACTORS
Statement of Capital
For the Month Ending May 31, 1976

Capital at May 1, 1976.		$ –0–
Add:		
Investment.	$10,000	
Income for May.	1,300	11,300
Deduct:		
Withdrawal		(1,000)
Capital at May 31, 1976		$10,300

of the company which took place during the month of May. These journal entries were then posted to the ledger accounts. At the end of the month, a trial balance was prepared and the transactions and the status of the company at that point in time were reviewed. All adjustments which were necessary to bring the accounts up to date were made.

The next step in the process was the preparation of a trial balance after adjustment. Again, it is important to note that any trial balance only proves the equality of the totals of the debits and the credits; it gives no other assurance as to the absence of errors.

Entries were then prepared to "close-out" all temporary accounts, the revenues, expenses, and withdrawals for the period. These are the only accounts closed. The permanent accounts, assets, liabilities, and capital, which appear in the balance sheet, are not closed out. The closing entries summarize the balances of the revenue and expense accounts in an income summary account.[1] The balance in the withdrawals account is then closed out to the capital account. The closing entries were then posted to the ledger and the after-closing trial balance and then the financial statements were prepared.

AN OVERVIEW

This completes our overview of the recording process. The reader may find it helpful at this point to compare the process which is described in this chapter to the analysis by transaction which was presented in Chapter 2. At the same time, remember that the manual process described in this chapter was undertaken and is adequate for purposes of explanation. In larger firms, much of the recording process will be accomplished by the

---

[1] The reader will note that the income summary is, in fact, a duplication of the income statement itself. That is, the credits to the summary are the revenues for the period and the debits are the expenses for the period. The difference, or balancing figure, is, of course, the income (or loss) for the period.

use of mechanical or electronic data processing equipment. Even in smaller firms, with essentially manual recordkeeping, time saving devices such as the mechanical systems and special journals described in Chapter 6 will be used to reduce the time devoted to recordkeeping by a significant amount. In either case, however, the basic principles described in this chapter are still applicable.

This chapter presented a summary of the recording process. The steps involved in this process are as follows:

1. Recording transactions with journal entries.
2. Posting journal entries to the ledger.
3. Preparing a trial balance before adjustment.
4. Preparing adjusting journal entries.
5. Posting adjusting entries to the ledger.
6. Preparing an adjusted trial balance.
   Preparing closing journal entries.
8. Posting closing entries to the ledger.
9. Preparing an after-closing trial balance.
10. Preparing financial statements.

KEY DEFINITIONS

Account An account is a place or means of summarizing all of the transactions that affect a particular asset, liability, equity, revenue, or expense item.

Adjusting entries At the end of an accounting period, adjusting entries record the transactions which are in process or have been completed but not yet recorded. These entries are necessary in order to record revenues when they are earned and expenses when they are incurred, and not when cash is received or paid. This is in accordance with the accrual concept of accounting.

Closing entries The purpose of closing entries is to close out or transfer the balances in the temporary accounts (revenues, expenses, and withdrawals) into the capital account.

Credit "Credit" is the term used to identify the right-hand side of an account. A credit decreases an asset and increases a liability, equity, or revenue account.

Debit "Debit" is the term used to describe the left-hand side of an account. By debiting an asset or expense account, the account is increased and by debiting a liability or equity account, the account is decreased.

Double-entry method This method requires that for every transaction recorded, the total dollar amount of debits must be equal to the total dollar amount of the credits.

General journal entry The general journal entry is a means of recording the transactions of a firm chronologically in terms of debits and credits.

General ledger   The general ledger is a compilation of all the accounts of a firm and their balances.

Posting   Posting to ledger accounts is the process of transferring the information from the general journal to the individual accounts of the general ledger. This enables the accountant to review and summarize all changes in the accounts.

Trial balance   The trial balance is a listing of all the accounts in the general ledger. If the accounts are "in balance," the total of the accounts with debit balances will equal the total of those with credit balances. The trial balance only indicates that the accounts are in balance. It does not prove that errors have not been made in the recording process.

QUESTIONS

1.   What is the purpose of the double-entry system of recording business transactions?
2.   Explain the terms "debit" and "credit." What effect does each of these have on asset and liability accounts?
3.   What is the general rule of the double-entry system?
4.   Describe a general journal entry.
5.   What is a T-account?
6.   What is "posting"?
7.   What is the purpose of a trial balance?
8.   What concept of accounting requires adjusting entries? Explain.
9.   What type of accounts do closing entries affect? Why are these accounts closed?

EXERCISES

3–1   The first nine transactions of a newly formed business, Smart Company, appear in the T-accounts below. For each set of debits and credits, explain the nature of the transaction. Each entry is designated by the small letters to the left of the amount.

Cash		Accounts Receivable		Equipment	
(a) 10,000	(c) 2,000	(d) 6,000	(g) 2,000	(b) 3,000	
(g) 2,000	(e) 4,000				
(i) 2,500	(f) 1,000				
	(h) 1,500				

Accounts Payable		Unearned Fees	
(f) 1,000	(b) 3,000		(i) 2,500

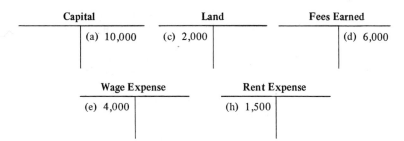

Capital		Land		Fees Earned	
	(a) 10,000	(c) 2,000			(d) 6,000

Wage Expense		Rent Expense	
(e) 4,000		(h) 1,500	

3–2   Assume that the ledger accounts given in Exercise 3–1 are for the Smart Company as of December 31, 1975. Prepare a trial balance for Smart Company as of that date.

3–3   Prepare the closing entries, the income statement for 1975, and the balance sheet as of December 31, 1975, for the Smart Company assuming the data given in Exercise 3–1.

3–4   Bob Feller opened a driving range and the following transactions took place in July, 1975:

July 1   The owner invested $10,000 cash in the business.
      5   Purchased fixed assets for $5,000; made a cash down payment of $2,000 and signed a 60 day note for the balance.
     10   The total revenue for the month was $1,500; $1,200 in cash was collected and the balance was owed on account by customers.
     15   The total expenses for the month were $1,100; $900 was paid in cash and the balance was owed on account.
     25   The owner withdrew $100 in cash.

Prepare the journal entries to record these transactions and enter the debits and credits in T accounts.

3–5   After recording and posting the transactions from Exercise 4, prepare a trial balance for Feller Company as of July 31, 1975.

PROBLEMS

Series A

3A–1   Presented below are the transactions of the Home Finder Realty Company for the month of May, 1975.

May 1   The owner invested $20,000 cash in the business.
     3   Purchased office equipment for $1,800 on account.
     5   Purchased a car for $3,000, giving $1,000 in cash and a note payable of $2,000.
    10   Purchased $500 of office supplies on account.
    15   Paid $300 office rent for the month of May.
    16   Paid for office supplies purchased on May 10.

May 18   Received a bill for $200 for radio advertising.

20   Earned and collected $1,500 commission for the sale of a house.

21   Paid bill for advertising that was received on May 18.

23   Earned but did not collect an $800 commission.

25   Paid salaries of $400.

27   Received payment in full from customer of May 23.

29   Paid the telephone bill, $50.

Prepare the general journal entries that would be required to record the above transactions.

3A–2   On September 1, 1975 Mark Walls, a bookkeeper, organized a bookkeeping service business. The following events occurred during September.

Sept. 1   Walls withdrew $10,000 from his personal savings and invested this amount in the business.

2   Paid September rent of $250.

4   Purchased office furniture for $2,000 on account.

6   Received and paid a bill for $200 for advertising in the local newspaper.

9   Received cash of $1,400 as payment for services to customers.

15   Paid the $300 salary of a part-time secretary.

17   Paid for office furniture purchased on account.

18   Purchased $150 of office supplies on account.

20   Received a utilities bill for $75.

21   Completed $600 of services on credit for customers.

23   Collected $200 of receivables for credit services provided.

27   Walls withdrew $600 from the business.

Required:

1. Prepare the general journal entries to record the above transactions.
2. Post the above journal entries to T-accounts.
3. Prepare a trial balance as of the end of September.

3A–3   The following transactions involving the Mantle Company occurred during the month of July:

July 1   Mantle organized the company, contributing $1,000 as an initial investment.

3   Purchased office supplies paying $100 in cash.

6   Performed services for his first customer and collected $500 in cash.

9   Performed services for another customer and agreed to accept his payment of $700 later in the month.

13   Contracted to perform certain services for a third customer and received the full payment of $1,000 in advance.

18   Received the payment from the customer for whom services were performed on July 9.

July 24   Paid the following operating items:

Salaries for July.	$250
Office rent for July and August.	300
Other July expense	75

(Mantle will prepare financial statements at the end of July.)

31   Noted that exactly one-fourth of the services contracted for on the thirteenth by a customer had been performed. Counted the office supplies on hand and ascertained that supplies with an original cost of $65 were still on hand.

Required:

1. Record the above transactions with general journal entries.
2. Post the journal entries by entering debits and credits in T-accounts.
3. Prepare a trial balance as of July 31, 1975.

3A–4 Below is the trial balance *after adjustment* of the Nittany Lion Company as of October 31, 1975:

Cash	$10,000	
Accounts receivable.	4,000	
Notes receivable.	2,500	
Supplies	1,000	
Accounts payable		$ 4,500
Note payable.		3,000
Unearned income		1,500
Capital		7,500
Withdrawals	500	
Revenues.		3,000
Expenses	1,500	
	$19,500	$19,500

Required:

1. Prepare the entries which are necessary to close the accounts as of October 31, 1975.
2. Prepare the following statements:
   a. Balance sheet
   b. Income statement
   c. Statement of capital

3A–5 Certain data relating to River Corporation are presented below: Trial balance data as of June 30, 1975.

Advertising expense.	$ 75
Capital	3,195
Cash	895
Commissions earned	1,900
Commissions receivable	950
Interest earned	5
Land	2,000
Mercantile Company bonds	1,000
Notes payable	700
Office rent	80
Salaries expense	800

Adjusted trial balance data as of June 30, 1975.

Accrued interest receivable	5
Accrued interest payable	7
Accrued rent receivable	55
Accrued salaries payable	100
Advertising expense	75
Capital	3,195
Cash	895
Commissions earned	1,960
Commissions receivable	1,010
Interest earned	10
Interest expense	7
Land	2,000
Mercantile Company bonds	1,000
Notes payable	700
Office rent	80
Rent earned	55
Salaries expense	900

Compare the unadjusted and adjusted account balances and prepare the adjusting journal entries made by River Corporation as of June 30, 1975. Also prepare the closing entries as of June 30, 1975. (No withdrawals were made during the period ending June 30, 1975.)

3A–6   The following information has been developed by the bookkeeper of the Sneed Company. It relates to the company's operations for 1975.

Cash receipts
From customers $46,100
Cash disbursements
For expenses 10,600

Account balances as of December 31	*1974*	*1975*
Accounts receivable from customers, (all collectible)	$10,400	$9,600
Accrued expenses payable	1,900	1,600

Required:

Prepare the company's income statement for the year ended December 31, 1975.

3A–7   On June 30, 1975, the Repertory Theater Co. was organized. On that date the owners invested $25,000 in cash and the company manager signed a 10-year lease on a building. The lease called for a monthly rental of $4,000. The first payment under the lease was made immediately; all future rentals were to be paid on the last day of each month. The theater capacity was 800 seats which were to be sold for $3 at each performance. A 3-year comprehensive insurance policy was paid for on July 1, 1975, at a cost of $600.

The theater opened on August 1, 1975. There were 8 performances each week (each evening Monday through Saturday and matinees on Wednesday and Saturday). Through December 31, 1975, there had been exactly 22 full weeks of performances. The player companies who were engaged to perform received 40 percent of the gate with settlement to be made after each Saturday evening performance for the 8 performances of the week then ending. At the beginning of the 19th week of business a smash hit opened. This show played to capacity crowds and was sold out through the first 7 weeks of 1976.

A refreshment counter in the lobby dispensed soft drinks, candy, etc., and proved to be most lucrative. This was the only source of revenue other than ticket sales. Refreshments with an invoice cost of $19,000 had been purchased during 1975. The inventory of refreshments on hand at December 31, 1975, had an invoice price of $2,200. All purchases had been paid for except one made on December 27, 1975, at a cost of $1,200.

Prior to the opening of the smash hit, the theater enjoyed good success, averaging exactly 75 percent of capacity for all performances. All receipts during the year had been deposited intact and deposit slips showed a total of $517,400 deposited through December 31, 1975.

Salaries for ushers, ticket-takers, the manager, and other employees were paid after each Friday evening performance for work done through that performance. These salaries averaged $900 per week. Advertising had been run in local newspapers and $2,900 had been paid for as of December 31, 1975. The bill for ads run during the last week of 1975 had not been received by December 31, but based upon knowledge of the rates it was estimated that it would be $150. Utilities bills through December 31 totaled $2,700 and had been paid.

There were no liabilities at December 31, 1975, other than those which have been specifically mentioned or alluded to above. No additional investments by the owners had been made and no withdrawals were made.

Required:

1. A statement of financial position as of December 31, 1975.
2. An income statement for the six months ended December 31, 1975.

PROBLEMS

Series B

3B–1 Presented below are the transactions of the Goodson Realty Company for the month of June, 1975.

June 2 The owner invested $15,000 cash in the business.
     5 Purchased office furniture for $1,500 cash.
     7 Paid $300 in cash for June rent.
     9 Office supplies of $200 were purchased on account.
    10 Received and paid a bill for $300 for advertising in a local newspaper during June.

June 13   Paid wages of $200 in cash for the month of June.

15   Received a cash advance of $500 from a customer for services to be rendered during July.

16   Sold a house and collected $800 commission.

17   Sold a house and will collect the $600 commission in July.

21   The owner withdrew $500 from the business.

23   Received and paid the June telephone bill for $100.

25   Paid for office supplies purchased on June 9.

27   Paid the utilities bill for the month, $35.

Prepare the general journal entries necessary to record the above transactions.

3B-2   On August 1, 1975 Bill King began operating a bicycle repair shop. The transactions of the business during the month of August were as follows:

Aug. 2   King began the business by investing $15,000 in cash and repair equipment with a fair value of $2,000.

4   Purchased land for $4,000 cash.

7   Purchased a building for $20,000. The terms of the purchase required a cash payment of $5,000 and the issuance of a note payable for $15,000.

11   Purchased supplies on account in the amount of $700.

13   Completed repair work for customers and collected $700 cash.

15   Paid the $400 salary of an employee.

17   Completed repair work of $500 on credit.

19   Paid for supplies purchased on account.

21   Withdrew $300 from the business to be used for personal expenses.

25   Received $500 cash for repair work previously completed.

27   Paid a $50 utility bill.

30   Made first payment of $1,000 on the note payable.

Required:

1.   Prepare the general journal entries to record each of the above transactions.

2.   Post the above journal entries to T-accounts.

3.   Prepare a trial balance as of the end of August.

3B-3   Bea Toven has just begun the operation of a piano lesson studio. During the month of June she completed the following transactions:

June 1   Toven invested $30,000 cash in the business.

2   The business acquired land for $5,000 and a building for $10,000 in cash.

3   The business purchased equipment for $6,000 on account.

4   Supplies of $4,000 were purchased on account.

7   Fees of $7,000 were received for services to be performed at a later date.

June 9 Services of $5,000 were provided on credit.
21 Completed services of $3,000—the fee had been collected
15 Paid one-half of the accounts payable.
in advance.
25 Toven withdrew $1,000 cash from the business.
30 Paid wages of $3,000 in cash.
30 It was determined that $1,000 of supplies remained on hand.

Required:

1. Record the above transactions with general journal entries.
2. Post the journal entries to the ledger by entering the debits and credits in the T-accounts.
3. Prepare a trial balance as of June 30.

3B–4 Below are the balances of the Gobbler Company as of November 30, 1975:

Accounts receivable.	$ 1,800
Capital	20,000
Cash	19,800
Note payable	3,000
Painting fees.	5,400
Salaries.	1,000
Supplies	4,000
Supplies used	2,000
Unearned income	2,200
Withdrawals	2,000

Required:

1. Prepare the necessary entries to close the temporary accounts at November 30, 1975.
2. Prepare a balance sheet, income statement, and statement of capital as of November 30, 1975.

3B–5 Below are given the *total debits and total credits* for the year (which include beginning-of-the-year balances) in certain accounts of the Ace Company, *after the closing entries have been posted to the accounts* as of December 31, 1975.

	Debits	Credits
Advertising expense.	$ 210	$ 210
Salaries expense.	700	700
Telephone expense	48	48
Prepaid insurance	90	15
Insurance expense.	15	15
Fees earned	1,880	1,880
Drawings.	600	600
Income summary	1,880	1,880
Accounts receivable.	2,330	2,330
Capital	600	19,257

Required:

1. Reconstruct the December 31, 1975, *closing entries* (in general journal form).

3B–6 The Maryland Wholesale Company has kept no formal books of accounts. The owner has, however, made up a statement of assets and liabilities at the end of each year. For 1975 and 1976, a portion of this statement appears as follows, as of December 31:

	1975	1976
Cash	$3,000	$ 5,000
Accounts receivable.	7,000	5,000
Accounts payable for expenses	8,000	10,000

An analysis of the checkbook for 1976 shows (1) deposits of all amounts received from customers totaling $50,000 and (2) cash payments to creditors for expenses amounting to $33,000.

Required:

Prepare the company's income statement for the year ended December 31, 1976.

4

The Worksheet and Adjustments

THE WORKSHEET

MOST BUSINESSES prepare annual reports for the use of their owners, creditors, and other interested parties. In addition to these reports, many companies also provide interim reports which cover periods of less than a year
such as a month or a quarter. In order to prepare financial statements
at a date other than at the end of the accounting period, a worksheet is
often used. The use of a worksheet avoids the necessity of many of the
detailed procedures which are normally required in the adjustment and
closing process. A worksheet summarizes the trial balance, adjusting entries, and, in effect, closing entries in one simple document. It facilitates
the preparation of interim financial statements without recording the adjusting entries in the accounts, if the accountant so desires. A worksheet
may also be prepared and used in conjunction with the regular year-end
closing process. Even if the accountant intends to record adjusting and
closing entries in the accounts, as would be the case at year-end, a worksheet may still be used as a valuable check on the recording process.

An understanding of the worksheet is also important for quite a different
reason; it provides an excellent perspective as to the preparation of the
income statement, statement of capital, and balance sheet. In short, a critical review and understanding of the worksheet will provide the reader with
an excellent overview of the entire reporting process and is particularly
useful in developing an understanding of the adjusting and closing process
as well as the preparation of the basic financial statements. The worksheet,
then, is a tool which is useful in both a practical and a conceptual sense.

AN ILLUSTRATION

In order to illustrate the preparation of a worksheet we will return again to the Kilmer Contractors example used in the previous chapters. Note that a trial balance before adjustment as of May 31, 1976, appears in the first two columns of the worksheet in Illustration 4–1 on page 83.[1] This trial balance before adjustment is the starting point in the preparation of a worksheet. The steps which are involved in the preparation of a worksheet are described below and depicted in Illustrations 4–1 through 4–7.

Step 1. As indicated above, the initial step in the preparation of the worksheet is to insert the trial balance before adjustment in the first two columns of the worksheet. This has been done in Illustration 4–1. Note that the worksheet includes six pairs of columns with each set divided into a debit and credit column.

Step 2. This step involves recording the adjusting journal entries in the second set of columns of the worksheet, the adjustment columns. Recall that the adjusting entries which were required for Kilmer Contractors included recording: (*a*) the revenue which was earned from painting one of the two houses contracted for on May 10; and (*b*) the painting supplies which were used during the month of May. The Company received an advance payment of $2,200 from one of its customers on May 10 for the painting of two houses at some future date. At the end of May, Kilmer had painted one of the two houses and therefore half of the $2,200 had been earned but not recorded in the accounts as earned revenue. On May 2, Kilmer had purchased painting supplies at a cost of $3,000. At May 31, the unused painting supplies on hand had an original cost of $2,000 indicating that supplies with a cost of $1,000 (supplies costing $3,000 originally purchased less the supplies still on hand with an original cost of $2,000) had been used during the month of May and should therefore be charged to expense. The adjusting entries required in order to record these events have been made and recorded in the second set of columns of Illustration 4–2. Accounts which are affected by the adjusting entries but which do not appear in the trial balance before adjustment must be added below the original listing of accounts in the worksheet. For example, in adjustment (*b*) there was no account for supplies used in the trial balance before adjustment. Therefore, the account title "supplies used" was entered on the worksheet below the original trial balance accounts.

For purposes of reference, the debit and the credit amounts of each entry have been associated with an identifying letter to the left of each amount. For example, note that the debit to unearned fees and the related credit to painting fees recorded in the adjustments columns are labeled with the identifying letter (*a*). This notation indicates that this particular

---

[1] This trial balance is the one that appeared in Illustration 3–2 of Chapter 3.

Illustration 4–1

KILMER CONTRACTORS
Worksheet
For the Month Ended May 31, 1975

	Trial Balance Before Adjustments		Adjustments		Trial Balance After Adjustments		Income Statement		Statement of Capital		Balance Sheet	
Cash	10,000											
Accounts receivable . . .	900											
Supplies	3,000											
Notes payable.		1,500										
Unearned fees.		2,200										
Capital.		10,000										
Withdrawals.	1,000											
Painting fees		1,600										
Salaries	400											
	15,300	15,300										

Illustration 4–2

KILMER CONTRACTORS
Worksheet
For the Month Ended May 31, 1975

	Trial Balance Before Adjustments		Adjustments		Trial Balance After Adjustments		Income Statement		Statement of Capital		Balance Sheet	
Cash	10,000											
Accounts receivable . . .	900											
Supplies	3,000			(b)1,000								
Notes payable.		1,500										
Unearned fees.		2,200	(a)1,100									
Capital.		10,000										
Withdrawals.	1,000											
Painting fees		1,600		(a)1,100								
Salaries	400		(b)1,000									
Supplies used												
	15,300	15,300	2,100	2,100								

Key to Adjustments:
(a) To record revenue from one of the two houses contracted for on May 10.
(b) To record the cost of the supplies used during the month of May.

debit and credit represents a single journal entry. Also observe that each adjusting journal entry is explained at the bottom of the worksheet with the same notation used as a reference.

Step 3. The third step in the worksheet process is the preparation of an adjusted trial balance. The adjusted trial balance is completed by combining the trial balance before adjustment (in the first two columns of the worksheet) with the related adjustments which were made in the second set of columns. This has been done in Illustration 4–3 and the resulting adjusted trial balance appears in the third set of columns of the worksheet. Note that the debit and credit columns of the trial balance after adjustment columns have been totaled in order to check the arithmetic accuracy of this step.

The preparation of an adjusted trial balance indicates how the adjusting entries affect the various accounts which are included in the trial balance before adjustment.

Step 4. The next step involves the distribution of each amount which appears in the adjusted trial balance to the appropriate columns of the income statement, statement of capital, or the balance sheet columns of the worksheet. Note that the balances in the cash, accounts receivable, supplies, notes payable, and unearned fees accounts were transferred directly to the balance sheet columns of the worksheet. The balances in the capital account and the withdrawals account were transferred to the statement of capital columns. The remaining accounts—painting fees, salaries, and supplies—were transferred to the income statement columns. All asset and liability accounts are transferred to the balance sheet columns; equity accounts (including withdrawals) are transferred to the statement of capital columns; and all revenue and expense accounts are transferred to the income statement columns. The worksheet after the transfer of each of the items which were included in the adjusted trial balance is shown in Illustration 4–4. Observe that each amount in the adjusted trial balance is transferred to only one of the six remaining columns, as indicated above.

Step 5. The fifth step in the preparation of the worksheet involves the "balancing" of the income statement columns of the worksheet. Note that an amount which is equal to the difference between the credit (revenue) column and the debit (expense) column ($2,700 − $1,400 = $1,300) is entered in both the debit column of the income statement (as a balancing figure) and the credit column of the statement of capital set of columns. This amount is the net income for the period. The purpose of entering net income as a credit in the capital set of columns is that the excess of the revenues over the related expenses for the period is income and results in an increase in owner's equity. Of course, an increase in capital is recorded by a credit. If the balance in the debit (expense) column exceeds the balance in the credit (revenue) column of the income

Step 3 (handwritten)

Illustration 4-3

KILMER CONTRACTORS
Worksheet
For the Month Ended May 31, 1975

	Trial Balance Before Adjustments		Adjustments		Trial Balance After Adjustments		Income Statement		Statement of Capital		Balance Sheet	
Cash	10,000				10,000							
Accounts receivable	900				900							
Supplies	3,000			(b)1,000	2,000							
Notes payable.		1,500				1,500						
Unearned fees.		2,200	(a)1,100			1,100						
Capital.		10,000				10,000						
Withdrawals.	1,000				1,000							
Painting fees		1,600		(a)1,100		2,700						
Salaries	400				400							
Supplies used			(b)1,000		1,000							
	15,300	15,300	2,100	2,100	15,300	15,300						

Key to Adjustments:
(a) To record revenue from one of the two houses contracted for on May 10.
(b) To record the cost of the supplies used during the month of May.

Step 4

Illustration 4-4
KILMER CONTRACTORS
Worksheet
For the Month Ended May 31, 1975

	Trial Balance Before Adjustments		Adjustments		Trial Balance After Adjustments		Income Statement		Statement of Capital		Balance Sheet	
Cash	10,000				10,000						10,000	
Accounts receivable . .	900				900						900	
Supplies	3,000			(b)1,000	2,000						2,000	
Notes payable.		1,500				1,500						1,500
Unearned fees.		2,200	(a)1,100			1,100						1,100
Capital.		10,000				10,000				10,000		
Withdrawals.	1,000				1,000				1,000			
Painting fees		1,600		(a)1,100		2,700		2,700				
Salaries	400				400		400					
Supplies used			(b)1,000		1,000		1,000					
	15,300	15,300	2,100	2,100	15,300	15,300						

Key to Adjustments:
(a) To record revenue from one of the two houses contracted for on May 10.
(b) To record the cost of the supplies used during the month of May.

statement set of columns, the difference between the two totals would represent a net loss for the period. This amount would be entered as a credit in the income statement columns as the balancing figure and in the debit column of the statement of capital set of columns as a reduction of the owner's equity. It is also important to note that the income statement columns of the worksheet are identical to: (1) the income summary account used in the closing process; (2) the summary entry which may be used in order to close out revenues and expenses for the period; and (3) the income statement for the period. Step 5 of the worksheet process is presented in Illustration 4–5.

Step 6. This step involves the determination of the ending balance in the capital account for the period by adjusting the capital balance for the income (or loss) of the business and for any investments or withdrawals which were made by the owner. This ending balance in the capital account is entered in both the credit column of the balance sheet set of columns and the debit column of the statement of capital columns (as a balancing figure). The latter set of columns is, of course, identical to the formal Statement of Capital. Illustration 4–6 presents this step.

Step 7. The final step in the process of preparing a worksheet is the balancing of the final two columns, the balance sheet, as a test of the arithmetic accuracy of the process. These two columns are now identical to the balance sheet of the firm. The step is shown in Illustration 4–7.

As previously indicated, the completed worksheet is a one-page summary of the adjusting and closing procedures. A critical review of Illustration 4–7 will provide the reader with an excellent overview of this process. Observe that preparing the financial statements from the completed worksheet would be a simple process since all of the necessary information has already been sorted into the appropriate worksheet columns.

When the worksheet is used at the end of the period, it permits the preparation of financial statements before adjusting and closing entries are recorded in the accounts. At year-end, after the statements are prepared, the adjusting entries indicated on the worksheet and the normal closing entries must still be entered into the journal and then posted to the ledger. When a worksheet is used in the preparation of financial statements at the end of the period, the steps involved in the accounting process described in Chapter 3 will be modified as follows:

1. Record the transactions with journal entries.
2. Post journal entries to the ledger.
3. Prepare the worksheet.
4. Prepare the financial statements.
5. Record the adjusting entries in the journal and post to the ledger.
6. Record the closing entries in the journal and post to the ledger.

Illustration 4-5

KILMER CONTRACTORS
Worksheet
For the Month Ended May 31, 1975

	Trial Balance Before Adjustments		Adjustments		Trial Balance After Adjustments		Income Statement		Statement of Capital		Balance Sheet	
Cash	10,000				10,000						10,000	
Accounts receivable . . .	900				900						900	
Supplies	3,000			(b)1,000	2,000						2,000	
Notes payable.		1,500				1,500						1,500
Unearned fees.		2,200	(a)1,100			1,100						1,100
Capital.		10,000				10,000				10,000		
Withdrawals.	1,000				1,000				1,000			
Painting fees		1,600		(a)1,100		2,700		2,700				
Salaries	400				400		400					
Supplies used			(b)1,000		1,000		1,000					
	15,300	15,300	2,100	2,100	15,300	15,300	1,400	2,700				
							1,300			1,300		
							2,700	2,700				

Key to Adjustments:
(a) To record revenue from one of the two houses contracted for on May 10.
(b) To record the cost of the supplies used during the month of May.

Step 6

Illustration 4–6

KILMER CONTRACTORS
Worksheet
For the Month Ended May 31, 1975

	Trial Balance Before Adjustments		Adjustments		Trial Balance After Adjustments		Income Statement		Statement of Capital		Balance Sheet	
Cash	10,000				10,000						10,000	
Accounts receivable	900				900						900	
Supplies	3,000			(b)1,000	2,000						2,000	
Notes payable		1,500				1,500						1,500
Unearned fees		2,200	(a)1,100			1,100						1,100
Capital		10,000				10,000				10,000		
Withdrawals	1,000				1,000				1,000			
Painting fees		1,600		(a)1,100		2,700		2,700				
Salaries	400				400		400					
Supplies used			(b)1,000		1,000		1,000					
	15,300	15,300	2,100	2,100	15,300	15,300	1,400	2,700				
							1,300		1,300			
							2,700	2,700	1,000	11,300		
									10,300		10,300	
									11,300	11,300		

Key to Adjustments:
(a) To record revenue from one of the two houses contracted for on May 10.
(b) To record the cost of the supplies used during the month of May.

Step ?

Illustration 4-7
KILMER CONTRACTORS
Worksheet
For the Month Ended May 31, 1975

	Trial Balance Before Adjustments		Adjustments		Trial Balance After Adjustments		Income Statement		Statement of Capital		Balance Sheet	
Cash.	10,000				10,000						10,000	
Accounts receivable . . .	900				900						900	
Supplies.	3,000			(b)1,000	2,000						2,000	
Notes payable.		1,500				1,500						1,500
Unearned fees.		2,200	(a)1,100			1,100						1,100
Capital.		10,000				10,000				10,000		
Withdrawals.	1,000				1,000				1,000			
Painting fees		1,600		(a)1,100		2,700		2,700				
Salaries	400				400		400					
Supplies used			(b)1,000		1,000		1,000					
	15,300	15,300	2,100	2,100	15,300	15,300	1,400	2,700	1,000	11,300	12,900	10,300
							1,300		10,300			1,300
							2,700	2,700	11,300	11,300	12,900	12,900

Key to Adjustments:
(a) To record revenue from one of the two houses contracted for on May 10.
(b) To record the cost of the supplies used during the month of May.

In addition to the end-of-period financial statements, many companies prepare interim financial statements which cover shorter periods of time such as a month or a quarter. The worksheet is a valuable aid to the accountant in preparing these interim statements since the adjustments made on the worksheet need not be journalized and posted to the accounts. If a worksheet is used, the journalizing and posting of the adjustments will usually be done only at the end of the accounting period.

ADJUSTING ENTRIES

As previously indicated, the accrual basis of accounting requires that all revenues be recorded as they are earned and that expenses be recorded as they are incurred. That is, there is a proper matching of revenues and expenses only if the income statement for the period includes all of the revenues and expenses which are applicable to the accounting period without regard to the timing of either the receipt or the disbursement of cash. At the end of any accounting period, then, there will usually be certain transactions which are still in the process of completion or which have occurred but which have not been recorded in the accounts. These transactions require adjusting entries in order to record revenues and expenses and to allocate them to the proper period or periods. In the case of Kilmer Contractors, adjustments were required for the revenue which was earned by painting one of the two houses for which payment had been received in advance and in order to record the cost of the painting supplies which were used during the month of May. In general, the types of transactions which require end-of-period adjusting entries fall into the following groups:

1. Allocation of prepaid expenses to the proper periods.
2. Recognition of unrecorded expenses.
3. Allocation of a portion of the recorded cost of a fixed asset to the accounting periods which benefit from its use.
4. Allocation of recorded revenue to the proper periods.
5. Recognition of unrecorded revenues.

The remainder of this chapter will discuss these types of adjusting journal entries. In order to illustrate the different types of adjusting entries, the trial balance before adjustment of Brown Company as of December 31, 1976, will be used. This trial balance appears in Illustration 4–8.

Prepaid Expenses

Certain goods and services, such as insurance, rent, and supplies, are purchased prior to their use by the business. If these goods have been used or the services have expired during the accounting period, these costs should be classified as expenses. However, the portion of the goods which

Illustration 4–8

BROWN COMPANY
Trial Balance Before Adjustment
December 31, 1976

	Debit	Credit
Cash	$ 2,760	
Accounts receivable.	4,000	
Supplies	3,000	
Office furniture	3,600	
Accumulated depreciation—		
office furniture		$ 360
Accounts payable		2,000
Unearned rent		3,000
Capital		5,000
Withdrawals	1,000	
Service revenues.		20,000
Rent expense	9,000	
Salaries	6,000	
Other expense	1,000	
	$30,360	$30,360

is unused or the services which have not expired should be included in the balance sheet and classified as an asset, referred to as a prepaid expense. A prepaid expense will be reclassified as an expense in a subsequent accounting period (or periods) as it is used or expires. Adjusting entries are necessary in order to allocate the cost of each item between the asset account and the expense account.

To illustrate, assume that Brown Company purchased supplies at a cost of $3,000 on June 30. This transaction was recorded by the following journal entry:

Supplies 3,000
    Cash   3,000

This entry indicates that an asset has been acquired by the company. Supplies will be carried in the accounts as an asset until they are used, at which time they will become an expense and be reclassified as such. Note that the trial balance before adjustment reflects the $3,000 balance in the supplies account as an asset.

At the end of December the supplies which were still on hand had a cost of $2,000. Subtracting the cost of the supplies on hand at December 31 ($2,000, as indicated above) from the cost of the supplies which were available for use during the year ($3,000 of supplies purchased on June 30) indicates that it is necessary to record the difference of $1,000, the cost of the supplies used during the year, as an expense. This would be accomplished by means of the following entry:

Supplies Used 1,000
    Supplies   1,000

Alternatively, a prepaid expense may be initially recorded as an expense. For example, Brown Company could have recorded the purchase of the supplies on June 30 with the following journal entry:

```
Supplies Used ...............................  3,000
     Cash ....................................           3,000
```

Since only $1,000 of the supplies were actually used and should be considered as an expense, the following entry would be necessary at the end of the accounting period in order to reclassify the $2,000 of supplies which were still on hand as an asset.

```
Supplies ....................................  2,000
     Supplies Used ...........................           2,000
```

Note that this alternative method results in identical balances at the end of the period in both the Supplies account ($2,000) and the Supplies Used account ($1,000). Thus, either method is acceptable as long as the appropriate adjusting entries are made at the end of the period.

In some instances, companies will purchase supplies or prepay expenses which will be entirely used or consumed prior to the preparation of financial statements. In these instances, the amounts paid may be charged directly to expense when the outlay is made simply as a matter of convenience. For example, assume that Brown Company pays the monthly rent on its office space in advance on the first day of each month. This outlay could be recorded on December 1 as follows:

```
Prepaid Rent. ...............................  750
     Cash ....................................           750
```

If the transaction is recorded in this manner, the following adjusting entry would be required at the end of December in order to reclassify the outlay which was made for rent as an expense:

```
Rent Expense ................................  750
     Prepaid Rent ...........................            750
```

Alternatively, it might be expedient to record the expenditure as follows, since the rent is paid and the benefit is received during the month:

```
Rent Expense ................................  750
     Cash ....................................           750
```

Assuming that Brown Company recorded the transaction in this manner, an adjusting entry would not be required at the end of the month since the expense has been fully incurred and the "prepayment" has been fully used by December 31.

Accrued Expenses

At the end of an accounting period there are usually expenses which have been incurred but which have not been paid because payment is not due until a subsequent period. Many expenses, such as wages and salaries, or interest on loans, may be incurred during a period but not recorded in the accounts because they have not been paid. These expenses are re-ferred to as accrued expenses. Adjusting entries are necessary at the end of an accounting period in order to record all accrued expenses. For ex-ample, assume that Brown Company placed a newspaper advertisement which appeared during the month of December, but was not billed for the expense until some time in January. Since Brown Company did not pay for the advertisement during December, this amount does not appear on the trial balance before adjustment. Therefore, the following adjusting entry would be required at the end of December:

```
Advertising Expense . . . . . . . . . . . . . . . . . . . . . . . . . . . . . . . . . 75
    Accounts Payable. . . . . . . . . . . . . . . . . . . . . . . . . . . . . . .          75
```

This adjusting entry records the expense which was incurred but not paid during December and the corresponding liability which exists at the end of the month.

When the bill is received in January and is paid, the payment would be recorded by the following journal entry:

```
Accounts Payable . . . . . . . . . . . . . . . . . . . . . . . . . . . . . . . . . . 75
    Cash . . . . . . . . . . . . . . . . . . . . . . . . . . . . . . . . . . . . . . .        75
```

This entry records the fact that the liability has been satisfied (and assets reduced) by the cash payment. The timing of the recognition of the ex-pense is not determined by the date of the payment; the expense was recorded during the previous month when it was incurred.

Depreciation

Businesses normally acquire assets which are used in their operations over a number of years. Buildings and equipment are examples of this type of asset. A business may purchase equipment and use it for a number of years. For example, assume that Brown Company acquired office furni-ture on January 1, 1975, and expects to use this furniture for ten years before it will be replaced. Assuming that the cost of this furniture was $3,600, the purchase would have been recorded as follows:

```
Office Furniture. . . . . . . . . . . . . . . . . . . . . . . . . . . . . . . . . . . 3,600
    Cash . . . . . . . . . . . . . . . . . . . . . . . . . . . . . . . . . . . . . . .      3,600
```

The office furniture is an asset of the business and is recorded as such. Its cost should be charged to expense over the period that it is used, in this case ten years. The process of allocating the cost of an asset to expense over its useful life is referred to as depreciation. Depreciation is the sys-tematic allocation of the cost of an asset to the periods which benefit from its use. The primary difference between allocating the cost of a fixed asset to expense (i.e., depreciation) and the allocation of the cost of a prepaid item such as supplies or insurance to expense is that it is normally much more difficult to measure the portion of the cost of a fixed asset which has been used during an accounting period. Therefore, the allocation of the cost of a fixed asset to expense during an accounting period is only an *estimate* of the part of the usefulness of the asset which has expired or been used during the year. Since the cost of the furniture was $3,600 and the expected useful life of this asset was 10 years or 120 months, depreciation in the amount of $360 ($3,600 divided by 10) should be recorded annually. Assuming that Brown Company did not make monthly entries to record the depreciation, the adjusting entry which should be made on December 31 in order to record depreciation expense would be as follows:

```
Depreciation Expense  . . . . . . . . . . . . . . . . . . . . . . . . . . . . . .  360
    Accumulated Depreciation  . . . . . . . . . . . . . . . . . . . . . . . .         360
```

The debit to depreciation expense records the portion of the cost of the asset which is recorded as an expense of the year. The credit is to accumulated depreciation, a contra account which would appear as an offset or deduction from the related asset account in the balance sheet. As the title accumulated depreciation implies, the depreciation taken over the useful life of the asset is accumulated in this account. Usually a reduction in an asset account is recorded with a credit made directly to the account. However, a contra account is used for fixed assets in order to provide additional information concerning the asset—that is, both the original cost and the depreciation expense which has been taken to date may be recorded and reported in the balance sheet. The asset and the related accumulated depreciation account would appear in the balance sheet as follows at the end of 1976:

```
Office Furniture. . . . . . . . . . . . . . . . . . $3,600
Less: Accumulated Depreciation . . . . . . . .    720   $2,880
```

A more complete discussion of the procedures which are involved in determining depreciation expense is presented in Chapter 10.

Unearned Revenues

Revenue which is collected before a business actually performs a service or delivers goods to a customer is referred to as unearned revenue. Since cash is received prior to the performance of the service or delivery of the goods, the amount received represents a liability to the firm. Unearned revenues are not a liability in the sense that the company will be required to repay the money. Rather they represent an obligation of the company to perform a service or deliver goods at some future date, i.e., revenues that have been received but not earned. Examples of unearned revenues include rent collected in advance and subscription fees received prior to delivery of a magazine or newspaper.

To illustrate, assume that Brown Company subleased a portion of its office space to Smith for a rental of $3,000 per year. Terms of the lease agreement specify that Smith will pay the yearly rental in advance on July 1. The entry to record the receipt of the $3,000 advance payment on July 1, 1976 would be as follows:

Cash	3,000	
Unearned Rent		3,000

Note that the trial balance before adjustment includes the $3,000 balance in the unearned rent account. Since no service had been performed at the time the cash was received, the entire amount was initially recorded in a liability account, unearned rent. Since rent is earned over the 12 month period that Brown Company provides office space to Smith, exactly one-half of the service will be rendered during the period July 1 to December 31, 1976. Thus $1,500 ($\frac{1}{2} \times$ $3,000) of the rent has been earned and would be recorded by the following adjusting entry on December 31:

Unearned Rent	1,500	
Rental Income		1,500

The liability account, unearned rent, has been reduced by $1,500 and revenue for the period has been increased by this amount. The remaining balance in the unearned rent account represents an obligation to provide office space to Smith during the first six months of 1977. This adjusting entry made on December 31 emphasizes the fact that income is recorded as it is earned, not as cash is received.

Accrued Revenues

Accrued revenues are revenues that have been earned but not recorded in the accounts during an accounting period because cash has not yet been received. As such, accrued revenues are the opposite, so to speak, of un-earned revenues. Therefore, adjusting entries are necessary in order to record any revenue which has been earned but not recorded in the accounts as of the end of the accounting period. To illustrate, assume that Brown Company entered into an agreement with the Fooler Brush Company on December 1, 1976. Brown Company agreed to display a line of brushes at their offices in return for a commission of 10 percent on any sales made by Fooler if the initial contact with the customer was made by Brown Company. The commissions are payable on a quarterly basis. Assume that Brown Company earned commissions of $100 during the month of Decem-ber. The following adjusting journal entry would be made on December 31:

Commissions Receivable	100	
Commissions Earned		100

This entry increases the assets (commissions receivable) of Brown Company by the $100 due from Fooler Brush Company and records the revenue which has been earned to date by providing the agreed-upon service. When payment is received from the Fooler Brush Company, the following journal entry would be made:

```
Cash . . . . . . . . . . . . . . . . . . . . . . . . . . . . . . . . . . . . . . . . . . . . . . . 100
     Commissions Receivable. . . . . . . . . . . . . . . . . . . . . . . . . . . . .        100
```

It is important to note that this second entry simply records the fact that one asset, cash, was received in exchange for another, commissions receivable; revenues were not affected. The revenues were recorded at the time the service was performed, which was when they were earned by Brown Company.

ACCRUAL BASIS OF ACCOUNTING

When a company records revenues as they are earned and records its expenses as they are incurred, the company is using the *accrual* basis of accounting. Under the accrual basis, revenues must be recorded as they are earned and expenses recorded as they are incurred without regard to the timing of either the receipt or disbursement of cash. Thus, the purpose of end-of-period adjusting entries is to update the accounting records of a business so that they are on the accrual basis.

Preparation of the Worksheet

In order to illustrate the different types of adjustments which typically are made in the preparation of a worksheet, we will prepare the worksheet for Brown Company at December 31, 1976. The trial balance before adjustment as of December 31, 1976 (see Illustration 4–8), appears in the first two columns of the worksheet in Illustration 4–9 on page 99.

The procedures followed in preparing the worksheet for Brown Company included the following:

1. The adjustments were entered in the adjustments columns.
2. Each amount in the trial balance was combined with the adjustment to that account, if any, and was entered in the trial balance after adjustment columns.
3. Each amount in the trial balance after adjustment columns was transferred to either the income statement columns, the statement of capital columns, or the balance sheet columns. The revenue and expense accounts were extended to the income statement columns; the capital and withdrawal accounts were extended to the statement of capital

Illustration 4–9
BROWN COMPANY
Worksheet
For the Year Ended December 31, 1976

	Trial Balance Before Adjustments Dr	Cr	Adjustments Dr	Cr	Trial Balance After Adjustment Dr	Cr	Income Statement Dr	Cr	Statement of Capital Dr	Cr	Balance Sheet Dr	Cr
Cash	2,760				2,760						2,760	
Accounts receivable	4,000				4,000						4,000	
Supplies	3,000			(a)1,000	2,000						2,000	
Office furniture	3,600				3,600						3,600	
Accumulated depreciation—office furniture		360		(c)360		720						720
Accounts payable		2,000		(b)75		2,075						2,075
Unearned rent		3,000	(d)1,500			1,500						1,500
Capital (1/1/76)		5,000				5,000				5,000		
Withdrawals	1,000				1,000				1,000			
Service revenues		20,000				20,000		20,000				
Rent expense	9,000				9,000		9,000					
Salaries	6,000				6,000		6,000					
Other expense	1,000				1,000		1,000					
Supplies used			(a)1,000		1,000		1,000					
Advertising expense			(b)75		75		75					
Depreciation expense			(c)360		360		360					
Rental income				(d)1,500		1,500		1,500				
Commissions earned				(e)100		100		100				
Commissions receivable			(e)100		100						100	
	30,360	30,360	3,035	3,035	30,895	30,895	17,435	21,600				
Net income							4,165			4,165		
							21,600	21,600	1,000	9,165	12,460	8,165
Capital, 12/31/76									8,165			
									9,165	9,165	12,460	12,460

Key to Adjustments:
(a) To adjust for supplies used.
(b) To adjust for accrued advertising expense.
(c) To adjust for depreciation on office furniture.
(d) To adjust for portion of rent collected in advance which was earned.
(e) To adjust for accrued commissions earned.

columns; and the asset and liability accounts were extended to the balance sheet columns.

4.   The income statement columns were totaled, and the difference between the debit and credit totals was entered as a balancing figure in the income statement debit column and in the credit column of the statement of capital columns. This difference is, of course, equal to the net income for the year.

5.   The statement of capital columns were totaled, and the difference between the debit and credit totals was entered as a balancing figure in the statement of capital debit column and in the credit column of the balance sheet columns. This difference is equal to the owners' equity at the end of the year.

6.   The balance sheet columns were totaled as a test of the arithmetic accuracy of the process. If the debit and credit balance sheet columns had not been equal, this would have indicated that the worksheet was prepared inaccurately.

At this point, the completed worksheet would be used in preparing the formal financial statements for Brown Company. All necessary information is included in the income statement columns, statement of capital columns, and the balance sheet columns of the worksheet.

After the preparation of financial statements, all adjustments appearing in the adjustments columns of the worksheet would be entered in the journal and then posted to the ledger accounts. Then, the entries to close the revenue and expense accounts would be journalized and posted to the ledger.

AN OVERVIEW

This chapter introduced the worksheet, a device which is used to facilitate the preparation of financial statements. The worksheet may also be used to assist the accountant in preparing financial statements at a date other than the end of the accounting period or at year-end as a valuable test or check on the usual recording process. The worksheet summarizes the trial balance, adjusting entries and, in effect, closing entries in one document. A critical review of the worksheet provides the student with an excellent overview of the adjusting and closing process.

The accrual basis of accounting requires that revenues be recorded as they are earned and expenses be recorded as they are incurred. At the end of any accounting period there are usually transactions which are in the process of completion or which have occurred but have not been recorded. These transactions require adjusting entries. Adjusting entries for prepaid expenses, accrued expenses, depreciation, unearned revenues, and accrued revenues were discussed and illustrated in this chapter.

KEY DEFINITIONS

Accrual basis of accounting The accrual basis of accounting is the process of recording revenues in the period in which they are earned and recording expenses in the period in which they are incurred.

Accrued expenses Accrued expenses are expenses such as wages and salaries or interest on loans which have been incurred during a period but not yet recorded in the accounts because they have not yet been paid.

Accrued revenues Accrued revenues are revenues which have been earned but not yet recorded in the accounts during the accounting period because cash has not yet been received.

Accumulated depreciation Accumulated depreciation is a contra account which appears as an offset or deduction from the related asset account in the balance sheet. The depreciation taken over the useful life of the asset is accumulated in this account.

Adjusted trial balance The adjusted trial balance is prepared by combining the trial balance before adjustments with the related adjusting entries.

Adjusting entries At the end of any accounting period there will usually be certain transactions which are still in the process of completion or which have occurred but which have not yet been recorded in the accounts. These transactions require adjusting entries in order to record revenues and expenses and to allocate them to the proper period.

Closing entries Closing entries are entries which are prepared in order to close out or transfer the balances in temporary accounts to the capital account.

Contra account A contra account is an account which is offset against or deducted from another account in the financial statements.

Depreciation Depreciation is the systematic allocation of the cost of an asset to the periods which benefit from its use.

Interim financial statements These are financial statements which cover periods of less than a year such as a month or a quarter.

Prepaid expenses Certain goods and services, such as insurance, rent, and supplies, are often paid for prior to their use by the business. The portion of the goods which has not been used up or the services which have not expired should be included in the balance sheet and classified as an asset.

Unearned revenues Unearned revenues are revenues which are collected before a business actually performs a service or delivers goods to a customer.

Worksheet A worksheet summarizes the trial balance, adjusting entries, and closing entries in one simple document. It also permits the preparation of interim financial statements without recording the adjusting entries in the accounts. The worksheet may also be prepared and used in conjunction with the regular year-end closing process. Even if the accountant intends to record the adjusting and closing entries in the accounts, such as would be the case at year-end, the worksheet may still be used as a valuable check on the recording process.

QUESTIONS

1. What is the purpose of the worksheet?
2. How is the adjusted trial balance prepared?
3. Which accounts are closed at the end of the period?
4. Explain how the net income for the period is calculated and presented on the worksheet.
5. How are the adjusting entries for the period included in the worksheet?
6. Explain the relationship of the worksheet to the financial statements.
7. Are prepaid expenses reclassified as expenses in future periods? Why?
8. How is revenue which is collected before a business actually performs a service classified in the financial statements?
9. Explain the accrual basis of accounting. How does it differ from the cash basis?
10. What check may be used in order to determine if the worksheet was prepared accurately?

EXERCISES

4–1   Boyd Company purchased a two-year insurance policy on June 30 for $900 and recorded the transaction with a debit to the Prepaid Insurance account. Give the adjusting journal entry necessary to record the insurance that has expired as of December 31.

4–2   Below are the 1975 adjusting entries for Branson Shoe Repairs.

a.	Supplies Expense	275	
	Supplies		275
b.	Rent Expense	500	
	Prepaid Rent		500
c.	Interest Receivable	150	
	Interest Income		150
d.	Wage Expense	75	
	Wages Payable		75
e.	Repair Fees	25	
	Unearned Fees		25
f.	Fees Receivable	33	
	Repair Fees		33

Give a possible explanation for each of the above adjusting entries.

4–3   Gardner Company leases a building to a client at a rental of $2,400 per year on June 1, 1975. Give the required December 31, 1975, adjusting entry on the books of Gardner Company under each of the following assumptions.

   a. The rent is paid in advance on June 1, 1975, and is recorded by crediting Unearned Rent.

b. The rent is paid in advance on June 1, 1975, and is recorded by crediting Rental Income.

c. The rent for the period of June 1, 1975, to May 31, 1976, is to be paid on May 30, 1976.

4-4   Prepare the adjusting entries required at December 31, 1975, in each of the following cases:

a. Herman Company was assessed property taxes of $350 for 1975. The taxes were due April 15, 1976.

b. Norton Company's payroll was $6,000 per month and wages were paid on the 15th of the following month. The company closes its books on December 31.

c. Frazier Company has $3,000 of savings bonds. Interest receivable on these bonds was $180 at December 31.

d. Foreman Company owns a building costing $30,000. $1,000 of the cost is to be allocated to expense in 1975.

4-5   The income statement for 1975 for the Lang Company reflected wage expense of $80,000. The year-end balances in the wages payable account were $10,000 at December 31, 1974, and $12,000 at December 31, 1975. Determine the amount of cash paid for salaries during 1975.

PROBLEMS

Series A

4A-1   The following information for adjustments was available at December 31, the end of the accounting period. Prepare the necessary adjusting entry for each item of information.

a. Annual office rent of $1,200 was paid on July 1, when the lease was signed. This amount was recorded as prepaid rent.

b. The office supplies account had a $100 balance at the beginning of the year and $600 of office supplies were purchased during the year. An inventory of unused supplies at the end of the year indicated that $150 of supplies were still on hand.

c. Wages earned by employees during December but not yet paid amounted to $700 on December 31.

d. The company subleased part of its office space at a rental of $50 per month. The tenant occupied the space on September 1 and paid six months rent in advance. This amount paid was credited to the unearned rent account.

e. Equipment was purchased on January 1 for $5,000. The useful life was estimated to be ten years with no salvage value.

f. Services provided for clients which were not chargeable until January amounted to $800. No entries had yet been made to record these earned revenues.

4A-2   From the information given below concerning the College Inn Ski Resort, prepare the adjusting entries required at December 31, 1975.

1. Accrued property taxes at December 31, 1975, were $500.
2. Accrued wages payable at December 31, 1975, were $2,400.
3. Interest receivable on United States government bonds owned at December 31, 1975, was $75.
4. A tractor had been obtained on October 31 from Equipment Rentals, Inc., at a daily rate of $4. No rental payment had yet been made. Continued use of the tractor was expected through the month of January.
5. A portion of the land owned by the resort had been leased to a riding stable at a yearly rental of $3,600. One year's rent was collected in advance at the date of the lease (November 1) and credited to Unearned Rental Revenue. 600
6. Another portion of the land owned had also been rented on October 1 to a service station operator at an annual rate of $1,200. No rent had as yet been collected from this tenant. 300
7. On December 31, the College Inn Ski Resort signed an agreement to lease a truck from Gray Drive Ur-Self Company for the next calendar year at a rate of 10 cents for each mile of use. The Resort estimates that they will drive this truck for about 1,000 miles per month. 100
8. On September 1, the Company purchased a three-year fire insurance policy for $360. At the time the policy was acquired, the Company debited insurance expense and credited cash. 30

4A–3 Below is given the September 30, 1975, trial balance *before* adjustment of the Cavilier Company.

CAVILIER COMPANY
Trial Balance
September 30, 1975

Cash	$ 2,700	
Supplies	1,250	
Prepaid rent	1,800	
Land	10,000	
Accounts payable		$ 3,500
Fees received in advance		2,500
Capital		7,250
Drawings	500	
Commissions earned		5,800
Fees earned		2,200
Wages and salaries expense	4,000	
Utilities expense	550	
Miscellaneous expense	450	
	$21,250	$21,250

Other data:

1. Supplies on hand at the end of September totaled $750.
2. In accordance with the terms of the lease, the annual rental of $1,800 was paid in advance on April 1, 1975.

3. Wages and salaries earned by employees but unpaid at September 30, 1975, amounted to $450.
4. Of the balance in the Fees Received in Advance account, $1,500 had not been earned as of September 30.
5. On September 1, 1975, Cavilier Company rented certain equipment to the Alpha Fraternity under the following terms: $50 per month payable on the first day of each month following the start of the rental arrangement.

Required:

Prepare all journal entries necessary to: (1) adjust the accounts and (2) close the books as of September 30, 1975.

4A–4   Given below is the trial balance before adjustment and the adjusted trial balance for Doak Company at December 31, 1975.

DOAK COMPANY
Trial Balance and Adjusted Trial Balance
December 31, 1975

	Trial Balance		Adjusted Trial Balance	
Cash	$ 3,000		$ 3,000	
Accounts receivable	2,500		2,500	
Rent receivable	-0-		200	
Prepaid insurance	1,000		600	
Supplies	1,200		400	
Office furniture	3,000		3,000	
Accumulated depreciation— office furniture		$ 900		$ 1,200
Land	7,000		7,000	
Accounts payable		1,500		1,500
Notes payable		2,000		2,000
Interest payable		-0-		100
Unearned fees		800		300
Wages payable		-0-		600
Withdrawals	500		500	
Capital		9,000		9,000
Service fees		10,000		10,500
Rental income		600		800
Wage expense	6,000		6,600	
Insurance expense	-0-		400	
Depreciation expense	-0-		300	
Interest expense	100		200	
Supplies expense	-0-		800	
Other expenses	500		500	
	$24,800	$24,800	$26,000	$26,000

Prepare the adjusting journal entries made by Doak Company on December 31, 1975.

4A-5   Below is the trial balance for the Martin Company:

MARTIN COMPANY
Trial Balance
December 31, 1975

Cash	$ 800.00	
Notes receivable.	2,500.00	
Prepaid insurance	750.00	
Land	21,000.00	
Service revenue received in advance		$ 3,500.00
Mortgage payable		5,000.00
Capital		14,700.00
Commissions earned		9,000.00
Salaries expense	6,500.00	
Miscellaneous expense	650.00	
	$32,200.00	$32,200.00

Data for adjustments:

a. Accrued salaries at December 31, 1975, were $220.
b. Accrued interest on the mortgage at December 31, 1975, was $250.
c. At year-end, one-half of the service revenue received in advance had been earned.
d. Insurance expense for 1975 was $375.
e. Accrued interest on the notes receivable at December 31, 1975, was $20.

Required:

a. Prepare a worksheet for Martin Company at December 31, 1975.
b. Prepare an income statement for the year and the balance sheet as of December 31, 1975.

4A–6 As chief accountant for Ford Company, it is your job to prepare end-of-period financial statements for the firm. You had an assistant prepare the following unadjusted trial balance from the books of the company.

FORD COMPANY
Trial Balance
December 31, 1975

Cash	$ 1,100	
Accounts receivable	800	
Prepaid insurance	900	
Office furniture	4,000	
Accumulated depreciation–office furniture		$ 400
Land	8,000	
Accounts payable		900
Unearned revenues		1,500
Note payable		2,500
Capital		9,600
Withdrawals	400	
Service revenues		4,100
Rent expense	600	
Salaries expense	1,000	
Supplies expense	2,000	
Other expenses	200	
	$19,000	$19,000

The following information was also gathered from the books of the Ford Company:

a.   The company paid $900 for a three-year insurance policy on June 30, 1975.

b.   The office furniture was purchased January 1, 1974, and is expected to have a 10-year life and no salvage value. Depreciation for 1975 has not been recorded.

c.   The unearned revenues account was created when Ford Company was paid $1,500 for services to be rendered. One-third of these services were rendered on December 1, 1975.

d.   Interest of $20 has accrued on the note payable at December 31.

e.   Ford Company paid $600 on August 1 as annual rent for their warehouse. This amount was debited to rent expense.

f. $100 of salaries have been earned by employees but not yet paid or recorded on the books.

g.   Supplies on hand at December 31 had a cost of $500.

Required:

a.   Prepare a worksheet for Ford Company at December 31, 1975.

b.   Prepare the company's balance sheet, income statement, and statement of capital.

4A–7 Given below is a trial balance before adjustment for Holmes Company.

HOLMES COMPANY
Trial Balance Before Adjustment
December 31, 1975

Cash	$1,100	
Accounts receivable	800	
Notes receivable	1,500	
Office furniture	2,000	
Accumulated depreciation—office furniture		$ 400
Accounts payable		1,250
Unearned fees		500
Capital		4,350
Withdrawals	400	
Service fees		2,000
Rent income		300
Supplies expense	1,500	
Insurance expense	900	
Wage expense	600	
	$8,800	$8,800

After preparing the worksheet, the accountant for Holmes Company produces the following balance sheet for the year.

HOLMES COMPANY
Balance Sheet
As of December 31, 1975

ASSETS

Cash		$1,100
Accounts Receivable		800
Interest Receivable		20
Supplies		250
Prepaid Insurance		600
Notes Receivable		1,500
Office Furniture	$2,000	
Less: Accumulated Depreciation	600	1,400
Total Assets		$5,670

LIABILITIES AND OWNERS' EQUITY

Accounts Payable		$1,250
Unearned Fees		300
Unearned Rent		100
Total Liabilities		$1,650
Capital		4,020
Total Liabilities and Owners' Equity		$5,670

Required:

Reproduce the worksheet generated by the accountant for Holmes Company.

Series B

4B–1   Liston Rent-All uses the calendar year for its accounting period. Prepare the adjusting entries required at December 31, 1975, given the following information:

    a. Liston received $1,000 on November 1, 1975 as payment for the rental of a truck. The rental agreement expires August 31, 1976. The amount was credited to rental income.

    b. Van Zandt Ad Agency prepared a commercial for Liston which was run in December. The agency fee is $200, but Liston has not yet received the bill.

    c. Liston paid $900 for a three-year insurance policy on January 1, 1975, and debited the amount to prepaid insurance.

    d. A regular customer was given a rubber raft on December 1, 1975, with rent to be paid when the raft was returned. The raft had not been returned as of December 31, 1975. Rent is $25 per month.

    e. Liston Rent-All rented a bird cage to a customer on August 1 for two months. The customer paid the $50 rent charge for August and September on August 3 and it was credited to rental income.

4B–2   The trial balance of the Aggie Company as of September 30, 1975, was as follows:

AGGIE COMPANY
Trial Balance
September 30, 1975

Cash	$ 6,000	
Supplies	500	
Prepaid rent	900	
Land	8,500	
Accounts payable		$ 4,000
Unearned revenues		1,050
Capital		10,000
Withdrawals	1,000	
Commissions earned		10,100
Salaries expense	7,500	
Miscellaneous expense	750	
	$25,150	$25,150

Other financial data:

1. The cost of supplies on hand at the end of September was $100.
2. In accordance with the terms of its lease, the company paid its annual rent of $900 on September 1st.
3. Salaries earned by employees but not paid as of September 30, 1975, totaled $500.
4. Of the balance in the unearned revenues account, $450 had not been earned as of September 30, 1975.
5. Included in the miscellaneous expense account was the cost of a fire insurance policy purchased on August 31, 1975, at a cost of $180. The policy expires on August 31, 1977.

Required:

Prepare adjusting journal entries for the above data.

4B–3   Below is the trial balance for the Thomas Company:

THOMAS COMPANY
Trial Balance
December 31, 1975

Cash	$ 800	
Notes receivable.	2,500	
Prepaid insurance	750	
Land	21,000	
Service revenue received in advance		$ 3,500
Mortgage payable		5,000
Capital		14,750
Commissions earned		9,000
Salaries expense.	6,500	
Miscellaneous expense	700	
	$32,250	$32,250

Data for adjustments:

a.   Accrued salaries at December 31, 1975 were $220.

b.   Accrued interest on the mortgage at December 31, 1975 was $250.

c.   At year-end, one-half of the service revenue received in advance had been earned.

d.   Insurance expense for 1975 was $375.

e.   Accrued interest on the notes receivable at December 31, 1975 was $20.

Required:

Prepare adjusting journal entries for the above data.

4B–4   Below is given a trial balance before and after adjustment for Bonham Company at December 31, 1974.

BONHAM COMPANY
Trial Balance Before Adjustment
December 31, 1974

Cash	$ 800	
Accounts receivable.	1,100	
Prepaid insurance	600	
Supplies	2,250	
Office furniture	2,500	
Accumulated depreciation – office furniture		$ 500
Land	4,000	
Accounts payable.		700
Unearned fees		750
Note payable		2,000
Capital		5,450
Withdrawals	150	
Service fees		3,750
Rent income		200
Salaries expense.	1,200	
Other expenses	750	
	$13,350	$13,350

BONHAM COMPANY
Trial Balance After Adjustment
December 31, 1974

Cash	$ 800	
Accounts receivable	1,100	
Rent receivable	200	
Prepaid insurance	300	
Supplies	750	
Office furniture	2,500	
Accumulated depreciation—office furniture		$ 1,000
Land	4,000	
Accounts payable		775
Interest payable		20
Unearned fees		500
Unearned rent		50
Note payable		2,000
Capital		5,450
Withdrawals	150	
Service fees		4,000
Rent income		350
Salaries expense	1,200	
Advertising expense	75	
Insurance expense	300	
Depreciation expense	500	
Interest expense	20	
Supplies expense	1,500	
Other expenses	750	
	$14,145	$14,145

Required:

Prepare the adjusting entries for Bonham Company for 1974.

4B–5 The trial balance of the Blanchard Company as of September 30, 1975, was as follows:

BLANCHARD COMPANY
Trial Balance
September 30, 1975

Cash	$ 8,450	
Supplies	900	
Prepaid rent	1,800	
Land	16,450	
Accounts payable		$ 9,750
Unearned revenues		900
Capital		21,850
Withdrawals	500	
Commissions earned		5,500
Salaries expense	9,000	
Miscellaneous expense	900	
	$38,000	$38,000

Other financial data:

a. The cost of supplies on hand at the end of September was $150.
b. In accordance with the terms of its lease, the company paid its annual rent of $1,800 on September 1.
c. Salaries earned by employees but not paid as of September 30, 1975, totaled $725.
d. Of the balance in the unearned revenues account, $250 had not been earned as of September 30, 1975.
e. Included in the miscellaneous expense account was the cost of a fire insurance policy purchased on August 31, 1975, at a cost of $360. The policy expires on August 31, 1977.

Required:

a. Prepare a worksheet for Blanchard Company at September 30, 1975.
b. Prepare an income statement and a balance sheet from the above information.

4B–6   Below is given the September 30, 1975, trial balance *before* adjustment of the Duren Company.

DUREN COMPANY
Trial Balance
September 30, 1975

Cash	$ 2,571.07	
Supplies	1,410.60	
Prepaid rent	1,200.00	
Land	15,000.00	
Accounts payable		$ 7,325.25
Fees received in advance		2,600.00
Capital		10,175.03
Drawings	120.00	
Commissions earned		4,925.00
Fees earned		1,110.00
Wages and salaries expense	5,315.75	
Utilities expense	200.00	
Miscellaneous expense	317.86	
	$26,135.28	$26,135.28

Other data:

a. Supplies on hand at the end of September totaled $840.
b. In accordance with the terms of the lease, the annual rental of $1,200 was paid in advance on April 1, 1975.
c. Wages and salaries earned by employees but unpaid at September 30, 1975, amounted to $211.
d. Of the balance in the Fees Received in Advance account, $2,100 had not been earned as of September 30.
e. On September 1, 1975, Duren Company rented certain equipment to the Alpha Fraternity under the following terms: $75 per month

payable on the first day of each month following the start of the rental arrangement.

Required:

Prepare a worksheet for Duren Company at September 30, 1975.

4B–7 The accountant for Reynold's Repair Service debited all cash expenditures for 1975 to expense accounts and credited all cash receipts to revenue accounts. On December 31, he prepared the following trial balance.

REYNOLD'S REPAIR SERVICE
Trial Balance
December 31, 1975

Cash	$ 1,500	
Notes receivable.	2,000	
Land	6,000	
Accounts payable		$ 1,050
Notes payable		4,000
Capital		8,650
Withdrawals	200	
Service revenues.		5,000
Rent expense	300	
Insurance expense	800	
Salaries expense	2,000	
Supplies expense	2,500	
Furniture expense	3,000	
Miscellaneous expense	400	
	$18,700	$18,700

As Reynold's new accountant, you review the books and find the following information:

a. $60 of interest has accrued on the note receivable.
b. $160 of interest has accrued on the note payable.
c. Joe Strong paid $500 for a repair job to be performed next month.
d. The $300 rent expense was for a moving van rented from June 1 to June 30.
e. The company paid $800 for a four-year insurance policy on April 1.
f. The employees were given one week's advance salary of $100 on December 31.
g. $1,000 of supplies were on hand at December 31.
h. The company purchased $3,000 of furniture with a ten-year useful life and no salvage value on January 1, 1975. No depreciation expense has been recorded on the furniture.

Required:

Prepare a worksheet for Reynold's Repair Service at December 31, 1975, adjusting all accounts to their proper amounts.

Operational Differences
in Companies

THERE ARE many different types of organizations engaged in both profit-
making and not-for-profit activities. The vast majority of companies
involved in profit-oriented industries are engaged in operations such as retailing, manufacturing, service, agriculture, or a combination of these
activities. The operating cycle for these industries and, on occasion, even
for companies within a particular industry, will vary somewhat. In Chapters 2 through 4 we discussed the accounting procedures for Kilmer Contractors, a service organization. The operations of a service organization differ from those of companies engaged in other types of activities.
For example, in order for a retailer or wholesaler to earn a profit, the
revenue earned from selling merchandise must exceed the total of the cost
of goods sold and operating expenses. The operating cycle for a retailer
or wholesaler includes purchasing goods, making them available for sale
to customers, selling goods, and collecting the proceeds from the sale. The
cycle is then repeated. This operating cycle may be illustrated as follows:

A manufacturer, in order to earn a profit, must add an additional step
to this cycle—the production of goods to be sold. Similarly, a farmer must

grow his products before he can take them to market. Although slightly different in format, the accounting for organizations engaged in these different industries follows the basic concepts and procedures which were illustrated and discussed in Chapters 1 through 4.

Although all firms earn revenue from activities such as selling a product or providing a service, the point in time at which these revenues are recognized may differ among industries. In general, most businesses recognize revenue at the time a sale is made. There are exceptions to this rule, however. Many types of agricultural products are sold on the market in the form of "futures" even before the crops are planted. In the case of futures, the farmer makes a promise of future delivery at a specified price. Therefore, when the crop is harvested, revenues are recognized at that point in time since the sale of the crops at a fixed price is known with certainty.

The flow of costs in different industries can also vary substantially. For example, the function of a retailer is to purchase finished goods and sell this merchandise to his customers at a profit. In contrast, a farmer growing trees must begin with seedlings. He incurs various costs and expenses over a number of years before the trees are ready to be marketed. Likewise, a manufacturer must purchase raw materials and convert these materials into a finished product before the goods produced can be sold to customers in the normal business process.

ALLOCATION OF COSTS

The cost of an asset is considered to be an expense of the accounting period or periods which benefit from its use. In other words, assets become expenses of the periods in which they are used or consumed in the process of generating revenues. It should be noted that the determination of the portion of the cost of an asset which should be considered an expense of a particular period is usually somewhat subjective. This subjectivity is caused primarily by the concept of the accounting period or periodicity of accounting, that is, the concept of determining the income earned during a specified period of time. For example, assume that a firm purchases an asset which is used in its operations for a period of ten years. Obviously, the cost of that asset represents an expense to the firm over ten years since the business will benefit from the use of the asset during this time. However, a subjective estimate is required in order to determine the expense during each separate year of that period.

In absolute terms, the earnings of a business can only be determined with certainty over its entire lifespan—from the date of inception of the business to its termination at the time of its liquidation. It is important, however, to measure income and financial position at various points in time throughout the life of the business in order to provide interested users such as managers, investors, creditors, and the public with relevant economic information for decision making. Therefore, the accountant has divided the life of the business into accounting periods which are usually defined as one year for reporting purposes. This aids the accountant in matching the revenues earned and the expenses incurred during a particular accounting period, even though the actual receipt of cash relating to revenues or the payment of cash relating to expenses may take place over a number of accounting periods.

Accountants have developed procedures which may be used in order to determine the portion of the cost of an asset which should be considered as an expense during a particular accounting period. For example, assume that a company paid cash for a building. At the time of its purchase, it was estimated that the building had a useful life of 25 years and would have no value at the end of its useful life. Since the building is expected to be of benefit to the company for more than one period, a portion of its cost should be recognized an an expense during each accounting period that the building is used by the firm. The total expense recognized by the firm during the useful life of the building should equal the cost of the asset since it was assumed that it would have no value at the end of 25 years. The net book value of the building included in the balance sheet (the original cost of the building less that portion of the cost of the building which has been recognized as an expense) will decrease each year since a portion of the cost is charged to expense during each period. There are certain expenditures for which the estimation of future benefit is so subjective that accountants usually make no attempt to allocate these costs to future accounting periods. Instead, costs are recognized as expenses in the period in which they are incurred because the measurement of a future benefit with any degree of accuracy is either impossible or impractical. For example, assume that Chevrolet purchased a 60-second advertising spot during the Redskins vs. Dolphins football game at a cost of $25,000. It would be extremely difficult, if not impossible, to determine the periods which would benefit from this advertising expenditure. Therefore, the usual accounting treatment would be to consider the outlay for advertising as an expense of the period in which the advertising was broadcast since the benefits to future periods usually are not measurable with a reasonable degree of accuracy.

Period Costs and Product Costs

Two general classifications of cost are used for purposes of income determination: *product cost* and *period cost*. A product cost is a cost that can be directly identified with the purchase or production of goods that are available for sale. These costs are carried as assets until the goods are sold. For example, inventory purchased by a retailer would be considered to be an asset until it is sold. This cost, referred to as cost of goods sold, is included as an expense in the income statement in the period in which the inventory is actually sold.

Period costs, on the other hand, cannot be easily identified with the purchase or manufacture of a product. For the most part, period costs are costs which are incurred with the passage of time. Examples of typical period costs include interest expense, rent expense, administrative employee salaries, and certain types of insurance expense. For a manufacturing company, period costs include all costs which would continue to be incurred if the company abandoned all of its manufacturing activities and instead purchased a product for resale to its customers.

ACCOUNTING FOR RETAILING OPERATIONS

In order to illustrate the application of accounting to retailing operations, assume that Kilmer Contractors decided to expand its decorating operations by selling carpet to its customers in addition to its painting activities. Recall that its balance sheet at May 31, 1976, was as follows:

Illustration 5–1
KILMER CONTRACTORS
Balance Sheet
May 31, 1976

ASSETS		LIABILITIES AND OWNER'S EQUITY	
Cash	$10,000	Note payable	$ 1,500
Accounts receivable.	900	Unearned fees	1,100
Supplies	2,000	Capital	10,300
	$12,900		$12,900

On June 1, the company purchased 1,000 square yards of carpet, paying $5 per yard in cash. The cost of items purchased for resale is frequently charged or debited to a Purchases account. The Purchases account is used to accumulate the cost of all merchandise acquired for resale during an accounting period. The journal entry to record the purchase of this carpet would be as follows:

Purchases.	5,000	
Cash		5,000

This transaction represents an exchange of one asset for another. The debit to the Purchases account records the acquisition of the carpet, and the credit to cash indicates the cash expenditure. Because the carpet has not been sold, its cost is considered to be an asset and will not be reclassified as an expense until the year that the carpet is sold.

During June, Kilmer sold 800 square yards of this carpet at a selling price of $9 per yard. These sales would be recorded as follows, assuming that they were made for cash:

```
Cash  . . . . . . . . . . . . . . . . . . . . . . . . . . . . . . . . . . . . . .  7,200
    Sales . . . . . . . . . . . . . . . . . . . . . . . . . . . . . . . . . . . .        7,200
```

This transaction was a sale of a product for cash. The debit to the cash account records the increase in cash, and the credit to sales records the total amount of revenue generated from the sale of the carpet. If this sale had been made on a credit basis, the entry would have been a debit to accounts receivable and a credit to sales. For purposes of illustration, the cost of the carpet sold will be recorded as an expense by means of an adjusting entry made at the end of the period. Therefore, the balance in the Purchases account during the period does not normally indicate whether the goods purchased during the period are still on hand or were sold.

We will assume that the only expense (other than the cost of the carpet itself) incurred by Kilmer Contractors during the month of June was the payment of salaries to the crew which was hired to install carpet. This outlay of $1,500 would be recorded as follows:

```
Salaries Expense. . . . . . . . . . . . . . . . . . . . . . . . . . . . . . . . .  1,500
    Cash . . . . . . . . . . . . . . . . . . . . . . . . . . . . . . . . . . . . . .        1,500
```

This journal entry reflects the fact that period expenses of $1,500 were incurred and paid in cash. This cost is a period cost since it cannot be associated with the purchase or manufacture of a product and since the benefits were obtained by the firm from this outlay (that is, installation of the carpet sold) during the current accounting period.

The next step in the recording process would be to post the journal entries to appropriate ledger accounts in order to summarize the transactions which have occurred. This process would be identical to that described in Chapter 3 and will not be repeated here.

After the posting process is completed, the trial balance would appear as follows:

Illustration 5–2

KILMER CONTRACTORS
Trial Balance Before Adjustment
June 30, 1976

Cash	$10,700	
Accounts receivable.	900	
Supplies	2,000	
Note payable		$ 1,500
Unearned fees		1,100
Capital		10,300
Sales		7,200
Purchases.	5,000	
Salaries expense	1,500	
	$20,100	$20,100

An adjusting journal entry would now be required in order to determine the product cost for the month. Note that the balance in the Purchases account is $5,000, representing the cost of the 1,000 square yards of carpet which were purchased during the month of June. It is necessary to allocate this balance to record the cost of carpet which was still on hand as of June 30 and the cost of the carpet which was sold during the month of June. The cost of the items still on hand at the end of the period represents an asset referred to as Inventory. The cost of the items sold during the period is an expense called Cost of Goods Sold. The adjusting entry neces- sary to record the cost of the 800 square yards of carpet sold during June and the cost of the 200 square yards of carpet still on hand at June 30, 1976, would be as follows:

Inventory	1,000	
Cost of Goods Sold	4,000	
Purchases		5,000

The debit to Cost of Goods Sold records the cost of the carpet which was sold during June (800 yards × $5) and the debit to Inventory records the cost of the carpet still on hand at June 30 (200 yards × $5). Since the Purchases account is closed out, it has a zero balance at the beginning of the next accounting period, July 1. The balance in the Inventory account at June 30 is also the inventory at the beginning of the next period. Thus, the cost of goods available for sale during the next accounting period will include the beginning inventory plus any purchases made during July. Note that cost of goods available for sale is divided into two components at the end of the period—the cost of goods sold and the inventory on hand. This is done by means of an adjusting entry which would then be posted to the ledger accounts. The next step in the recording process would be the preparation of a trial balance *after* adjustment. This trial balance is presented in Illustration 5–3 below:

Inventory + Cost of Goods Sold = Purchases

Illustration 5–3

KILMER CONTRACTORS
Trial Balance After Adjustment
June 30, 1976

Cash	$10,700	
Accounts receivable	900	
Supplies	2,000	
Inventory	1,000	
Note payable		$ 1,500
Unearned fees		1,100
Capital		10,300
Sales		7,200
Salaries expense	1,500	
Cost of goods sold	4,000	
	$20,100	$20,100

Again, the only difference between the trial balance above and the one presented in Illustration 5–2 is the inclusion of the effect of the adjusting entry which was made to record the cost of goods sold for June.

The next step in the recording process would be to prepare closing entries. The journal entries required to close out the revenue and expense accounts of Kilmer Contractors are as follows:

```
Sales .................................... 7,200
    Income Summary. ...........................        7,200
Income Summary. ............................. 5,500
    Salaries Expense .............................        1,500
    Cost of Goods Sold. ..........................        4,000
```

The balance in the income summary account is then transferred to Kilmer's capital account by the following entry:

```
Income Summary. ............................. 1,700
    Capital. ...................................        1,700
```

The closing entries would then be posted to the general ledger. The reader should note that the closing entries for a retailing concern are almost identical to those for a service organization.

After the closing entries have been made and posted to the ledger, the financial statements would then be prepared as follows:

Illustration 5–4

KILMER CONTRACTORS
Balance Sheet
June 30, 1976

ASSETS		LIABILITIES AND OWNER'S EQUITY	
Cash	$10,700	Note payable	$ 1,500
Accounts receivable.	900	Unearned fees	1,100
Supplies	2,000		
Inventory.	1,000	Capital	12,000
	$14,600		$14,600

Illustration 5–5

KILMER CONTRACTORS
Income Statement
For the Month Ending June 30, 1976

Sales			$7,200
Less: Cost of goods sold			
Beginning inventory.		$ –0–	
Purchases.		5,000	
Goods available for sale		$5,000	
Ending inventory		1,000	4,000
Gross profit			$3,200
Salaries			1,500
Income....................			$1,700

Note that the difference between the balance sheet for a service business and that of a retailing firm is that the latter includes inventory as an asset. The primary difference between the financial statements of the two types

Illustration 5–6

KILMER CONTRACTORS

Statement of Capital

For the Month Ending June 30, 1976

Capital at June 1, 1976.	$10,300
Add: Income for the month of June	1,700
Capital at June 30, 1976	$12,000

of organizations is in the income statement. The income statement for a service business (see Illustration 3–8) usually includes a revenue account for each major source of revenue followed by a grouping of expenses which are deducted, in total, from the total revenues for the period in order to determine income. The income statement for a retailing firm (see Illustration 5–5) includes two major segments or sections. The revenue from the sale of goods is shown first. The determination of the cost of the goods sold (product cost) is then made and is deducted from sales in order to disclose the gross profit from sales for the period (sales less cost of goods sold). The other expenses (period costs) are then subtracted from the gross profit figure in order to determine the net income for the period.

THE MANFACTURING COMPANY—COST FLOWS

The cost flows of a manufacturing company differ substantially from those of a retail company. The manufacturer acquires raw materials and converts them into a finished product. In this conversion process, the manufacturer purchases labor and services, utilizes manufacturing facilities, and usually employs unique processes. All of these factors are combined in order to produce a finished product. Thus, value has been added to the raw material by the production process in order to produce a product which is marketable at a price in excess of its cost. The manufacturer must add the production costs to the cost of raw materials used during a period in order to determine the cost of goods manufactured for sale during a period.

All of the costs which can be identified with the manufacturing process are considered to be product costs. These costs will not appear as an expense in the income statement until the products with which the costs are identified are sold. Costs which cannot be related to the manufacturing process are considered to be period costs; that is, expenses of the period in which they are incurred.

Product Cost Flows in Manufacturing

The three general elements of product cost in a manufacturing company are: (1) direct materials, (2) direct labor, and (3) manufacturing overhead. *Direct materials* are raw materials which are used in the production process and which can be directly identified with finished products. For example, lumber would be a direct material in the production of furniture. *Direct labor* includes the wages of production employees who work directly on a product and whose efforts may be directly traced to specific units or batches of output. Thus, wages of an employee who applies varnish to a product would be a direct labor cost in the production of furniture. Manufacturing costs which are associated with production but not directly traceable to specific units of output as either direct materials or direct labor are classified as *manufacturing overhead*. Examples of manufacturing overhead include depreciation on plant, building, and equipment; maintenance; indirect labor; factory supplies; and salaries of production foremen.

The product cost flows in a manufacturing business are traced in the following diagram.

Product Cost Flows

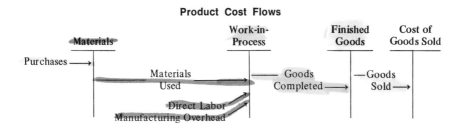

These cost flows may also be summarized as follows:

```
      Beginning Raw Materials Inventory
    + Purchases of Raw Materials
    ─────────────────────────────────────
      Raw Materials Available for Use
    − Ending Raw Materials Inventory
    ─────────────────────────────────────
      Cost of Raw Materials Used
    + Direct Labor Costs
    + Manufacturing Overhead Costs
    ─────────────────────────────────────
      Total Manufacturing Costs
    + Beginning Work-in-Process Inventory
    ─────────────────────────────────────
      Total Cost of Work-in-Process during the period
    − Ending Work-in-Process Inventory
    ─────────────────────────────────────
      Cost of Goods Manufactured and Completed during the period
    + Beginning Inventory of Finished Goods
    ─────────────────────────────────────
      Cost of Goods Available for Sale
    − Ending Finished Goods Inventory
    ─────────────────────────────────────
      Cost of Goods Sold during the period
```

The cost of direct materials, direct labor, and manufacturing overhead are combined and accumulated in a Work-in-Process Inventory account. As goods are completed, the production costs of the goods are transferred to a Finished Goods account. The Raw Materials, Work-in-Process, and Finished Goods accounts are all inventory accounts. The Raw Materials inventory account reflects the cost of the materials on hand but not used in production during the period. The Work-in-Process inventory represents the cost of partially completed products on hand at the end of the period. Finished Goods inventory indicates the cost of completed but unsold goods on hand at the end of the period. The three inventory accounts appear as current assets in the balance sheet. As sales are made from the finished goods inventory, the costs are transferred to the Cost of Goods Sold account.

The following example will be used in order to illustrate the accounting procedures for manufacturing costs. The Standard Broom Company produces street-sweeping brooms in an old factory building. The company's general ledger accounts that are pertinent to the manufacturing process, and the beginning balances in these accounts as of January 1, 1976, are as follows:

Raw Materials Inventory		Work-in-Process Inventory	
1/1/76 2,000		1/1/76 4,800	

Finished Goods Inventory		Miscellaneous Manufacturing Overhead	
1/1/76 10,200		1/1/76 -0-	-0-

Wages Payable—Direct Labor		Cost of Goods Sold	
1/1/76 -0-	-0-	1/1/76 -0-	-0-

During 1976 numerous transactions took place. The transactions which affected the product cost flows are summarized and presented below:

a) Raw materials with a cost of $23,000 were purchased for cash in 1976.
b) Transfers of raw materials to production totaled $21,000 during 1976.
c) Direct labor costs for the year totaled $38,000, of which $37,200 has been paid in cash by the end of 1976.
d) The total manufacturing overhead incurred and applied to the work-in-process was $41,000 in 1976.
e) The total production cost of the goods completed was $96,000.
f) The total cost of the goods sold during 1976 was $103,000.

The journal entries necessary to record these transactions, given the information available above, would be as follows:

a) Raw Materials.   23,000
      Cash   23,000

b) Work-in-Process Inventory   21,000
      Raw Materials Inventory   21,000

c) Work-in-Process Inventory   38,000
      Cash   37,200
      Wages Payable—Direct Labor   800

d) Misc. Manufacturing Overhead Accounts   41,000
      Cash, Accumulated Depreciation, etc..   41,000
    Work-in-Process Inventory   41,000
      Misc. Manufacturing Overhead Accounts   41,000

e) Finished Goods Inventory.   96,000
      Work-in-Process Inventory   96,000

f) Cost of Goods Sold   103,000
      Finished Goods Inventory   103,000

These journal entries, when posted to the appropriate ledger accounts pertinent to the manufacturing process, appear as follows:

Raw Materials Inventory

1/1/76	2,000		
a)	23,000		
		b)	21,000
12/31/76	4,000		

Work-in-Process Inventory

1/1/76	4,800		
b)	21,000		
c)	38,000		
d)	41,000		
		e)	96,000
12/31/76	8,800		

Finished Goods Inventory

1/1/76	10,200		
e)	96,000		
		f)	103,000
12/31/76	3,200		

Miscellaneous Manufacturing Overhead Accounts

1/1/76	-0-		
d)	41,000	d)	41,000

Wages Payable—Direct Labor

1/1/76	-0-		-0-
		c)	800
12/31/76			800

Cost of Goods Sold

1/1/76	-0-		-0-
f)	103,000		
12/31/76	103,000		

The balance sheet presentation as of December 31, 1976, would include the three ending inventory balances as current assets: raw material inventory of $4,000, work-in-process inventory of $8,800, and finished goods inventory of $3,200. Wages payable of $800 would be shown as a current liability.

Manufacturing overhead accounts also have an impact on the balance sheet. For example, depreciation on the plant would be a part of the $41,000 charge to the Miscellaneous Manufacturing Overhead account, and the offsetting credit would have been made to the Accumulated Depreciation account. The result of this transaction would be to decrease the net fixed asset balance, plant and equipment, on the balance sheet since accumulated depreciation is deducted from the cost of fixed assets. Any overhead items that required payments of cash would increase the work-in-process inventory and decrease the cash balance. In other instances, work-in-process would have been increased as liabilities, such as wages payable, were incurred.

FINANCIAL STATEMENT DIFFERENCES— RETAILING VERSUS MANUFACTURING

The only significant difference between the balance sheets of retailers and those of manufacturers is in the inventory accounts. On the balance sheet of a retail firm, inventory will usually include only a single balance or amount, merchandise inventory. Thus, the costs of all types of inventory items are aggregated in a single total amount. This procedure can be justified because of the ready marketability of inventory in the normal business process. The inventory is ready for the buyer and does not require any further processing by the seller.

The manufacturer's inventory balances are usually classified into three general categories: raw materials, work-in-process, and finished goods. The cost of *all* different types of raw materials are aggregated and reported as raw materials inventory. Similarly, *all* work-in-process will be classified as work-in-process inventory and *all* finished goods will be classified as finished goods inventory. These classifications are made on the basis of the form of the inventory.

Except for the substitution of "cost of goods manufactured" for "purchases" in the calculation of the cost of goods sold, the income statements of the manufacturer and retailer will not be significantly different as long as the manufacturer presents the cost of goods manufactured as a single figure that was developed in cost of goods manufactured statement (see Illustration 5–7). The closing entries for a manufacturing firm are also very similar to those of a retail business. There are no differences in the statements of capital of the two types of organizations.

Cost of Goods Manufactured and Cost of Goods Sold Statements

The manufacturing company usually prepares a cost of goods manufactured statement. This statement is an analysis of the manufacturing costs of the company for the period. Illustration 5–7 presents a cost of goods manufactured statement which was prepared for the Standard Broom Company for 1976.

Illustration 5–7
STANDARD BROOM COMPANY
Statement of Cost of Goods Manufactured
For the Year Ending December 31, 1976

Raw materials used:

Beginning raw materials inventory	$ 2,000	
Add: Purchases	23,000	
Raw materials available for use	$ 25,000	
Less: Ending raw materials inventory.	4,000	
Raw materials used in production.	$ 21,000	
Direct labor used in production	38,000	
Manufacturing overhead used in production.	41,000	
Total manufacturing costs	$100,000	
Add: Beginning work-in-process inventory.	4,800	
Less: Ending work-in-process inventory	8,800	
Cost of Goods Manufactured in 1976	$ 96,000	

The cost of goods manufactured for an accounting period is the equivalent of the net inventory purchases in the cost of goods sold statement of a retail company. Illustration 5–8 includes a cost of goods sold statement for both a manufacturer and a retailer. The statement formats are identical. The purpose of this statement is to provide an analysis of the cost of goods sold account.

Illustration 5–8
STANDARD BROOM COMPANY
Cost of Goods Sold Statement
For the Year Ending December 31, 1976

Manufacturer		Retailer	
Beginning finished goods inventory.	$ 10,200	Beginning merchandise inventory.	$ 10,200
Cost of goods manufactured (from Illustration 5–7)	96,000	Net inventory purchases	96,000
Goods available for sale	$106,200	Goods available for sale	$106,200
Ending finished goods inventory.	3,200	Ending merchandise inventory.	3,200
Cost of Goods Sold	$103,000	Cost of Goods Sold	$103,000

INVENTORY COSTS

The inventory costing process for manufacturing companies is consistent with the cost concept of inventory valuation. Inventory values should reflect all costs that are required in order to manufacture a product (manufacturer) or to obtain merchandise (retailer or wholesaler) in the desired condition and location. If any costs of obtaining inventory (in addition to the purchase price) are not included as product costs and instead are considered to be costs of the period, inventory values on the balance sheet would be understated and expenses on the income statement would be overstated. When these goods are sold in a later period, expenses on the income statement of that period would be understated.

All indirect costs that were incurred by the business in obtaining and placing the goods in a marketable condition should be included as a part of inventory cost if it is possible and practical to identify these costs with inventory purchases. Examples of these costs would include such items as sales taxes, duties, freight-in, and insurance.

AN OVERVIEW

Although the basic concepts and procedures of accounting are the same for profit-oriented companies in different industries, the operating cycle, cost flows, and revenue recognition points may differ substantially.

Two basic general classifications of cost used for purposes of income determination are product costs and period costs. A product cost is a cost which can be directly identified with the purchase or manufacture of goods that are available for sale. A period cost, which is usually associated with the passage of time, is recognized on the income statement as an expense of the period in which it is incurred.

Three general categories of product cost in a manufacturing company are direct materials, direct labor, and manufacturing overhead. These costs are accumulated in the Work-in-Process account. There are three inventory accounts, Raw Materials, Work-in-Process, and Finished Goods, which may appear on the balance sheet of the manufacturing company. The retail concern usually has only a single form of inventory—merchandise inventory.

A manufacturing company usually prepares a cost of goods manufactured statement, in addition to the basic statements prepared by all firms. This statement is intended to be an analysis of the manufacturing accounts for the period which it covers. A cost of goods sold statement may be prepared for any type of business that sells a product. The purpose of this statement is to provide an analysis of the cost of goods sold and to determine the gross profit or gross margin on sales (sales less cost of goods sold).

KEY DEFINITIONS

Cost of goods manufactured statement   This statement is an analysis of the manufacturing costs incurred during the accounting period.

Cost of goods sold statement   This statement is an analysis of the cost of goods sold for the accounting period.

Direct labor   Direct labor is one of the three general categories of product costs. It includes the wages of the production employees which can be specifically identified or associated with the goods being produced.

Direct materials   Direct materials, another of the three general categories of product costs, are the raw materials which are used directly in the production of the goods being manufactured.

Manufacturing overhead   Manufacturing overhead includes costs which are incurred in the production process but which cannot be identified with any specific unit of product. These costs are allocated to production according to subjective management decisions.

Operating cycle   The operating cycle includes the steps that take place from the purchase of inventory or raw materials to its sale and conversion into cash.

Period cost   A period cost is a cost which cannot be directly identified with the production of a specific product or products. It is usually more closely associated with the passage of time.

Product cost   A product cost is a cost which is directly associated with the production or purchase of goods that are available for sale.

QUESTIONS

1. Describe the operating cycle for a retailer.
2. Explain the difference between product costs and period costs. Give examples of each type of cost.
3. The determination of the portion of the cost of an asset which should be allocated to expense during a period may be somewhat subjective. Explain.
4. Describe the three input categories of manufacturing costs. How are they recorded in the financial statements?
5. What is the major difference between the balance sheet of the retailer and that of the manufacturer?
6. What is the purpose of the cost of goods manufactured statement?
7. What costs should be included in the cost of inventory?
8. What is the importance of the cost of goods sold statement?
9. Why would a company want to prepare a cost of goods manufactured statement?

EXERCISES

5-1   Using the following information, calculate the total sales.

Inventory purchases	$50,200
Beginning inventory	10,350
Wage expense	9,300
Rent expense	1,500
Interest expense	700
Ending inventory	9,350
Net income	12,000

5–2   The following balances were taken from the accounts of Norris Company. Using this information, calculate the beginning inventory.   *B.I = 294,000*

Sales	$510,000
Ending inventory	84,000
Purchases	300,000
Net income	162,000
Other expenses	108,000

5–3   Fill in the blanks:

Beginning inventory	$ 20,000
Purchases	(a) *56,000*
Ending inventory	22,000
Cost of goods sold	54,000
Expenses	(d) *28,000*
Net income	(c) *26,000*
Beginning owners' equity	200,000
Owners' additional investments	12,000 *204,000*
Owners' withdrawals	8,000 *NI = 26,000*
Ending owners' equity	230,000
Gross margin	(b) *54,000*
Net sales	108,000

5–4   Determine and fill in the missing amounts in the following situations. Each column of figures is a separate situation.

	A	B	C	D
Sales	$100,000	$100,000	$200,000	?
Beginning inventory	10,000	?	30,000	$15,000
Purchases	?	70,000	100,000	75,000
Ending inventory	20,000	10,000	?	10,000
Cost of goods sold	50,000	?	110,000	?
Gross profit	?	25,000	?	40,000
Expenses	?	?	60,000	25,000
Net income	20,000	10,000	?	?

5–5   Determine the missing amounts:

Raw materials, January 1, 1974	$ 1,000
Raw materials, December 31, 1974	3,000
Raw materials used	20,000
Raw materials purchased	(a) *18,000*
Direct labor used	(b) *39,000*
Manufacturing overhead	40,000
Total manufacturing costs	99,000
Beginning work-in-process inventory	3,800
Costs of goods manufactured in 1974	95,000
Ending work-in-process inventory	(c) *7,800*

PROBLEMS

Series A

5A–1   The following transactions took place during October, 1974. Prepare the journal entries to record these transactions.

October 1   Purchased merchandise from supplier A on account, $5,000.
         2   Merchandise was sold on account to R. P. Jones for $1,000.
         3   A $1,500 credit sale was made to J. R. Lowry.
         6   Purchased merchandise from supplier B on account, $3,000.
         9   Received payment from R. P. Jones.
        15   Sales on account of $2,000 and $2,500 were made to K. L. Putnam and A. R. Hardy, respectively.
        17   Paid supplier A in full.
        18   Received payment from J. R. Lowry.
        23   Sold merchandise on account to M. S. Fletcher for $2,500.
        24   Received payment of half of K. L. Putnam's account.
        25   Paid supplier B half of the amount owed to him.
        26   Received full payment from A. R. Hardy.
        30   Received balance of payment from K. L. Putnam.
        31   Paid supplier B the balance of the account.

5A–2   A trial balance of the Sport Shop at the end of the first year of its operations is shown below.

SPORT SHOP
Trial Balance
December 31, 1975

Cash	$ 7,000	
Accounts receivable	9,000	
Supplies	3,000	
Inventory, January 1	–0–	
Accounts payable		$ 1,000
Notes payable		4,000
Capital		15,000
Sales		20,000
Purchases	15,000	
Wage expense	4,000	
Other expense	2,000	
	$40,000	$40,000

The inventory on hand at December 31, 1975 was determined to be $3,000.

Required:

Prepare the income statement for the year ended December 31, 1975.

5A–3   Paul Peach opened a small office supply store on January 1, 1975. The following trial balance was taken from the ledger at the end of the first year of operation.

PEACH OFFICE SUPPLY
Trial Balance
December 31, 1975

Cash	$ 3,500	
Accounts receivable	13,500	
Inventory	-0-	
Prepaid insurance	1,000	
Equipment	20,000	
Accounts payable		$ 5,000
Unearned revenue		15,000
Peach, capital		13,000
Sales		75,000
Purchases	40,000	
Wage expense	10,000	
Rent expense	12,000	
Other expense	8,000	
	$108,000	$108,000

A physical count taken on December 31, 1975, showed merchandise on hand in the amount of $7,000. Other information available on December 31 included the following:

a. The equipment was purchased on January 1, 1975, and had an estimated useful life of 10 years and no salvage value.

b. The amount of insurance that expired during the year was $400.

c. Certain customers paid in advance for regular deliveries of supplies. The amounts collected were credited to Unearned Revenue. As of December 31, $5,000 of the supplies purchased had been delivered.

d. Accrued wages payable amounted to $500.

Required:

1. Prepare the necessary adjusting journal entries at December 31, 1975.
2. Prepare the entries required to close the books.
3. Prepare an income statement for the year ended December 31, 1975.

5A–4 The following account balances pertaining to 1974 were taken from the general ledger of Norris Company. Using this information, prepare a statement of cost of goods manufactured.

	Beginning Account Balance	Ending Account Balance
Raw materials inventory	$15,300	$12,200
Work-in-process inventory	8,400	14,500
Accounts payable	11,600	9,400
Finished goods inventory	13,800	14,700
Raw materials purchases		10,900
Direct labor used in production		15,250
Manufacturing overhead used in production		18,350
Sales		65,300

5A–5 Use the following information to answer the questions below.

Finished goods inventory–January 1, 1974	$162,000
Cost of goods sold–1974	230,300
Total production costs–1974	208,500
Work-in-process–January 1, 1974	98,400
Sales	450,600
Selling expenses	68,000
Withdrawals	5,000
Depreciation expense–plant and equipment	30,000
Cost of goods manufactured	200,400

1. What is the work-in-process at December 31, 1974?
2. What is the ending finished goods inventory?
3. What is the gross profit for the year?
4. What is the net operating income for 1974?

5A–6 At the beginning of the current accounting period the records of a local manufacturer showed the following balances:

Cash	$23,000
Raw materials	58,250
Work-in-process	82,900
Finished goods	98,300
Wages payable	3,000

Required: Open the appropriate T-accounts and post the following transactions to them.

1. Purchased $13,000 of raw materials.
2. Transferred $30,000 of raw materials to work-in-process.
3. Paid insurance of $300 on the plant.
4. Paid two-thirds of the $3,000 wages payable.
5. Recorded depreciation on the plant of $7,500.
6. Cost of goods manufactured was $68,000.
7. Paid selling and administrative salaries of $4,800.
8. Paid supplier for the raw materials (1 above).
9. Cost of goods sold was $108,500. C.6.S. / Fi~ Goods

Series B

5B–1 Prepare the general journal entries required to record the following transactions:

June   1   Purchased merchandise on account from the Acme Co., $2,000.

       5   Purchased merchandise on account from Baker Brothers Company, $6,000.

       9   Sold merchandise on account to Smith Company for $4,000.

       11 Sold merchandise for $3,000 cash.

       13 Paid for merchandise purchased on June 1.

       17 Sold merchandise on credit to Jones Company for $6,000.

20   Received payment in full from Jones Company.

24   Purchased merchandise on account from Acme Company, $1,000.

27   Received a $1,000 partial payment on the Smith Company account.

30   Paid balance due to Baker Brothers Company.

5B–2   The trial balance for Mitchell Supply Company at the end of the first year of operation is shown below.

MITCHELL SUPPLY COMPANY
Trial Balance
December 31, 1975

Cash	$ 6,000	
Accounts receivable	13,000	
Inventory	–0–	
Accounts payable.		$ 2,000
Note payable		10,000
Capital		18,000
Sales		100,000
Purchases	80,000	
Salaries.	20,000	
Rent expense	6,000	
Other expense.	5,000	
	$130,000	$130,000

The inventory of merchandise at December 31, 1975, determined by a physical count, was $15,000.

Required:

Prepare the income statement for the year ended December 31, 1975.

5B–3   Paul Shank opened a men's clothing store on January 1, 1975. The following trial balance was taken from the ledger at the end of the initial year of its operations.

SHANK'S MENS STORE
Trial Balance
December 31, 1975

Cash	$ 4,000	
Accounts receivable	6,000	
Inventory	–0–	
Prepaid insurance	1,500	
Equipment	30,000	
Accounts payable.		$ 6,000
Shank, capital		35,500
Sales		100,000
Purchases	60,000	
Rent expense	13,000	
Wage expense	20,000	
Other expense.	7,000	
	$141,500	$141,500

The inventory of merchandise on hand at December 31 was determined to be $14,000. Other information available at December 31 included the following:

a. The equipment had an estimated useful life of 10 years.
b. The amount of insurance that expired during the year was $600.
c. Accrued wages payable at December 31 amounted to $1,000.
d. The monthly rent on the building is $1,000. Two months' rent was paid in advance on December 1 and debited to the rent expense account.

Required:

1. Prepare the necessary adjusting journal entries at December 31, 1975.
2. Prepare the closing entries required at December 31, 1975.
3. Prepare an income statement for 1975.

5B–4   Given the following information for Marshall Manufacturing Company, prepare a cost of goods manufactured statement for 1974.

Work in process, January 1, 1974.	$ 3,200
Raw materials inventory, January 1, 1974.	14,200
Direct labor used	40,000
Total manufacturing costs.	112,000
Raw materials, December 31, 1974.	12,100
Raw materials available for use	27,000
Work in process, December 31, 1974.	5,400

5B–5   Using the information below, calculate:

1. The cost of goods manufactured,
2. The manufacturing overhead used in production,
3. The cost of raw materials used.

	Beginning Account Balance	Ending Account Balance
Raw materials inventory.	$58,000	$ 64,000
Work-in-process.	19,500	21,400
Finished goods inventory	33,200	36,300
Cost of goods sold		168,700
Direct labor		74,000
Raw materials purchases		38,000

6

Accounting Systems
and Internal Control

FINANCIAL ACCOUNTING SYSTEMS

A PRIMARY function of accounting is to accumulate the information which is required by decision makers and communicate this data to them. A financial accounting system must communicate data to users in such a way that the operating performance and current financial position of a company is reported in a manner that is both meaningful and useful. All pertinent information which is required for decision making and planning and control purposes must be made available to the user on a timely basis. There are also certain other basic housekeeping functions that the system should accomplish. For example, detailed information must be made available in order to identify the specific accounts receivable balance of each customer, detailed information regarding payroll and deductions is required in order to pay employees and satisfy government regulations, and inventory balances must be available on a current basis for purposes of inventory planning and control. The accounting system of an organization should be designed to handle all of the many facets of accounting and the system must operate in a manner which is efficient, effective, accurate, and timely.

Model of a Financial Accounting System

A model of a basic financial accounting system is presented in tabular form in Illustration 6–1 and in the form of a diagram in Illustration 6–2.

Illustration 6–1
The Financial Accounting System

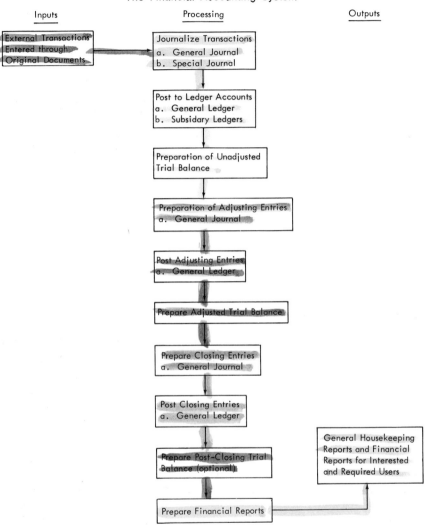

Inputs	Processing	Outputs

External Transactions Entered through Original Documents

Journalize Transactions
a. General Journal
b. Special Journal

Post to Ledger Accounts
a. General Ledger
b. Subsidary Ledgers

Preparation of Unadjusted Trial Balance

Preparation of Adjusting Entries
a. General Journal

Post Adjusting Entries
a. General Ledger

Prepare Adjusted Trial Balance

Prepare Closing Entries
a. General Journal

Post Closing Entries
a. General Ledger

Prepare Post-Closing Trial Balance (optional)

General Housekeeping Reports and Financial Reports for Interested and Required Users

Prepare Financial Reports

The financial accounting system shown in these illustrations indicates the procedures which are followed during the accounting cycle. Presentation of the system in these illustrations is intended to provide a comprehensive picture or overview of the information flows that are required in a typical organization. Note that Illustration 6–1 is a summarization of the steps in the recording process which was discussed in Chapters 3 and 4. Illustration 6–2 diagrams the same general data flows in a financial accounting system.

Illustration 6–2
Information Flows in the Financial Accounting System

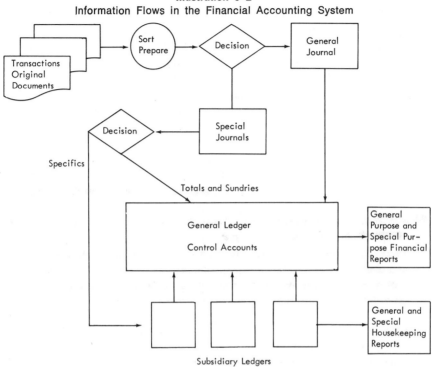

The basic components of the system are as follows:

1. A Chart of Accounts
2. A Coding System
3. A General Journal
4. A General Ledger
5. Subsidiary Ledgers
6. Special Journals
7. Internal Control
8. An Audit Trail

These components of the financial accounting system are discussed in the following paragraphs.

The Chart of Accounts

A chart of accounts is a listing of all of the accounts that an organization may use in its accounting system. The scope of the chart of accounts and the ability to adapt new account titles to the existing listing is a very important factor to be considered in the process of designing and installing an accounting system. The design of the chart of accounts will affect the manner in which accounting information will be accumulated, summarized, and used by the organization.

At a minimum, the chart of accounts should include all of the accounts that appear on the balance sheet, income statement, and statement of capital or retained earnings. In most cases, however, limiting the chart to only these accounts would be inadequate since management often requires information which is more detailed than that which is included in the basic financial statements. This detailed information is required in order to manage the day-to-day operations of the business. Also, external users such as governmental agencies frequently require information not included in the financial statements, often in detailed and specified formats. In addition to the basic functional classifications, management normally requires:

1. Accounting information which is based on cost behavior patterns for purposes of planning and control.
2. Accounting information which is based on areas of responsibility for purposes of performance measurement and control. For example, information regarding divisions or geographical regions may be used in order to measure the performance of these segments.

Many of the accounts used by the organization will be utilized for multiple purposes in the management and operations of the business. For example, production cost data is required in the process of inventory valuation, but it is also necessary for evaluating the performance of the specific departments which are involved in the production process.

Coding the Chart of Accounts

In order to facilitate the use of data and to provide a unique identity for each account, the chart of accounts is normally coded numerically. A normal pattern of arrangement and coding of the chart of accounts is in the format and the order of the financial statements and the accounts included in these statements. A simplified example of the broad categories of accounts which might be included in a typical chart of accounts is presented below.

1000–1999	Asset Accounts
2000–2999	Liability Accounts
3000–3999	Owners' Equity Accounts
4000–4999	Revenue Accounts
5000–5999	Manufacturing Cost Accounts
6000–6999	Distribution Expense Accounts
7000–7999	Administrative Expense Accounts
8000–8999	Other Income Accounts
9000–9999	Other Expense Accounts

To illustrate the usefulness of coding and the means of identifying specific items using numerical codes, a code for asset accounts will be expanded and explained. The first digit in the code may be used to identify the general account classification. Any search of the accounts is then limited to one thousand possible accounts in that category. The second digit could be used to identify an asset's location; that is, for example, whether the asset is located at the home office or at a division. The third digit could be used to identify the classification of the asset; that is whether the asset is a current asset, a long-term asset, an intangible asset, etc. The fourth digit might be used to identify the specific asset itself.

Obviously, in a large organization the coding structure may be very complex. In order to deal with the complexity of the coding structure, a code dictionary, identifying the specific account and its code, is often employed. In situations where automated equipment with sensing or scanning capability is used, numerical characters are usually considered necessary for reasons of both economy and efficiency.

The General Journal and General Ledger

Until this point, the mechanics of recording and handling transactions described in this text has been limited to the general journal and the general ledger. As previously indicated, each transaction is recorded in the general journal chronologically, and then the debits and credits from the general journal are posted to the appropriate accounts in the general ledger.

In the accounting procedures illustrated to this point, the general journal was used as the book of original entry while the general ledger served as the book of final entry. Financial statements were usually prepared from an adjusted trial balance or worksheet. The mechanics of this system would make it almost impossible for all but the smallest business to operate effectively or, at least, efficiently. This type of system is simply unable to process large volumes of transactions on a timely basis, primarily because no effective division of labor is possible since each and every journal entry must be written out on an individual basis.

In addition, this system might not provide the detailed information necessary to operate a business efficiently. For example, the system previously described did not always identify the specific individual who purchased goods on account. Likewise, it did not provide information as to the identity of individual creditors. Division of labor and necessary detail may be accomplished in this basic system by the addition and use of special journals and subsidiary ledgers in addition to the general journal and general ledger.

Subsidiary Ledgers

Subsidiary ledgers are supplemental detailed records which provide underlying support for the amounts recorded in control accounts included in the general ledger. An example of a subsidiary ledger is the accounts receivable subsidiary ledger. An individual record must be maintained on a current basis for every customer for purposes of control, billing, and for handling any inquiries.

The use of individual customer records eliminates the problem of including large numbers of detailed accounts receivable accounts in the general ledger. There are also many other obvious advantages to the use of subsidiary ledgers other than the accumulation of necessary detail. Subsidiary ledgers permit a division of duties among employees by allowing a number of different individuals to assist in the preparation of the records. In addition, personnel with less experience may be used. Also, an error in a trial balance may be localized to a subsidiary ledger, thus reducing the effort necessary to locate the error.

The total of the balances in a subsidiary ledger should be equal to the total in the corresponding control account which is included in the general ledger. This control feature will be illustrated in the example included in a later section of this chapter.

Subsidiary ledgers are necessary in order to permit the classification of a large group of accounts under a single control account in the general ledger. The subsidiary ledgers found in most systems include: accounts receivable, accounts payable, inventories, employee pay records, property records, and the stockholders' register.

Special Journals

Illustration 6–2 indicates that the initial step in the flow of information through the financial accounting system is identifying the transactions that will be processed. A decision is then made as to whether the transaction falls into a class that should be entered in a special journal or is an infrequently occurring transaction that should be entered directly in the general journal. A special journal is useful in those instances where there is a large volume of transactions which result in debits and credits to the same accounts. For such transactions, the recording process is facilitated by entering the amounts in the columns of a special journal and posting the totals periodically to the general ledger. The types of transactions which normally occur with sufficient frequency to justify the use of special journals include receipts of cash, disbursements of cash, sales of merchandise on credit, and the purchase of merchandise on account. Of course, transactions not recorded in any of the special journals are recorded in the general journal.

The accounts receivable example which was employed in order to illustrate the use of subsidiary ledgers is also applicable to special journals. When goods are sold on account, the sale is made and should be recorded at that time. The relevant aspects of credit sales from a data gathering standpoint include: identity of the customer; amount of the sale; nature of any credit terms;[1] date of the sale; and, for any future inquiries, the invoice number. This is repetitive data which will be accumulated for each and every sale.

Special journals permit a division of labor, allow the use of less experienced personnel, employ preprinted account columns or summaries which reduce the incidence of error, and allow special transactions of like kind to be easily analyzed since the original data was accumulated by category rather than on an individual basis.

If a specific type of transaction occurs frequently in the business, a special journal should be designed and used for these transactions. As previously indicated, the types of special journals most frequently used by a business normally include: sales, cash receipts, cash disbursements, and purchases.

An Example—Special Journals and Subsidiary Ledgers

Before considering the following example, the reader should review Illustrations 6–1 and 6–2 in order to make certain that the general steps included in 6–1 and the information flows illustrated in 6–2 are understood.

The credit sales and cash collections for the Yello Brewery for January are presented below in order to illustrate the interrelationships of special journals, subsidiary ledgers, and the general ledger.

January   2   Sold 200 cases at $4 per case to Harry the Hat's Bar & Grill (on account)—Invoice #101.

5   Sold 50 cases at $4 per case to Big Brother's Place (on account)—Invoice #102.

7   Received a check from Harry the Hat's Bar & Grill for $800.

11   Sold 200 cases at $4 per case to Harry the Hat's Bar & Grill (on account)—Invoice #103.

13   Sold 10 cases at $4.50 per case to the Bachelor's Club (on account)—Invoice #104.

15   Sold 20 cases at $4.10 per case to Dink's Place (on account) —Invoice #105.

25   Received a check from Big Brother's Place for $200.

31   Received a check from the Bachelor's Club for $45.

31   Received a dividend check of $50 on marketable securities.

---

[1] Credit terms include the time allowed for payment and any discounts allowed. Payment required within 30 days would be shown by the notation N/30 indicating that the full amount is due in 30 days. A discussion of discounts is included in Chapter 9.

The transactions for the Yello Brewery are journalized and posted in the special journals, subsidiary ledgers, and general ledger in Illustration 6–3.

Note that each individual credit sale is recorded in the sales journal. Any merchandise sold for cash would be recorded directly in the cash receipts journal. The amount of each credit sale is posted daily to the individual customer account in the accounts receivable subsidiary ledger. This procedure assures that each customer's account will be kept up-to-date for purposes of responding to inquiries from customers and for making decisions regarding future extensions of credit to individual customers. The check mark ($\sqrt{}$) in the sales journal indicates that the posting to the subsidiary ledger has been made. Then, at the end of the month, the total of the sales journal column ($1,927) is debited to Accounts Receivable-Control and credited to Sales Revenue.

Similarly, a cash receipts journal is used to record all transactions involving the receipt of cash. The cash receipts journal must include several columns for recording transactions since the source of the receipts may differ. For example, note that the cash receipts journal in Illustration 6–3 includes credit columns for collections on accounts receivable, sales of merchandise for cash, and all other (sundry) transactions. Thus, a receipt of cash is recorded by entering the amount received in the debit column for cash and in the appropriate column to record the credit.

As in the case of the sales journal, the individual credits in the accounts receivable credit column are posted daily to the customer accounts in the accounts receivable subsidiary ledger. The check mark ($\sqrt{}$) in the cash receipts journal indicates that the posting has been made to the subsidiary ledger.

At the end of the month, the column totals are posted to the appropriate general ledger accounts. Prior to this posting, it is necessary to prove that the total of the debit columns is equal to the total of the credit columns. After the totals in the cash receipts journal have been checked, the total in the cash column is posted as a debit to the cash account and the total of the accounts receivable column is posted as a credit to the accounts receivable-control account. Similarly, the total of the credits in the column for cash sales would be posted to the sales account in the general ledger. The individual items in the sundry account column are posted to the appropriate general ledger accounts.

Cash Disbursements Journal. A cash disbursements journal may be used to record all expenditures of cash made by the business. Normally, a journal of this type will include individual credit columns for cash and purchase discounts and a sundry or other credit column. The total of the credits to cash and purchase discounts would be posted directly to these accounts on a monthly basis while the amounts included in the other credit-column would be posted to the individual accounts at any time that it is

Illustration 6–3
Special Journals and Subsidiary Ledgers

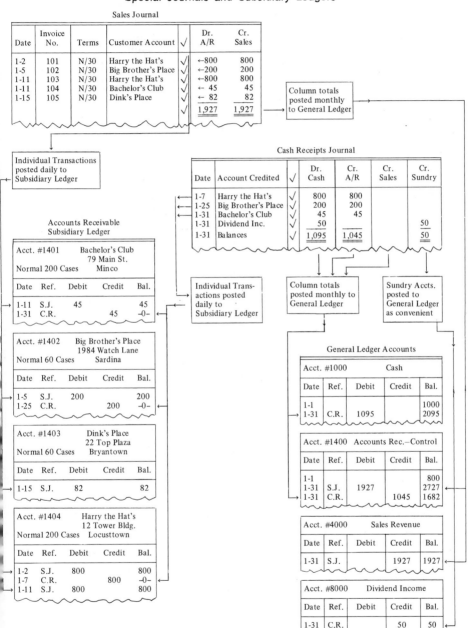

convenient to do so. Debit columns are normally included for accounts frequently affected by cash disbursements such as purchases and accounts payable. The totals of these account columns are posted directly to the purchases and accounts payable control accounts on a monthly basis. The individual debits in the accounts payable debit column must be posted daily to the accounts payable subsidiary ledger. There will be a sundry or other debit column where debits to accounts other than purchases and accounts payable may be recorded. These entries would be posted to the appropriate general ledger accounts as it is convenient to do so. The mechanics of the cash disbursements journal are almost identical to those of the cash receipts journal. Like any other special journal, the cash disbursements journal should be designed in a manner that meets the specific requirements of its user. It should include debit and credit columns for the accounts most often affected by the payment of cash. The columns suggested above are typical of those included in the cash disbursements journals of many businesses, but others may be required in particular circumstances. An example of a cash disbursements journal is included in Illustration 6–4.

Illustration 6–4

Cash Disbursements Journal

Date	Account	√	Credit Cash	Credit Purchase Discounts	Credit Sundry	Debit Accounts Payable	Debit Purchases	Debit Sundry
1-5	Miller Supply Co.	√	686	14		700		
1-9	Cantwell Sales Co.	√	388	12		400		
1-15	January Rent		500					500
1-18	Purchased Goods		250				250	
1-27	Paid Note		1000					1000
		√	2824	26		1100	250	

Individual Transactions posted daily to Subsidiary Ledger

Column Totals posted monthly to General Ledger

Sundry Accounts posted to General Ledger as convenient

Payroll Journal. A payroll journal is a specialized form of a cash disbursements journal. As its name implies, it is used exclusively to record the payment of salaries and wages to employees. A payroll journal will normally include credit columns for cash, federal income taxes withheld, state income taxes withheld, social security taxes withheld (employees' share), and other deductions such as union dues, employee hospitalization, etc. A debit column will be included for payroll expense, gross salaries, and the employer's share of social security taxes and federal and state unemployment taxes. Summary entries are made to record total payroll expense, payment of the salaries and wages, and the incurring of the liabilities related to the payroll. Information for individual employees is posted to the separate payroll records maintained for each employee. These records are, in effect, subsidiary records for payroll from which various reports and tax returns are prepared and filed.

Purchases Journal. A purchases journal is very similar to the sales journal. Credit purchases are entered in the journal, with a notation made of such information as the date of purchase, the name of the vendor, date of the invoice, terms of the purchase, and the purchase amount. As individual purchases are made, they are recorded in the accounts payable subsidiary ledger which would include a separate account for each of the suppliers of the business. Periodically, the total amount of the purchases is posted as a debit to the purchases account and a credit to the accounts payable control account. At this time, the balance in the control account should be equal to the total of the balances in the accounts payable subsidiary ledger. This information included in the accounts payable subsidiary ledger is used for making decisions regarding future purchases from particular suppliers, for checking prices, for testing the accuracy of billings made by suppliers, etc.

An example of a purchases journal is shown in Illustration 6–5. This journal includes an entry for each credit purchase of merchandise made during the month.

Form of Special Journals. There is no specified format for special journals nor is there any limit as to the number of types of special journals and subsidiary ledgers that are necessary. As mentioned previously, special journals and subsidiary ledgers should be designed so as to meet the individual needs of the particular company that will use them.

The check marks found in the special journals are made for purposes of control. The bookkeeper will check the transactions as he posts them to the appropriate ledger accounts.

INTERNAL CONTROL

Certain accounting controls are necessary within a business in order to safeguard the assets and check the accuracy and reliability of the accounting data. Generally, these accounting controls include a specified system of authorization and approval of transactions, separation of the record keeping and reporting functions from the duties concerned with asset custody and operations, physical control over assets, and internal auditing.

Illustration 6–5

Purchases Journal

Date	Invoice Date	Account	√	Amount
1/3	1/2	Miller Supply Co.	√	700
1/7	1/6	Cantwell Sales Co.	√	400
1/15	1/15	Harwell Co.	√	600
1/20	1/17	Walter & Son	√	300
1/27	1/26	Burton Inc.	√	900
			√	2900

General Ledger	Accounts Payable Subsidiary Ledger	

Purchases

Miller Supply Co. **Cantwell Sales Co.**

1/31 2900 | 1/3   700 | 1/7   400

Accounts Payable **Harwell Co.** **Walter & Son**

1/31   2900 | 1/15   600 | 1/20   300

Burton Inc.

1/27   900

A subdivision of responsibility in a financial accounting system is necessary in order to provide adequate checks on the work of company personnel. When one transaction is handled from beginning to end by a single individual and that person makes an error, the mistake will probably be carried through in the mechanics of recording the transaction and will be very difficult to locate. On the other hand, if different aspects of a transaction are processed by different people, each acting on an independent basis, an error will be much more readily identifiable. Many of the errors that would have affected the accounts will never occur because the mistake may be identified and corrected on a timely basis.

A division of responsibility among employees is also necessary for control purposes. In a properly designed accounting system, with adequate division of duties, fraud and embezzlement should be very difficult and require the collusion of two or more people. However, even in a properly designed system, the possibility of errors and embezzlement cannot be completely eliminated.

The division of duties should, of course, be logically based on the desired purposes of the system. For example, the person who maintains the subsidiary ledger of accounts receivable should not have access to cash. This will prevent him from being able to manipulate the accounts receivable and retain the cash. Likewise, a single individual should not be given the responsibility of both approving purchases and then signing the checks that are used to pay for them. Payments made to nonexistent companies for fictitious purchases would be difficult to prevent if one person is able to approve both the purchase and the payment.

A system of internal control is frequently justified because it assists the business in the detection of errors and the prevention of embezzlement. Another major benefit of a system of internal control is that it provides an atmosphere and system which are deterrents to inefficient utilization of the company's resources, fraudulent conversion of assets, and inefficient and inaccurate handling of the company's accounts.

The Audit Trail

An audit trail is the traceability factor that is built into an accounting system. It permits a person, normally an independent certified public accountant referred to as an auditor, to follow the processing of a specific transaction from the beginning of the system described in Illustration 6–1 or 6–2 to the final output of the system. This procedure should also be reversible, that is, the final output of the system should be traceable back to the original source documentation that represents the transactions which caused the final output. An audit trail provides a path that can be followed in order to verify the accuracy with which transactions were handled as well as their legitimacy. The audit trail relies on a good system of internal control and documentation of transactions.

Illustration 6–6 presents a flowchart of the purchase, receipt, payment, and use of office supplies for the Brown Grass Seed Company. This flowchart describes both the internal control and audit trail for these types of transactions.

Note that only three sets of forms are used in Illustration 6–6: a purchase requisition, the invoice prepared by purchasing (which is the first of a series of invoices in this case), and the bill of lading and the invoice received from the vendor. Multiple copies of these documents are used by the business for internal control purposes. The entire transaction may be traced from the financial statements to any point in the accounting system.

FORMS OF AUTOMATED ACCOUNTING SYSTEMS

Until this point, the manual processing of data was emphasized in our discussion. The introduction of equipment into this system does not alter

Illustration 6–6
BROWN GRASS SEED COMPANY
Purchase Order Flows

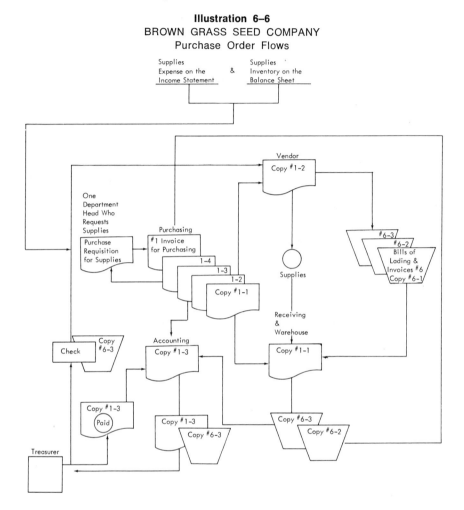

the data flows found in Illustration 6–2, but it can affect factors such as the following:

1. Methods of establishing source documents
2. Methods of transmitting data
3. Techniques of data preparation
4. Amount of data handled
5. Speed and accuracy
6. Processing of the data
7. Methods of data storage
8. Methods of information retrieval
9. Number of accounting reports used
10. Types of controls necessary for adequate internal control

Three basic automated systems are mechanical, punched card, and computer systems. Because of the basic nature of this text, it is impractical to do more than briefly describe each of these systems and to discuss the changes in the accounting process which have occurred because of the introduction of this type of equipment and capability. Remember that the distinctions made are somewhat arbitrary. The levels described are artificial distinctions and each will normally include certain aspects of the lower levels.

Mechanical Systems

The accounting system progresses to the mechanical level when a bookkeeping machine is employed in a situation where all journalizing and posting was previously done by hand and calculations were made on an adding machine or calculator. There are a number of bookkeeping machines available that have peripheral equipment attachments; but, in general, the basic machine is a combination adding machine/calculator and typewriter. Through the use of specially prepared forms with proper spacing and carbon paper, bookkeeping machines can perform multiple steps in the accounting cycle such as simultaneously journalizing and posting. Many bookkeeping machines are quite sophisticated and may be programmed to perform many functions automatically.

Punched Card Systems

Punched card systems may be either mechanical or electronic. Data preparation will require coding the data on a computer card with a keypunch machine. Once the data are prepared, the actual processing requires moving from one card-handling machine to another in order to complete all of the steps in the financial accounting process. The equipment can normally be programmed to perform specific functions. The major advantages of the punched card system in comparison to the mechanical system are its speed and accuracy.

Computer Systems

Possibly the only general statement which can be made about computerized accounting systems that holds true for each and every system is that the equipment will use electricity. The configurations of equipment, the uses of equipment, and the reasons that a business decides to use a computer system are unique to almost every company. The improvement of financial accounting is not usually one of the reasons for changing to a computer system. However, financial accounting will no doubt remain as one of its basic applications. Financial accounting is relatively simple to adapt to a computerized system. The large amounts of input data and extensive file structures required for financial accounting alone often provide a justification for the use of a computer. Speed of processing financial accounting transactions with a computerized system is limited only by the speed of the input-output devices. Accuracy is limited only by the accuracy of the data inputs. After the data have been prepared, a computer system functions as a processing unit, storage unit, information retrieval unit, and printer.

Illustration 6–7 diagrams the general processing flows of a simple computer system used for financial accounting. The reader will note that this illustration is very similar to Illustration 6–2.

Illustration 6–7
Computer Data Flows

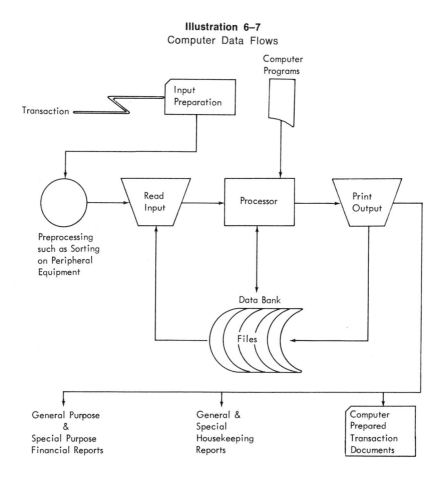

AN OVERVIEW

A financial accounting system must communicate economic information efficiently, effectively, accurately, and on a timely basis. Basic components of the system include: (1) a chart of accounts, (2) a coding system, (3) a general journal, (4) a general ledger, (5) special journals, (6) subsidiary ledgers, (7) a system of internal control, and (8) an audit trail.

A chart of accounts is a listing of all the accounts that may be used by a company. The basic design of the chart of accounts determines how accounting information will be accumulated, summarized, and used. A coding system is necessary in order for the chart of accounts to provide a unique identity for each account included in the chart of accounts. A general journal is used to record those transactions which occur on an infrequent basis. A general ledger contains the control accounts for the system. Special journals will be used for recording transactions which occur frequently. Subsidiary ledgers are supplemental detailed records which provide underlying support for the control accounts included in the general ledger. An effective system of internal control serves as a deterrent to the inefficient utilization of a company's resources; it discourages the fraudulent conversion of assets and the inefficient and inaccurate handling of a company's accounts. An audit trail is necessary to allow traceability of transactions after the fact.

The use of automated equipment in the financial accounting system does not alter the data flows in the system per se; but the equipment may cause significant changes in: (1) the source documents, (2) methods of transmitting data, (3) techniques of data preparation, (4) amount of data handled, (5) speed and accuracy, (6) processing of data, (7) methods of data storage, (8) methods of information retrieval, (9) the number of accounting reports used, and (10) the controls necessary for adequate internal control.

KEY DEFINITIONS

Audit trail The audit trail is the traceable sequence of steps through which a transaction is processed from the beginning of the accounting system to the final output. The procedures and documentation should be clear so as to provide traceability from the output back to the original documents.

Cash disbursements journal A cash disbursements journal is a special journal which may be used to record all expenditures of cash made by the business.

Cash receipts journal A cash receipts journal is a special journal which may be used to record all transactions involving the receipt of cash.

Chart of accounts The chart of accounts is the list of all accounts that a company will use in conducting its business. It includes all accounts used in the preparation of the balance sheet, income statement, and statement of capital, and in addition, all accounts that management needs for planning and control purposes. The design of the chart of accounts will determine how the information will be gathered, summarized, and used in its accounting system.

Coding   Coding is the process of assigning a system of numbers to the various accounts included in the chart of accounts.

Coding dictionary   The coding dictionary identifies an account with its coding number to simplify use of the coding system and the accounts.

Control account   A control account is a general ledger account which is supported by detailed information included in subsidiary accounts.

Internal control   Internal control comprises the plan of organization and all of the coordinate methods and measures adopted within a business to safeguard its assets, check the accuracy and reliability of its accounting data, promote operational efficiency, and encourage adherence to prescribed managerial policies.

Payroll journal   A payroll journal is a specialized form of a cash disbursements journal used exclusively to record the payment of salaries and wages to employees.

Purchases journal   A purchases journal is a special journal which may be used to record credit purchases.

Special journals   Special journals are designed to record the type of transactions where there is a large volume of transactions that occur on a frequent basis. Special journals are often used for accounts receivable, accounts payable, and cash receipts and disbursements.

Subsidiary ledgers   A subsidiary ledger is a supplementary record which provides underlying support for control accounts which are included in the general ledger. A subsidiary ledger will include more detail than the related general ledger account, and the total of all subsidiary accounts will equal the balance of the applicable control account.

QUESTIONS

1. What are the functions of a financial accounting system?
2. Explain the importance of the chart of accounts.
3. What does coding accomplish?
4. List some shortcomings of the general journal and ledger.
5. What are some advantages of subsidiary ledgers?
6. Explain how a special journal and subsidiary ledger can be used with accounts receivable.
7. What are some important components of internal control?
8. How clear should an audit trial be?
9. Why are automated systems introduced?

EXERCISES

6–1   Arrange the following activities in the order in which they normally occur.

1. Prepare adjusting entries
2. Make journal entries
3. Prepare financial statements
4. Transactions
5. Prepare adjusted trial balance
6. Post to ledger accounts
7. Prepare closing entries
8. Prepare post-closing trial balance
9. Prepare unadjusted trial balance
10. Post closing entries
11. Post adjusting entries

6–2 The Huffman Company uses 5 special journals: sales (S), cash receipts (CR), cash disbursements (CD), purchases (Pu), and payroll (P). The following transactions occurred during November 1975. Classify each account according to the special journal in which it would be entered.

1. Purchased $1,000 of merchandise from Q. R. Trucker on account.
2. Sold land for $10,500.
3. Sold $50 of merchandise to Anne Rutledge on account.
4. Purchased $300 insurance to cover the next 3 years.
5. Paid $1,500 rent in advance.
6. Paid back wages of $2,200.
7. Purchased $3,000 of merchandise from K. O. Snyder on credit.
8. Sold $300 of merchandise to Harry Benson, cash.
9. Received payment in full from Anne Rutledge.
10. Paid Q. R. Trucker the full amount due.
11. Sold merchandise on account to Jane Donner, $450.
12. Paid $38 shipping charges on merchandise purchased from K. O. Snyder.
13. Paid Best, Blake and Bader $500 in legal fees.
14. Received payment in full from Harry Benson.
15. Paid $4,000 in wages.

6–3 Bond Company had the following credit sales during the month of March:

March 1	Walter Manning	$ 600
5	Carl Stolle	900
9	Larry Pointer	400
16	Phil Youngdahl	700
25	Earl Bennett	300
29	Dan Lowe	1,100
		$4,000

The company records these transactions in a sales journal.

Required:

a. Prepare an accounts receivable ledger and post the above amounts to the subsidiary ledger.

b. Prepare an accounts receivable control account and a sales account and post the sales for the month to these accounts.

c. Prove the accounts receivable subsidiary ledger to the accounts receivable control account.

6-4 The following credit sales were made by the White Lightning Distillery in January:

January 5 Sold 15 cases at $50 per case to the Tip-Top Saloon (on account)—invoice #10.

16 Sold 20 cases at $50 per case to Sam's Alley Cat (on account)—invoice #11.

20 Sold 5 cases at $52 per case to Ferguson A-Go-Go (on account)—invoice #12.

22 Sold 17 cases at $50 per case to the Tip-Top Saloon (on account)—invoice #13.

25 Sold 1 case at $55 per case to Mabel Tucker (on account)—invoice #14.

Collection terms are n/30. Indicate the effects of these transactions on the sales journal, accounts receivable subsidiary ledger, and the general ledger.

PROBLEMS

Series A

6A-1 Below are listed certain transactions of Sorrenson Sales Company for the month of June 1975.

June 1 Sold goods on credit to J. P. Nelson, $1,500, Invoice #328, terms n/30.

3 Sold merchandise on credit to Joe's Bar and Grill, $2,300, Invoice #329, terms n/30.

4 Cash sales of merchandise, $900.

5 Sold merchandise to J. A. Baker, $1,300, Invoice #330, terms n/30.

7 Received payment in full on J. P. Nelson account.

11 Received dividend of $35 on marketable securities.

14 Received a check from Joe's Bar and Grill in full payment of account.

17 Sold merchandise to T. W. Stark, $1,700, Invoice #331, terms n/30.

19 Received full payment from J. A. Baker.

20 Sold merchandise to B. A. Spendler, $1,900, Invoice #332, terms n/30.

25 Cash sales of merchandise, $600.

26 Received payment in full from B. A. Spendler.

28 Received payment in full from T. W. Stark.

30 Cash sales of merchandise, $3,200.

Required:

a. Prepare a sales journal and a cash receipts journal.

b. Open general ledger accounts for accounts receivable, cash, and sales.

c. Open subsidiary accounts receivable ledger accounts for the credit customers.

d. Enter the above transactions in the sales and cash receipts journals and post to the appropriate ledger accounts.

6A–2   During the month of May, 1975, the Williamson Company purchased merchandise from the following suppliers on account for the respective amounts.

Date	Creditor	Amount
May 1	G & S Electronics	$ 3,000
3	T. R. Lowry	2,500
7	Western Enterprises	5,300
8	Barnard and Ralph, Inc.	7,200
10	Dobson and Heath Associates	1,500
13	W. R. Blakely	4,700
16	T. W. Barlett and Company	10,250
18	J. Presser Richards	1,100
22	Karen Prichard	500
25	Shippers National Company	350
27	Time Tickers Corporation	2,100
30	J. W. Redford	750

Cash disbursements to creditors during the month were as follows:

Date	Creditor	Amount
May 10	G & S Electronics	$3,000
12	Western Enterprises	2,300
15	Barnard and Ralph, Inc.	7,200
21	W. R. Blakely	4,700
23	T. W. Barlett and Company	5,000
27	Karen Prichard	500
28	Dobson and Heath Associates	1,500
30	Western Enterprises	3,000

The company had the following cash purchases of merchandise during May:

Date	Amount
May 5	$600
13	800

Required:

a. Prepare a purchases journal and a cash disbursements journal.

b. Prepare general ledger accounts for accounts payable, cash, and purchases.

    c. Open subsidiary accounts payable ledger accounts for the suppliers listed above.

    d. Enter the above transactions in the purchases and cash disbursements journal and post to the appropriate ledger accounts.

    e. Prove the balance in the accounts payable control account with a schedule of accounts payable.

6A–3   Condor Company uses a cash receipts journal and a cash disbursements journal. Selected transactions during the month of April are listed below.

April 1	Purchased merchandise on account from S. Klien, $600.
2	Paid April rent, $500.
3	Sold merchandise on credit to D. Gilman, $375. Received
4	Sold merchandise on credit to W. Cox, $280.
	$200 rent for subleased office space.
5	Paid $180 for advertisement in local newspaper.
6	Received $105 dividend on marketable securities.
8	Paid S. Klien $600 on account.
9	Received payment in full from D. Gilman.
10	Cash sales of merchandise, $6,250.
11	Purchased merchandise on account from Main Supply Company, $7,100.
12	Received payment in full from W. Cox.
13	Paid $100 interest on loan from City National Bank.
14	Sold merchandise on account to K. Telg, $625.
15	Purchased equipment from Barton Brothers, $3,250 cash.
17	Purchased merchandise for cash, $1,150.
18	Cash sales of merchandise, $6,100.
19	Sold a plot of land for $15,000 cash.
24	Paid Main Supply Company $7,100 on account.
27	Received payment in full from K. Telg.
28	Cash sales of merchandise, $4,300.
29	Paid salaries and wages, $6,750.

Required:

Prepare a cash receipts journal and a cash disbursements journal. Enter the above transactions in these journals as appropriate.

6A–4   The special journals for a merchandising business are listed below.

Sales Journal

Date	Account	Amount
1-1	E. R. Smith	400
1-7	J. B. Conn	600
1-13	Robert Jones	300
1-17	Bart Banner	480
1-25	Pete Zapie	120

Purchases Journal

Date	Account	Amount
1-1	Smith Co.	200
1-12	Payne Brothers	350
1-19	Donnely & Sons	420
1-24	Barton Co.	175

Cash Receipts Journal

		Debits		Credits		
Date	Account	Cash	Sales Discounts	Sales	Accounts Receivable	Sundry Accounts
1-5	Cash Sales	1000		1000		
1-8	E. R. Smith	380	20		400	
1-11	Notes Payable	2000				2000
1-16	J. B. Conn	600			600	
1-21	Cash Sales	200		200		
1-27	Robert Jones	300			300	

Cash Disbursements Journal

		Credit	Debits		
Date	Account	Cash	Accounts Payable	Purchases	Sundry Accounts
1-1	Cash Purchases	700		700	
1-9	Prepaid Insurance	300			300
1-10	Smith Co.	200	200		
1-16	Payne Brothers	600	600		
1-25	Cash Purchases	250		250	

Required:

a. Prepare T-accounts for the following general ledger accounts with the indicated balances on January 1: Cash, $3,000; Accounts Receivable, $800; Sales, 0; Purchases, 0; Accounts Payable, $400; Notes Payable, $1,000; Prepaid Insurance, $100; Sales Discounts, 0.

b. Prepare the necessary subsidiary accounts receivable ledger accounts. Balances at January 1 were: E. R. Smith, $500 and Bart Banner, $300.

c. Prepare the necessary subsidiary accounts payable ledger accounts. Balances at January 1 were: Payne Brothers, $250 and Donnely & Sons, $150.

d. Post the entries from the journals listed above to the proper T-accounts.

e. Prove the balances in accounts receivable and accounts payable with the subsidiary ledgers at January 31.

6A-5 During the month of August, Harcourt Company completed the following transactions.

August 2 Purchased merchandise on accounts from Sands Company, $1,800.

3 Sold merchandise on credit to Tom Beams, $350 (Invoice #101).

5 Sold merchandise for cash, $2,200.

6 Purchased merchandise on accounts from Bryan Supply Company, $1,400.

August   7   Purchased office equipment on accounts from Town Supply Company, $300.

9   Received payment from Tom Beams for Invoice #101.

10   Sold merchandise on credit to Gene Seago, $225 (Invoice #102).

11   Paid the Sands Company Invoice dated August 2.

12   Sold merchandise for cash, $1,600.

13   Paid cash for a two-year fire insurance policy, $800.

14   Sold merchandise on credit to Wayne Lenner, $600 (Invoice #103).

15   Purchased merchandise on account from Hardy Company, $2,100.

16   Received payment from Gene Seago for Invoice #102.

17   Sold merchandise for cash, $1,300.

18   Sold merchandise on credit to Al Sheppard, $200 (Invoice #104).

19   Borrowed $3,000 by giving the City National Bank a six-month note payable.

20   Paid the Bryan Supply Company invoice dated August 6.

21   Received payment from Wayne Lenner for Invoice #103.

22   Paid August rent in cash, $350.

23   Sold merchandise on credit to Jerry Connors, $400 (Invoice #105).

24   Purchased merchandise on account from Eastside Supply Company, $1,600.

25   Paid Town Supply Company invoice dated August 7.

26   Purchased merchandise on account from Martin Company, $700.

27   Sold merchandise for cash, $900.

28   Sold merchandise on credit to Sam Lynch, $350 (Invoice #106).

29   Purchased merchandise on account from Winters Company, $1,000.

30   Paid monthly salaries, $1,500.

31   Purchased merchandise for cash, $900.

Required:

a.   Prepare a sales journal, a purchases journal, a cash receipts journal, a cash disbursements journal, and a general journal.

b.   Enter the above transactions in the appropriate journals.

c.   Open the necessary general ledger and subsidiary ledger accounts. Post the amounts from the journals to the appropriate ledger accounts.

Series B

6B–1   Selected transactions of Pinto Company for the month of March 1975 are listed below.

March 1 Sold merchandise on credit to Harry Hondo, $700, Invoice #101.

       2 Sold merchandise on credit to Dick Ducat, $1,600, Invoice #102.

       4 Sold merchandise on credit to Arnold Abbott, $400, Invoice #103.

       7 Cash sales of merchandise, $925.

       8 Received payment from Harry Hondo for Invoice #101.

     10 Borrowed $1,000 from National Bank giving a 60-day note payable.

     11 Received payment from Dick Ducat for Invoice #102.

     12 Sold merchandise on credit to Paul Cabot, $375, Invoice #104.

     14 Cash sales of merchandise, $700.

     16 Received payment from Arnold Abbott for Invoice #103.

     18 Sold merchandise to Bob Roberts, $620, Invoice #105.

     20 Received payment from Paul Cabot for Invoice #104.

     23 Cash sales of merchandise, $900.

     26 Sold merchandise to Ed Sanders, $180, Invoice #106.

     28 Sold merchandise to Tom Jenner, $220, Invoice #107.

     30 Received payment from Bob Roberts for Invoice #105.

Required:

a. Prepare a sales journal and a cash receipts journal.

b. Open general ledger accounts for accounts receivable, cash, and sales.

c. Open subsidiary accounts receivable ledger accounts for the credit customers.

d. Enter the above transactions in the sales and cash receipts journals and post to the appropriate ledger accounts.

e. Prove the balance in the accounts receivable control account with the accounts receivable subsidiary ledger.

6B–2 During the month of September, Danner Company purchased merchandise on account from the following suppliers:

Date	Creditor	Amount
September 1	Allen Inc.	$1,600
5	Anthony Garage	900
7	Chapman Co.	875
9	Ace Glass Co.	350
11	L & M Company	640
15	Barnes Garage	1,125
17	Joe's Furniture Co.	1,350
19	Loke's Furniture Co.	890
21	Beal Sales	1,675
22	Bryan Supply Co.	1,100
24	Daniel & Son	900

Cash disbursements to suppliers during the month were as follows:

Credit Purchases:

Date	Supplier	Amount
September 8	Allen Inc.	$1,600
17	Chapman Co.	875
19	L & M Co.	350
25	Barnes Garage	1,125
29	Beal Sales	1,675

Cash Purchases:

Date	Supplier	Amount
September 7	Snyder Company	$2,500
19	Franklin Inc.	3,000

Required:

a. Prepare a purchases journal and a cash disbursements journal.

b. Prepare general ledger accounts for accounts payable, cash, and purchases.

c. Open subsidiary accounts payable ledger accounts for the suppliers listed above.

d. Enter the above transactions in the purchases and cash disbursements journals and post to the appropriate ledger accounts.

e. Prove the balance in the accounts payable control account with a schedule of accounts payable.

6B–3 Parker Company uses only two special journals, cash receipts and cash disbursements. Selected transactions during the month of February were as follows:

February 1   Purchased merchandise from M. Manco on credit, $100.

2   Paid $5,000 rent for February.

2   Sold merchandise on credit to K. S. Stacey, $150.

4   Received $4,300 rent from office space rented in the building.

5   Sold merchandise on credit to H. G. Wellar, $420.

6   Paid $230 advertising expense.

7   Received $155 in dividends on marketable securities held.

8   Paid $100 to M. Manco on account.

9   Received payment in full from K. S. Stacey.

10   Cash sales of merchandise, $11,250.

12   Ordered merchandise on account from Klein Bros., $12,500.

14   Received payment in full from H. G. Wellar.

15   Paid $50 interest on loan from Quantity First Bank.

17   Sold merchandise on account to R & R Enterprises, $7,800.

18   Purchased a new delivery truck from Brand Motors, $5,870 cash.

February 20   Purchased merchandise for cash, $2,300.
         20   Cash sales of merchandise, $9,830.
         22   Sold marketable securities for $2,700, cash at cost.
         23   Sold land for $35,300 at cost.
         24   Received the goods ordered from Klein Bros. and paid
              the account in full.
         26   Collected full amount from R & R Enterprises.
         28   Cash sales of merchandise, $15,720.
         28   Paid wages of $7,780.

Required:

a.   Prepare a cash receipts journal and a cash disbursements journal.
     Enter the above transactions in the journals as appropriate.
b.   Determine the equality of the debits and credits in the column
     totals.

6B–4   The special journals for a merchandising business for the month of
       January are listed below.

Sales Journal

Date	Account	Amount
1-1	J. A. Haynes	500
1-7	W. Russell	300
1-11	C. Andrews	700
1-18	D. Parker	900
1-25	J. Sutton	600

Purchases Journal

Date	Account	Amount
1-3	B & K Supply	400
1-10	Stan's Sport Shop	300
1-13	Bradford Co.	100
1-19	Blocker Co.	700
1-28	Jones Sales	600

Cash Receipts Journal

		Debits		Credits		
		Cash	Sales Discounts	Sales	Accounts Receivable	Sundry Accounts
1-6	Cash Sales	1200		1200		
1-9	J. A. Haynes	495	5		500	
1-12	Notes Payable	1000				1000
1-20	W. Russell	297	3		300	
1-22	Cash Sales	1700		1700		
1-27	C. Andrews	693	7		700	

Cash Disbursements Journal

		Credit	Debits		
Date	Account	Cash	Accounts Payable	Purchases	Sundry Accounts
1-3	Cash Purchases	600		600	
1-8	Prepaid Insurance	400			400
1-16	B & K Supply	400	400		
1-21	Stan's Sport Shop	300	300		
1-28	Cash Purchases	750		750	

Required:

a. Prepare T-accounts for the following general ledger accounts with the indicated balances on January 1: Cash, $4,000; Accounts Receivable, $600; Accounts Payable, $200; Prepaid Insurance, 0; Notes Payable, 0; Sales, 0; Purchases, 0; Sales Discounts, 0.

b. Prepare the necessary accounts receivable ledger accounts. Balances at January 1 were: Paul Basi, $400; Art Smith, $200.

c. Prepare the necessary subsidiary accounts payable ledger accounts. Balances at January 1 were: Hooton Company, $200.

d. Post the amounts listed in the journals above to the appropriate T-accounts.

e. Prove the balances in Accounts Receivable and Accounts Payable with the subsidiary ledgers at January 31.

6B-5   Blake and Hoss Company completed the following transactions during September 1975.

September 2 Purchased merchandise for $3,000 on credit from Thompson Suppliers.

3 Purchased office equipment for $75 on credit from Franklin Office Supply.

4 Sold merchandise on credit to J. K. Allred, $350, Invoice #1, terms n/30.

5 Sold merchandise on credit to N. M. Snyder, $175, Invoice #2, terms n/30.

6 Purchased merchandise for $1,200 on credit from Jackson, Inc.

7 Borrowed $2,000 by giving the University National Bank a 60-day note payable.

8 Sold merchandise on credit to T. S. Wheelwright, $230, Invoice #3, terms n/30.

9 Paid $1,500 on account to Thompson Suppliers.

10 Received payment in full from J. K. Allred.

11 Paid cash for a two-year fire insurance policy, $300.

12 Sold merchandise on account to M. W. Scavely, $450, Invoice #4, terms n/30.

13 Received payment in full from N. M. Snyder.

14 Sold merchandise on credit to C. R. Anderson, $780, Invoice #5, terms n/30.

15 Paid Franklin Office Supply in full.

16 Received payment in full from T. S. Wheelright.

17 Purchased merchandise for $3,300 on credit from Thompson Suppliers.

18 Sold merchandise on credit to D. W. Landale, $1,000, Invoice #6, terms n/30.

19 Sold merchandise on credit to J. K. Allred, $475, Invoice #7, terms n/30.

20 Paid $1,500 to Thompson Suppliers.

September 21 Received payment in full from M. W. Scavely.
         22 Received $400 on C. R. Anderson's account.
         23 Paid Jackson, Inc., total on account.
         24 Sold merchandise on credit to N. M. Snyder, $250, Invoice #8, terms n/30.
         26 Received payment in full from D. W. Landale.
         28 Purchased office supplies from Franklin Office Supply, $75 on credit.

Required:

a. Prepare a sales journal, a purchases journal, a cash receipts journal, a cash disbursements journal, and a general journal.
b. Enter the above transactions in the appropriate journals.
c. Open the necessary general ledger and subsidiary ledger accounts. Post the amounts from the journals to the appropriate ledger accounts.

Cash and Temporary Investments

ALMOST every transaction of any business organization will eventually result in either the receipt or disbursement of cash. The accounting procedures which enable a business to establish effective control over its cash transactions are among the most important, if not *the* most important, "controls" necessary for the operation of a business. While it is certainly true that cash is no more important than any of the other individual assets of the business, cash is more susceptible to misappropriation or theft because it can easily be concealed and because it is not readily identifiable. It is essential, therefore, that the company institute procedures or controls throughout every phase of its operations in order to safeguard cash from the time of its receipt until the time it is deposited in the company's bank account.

CASH RECEIPTS

The effective control of cash transactions begins at the moment cash is received by the business. Among the basic principles to be followed in controlling cash receipts are the following:

1. A complete record of all cash receipts should be prepared as soon as cash is received. This involves the listing of all cash items received by mail (often accomplished by the use of EDP equipment) and the use of devices such as cash registers to record "over-the-counter" sales. The immediate recording of each cash transaction is important because the likelihood of misappropriations of cash receipts occurring is usually greatest

before a record of the receipt has been prepared. Once the receipt of cash has been properly recorded, misappropriation or theft is much more difficult to accomplish and conceal.

2.   Each day's cash receipts should be deposited intact in the company's bank account as soon as possible. Disbursements should never be made directly from cash receipts; each and every cash item received should be promptly deposited in the bank. All major disbursements should be made by check, while outlays of smaller amounts may be made from controlled petty cash funds (described in a later section of this chapter). Adherence to these procedures will provide the firm with a valuable test of the accuracy of its cash records since every major cash transaction will be recorded twice: by the firm in its accounting records and by the bank. The periodic comparison or reconciliation of the accounting records of the business with those maintained by an independent, external source (the bank) is an important control feature in itself and will be discussed in detail in a later section of this chapter.

3.   The employees charged with the responsibility of handling cash receipts should not be involved in making cash disbursements. This is a normal procedure employed by most firms of any size. Insofar as possible, the internal functions of receiving and disbursing cash should be kept separate in order to prevent the possible misappropriation or theft of cash. The employees handling cash receipts should not have access to the other accounting records of the firm for the same reasons.

"Over-The-Counter Sales."   The cash proceeds received at the time a sale is made should be recorded by means of a cash register. In larger firms, it may be preferable to have all sales recorded by a cashier at a centrally located cash register. One employee may "make the sale" and prepare a pre-numbered sales slip which is given to the cashier who then records the sale on the cash register and accepts the customer's payment. Involving two (or more) employees in each sales transaction, rather than permitting a single employee to handle a transaction in its entirety, increases the control over cash. The use of a cash register also provides certain other benefits. Customers will observe that their purchases are recorded at the proper amount (another form of control). You may recall making a purchase where your money was refunded "if a star appears on your receipt" or where your drink was free if the waiter failed to give you a receipt. These are simple, yet effective examples of control procedures which are intended to encourage customers to note whether the sale has been properly recorded at the correct amount. The cash register may also be used as a means of classifying the sources of receipts, such as sales by departments.

At the end of each day, or more often if necessary (for example at the end of each cashier's shift), the cash in the register should be counted and recorded on a cash register summary or other report by an employee who does not have access to the sales slips. A second employee should total the sales slips and reconcile the total of the sales slips to the cash register total. As previously indicated, all cash received should be deposited intact in the bank and the receipts recorded in the accounting records.

In certain circumstances, it may not be feasible to use prenumbered sales slips. If this is the case and a cash register is used, the above procedures should still be followed to the extent applicable. The major difference will be that the cash in the register will be reconciled to the totals contained in the register rather than to totals obtained from sales slips.

Receipts from Charge Sales. Remittances from customers for sales which were made on account may be received either by mail or by payment in person. In either case, procedures should be employed so that the receipt and the recording of the cash is performed by different employees whenever it is possible and practical to do so. If this separation of duties can be effectively maintained, the misappropriation of cash would require the collusion of two or more employees, thus diminishing the likelihood of the occurrence of any irregularity.

The employee who opens the mail should immediately prepare a listing of all cash items received. Of course this can be done "automatically," such as by the use of punched cards as remittance forms and EDP equipment. This listing, along with a summary of over-the-counter receipts described previously, may be used to record each day's receipts in the cash receipts summary. Mail remittances are then combined with over-the-counter receipts, and the daily bank deposit is prepared and made. The amount deposited will be equal to the total cash receipts for the day. The employee making the bank deposit should obtain a duplicate deposit slip or other receipt from the bank for subsequent comparison to the cash receipts book.

The advantages of the procedures described above are many. The most important of these benefits may be summarized as follows:

1. The possibility of irregularities with respect to cash transactions are reduced, since any misappropriation will generally require the collusion of two or more employees.
2. The prompt deposit of each day's receipts intact (along with the disbursement procedures described in a later section of this chapter) provides the basis for an independent, external check on the internal records of the firm by reconciliation with bank statements.
3. Frequent deposits of receipts minimizes the idle cash and thereby reduces interest or other carrying charges which might otherwise be incurred by the business.

Several sections of this chapter have discussed the possible misappropriations of cash and outlined certain procedures which are intended to minimize these occurrences. It is obvious that the owners and/or management of any organization are naturally concerned with establishing effective controls that will prevent irregularities, but it may not be as apparent that every employee of the business also has a definite interest in these safeguards. If, for example, cash is misappropriated in an instance where the control procedures are ineffective or not in existence, any employee who might possibly be involved will be under suspicion. Although it may not be possible to identify the guilty person, no employee will be able to prove his (or her) innocence. Employee morale and efficiency will be adversely effected. An effective system of internal control avoids this situation; responsibilities are well-defined, definite, and fixed. Internal control is often an excellent preventive measure, as it often removes the temptation which might cause an otherwise good employee to succumb.

CASH DISBURSEMENTS

As previously indicated, one of the basic rules of effective internal control over cash transactions is that each day's receipts should be deposited intact in the bank and that all disbursements should be made by check. The functions of handling cash receipts and cash disbursements should be separated or divided among employees to the greatest extent practical. Other procedures which may be used to establish effective control over cash disbursements include the following:

1.   All checks should be prenumbered consecutively and should be controlled and accounted for on a regular basis. Checks which are voided or spoiled should be retained and mutilated to prevent any possible unauthorized use.

2.   Each disbursement should be supported or evidenced by an invoice and/or a voucher which has been properly approved.

3.   Invoices and vouchers should be indelibly marked as "paid" or otherwise cancelled in order to prevent duplicate payments.

4.   The bank statement and returned checks should be routed to the employee charged with the preparation of the bank reconciliation statement (described below). This employee should be someone other than the person who is responsible for making cash disbursements.

THE BANK RECONCILIATION STATEMENT

As was indicated earlier, if all receipts are deposited intact in the bank and all major disbursements are made by check, each cash transaction will be recorded twice: by the business in its accounting records, and in the records of the bank. It might seem logical, then, that at any given time the cash balance obtained from the accounting records of the firm should be identical to (i.e., equal to) the balance in the business's checking account at the bank. This is very seldom the case, however. Comparison of the balance shown in the firm's records with the balance shown at the same date by the bank statement usually reveals a difference in the two amounts. One reason for the difference could, of course, be erroneous entries made either by the firm or by the bank. A more frequent cause for the difference is, however, attributable to the difference in the timing of the recording of the transactions by the firm and the bank. If all transactions were recorded simultaneously by the business and by the bank no differences would result (except in the case of errors), but this is almost never the case. The firm, for example, will write a check and immediately deduct the amount of the expenditure from the cash balance in its checkbook. The bank will not deduct this same disbursement from the firm's account until the check is presented to it for payment, perhaps several days later. Until the disbursement is deducted by the bank, the balance in the firm's account at the bank will exceed the firm's cash balance in its checkbook by the amount of the check. Similarly, the bank may levy a service charge against the firm's bank account from time to time. The business is usually unaware of the amount of this charge until it receives its monthly statement from the bank. Until the bank statement is received and the service charge is deducted, the balance on the firm's records will exceed the bank statement balance by the amount of the service charge. The above examples are but two of the many items which may cause a difference between the bank statement balance and the cash balance as shown on the accounting records of the business.

A bank reconciliation is prepared in order to identify and account for all items which cause a difference between the cash balance as shown on the bank statement and the balance as it appears in the firm's accounting records. One format of this statement which is often used is such that both the book and bank balances are adjusted to the actual amount of cash which is available to the business. This amount is often referred to as the "adjusted cash balance" or "true cash." A typical bank reconciliation statement is presented in Illustration 7–1 on page 169.

The initial step in preparing a bank reconciliation statement is to examine the bank statement and any debit and credit memoranda accompanying it. A debit memorandum is evidence of a deduction made by the bank from a depositor's account which arises from a transaction other than the normal payment of a check by the bank. Likewise, a credit memorandum is an addition to the depositor's account which arises from a transaction other than a normal deposit. These documents should be compared with the firm's accounting records in order to determine whether or not they have been previously (and properly) recorded by the business. If these transactions have not been recorded, they will be included as additions or deductions in the bank reconciliation statement and then recorded

Illustration 7–1

CAROL'S BAKERY
Bank Reconciliation Statement
June 30, 1976

Balance per the bank statement, June 30, 1976.		$4,590
Add: Deposit in transit		500
Bank error, check drawn by Carrol's Tavern charged to the account of Carol's Bakery		10
Less: Outstanding checks:		
Number 95–$50		
Number 101– 15		
Number 106– 30		
Number 110– 5		(100)
"True" cash balance, June 30, 1976		$5,000
Balance per the books, June 30, 1976		$4,000
Add: Note collected by the bank		1,000
Error made by the accountant in recording check #100		45
Less: Bank charges		(5)
NSF check.		(40)
"True" cash balance, June 30, 1976		$5,000

at a subsequent time. Examples of these types of reconciling items which were included in Illustration 7–1 are as follows:

1.   The $1,000 addition to the book balance represents the proceeds from a note payable to Carol's Bakery which was collected by the bank and added to Carol's bank account.
2.   The bank charges of $5 for the month of June were deducted from Carol's account by the bank.
3.   The N.S.F. (Not Sufficient Funds) check of $40 represents a check received from a customer and deposited by Carol. The check was returned unpaid by the customer's bank.

The second step in preparing the reconciliation is to arrange the paid checks returned with the bank statement in numerical sequence. The checks returned by the bank are then compared with the checks issued as listed in the business checkbook or cash disbursements journal. Distinctive "tick marks" or symbols (such as a $\sqrt{}$) may be used in the checkbook in order to indicate those checks which have been returned by the bank. The amount of each check should be compared to the amount listed in the checkbook during this process. The outstanding checks are those which have been issued but not yet returned by the bank.

Checks which were outstanding at the beginning of the month and which cleared the bank during the month may be traced to the bank reconciliation statement prepared at the end of the previous month. Any checks which were outstanding at the beginning of the month and which did not clear the bank will, of course, still be included as outstanding in the current month's reconciliation. In the example, the $100 total of outstanding checks included in the bank reconciliation statement was determined by comparing the cancelled checks returned with the bank statement with the checkbook and the listing of outstanding checks included in the previous month's bank reconciliation.

In our example, examination of the cancelled checks returned with the bank statement disclosed the fact that the bank had deducted a check of Carrol's Tavern in the amount of $10 from the Carol's Bakery account. This item is shown as an addition to the balance per bank in the reconciliation and would be called to the attention of the bank for correction.

The next step in the reconciliation process is to ascertain whether or not there are any deposits in transit. A deposit in transit is a receipt which has been included in the cash balance per books and deposited in the bank (for example, in a night depository or by mail) but which has not yet been processed by the bank and credited to the depositor's account. In the illustration, the total receipts of $500 for June 30th were deposited in the bank's night depository on that date. The bank, however, did not credit the firm's account until the next day, July 1st. The $500 amount is therefore shown as a deposit in transit in the June 30, 1976, bank reconciliation statement.

An excellent test of the accuracy of the firm's cash receipts records is to reconcile the total receipts for the month (or other period) to the total deposits credited to the bank account in the bank statement. In order to perform this test, the following information would be required:

1. The total deposits which are included in the bank statement for the month of June (including a deposit in transit at the beginning of the month [May 31, 1976] of $700) $15,000
2. The total cash receipts shown in the firm's accounting records for the month of June (including the receipts of June 30th of $500). $14,800

The receipts as per the books for the month of June would be reconciled with the deposits as per the June 30, 1976, bank statement as follows:

Deposits per bank statement. $15,000
Less: Deposit in transit at the end of
       the prior month   700
                                                              $14,300
Add: Deposit in transit at the end of
       the current month   500
Cash receipts per the books $14,800

In many instances, deposits in transit, outstanding checks, service charges, and errors will be the only reconciling items between the book and the bank balances. Omissions from, or errors in, the accounting records of the firm should, of course, be corrected immediately. If errors made by the bank are discovered in the reconciliation process (such as a check charged to the wrong account), they should be called to the attention of the bank for immediate correction.

In the example, several adjusting or correcting entries would be required. These are as follows:

Note collected by the bank

Cash 1,000
    Notes Receivable   1,000

Error

Cash   45
    Accounts Receivable 45*

Bank service charges

Service charge expense   5
    Cash   5

N.S.F. check

Accounts Receivable   40
    Cash   40

    * The receipt of a payment on account of $572 was erroneously recorded as $527 by the firm. This entry reduces the customer's account in order to reflect the actual amount which was paid and increases cash to the proper amount.

The effect of these three entries will be to adjust the balance per books as of June 30, 1976, to the "true cash" balance as of that date. This adjustment procedure may be illustrated as follows:

Cash	
4,000	
1,000	5
45	40
5,000	

It should be noted that only those items which are adjustments of the "balance per books" in the bank reconciliation statement will require adjusting or correcting entries. This is because these items have either not been previously recorded on the books of the firm (in the example, the note collected by the bank, the bank charges, and the check which was returned N.S.F.) or have been recorded erroneously (in the example, the receipt of $572 which was recorded by the firm as $527[1]). Items which are included as adjustments of the "balance per the bank statement" do not require adjustment on the firm's books since these items are either

---

[1] Transposition errors (i.e. $572 − $527) are always divisible by nine. This fact may be helpful in locating differences, errors, etc.

transactions which have been already recorded by the firm but not by the bank (in the example, the deposit in transit and the outstanding checks) or errors which were made by the bank (in the example, the check of Carrol's Tavern which was erroneously charged to the account of Carol's Bakery).

The bank reconciliation procedure may be summarized as follows:

Balance per the bank statement—Adjust for:

1. Transactions recorded by the firm but not by the bank (deposits in transit, outstanding checks, etc.).
2. Errors made by the bank.

───────────
True Cash
═══════════

Balance per the books—Adjust for:

1. Transactions recorded by the bank but not by the firm (collections made for the firm by the bank, service charges, N.S.F. checks, etc.).
2. Errors made by the firm.

───────────
True Cash
═══════════

PETTY CASH FUNDS

As previously indicated it is best to make all major disbursements by check. This is not practicable, however, in instances where small expenditures are required for postage, freight, carfare, employees' "supper money," etc. In circumstances such as these, it is usually more convenient to make payments in currency and/or coin. This can be accomplished and effective control over cash still maintained by the use of a petty cash fund.

A petty cash fund is established by drawing a check on the regular checking account, cashing it, and placing the proceeds in a fund. The amount of the fund depends upon the extent to which petty cash will be used and how often it will be reimbursed. As a practical matter it should be large enough to cover petty cash disbursements for a reasonable period of time—for example, a week. A single employee should be placed in charge of the fund and made responsible for its operation.

A major difference between making disbursements from a petty cash fund and from a regular checking account is that disbursements from petty cash funds are recorded in the accounting records not as they are made, but when the fund is reimbursed. At the time each expenditure is made from the fund, a petty cash voucher, such as the one in Illustration 7–2 is prepared. If an invoice or other receipt is available in support of the disbursement, it should be attached to the voucher. In any event the person receiving the cash should always be required to sign the petty

Illustration 7–2

```
┌─────────────────────────────────────────────────────────────────┐
│                                                                   │
│               Petty Cash Voucher #53                              │
│                                                                   │
│   TO    Vince Brenner        DATE   May 1        1976             │
│                                                                   │
│   EXPLANATION          ACCOUNT              AMOUNT                │
│            Postage         119               $5.00               │
│                                                                   │
│                                                                   │
│   APPROVED                       RECEIVED                         │
│   BY          P D                PAYMENT      V. B.               │
│                                                                   │
└─────────────────────────────────────────────────────────────────┘
```

cash voucher as evidence of his or her receipt of the disbursement. If this procedure is followed, at any given time the total of the cash on hand in the petty cash fund plus the total of the unreimbursed receipts should be exactly equal to the original amount of the fund.

The fund would be reimbursed on a periodic basis or whenever necessary. In order to obtain reimbursement of the fund, the employee acting as petty cashier would bring the paid petty cash vouchers to the person who is authorized to write checks on the firm's bank account and exchange them for a check equal to the total of the vouchers. At this point, the petty cash vouchers would be separated and summarized according to the appropriate expense category for recording in the firm's accounting records. Before the check is issued, the vouchers would be reviewed in order to ascertain that all the expenditures made were for valid business purposes. After the petty cash vouchers are approved and the fund replenished, the vouchers and the underlying support should be marked as "paid" or otherwise mutilated in order to prevent their reuse, either intentionally or unintentionally.

To illustrate the operation of a petty cash fund, assume that Barney Company establishes a $100 petty cash fund on January 1, 1976, by cashing a check in the amount of $100 and placing the proceeds in the fund. The entry to record this transaction would be as follows:

```
January 1   Petty Cash . . . . . . . . . . . . . . . . . . . . . . . . . . . . .   100
                 Cash . . . . . . . . . . . . . . . . . . . . . . . . . . . . . .          100
```

Assume further that during the month of January, disbursements from the fund (supported by vouchers) totaled $85. In order to replenish the fund on January 31, the employee responsible for the fund would exchange the vouchers for a check drawn on the regular cash account for $85. This check would be cashed and the $85 proceeds would be used to restore the fund to its original cash balance of $100. This transaction would be recorded by the following entry:

```
January 31   Various Expenses . . . . . . . . . . . . . . . . . . . . . . . .   85
             Cash  . . . . . . . . . . . . . . . . . . . . . . . . . . . . .        85
```

Note that no entry is made to the "petty cash" account after the fund is established (unless the firm wishes to increase or decrease the fund balance).

Effective control over petty cash operations is accomplished in two ways: at any time the cash on hand in the fund plus the unreimbursed petty cash vouchers must be equal to the fund balance, and the expense vouchers are examined and approved upon reimbursement by a person other than the employee who made the disbursement. If considered necessary or desirable, surprise counts of the petty cash fund also may be made in order to insure that the fund is operating according to its intended purpose.

INVESTMENTS

Investments are the temporary or long-term conversion of cash into productive use by the purchase of securities. Investments are found among the assets of almost all businesses. In general, investments are classified as either temporary or long-term depending on the nature of the security and the intention of the investor firm. Temporary investments will be discussed in this chapter and long-term investments in Chapter 15.

Temporary Investments

Temporary investments, usually referred to as marketable securities, normally arise from seasonal excesses of cash and represent its conversion to productive use (earning interest or dividends) on a short-term basis. In order to be classified as a temporary investment, a security must be readily salable and the volume of trading of the security should be such that the sale does not materially affect the market price. In addition, there is general agreement that there should be an intention on the part of the investor firm to sell the securities in the short run as the need for cash arises. Temporary investments include both stocks and bonds.

Control over Investments

The effective control over marketable securities includes the physical safeguarding of the certificates. This usually means that the securities should be kept in a safe if they are retained by the firm, and the access to the certificates controlled. In many instances, the firm will leave its investments in the custody of its broker. The authority to purchase and sell is usually vested in the Board of Directors of the firm or in a specifically designated investments committee. In either case, requiring written authorization in order to either acquire or dispose of investments is another important control feature. Finally, the accounting records themselves are important in establishing control over investments. The periodic reconciliation of the accounting records to the securities on hand or in the custody of the broker and the reconciliation of the recorded income to the income which should have been earned (as determined by calculation and reference to sources such as *Standard & Poor's Dividend Record*) help to provide effective control over investments.

Accounting for Acquisition of Temporary Investments

The basis for recording temporary investments in the accounts is the cost of the investment. Cost includes all outlays which are required to acquire the investment including the quoted price of the security, brokerage commissions, transfer taxes, etc. When bonds are purchased between interest dates, the purchase price of the bonds usually includes the accrued interest to the date of purchase. As will be discussed in more detail in Chapter 14, the amount of the accrued interest purchased is recorded in a separate asset account and not as a part of the cost of the investment. To illustrate the accounting for the acquisition of marketable securities, assume that Jones Company purchased 100 shares of the stock of IBM Corporation at a price of $200 per share on January 1, 1976. The entry to record this purchase would be as follows:

```
Investment in Stock  . . . . . . . . . . . . . . . . . . . . . . . . . . . . 20,000
    Cash . . . . . . . . . . . . . . . . . . . . . . . . . . . . . . . . . . . . .          20,000
```

When a temporary investment is sold, the difference between the selling price and carrying value of the investment is recorded as a gain or loss of the period in which the sale took place.

Valuation of Temporary Investments

As indicated above, investments in marketable securities are generally valued at cost. A gain or loss is recognized when the investment is sold according to the difference between the selling price and the acquisition cost. Alternatively, marketable securities may be valued at cost or market, whichever is lower. When using this method, if the market value of a security is lower than its cost, the security is written down to its market value. In other words, the securities are carried at the lower of the original cost or their current market value. Therefore, if the maket price falls below cost, the asset value is decreased and a loss is recognized, but if market is higher than cost, the cost is not adjusted and no gain is recognized. Obviously, such treatment results in investments being conservatively presented in the balance sheet and a conservative treatment of investment income in the income statement. There does not appear to be any justification other than conservatism for the practice of recognizing decreases but failing to recognize increases in the value of marketable securities.

In applying the lower of cost or market method, a reduction in the amount at which a security is carried in the accounts may be recorded by an adjusting entry debiting a "loss on temporary investments" account and crediting the "investments" account. The loss would be included in the income statement of the accounting period in which it occurred. To illustrate, assume that the market price of the IBM stock held by Jones Company was $190 per share on December 31, 1976. Using the lower of cost or market rule, the following entry could be made in order to record the decline in market value of the IBM stock:

Loss on Temporary Investments 1,000
    Investment in Stock   1,000

Accordingly, the balance sheet at December 31, 1976, would report the investment at a carrying value of $19,000.

If a company owns several different types of temporary investments, the lower of cost or market procedure may be applied to the securities as a group or it may be applied to individual securities. For example, assume that a company holds the following marketable securities on December 31, 1976:

	Original Cost	Market Value
IBM Stock	$20,000	$19,000
MMM Stock	10,000	10,500
	$30,000	$29,500

The lower of cost or market rule applied to the securities as a group would result in recognition of a $500 loss ($30,000 original cost less $29,500 market value) and result in a balance sheet carrying value of $29,500. Application on an individual securities basis would result in the recognition of the $1,000 decline in the value of the IBM stock since the increase in the value of the MMM stock would be ignored. The balance sheet would show a carrying value of $29,000 for marketable securities. Obviously, application of the lower of cost or market rule to individual securities will always yield a lower carrying value since increases in market values are not considered and therefore do not offset any decreases in the market value of other securities.

Disclosure of Temporary Investments

Temporary investments are by their nature current assets and are carried in the financial statements as such. The current market value of marketable securities is usually disclosed, either parenthetically or by footnote. The income earned from temporary investments, in the form of dividends and interest or gains or losses on sales, is usually shown on the income statement in a "miscellaneous" or "other" income classification.

Comprehensive Illustration—Bank Reconciliation

A bank statement for Kilbourne, Inc., shows a balance as of December 31, 1976, of $3,691.18. The cash account for the company as of this date shows an overdraft of $611.48. In reconciling the bank statement with the book balance, the following items are discovered:

a. The balance in the cash account includes $400.00 representing a change fund on hand. When this change fund is counted, only $374.70 is found to be on hand.

b. The cash balance includes $500.00 representing a petty cash fund. An inspection of this fund reveals cash of $420.00 on hand and a replenishing check drawn on December 31, 1976 for $80.00.

c. Proceeds from cash sales of December 27, 1976 were stolen. The company expects to recover the full amount stolen ($690.00) from its insurance company and has made no entry for the loss.

d. The bank statement shows that the company was charged with a customer's N.S.F. check for $125.84, bank services charges of $39.50, and a check drawn by another firm for $136.00 which was incorrectly charged to Kilbourne's account.

e. The bank statement does not show receipts of December 31, 1976, totaling $1,837.00, which were mailed to the bank on that date but not received by the bank and credited to Kilbourne's account until January 2, 1977.

f. Checks outstanding were found to be $8,031.00. This includes the check transferred to the petty cash fund and also two checks, each for $182 and payable to I. M. Acrook. Acrook had notified Kilbourne that he had lost the original check and had been sent a second one; Kilbourne stopped payment on the first check. Also among the checks outstanding was one for $120.00 which has been outstanding for 17 years. This check was originally issued as final payment for the company's African Puma, which is still being used to guard the company's shop at nights. It is decided to cancel this item since the payee, P. U. Maroper, cannot be found and payment will never be claimed.

Required:

1. Prepare a bank reconciliation, using the format where both bank and book balances are adjusted to a corrected cash balance.
2. Give any correcting or adjusting entries required by the foregoing information.
3. List the cash items as they should appear on the Balance Sheet on December 31.

(AICPA Adapted)

Solution for Comprehensive Illustration

Balance per bank statement		$3,691.18
Add: Deposit in transit		1,837.00
Bank error		136.00
		$5,664.18
Less: Outstanding checks		7,729.00
		($2,064.82)
Balance per books		($ 611.48)
Add: Stop payment		182.00
Check canceled		120.00
		($ 309.48)
Less: Change fund	$400.00	
Petty cash fund	500.00	
Loss from theft	690.00	
N.S.F. check	125.84	
Service charges	39.50	1,755.34
		($2,064.82)
Correcting entry:		
Cash change fund	$374.70	
Petty cash	500.00	
Cash shortage	25.30	
Receivable from ins. co	690.00	
Accounts receivable	125.84	
Expense	39.50	
Accounts payable		$ 182.00
Puma		120.00
Cash		1,453.34
Statement presentation:		
Current assets:		
Cash on hand		$ 874.70
Current liabilities:		
Cash overdraft		$2,064.82

KEY DEFINITIONS

Balance per bank statement   This balance is the amount in the cash account of the business according to the bank's records.

Balance per books   This amount is the balance in the cash account according to the firm's records.

Bank reconciliation   A bank reconciliation is an analysis made to identify and account for all items which cause differences between the cash balance as shown on the bank statement and the cash balance as it appears in the firm's accounting records.

Cash   Cash consists of currency, coins, checks and certain other forms of negotiable paper.

Cash disbursement   A cash disbursement is an outlay of cash made by the firm.

Cash receipt   A cash receipt is an inflow of cash into the firm.

Cash transaction   A cash transaction is an accounting transaction that involves either a cash receipt or a cash disbursement.

Charge sales   Charge sales are sales in which the firm provides a customer with goods or services in exchange for the customer's promise to pay at a later date.

Credit memorandum   This memorandum is an addition which is made by the bank to a depositor's account. The addition arises from a transaction other than a normal deposit.

Debit memorandum   This memorandum is a deduction which is made by the bank from a depositor's account. The deduction arises from a transaction other than the normal payment of a check by the bank.

Deposit in transit   This deposit is a receipt which has been included in the cash balance per books and deposited in the bank, but not yet processed by the bank and credited to the depositor's account.

Investments   Investments are the temporary or long-term conversion of cash into productive use by the purchase of securities.

Outstanding check   This is a check which has been issued by the business but not yet presented to the bank for payment.

Over-the-counter sales   These sales are consummated by the immediate payment of cash for the goods or services purchased.

Petty cash fund   The petty cash fund is a fund established to make cash disbursements for small expenditures.

Petty cash voucher   This voucher is an authorization to disburse cash from the petty cash fund and is usually retained as a receipt for the expenditure.

Temporary investments   A temporary investment is a security that is readily salable, and the volume of trading of the security should be such that the sale does not materially affect the market price. In addition, there should be an intention on the part of the investor firm to sell the security in the short run as the need for cash arises.

True cash   True cash is the amount of cash that is actually available to the entity. One format for the bank reconciliation statement adjusts both the book and bank balances to true cash.

Voucher   A voucher is an authorization to make a cash disbursement.

QUESTIONS

1. Why is control over cash transactions considered to be more important than other assets of a business?

2. List a few basic principles in connection with cash control. You may wish to organize your discussion along the line of the normal cash flow.

3. What are the principal advantages of maintaining a separation of duties involving cash transactions?

4. In order to establish control over the cash receipts from over the counter sales, a small firm installs a cash register with each sales clerk responsible for ringing up his or her own sales. Discuss.

5. List some procedures other than separation of duties which may be employed in order to establish effective control over cash disbursements.

6. What is the purpose of a bank reconciliation statement?

7. What are the necessary adjustments in the bank reconciliation statement to the balance per the bank statement? To the balance per the books?

8. The petty cash account has a debit balance of $300. At the end of the accounting period there is $35 in the petty cash fund along with petty cash vouchers totaling $265. Should the fund be replenished as of the last day of the period? Discuss.

9. How are investments classified for financial statement purposes?

10. What is the basis for recording investments in the accounts?

EXERCISES

7-1 State whether the following bank-reconciliation items would need an adjusting or correcting entry on the *depositor's* books:

1. Checks totaling $1,850 were issued by the depositor but not paid by the bank.

2. A $1,000 note was collected for the depositor by the bank and was deposited in his account. Notice was sent to the depositor with the bank statement.

3. The last day's receipts ($1,750) for the month were not recorded as a deposit by the bank until the following month.

4. The depositor issued a check for $180 but entered it in his records as $810.

5. The bank paid a check for $150 but entered it as $510 on their records.

6. The bank charged a bad check that it received in a deposit back against the depositor's account. Notice to the depositor was made by the bank with the bank statement.

7. The bank charged $21 for service charges and notified the depositor with the bank statement.

8. The bank had erroneously charged a check, drawn by another depositor with a similar name, to the depositor's account.

7-2 Prepare the journal entries that are necessary to adjust the cash account on the depositor's books, based on the information included in Exercise 7-1 above.

7-3 The following information is taken from the books and records of the Terp Company.

```
Balance per the cash account (before adjustment) . . . . . . .    $2,860
Outstanding checks. . . . . . . . . . . . . . . . . . . . . . .       820
Deposit in transit . . . . . . . . . . . . . . . . . . . . . . .      208
Bank service charges . . . . . . . . . . . . . . . . . . . . . .       18
Cash on hand—unrecorded on the books and not yet
    deposited in the bank  . . . . . . . . . . . . . . . . . . .      180
Balance per the bank statement. . . . . . . . . . . . . . . . . unavailable
```

Required:

Prepare a bank reconciliation showing the "true" cash balance.

7–4 Prepare, in general journal form, the entries that Terp Company should make to adjust its cash balance as a result of the bank reconciliation in Exercise 7–3 above.

7–5 Test the accuracy of Willard Company's cash receipts records for August given the following information:

Total cash receipts as shown in the firm's records were $14,910.
Payment of $1,110 was received on August 31 but the deposit was not yet recorded by bank.
Total deposits included in the August bank statement were $14,700.
Deposit in transit at end of July was $900.

7–6 The Gibbons Company reconciles its one bank account on a monthly basis. The company follows the procedure of reconciling the balance as reported on the bank statement and the balance per books *to a corrected balance*. The corrected balance appears on the balance sheet.

The facts stated in items 1 through 10 below are involved in the reconciliation for the month of December. Decide which of the five answer choices best indicates how each fact should be handled in the December 31 bank reconciliation.

Answer choices for items 1 through 9:

(1) An addition to the balance per books.
(2) A deduction from the balance per books.
(3) An addition to the balance per bank.
(4) A deduction from the balance per bank.
(5) Should not appear in the reconciliation.

1. A deposit of $100 made on December 31 did not appear in the December bank statement . . . . ( )
2. A deposit of $130 made on November 30 was recorded by the bank on December 1 . . . . ( )
3. Three checks totalling $180 drawn in December did not clear the bank . . . . ( )
4. A check from customer Kay for $75 was returned by the bank marked N.S.F. . . . . ( )
5. The bank statement was accompanied by a credit memo

dated December 30 for the proceeds of a note ($198) which
Gibbons Company had left with the bank for collection ....   ( )

6. Gibbons Company discovered that a December check recorded in the check register as $150 was actually drawn for
$105. This check was cleared by the bank in December ....   ( )

7. Two checks totalling $120 drawn in November had cleared
the bank in December ....   ( )

8. Accompanying the December bank statement was a cancelled check for $60 of Gibson Company ....   ( )

9. The bookkeeper of Gibbons Company had recorded a $90
check received from customer Fay on December 29 as
$190 ....   ( )

10. Which of the facts disclosed in items 1 through 9 above
require adjusting entries on the books of the Gibbons
Company?

(1) 1, 3, 8   (2) 6, 8, 9
(3) 1, 2, 3, 7   (4) 4, 5, 6, 9
(5) Some other group

7–7 Show in general journal form all entries that should be made to reflect
the operation of the Eljon Corporation's petty cash fund:

May 10 The company established a petty cash fund of $225.
    12 Paid miscellaneous office expenses amounting to $52.
    14 Paid $15 to messengers for cab fares.
    19 Paid telephone bill of $63.
    25 Paid $21 in postage.
    30 The petty cash fund was reimbursed for the first time.
    31 Eljon Corporation increased its petty cash fund to $300.

7–8 Ames Company had the following transactions relating to marketable
securities during the last three months of 1975:

September 1 Purchased 100 shares of Burden Company common stock
             for $27 per share plus commission of $100.
November 1   Received a $1 per share dividend on the Burden Com-
             pany stock.
December 1   Sold 50 shares of Burden Company stock at $32 per
             share net of commissions.

Required:

a. Prepare the journal entries necessary to record the above
    transactions.
b. Determine the cost basis for marketable securities at December 31,
    1975.

PROBLEMS

Series A

7A–1   Red, Inc.'s bank statement for the month ending June 30 shows a balance of $231. The cash account as of the close of business on June 30 indicates a credit balance or overdraft of $123. In reconciling the balances, the auditor discovers the following:

Receipts on June 30 of $1,860 were not deposited until July 1.
Checks outstanding on June 30 were $2,215.
The bank has charged the depositor $10 for service charges.
A check payable to S. S. Dohr for $56 was entered in Red's cash payments journal in error as $65.

Prepare a bank reconciliation.

7A–2   *a.*   Prepare a bank reconciliation showing the "true" cash balance for Ginger's Floral Shop for July 1974 given the following information:

1.   Balance per bank statement at July 31, $4,610.
2.   Balance per books at July 31, $3,900.
3.   Deposits in transit not recorded by banks, $445.
4.   Bank error, check drawn by the Ginger Bread Shop debited to account of Ginger's Floral Shop, $20.
5.   Note collected by bank, $1,025.
6.   Debit memorandum for bank charges, $10.
7.   NSF check returned by bank, $35.
8.   Accountants credited cash account for $175 rather than the correct figure of $100 in recording check #55.
9.   Outstanding checks of $120 on July 31.

b.   Prepare the adjusting or correcting entries required.

7A–3   You have been engaged to audit the Able Company. In the course of your examination, you gather the following information:

1.   Balance per cash account, July 31, 1975, $2,750.
2.   Bank service charges for the month included as a debit memo with the bank statement, $22.
3.   Outstanding checks at June 30, $195.
4.   Deposits received on July 31 and sent to bank but not yet recorded by bank, $216.
5.   Checks written in month of June and returned with July statement, $135.
6.   Checks written in July but not returned with July 31 bank statement, $535.

Required:

Compute the balance reported on July 31, 1975 bank statement.

7A–4   In connection with an examination of the cash account you are given the following worksheet:

Bank Reconciliation
December 31, 1974

Balance per books at December 31, 1974		$17,174.86
Add: Collections received on the last day of December and charged to "cash in bank" on books but not deposited		2,662.25
Debit memo for customer's check returned unpaid (check is on hand but no entry has been made on the books)		200.00
Debit memo for bank service charge for December		5.50
		$20,142.61
Less: Checks drawn but not paid by bank (see detailed list below)	$2,267.75	
Credit memo for proceeds of a note receivable which had been left at the bank for collection but which has not been recorded as collected	400.00	
Check for an account payable entered on books as $240.90 but drawn and paid by bank as $419.00.	178.10	2,945.85
Computed balance		$17,196.76
Unlocated difference		200.00
Balance per bank		$16,996.76

Checks Drawn but Not Paid by Bank

No.	Amount
573	$ 67.27
724	9.90
903	456.67
907	305.50
911	482.75
913	550.00
914	366.76
916	10.00
917	218.90
	$2,267.75

BAl. correct in correct   *2467.75*

Required:

a. Prepare a corrected reconciliation.

b. Prepare journal entries for items which should be adjusted prior to closing the books.

7A–5 The Backward Company decided to create a petty cash fund because of the increase in small cash disbursements such as supplies and postage. The following transactions took place in the month of May.

Postage.	$13
Delivery costs	9
Supplies	25
Tapes for recorder	3

The petty cash fund was established at $300 on May 1. It was replenished on May 30 and then increased by $50 on May 31.

Required:

Prepare all journal entries related to the petty cash fund for the month of May.

7A–6 The transactions of Sandy Company relating to marketable securities during 1975 are listed below.

January 10	Purchased 500 shares of Smith Corporation common stock at a price of $21 per share plus a $200 commission.
February 5	Purchased 100 shares of Dade Corporation common stock at a price of $40 per share plus an $80 commission.
March 1	Received a cash dividend of $1 per share on Smith Corporation common stock.
April 16	Purchased 200 shares of Consolidated Company common stock at $80 per share plus $120 commission.
June 1	Received a cash dividend of $2 per share on Dade Corporation common stock.
August 20	Sold 100 shares of Dade Corporation stock at $42 per share, net of sales commissions.
September 1	Received a $1 per share dividend on Consolidated Company common stock.

Required:

a. Prepare the journal entries necessary to record the above transactions.
b. Determine the cost basis for marketable securities at December 31, 1975.

Series B

7B–1 The following data are accumulated for use in reconciling the bank account of Montgomery Company for the month of May.

a. Balance per bank statement at May 31, $4,870.30.
b. Balance per books at May 31, $4,678.27.
c. Deposit in transit not recorded by bank, $402.00.
d. Checks outstanding, $589.93.
e. A check for $156.00 in payment of rent expense was erroneously recorded on the company's books at $165.00.
f. Bank debit memorandum for service charges, $4.90.

Prepare a bank reconciliation and the journal entries necessary to adjust the cash account as of May 31.

7B–2 On December 31, 1973, the accounting records of the Cavilier Sales Company showed a cash balance of $6,600. A review of its bank reconciliation as of that date disclosed that a deposit of $7,200 was in transit and that checks of $6,350 were outstanding. Cavilier's books showed cash receipts of $108,700 and cash disbursements of $115,250 during the year. The company's bank paid checks totaling $121,000 during 1973. A deposit of $9,000 was in transit at the beginning of the year.

Required:

Reconstruct the December 31, 1972 bank reconciliation of the Cavilier Sales Company.

7B–3   Use the following data concerning King Company to prepare a bank reconciliation statement.

Balance per bank	$10,500
Balance per books.	9,250
Deposit in transit	1,015
Refund of cash for damaged material (not deposited)	35
Outstanding checks.	175
Bank service charge.	3
NSF check received by bank from the Goodman Company (a customer).	62
Interest collected by the bank for King Company on a note receivable	1,111
$400 deposit from King Company recorded as $410 by bookkeeper.	

Hint: Watch for cash overage or shortage.

7B–4   The Patrick Company had poor internal control over its cash transactions. Information about its cash position at November 30, 1974 was as follows:

The cash books showed a balance of $18,901.62, which included undeposited receipts. A credit of $100 on the bank's records did not appear on the books of the company. The balance per bank statement was $15,550. Outstanding checks were: No. 62 for $116.25, No. 183 for $150.00, No. 284 for $253.25, No. 8621 for $190.71, No. 8623 for $206.80, and No. 8632 for $145.28.

The cashier embezzled all undeposited receipts in excess of $3,794.41 and prepared the following reconciliation:

Balance, per books, November 30, 1974		$18,901.62
Add: Outstanding checks:		
8621	$190.71	
8623	206.80	
8632	145.28	442.79
		$19,344.41
Less: Undeposited receipts		3,794.41
Balance per bank, November 30, 1974		15,550.00
Deduct: Unrecorded credit.		100.00
True cash, November 30, 1974		$15,450.00

(AICPA Adapted)

Required:

a. Prepare a supporting schedule showing how much the cashier embezzled

b. How did he attempt to conceal his theft?

c. Taking only the information given, name two specific features of internal control which were apparently missing.

7B–5 Listed below are all transactions affecting the Stupark Company petty cash fund in April.

April 1 The company created a petty cash fund of $150.
5 Bought paper clips for $3.
8 Bought lunch for a prospective customer, $5.
15 Paid bill for a palm tree for the new office, $23.
19 Paid $20 cab fare for president stranded at airport.
25 Increased the amount of the fund from $150 to $200.
27 Paid $33 cash for postage.
30 Reimbursed the petty cash fund.

Required: Prepare the journal entries necessary to reflect the above transactions.

7B–6 Handy Company had the following transactions relating to marketable securities during 1975:

January 20 Purchased 100 shares of Bear Corporation common stock at $50 per share plus a $105 commission.

April 16 Purchased 400 shares of River Corporation common stock at $10 per share plus a commission of $95.

May 1 Received a cash dividend of $1 per share on Bear Corporation common stock.

June 5 Purchased 100 shares of Gunner Corporation common stock at $75 per share plus a $160 commission.

August 11 Received a cash dividend of $2 per share on River Corporation common stock.

November 1 Sold 100 shares of Bear Corporation common stock at $55 per share, net of commissions.

December 1 Received a $1 per share dividend on Gunner Corporation common stock.

Required:

a. Prepare the journal entries to record the above transactions.

b. Determine the cost basis for marketable securities at December 31, 1975.

8

Receivables

RECEIVABLES are assets representing the claims that a business has against others. Normally these assets will be realized or converted into cash by the business. Receivables are classified according to the timing of their expected realization (i.e.—as current assets if realization is anticipated within a year, or as noncurrent assets if collection is expected subsequent to the current period). Receivables are also classified according to their form. Notes receivable are claims against others which are supported by "formal" or written promises to pay. These may or may not be negotiable instruments, depending on such factors as the terms, form, and content of the note. An example of a note receivable would be the written promise by a borrower to repay a loan, with interest, at a stated date. Accounts receivable, on the other hand, are not supported by "formal" or written promises to pay. An example of an account receivable would be the claim of a business against a customer who makes a purchase on account.

The purpose of this chapter is to describe and discuss the procedures which are necessary in order to establish effective control over receivables and to illustrate the accounting practices and procedures which are employed with regard to these assets.

CONTROL OVER RECEIVABLES

At the time an over-the-counter sale is made, it should be recorded by means of a cash register whether it is a cash sale or a charge sale. The controls described in Chapter 7 apply to both charge or credit sales as well as to cash sales. If a sale is made on account, a prenumbered sales ticket should be prepared and signed by the customer making the purchase. As a minimum, this charge ticket should include the following information:

1. The date.
2. The customer's name and account number.
3. A description of the item(s) purchased by the customer.
4. The total amount of the sale.
5. The customer's signature.

Effective control procedures require that the sales slip be prepared in triplicate: one copy would be given to the customer; a second copy would be placed in the cash register; and a third copy would be retained by the salesperson. An invoice dispenser which automatically retains a copy in a locked container is an ideal control device for this purpose.

At the end of each day, or more often if necessary, the charge slips accumulated in the register would be used in the reconciliation of the cash register receipts as previously described in Chapter 7.

The charge slips will serve as the basis for recording credit purchases in customers' accounts. A "control" account, trade accounts receivable for example, would be used to record the total charge sales and the total payments which are received from customers. Individual ledger accounts, referred to as "subsidiary" accounts, would be maintained for each customer. The amount of each charge sale would be recorded individually in the particular customer's account, and the total sales would be recorded in the control account. Bills would be prepared from the individual customers' ledger accounts and mailed out periodically, usually on a monthly basis. As payments are received from customers, the remittances would be recorded individually in the customer's account and in total in the "control" account. Cash receipts, received either by mail or "over-the-counter," would be controlled according to the procedures outlined in Chapter 7. At any point in time, the balance in the "control" account should be equal[1] to the total of the balances in the individual customers' accounts. Therefore, a periodic reconciliation should be made of the control and the subsidiary accounts.

ACCOUNTING FOR RECEIVABLES

As credit sales are made, entries are recorded in both the "control" and the "subsidiary" accounts. For purposes of illustration, assume that

---

[1] If a special journal is used, they may be equal only at the end of the period.

a department store makes the following sales during the month of June, 1976:

To Larry Killough.	$ 100
To Gene Seago	150
To Pat Kemp.	200
To all other charge customers	10,000
	$10,450

These sales would be recorded in the "control" account, trade accounts receivable, by the following entry: .

Accounts Receivable	10,450	
Sales		10,450

At the same time, these sales would also be recorded in the individual customers' accounts, so that at all times the balance in the "control" account (accounts receivable) would be equal to the total of all the balances in the "subsidiary" accounts (individual customers' accounts). Using T-accounts, this process is illustrated as follows:

Control Accounts · *Subsidiary Accounts*

Accounts Receivable = **Killough**   **Seago**

Accounts Receivable		Killough		Seago	
100		100		150	
150					
200					
10,000		Kemp		All Others	
Bal. 10,450		200		10,000	

Sales	
	100
	150
	200
	10,000
	10,450 Bal.

Now assume that the collections received from customers are as follows:

From Killough.	$ 100
From Seago	100
From other customers	8,000
	$8,200

These collections would also be recorded in the control account by the following entry:

```
Cash ......................................  8,200
    Accounts Receivable ...........................          8,200
```

At the same time, the collections would also be recorded in the subsidiary accounts, thereby maintaining a balance with the control account. This procedure is illustrated as follows:

Control Account		Subsidiary Accounts			
Accounts Receivable		**Killough**		**Seago**	
Bal. 10,450	8,200	100	100	150	100
2,250		0		50	

Kemp		**All Others**	
200		10,000	8,000
		2,000	

BAD DEBT EXPENSE

One of the costs of making sales on a credit basis is the expense that results from the fact that some of the customers who make purchases on account may never pay the amounts which are owed to the firm. This is to be expected and should be considered a normal cost of doing business. Obviously, if a firm were able to identify the particular customers who would ultimately fail to pay their accounts, it would not sell to them on a credit basis. Unfortunately, although credit investigations of varying degrees of effectiveness are made by firms, some bad debts will still result. In fact, if a firm had no bad debts whatsoever, this might be an indication that its credit department was performing unsatisfactorily. If credit standards were set so high as to eliminate *all* those potential customers whose credit rating was judged to be marginal, the revenue lost from refusing credit to these customers would no doubt exceed the potential losses, thus decreasing the firm's net income. From a theoretical viewpoint, the firm should grant credit to its customers up to that point where the marginal revenue from the granting of credit sales is exactly equal to the marginal expense, including the cost of bad debts. Of course this goal is impossible to attain in actual practice, but a firm's credit policy should attempt to approximate this objective to the extent possible and/or practical.

Bad debt expense, then, is a normal business expense which should be expected by those firms selling goods or services on a credit basis. The proper determination of income requires that bad debt expense be matched against revenue in the period in which the revenue is earned. Most accountants agree that this is the period in which the sale was originally made, and not the period in which a particular account is determined to be uncollectible. Since the particular accounts which will ultimately prove to be uncollectible are unknown, bad debt expense must be estimated. There are two general approaches to the estimation of bad debts: (1) use of a percentage of credit sales with the percentage determined by the firm's past credit experience; and (2) analysis of the receivable balance at the end of the period. Although these two methods will be discussed in turn, they should be regarded as complementary since both are used in combination by most firms.

As a firm makes credit sales during a period, it will normally record the estimated bad debt expense which is related to these sales on a periodic basis. Assume, for purposes of illustration, that the credit experience of a small firm has been as follows:

Year	Credit Sales	Losses from Bad Debts
1973	$120,000	$2,300
1974	130,000	2,650
1975	150,000	3,050
	$400,000	$8,000

For 1976, it might be reasonable for the firm to estimate that its losses from uncollectible accounts would be similar to its experience in prior-years. A percentage which could be used in estimating bad debts would be $8,000 divided by $400,000 or 2 percent of credit sales. In practice, of course, this percentage would be adjusted for any expected changes in general economic conditions, credit policies, etc.

Returning to the example used earlier in the chapter, recall that credit sales for the period were $10,450. The estimated bad debts from these sales would be calculated by multiplying $10,450 by 2 percent or $209. This estimated bad debt expense would be recorded in the accounts by the following journal entry: *To Record Bad Debts*

Bad Debt Expense	209	
Allowance for Bad Debts		209

Note that the credit portion of this entry is to an Allowance for Bad Debts account and not to Accounts Receivable. While the firm's best estimate of its bad debt expense, based on its past experience, indicates that approximately $209 will not be collectible, it is unable to identify the individual accounts that may not be paid at this time. Note the effect of this entry on the control and subsidiary accounts:

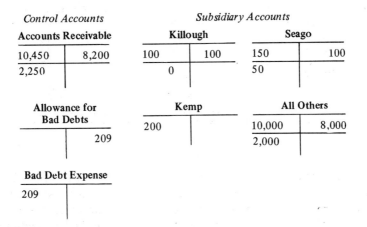

Control Accounts		Subsidiary Accounts			

Control Accounts

Accounts Receivable

10,450	8,200
2,250	

Allowance for Bad Debts

	209

Bad Debt Expense

209	

Subsidiary Accounts

Killough

100	100
0	

Seago

150	100
50	

Kemp

200	

All Others

10,000	8,000
2,000	

Since the particular individual whose account may ultimately prove to be uncollectible cannot be identified at this time, a direct credit to accounts receivable is inappropriate since such a procedure would eliminate the equality of the control and the subsidiary accounts.

A second approach to the estimation of bad debts is the analysis of the receivable balance at the end of a period in order to make a judgment as to which accounts are likely to prove to be uncollectible. An "aging" of the accounts is usually a part of this procedure. Aging involves the classifying or grouping of accounts according to the period of time that the accounts have been outstanding. The basic assumption is that, all other factors being equal, the collectibility of receivables decreases as the account remains outstanding. An example of the "aging" process is presented below:

Account	Balance	Number of Days Outstanding			
		0-30	31-60	61-90	91 and Older
Killough	$ 0	$ 0	$ 0	$ 0	$ 0
Seago	50	50	0	0	0
Kemp.	200	200	0	0	0
All others	2,000	1,350	400	50	200
	$2,250	$1,600	$400	$50	$200

Based on the experience of the firm, different percentages may be applied to the different classifications of accounts in order to estimate the amount of uncollectible receivables. For example, the following calculation might be appropriate:

Number of Days Outstanding	Amount	Percentage*	Estimated to be Uncollectible
0–30	$1,600	1%	$ 16
31–60	400	10	40
61–90	50	50	25
91 and older.	200	75	150
	$2,250		$231

* The percentage used would be determined by the credit experience of the firm, adjusted as considered necessary for such factors as changes in economic conditions, credit policies, etc.

The older accounts, as well as those which are known to be in financial difficulty, should also be reviewed on an individual basis as an additional test of the amount which is estimated to be uncollectible. Assume that, after this review, the firm decided that the allowance for bad debts should be increased to $231. The following journal entry would be required:

Bad Debt Expense 22
    Allowance for Bad Debts   22

After this entry has been posted to the allowance account, the balance in the account would be $231.

Allowance for Bad Debts

	209
	22
	231

In the balance sheet, the allowance for bad debts would appear as an offset to, or deduction from, accounts receivable. For example, the receivables of the firm would be shown as follows:

ASSETS

Cash		$ 5,000
Accounts receivable.	$2,250	
Less: Allowance for bad debts	231	2,019
Other assets		10,000
Total Assets		$17,019

When a particular account balance is determined to be uncollectible, an entry is made in the accounts in order to recognize this fact. Returning to the example used earlier in the chapter, assume that the $50 balance owed by Seago proves to be uncollectible. The following entry would be required:

Allowance for Bad Debts	50	
Accounts Receivable		50

After this entry has been posted to the accounts, the control[2] account would appear as follows:

Accounts Receivable		Allowance for Bad Debts	
2,250	50	50	231
2,200			181

In the balance sheet, the receivables would appear as follows:

Accounts receivable	$2,200	
Less: Allowance for bad debts	181	$2,019

It is important to note that the entry for the write-off of the uncollectible receivable affects neither expense nor total assets. The net receivable balance (accounts receivable less the allowance for bad debts) remains the same since both accounts receivable and the allowance for bad debts are reduced by the same amount. The expense related to bad debts is recorded when the estimated bad debts are recorded (i.e., when the provision for bad debts is made). The entry to record bad debts expense is normally made during the year-end adjustment process.

Even though a company writes off an account as uncollectible, it will still attempt to collect the balance due. In some instances, it may continue its own efforts to collect the account, in others it may turn the account over to a collection agency. In any event, if the collection efforts prove to be successful, the company will receive cash and two entries are required in order to record this receipt. The first entry reinstates the balance which has been written off by reversing the original entry which was made at the time of the write off. The second entry records the collection of the account balance.

In order to illustrate the recovery of an account which had previously been written off, we will return to the example used above. Assume now that the $50 balance owed by Seago which was written off as uncollectible

---

[2] The effect on the subsidiary accounts would be to reduce the balance in Seago's account from $50 to zero, thus maintaining the equality between the control and the subsidiary accounts.

is subsequently collected. The collection would be recorded by the following entries:

```
Accounts Receivable . . . . . . . . . . . . . . . . . . . . . . . . . . . . . . . . . . . .  50
    Allowance for Bad Debts . . . . . . . . . . . . . . . . . . . . . . . . . . .          50

Cash  . . . . . . . . . . . . . . . . . . . . . . . . . . . . . . . . . . . . . . . . . . .  50
    Accounts Receivable . . . . . . . . . . . . . . . . . . . . . . . . . . . . . .          50
```

Again, note that the first entry simply reverses the previous write-off. The second entry records the collection of the balance.

NOTES RECEIVABLE

As previously indicated, notes receivable are claims against others which, unlike accounts receivable, are supported by formal or written promises to pay. A typical note receivable is shown in Illustration 8–1.

Illustration 8–1

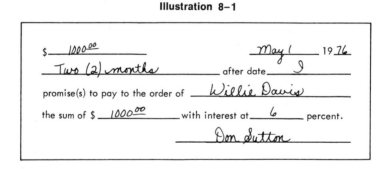

The note shown above is an interest-bearing note: Don Sutton (the maker of the note) agrees to pay Willie Davis (the payee) $1,000 (the principal amount of the note) plus interest at six percent on July 1, 1976 (the maturity date). The six percent annual interest is the charge that Sutton pays for the use of Davis's funds. Interest, which is an expense for Sutton and income for Davis, is calculated by the following formula:

$$\text{Principal} \times \text{Rate} \times \text{Time} = \text{Interest}$$
$$\$1,000 \quad \times \quad .06 \quad \times \quad {}^{2}\!/_{12} \quad = \quad \$10$$

The maturity value of this note is $1,010 (the principal amount of $1,000 plus interest at $10); this is the amount that Sutton must pay Davis on July 1, 1976, when the note becomes due and payable (matures).

Note that for ease of calculation, the six percent interest rate was expressed as a decimal, .06. Alternatively, a fraction $^{6}\!/_{100}$ could have been used in the computation. The interest rate stated in a note is usually expressed in terms of an annual or yearly rate. Since the note used in the illustration was for a duration of two months, time was expressed as a fraction of a year, $\frac{2}{12}$. In some instances, time may be stated in days. If this is the case, a year is usually considered to have 360 days in order to simplify the computation of interest. For example, if the note in the illustration was for a period of 30 days, the calculation of interest would be as follows:

$$\$1,000 \times .06 \times \frac{30}{360} = \$5$$

In order to illustrate the accounting for notes receivable, the entries necessary to record the transactions regarding the Sutton-Davis note will be presented in the sections which follow.

Issuance of the Note

On May 1, 1976, when Sutton borrowed the $1,000 from Davis, the following entry would be made on Davis' books to record the loan:

Notes Receivable	1,000	
Cash		1,000

This entry indicates that Davis has exchanged one asset (cash of $1,000) for another asset of equal value (a note receivable of $1,000).[3]

Accrual of Interest

Interest is the cost of borrowing to the maker of the note or, from the payee's (lender's) viewpoint, the income which is earned. In the example, Davis' earnings during the month of May would be calculated as follows:

$$\$1,000 \times .06 \times \frac{1}{12} = \$5$$

If Davis wished to accrue the interest earned during the month of May, (i.e.,—record it on his books) the following entry would be necessary:

Interest Receivable	5	
Interest Earned		5

This entry recognizes the fact that Davis' assets have increased by $5 because of the interest earned during the month of May. This entry would be necessary only if Davis prepares financial statements as of the end of May.

---

[3] In some instances, a note may be taken in settlement of an open account receivable (dr. note receivable, cr. accounts receivable) or at the time of sale (dr. notes receivable, cr. sales). Except for the initial entry, these circumstances do not change the accounting or recording considerations illustrated and discussed.

Payment of the Note

On July 1, 1976, the maturity date of the note, it becomes due and payable. As previously indicated, the interest for the two-month period was:

$$\$1,000 \times .06 \times \frac{2}{12} = \$10$$

and the maturity value, i.e., the total amount that Sutton should pay to Davis, is $1,000 plus $10 or $1,010. Since we have assumed that Davis had previously recorded or accrued the $5 of interest earned during the month of May, the entry which would be required on Davis's books in order to record the receipt of the $1,010 from Sutton at the maturity date of the note would be as follows:

```
Cash ......................................... 1,010
    Notes Receivable .............................         1,000
    Interest Receivable...........................             5
    Interest Earned ..............................             5
```

Analyzing this entry, the debit to cash of $1,010 records the total proceeds of the note, i.e., its maturity value. This maturity value includes both the principal amount and the total interest earned by Davis during the two-month period that he held the note. The credit to notes receivable removes the note balance from Davis's books since it has been paid at maturity. The credit of $5 to interest receivable eliminates the receivable which had been set up at the end of May when Davis accrued the interest earned for that month. The $5 credit to interest earned is made in order to record the interest income on the note for the month of June.

Dishonored Note

If Sutton had not paid the note at maturity, the note would be said to be dishonored. Of course, Davis would continue his efforts to collect the amount due him and Sutton would still be liable for his obligation. In the event that the note was not paid at maturity, Davis would make an entry to remove the note from the notes receivable account as follows:

```
Receivable from Dishonored Note .................... 1,010
    Notes Receivable .............................         1,000
    Interest Receivable...........................             5
    Interest Earned ..............................             5
```

This entry would remove the note from the notes receivable account and place it in a separate receivable classification—receivable from dishonored notes. If Sutton subsequently pays the note, Davis would record the receipt by debiting cash and crediting "receivable from dishonored note." If Davis is unable to collect the $1,010 from Sutton, he would eventually write off the receivable as an uncollectible account against the allowance for bad debts account.

Notes Issued at a Discount

In some circumstances, the interest on notes is deducted in advance, i.e., at the time the note is issued. The difference between the amount due at maturity and the amount loaned is classified as unearned interest at the date of issuance on the books of the lender. As the note matures, this unearned interest is earned and is reclassified as interest income. For example, assume that on November 1, 1976, Wynn Company borrows $1,000 from Osteen Company on a three-month note with a six percent rate of interest. The entry made on November 1, 1976, by Osteen Company to record the loan of $985 [$1,000 − ($1,000 × $\frac{3}{12}$ × $\frac{6}{100}$) would be as follows:

Notes Receivable	1,000	
Unearned Interest		15
Cash		985

At December 31, the following adjusting entry is necessary in order to record the interest earned of $10 ($1,000 × $\frac{2}{12}$ × $\frac{6}{100}$) for the months of November and December:

Unearned Interest	10	
Interest Income		10

When the note matures and is paid, the entry to record the receipt is as follows:

Cash	1,000	
Unearned Income	5	
Note Receivable		1,000
Interest Income		5

The total interest income earned on the note and recorded in the accounts is $15—$10 in 1976 and $5 in 1977. Although a rate of 6 percent was used in determining the original discount on the note, the effective interest rate is actually 6.09 percent since the borrower paid $15 for the use of $985 (not $1,000) for a period of three months.

Discounting Notes Receivable

Notes receivable are sometimes sold by the payee to a third party in order to obtain funds prior to the maturity date of a note. The process of selling a note in this manner is referred to as discounting a note. The payee endorses the note, delivers it to the purchaser (usually a bank) and receives his funds. The payee discounting the note is usually contingently liable on the note, i.e., he must pay the note at the maturity if the maker fails to do so.

The calculation of the discount charged by the purchaser is somewhat similar to the calculation of interest:

$$\frac{\text{Maturity}}{\text{Value}} \times \frac{\text{Discount}}{\text{Period}} \times \frac{\text{Discount}}{\text{Rate}} = \text{Discount}$$

As previously indicated, the maturity value is the total amount, both principal and interest, due at the maturity of a note. The discount period is the period of time from the date a note is discounted to the maturity date of the note. The discount rate is the rate charged by the purchaser to discount a note. The amount received by the payee, referred to as the proceeds of the note, is calculated as follows:

$$\text{Maturity Value} - \text{Discount} = \text{Proceeds}$$

To illustrate the procedures which are involved in discounting a note, we will assume that after recording the interest earned for the month of May, Davis sold or discounted the Sutton note on June 1 and was charged a discount rate of ten percent. The calculation of the amount of the discount and the net proceeds to Davis from the note would be as follows:

$$\$1,000 \times .06 \times \tfrac{2}{12} = \$10 \text{ (interest)}$$
$$\$1,000 + \$10 = \$1,010 \text{ (maturity value)}$$
$$\$1,010 \times .10 \times \tfrac{1}{12} = \$8.42 \text{ (discount)}$$
$$\$1,010 - \$8.42 = \$1001.58 \text{ (proceeds)}$$

The discounting of the note will be recorded in the accounts by Davis as follows:

Cash	1,001.58	
Interest Expense	3.42	
Interest Receivable		5.00
Notes Receivable Discounted		1,000.00

The debit of $1,001.58 to cash records the proceeds received from the sale of the note. The charge to interest expense of $3.42 was calculated as follows:

Principal		$1,000.00
Interest earned during May		5.00
Book value of the note at the date of sale		$1,005.00
Principal	$1,000.00	
Total interest for the note to maturity	10.00	
Maturity value of the note	$1,010.00	
Discount	8.42	
Net proceeds		1,001.58
Interest expense		$ 3.42

As the above calculation indicates, interest expense represents the difference between the cash proceeds and the total of the: (1) face or principal amount of the note; and (2) interest earned up to the date the note was discounted.[4] The credit to interest receivable removes the interest which had been previously accrued at the end of May from the accounts. It should be noted that the credit in the entry is to notes receivable *discounted*, rather than to notes receivable. The credit to notes receivable discounted indicates that Davis is contingently liable for the note—i.e., in the event that Sutton fails to pay the note at maturity, Davis must pay it. On Davis's balance sheet the notes receivable would appear as follows:

Cash		$10,000
Notes receivable	$1,000	
Less: Notes receivable discounted	1,000	0
Other assets		50,000
Total Assets		$60,000

Offsetting the notes receivable discounted account against the notes receivable account discloses the contingent liability of Davis with regard to the Sutton note. An alternative to this presentation would be to disclose the contingent liability by means of a footnote to the balance sheet. Such a footnote might be worded as follows: "Davis is contingently liable for notes receivable discounted in the amount of $1,000."

If Sutton pays the note at its maturity, Davis would be notified of this payment and the following entry would be made on Davis's books:

Notes Receivable Discounted	1,000	
Notes Receivable		1,000

By removing both the notes receivable discounted and the notes receivable balances from the accounts, the effect of this entry is to recognize the fact that the contingent liability for the note no longer exists.

If Sutton fails to pay the note at maturity, Davis' *contingent* liability becomes a *real* liability that he must now pay. He would recognize this fact by the same entry as that which was made above:

Notes Receivable Discounted	1,000	
Notes Receivable		1,000

---

[4] Had the discount rate been four percent, the entry would have been as follows:

Cash	1,006.63	
Notes Receivable Discounted		1,000.00
Interest Receivable		5.00
Interest Income		1.63

In this instance the credit of $1.63 to interest income represents the excess of the proceeds over the principal amount of the note plus interest earned to date.

It should be noted that both the contingent liability and the notes receivable balance are removed from the books at the maturity date of the note whether or not it is paid by the maker. If it is paid, that is all that is required—no further action on the part of Davis is necessary. If it is not paid, Davis must pay the full amount due (principal plus interest, or full maturity value) to the holder of the note. This payment would be recorded as follows:

Receivable from Dishonored Note	1,010	
Cash		1,010

Davis would then attempt to recover the $1,010 from Sutton.

STATEMENT PRESENTATION OF RECEIVABLES

Receivables are classified first according to their form: notes receivable and accounts receivable. Generally, those which are expected to be converted into cash within a year are classified as current assets while those which will be realized in subsequent periods are included in a noncurrent category. Any interest receivable from interest-bearing notes will also be classified according to the timing of its expected collection. The income from interest appears on the income statement, usually as an addition to net income from operations, as follows:

DAVIS COMPANY
Income Statement
For the Year Ended December 31, 1976

Sales	$100,000
Cost of sales	60,000
Gross profit on sales	$ 40,000
Expenses	25,000
Net income from operations	$ 15,000
Other income:	
Interest income	100
Net income	$ 15,100

If there are receivables from sources other than normal operations, such as from officers, employees, affiliated companies, etc., these would be shown as separate items rather than included as a part of regular accounts or notes receivable in the balance sheet.

Comprehensive Illustration

Listed below are certain transactions of A Company during 1976.

January 10   Sold merchandise on account to B Company for $10,000. The terms of the sale required payment within 10 days.

January 15	Sold merchandise on account to C Company for $5,000. The terms of the sale required payment within 10 days.
January 25	Accepted a $10,000, 10%, 3-month note from B Company in settlement of the past due account.
February 25	Discounted the B Company note at City National Bank at 12%.
March 1	The account receivable from C Company was written off as uncollectible.
April 25	The Bank notified A Company that B Company's note was dishonored. A Company paid the bank the maturity value of the note plus a protest fee of $25.
May 1	Received $5,000 payment from C Company on account previously written off.
May 5	Collected maturity value of dishonored note plus the protest fee from B Company.
December 31	Determined that the allowance for bad debts account should have a $12,000 balance. The account had a $700 debit balance prior to adjustment.

Required:

Prepare all the journal entries to record the above transactions on the books of A Company.

Solution to Comprehensive Illustration

January 10	Accounts Receivable	10,000	
	Sales		10,000
January 15	Accounts Receivable	5,000	
	Sales		5,000
January 25	Note Receivable	10,000	
	Accounts Receivable		10,000
February 25	Cash	10,045	
	Notes Receivable Discounted		10,000
	Interest Income		45
March 1	Allowance for Bad Debts	5,000	
	Accounts Receivable		5,000
April 25	Notes Receivable Discounted	10,000	
	Notes Receivable		10,000
	Receivable from Dishonored Note	10,275	
	Cash		10,275
May 1	Accounts Receivable	5,000	
	Allowance for Bad Debts		5,000
	Cash	5,000	
	Accounts Receivable		5,000
May 5	Cash	10,275	
	Receivable from Dishonored Note		10,275
December 31	Bad Debt Expense	12,700	
	Allowance for Bad Debts		12,700

KEY DEFINITIONS

Accounts receivable   Accounts receivable are receivables not supported by formal or written promises to pay.

Aging of accounts receivable   Aging of accounts receivable is the process of classifying accounts according to the period of time that the accounts have been outstanding.

Allowance for bad debts   Allowance for bad debts is a contra account to accounts receivable that reflects the portion of the total dollar amount of accounts receivable that is expected to be uncollectible.

Bad debt expense   Bad debt expense is the expense that occurs from customers' failure to pay debts to the firm.

Contingent liability   A contingent liability is an amount which may become a liability at some future date, depending on the occurrence of some future event. For example, the payee who discounts a note is contingently liable if the maker of the note fails to pay it at maturity.

Contra account   A contra account is an account which is offset against or deducted from another account in the financial statements.

"Control" account   A "control" account is used to record the total charge sales and the total payments which are received from customers.

Discount (D)   Discount is the charge made by the purchaser of a note prior to its maturity. ($MV \times DR \times DP = D$)

Discount period (DP)   The discount period is the period from the date a note is discounted until its maturity.

Discount rate (DR)   The discount rate is the rate charged to discount a note. This percentage is expressed in an annual rate and is used to calculate a discount.

Discounting   Discounting is the sale of a note by the payee prior to its maturity date.

Dishonored notes receivable   Dishonored notes receivable are notes which are not paid at their maturity.

Interest expense (I)   Interest expense is the cost to the borrower of borrowing funds. ($P \times R \times T = I$)

Interest income   Interest income is the income to the lender from the lending of funds. ($P \times R \times T = I$)

Interest receivable   Interest receivable is interest earned but not yet received.

Maker   A maker is the borrower of funds on a note receivable.

Maturity date   The maturity date is the date a note becomes due and payable.

Maturity value (MV)   Maturity value is the value of a note at its maturity, i.e., principal plus interest.

Note receivable   A note receivable is a receivable supported by a formal or written promise to pay.

Payee   The payee is the lender of funds on a note receivable.

Principal (P)   The principal is the face amount of a note receivable.

Proceeds   Proceeds are the net amount received by a payee selling or discounting a note prior to its maturity. Maturity value less discount equals proceeds.

Rate (R)   Rate is the percentage usually expressed as an annual rate used to calculate interest.

Receivable   A receivable is an asset representing the claim that a firm has against others.

Receivable from dishonored note   This receivable is equal to the maturity value of a note arising from the failure of the maker to pay it at maturity.

Time (T)   Time is the period usually expressed in years or a fraction thereof used to calculate interest. It is normal to assume a 360-day year when calculating simple interest.

QUESTIONS

1. Compare and contrast accounts receivable and notes receivable.
2. Why is control over receivables important? How can control be achieved?
3. Explain how the control account, accounts receivable, is related to the individual subsidiary ledger accounts. What could make the two be out of balance?
4. Theoretically, when should a firm cease to grant credit to its customers?
5. Another method for handling bad debt expense—called the direct write-off method—is to wait until the account is known to be uncollectible. The journal entry then is a debit to bad debt expense and a credit to accounts receivable. Compare and contrast this with the allowance method. Which method is theoretically correct? Why?
6. What accounting principle does the allowance method rest upon?
7. What are the two methods for estimating bad debts?
8. Could an allowance method be used with notes receivable? Would it be feasible?
9. What is the entry to increase Allowance for Bad Debts? To decrease it?
10. Suppose an account is written off as uncollectible, but later the customer remits payment. What would the entry be?
11. Calculate the interest on a $10,000, 6-month note, with interest at 6 percent.
12. What adjusting entries may be required with regard to notes receivable at the end of the period?
13. What is the nature of the note receivable discounted account?
14. Why is an entry on the books of the payee necessary whether or not a discounted note is paid by the maker at maturity?
15. Explain how the proceeds from the discounting of a note receivable are calculated.

EXERCISES

8-1   By reviewing their past credit experience, Brown Company estimated that its losses from uncollectible accounts would be three percent of credit sales for 1975. Sales for 1975 amounted to $360,000, of which

$100,000 were in cash. Make the entry recording bad debt expense for the year in the books of the Brown Company.

8–2   Based on an aging of receivables, Blue Company estimated doubtful accounts to be a total of $5,000. Give the adjusting entry for bad debts under each of the following independent situations:

a.   The Allowance for Bad Debts has a zero balance.
b.   The Allowance for Bad Debts has a debit balance of $400.
c.   The Allowance for Bad Debts has a credit balance of $700.

8–3   Bobby Mitchell's 6%, 60-day note for $600 (principal amount) was discounted by the Washington Deadskunks to the Second National Bank after it was held for 30 days. The Deadskunks received $603.96 as proceeds from the sale.

Required:

1.   Calculate the discount rate on the sale.
2.   Prepare the journal entry to record the sale of the note on the books of the Washington Deadskunks.
3.   Prepare the entry necessary if Mitchell fails to pay the note at maturity.

8–4   On February 1, 1975, Alex Grammas borrowed $700 from Vic Wertz and signed a note in evidence of the loan. Grammas agreed to pay Wertz $700 plus 10 percent interest on August 31, 1975. Wertz's accounting period ends June 30. Make all entries related to the note on the books of Wertz (assume Grammas does not default on payment).

8–5   Dallas Company discounted three separate notes receivable at a bank on August 1, 1975. Each note is in the amount of $1,000. The bank charged a discount rate of 10 percent. Compute the proceeds of each note from the following data.

	Date Note Received	*Interest Rate*	*Life of Note*
1.	July 1	8%	3 months
2.	June 1	6%	6 months
3.	July 15	9%	1 month

8–6   Give the journal entries to record the following transactions:

March 15   Accepted a $2,000, 3-month, 10% note from Bob Hanson in settlement of a past due account.

April 15   Discounted the Hanson note at the bank at a discount rate of 12%.

June 15   Received notice from the bank that the Hanson note was in default. Paid the bank the maturity value of the note.

July 15   Received a check from Hanson for the maturity value of the note plus 10% interest on the maturity value of the note for the 30-day period subsequent to maturity.

PROBLEMS

Series A

8A–1 When aging their accounts receivable, the Wingfoot Company drew up the following schedule.

Accounts Receivable Balance	Number of Days Outstanding			
	0–30	31–60	61–90	91 and older
$5,250	$3,450	$900	$650	$250
	Estimated % Uncollectible			
	1%	5%	15%	50%

Prepare a table calculating the estimated bad debt expense for the period and make the appropriate journal entry on the books of the Wingfoot Company, assuming that there is a credit balance of $100 in the Allowance for Bad Debts before adjustment.

8A–2 During 1976 Squeeze, Inc. had $800,000 of sales on credit. Also during 1976 the company wrote off $14,000 of accounts receivable as definitely uncollectible and collected $700 from individuals whose accounts had been written off during previous years. The company estimates its bad debts each year to be 2% of credit sales. On January 1, 1976, the accounts receivable balance was $60,000. Collections on account for 1976 totaled $775,000 and customers returned goods for credit in the amount of $20,000. The company offers no cash discounts. On December 31, 1976, after all adjustments and accruals, accounts receivable net of the allowance for uncollectible accounts amounted to $45,400.

Required:

1. Journal entries for *all* transactions during 1976 involving accounts receivable and the related allowance account.
2. The balance in the allowance account at:
   a. January 1, 1976.
   b. December 31, 1976 (after all adjustments).

8A–3 Charlie Tuna, owner of Tuna's Fish Wholesalers, has instructed his accountant, Jack D. Ripper, to make sure the Allowance for Bad Debts account is at least 10 percent of total accounts receivable at the end of each calendar year. The January 1, 1976, balance in Allowance for Bad Debts is $10,000.
During 1976, the following transactions took place:

January 13	Notice was received that I. M. Acrook, who owed the company $4,000, was in bankruptcy and no payment could be expected.
May 13	Wheel & Deal, Inc. paid $14,000 applicable to its account which totaled $20,000. Its treasurer was last seen boarding a steamer for South America (with all the company's funds), so no other payments would be forthcoming.
July 10	Received a check for $2,000 from A. Lincoln whose account had been written off as uncollectible in 1974.
October 13	H. E. Asucker, a customer, notified Charlie that his partner had absconded with all the company funds. Asucker stated that their business had folded and he was unable to pay Charlie the $8,000 he owed him.
December 31	The balance of accounts receivable, as of the close of today's business, was $200,000.

Required:

Prepare general journal entries to record the above transactions.

8A–4 On January 1, 1967 H. E. Asucker made a loan of $1,000 to S. H. Esacrook. Asucker accepted a one (1)-year, 6 percent note as evidence of this transaction. On July 1, 1967, Asucker, in need of funds, sold (discounted) Esacrook's note to the Piggy Bank. Piggy charged a discount rate of 10 percent. On January 1, 1968, Piggy notified Asucker that the note had not been paid by Esacrook. Asucker paid the note.

Required:

Prepare journal entries for H. E. Asucker to record all of the above information.

8A–5 The Marrion Company purchases and sells merchandise on account. The following transactions occurred in 1975.

April 1	Sold $2,000 worth of merchandise to Jack Palmer on account.
May 17	Purchased $275 of merchandise from the Colonial Company on account.
June 1	Jack Palmer signed a 3 percent two-month note in payment on his account.
June 15	Paid for merchandise purchased from Colonial Company.
July 15	Discounted Palmer's note at the Republic Bank. The discount rate was 6 percent.
August 1	Palmer dishonors his note. Marrion Company pays the bank the required amount.

Required:

Prepare journal entries to record the above transactions on the books of Marrion Company.

8A–6 Listed below are selected transactions of Eastern Company for a six-month period ending March 31, 1976. Eastern's accounting period ends on December 31.

October 1
Sold merchandise on account to Ed Jackson for $1,600. The terms of the sale were n/30.

November 1
Loaned $4,000 to Roger Herman on a three-month, 10 percent note.

November 5
Accepted a $1,600, 90-day, 10 percent note from Ed Jackson in settlement of his past due account.

December 5
Discounted the Jackson note at 12 percent at the bank.

December 15
Sold merchandise on account to Bill Martin for $400; the terms of the sale were n/30.

December 31
Determined by aging of accounts receivable that a $6,500 credit balance in the allowance for bad debts is required. There was a $300 debit balance in the allowance account prior to an adjusting entry.

December 31
Made an adjusting entry to record the accrued interest on the note receivable from Roger Herman.

January 24
Determined that the account receivable from Bill Martin was uncollectible, and it was then written off.

February 5
Received notice from the bank that the Jackson note was in default. Paid the bank the maturity value of the note plus a $10 protest fee.

March 5
Collected from Jackson the maturity value of the dishonored note plus 10 percent interest on that amount since the date of default and the protest fee.

March 20
Full payment of $400 was received from Bill Martin on an account previously written off.

Required:

Prepare general journal entries to record the transactions and adjustments listed above.

Series B

8B–1
The Laguna Company's sales on account and the related losses from bad debts for previous years were as follows:

Year	Sales on Account	Losses from Bad Debts
1974	$100,000	$ 9,000
1975	$200,000	$21,000
1976	$300,000	$30,000

Sales for the current year are $600,000.

Required:

Use the percentage of credit sales method to estimate the losses from bad debts for the current year and make the journal entry to record bad debt expense for the year.

8B–2   The El Ropo Company uses the allowance method of recording bad debt expense. On January 1, 1975, the Allowance for Bad Debts had a credit balance of $14,000. The following events occurred during the year.

1.   On March 1, the Get Rich Quick Company was declared bankrupt with no assets to satisfy creditors' claims. The company owed El Ropo $6,000.
2.   On September 30, I. M. Crook Company folded operations and was declared bankrupt. As a partial remittance on their bill, they forwarded $1,000 to El Ropo—which left an unsatisfied claim of $6,400.
3.   El Ropo aged their ending balance in accounts receivable and estimated that $13,000 of its accounts would be uncollectible.

Required:

Prepare journal entries to record the above items.

8B–3   The following balances relate to the Grub Company:

	(all balances are credits)
Allowance for bad debts (*before* the provision for bad debts), 12/31/74.	$ 700
Allowance for bad debts (*after* the provision for bad debts), 12/31/75.	2,950
Credit sales, 1975.	152,450

The Grub Company estimates its annual bad debts to be 2 percent of credit sales. During 1975 various customer's accounts were adjudged uncollectible and were written off. The total of such write-offs was $3,300. Also in 1975 money totaling $500 was received from several customers whose accounts had previously been written off; some of these had been written off as far back as 1971.

Required:

1.   What was the balance in the Allowance for Bad Debts account at December 31, 1974 *after* the provision for bad debts?
2.   What was the 1974 provision for bad debts?
3.   What was the balance in the Allowance for Bad Debts account at December 31, 1975, before the 1975 provision for bad debts?

8B–4   Calculate the proceeds from discounting the notes described in the following cases.

1.   Four-month, 9-percent, $1,000 note discounted one month before maturity. Discount rate is 11 percent.
2.   One-year, 7-percent, $5,000 note discounted three months before maturity. Discount rate is 11 percent.
3.   Eighteen-month, 7-percent, $2,000 note discounted four months before maturity. Discount rate is 9 percent.

8B–5 Make all necessary journal entries for the Allen Company based on the following information:

January 1   Mr. Allen lends the Acme Company $4,000, accepting Acme's 3-month, 8-percent interest-bearing note for that amount.

February 1   Mr. Allen discounts the Acme Company's note at the bank. The rate of discount charged is 11 percent.

April 1   Mr. Allen receives notice that the note has been dishonored. He pays the bank the amount due them.

July 1   Mr. Allen gives the Cable Company $10,000 in cash, accepting a note requiring Cable Company to pay $10,500 to Allen Company on July 1 of next year.

December 31 Allen Company closes its books.

8B–6 Listed below are selected transactions of Western Company during the last seven months of 1975.

June 5   Sold $1,000 of merchandise on credit to Buster Benson, terms n/30.

July 6   Accepted a $1,000, 60-day, 9-percent note from Buster Benson in settlement of his past due account.

July 31   Loaned $10,000 to Carl Bennett on a 6-month, 10-percent note.

August 6   Discounted the Benson note at 12 percent at the bank.

August 25   Sold $500 of merchandise to Paul Blair on credit, terms n/30.

September 6 Received notice from bank that Benson note was in default. Paid the bank the maturity value of the note.

September 15 Accepted a $2,000, 120-day, 9-percent note from Bill Smith in settlement of a past due account.

October 15   Determined that the account receivable from Paul Blair was uncollectible and it was written off.

November 1   Full payment of $500 was received from Paul Blair on an account previously written off.

November 15 Accepted a $800, 60-day, 9-percent note from Tom Hubbard in settlement of a past due account.

December 1   Discounted the Hubbard note at 10 percent at the bank.

December 31 Determined by aging of accounts receivable that a $5,000 credit balance in the Allowance for Bad Debts account is required. The Allowance for Bad Debts prior to any adjustment has a credit balance of $4,500.

December 31 Made an adjusting entry to record the accrued interest on the notes receivable.

Required:

Prepare general journal entries to record the transactions and adjustments listed above.

9

Inventories

THE INVENTORIES of a firm are those assets which are acquired and/or produced for ultimate sale in the continuing operations of a business. With the exception of relatively small inventories of materials and supplies which are used in the operations of the business, inventories are intended for resale to customers of the firm. In an accounting sense, therefore, inventories include all goods which are held for sale to customers (finished goods inventory), goods which are in the process of being produced for sale (work-in-process inventory), and goods which are to be used in the production of inventories for sale (raw materials, manufacturing supplies, etc.).

In this chapter we will discuss the objectives of inventory accounting, the basis for recording inventories in the accounting records, the procedures which are required in order to establish control over inventories, and the procedures and techniques which may be employed in the valuation of these assets as well as in the determination of the expenses which are related to their use.

CONTROL OVER INVENTORIES

An important function in maintaining effective control over a company's inventories is establishing physical control over its raw materials, purchased parts, work-in-process, finished goods, and supplies. Each category of inventory should be placed under the responsibility of a designated stores keeper who should notify the accounting department of all receipts of merchandise by means of receiving or production reports. Issues of goods should be made only against signed requisitions or shipping orders. Every item included in the inventory should be counted at least once a year, either periodically during the year or at the end of the year.

Accounting control is also an effective means of establishing internal control over inventories. These controls, such as the use of the net method of recording inventories and the perpetual inventory method, will be described in subsequent sections of this chapter.

OBJECTIVE OF INVENTORY ACCOUNTING

The objective of inventory accounting is two-fold. First, it is concerned with valuation of the asset inventory. Valuation of the asset account is important because the funds invested by a firm in its inventories are usually quite significant; the inventory of a business is often the largest of its current assets. Second, and at least of equal importance, is the proper determination of net income of the business for the period by matching the appropriate costs (the cost of the inventory sold) against the related revenue (the revenue received from the sale of the inventory). In other words, the matching process requires that costs be assigned: (1) to those goods which were sold during the period and (2) to those goods which are still on hand and available for sale at the end of a period. It should be noted that this is really a single process; the procedures which are employed in the valuation of inventories also simultaneously determine the cost of goods sold. In order to illustrate this general process, consider the following activities of Art's Wholesalers for the month of June:

1. Purchased 100 cases of Lone Star beer at a cost of $3.00 per case.
2. Sold 80 cases of Lone Star at a price of $5.00 per case.
3. Selling expenses for June totaled $25.00.
4. On June 1, Art had 10 cases of beer which had also cost him $3.00 per case on hand. At June 30, Art's inventory consisted of 30 cases of Lone Star.

If Art were to prepare an income statement for the month of June, it would appear as follows:

ART'S WHOLESALERS
Income Statement
For the Month of June

Sales (80 cases @ $5)		$400
Less: Cost of goods sold		
Beginning inventory, June 1 (10 cases @ $3).	$ 30	
Add: Purchases (100 cases @ $3)	300	
Goods available for sale	$330	
Deduct: Ending inventory, June 30 (30 cases @ $3)	90	
Cost of goods sold		240
Gross profit from sales		$160
Selling expenses		25
Income		$135

Several points should be noted from the analysis of the above income statement. The total inventory of beer which was available for sale, identified in the income statement as the *goods available for sale,* was accumulated by combining the cost of goods which were on hand at the start of the period (*beginning inventory*) with the cost of beer purchased during the period (*purchases*).

Goods available for sale was then divided into its two components: (1) the cost of beer which was still on hand and available for sale at the close of the period (*ending inventory*) and (2) the cost of beer which was sold during the period (*cost of goods sold*). *Cost of goods sold* was subtracted from the sales revenue for the period (*sales*) in order to determine *gross profit from sales.* Note that the gross profit from sales is determined and presented before the other costs and expenses incurred during the period are considered. The next step in the preparation of the income statement is the deduction of these expenses, in this example *selling expenses,* in order to arrive at the income for the period.

Of course the example used above was very simple for purposes of illustration. All beer was assumed to be acquired at a single price and no discounts, returns, or losses were encountered. Our purpose was to illustrate the general concepts of inventory accounting; we will now consider some of the detailed procedures which are normally involved in this process.

BASIS OF ACCOUNTING

Historical cost is the primary basis used in accounting for inventories. This cost includes not only the price of the asset itself, but also any direct or indirect outlays which were made or incurred in order to bring the inventory to the firm's location in the desired form and condition. For example, shipping costs would be considered a part of the cost of the inventory if they were paid by the purchaser.

PURCHASE DISCOUNTS

Sellers of goods frequently offer discounts to their customers to recognize quantity purchases and to encourage prompt payment for goods sold on account. Quantity discounts, often referred to as trade discounts, usually represent an adjustment of a catalog or list price which is made to arrive at the selling price of merchandise to a particular customer. For this reason, trade discounts are not usually reflected in the accounts. For example, assume that the distributor offered beer at a list price of $4 per case and allowed Art's Wholesalers a trade discount of 25 percent. From an accounting viewpoint, Art would determine the cost to be employed in his accounts as follows:

List price per case.	$4
Less: Trade discount	
(25% of $4)	1
Cost per case	$3

Art would use the $3 figure as his cost; the $4 list price and the $1 discount would not appear anywhere in the accounts.

Discounts which are offered to encourage the prompt payment of purchases made on a credit basis are another matter. These discounts usually are reflected in the accounts. Such discounts, often referred to as purchase discounts, are usually stated in terms such as 2/10; n/30. This notation means that a 2 percent discount is offered to the customer if his account is settled within 10 days of the date of sale, the full amount is due at the end of the 30 day period. Two methods may be used in accounting for these discounts, the *net* method and the *gross* method. In order to illustrate these two methods, we will return to the transactions of Art's Wholesalers for the month of June and record the purchase of the 100 cases of beer at $3 per case in Art's books and in the distributor's accounts using both the net and gross methods. We will assume that the terms offered were 2/10; n/30.

Note that the seller of merchandise normally records the sale at the gross amount. One reason for this procedure lies in the fact that the seller has no control over whether or not the purchaser will make payment during or after the discount period. If payment is made by the purchaser during the discount period, the difference between the cash payment and the amount of the receivable (which was set up for the gross amount of the sale) is recorded by the seller as a *sales discount*. Of course, if payment is made after the expiration of the discount period there is no problem since the purchaser will be required to pay the gross amount in full. If this is the case, the seller will simply debit cash and credit accounts receivable for the amount of cash received.

In the purchaser's accounts, the sales price *less* the purchase discount will be recorded at the time of the purchase if the net method is used. If payment for the goods is made during the discount period, there is no problem. The purchaser will simply debit accounts payable and credit cash for the amount paid. On the other hand, if payment is made after the discount period has passed, the purchaser will be required to pay the full or gross price. Since the payable was originally recorded at the net amount, the entry for payment will require a debit to accounts payable for the net amount and a credit to cash for the amount paid (gross price); the differ-

Illustration 9-1

Transaction	Lone Star Distributor		Art—Net Method		Art—Gross Method	
Sale of 100 cases of Lone Star Beer; terms: 2/10; n/30.	Accounts Receivable. . . .	300	Purchases.	294	Purchases.	300
	Sales	300	Accounts Payable. . .	294	Accounts Payable. . .	300
Payment made *during* the discount period.	Cash	294	Accounts Payable.	294	Accounts Payable.	300
	Sales Discounts	6	Cash	294	Cash	294
	Accounts Receivable. .	300			Purchase Discount . .	6
Payment made *after* the discount period.	Cash	300	Accounts Payable.	294	Accounts Payable.	300
	Accounts Receivable. .	300	Discounts Lost	6	Cash	300
			Cash	300		

ence between the gross and the net price will be debited to a *Discounts Lost* account. Discounts Lost is considered to be an expense of the period and is included as such in the income statement.

Under the gross method of recording purchases, the initial entry will be for the buyer to debit purchases and credit accounts payable for the full (gross) price. If payment is made during the discount period, the entry will consist of a debit to accounts payable for the original amount recorded as a liability (gross price), a credit to cash for the amount actually paid (net price), and the difference will be credited to a Purchase Discounts account. Purchase Discounts is reported as a deduction from the purchases made during the period. If the payment is made after the discount period has passed or expired the entry will simply consist of a debit to accounts payable and a credit to cash for the full or gross price.

Note that the difference between the two methods lies in the information which is provided by each. The net method provides information as to the discounts which were lost but gives no data as to those which were taken. The gross method indicates the amount of discounts taken but gives no information as to the discounts which were lost. Because of the significance[1] of discounts lost to the business, the authors feel that information regarding the discounts not taken is critical and for this reason believe that the net method should be used by purchasers. We feel that any discounts lost are, in fact, interest costs and should be disclosed as such and not included as a part of the cost of inventories.

FREIGHT-IN, RETURNS, AND ALLOWANCES

The purchase of merchandise often involves payment of shipping costs. Frequently purchasers of goods will also find it necessary to return goods to their suppliers. In other instances, the goods will be retained by the purchaser and the supplier will allow him an adjustment of the purchase price, known as an allowance. In order to illustrate these occurrences, we will assume the following facts:

1. Art ordered 100 cases of Lone Star, 50 cases of Pearl, and 50 cases of Coor's beer, all at a price of $3 per case. The terms were F.O.B. shipping point,[2] 2/10; n/30, and Art uses the net method for recording purchases. Art pays the freight of $10.

---

[1] Failure to take a discount when the terms are 2/10; n/30 represents an interest cost in excess of 36 percent per annum. ($294 \times R \times 20/360 = 6; solving for R, the interest rate is 36.7 percent.)

[2] The initials F.O.B. stand for free on board. F.O.B. shipping point means that the seller pays the costs *to* the shipping point only; the buyer pays the cost of transit from the shipping point to the destination. Alternatively, F.O.B. destination terms would require the seller to pay all shipping costs.

2. Art's distributor ships him 100 cases of Lone Star, 50 cases of Pearl, and, by mistake, 50 cases of Rolling Rock instead of the Coor's.
3. Art returns 50 cases of the Lone Star, agrees to keep the Rolling Rock in lieu of the Coor's since the distributor gave him a $5 allowance, and pays the balance in full within the discount period.

The entries to record these transactions would be as follows:

Art			*Distributor*		
Purchases	588		Accounts Receivable	600	
Freight-in	10		Sales		600
Accounts Payable.		588			
Cash		10			
Accounts Payable	588		Cash	436	
Purchase Returns		147	Sales Returns	150	
Purchase Allowance . . .		5	Sales Allowance	5	
Cash		436	Sales Discount	9	
			Accounts Receivable . . .		600

Art debits Purchases and credits Accounts Payable for the net amount of the purchase ($600 less 2 percent of $600 or a net amount of $588). He debits Freight-in and credits Cash for the $10 freight charge that he paid in cash, since according to the terms of the purchase (F.O.B. shipping point) this is his responsibility. The seller, using the gross method, simply debits Accounts Receivable and credits Sales for the full price of the sale (200 cases @ $3).

At the time payment is made, Art would debit Accounts Payable for the amount of the liability originally recorded (net price). He would credit Purchase Returns for the net cost of the 50 cases of Lone Star that he returned to the seller (50 cases @ $3 or $150, less 2 percent of $150, or a net of $147) and credit Purchase Allowances for the $5 adjustment made to Art for keeping the Rolling Rock rather than the Coor's that he ordered. The credit to Cash would be for the net cash paid ($588 less the $147 return, less the $5 allowance, or a net amount of $436).

When the seller receives Art's payment, he would debit Cash for the $436 received, debit Sales Returns for $150 (the 50 cases of Lone Star returned @ $3), debit Sales Allowance for the $5 adjustment, and debit Sales Discounts for $9 (150 cases @ $3 or $450 multiplied by 2%). The distributor would credit Accounts Receivable for the amount he originally recorded, the gross amount of $600.

The partial income statement presented in Illustration 9–2 indicates how these items would be disclosed in the statements.

The reader should note that the account Purchase Discounts does not appear in the statements since we assumed that Art is using the net method of recording purchases. If the gross method was used, purchases would

Illustration 9–2

ART'S WHOLESALERS
(Partial) Income Statement
For the Year Ending December 31, 1976

Sales			$102,800
Less: Sales returns.	$ 500		
Sales allowances.	300		
Sales discounts	2,000		2,800
Net sales			$100,000
Less: Cost of goods sold			
Beginning inventory		$10,000	
Purchases	$70,000		
Less: Purchase returns	$1,000		
Purchase allowances	100	1,100	
Net purchases		$68,900	
Add: Freight-in		600	$69,500
Goods available for sale			$79,500
Ending inventory			15,500
Cost of goods sold			64,000
Gross profit on sales			$ 36,000
Discounts lost	$ 100		
All other expenses	20,000		$ 20,100
Income.			$ 15,900

be included at their gross rather than net amount and purchase discounts would appear along with purchase returns and purchase allowances as a deduction in arriving at the net purchases for the period. Discounts lost would not appear in the statements when using the gross method.

PERIODIC AND PERPETUAL INVENTORIES

There are two general methods of recordkeeping which are used in accounting for inventories: the periodic and the perpetual inventory methods. The basic difference between these two methods is in the timing of the recording of the cost of sales.

Under the periodic method the cost of goods sold is determined at the end of the period by making a physical count of the goods on hand and subtracting the cost of the goods which are still on hand from the total cost of goods which were available for sale. Using the perpetual method, an entry recording the cost of goods sold is usually made at the time a sale is made. A physical inventory is still taken, either at the end of the year or periodically during the year, and the inventory amounts on the books are then adjusted, if necessary, in order to reflect the cost of the actual goods which are on hand.

The above procedures describe periodic and perpetual systems in terms of dollar amounts. Either of these inventory systems can also be maintained on a quantity basis. For example, with a perpetual system on a quantity basis, a "running count" of each class or category of inventory item may be maintained, either manually or by the use of electronic data processing equipment, in order to provide information with regard to the quantity of a particular inventory item on hand at any particular point in time.

The basic difference between the two methods is illustrated by the following example:

1. Purchased 10 cases of beer @ $3 per case (assume that the firm had no inventory at the beginning of the period).

	Perpetual			*Periodic*	
Inventory	30		Purchases.	30	
Cash		30	Cash		30

2. Sold 7 cases of beer for $5 per case.

	Perpetual			*Periodic*	
Cash	35		Cash	35	
Sales		35	Sales		35
Cost of Goods Sold	21				
Inventory		21			

3. Ending inventory is 2 cases of beer.

	Perpetual			*Periodic*	
Loss	3		Cost of Goods Sold	24	
Inventory		3	Inventory	6	
			Purchases		30

An analysis of the entries presented above indicates that using the perpetual system the cost of goods sold is $21 and a loss of $3 is shown for the missing case of beer (10 cases purchased minus 7 cases sold minus 2 cases in the ending inventory indicates that 1 case was "missing"). Using the periodic method, the $3 cost of the missing case would be included in the cost of goods sold since the cost of goods sold under this method was determined by subtracting the $6 cost of ending inventory from goods available for sale of $30 and assuming that the difference represented inventory that was sold. This is a disadvantage of the periodic method, because the cost of sales under this method will include not only the cost of the goods actually sold, but also the cost of any merchandise lost or stolen as well. More effective control over inventories may be established by using the perpetual method, either on a dollar or a quantity basis.

INVENTORY COST FLOW METHODS

Once the quantities of goods on hand at the end of the period and the quantity of goods sold during the period are determined, the next step is to decide how costs should be allocated between cost of goods sold and ending inventory. If all purchases of inventory were made at the same unit price (as in the previous example), this allocation does not create any problems. However, if the inventory items were acquired at different unit costs, it is necessary to determine which costs should be assigned to each inventory item. One method of determining the cost of the inventory on hand would be to maintain records of the exact cost of each item sold during the period and each item on hand at the end of the period. In many cases, this procedure would require excessive record keeping costs, while in other instances it would be impossible to do so. Consequently, some arbitrary method for assigning costs to inventory must be used. The three most common methods used in pricing inventories (and therefore determining cost of goods sold for the period) are the average method; the first-in, first-out (Fifo) method; and the last-in, first-out (Lifo) method. These methods are assumptions regarding the flow of inventory *costs* and not about the actual *physical* flow of goods. The following data relating to a special brand of foreign beer, again taken from the inventory records of Art's Wholesalers, will be used to illustrate these methods:

January 1–Beginning inventory (100 cases @ $2).	$200
February 7–Purchase (150 cases @ $3)	450
March 25–Purchase (200 cases @ $4)	800
October 6–Purchase (150 cases @ $5)	750
November 10–Purchase (100 cases @ $6)	600

Thus, the goods available for sale during the year were 700 cases at a total cost of $2,800. Art's records indicate that 500 cases were sold during the year. The accounting problem is in assigning or allocating the $2,800 cost of goods available for sale between the ending inventory and the cost of goods sold. The valuation of the ending inventory (and therefore the determination of the cost of goods sold) under each of the alternative methods of inventory valuation is illustrated in the paragraphs which follow.

Average Method

The average cost method assumes that no definite relationship exists between the receipt and the usage of quantities of inventory. This method averages costs on the assumption that one unit cannot be distinguished from another. One feature of the average method is the assignment of cost on an equal unit basis to both the ending inventory and cost of goods sold. The average cost is computed by dividing the total cost of the beginning inventory plus purchases by the total number of units included in the inventory.

In the example stated above, the average cost would be calculated as follows:

January 1–Inventory (100 cases @ $2).	$ 200
February 7–Purchase (150 cases @ $3)	450
March 25–Purchase (200 cases @ $4)	800
October 6–Purchase (150 cases @ $5)	750
November 10–Purchase (100 cases @ $6)	600
Total 700 cases	$2,800

The total cost of the goods available for sale ($2,800) would be divided by the number of cases (700) and the result of $4 would be the average cost of the inventory. This average cost figure would be used both in valuing the ending inventory (200 × $4 = $800) and in determining the cost of goods sold for the period (500 × $4 = $2,000).

First-in, First-out (Fifo) Method

Fifo is the most widely used method of determining inventory cost. This method assumes that the cost of the first item acquired or produced is the cost of the first item used or sold. Its use is advantageous because it assigns a current cost to inventories on the balance sheet and is relatively easy to apply. In many cases, the assumption is also consistent with the actual flow of goods. Fifo inventories are priced by using the actual invoice costs or production costs for the latest quantities purchased or produced to the extent of the stock on hand. It is a good method to use in those instances where the inventory turnover is rapid or where changes in the composition of the inventory are frequent since the costs associated with the oldest inventory are always transferred to cost of goods sold first. Its disadvantage is that it does not match the most recent costs with current revenues. On the other hand, it does give a fairly current valuation of the ending inventory balance. The Fifo inventory and the related cost of goods sold for Art's Wholesalers would be calculated as follows:

Fifo Cost of Goods Sold–the First 500 Units

January 1–Inventory (100 cases @ $2)	$ 200
February 7–Purchase (150 cases @ $3)	450
March 25–Purchase (200 cases @ $4)	800
October 6–Purchase (50 cases @ $5)	250
Fifo Cost of Goods Sold	$1,700

Fifo Ending Inventory—the Last 200 Units

October 6—Purchase (100 cases @ $5) . . . . $ 500
November 10—Purchase (100 cases @ $6)   600

Fifo Cost of Ending Inventory $1,100

Last-in, First-out (Lifo) Method

This method assumes that the cost of the last item received or produced is the cost of the first item used or sold.

A principal advantage of the Lifo method is that it matches current costs more nearly with current revenues. Another advantage of Lifo is the fact that in periods of price increases, net income computed using Lifo is less than the amount that would result from using Fifo or the average cost method. Therefore, it reduces federal income taxes. Providing that prices do not decline below the prices of the year in which Lifo was adopted, the method results in a postponement of income taxes.

Its disadvantages are that it gives a "noncurrent" value to inventories in the balance sheet and it reduces reported income in periods of rising prices.

When there is an increase in the quantity of inventory, the year-end Lifo inventory consists of the prior year-end inventory plus the earliest additions at cost in the current year. The cost of the Lifo inventory and the related cost of goods sold would be calculated as follows:

Lifo Ending Inventory—the First 200 Units

January 1—Inventory (100 cases @ $2) $200
February 7—Purchase (100 cases @ $3)   300

Lifo Cost of Ending Inventory $500

Lifo Cost of Goods Sold—the Last 500 Units

February 7—Purchase (50 cases @ $3) . . . . $ 150
March 25—Purchase (200 cases @ $4)   800
October 6—Purchase (150 cases @ $5)   750
November 10—Purchase (100 cases @ $6)   600

Lifo Cost of Goods Sold $2,300

Differences in Methods

The effect of the differences in the three methods which we described above are illustrated by the following summary (shown at the top of page 224):

	Average	Fifo	Lifo
Sales (500 cases @ $10)	$5,000	$5,000	$5,000
Less: Cost of goods sold			
Beginning inventory (100 cases)	$ 200	$ 200	$ 200
Purchases (600 cases)	2,600	2,600	2,600
Goods available for sale (700 cases)	$2,800	$2,800	$2,800
Ending inventory (200 cases)	800	1,100	500
Cost of goods sold (500 cases)	$2,000	$1,700	$2,300
Gross profit on sales	$3,000	$3,300	$2,700

The total cost of goods available for sale ($2,800) was allocated either to cost of goods sold or ending inventory in every case. The sales, beginning inventory, and purchases included in the example are identical irrespective of the inventory method chosen. An inventory method is only used to cost the ending inventory and determine the cost of goods sold. It does not necessarily reflect the actual physical flow of goods. That is, a bakery could use the Lifo method for accounting purposes although obviously the physical flow would be Fifo—who wants a ten-year-old cake!

Although a firm may select any one of several acceptable methods, the consistency principle requires that a firm use the same method over time. The selection of the method to be used should depend upon such factors as the potential effect upon the balance sheet and the income statement, and the effect on taxable income.

LOWER OF COST OR MARKET

As previously indicated, the primary basis for accounting for inventories is historical cost. Therefore, if the value of the item increases or decreases prior to its sale, no record of this fact is normally entered in the books. However, an exception to this rule may occur when the market price, which is defined as the current replacement cost of the goods, is less than their historical cost. In this case the inventory may be carried at its replacement cost. In other words inventories may be carried at the lower of their cost or their market value. If the market price for a firm's inventory falls below its original cost, an entry is made recognizing the difference between cost and market as a loss and reducing the carrying value of the inventory to market. The reduced figure becomes the new "cost" of the inventory for accounting purposes. However, if the market price exceeds the original cost, no entry is made in the accounts. The recognition of losses but not gains prior to sale is based on the principle of conservatism. To illustrate the lower of cost or market method, assume the same facts as presented above—that a firm had 700 cases of beer available for sale and that this beer had been purchased at an average price of $4 per case. Sales for the period were 500 cases at a selling price of $10 per case. If the business used the "average" inventory method, the gross profit on sales would be calculated as follows:

Sales (500 cases @ $10)	$5,000
Less: Cost of goods sold	
Beginning inventory (100 cases)	$ 200
Purchases (600 cases)	2,600
Goods available for sale (700 cases)	$2,800
Ending inventory (200 cases)	800
Cost of goods sold	$2,000
Gross profit on sales	$3,000

If the replacement cost of the ending inventory had declined to $750 as of the end of the period, the ending inventory might be written down from its original cost of $800 to its current replacement cost of $750 by the following entry:

Loss on Inventory Decline	50	
Inventory		50

The effect of the write-down of inventory would be to reduce income for the period by $50 by recognizing the reduction in the replacement cost of the inventory below its original cost. In subsequent periods, inventory would be carried at a "cost" of $750 in the balance sheet and this amount would be used in determining the cost of goods sold when the inventory was sold.

METHODS OF ESTIMATING INVENTORIES

In many instances, such as in the case of the preparation of interim financial statements, it may be desirable simply to estimate the amount of the ending inventory rather than go to the time and trouble of taking a physical inventory. Two methods which are often used in estimating inventories, the retail method and the gross profit method, will be described in the remaining sections of this chapter.

Retail Method. As its name implies, this method is based on retail prices. It is an averaging method which assumes that the cost of merchandise on hand at any time bears the same relationship to total retail prices as the total cost of all goods handled during the period bears to original selling prices. In using this method, when sales are subtracted from goods available for sale at retail selling prices, the result is the estimated ending inventory at retail prices. Then, this amount is multiplied by the average ratio of cost to selling prices to give an estimate of ending inventory at cost. Its principal advantages are: it provides a clerically feasible means of determining inventories on hand; it provides a measure of control over inventories and a means of computing the cost of merchandise sold at any time, even though the store handles a large number of items and has a very high volume of sales transactions; it simplifies the taking and pricing of physical inventories; it provides information for a monthly determination of gross profit for each department and store; and it helps control inventory by disclosing shortages which may indicate either thefts or sales made at unauthorized prices.

As goods are purchased, information regarding the goods is accumulated on both a cost and a selling price basis. For example, assume the following information:

	Cost	Selling Price
Beginning inventory	$ 1,500	$ 2,000
Add: Purchases	10,000	18,000
Freight	500	
	$12,000	$20,000
Deduct: Sales		16,000
Ending inventory, at retail		$ 4,000

Cost percentage: $\dfrac{\$12,000}{\$20,000} = 60\%$

Ending inventory, at cost: $4,000 \times 60\% = \$2,400$

Gross Profit Method. Another method of estimating the cost of the ending inventory is by the use of the gross profit method. This method assumes that the relationship between sales, the cost of goods sold, and gross profit will remain relatively constant. This relationship is expressed as a percentage and is used in estimating the cost of the ending inventory, as indicated in the following example for Art's Wholesalers for the month of January 1976.

Sales	$10,500
Sales returns	500
Purchases	5,500
Purchase returns	100
Purchase allowances	50
Freight	150

In addition to the data summarized above, information concerning the inventory at the beginning of the year ($15,500) was obtained from the 1975 income statement as was the gross profit percentage (gross profit of $36,000 divided by net sales of $100,000 or 36%). This information would be used as follows:

Beginning inventory			$15,500
Purchases		$ 5,500	
Less: Purchase returns.	$100		
Purchase allowances	50	150	
Net purchases		$ 5,350	
Freight-in		150	5,500
Goods available for sale			$21,000
Less: Estimated cost of goods sold			
Sales		$10,500	
Less: Sales returns.		500	
Net sales		$10,000	
Multiply by the reciprocal of the gross profit percentage			
(100% − 36%)		✕ 64%	
Estimated cost of goods sold			6,400
Estimated cost of January 31, 1976 inventory			$14,600

The gross profit method can be used in order to estimate inventories for interim statement purposes; to test the accuracy of inventories determined by physical count; and to estimate inventory destroyed by fire, lost by theft, etc.

The reader should keep in mind that the retail method and the gross profit method are methods of *estimating* inventories, not *costing* inventories.

KEY DEFINITIONS

Average inventory method   The average inventory method is a method based on the theory that one unit cannot be distinguished from another. The average cost is computed by dividing the total cost of the beginning inventory plus purchases by the total number of units.

Beginning inventory   Beginning inventory includes the goods which are on hand and available for sale at the beginning of the period.

Cost of goods sold   Cost of goods sold is the cost of the inventory sold during the period. Beginning inventory plus purchases minus the ending inventory equals the cost of goods sold.

Cost of inventory   Cost of inventory is the price of the inventory itself plus all direct and indirect outlays incurred in order to bring it to the firm's location in the desired form.

Cost percentage   Cost percentage is the percentage obtained from the ratio of the goods available for sale at cost to the goods available for sale at selling price. This percentage is used in the retail method in order to calculate the estimated cost of the ending inventory.

Discounts lost   Discounts lost is an account used under the net method of recording purchases to record the amount of the discounts which were not taken.

Ending inventory   Ending inventory is goods which are still on hand and available for sale at the end of the period.

Finished goods inventory   Finished goods inventory includes completed goods which are held for resale.

First-in, first-out (Fifo)   Fifo is an inventory method which assumes that the cost of the first item acquired or produced is the cost of the first item used or sold.

F.O.B.   F.O.B. means "free on board."

F.O.B. destination   F.O.B. destination terms would require the seller to pay all shipping costs.

F.O.B. shipping point   F.O.B. shipping point means that the seller pays the costs to the shipping point only. The buyer pays the cost of transit from the shipping point to the destination.

Freight-in   Freight-in is the shipping costs incurred for goods purchased.

Goods available for sale   Goods available for sale includes the beginning inventory plus the net purchases for the period.

Gross method   Gross method is a method of recording purchases whereby purchases are recorded at the gross price.

Gross profit from sales   Gross profit from sales is the difference between the revenue from sales and the cost of the goods sold.

Gross profit method   This is a method which estimates the cost of the ending inventory by assuming that the relationship between sales, cost of goods sold and gross profit remains constant.

Gross profit percentage   Gross profit percentage is the gross profit or gross margin (sales minus cost of goods sold) divided by sales.

Inventories   Inventories include those assets which are acquired and/or produced for sale in the continuing operations of a business.

Last-in, first-out (Lifo)   Lifo is an inventory method which assumes that the cost of the last item received or produced is the cost of the first item used or sold.

Lower of cost or market   Lower of cost or market is a method of pricing inventory whereby the original cost or the market value, whichever is lower, is used to value inventory for financial statement purposes.

Materials   Materials are goods which are to be used in the production of inventories for sale.

Net method   The net method is a method of recording purchases whereby purchases are recorded at the net price—that is, the gross price less the purchase discount.

Periodic inventories   Under the periodic method, the cost of goods sold is determined at the end of the period by making a physical count of the goods on hand and subtracting the cost of the goods which are still on hand from the total cost of goods available for sale. This inventory system may also be maintained on a quantity basis.

Perpetual inventories   Under the perpetual method, an entry recording the cost of goods sold is usually made at the time a sale is made. This inventory system may also be maintained on a quantity basis.

Purchases   Purchases include all inventory acquired by purchase during the period.

Purchase allowances   Purchase allowances is an adjustment of the purchase price allowed the buyer by the seller. See sales allowances.

Purchase discounts   Purchase discounts are discounts which are offered to encourage the prompt payment of purchases made on account. Purchase discounts are reflected in the accounts. It is also an account used under the gross method to record purchase discounts taken. See sales discounts.

Purchase returns   Purchase returns is the account used by the buyer to record the cost of goods returned to the seller. See sales returns.

Retail method   This is a method of estimating inventories which assumes that the cost of merchandise on hand at any time bears the same relationship to total retail prices as the total cost of all goods handled during the period bears to the original selling prices.

Sales allowances   Sales allowances are adjustments of the purchase price allowed the buyer by the seller. See purchase allowances.

Sales discount   This is a discount offered by the seller to the purchaser. See purchase discounts.

Sales returns   Sales returns is the account used by the seller to record the goods returned by the buyer. See purchase returns.

Trade discount   A trade discount is a quantity discount that represents an adjustment of a catalog or list price which is made in order to arrive at the selling price to a particular customer. Trade discounts are not reflected in the accounts.

Work-in-process inventory   Work-in-process inventory represents goods which are in the process of being produced for resale.

QUESTIONS

1. Why should a company have accounting control over its inventory?
2. What are goods available for sale?
3. Explain the term "cost" with respect to accounting for inventories.
4. Why do businesses offer discounts and how are they recorded in the accounts?
5. Explain how the gross price method and the net price method each provide an evaluation of management. Which method is preferred?
6. Explain F.O.B. shipping point and F.O.B. destination. What effect do these have on the valuation of inventory?
7. What are two methods of inventory recordkeeping? Describe these methods.
8. How is the cost of goods sold figure arrived at under the periodic inventory method?
9. How does the perpetual inventory method act as a control?
10. Briefly discuss the three inventory cost flow methods.
11. Give examples of some kinds of inventories in which average cost, Fifo, and Lifo would actually match the flow of goods.
12. What problems of valuation occur with Fifo? With Lifo?
13. What is the main advantage of Lifo?

14. Explain the exception to the general historical cost rule for inventories.
15. What are some reasons why a company would want to estimate its inventory?
16. What is the basic assumption of the retail method of estimating inventory? What are some advantages of this method?
17. What is the gross profit method? When is it especially useful?

EXERCISES

9–1 Given below are the pertinent data for Griswold's Bookkeeping Services for August.

1. Purchased 100 cartons of ledger tablets @ $5 per carton during August.
2. Sold 90 cartons of tablets at $7.50 per carton during the month.
3. Incurred selling expenses of $35 during August.
4. On August 1, Griswold had 15 cartons of tablets on hand which had cost $5 per carton.

From the above information, prepare an income statement for Griswold's Services for the month of August.

9–2 Prepare journal entries to record the following transactions under both a perpetual and a periodic inventory system.

1. Purchased 15 dozen apples @ $2 per dozen (assume that the firm had a beginning inventory of 3 dozen apples which were purchased at $2 per dozen).
2. Sold 14 dozen apples @ $3 per dozen.
3. Counted the remaining apples and discovered that 3 dozen were on hand.

9–3 Determine the missing figures in each of the following independent cases.

	Sales	Beginning Inventory	Ending Inventory	Gross Profit	Expenses	Net Income	Purchases	Cost of Goods Sold
1.	$1,000	$300	a	b	$100	c	$500	$600
2.	a	100	$200	$400	b	$200	700	c
3.	800	a	150	100	100	b	400	c

9–4 Grasso, Inc. began its operations on January 1, 1975. It purchased goods for resale during the month as follows:

January 3 . . . . 3 units @ $3
January 11. . . . . 2 units @ $4
January 20. . . . . 3 units @ $5
January 30. . . . . 2 units @ $6

Sales for the month totaled 6 units. The selling price per unit was $10. A count of the units as of January 31, 1975, shows four (4) units on hand.

Required:

The inventory at January 31, 1975 would be carried at the following amounts (for each method listed below):

Fifo . . . . _____
Lifo . . . . _____
Weighted Average . . . . _____

All computations should be shown.

9–5 On December 31, 1975, the end of its first year of operations, the management of the Busby Company is trying to decide whether to use the Fifo or Lifo method of measuring inventory. It determines that the Lifo method would produce the lower asset amount.

Required:

a. Which method would produce the higher cost of goods sold?
b. Which method would produce the higher net income for 1975?
c. Which method would produce the higher cost of goods available for sale for 1975?
d. In what direction do you think prices have been moving during the year?

9–6 The following information was available from the records of a merchandising company at the end of an accounting period.

	At Cost	At Retail
Beginning inventory	$10,000	$ 20,000
Net purchases	69,000	100,000
Freight-in	1,000	–
Sales	–	90,000

Estimate the cost of the ending merchandise inventory using the retail inventory method.

9–7 Bando Company determines its ending inventory by taking a physical inventory at the end of each accounting period. On June 15, the merchandise inventory was completely destroyed by a fire. In the past, the normal gross profit rate was 20 percent. The following data were salvaged from the accounting records.

Inventory, January 1 . . . . $ 20,000
Purchases, January 1 to June 15 90,000
Sales, January 1 to June 15 100,000

Estimate the cost of the merchandise destroyed by the fire.

PROBLEMS

Series A

9A–1 The following transactions took place between Flintstone's Friendly Fish Market and Barney's Beanery during June of 1975.

June   1   Barney buys the following items from Flintstone:

>   10 cases of Charlie the Tuna Fish @ $10 per case
>   1 Fishing submarine @ $2,000,000

Terms of the sale are 2/10; n/30. The purchase was made on account.

June   9   Barney notifies Flintstone that the shipment included eight cases as ordered, one case of horse meat, and one case of caviar. The submarine was O.K. Barney proposes that he keep the caviar and deduct 50¢ from the net amount which would otherwise be due. He plans to return the horse meat. Flintstone agrees and Barney mails him a check for the net amount after making the agreed-on deductions.

June 15   Barney pays for the submarine.

Required:

1.   Record the above transactions on Flintstone's books assuming that he records sales using the gross method.
2.   Record the above transactions on Barney's books assuming he uses:
    a.   the net method of recording purchases.
    b.   the gross method of recording purchases.

9A-2   Peterson Company sells a single product. The company began 1975 with 20 units of the product on hand with a cost of $4 each. During 1975 Peterson made the following purchases:

February 3, 1975	10 units @ $5
April 16, 1975.	25 units @ $6
October 6, 1975	10 units @ $7
December 7, 1975	10 units @ $8

During the year 50 units of the product were sold. The periodic inventory method is used.

Required:

Compute the ending inventory balance and the cost of goods sold under each of the following methods:

a.   Fifo.
b.   Lifo.
c.   Weighted Average.

9A-3   Dente Company began business on January 1, 1975. Purchases of merchandise for resale during 1975 were as follows:

January 1	300 units @ $3.00	$ 900.00
February 7.	600 units @ $3.50	2,100.00
March 25.	400 units @ $3.00	1,200.00
October 6	800 units @ $2.50	2,000.00
November 10	300 units @ $2.50	750.00
November 16	300 units @ $2.25	675.00
Total	2,700 units	$7,625.00

A total of 2,200 units were sold during 1975.

Required:

a. Compute the ending inventory at December 31, 1975 under each of the following methods: (1) Fifo; (2) Lifo; (3) Average.
b. Considering the information given above and your computations for Dente Company, answer the following:

    1. Would the net income for 1975 have been greater if the company had used (a) Fifo or (b) Lifo in computing its inventory?
    2. Assume that the market cost of the merchandise sold by Dente Company was $2.15 per unit at December 31, 1975. Assuming the Fifo method of inventory valuation, what would the *total* carrying value of the inventory be if the lower of cost or market method is used?
    3. Give the journal entry necessary to reduce the inventory to market in (2) above.

9A–4 On February 1, 1975, the Sporting Goods Department of the Most Store had an inventory of $11,000 at retail selling price; the cost of this merchandise was $8,000.

During the three months ended April 30, purchases of $18,000 were made for that department and were marked to sell for $25,000. Freight-in on this merchandise was $1,000. Sales for the period amounted to $25,000. Sales returns and allowances were $900.

The physical inventory at retail amounted to $2,500. Estimate the cost of theft or shrinkage.

9A–5 The McDermott Company had a fire on June 30, 1975, which completely destroyed its inventory. No physical inventory count had been taken since December 31, 1974. The company's books showed the following balances at the date of the fire:

Sales		$180,000
Sales returns and allowances.	$ 1,400	
Inventory, December 31, 1974	40,000	
Purchases	130,000	
Purchases returns and allowances		2,000
Transportation in	1,600	
Selling expenses	50,000	
Administrative expenses	30,000	

Assume that the company's records show that in prior years it made a gross profit of approximately 25 percent of net sales, and there is no indication that this percentage cannot be considered to have continued during the first six months of this year.

Required:

Determine the cost of inventory destroyed by fire on June 30, 1975.

9A–6 A condensed income statement for the year ended December 31, 1975, for Murcer Products shows the following:

Sales	$80,000
Cost of goods sold	50,000
Gross profit on sales	$30,000
Expenses.	20,000
Net income	$10,000

An investigation of the records discloses the following errors in summarizing transactions for 1975.

a.   Ending inventory was overstated by $3,100.

b.   Accrued expenses of $400 and prepaid expenses of $900 were not given accounting recognition at the end of 1975.

c.   Sales of $250 were not recorded although the goods were shipped and excluded from the inventory.

d.   Purchases of $3,000 were made at the end of 1975 but were not recorded although the goods were received and included in the ending inventory.

Required:

1.   Prepare a corrected income statement for 1975.

2.   Prepare the entries necessary to correct the accounts in 1975, assuming the books have not been closed.

Series B

9B–1   Rink, Inc. uses the gross method of recording sales. Its major customer, Dink, Inc., uses the net method of recording all its purchases. The following transactions between the two companies occurred during the month of July, 1975.

July   1   Dink buys the following items from Rink:

> 10 cases of Burpo beer @ $2 per case.
> 1 African puma @ $1,000.
> 5 crates of puma food @ $10 per case.

The purchase was made on account. Terms of the sale were 1/10;n/30.

July   8   Dink notifies Rink that the shipment received on July 2d was not entirely satisfactory as it included 8 cases of Burpo beer in good condition, 1 case of Burpo which was in bottles rather than in pop-top cans (as ordered) and 1 case of Burpo from which the pop-tops had been removed and the contents consumed.

Rink informs Dink that it should keep the case of Burpo and deduct $1 from the net price agreed upon. Rink also requests that Dink return the case of pop-top-less Burpo to Rink's warehouses and promises that Dink's account will be credited for the purchase price.

July   9   Dink accepts Rink's offers (outlined above) and gives Rink a check for the proper amount after deducting an additional $1 for freight charges incurred in returning the Burpo.

July 20   Dink pays for the puma and the food.

Required:

Record the above transactions in proper general journal form, on the books of *both* Rink and Dink.

9B–2   Walls Company, a merchandising concern that sells a single product, began the accounting period with 25 units of product on hand with a cost of $10 each. During the year, the company made the following purchases:

> January 15. . . . . 30 units @ $11
> April 15 . . . . 40 units @ $12
> October 15 . . . . 20 units @ $13
> November 30 . . . . 50 units @ $14

It was determined that 130 units of the product were sold during the year. The company uses the periodic inventory method.

Required:

Compute the ending inventory and the cost of goods sold under each of the following methods:

a.   Fifo.

b.   Lifo.

c.   Weighted Average.

9B–3   The Yost Company began business on January 1, 1975. Its reported net losses for the calendar years 1975 and 1976 were as follows:

> 1975 . . . . $95,000 loss
> 1976 . . . . $40,000 loss

Selected information from its accounting records is presented below.

Purchases of Goods for Resale

Date	Units		Price
February 1, 1975	10,000	at	$10
May 1, 1975.	10,000	at	$12
September 1, 1975	10,000	at	$15
December 1, 1975	10,000	at	$18
January 1, 1976.	10,000	at	$20
March 1, 1976.	10,000	at	$24
June 1, 1976	10,000	at	$25
November 1, 1976	10,000	at	$26

Sales

> 1975 . . . . 25,000 units
> 1976 . . . . 40,000 units

Other data:

The company uses the last-in, first-out (Lifo) method of inventory valuation.

Required:

1. Using the company's present inventory method (Lifo) compute:

   a. Ending inventory for the calendar years 1975 and 1976.
   b. Cost of goods sold for the calendar years 1975 and 1976.

2. Determine what the net income or net loss for each year would have been if the company had used the first-in, first-out (Fifo) method of inventory valuation.

9B–4   The Michaels Sales Company uses the retail inventory method. From the following information estimate the cost of goods sold during the period and the amount at which the inventory would be shown in the financial statements.

The beginning inventory at cost was $12,000.
Goods available for sale at retail was $98,000.
Sales for the year totaled $79,000.
The beginning inventory at retail included a gross profit of 66⅔ percent of cost.
Goods purchased during the year were marked up so that the gross profit was one third of the retail selling price.
A physical count of inventory taken at the end of the period showed goods on hand at retail amounting to $10,000.

9B–5   The profit and loss data for the Vernon Co., is as follows:

	Sales	*Purchases*
October	$10,000	$ 8,000
November	12,000	8,000
December	13,000	10,000

The inventory on hand at October 1st had a cost of $4,000. Goods are sold at a gross profit of 20 percent on sales.

Required:

Estimate the cost of the inventory on hand at October 31, November 30, and December 31.

9B–6   The condensed income statement for the Ruth Corporation for the year ending December 31, 1975, is as follows:

Net sales	$120,000
Cost of goods sold	85,000
Gross profit on sales	$ 35,000
Expenses.	37,500
Net loss	$ 2,500

An investigation of the accounting records disclosed that the following errors had been made during 1975:

a. The January 1, 1975 inventory was overstated by $2,600.
b. Purchases of $6,000 made in December of 1975 had not been recorded although the goods were received and included in the ending inventory figure used in the financial statements. (Ruth uses the periodic inventory system.)
c. Miscellaneous items of maintenance and repair expense totaling $1,000 were recorded as additions to the machinery account. Depreciation at 5 percent was recorded on these items during the year.

Required:

1. Prepare a corrected income statement for the year ended December 31, 1975.
2. Make the journal entries necessary to correct the accounts in 1976. (You are to assume that the books had not been closed for 1975.)

10

Long-Term Assets

THE LONG-TERM or fixed assets of a firm are those resources which are used in the continuing operations of a business over a number of years. They are the assets which are acquired for *use* in the firm's operations as contrasted to those assets which are purchased for *resale* to the customers of a business.

Fixed or long-term assets are generally classified into two general classifications: tangible fixed assets and intangible fixed assets. Tangible fixed assets are those assets which have physical substance—for example, land, buildings, equipment, furniture, and fixtures. Intangible fixed assets are usually property rights rather than property itself—for example, patents, copyrights, franchise rights, and goodwill.

In this chapter we will discuss the procedures which are necessary to establish control over the use of long-term assets and some of the accounting practices and techniques which may be employed with regard to these resources as well as the expenses related to their use.

CONTROL OVER TANGIBLE LONG-TERM ASSETS

A fixed asset ledger card should be prepared and maintained for each individual asset purchased. This card should include all of the pertinent information relating to the asset and its use. This data will enable the management of the firm to establish and maintain control over each individual asset (for example, by providing the basis for taking a physical inventory of all fixed assets owned by the firm). It will also assist in accounting for all transactions relating to fixed assets. For example, the fixed asset ledger card will provide the information which is required in order to calculate the periodic depreciation expense for the asset and the data required to adjust the accounts as assets are sold or retired.

Using a ledger card for an automobile as an illustration, the following information should ordinarily be provided.

Asset Ledger Account

Description	Cost	Depreciation	Other Information
Name of asset	Date acquired	Estimated life	Repairs
Account number	Invoice cost	Estimated salvage	Date
Asset number	Other costs	value	Amount
Manufacturer's		Depreciation to	Actual life
serial number		date	Data on disposal:
Horsepower			Date
Insurance carried			Sales price
Property tax			(if any)
valuation			Gain or loss
			To whom sold

ACCOUNTING FOR TANGIBLE FIXED ASSETS

Fixed assets are initially recorded at their acquisition cost. The cost of a fixed asset includes not only the invoice cost (i.e., the cost of the asset itself), but also all expenditures which may be necessary to place the asset in use. This latter type of expenditure would include expenditures for freight, installation, testing, sales taxes, and any other costs which are incurred in the process of acquiring an asset and preparing it for use at the intended time and place. A proper determination of the total cost of a fixed asset is important because the cost of an asset (less any salvage value, i.e., the amount the firm can recover when the firm has finished using it) becomes an expense which should be charged against the income of the business during the periods the asset is used by the firm.[1] This process of allocating the cost of an asset to expense is known as depreciation.

The basic nature of and the problems involved in depreciation accounting may be illustrated by the use of a simple example. Assume that you decide to purchase a Chevrolet Impala for use as a taxi cab. The cost of the auto is $4,000. You feel that you will be able to earn approximately $12,000 each year in fares, and the estimated operating costs (gas, oil, repairs, insurance, etc.) will be approximately $4,000 per year. You further estimate that the auto will last for four years at which time it will probably have to be replaced. At the end of the four-year period you esti-

---

[1] The cost of certain fixed assets which are not used up in the generation of revenue, such as land, are not allocated to expense. Instead, the original cost of the asset is maintained in the accounts until the asset is disposed of.

mate that your used Chevrolet may be sold for about $400. What would your earnings be over the four years if your estimates prove to be accurate? Total income for the four-year period might be calculated as follows:

YOUR TAXI COMPANY
Income Statement
For Four Years

Revenues ($12,000 per year for 4 years).	$48,000
Operating costs ($4,000 per year for 4 years)	$16,000
Cost of the taxi ($4,000 cost less $400 received from its sale at the end of the four-year period)	3,600
Total costs	$19,600
Net Income	$28,400

Assume now that you wished to prepare separate income statements for each of the four years. You could do the following:

YOUR TAXI COMPANY
Income Statements

	For the Year				
	1	*2*	*3*	*4*	*Total*
Revenues.	$12,000	$12,000	$12,000	$12,000	$48,000
Operating costs	$ 4,000	$ 4,000	$ 4,000	$ 4,000	$16,000
Cost of the taxi	4,000	0	0	(400)*	3,600
	$ 8,000	$ 4,000	$ 4,000	$ 3,600	$19,600
Net Income	$ 4,000	$ 8,000	$ 8,000	$ 8,400	$28,400

* The negative four hundred dollars shown as "cost of the taxi" represents the proceeds received from its sale at the end of the fourth year—i.e., its salvage value.

But do these statements really reflect the actual facts of the situation? Is it reasonable to report that your income doubled during year 2, remained constant during the third year and then increased slightly in year 4? Of course not. The total for the four years seems to be reasonable, but the problem lies in attempting to measure the income for *each* individual year. This difficulty arises because you purchased the car and paid for it at the beginning of year 1, used it for four years and sold it at the end of the fourth year. In order to measure the income for each year properly, it is necessary to allocate, in a rational and systematic manner, the net cost of owning the auto (i.e., the purchase price of the car less its estimated salvage value) over the periods which benefit from its use.

As previously indicated, the process of amortizing or charging the cost of a fixed asset to expense over the period of its useful life is referred to as depreciation. A more formal definition of depreciation is ". . . the systematic allocation of the cost of an asset, less salvage value (if any) over its estimated useful life."

From a theoretical viewpoint, depreciation expense for a particular period represents an estimate of the portion of the cost of an asset which is used up or which otherwise expires during that period. A precise determination of the depreciation expense related to an individual asset for any given year is difficult because it is almost impossible to accurately predict the exact useful life of an asset. The life of an asset, and therefore its depreciation, is affected by a combination of factors such as the passage of time, normal wear and tear, physical deterioration, and obsolescence. Even though the various techniques which can be employed in determining the depreciation may appear to be precise, and from a mathematical viewpoint they are, it should be noted that because of the estimating of useful life, salvage value, etc., depreciation is always an estimate or approximation. However, periodic measurement of that portion of the cost of an asset which has been used up or has expired during a period is a necessary element in determining the income of the firm for that period. Depreciation accounting is a method of allocation by which an attempt is made to "match" the cost of an asset against the revenue which has been generated or produced from using the asset.

DEPRECIATION METHODS

In recording the periodic depreciation for fixed assets, three basic factors must be considered:

1. The cost of the asset—the invoice cost plus all costs which are necessary to place it in use.
2. The estimated useful life of the asset.
3. The estimated salvage or scrap value of the asset—the amount which will be recovered when the asset is retired.

There are several methods which may be employed in computing and recording the periodic cost, depreciation expense, which is associated with the use of the fixed assets of a firm. This section of the chapter will discuss three of the methods which are often used in accounting for the use of long-term tangible assets in the operations of businesses: the straight-line method, the declining balance method, and the sum-of-the-years'-digits method. Each of these methods results in identical total depreciation over the life of a fixed asset—an amount equal to the original cost of the asset less its estimated salvage value. The methods differ, however, in the amount of cost which is allocated to expense during each year of the life of the asset.

Although each of these methods is acceptable, the consistency principle requires that once a method has been adopted for a particular type of asset, the firm must continue to use this method. In order to illustrate these techniques, the following data will be used:

```
Type of asset. . . . . . . . . . . . . . . . . . . . . . .    Chevrolet Impala
Date acquired . . . . . . . . . . . . . . . . . . . . . .    January 1, 1974
Cost (including delivery,
    sales tax, etc.). . . . . . . . . . . . . . . . . . . .    $4,000
Estimated useful life . . . . . . . . . . . . . . . . .    4 years
Estimated salvage value  . . . . . . . . . . . . . .    $400
```

Straight-Line Depreciation. One of the simplest, and most commonly used, methods of computing depreciation is the straight-line method. This method considers the passage of time to be the most important single factor or limitation on the useful life of an asset. It assumes that other factors such as wear and tear and obsolescence are somewhat proportional to the elapsed time; this may or may not be the case in fact. The straight-line method allocates the cost of an asset, less its salvage value, to expense equally over its useful life. A formula which may be employed in calculating depreciation using the straight-line method is as follows:

$$\frac{\text{Cost of the Asset} - \text{Estimated Salvage Value}}{\text{Estimated Useful Life}} = \text{Depreciation for the Period}$$

Substituting the illustrative data presented above in the formula, we obtain the following calculation of depreciation for 1974:

$$\frac{(\$4,000 - \$400)}{4 \text{ years}} = \$900 \text{ per Year}$$

Since the straight-line method of depreciation allocates an identical dollar amount of depreciation expense to each period, depreciation for the years 1975, 1976, and 1977 (the remaining useful life of the automobile) would also be $900 each year.

Accelerated Methods of Depreciation. Businessmen recognize that the benefits obtained from the use of a fixed asset frequently may not be uniform over its useful life. Both the revenue-producing ability of an asset and its value may decline at a faster rate during the early years of its life. Also, the costs of repairing and maintaining the asset may increase during the later years of its life. Furthermore, accelerated depreciation methods are permitted for income tax purposes and may benefit the taxpayer by postponing or deferring the payment of taxes to a later year. Although a business may use different methods of computing depreciation for accounting and tax purposes, firms often wish to simplify their record-keeping by using the same method for both purposes. For these reasons many businesses have adopted accelerated methods of calculating depreciation expense. In general these methods allow the recording of larger amounts of depreciation in the early periods of an asset's life than in later years. As indicated above, a business may choose to employ accelerated depreciation methods for computing the expense relating to the use of its fixed assets for tax purposes because the increased depreciation charges (which do not require the outlay of cash, since the cash expenditure was made at the time the asset was acquired) reduce taxable income and therefore reduce the amount of income tax currently payable. By postponing or deferring the payment of income taxes from an earlier to a later year of an asset's life, the business has obtained, in effect, an interest-free loan from the taxing authority.[2]

Two commonly used methods of accelerated depreciation will be illustrated: the double-declining balance method and the sum-of-the-years'-digits method.

The Double-Declining Balance Method.   The procedures used in applying the double-declining balance method arbitrarily double the depreciation rate which would be used in calculating depreciation under the straight-line method.[3] This increased rate is then applied to the book value (i.e., the cost of the asset less the total depreciation taken to date) of the assets. The formula used in calculating double-declining balance depreciation is as follows:

$$(2 \times \text{Straight-line rate}) \times (\text{Cost} - \text{Depreciation Taken in Prior Periods})$$
$$= \text{Depreciation for the Period}$$

Salvage value is ignored in the computation of depreciation under the double-declining balance method with the exception of the final year. In the final year of the asset's life, the formula is ignored and the depreciation taken is simply whatever amount is necessary to reduce the book value of the asset to its salvage value.

Using the same data as in the previous example, the calculation of double-declining balance depreciation may be illustrated as follows:

$$(2 \times 25\%) \times (\$4,000 - \$0) = \$2,000 \text{ Depreciation for 1974.}$$

The straight-line rate is 25 percent; since the asset has a useful life of four years, one-fourth (or 25 percent) of the cost is expensed each year using the straight-line method. The doubled rate (2×25 percent) is applied to the full cost of $4,000 since the salvage value is ignored in the initial years of the asset's life and there is, of course, no depreciation from prior years.

---

[2] See Chapter 19 for a detailed discussion of income tax allocation.

[3] The straight-line rate may be calculated by dividing the useful life of the asset (in years) into 100%. For the example used, the straight-line rate would be 100% divided by 4 or 25%.

The depreciation charge for 1975 would be calculated as follows:

$$(2 \times 25\%) \times (\$4,000 - \$2,000) = \$1,000 \text{ Depreciation for 1975.}$$

The only change from the previous year is that $2,000, the depreciation taken in 1974, is substituted for $0 in the first calculation.

Depreciation for 1976 would be:

$$(2 \times 25\%) \times (\$4,000 - \$3,000) = \$500 \text{ Depreciation for 1976.}$$

Again, the only change in the formula is in the depreciation taken in prior years. The $3,000 amount used in the computation of depreciation for 1976 is the 1974 depreciation of $2,000 plus the 1975 depreciation of $1,000.

The formula would not be used to calculate the depreciation expense for 1977, since this is the final year of the asset's useful life. Depreciation for 1977 would be computed as follows:

Cost of the asset.		$4,000
Less: Depreciation taken in prior years:		
1974.	$2,000	
1975.	$1,000	
1976. . . . . :	$ 500	$3,500
Net book value of the asset at January 1, 1977		500
Less: Estimated salvage value		400
Depreciation for 1977		$ 100

Income tax regulations permit the use of the double-declining balance method only when assets are acquired new. If a used asset is purchased, a similar method, referred to as the 150-percent declining balance method, may be used. The only difference between the two methods is the substitution of 150% for 200% in determining the rate. Using the same data as above, depreciation expense using the 150 percent-declining balance method would be as follows:

$$1974: \quad (1.5 \times 25\%) \times (\$4,000 - \$0) \qquad = \$1,500.00$$
$$1975: \quad (1.5 \times 25\%) \times (\$4,000 - \$1,500.00) = \$\ 937.50$$
$$1976: \quad (1.5 \times 25\%) \times (\$4,000 - \$2,437.50) = \$\ 585.93$$

Depreciation for 1977 would be computed as follows:

Cost of the asset.		$4,000.00
Less: Depreciation taken in prior years:		
1974.	$1,500.00	
1975.	937.50	
1976.	585.93	3,023.43
Book value of the asset at January 1, 1977		976.57
Less: Estimated salvage value		400.00
Depreciation for 1977		$ 576.57

The Sum-of-the-Years'-Digits Method. The use of the sum-of-the-years'-digits method also produces greater charges for depreciation in the early years of an asset's useful life. The life-years of an asset are totaled[4] and utilized as the denominator of a fraction that uses the number of years of life remaining from the beginning of the year (i.e., the years in reverse order) as the numerator. This fraction is then applied to the cost of the asset less its estimated salvage value in order to compute the depreciation for the period.

Again, using the same data as in the previous illustrations, the depreciation expense for each of the four years, 1974 through 1977, using the sum-of-the-years'-digits method, would be calculated as follows:

Sum-of-the-years'-digits:

$$1 + 2 + 3 + 4 = 10$$

Depreciation for each period: ~~Life of Asset~~ , Salvage Value

1974: $\frac{4}{10} \times (\$4,000 - \$400) = \$1,440$
1975: $\frac{3}{10} \times (\$4,000 - \$400) = \$1,080$
1976: $\frac{2}{10} \times (\$4,000 - \$400) = \$\ 720$
1977: $\frac{1}{10} \times (\$4,000 - \$400) = \$\ 360$

As is now apparent, the *total* amount of depreciation taken for a fixed asset over its useful life will be identical regardless of the method used, although the timing and pattern of the depreciation charges vary widely according to the particular method chosen. The effects of the three methods on the example data are illustrated below.

Year	Straight-line	Double-Declining Balance	Sum-of-the-years'-digits
1974	$ 900	$2,000	$1,440
1975	900	1,000	1,080
1976	900	500	720
1977	900	100	360
Total	$3,600	$3,600	$3,600

The differences in the depreciation expense depending on the method chosen are illustrated graphically in Illustration 10–1.

---

[4] The sum of the numbers from one to the estimated life of an asset in years. For example, the life-years of an asset with a 3-year estimated life would be $1 + 2 + 3 = 6$.

Illustration 10–1

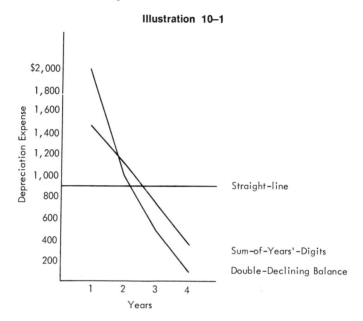

Because depreciation expense is an important factor which enters into the determination of the income of a firm for a period, the reported income will also vary according to the depreciation method selected. The effect of depreciation on the reported income of the firm (and therefore its income taxes) is an important factor in the selection of the depreciation method(s) a firm will use.

RECORDING LONG-TERM ASSETS

Using the Chevrolet Impala acquired by Your Taxi Company (described on page 242) as an example, the accounting procedures for recording the acquisition and use of fixed assets will be illustrated.

On January 1, 1974, the acquisition of the automobile would be recorded as follows:

```
Automobile . . . . . . . . . . . . . . . . . . . . . . . . . . . . . . . .    4,000
     Cash . . . . . . . . . . . . . . . . . . . . . . . . . . . . . . . . .            4,000
```

It should be noted that the debit to the asset account was for the total cost of the Chevrolet including delivery charges, sales tax, etc. In this instance the car was paid for in cash. Had a liability been incurrrd it would have been recorded by a credit. The procedures required when an old asset is traded in on a new asset are discussed in a later section of this chapter.

At the end of 1974, it would be necessary to record depreciation on the asset in order to charge to expense the portion of the cost of the asset which had been "used up" during the period. For purposes of illustration, we will assume that the straight-line method of depreciation was used. On December 31, 1974, depreciation would be recorded in the books of Your Taxi Company by the following entry:

```
Depreciation Expense .............................. 900
    Accumulated Depreciation ..........................        900
```

The debit to depreciation expense records the portion of the cost of the asset which is to be charged as an expense of the period. The credit to the accumulated depreciation account adds the current period's depreciation to that which was taken in prior years (in this case zero since this is the initial year of the asset's useful life); the total of this account indicates the total amount of depreciation taken to date at any given point in time. The depreciation expense of $900 would appear in the income statement along with the other expenses of the period and would be deducted from revenue in the determination of income. Accumulated depreciation would appear as an offset (called a contra account) against the related asset account in the balance sheet as follows:

```
Current assets ......................        $10,000
Automobile .......................  $4,000
Less:  Accumulated depreciation...........    900      3,100
    Total Assets ......................        $13,100
```

Since the straight-line method of depreciation was used, the entries which are required in order to record depreciation expense for the years 1975, 1976, and 1977 will be the same as the one which was made on December 31, 1974, shown above. The automobile and accumulated depreciation accounts would appear as follows:

Automobile		Accumulated Depreciation	
(a) 4,000		(b) 900	
		(c) 900	
		(d) 900	
		(e) 900	
		(f) 3,600	

Key:
(a)   Cost of the automobile on January 1, 1974.
(b)   Depreciation for 1974.
(c)   Depreciation for 1975.
(d)   Depreciation for 1976.
(e)   Depreciation for 1977.
(f)   Balance in the account at December 31, 1977.

Assets Acquired during the Period

In the example used in the previous section, the automobile was acquired at the beginning of the period. In practice, assets will be acquired throughout the accounting period and this will require that depreciation be recorded for a part of a period in the year of acquisition. For example, the purchase of the automobile on June 1, 1974 would be recorded as follows:

```
Automobile . . . . . . . . . . . . . . . . . . . . . . . . . . . . . . . . . .  4,000
    Cash . . . . . . . . . . . . . . . . . . . . . . . . . . . . . . . . . .          4,000
```

At the end of 1974, it would be necessary to record depreciation on the asset for the seven (7)-month period that it was used during the year (June 1, 1974, to December 31, 1974). Again, we will assume the same facts as before (4-year life, $400 salvage value) and that the straight-line method of depreciation was used, so the calculation would be as follows:

$$\frac{(\$4,000 - \$400)}{4 \text{ years}} = \$900 \text{ per Year}$$

$$\frac{\$900}{12 \text{ months}} = \$75 \text{ per Month}$$

Depreciation for the period June 1, 1974, to December 31, 1974, would be 7 months $\times$ $75 per month or a total of $525. At December 31, 1974, depreciation for the period would be recorded by the following entry:

```
Depreciation Expense  . . . . . . . . . . . . . . . . . . . . . . . . . . . . . 525
    Accumulated Depreciation  . . . . . . . . . . . . . . . . . . . . . . . .         525
```

The entries to record depreciation expense for the years 1975, 1976, and 1977 would each cover a full year and each would be as follows:

```
Depreciation Expense  . . . . . . . . . . . . . . . . . . . . . . . . . . . . . 900
    Accumulated Depreciation  . . . . . . . . . . . . . . . . . . . . . . . .         900
```

In 1978, depreciation would be recorded for the final five (5) months of the life of the asset (5 months $\times$ $75 per month or $375) by the following entry:

```
Depreciation Expense  . . . . . . . . . . . . . . . . . . . . . . . . . . . . . 375
    Accumulated Depreciation  . . . . . . . . . . . . . . . . . . . . . . . .         375
```

The automobile and accumulated depreciation accounts would appear as follows:

Automobile		Accumulated Depreciation	
(a) 4,000		(b) 525	
		(c) 900	
		(d) 900	
		(e) 900	
		(f) 375	
		(g) 3,600	

Key:
(a) Cost of the automobile on June 1, 1974.
(b) Depreciation for 1974 (7 months).
(c) Depreciation for 1975 (12 months).
(d) Depreciaton for 1976 (12 months).
(e) Depreciation for 1977 (12 months).
(f) Depreciation for 1978 (5 months).
(g) Balance in the account at May 31, 1978.

In the above example, depreciation was calculated from the exact date of acquisition until the end of the useful life of the asset. In practice, as a matter of convenience, a business may establish a procedure whereby it will always take six months' depreciation in the year an asset is acquired and six months' depreciation in the year it is disposed of (see next section) irrespective of the exact dates of acquisition or disposal. Alternatively, a firm might take a full year's depreciation in the year of acquisition and no depreciation in the year of disposal, or vice-versa. The use of procedures such as those described above do not change the entries illustrated and are generally acceptable as long as there is no significant distortion of depreciation expense or income.

Disposition of Assets

At some point in time, the cost of continuing to use a particular asset will exceed the benefits derived from its use and it will be to the advantage of the firm to dispose of it. For example, assume that after using the Chevrolet as a taxi for four years, it was sold for $400, its book value at that time. (Recall that the auto had an original cost of $4,000, an estimated life of four years, and an anticipated salvage value of $400.) The entry to record the sale of the Chevrolet would be as follows:

Cash   400
Accumulated Depreciation.   3,600
    Automobile   4,000

The debit to cash records the amount of cash received while the debit to accumulated depreciation and the credit to automobile remove the automobile and its related accumulated depreciation account from the books of Your Taxi Company. In this example, the estimate of useful life and salvage value were precise. This would occur only infrequently in actual practice. For example, if the same Chevrolet were sold at the end of the fourth year for $500, the entry to record this transaction would be as follows:

```
Cash ......................................    500
Accumulated Depreciation. .....................  3,600
    Automobile ...............................             4,000
    Gain ....................................              100
```

The only difference between this entry and the preceding entry is that the amount of cash received increased from $400 to $500. This amount exceeds the book value of the asset (original cost of $4,000 less accumulated depreciation of $3,600 or $400) and therefore a gain ($500 minus $400 or $100) is realized. On the other hand, if the car had been sold for $350, a loss would have been incurred. The calculation of the gain and/or loss on the disposal of the automobile in all three cases mentioned above may be summarized as follows:

		A	B	C
Selling price		$400	$500	$350
Cost of automobile	$4,000			
Accumulated depreciation	(3,600)			
Book value		(400)	(400)	(400)
Gain (loss) on the sale of the automobile		0	$100	($50)

The entries for the disposal of the asset under Cases A and B have been presented above. The entry for Case C, the loss situation, is as follows:

```
Cash ......................................    350
Accumulated Depreciation. .....................  3,600
Loss ......................................     50
    Automobile ...............................             4,000
```

Again, the only difference between this entry and the two preceding entries is the amount of cash received, $350. Since the cash received was less than the book value of the automobile ($4,000 less $3,600 or $400) a loss equal to the difference ($400 less $350 or $50) occurred and should be recorded in the accounts.

In some instances, an asset may be discarded prior to the end of its useful life. For example, assume that the automobile was involved in an accident at the end of its third year of use and was damaged to the extent that repairs were not considered to be feasible. The entry to record the loss from the accident would be as follows:

```
Loss ......................................   1,300
Accumulated Depreciation. .....................  2,700*
    Automobile ...............................             4,000
```

* For purposes of the example, it was assumed that the straight-line method of depreciation was used.

Of course, the taxi would probably be insured. If this was the case and $1,000 was received from an insurance policy on the automobile, the entry would be as follows:

```
Cash  . . . . . . . . . . . . . . . . . . . . . . . . . . . . . . . . . . 1,000
Accumulated Depreciation. . . . . . . . . . . . . . . . . . . . . . . 2,700*
Loss  . . . . . . . . . . . . . . . . . . . . . . . . . . . . . . . . . .  300
    Automobile . . . . . . . . . . . . . . . . . . . . . . . . . . . .          4,000
```
* For purposes of the example, it was assumed that the straight-line method of depreciation had been used.

In any case, cash is debited for the amount received (if any), accumulated depreciation is debited for the depreciation taken to the date of disposal, and the asset is credited for its original cost in order to remove these accounts from the books. A loss (or gain) is recorded for the difference between the book value of the asset and the cash received (if any).

In each of the illustrations included above, it was assumed that the disposal of the asset took place at the end of the period. If the disposal is made during the period, the only difference would be that an entry would be required to record the depreciation for the period from the end of the preceding year up to the date of the disposal. The entry to record the disposal itself would be exactly the same as those illustrated above.

Trade-Ins

In acquiring assets, a firm will frequently trade in an old asset in purchasing the new asset. Assume that Your Taxi Company traded in its Chevrolet Impala on a Plymouth Fury on January 1, 1978. The following data will be used in the example:

```
List-Price of the Plymouth Fury. . . . . . . . . . . . . . $4,600
Cost of the Chevrolet Impala
    (at January 1, 1974) . . . . . . . . . . . . . . . . . . .  4,000
Accumulated depreciation on the Chevrolet
    (at December 31, 1977) . . . . . . . . . . . . . . . . . .  3,600
Trade-in allowance . . . . . . . . . . . . . . . . . . . . . .   500
Fair market value of the Chevrolet
    (at January 1, 1978) . . . . . . . . . . . . . . . . . . .   200
Cash difference paid . . . . . . . . . . . . . . . . . . . . .  4,100
```

The entry to record the acquisition of the Plymouth Fury could be as follows:

```
Automobile . . . . . . . . . . . . . . . . . . . . . . . . . . . . . . . 4,300
Accumulated Depreciation. . . . . . . . . . . . . . . . . . . . . . . 3,600
Loss  . . . . . . . . . . . . . . . . . . . . . . . . . . . . . . . . . .  200
    Automobile . . . . . . . . . . . . . . . . . . . . . . . . . . . .          4,000
    Cash . . . . . . . . . . . . . . . . . . . . . . . . . . . . . . . .          4,100
```

The debit to automobile records the $4,300 "cost" of the new Plymouth Fury as the $4,100 cash paid plus the $200 fair market value of the Chevrolet traded in. The debit to accumulated depreciation of $3,600 and the credit to automobile of $4,000 remove the original cost of the Chevrolet and its related accumulated depreciation from the accounts. The debit to loss of $200 records the loss on the disposal of the Chevrolet and was calculated as follows:

Original cost of the Chevrolet	$4,000
Less: Accumulated depreciation as of the date of trade-in	3,600
Book value of the Chevrolet at the date of the trade-in	$ 400
Less: Fair market value of the Chevrolet at the date of the trade-in	200
Loss	$ 200

The credit to cash of $4,100 records the cash outlay which was made in order to acquire the Plymouth. This method is referred to as the "fair market value" method.

An alternative procedure would be to record a gain or loss on the asset traded in based on the amount of the trade-in allowance rather than the fair market value of the asset traded, and to record the new asset in the accounts at its list price.

Using the same facts as were employed in the example above, the entry to record the acquisition of the Plymouth using this method would be:

Automobile	4,600	
Accumulated Depreciation	3,600	
Automobile		4,000
Cash		4,100
Gain		100

In this entry, the "gain" of $100 is simply the excess of the trade-in allowance of $500 over the book value of the Chevrolet of $400. This method is often referred to as the "accounting" method.

A third method, known as the "income tax" method would record the acquisition of the Plymouth Fury as follows.

Automobile	4,500	
Accumulated Depreciation	3,600	
Automobile		4,000
Cash		4,100

The debit to accumulated depreciation and the credit to automobile in the entry remove the original cost of the Chevrolet and its related accumulated depreciation from the accounts. The credit to cash records the cash outlay which was made to acquire the Plymouth. The debit to automobile records the "cost" of the new Plymouth Fury and was calculated as follows:

Cash paid.		$4,100
Add: Book value of trade-in:		
Cost	$4,000	
Accumulated depreciation.	3,600	
Book value.		$ 400
Cost of Plymouth Fury.		$4,500

This method assumes that the cost of a new asset is equal to the cash paid plus the undepreciated cost (book value) of the asset which was traded in. Since this method is the only procedure which is acceptable for federal income tax purposes, it is often referred to as the "income tax" method.

Of the three methods illustrated above, the "fair market value" method is the most correct from a theoretical point of view. This is because it records the cost of the new asset as the amount of the cash paid plus the fair market value of the trade-in and measures the loss as the difference between the book value of the asset and its fair market value.

Natural Resources

In addition to fixed assets such as property, plant, and equipment described in the earlier sections of this chapter, a firm may also own assets in the form of natural resources. These resources include such items as oil deposits, tracts of timber, and coal deposits. Like the other long-term assets of the firm, the basis for accounting for these resources is primarily historical cost. As these resources are converted into salable inventory by drilling, cutting, and mining operations, the cost of these operations along with the cost of the resources themselves are accumulated.

The process of writing off or amortizing the cost of these natural resources is generally referred to as depletion. Consider the following illustration, for example:

1. An oil field is acquired at a cost of $1,000,000. Geological surveys indicate that a total of approximately 400,000 barrels of oil will ultimately be taken from the field.
2. The estimated residual value of the field after the oil has been extracted is approximately $200,000.
3. During the first year of operations, the drilling costs total $50,000. A total of 50,000 barrels of oil are taken and sold at a price of $5 per barrel.

These transactions would be recorded as follows:

Acquisition of the Field

Oil Field	1,000,000	
Cash		1,000,000

Drilling during the First Year

Inventory of Oil.	50,000	
Cash		50,000
Inventory of Oil.	100,000	
Accumulated Depletion-Oil Field.		100,000

The $50,000 cost of drilling was assumed to be entirely applicable to the oil taken during the year and was therefore assigned to the inventory of oil as a part of its cost. The depletion of $100,000 was calculated as follows:

Cost of the field.	$1,000,000
Estimated residual value of the field	200,000
Cost of the 400,000 barrels of oil.	$ 800,000
Divide by 400,000 in order to obtain the	
cost per barrel.	$2

The total cost per barrel would be the cost of the oil, that is the depletion per barrel, of $2 plus the drilling cost of $1 per barrel[5] or $3.

Sale of the 50,000 Barrels of Oil

Cash	250,000	
Sales		250,000
Cost of Goods Sold.	150,000	
Inventory of Oil		150,000

The procedures described above are known as cost depletion and are required for accounting and financial reporting purposes. For income tax purposes, firms may choose to use either depletion based on cost or percentage depletion. It is often advantageous from a tax standpoint to use the percentage depletion method, since depletion calculated by this method frequently exceeds depletion on a cost basis. Furthermore, in many cases it allows the taxpayer to deduct more than the cost of the field over its useful life. The percentage depletion method allows the firm to deduct from sales a given percentage of sales as depletion[6] in lieu of cost depletion.

---

[5] Drilling costs of $50,000 divided by the 50,000 barrels taken, or $1 per barrel.

[6] The current percentage depletion allowable is 22.5 percent for oil.

Intangible Assets

Intangible assets are resources such as organization costs, trademarks, patents, copyrights, and goodwill which have value but do not have physical substance. An intangible asset derives its value from certain special rights and privileges which accrue to the firm which owns it. For example, the ownership of a patent has value because it gives the owner of the patent exclusive right to the manufacture, sale, or other use of an invention or process for a period of 17 years.

A firm may obtain an intangible asset by purchase or by development within the firm. The objectives of accounting for intangible assets are similar to those for tangible assets which were described earlier in the chapter—the cost of the asset is recorded upon acquisition and this cost is allocated to expense over the useful life of the intangible. The cost of an intangible asset includes all expenditures which are incurred in the development or acquisition of the rights or privileges. The cost of an intangible asset acquired by purchase can usually be measured with little difficulty. The cost of internally developed intangibles is often more difficult to determine. For example, it may be quite difficult to estimate how much of the total research and development cost for a particular period should be allocated to the development of a single patent.

The costs of intangible assets are written off to expense over their estimated useful lives in a manner similar to the depreciation of tangible fixed assets. This is referred to as amortization. Amortization is recorded by a debit to amortization expense and a credit to the intangible asset account. Like tangible fixed assets, the cost of intangibles should be amortized over their estimated useful lives. However, according to Accounting Principles Board *Opinion No. 17,* the period of amortization should not exceed a maximum of 40 years. The Board also concluded that the straight-line method of amortization should be used unless the firm shows evidence that some other systematic method is more appropriate in the circumstances.

To illustrate the accounting for intangible assets, assume that Landry Company purchased a patent from Allen Company for $10,000 on January 1, 1975. The purchase would be recorded as follows:

```
Patents . . . . . . . . . . . . . . . . . . . . . . . . . . . . . . . . . .   10,000
    Cash . . . . . . . . . . . . . . . . . . . . . . . . . . . . . . . . .            10,000
```

If the remaining useful or economic life of the patent was ten years, the adjusting entry required to record the amortization of the patent at the end of each year (from 1975 to 1984) would be as follows:

```
Amortization Expense . . . . . . . . . . . . . . . . . . . . . . . . .   1,000
    Patents . . . . . . . . . . . . . . . . . . . . . . . . . . . . . . . .            1,000
```

Note that the amortization is credited directly to the asset account rather than to an accumulated amortization account as in the case of tangible fixed assets. There appears to be no logical reason for this procedure other than tradition.

Certain intangibles, such as patents, copyrights, and franchises, may be identified with a specific right or privilege. The costs of these intangibles, whether purchased or internally developed, can be measured and allocated to expense over their useful lives. Other intangibles, however, cannot be specifically identified. This type of intangible is usually referred to as good-will. The intangible asset goodwill represents the sum of all the special advantages which are not identifiable and which relate to the business as a whole. It encompasses such items as a favorable location, good customer relations, and superior ability of management. The existence of such factors enables the firm to earn an above normal rate of return.

Unlike tangible assets or identifiable intangible assets, goodwill cannot be sold or acquired separately from the business as a whole. Because of the uncertainty involved in estimating the goodwill of a business enterprise, goodwill is normally recorded only when a business is acquired by purchase. In a purchase transaction, goodwill may be measured as the excess of the purchase price of an entity over the sum of the fair values of all its identifiable assets less its liabilities. The source of this excess is the potential of the firm to earn an above average rate of return.

To illustrate, assume that Richard Smith purchased the Campus Book Store on January 1, 1975, for $100,000 cash. Further assume that the identifiable assets were determined to have a total fair value of $90,000 at the date of purchase (including inventory, $10,000; equipment, $20,000; building, $40,000; and land, $20,000). The liabilities assumed by the purchaser were accounts payable of $20,000. The $30,000 excess of the purchase price over the value of all the identifiable assets less the liabilities represents the value of the goodwill. The purchase would be recorded as follows:

Inventory	10,000	
Equipment	20,000	
Building	40,000	
Land	20,000	
Goodwill	30,000	
Accounts Payable		20,000
Cash		100,000

Once goodwill is recorded in a purchase transaction, it is amortized like all other intangible assets—the recorded cost is allocated to expense over its estimated life with a maximum of 40 years.

Long-Term Assets in the Financial Statements

Fixed assets are carried in the balance sheet at their acquisition cost, less any accumulated depreciation. The depreciation on long-term assets is included in the income statement as an expense and is deducted in determining income from operations. Gains or losses on the disposal of long-term assets would appear on the income statement in a special section after income from operations, since they are normally not considered to be a part of the normal operations of the firm. A typical presentation of long-term assets in the balance sheet might be as follows:

Current assets			$15,000
Long-term assets:			
Furniture and fixtures	$ 5,000		
Less: Accumulated depreciation	3,500	$ 1,500	
Equipment.	$ 8,000		
Less: Accumulated depreciation	3,600	4,400	
Buildings.	$50,000		
Less: Accumulated depreciation	17,000	33,000	
Land		5,000	
Patents.		2,500	
Goodwill.		18,000	64,400
Total assets			$79,400

KEY DEFINITIONS

Accelerated methods of depreciation   Accelerated methods of depreciation are techniques for computing depreciation that assume the rate of depreciation decreases with the passage of time.

Accumulated depreciation   Accumulated depreciation is a contra account which appears as an offset or deduction from the related asset account in the balance sheet. The depreciation taken over the useful life of the asset is accumulated in this account.

Book value of an asset   The book value of an asset is the cost of an asset less accumulated depreciation. The book value of an asset is the remaining undepreciated cost.

Contra account   A contra account is an account which is offset against or deducted from another account in the financial statements.

Declining balance method   The declining balance method is an accelerated method of depreciation that assumes the rate of depreciation to be some multiple of the rate which would be used in the straight-line method.

Depletion   Depletion is the process of writing-off or amortizing the cost of natural resources over the periods which benefit from their use.

Depreciation   Depreciation is the systematic allocation of the cost of an asset, less the salvage value (if any), over its estimated useful life.

"Fair market value" method   The "fair market value" method is used in accounting for the trade-in of an old asset on a new one. The cost of the new asset is assumed to be the cash paid plus the fair market value of the old asset traded in.

Fixed asset ledger card   A fixed asset ledger card is prepared for each individual asset purchased. It includes all of the important information relating to the asset and its use.

Goodwill   Goodwill may be measured as the excess of the purchase price of an entity over the sum of the fair values of all its identifiable assets less its liabilities.

"Income tax" method   The "income tax" method is used to account for the trade-in of an old asset on a new one. The cost of the new asset is assumed to be the cash paid plus the book value of the old asset.

Intangible fixed asset   An intangible fixed asset is one that does not have physical substance, usually a property right.

Long-term or fixed assets   Long-term or fixed assets are those resources of a firm which are used in the continuing operations of a business over a number of years.

Salvage value   Salvage value is the residual amount of a long-term tangible asset that the firm expects to recover at the end of the useful life of the asset.

Straight-line depreciation   This method of depreciation assumes that factors such as wear and tear and obsolescence are somewhat uniform over time. The method allocates the cost of an asset, less its salvage value, to expenses equally over its useful life.

Sum-of-the-years'-digits method   This is an accelerated method of depreciation where the life-years of an asset are totaled and utilized as the denominator of a fraction that uses the number of years of life remaining from the beginning of the year as the numerator.

Tangible fixed asset   A tangible fixed asset is a long-term asset that has physical substance.

QUESTIONS

1. What expenditures are included in the total cost of a fixed asset?
2. What is the purpose of depreciation accounting?
3. What factors should be considered when determining periodic depreciation?
4. Explain the equations used in calculating straight-line, double-declining balance, and sum-of-the-years'-digits depreciation.
5. Three basic depreciation methods are straight-line, sum-of-the-years'-digits, and double-declining balance. In what way are the three depreciation methods similar? In what way are they different?
6. What does the balance in the accumulated depreciation account indicate at any given point in time? What is the purpose of the accumulated depreciation account?
7. When accounting for a trade-in of one asset on another, which of the three methods is the most correct from a theoretical viewpoint? Why?

8. What is the basis for accounting for natural resources? Is this basis the same as that for other long-term assets?

9. What is depletion? Is it similar to depreciation, and if so, in what way?

10. What is the difference in the accounting for intangible assets and the accounting for tangible assets?

EXERCISES

10–1 A machine was purchased for an invoice price of $10,000, F.O.B. destination. The freight charges were $200. Costs of installation amounted to $500. At what cost should the machine be recorded?

10–2 Determine which of the following accounts is to be debited for each of the transactions below.

A. Buildings
B. Accumulated Depreciation
C. Land
D. Patents
E. Depreciation Expense

F. Machinery
G. Insurance Expense
H. Freight Expense
I. General Repairs
J. Legal Fees

_____Purchased land and unusable building.
_____Paid legal fees for above purchase.
_____Constructed new building on site.
_____Purchased machinery for building.
_____Paid freight on machinery.
_____Paid cost of installing machinery.
_____Paid minor repairs on building.
_____Recorded depreciation of equipment.
_____Paid insurance for year on building.
_____Obtained patent from U.S. Patent Office.

10–3 A machine was installed at a total cost of $8,000, assumed to have an estimated useful life of 5 years and a salvage value of $2,000. Calculate the initial year's depreciation assuming (a) the straight-line method is used, (b) the sum-of-the-years'-digits method is used, and (c) the double declining balance method is used.

10–4 The Get Rich Quick Mining Company obtained a uranium mine for $1,350,000 on February 1, 1975. It is estimated that approximately 335,000 pounds of uranium can be extracted from the mine. The residual value of the property after the uranium has been removed is approximately $10,000. In 1975, 74,000 pounds of uranium were extracted from the mine and in 1976, 90,000 pounds were extracted. Mining costs were $14,800 for 1975 and $22,500 for 1976. The uranium is sold for $10 per pound.

Required:

Record the above transactions on the books of the Mining Company.

10–5 The Bratton Company developed a new product at a cost of $56,000. A patent was acquired on the product on January 1, 1975. Additional legal costs of $4,000 were incurred in obtaining the patent. The patent was estimated to have a useful life of 10 years. (Its legal life is 17 years.) What will be the patent amortization expense for 1975?

PROBLEMS

Series A

10A–1   The Carson Carton Company purchased a new cutting machine at an invoice price of $13,000. It paid the seller in time to take advantage of a 3 percent discount. Carson Carton then paid $400 shipping charges and $550 installation costs. However, after the machine was installed it was discovered that the electrical wiring in the plant was not adequate to carry the additional current needed by the new asset. The company rewired that section of the building at a cost of $875. At what amount should Carson Carton Company value the new cutting machine on its books?

10A–2   Cutler Cutlery Company purchased a large storage cabinet on January 1, 1974, at a cost of $7,500. It was assigned an estimated useful life of 5 years and a salvage value of $500. Prepare a depreciation schedule for the cabinet under the straight-line, double-declining balance and sum-of-the-years'-digits methods.

10A–3   For each of the depreciation methods listed, complete the following schedule of depreciation over the first two years of life of a delivery truck costing $8,800.00 and having a salvage value of $800.00. The truck has an estimated life of 5 years.

Method	Year	Depreciation Expense	Accumulated Depreciation	Book Value
Straight-line	1	$ 1600	$ 1600	$ 7200
Straight-line	2	1600	3200	5600
Sum-of-years'-digits	1	2666.67	2666.67	6133.33
Sum-of-years'-digits	2	2133.33	4800.	4000
Double-declining balance	1	3520	3520	5280
Double-declining balance	2	2112	5632	3168

10A–4   During the course of your audit of Confused, Inc. for the year ended December 31, 1977, you find the following account:

Equipment

(a)	20,000	(c)	3,400
(b)	14,000	(d)	6,600

Key:
(a) Cost of machine A purchased on January 1, 1976.
(b) Cost of machine B purchased on January 1, 1976.
(c) Credit resulting from the recording of depreciation expense for 1976 (Debit was to "depreciation expense.")
(d) Credit resulting from the recording of the sale of machine B on April 1, 1977 (Debit was to cash.)

Each machine had an estimated life of ten years with no salvage value anticipated. The company uses the straight-line method of recording depreciation.

Required:

Give all the adjusting and correcting entries (or entry) required on April 1, 1977.

10A–5   Anderson Aerospace Company traded in its Boeing 707 for a new Boeing 747 on January 1, 1976. The following is the pertinent data for the transaction:

Cost of the 707 (at January 1, 1972).	$785,000
Accumulated depreciation on the 707	
(at December 31, 1975)	300,000
Fair market value of the 707.	325,000
List price of the 747	925,000
Trade-in allowance	350,000
Note payable given for difference.	575,000

Required:

Record the acquisition of the Boeing 747 using the three alternative methods discussed in the chapter. Which of the methods is most theoretically correct and why?

10A–6   Marshall Furniture Manufacturers purchased a new lathe on January 1, 1974, for $1,600. It has an estimated salvage value of $100 and estimated useful life of 3 years. The company uses the sum-of-the-years'-digits depreciation method and maintains records on a calendar year basis. Prepare the journal entries to record the disposal of the lathe under each of the following independent conditions:

1.   Sold for $725 cash on October 1, 1975.
2.   Destroyed by flood on July 1, 1976. Insurance proceeds were $200.
3.   Traded in on purchase of new lathe on January 1, 1975. List price of new lathe was $1,800, market value of old lathe was $1,200, and $700 cash was paid on the transaction. (Record transaction using "fair market value" method.)

10A–7   Snowden Manufacturing Company decided to construct a new plant in 1975 rather than continue to rent its present plant. On January 1, 1975, the company purchased 10 acres of land with two old buildings standing on it. The old buildings were demolished and construction of the new plant was begun. The company set up a Land and Buildings account to which all expenditures relating to the new plant were charged.

The balance in the Land and Buildings account after completion of the plant was $740,450. Entries in the account during the construction period were:

a.	Cost of land and old buildings (old buildings appraised at $17,000)	$137,000	L
b.	Legal fees involved in securing title to property	250	L
c.	Cost of demolishing old buildings	9,500	L
d.	Surveying costs	1,200	L
e.	Price paid for construction of new building	425,000	B
f.	Salary paid to Jim Seales, engineer, supervisor of construction of new plant	12,500	B
g.	Fencing of plant property	3,000	L I
h.	Machinery for new plant	113,000	F.P.
i.	Installation costs of new machinery	9,500	E.P.
j.	Landscaping of grounds	6,250	LF
k.	Office equipment	12,000	E.O.
l.	Payment to architect for designing plans and for services during construction	13,000	B.
m.	Paneling and finishing work done on executive offices	2,250	B.F.
	Total Debits	$744,450	
n.	Proceeds from sale of scrap from old buildings	4,000	L
	Total Credit	$ 4,000	
	Balance	$740,450	•γ

Required:

Reclassify the items presently in the Land and Buildings account to the proper general ledger accounts.

Series B

10B–1 On October 30, 1974, Thomas Brothers, Inc. purchased a used machine for $7,800 from a company in a neighboring state. The machine could not be shipped until November 15 so Thomas Brothers were forced to pay $150 storage costs and $35 insurance fees. After the asset was received and $250 shipping costs had been paid, it was overhauled and installed at a cost of $320, including parts costing $130. On December 21, additional repair work was performed at a cost of $180 in order to put the asset in working condition. At what value should this machine be recorded on the balance sheet on December 31?

10B–2 Jim Strong purchased a mini-submarine on January 1, 1975, for $22,000. The estimated life is 5 years and salvage value is expected to be $2,000.

Required:

a. Prepare a schedule of depreciation over the life of the asset using the following methods: (1) straight-line depreciation, (2) sum-of-the-years'-digits, and (3) double-declining balance.

b. Make the entry to record depreciation on Jim Strong's books for 1975 using the straight-line method.

10B–3 Blintz, Inc. has followed the practice of depreciating its building on a straight-line basis. The building has an estimated useful life of 20 years and a salvage value of $20,000. The company's depreciation expense for 1976 was $20,000 on the building. The building was purchased on January 1, 1974.

Required:

1. The original cost of the building.
2. Depreciation expense for 1975 assuming:
    a. The company had used the double-declining balance method.
    b. The company had used the sum-of-the-years'-digits method.

10B–4 On January 1, 1976, the Confused Company purchased a new truck for $5,600 paying cash. On May 1, 1977, the Company purchased a new truck which had a list price of $6,200. They were given a trade-in allowance of $2,000 for the old truck, the balance being paid in cash. On December 1, 1977, the second truck was completely destroyed by fire. Confused received $3,200 from their insurance company as full settlement for the loss. Truck operating expense for 1977 totaled $2,200.

You are called in by the company's accountant who states that in preparing the December 31, 1977, trial balance he noted that the truck account had a balance of $8,800 although the company does not own any trucks. He also tells you that he failed to record depreciation on either truck during 1977, although the company's accounting manual requires straight-line depreciation, two-year life, $800 salvage value for all automotive equipment.

You obtain a copy of the company's ledger account "Trucks," which shows the following:

Trucks

5,600	2,000
6,200	3,200
2,200	
8,800	

Required:

1. Prepare all journal entries regarding the trucks as they *should* have been made originally.
2. Prepare an entry to correct the accounts as of December 31, 1977. You may assume that the books have not yet been closed for 1977.

10B–5 King Company purchased a truck on January 1, 1974, at a cost of $4,200. The truck was depreciated using the straight-line method with an estimated useful life of four years and a salvage value of

$200. On January 1, 1976, the truck was traded in on a new truck with a list price of $6,000. The fair market value of the old truck was $1,500 and the truck dealer gave a trade-in allowance of $2,400 on the old truck. King Company gave a note payable for the balance of the purchase price.

Required:

Record the acquisition of the new truck using the three alternative methods discussed in the chapter: (1) the "accounting" method, (2) the income tax method, and (3) the "fair market value" method.

10B–6 A truck was purchased on October 1, 1971, at a cost of $29,400. The expected life of this truck was 4 years with an expected salvage value of $600. The company used the straight-line depreciation method and the accounting records are maintained on a calendar year basis. Prepare journal entries to record the disposal of the truck on *May 1, 1973* under *each* of the following *separate* conditions:

1. Sold for $18,000 cash.
2. Completely destroyed by fire, and the insurance company paid $6,000 as full settlement of the loss.
3. Traded in on the purchase of another truck which had a cash price of $34,000; trade-in allowance granted on the old truck was $20,000 and the balance was paid in cash. (Record this transaction in accordance with the manner required for federal income tax purposes.)

10B–7 The Silver Fox Company purchased a parcel of land on which was located a large home and a riding stable on January 7, 1975, for $87,500. Additional expenditures made at the time of settlement were as follows:

Attorney's fees in connection with the purchase	$ 500
Cost of property transfer taxes	1,000
Real estate taxes for 1974 (the seller was to repay Silver Fox for these taxes)	2,000
Title insurance	500
Broker's commission	500
Gardening equipment	1,000
	$5,500

Silver Fox had the property appraised by a professional appraiser on the purchase date. His appraisal showed the following valuations:

Land	$ 55,000
Home	45,000
Stable	10,000
Total appraised value of property	$110,000

Extensive remodeling and redecorating was undertaken immediately to ready the property for rental. The following outlays were made during the month of January:

Cost of tearing down the stable	$ 10,000
Cost of removing fourth story of home	35,000
Architect's fee.	15,000
Replacement of plumbing	11,000
New electrical wiring	14,000
Landscaping	25,000
Payment of hospital bill of passer-by injured by	
falling debris.	5,000
	$115,000
Less: Sale of materials salvaged from stable	1
	$114,999

Required:

Indicate the accounts which would be charged with the cost of each of the items listed below. If an item is to be allocated to more than one account, simply list each account that would be charged.

In indicating your answers use the following code.

Land	L	Any expense or loss account. . . .	E
Home.	H	Any revenue or gain account . . .	R
Stable.	S	Any other account	X
Any other asset account	A		

Purchase price of $87,500	( )	Cost of tearing down stable . . .	( )
Attorney's fees	( )	Cost of tearing down fourth	
Property transfer taxes	( )	floor of home	( )
Real estate taxes for 1974	( )	Architect's fee.	( )
Title insurance.	( )	Plumbing.	( )
Broker's commission	( )	Electrical wiring.	( )
Gardening equipment.	( )	Landscaping	( )
		Hospital bill	( )
		Sale of materials salvaged	
		from stable.	( )

11

Unincorporated
Business Organizations

THERE ARE three basic types of business organizations: (1) the sole proprietorship, (2) the partnership, and (3) the corporation. This chapter
considers the accounting for unincorporated business organizations—sole
proprietorships and partnerships. The following two chapters concentrate
on the accounting issues related to corporations.

THE SOLE PROPRIETORSHIP

The simplest form of business organization is the sole proprietorship, a
business owned by a single individual. In terms of the absolute number
of business firms, the sole proprietorship greatly outnumbers all other
forms of business organizations in the United States. Because of their size,
however, corporations account for the greatest dollar amount of both assets
and sales. Sole proprietorships are the dominant form of business organization among smaller firms, particularly among businesses engaged in retail
trade and in the rendering of services.

One of the principal advantages of the sole proprietorship is the ease
of establishing this type of business. Other than local and possibly state
licensing requirements, an owner need only have the necessary capital and
begin operations in order to establish his firm. Legal contracts are not
necessary and the proprietor is not required to comply with provisions of
certain regulations or laws which apply to corporations. A proprietor owns,
controls, and usually manages the firm's assets and receives the profits (or
losses) from its operations. All earnings of the business are taxable to the

owner whether he withdraws them from the firm or not. A sole proprietorship is not considered to be a separate entity for income tax purposes.

Usually, the primary disadvantage of a sole proprietorship as a form of business organization is its unlimited liability feature. If the assets of the business are insufficient to meet its obligations, a sole proprietor will be required to satisfy business creditors from his own personal resources. Other principle disadvantages of the sole proprietorship form of business organization include limitations on the availability of funds to the business and difficulties involved in the transferability of ownership. Funds or resources available to a sole proprietorship are limited to the personal assets of the owner and what he is able to borrow. Ownership may be transferred only by selling the entire business or by changing to another form of business organization.

Accounting for a Proprietorship

It is primarily in the accounting for owner's equity that the accounts of an unincorporated business differ significantly from those of a corporation. The owner's equity accounts of a sole proprietorship normally include only a capital account and a drawing account.

The capital account reflects the proprietor's equity in the assets of the business as of a specific point in time. Capital is credited for the investments made by the owner in the business and for the earnings of the period, and it is debited for a net loss during the period.

A separate drawing or withdrawals account may be maintained which is debited for the withdrawals of cash or other business assets made by the owner, or for any payments which are made from business funds in order to satisfy personal debts of the owner. The balance in the drawing account is closed or transferred to the capital account during the preparation of closing entries which are made at the end of the period. As an alternative, the drawing account may be omitted with all changes in the owner's equity recorded directly in the capital account. Either procedure accomplishes the same end result.

THE PARTNERSHIP

A somewhat more complicated form of business organization is the partnership. A major difference between the sole proprietorship and the partnership is that the partnership has more than a single owner. The partnership form of business organization is often used as a means of combining the resources and special skills or talents of two or more persons. In addition, state laws sometimes prevent the incorporation of certain businesses which provide professional services such as certified public accounting firms or associations of physicians. Although only two persons are required to form a partnership, there is no limit as to the number of partners. For example, in some CPA firms there are more than 800 partners.

The Uniform Partnership Act defines a partnership as "an association of two or more persons to carry on, as co-owners, a business for profit." Even though two or more persons may, in fact, operate a business as a partnership without a formal agreement, it is important that a written contract, known as the articles of co-partnership, be drawn up in order to clearly delineate the rights and duties of all partners and thereby avoid possible misunderstandings and disagreements. The partnership agreement serves as the basis for the formation and operation of the partnership. At a minimum, the partnership contract should usually include the following points:

1. Names of all partners.
2. Rights and duties of each partner.
3. Name of the partnership.
4. Nature and location of the business.
5. Effective date and the duration of the agreement.
6. Capital contribution of each partner.
7. Procedures for dividing profits and losses.
8. Any rights or limitations of withdrawals by partners.
9. Accounting period to be used.
10. Provisions for dissolution.
11. Procedures for arbitrating disputes.

Characteristics of a Partnership

The significant characteristics of the partnership form of organization are summarized briefly in the following paragraphs.

Ease of Formation.   Partnerships may be formed with little difficulty. As was the case with a sole proprietorship, there are few legal formalities or regulations (aside from local and possibly state licensing requirements) to be complied with.

Mutual Agency.   Normally, all partners act as agents of the partnership and as such have the power to enter into contracts in the ordinary course of business. These contracts bind the remaining partners. The concept of mutual agency provides an important reason for the careful selection of partners.

Unlimited Liability.   Usually each partner may be held personally liable to partnership creditors for all the debts of the partnership in the event that the partnership assets are insufficient to meet its obligations. If one partner is unable to meet his obligations under the partnership agreement, the remaining partners are liable for these debts.

If a new partner is admitted to a partnership, the partnership agreement should indicate whether he assumes a liability for debts which were incurred prior to his admission into the partnership. When a partner withdraws from a partnership, he is not liable for partnership debts incurred *after* his withdrawal if proper notice has been given to the public, for example, by a legal notice in a newspaper. He is, however, liable for all debts which were incurred prior to his withdrawal unless he is released from these obligations by the creditors of the partnership.

Since any partner may bind the entire partnership when making contracts in the normal scope of business, a lack of good judgment on the part of a single partner could jeopardize both partnership assets and the personal resources of the individual partners. The mutual agency and unlimited liability features may discourage certain individuals with substantial personal resources from entering into a partnership agreement.

Limited Life. Since a partnership is based on a contract, a partnership is legally ended by the withdrawal, death, incapacity, or bankruptcy of any of its partners. Addition of a new partner also terminates the old partnership. Although the entry of a new partner or the exit of an old partner legally dissolves the partnership, the business may be continued without interruption by the formation of a new partnership. This is done on a continual basis by firms of attorneys, doctors, and CPAs.

Co-ownership by Partners. Partners are the co-owners of both the assets and the earnings of a partnership. The assets invested by each partner in the partnership are owned by all of the partners collectively. The income or loss of a partnership is divided among the partners according to the terms which are specified in the partnership agreement. If the partnership agreement specifies a method of dividing profits among the partners but is silent as to the division of losses, losses will be shared in the same manner as profits. If the manner of dividing profits or losses is not specified in the partnership agreement, partners will share profits and losses equally.

Evaluation of the Partnership Form of Organization

The primary disadvantages of organizing a business as a partnership include the unlimited liability of the owners, the mutual agency of all partners, and the limited life of the partnership. However, a partnership has certain advantages over both the sole proprietorship and the incorporated forms of business organization. In comparison to a sole proprietorship, a partnership has the advantage of being able to combine the individual skills or talents of partners and of pooling the capital of several individuals, both of which may be required to carry on a successful business. A partnership is much easier to form than a corporation and is subject to much less governmental regulation. In addition, a partnership may provide certain tax advantages. Like the sole proprietorship, the partnership itself is not subject to taxes. Individual partners are, however, required to pay income taxes on their share of the income of the partnership, whether or not these earnings are withdrawn from the business.

Accounting for a Partnership

The accounting for a partnership is very similar to that of a proprietorship except with regard to specific transactions involving the accounting for owners' equity. Since a partnership is owned by two or more persons, a separate capital account must be maintained for each owner and a separate drawing account may also be used for each partner. Further, the net income or loss for a period must be divided among the partners as specified by the terms of the partnership agreement. Additional accounting problems which are unique to partnerships may occur with the formation of a partnership, admission of a partner, withdrawal or death of a partner, and liquidation of a partnership.

Formation of a Partnership

Upon the formation of a partnership, resources invested by the partners are recorded in the accounts. A capital account for each partner is credited for the amount of net assets invested (assets contributed less liabilities assumed by the partnership). Individual asset accounts are debited for the assets contributed and liability accounts are credited for any debts assumed by the partnership.

If the investments made by the partners are entirely in the form of cash, the entry required would be a debit to cash and a credit to the partner's capital account for the amount of cash invested. When noncash assets such as land, equipment, or merchandise are invested, these assets should be recorded at their fair market values as of the date of investment. The valuations assigned to these assets may differ from the cost or book value of the assets on the books of the contributing partner prior to the formation of the partnership. Of course, the amounts recorded by the partnership must be agreed upon by all partners. Amounts agreed upon represent the acquisition cost of the assets to the newly formed partnership. The recording of assets at their current market value as of the date they were contributed to the partnership is necessary in order to provide a fair presentation in the partnership financial statements, and to assure a fair distribution of the property among partners in the event a dissolution of the partnership occurs.

To illustrate the entries which are required at the formation of a partnership, assume that Mantle and Maris, who operate separate sporting goods stores as sole proprietorships, agree to form a partnership by combining their two businesses. It is agreed that each partner will contribute

$10,000 in cash and all of his individual business assets, and that the partnership will assume the liabilities of each of their separate businesses. Assuming that the partners have agreed upon the amounts at which noncash assets are to be recorded, the following journal entries on the books of the partnership would be necessary in order to record the formation of the M & M partnership:

```
Cash .....................................  10,000
Accounts Receivable ......................  15,000
Merchandise Inventory ....................  30,000
    Accounts Payable ....................          5,000
    Mantle, Capital .....................         50,000

Cash .....................................  10,000
Merchandise Inventory ....................  35,000
Building .................................  50,000
Land .....................................  15,000
    Notes Payable .......................         10,000
    Maris, Capital ......................        100,000
```

Division of Profits and Losses

The net income or loss of a partnership is divided among the partners according to the terms or procedures specified in the partnership agreement. As previously indicated, if provisions are made only for dividing profits, any losses are divided in the same manner as profits. In the absence of any provisions for sharing profits and losses in the partnership agreement, the law provides that they must be shared equally among the partners.

The specific method of dividing profits and losses selected in a partnership situation may be designed to recognize and compensate the partners for differences in their investments in the partnership, for differences in their personal services rendered, for special abilities or reputations of individual partners, or for some combination of these and other factors. The following are examples of some of the methods which may be given consideration in the division of partnership profits or losses:

1. A fixed ratio base.
2. A capital ratio base.
3. Interest on capital.
4. Salaries to partners.

The specific method chosen by the partners may incorporate one or more of the methods of dividing partnership profits and losses which are mentioned above and illustrated in the following paragraphs. As a basis for these illustrations, assume that the M & M partnership had net income of $30,000 for the year ended December 31, 1976. The following capital accounts reflect the investments made by Mantle and Maris during 1976.

Mantle, Capital		Maris, Capital	
	1/1/76 50,000		1/1/76 100,000
	7/1/76 20,000		4/1/76 60,000

Fixed Fractional Basis. Partners may agree on any fractional or percentage basis as a means of dividing partnership profits and losses. For example, assume that in order to reflect differences in their initial capital contributions, services provided, and abilities, Mantle and Maris agreed to allocate one fourth of any profits or losses to Mantle and three fourths to Maris. Consequently, at the end of 1976 the $30,000 net income would be allocated $7,500 to Mantle ($\frac{1}{4} \times$ $30,000) and $22,500 to Maris ($\frac{3}{4} \times$ $30,000). The division of net income is recorded with a closing entry—the income summary account is closed to each partner's individual capital account according to the terms of the partnership agreement. The entry required in order to divide the net income among the two partners is as follows:

```
Income Summary. . . . . . . . . . . . . . . . . . . . . . . . . . . . .  30,000
    Mantle, Capital . . . . . . . . . . . . . . . . . . . . . . . . . . .            7,500
    Maris, Capital . . . . . . . . . . . . . . . . . . . . . . . . . . . .           22,500
```

Additional closing entries are also necessary in order to transfer any balances in the partners' drawing accounts to their respective capital accounts.

Capital Ratio. When the invested capital of a partnership is a major factor in the generation of income, net income is often divided on the basis of the relative capital balances of the partners. If a capital ratio is used, the partners must agree whether the beginning capital balances or average capital balances should be used.

For example, the partners may agree to distribute net income on the basis of capital balances at the beginning of the period. Division of the $30,000 net income of the M & M partnership on the basis of the ratio of the partners' beginning capital balances would be as follows:

Partner	Capital Balance 1/1/76	Fraction of Total Capital	Division of Income
Mantle	$ 50,000	$50/$150 or 1/3	$10,000
Maris	100,000	$100/$150 or 2/3	20,000
Total	$150,000		$30,000

Thus, the income summary account would be closed to the partners' capital accounts at the end of the year by the following journal entry.

```
Income Summary. . . . . . . . . . . . . . . . . . . . . . . . . . . . .  30,000
    Mantle, Capital . . . . . . . . . . . . . . . . . . . . . . . . . . .           10,000
    Maris, Capital . . . . . . . . . . . . . . . . . . . . . . . . . . . .           20,000
```

In order to reflect any significant changes in the capital accounts which may occur during a period in the division of income, the partners may agree to use the average capital balance ratio as a means of sharing partnership income. The average capital balance for each partner is equal to the weighted average of the different balances in their capital account during a period. In order to compute the weighted average, each balance in a partner's capital account is multiplied by the number of months until the next transaction affected the balance or to the end of the period. The sum of these amounts is divided by 12 in order to yield the partner's average capital balance during the period.

For purposes of illustration we will assume that Mantle's capital balance at the beginning of the year was $50,000 and that Maris's was $100,000. Maris invested an additional $60,000 on May 1 and Mantle invested an additional $20,000 on July 1. The computation of the average capital balance for Mantle and Maris is as follows:

Partner	Date	Balance	× Time	Total	Weighted Average
Mantle	1/1/76	$ 50,000 ×	6	= $ 300,000	
	7/1/76	70,000 ×	6	= 420,000	
				$ 720,000 ÷ 12 =	$ 60,000

Partner	Date	Balance	× Time	Total	Weighted Average
Maris	1/1/76	$100,000 ×	4	= $ 400,000	
	5/1/76	160,000 ×	8	= 1,280,000	
				$1,680,000 ÷ 12 =	$140,000

After the average capital balances have been computed, the division of net income is based on the ratios of average capital per partner to total average capital. In the case of the M & M partnership, the calculation would be as follows:

Partner	Average Capital	Fraction of Total Average Capital	Division of Income
Mantle	$ 60,000	$60/$200 or 3/10	$ 9,000
Maris	140,000	$140/$200 or 7/10	21,000
Total	$200,000		$30,000

Interest on Capital. In some instances, only partial recognition may be given to unequal investments made by the partners in determining the division of income. This may be accomplished by allowing some fixed rate of interest on the capital balances, and dividing remaining profits on some other basis. As in the use of capital ratios, interest may be based on beginning or on average capital balances during the period.

To illustrate, assume that Mantle and Maris agreed to allow each partner interest at the rate of 8 percent on his beginning capital balance, with any remaining profit to be divided equally. Under this agreement, the $30,000 net income for 1976 would be divided as follows:

	Mantle	Maris	
Income.................			$30,000
Interest:			
8% × $50,000............	$ 4,000		$ 4,000
8% × $100,000...........		$ 8,000	8,000
			$12,000
Remainder:			$18,000
$18,000 × ½	$ 9,000		$ 9,000
$18,000 × ½		$ 9,000	9,000
Total..................	$13,000	$17,000	$30,000

Salaries to Partners. As a means of recognizing differences in the value of personal services contributed to the partnership by individual partners, the partnership agreement may provide for "salary" allowances in the division of income. For this purpose, the agreed-upon salaries are used in the allocation of income but need not actually be paid to the partners. The partnership agreement may also allow for withdrawals of cash by the partners described as salaries. These withdrawals are treated like all withdrawals made by partners and debited to the drawing accounts; they are *not* salary expenses similar to those paid to employees. Salary allowances may be used in the division of partnership income whether or not the partners make any cash withdrawals.

To illustrate, assume that Mantle and Maris are allowed annual salaries of $6,000 and $8,000 respectively, with any remaining profits divided equally. The following division of the $30,000 profit for 1976 would be made:

	Mantle	Maris	Total
Salaries...........	$ 6,000	$ 8,000	$14,000
Remainder.........	8,000	8,000	16,000
Total...........	$14,000	$16,000	$30,000

Salaries and Interest on Capital. Sometimes both the investments of the individual partners and the value of personal services contributed by each may be quite different. In these situations, partners may agree to take into consideration both salaries and interest on capital investments in determining the division of income. Any remaining profit or loss may then be allocated on any agreed-upon fractional basis.

For example, assume that Mantle and Maris agree on the following division of income:

1. Annual salaries of $6,000 to Mantle and $8,000 to Maris.
2. Eight percent interest on beginning capital balances.
3. Any remainder to be divided equally.

Under this agreement, the $30,000 net income for 1976 would be divided as follows:

	Mantle	Maris	Total
Salaries (per agreement)	$ 6,000	$ 8,000	$14,000
Interest:			
8% × $50,000.	4,000		4,000
8% × $100,000		8,000	8,000
Remainder.	2,000	2,000	4,000
Total	$12,000	$18,000	$30,000

Allowing salaries or interest on capital is simply a procedure or step in the process of dividing partnership profits. Since partners are owners, their contributions of capital and personal services are made in an attempt to earn profits. Therefore, these amounts are not considered to be expenses and do not reduce the income of the business.

Salaries And/Or Interest in Excess of Income.   In the previous illustrations, partnership net income exceeded the total salary and interest allowances to the partners, and the balance was divided between the partners according to the agreed-upon percentage. If net income is less than the sum of the allowable salaries and interest, or if there is a net loss for the period, the residual after the deduction of salaries and interest will be negative in amount. This negative amount must then be divided between the partners according to the agreed-upon fractional basis.

To illustrate this situation, assume the same salary and interest allowances as in the previous example. Further, assume that the M & M partnership had net income of only $20,000 for 1976. The salary and interest allowances total $10,000 for Mantle and $16,000 for Maris. The total interest and salary allowances of $26,000 exceed the net income of the partnership for the period by $6,000. This excess must be deducted in determining the partners' share of the income as follows:

	Mantle	Maris	Total
Salaries.	$ 6,000	$ 8,000	$14,000
Interest.	4,000	8,000	12,000
Remainder (divided equally).	(3,000)	(3,000)	(6,000)
Total	$ 7,000	$13,000	$20,000

Partnership Financial Statements

The income statement of a partnership is very similar to that of either a sole proprietorship or a corporation. The statement does not reflect income tax expense, however, because the partnership is not subject to an income tax on its earnings. (Partners are taxed as individuals on their share of the partnership income.) In addition, the allocation of the net income among the partners is often included in the income statement as a final item below the net income figure.

The balance sheet of a partnership differs from that of a sole proprietorship or a corporation primarily in the owners' equity section. The equity section of a partnership reflects the end-of-period capital balances of each individual partner.

A statement disclosing the nature and amount of changes in the partners' capital balances during a period is often prepared for a partnership. For example, the Statement of Partners' Capital for the M & M partnership might appear as follows:

M & M
Statement of Partners' Capital
For the Year Ended December 31, 1976

	Mantle	Maris	Total
Balances, January 1, 1976	$50,000	$100,000	$150,000
Add: Additional investments.	20,000	60,000	80,000
Net income	15,000	15,000	30,000
Total	$85,000	$175,000	$260,000
Less: Withdrawals	(5,000)	(15,000)	(20,000)
Balances, December 31, 1976	$80,000	$160,000	$240,000

Thus, the December 31, 1976 balance sheet for M & M would include capital balances of $80,000 for Mantle and $160,000 for Maris.

Admission of a Partner

. Although the admission of a new partner to a partnership legally dissolves the existing partnership, a new agreement may be created without disruption of business activities. An additional person may be admitted by purchasing an interest directly from one or more of the current partners or by making an investment in the partnership. When a new partner purchases his share of the partnership from a current partner, the payment is made directly to the selling partner(s). Therefore, there is no change in either the total assets or the total capital of the partnership. When a new partner invests in the partnership by contributing assets to the partnership, however, both the total assets and total capital of the partnership are increased.

Purchase of an Interest from Current Partner(s). When a new partner acquires his interest by purchasing all or part of the interest of one or more of the existing partners, the purchase price is paid directly to the selling partner(s). Therefore, the amount paid is not recorded in the partnership records. The only entry which is required in the accounts of the partnership is to transfer the interest sold from the selling partner's capital account(s) to a capital account for the new partner.

For example, assume that Mantle and Maris have capital balances of $80,000 and $160,000, respectively. Mantle agrees to sell one half of his $80,000 interest in the partnership directly to Berra for $50,000. The entry to record this transaction on the partnership books is as follows:

Mantle, Capital	40,000	
Berra, Capital		40,000

The effect of this transaction is to transfer one half of Mantle's current capital balance ($\frac{1}{2} \times \$80,000$) to the new capital account created for Berra. The total capital of the partnership, $240,000, is not affected by the transaction. The entry which was made was not affected by the amount paid by the incoming partner to the selling partner. The $50,000 payment made by Berra to Mantle reflects a bargained transaction between the two men acting as individuals, and as such does not affect the assets of the partnership.

Purchase of Interest by Investment in the Partnership. When the incoming partner contributes assets *to* the partnership for his interest, both the assets and the capital of the partnership are increased. To illustrate, again assume that Mantle and Maris are partners in the M & M Partnership with capital accounts of $80,000 and $160,000 respectively. They agree to admit Berra as a new partner with a one fourth interest in the partnership for an investment of $80,000. The admission of Berra would be recorded by the following journal entry:

Cash	80,000	
Berra, Capital		80,000

After the admission of Berra, the total capital of the new partnership is as follows:

Maris, capital	$160,000
Mantle, capital	80,000
Berra, capital	80,000
Total Capital	$320,000

Berra's capital balance of $80,000 represents a one fourth interest in the total partnership capital of $320,000. It does not necessarily follow, however, that the new partner is entitled to a one fourth share in the division of partnership income. Instead, the division of income or loss must be specified in the new partnership agreement.

Because balances in the asset accounts usually are not equal to their current values, the investment of the new partner may be more or less than the proportion of total assets represented by his agreed-upon capital interest. However, since the agreement concerning the new partner's relative capital interest should be reflected in the capital accounts, adjustments to the capital accounts will be necessary if the amount invested is not equal to the book value of the capital interest acquired. The adjustment required in recording the investment of the new partner is accomplished by using either the bonus method or the goodwill method.

When a new partner invests more than book value for his relative capital interest, a bonus or goodwill may be allocated to the old partners. To illustrate these two different methods, assume that Mantle and Maris, who share profits equally and have capital balances of $80,000 and $160,000 respectively, agree to admit Berra to a one fourth interest in the new partnership for $120,000.

Bonus to Old Partners.   The total net assets of the partnership after the $120,000 investment by Berra will be $360,000 ($240,000 + $120,000). In order to acquire a one fourth interest in the net assets of the partnership, or $90,000 ($\frac{1}{4} \times$ $360,000), Berra was required to invest $120,000. The excess of the investment over the amount of capital allocated to Berra may be regarded as a bonus to the old partners. The old partners share the bonus in their agreed-upon profit and loss ratio. Each partner's share of the bonus is credited to his capital account. The entry to record Berra's investment in the partnership (assuming an equal distribution of profits and losses between Mantle and Maris) is:

Cash	120,000	
Berra, Capital		90,000
Mantle, Capital		15,000
Maris, Capital		15,000

Thus, after the investment, Berra has a capital balance of $90,000 which represents one fourth of the total capital of $360,000.

Goodwill to Old Partners.   Alternatively, if the new partner's investment exceeds his relative share of the net assets of the new partnership, it may be assumed that the old partnership had goodwill. The amount of goodwill is determined by the initial investment of the new partner. To illustrate, the $120,000 investment made by Berra represented a one fourth interest in the partnership. The fact that a one fourth interest required an investment of $120,000 implies that the business is worth $480,000 (120,000 ÷ ¼). The amount of goodwill is computed as follows:

Investment by Berra for a ¼ interest		$120,000
Implied value of Business ($120,000 ÷ ¼)		$480,000
Net asset value exclusive of goodwill:		
Capital of old partners	$240,000	
Investment by Berra	120,000	360,000
Goodwill		$120,000

As was the case with the bonus, the goodwill is divided between the old partners in their profit and loss ratio unless a specific agreement is made to the contrary. The entries which are required in order to record the admission of the new partner (again assuming an equal distribution of profits and losses) are as follows:

Cash	120,000	
Berra, Capital		120,000
Goodwill	120,000	
Mantle, Capital		60,000
Maris, Capital		60,000

The capital balances of the partners after the admission of Berra are as follows:

Mantle, capital	$140,000
Maris, capital	220,000
Berra, capital	120,000
	$480,000

It can be seen that Berra's share of the total capital is the agreed-upon one fourth interest in the partnership ($120,000/$480,000).

Note that the choice between the bonus and goodwill methods results in different account balances (but the same relative capital interests). The goodwill method causes the total capital of the partners to be larger by the amount of the goodwill recorded. Thus, the choice between methods results in different financial statements.

When the new partner invests less than the book value of his relative capital interest, a bonus or goodwill may be allocated to the incoming partner. To illustrate, assume that Mantle and Maris agree to admit Berra with a one fourth interest in the partnership for an investment of only $60,000.

Bonus to New Partner. Based on this method, the excess of the new partner's share of total capital over his investment is allocated as a bonus to the new partner. The amount of the bonus is calculated as follows:

Total capital prior to admission:
Mantle, capital . . . . $ 80,000
Maris, capital 160,000 $240,000
Investment by Berra   60,000
   Total capital. $300,000
Berra's one-fourth interest . . . . $ 75,000
Investment by Berra   60,000
Bonus to Berra . . . . $ 15,000

The bonus may be treated as a reduction of the old partners' capital accounts on the basis of their profit and loss ratio and as a credit to the new partner's capital. The entry to record the admission of the new partner assuming an equal distribution of profits and losses between Mantle and Maris is:

Cash   60,000
Mantle, Capital   7,500
Maris, Capital   7,500
   Berra, Capital   75,000

Goodwill to New Partner.   If the new partner's investment is less than his agreed-upon capital interest, the difference may be due to goodwill brought to the partnership by the incoming partner. This goodwill may be attributable to the reputation or special skills of the new partner which might be imparted to increase the earning power of the partnership entity. The goodwill is recorded as an asset with a corresponding credit to the new partner's capital account in order to allow him the agreed-upon capital interest in the partnership. There is no change in the capital accounts of the old partners.

To illustrate, assume that Mantle and Maris had capital balances of $80,000 and $160,000 respectively prior to the admission of Berra with a one fourth interest in the partnership. Since the total capital of Mantle and Maris, $240,000, represents a three fourths interest in the total capital of the partnership after Berra is admitted, the implied value of the partnership is $320,000 ($240,000 ÷ ¾). However, the actual tangible assets of the firm after Berra's investment are $300,000, consisting of net assets of $240,000 prior to the admission of Berra plus the $60,000 investment. Therefore, the implied goodwill is $20,000 ($320,000 — $300,000). The entry required to record the admission of the new partner under the goodwill method is as follows:

Cash   60,000
Goodwill   20,000
   Berra, Capital   80,000

After his admission, Berra has the agreed upon one fourth interest in total capital ($80,000/$320,000).

Withdrawal of a Partner

When one partner withdraws from a partnership, he may dispose of his partnership interest in any one of several ways:

1. Sell his interest to a new partner.
2. Sell his interest to one or more of the remaining partners with the payment coming from the personal resources of the purchasing partner(s).
3. Sell his interest to the partnership with the payment from partnership funds.

In the first two cases, the sale and purchase is made among the partners themselves acting as individuals. Therefore, the accounting treatment is the same as for the admission of a new partner through the purchase of an interest from the existing partners. The journal entry required on the partnership books is simply to transfer the capital account balance by debiting the capital account of the retiring partner and crediting the capital account(s) of the purchasing partner(s). There is no effect on either the assets or the total capital of the partnership.

If the withdrawing partner is paid from partnership assets, both the total assets and total capital of the firm are decreased. Because the current value and the recorded book values of the partnership assets probably differ, the withdrawing partner may be paid either more or less than the amount of his capital balance. The difference may be attributable, for example, to the change in value of certain specific assets or alternatively to the existence of goodwill or to a combination of both factors. The change in the asset values or goodwill may be recorded in the accounts and shared by the partners in their profit and loss ratios.

For example, assume that Mantle, Berra, and Maris have capital balances of $100,000, $120,000, and $180,000 respectively, and share profits and losses on a one fourth, one fourth, one half basis. Further, assume that it is agreed to pay Mantle $120,000 from partnership funds upon his withdrawal from the partnership, and that the fair value of the partnership at that time is $480,000. Assuming that specific assets cannot be identified to account for the increase in value, the entries required in order to record the goodwill and the withdrawal of Mantle are as follows:

Goodwill.	80,000	
Mantle, Capital		20,000
Berra, Capital		20,000
Maris, Capital		40,000
Mantle, Capital	120,000	
Cash		120,000

Instead of an increase in the value of specific assets or the existence of goodwill, the difference between the payment to the withdrawing partner and his capital balance may be regarded as a bonus paid to the withdrawing partner by the remaining partners. This bonus is charged to the capital accounts of the old partners in the relative profit and loss ratios of the remaining partners. Under this assumption, the withdrawal of Mantle would be recorded as follows:

Mantle, Capital	100,000	
Maris, Capital	13,333	
Berra, Capital	6,667	
Cash		120,000

The $20,000 bonus to the retiring partner was deducted from the remaining partners' capital balances on the basis of their relative profit and loss ratios of $\frac{2}{3}$ for Maris (50%/75%) and $\frac{1}{3}$ for Berra (25%/75%).

If the payment made to the withdrawing partner is less than his capital balance, the difference may be attributable either to specific assets that have fair values which are less than their recorded book values, or to a bonus paid by the retiring partner to the remaining partners in order to retire from the partnership without undergoing a liquidation of the business. Again, the revaluation of the assets of the partnership or the bonus is divided among the partners according to their profit and loss sharing ratio.

For example, if Mantle agrees to retire for a payment of $85,000, and it is agreed that the assets of the partnership are not overvalued, the entry to record the withdrawal would be as follows:

Mantle, Capital	100,000	
Maris, Capital		10,000
Berra, Capital		5,000
Cash		85,000

Again, Maris and Berra would share the $15,000 difference ($100,000 — $85,000) on the basis of their relative profit and loss ratios of $\frac{2}{3}$ and $\frac{1}{3}$ (as above).

LIQUIDATION OF THE BUSINESS

When a partnership goes out of business, its assets are sold, it liabilities are paid, and any remaining cash is distributed to the partners. This process is referred to as a liquidation.

As a basis for illustration, assume that Mantle, Maris, and Berra agree to liquidate their partnership. Profits and losses are allocated one fourth to Mantle, one fourth to Berra, and one half to Maris. The balance sheet of the partnership just prior to the liquidation process appeared as follows:

M M & B
Balance Sheet
As of December 31, 1976

Cash	$ 20,000	Liabilities	$ 50,000
Noncash assets.	430,000	Mantle, capital	100,000
		Maris, capital	180,000
		Berra, capital	120,000
	$450,000		$450,000

Assume that all of the noncash assets of the partnership are sold for $330,000, a loss of $100,000 ($430,000 — $330,000).

Any gain or loss on the sale of the partnership assets must be divided among the partners according to their agreed-upon profit and loss ratios before any cash is distributed to the partners. Thus, the $100,000 loss on the sale of the noncash assets of the partnership would be distributed among the partners as follows:

	Total	Mantle	Maris	Berra
Capital balance	$400,000	$100,000	$180,000	$120,000
Distribution of loss	(100,000)	(25,000)	(50,000)	(25,000)
Capital balance after sale.	$300,000	$ 75,000	$130,000	$ 95,000

The entries required in order to record the sale of the assets and the distribution of the loss would be as follows:

Cash	330,000	
Loss on Sale	100,000	
Noncash Assets		430,000
Mantle, Capital	25,000	
Maris, Capital	50,000	
Berra, Capital	25,000	
Loss on Sale.		100,000

After the noncash assets of the partnership have been sold and the gain or loss has been divided among the partners, the cash will be distributed first to creditors and then to the partners. The amount of cash to be distributed to each partner is reflected in the capital balances after all gains or losses on the sale of noncash assets have been recorded. The balance sheet prior to the distribution of cash appears as follows:

M M & B
Balance Sheet
January 10, 1977

Cash	$350,000	Liabilities	$ 50,000
		Mantle, capital	75,000
		Maris, capital	130,000
		Berra, capital	95,000
	$350,000		$350,000

The distribution of the cash, first to the creditors of the partnership and then to the partners, is recorded by the following entries:

Liabilities	50,000	
Cash		50,000
Mantle, Capital	75,000	
Maris, Capital	130,000	
Berra, Capital	95,000	
Cash		300,000

In the previous example, the capital account of each partner had a credit balance after the loss on the sale of noncash assets was distributed. In some instances, one or more of the partners may have a debit balance in his capital account as a result of losses on the disposal of the assets. This debit balance is referred to as a capital deficit since the partnership has a legal claim against the partner. If this claim cannot be collected by the partnership, the deficit must be divided among the remaining partners' capital balances according to their profit and loss ratios.

To illustrate, assume that the M, M & B partnership has the same assets and liabilities as in the preceding example. Further assume that the capital balances prior to liquidation are Mantle, $40,000; Maris, $210,000; and Berra, $150,000; and that the noncash assets are sold for $230,000 (a loss of $200,000). The capital accounts after the distribution of the loss would be as follows:

	Total	Mantle	Maris	Berra
Capital balances	$400,000	$40,000	$210,000	$150,000
Loss on sale of noncash assets	(200,000)	(50,000)	(100,000)	(50,000)
Capital balance	$200,000	($10,000)	$110,000	$100,000

After payment of the $50,000 of liabilities, the balance sheet of M, M & B would appear as follows:

M, M & B
Balance Sheet
January 10, 1977

Cash	$200,000	Mantle, capital	$(10,000)
		Maris, capital	110,000
		Berra, capital	100,000
	$200,000		$200,000

If Mantle is able to pay his capital deficiency to the partnership, the following entry would be made:

```
Cash  . . . . . . . . . . . . . . . . . . . . . . . . . . . . . . . . . . . .  10,000
    Mantle, Capital . . . . . . . . . . . . . . . . . . . . . . . . . . .              10,000
```

At this point Mantle would have a zero capital balance, and the $210,000 cash on hand would be distributed to Maris and Berra in amounts equal to the balances in their capital accounts.

If the partnership is unable to collect the capital deficiency from Mantle, this loss would be absorbed by the remaining partners. Since the partnership agreement provides that Maris had a one half share and Berra a one fourth share of profits and losses, their current interest in profits and losses is Maris's two thirds (50%/75%) and Berra's one third (25%/75%). The loss should be written off against the capital accounts of the remaining partners as follows:

```
Maris, Capital . . . . . . . . . . . . . . . . . . . . . . . . . . . . . . .  6,667
Berra, Capital . . . . . . . . . . . . . . . . . . . . . . . . . . . . . . .  3,333
    Mantle, Capital . . . . . . . . . . . . . . . . . . . . . . . . . . .              10,000
```

Accordingly, the distribution of the $200,000 cash would be based on the amount of the partners' capital balances after allowances for the loss on the noncollection of the capital deficiency. These amounts are as follows:

	Mantle	Maris	Berra
Capital balances	($10,000)	$110,000	$100,000
Capital deficiency	10,000	(6,667)	(3,333)
	-0-	$103,333	$ 96,667

The entry to record the distribution of the cash would be:

```
Maris, Capital . . . . . . . . . . . . . . . . . . . . . . . . . . . . . . .  103,333
Berra, Capital . . . . . . . . . . . . . . . . . . . . . . . . . . . . . . .  96,667
    Cash  . . . . . . . . . . . . . . . . . . . . . . . . . . . . . . . . .              200,000
```

In the event that any cash is subsequently received from the deficient partner, it would be divided between the remaining partners in their profit and loss sharing ratio, since that is how they shared the deficiency.

KEY DEFINITIONS

Capital account The capital account of a partnership consists of a separate account for each partner which reflects the investments by the partners plus each partner's share of the earnings or losses from the operations of the business less any withdrawals made by the partners.

Division of profits and losses This agreement determines the method of dividing partnership profits or losses among the partners. In the absence of such an agreement, the law provides that profits or losses shall be divided equally among the partners.

Drawing account   Cash or other assets withdrawn by a partner during the period are reflected in the partner's drawing account. The drawing accounts are closed to the partners' capital accounts at the end of the period.

Interest on capital   This is a method which provides for partners' capital interests as a factor in the distribution of the partnership earnings.

Limited life   A partnership is legally dissolved upon the withdrawal, death, incapacity or bankruptcy of any of its partners.

Liquidation   The process of terminating a business in which its assets are sold, its liabilities are paid, and any remaining cash or other assets are distributed to its owners.

Mutual agency   Each partner may act as an agent of the partnership, with the power to enter into contracts within the scope of the normal business operations.

Partnership   An association of two or more persons to carry on a business under a contractual arrangement.

Partnership agreement   This written contract of partnership sets forth the agreement between the partners as to the conditions for the formation and operation of the partnership.

Salaries to partners   A method which provides for the division of a portion of the partnership income by allocating specified salaries to the partners.

Sole proprietorship   A business owned by one person.

Statement of partners' capital   This statement shows the nature and amount of changes in the partners' capital accounts during a period.

Uniform Partnership Act   This act, which has been adopted in most states, governs the formation, operation, and liquidation of partnerships.

Unlimited liability   Each partner is personally liable to the creditors of the partnership in the event that the partnership assets are insufficient to meet its obligations.

QUESTIONS

1. List the three basic types of business organizations.
2. What are the primary advantages of the partnership form of organization?
3. List and describe three important disadvantages of organizing a business as a partnership.
4. Explain the difference between admittance of a new partner to a partnership by making an investment in the partnership and admittance by purchasing an interest from a partner.
5. Smith is a partner in the Smith and Jones Partnership. At the end of the year, Smith's share of the partnership income is $20,000. During the year, Smith had withdrawals of $10,000. What amount of income should be included in Smith's taxable income for the year?
6. Upon the formation of a partnership, at what amount should the investments of noncash assets be recorded? Why is this necessary?

7. What factors are usually considered in determining the method for dividing partnership income?

8. In the absence of a specific agreement, how should the profit or loss of a partnership be allocated among the partners? If there is a specific method for allocating profits in the partnership agreement but no mention of losses, how should a net loss be divided among the partners?

9. Why does the agreement for division of partnership earnings often allow for salaries and interest on partners' capital balances?

10. When a new partner is admitted to a partnership and goodwill or a bonus is attributed to the old partners, how is the goodwill or bonus distributed to the capital accounts?

11. What is the effect of gains or losses resulting from the liquidation of a partnership on the partners' capital balances? How are the gains or losses divided among the partners?

12. After the distribution of a loss on liquidation, assume that one partner has a debit balance in his capital account. If the partner is unable to contribute any personal assets, how is the loss divided among the remaining partners?

EXERCISES

11–1 Bibby and Rowe formed a partnership on January 1, 1975. Bibby contributed $75,000 capital while Rowe contributed $50,000 capital. No additions to capital were made during the year. For the year ended December 31, 1975, the partnership had net income of $25,000. Prepare a schedule showing the division of income in each of the following cases:

    a. Partners agree to allocate ⅓ of profits or losses to Rowe and ⅔ to Bibby.

    b. Partners agree to distribute net income on the basis of their capital balances in the partnership.

    c. Bibby and Rowe agree to allow each partner 8 percent interest on his beginning capital balance and divide the remaining profits equally.

11–2 Assume that Bibby and Rowe made withdrawals of $5,000 and $7,000, respectively, during 1975. Give the entries to record the division of income in 11–1 (a) above and the entries to record the closing of the withdrawal account.

11–3 Assume that Erickson and Goodrich, who have capital balances of $160,000 and $320,000, respectively, and who divide profits equally, agree to admit Hazard to a ¼ interest in the new partnership for $200,000. Make the entry to record Hazard's investment in the partnership under both the bonus method and the goodwill method.

11–4 Martin is withdrawing from the partnership of Martin, Water, and Osmond. The capital accounts of the partnership are as follows: Martin, $10,000; Water, $10,000; and Osmond, $20,000. The partners share profits and losses equally. The partners agree that Martin will be paid $12,000 cash for his interest in the partnership. Give the entries to record the retirement of Martin using the bonus method.

11–5   The partnership of Jones, Clare, and Jackson is being liquidated on December 31, 1975. The balances in the capital accounts prior to liquidation of the assets were as follows: Jones, $25,000; Clare, $20,000; and Jackson, $5,000. The partners share profits and losses equally. On December 31, the partnership assets with a book value of $60,000 were sold for $39,000, and liabilities of $10,000 were paid.

Required:

How should the remaining $29,000 available cash be distributed if Jackson is unable to pay the amount he owes to the firm?

PROBLEMS

Series A

11A–1   Vallely and Patterson form a partnership with Vallely investing capital of $70,000 and Patterson investing capital of $30,000. The partners agree to allow 8 percent interest on each partner's beginning capital balance. Also, due to differences in services rendered, Patterson is to receive a salary of $8,000 while Vallely receives a salary of $4,500. Any remaining profits or losses are to be divided equally. Make a schedule showing the division of partnership net income assuming the partnership earned $16,000 for the first year of its operations.

11A–2   Johnson and Kennedy formed a partnership on January 1, 1974, with investments of $40,000 each. Kennedy made an additional investment of $20,000 on June 30, 1974. Given each of the following assumptions, determine the division of partnership net income of $27,000 for the year:

1. No method for division of income specified in the partnership agreement.
2. Divided in the ratio of the ending capital balance.
3. Divided in the ratio of the average capital balances.
4. Interest at a rate of 10 percent on the ending capital balance and the remainder divided equally.
5. Salary allowances of $10,000 to Johnson and $5,000 to Kennedy and any remainder divided ⅓ to Johnson and ⅔ to Kennedy.
6. Interest at a rate of 10 percent on the ending capital balances, salary allowance of $12,000 to Johnson and $8,000 to Kennedy, and any remainder divided equally.

11A–3   Hawk and Dove formed a partnership on January 1, 1975, combining their separate businesses that they had operated as sole proprietorships. The account balances of the noncash assets contributed, and their agreed-upon fair values are shown below:

Hawk	Book Value	Fair Value
Accounts receivable.	$20,000	$20,000
Inventory	10,000	15,000
Equipment.	20,000	25,000
Accounts payable	10,000	10,000
Dove		
Inventory	5,000	6,000
Building	25,000	32,000
Land	10,000	12,000

In addition, Hawk invested $5,000 in cash and Dove contributed $25,000 in cash. They agreed to share profits and losses equally.

Required:

1. Prepare the journal entries required on the books of the partnership to record the investments in the partnership on January 1, 1975.
2. Prepare a balance sheet for the partnership on January 1, 1975.
3. On December 31, 1975, the partnership income was calculated as $20,000. Hawk and Dove had $5,000 and $8,000 debit balances, respectively, in their drawing accounts. Prepare the entries to close the Income Summary and Drawing accounts on December 31.

11A–4 Able and Baker agree to admit Comer into their partnership with a one fourth interest. Currently, Able has capital of $20,000 and Baker has capital of $10,000. They share profits and losses equally. Give the journal entries necessary to record the admission of Comer for each of the following investments by Comer:

1. $10,000.
2. $20,000 using the bonus method.
3. $20,000 using the goodwill method.
4. $6,000 using the bonus method.
5. $6,000 using the goodwill method.

11A–5 Wilkes, Lee, and Curtis have capital balances of $60,000, $80,000, and $100,000, respectively, in their partnership. They share profits on a ¼, ¼, and ½ basis, respectively. Wilkes withdraws from the partnership, and it is agreed that he will be paid $70,000 for his share of the partnership. At the time of Wilkes's withdrawal, the fair value of the partnership is $280,000.

Required:

Make the entries to record the withdrawal of Wilkes under the goodwill and bonus methods.

11A–6 Kemp, Killough, and Kubin agree to liquidate their partnership on

January 1, 1974. The balance sheet of the firm as of that date is as follows:

Cash		$10,000
Accounts receivable.		15,000
Inventory		30,000
Equipment.	$60,000	
Less: Accumulated depreciation.	(30,000)	30,000
Total Assets		$85,000
Accounts payable		$ 5,000
Kemp, capital		40,000
Killough, capital.		30,000
Kubin, capital		10,000
Total Liabilities and Capital		$85,000

Profits and losses are distributed 50 percent to Kemp, 30 percent to Killough, and 20 percent to Kubin. On January 1, 1974, the noncash assets were sold as follows: Accounts Receivable, $10,000; Inventory, $20,000; and Equipment, $15,000.

Prepare a schedule showing the distribution of cash to the partners upon liquidation.

11A–7 Brown, Gray, and White agree to liquidate their partnership. Prior to beginning the liquidation process, they have cash, $15,000; other assets, $90,000; liabilities, $20,000; and capital balances of $50,000, $25,000, and $10,000, respectively. Profits and losses are divided among the partners in the ratio of 4:4:2, respectively. None of the partners had any personal assets outside of the firm. The realization and liquidation proceeded as follows:

1. $50,000 of other assets were sold for $30,000.
2. The liabilities were paid.
3. The remaining other assets were sold for $10,000.
4. The cash was distributed to the partners.

Prepare a schedule showing the effects of the liquidation process on the partners' capital accounts and the amounts distributed to the partners upon liquidation.

Series B

11B–1 Cooper, Taft, and Ferguson were partners. At January 1, 1974, their capital balances were $30,000, $22,500, and $21,000, respectively. Taft invested an additional $4,500 on March 1, and Cooper withdrew $11,250 on September 1. Under each of the following unrelated assumptions, indicate the amount of each partner's share of net income of the firm for 1974.

a. Net profit is $15,000. Ferguson is allowed a salary of $6,000, and each partner is allowed 6 percent interest on his end-of-year capi-

tal balance before distribution of net income. Any remainder is
then divided on a ratio of 2:2:1.

b. Same as (a) except net profit is only $7,500.
c. Interest of 9 percent is allowed on the partners' beginning-of-the-
year capital balances, and Cooper and Taft are allowed a salary
of $10,000 each. Any remaining profits are divided equally. Net
profit was $22,500.

11B-2 Taylor, Smith, and Jones are partners in the TSJ Partnership. The
partnership agreement provides for the following procedures for
division of income:

a. Each partner is allowed 5 percent interest on the average capital
balance.
b. Salary allowances of $10,000 to Taylor and $12,000 to Smith.
c. Remainder divided 50 percent to Taylor, 30 percent to Smith and
20 percent to Jones.

During the current year, the average capital balances were $60,000,
Taylor; $40,000, Smith; and $20,000, Jones.
Calculate the division of income among the partners in each of the
following cases:

a. Net income, $38,000.
b. Net income, $18,000.
c. Net loss, $2,000.

11B-3 Herm, Man, and Son are partners of the Hermanson Co. The partnership agreement specifies that partners shall divide income as follows:

1. Partners receive 5 percent interest on their average capital
balances.
2. Salary allowances of $5,000 to Herm, $10,000 to Man, and
$12,000 to Son.
3. Any remainder to be divided 50 percent to Herm, 30 percent to
Man, and 20 percent to Son.

The capital accounts reflected the following during the period:

	Herm	Man	Son
Balance, January 1	$50,000	$40,000	$30,000
Investments: April 1.			10,000
July 1		20,000	
Balance, December 31	$50,000	$60,000	$40,000

Compute the distribution of income among the three partners for
each of the following cases:

a. Net income is $60,000.
b. Net income is $12,000.
c. Net loss is $9,000.

11B–4   Olson and Wright are partners and agree to share profits and losses equally. Their capital balances are $50,000 and $25,000 respectively. Olson and Wright have agreed to admit Taff to a one third interest in the partnership. Give the journal entries to record the admission of Taff under the following circumstances:

    a.   Taff invests $30,000 and total capital is to be $105,000.
    b.   Taff invests $30,000 and goodwill is recorded.
    c.   Taff invests $45,000 with goodwill allowed.
    d.   Taff invests $45,000 with no change in the asset valuation.

11B–5   Cane is retiring from the partnership of Cane, Carter, and Custer. Prior to the retirement, the capital balances were Cane, $20,000; Carter $30,000; and Custer, $30,000. They share profits and losses in the ratio of 20 percent, 40 percent, 40 percent, respectively. Record the retirement of Cane under the following circumstances:

    a.   Cane withdraws for $20,000.
    b.   Cane withdraws for $18,000.
    c.   Cane withdraws for $22,000.

11B–6   Barley, Wheat, and Rye agree to liquidate their partnership on December 31, 1974. They share profits and losses equally. The balance sheet just prior to beginning the liquidation process appears as follows:

BARLEY, WHEAT, AND RYE
Balance Sheet
December 31, 1974

Cash	$ 5,000	Accounts payable	$10,000
Other assets	75,000	Barley, capital	25,000
		Wheat, capital	35,000
		Rye, capital	10,000
		Total Liabilities and	
Total Assets	$80,000	Capital	$80,000

Determine the amount of cash to be distributed to each partner after the sale of assets and payment of liabilities in each of the following cases:

    a.   The other assets were sold for $51,000.
    b.   The other assets were sold for $81,000.
    c.   The other assets were sold for $42,000, and the partner with a debit capital balance was able to pay the partnership an amount equal to the deficit.
    d.   The other assets were sold for $42,000, and the partner with a debit capital balance was bankrupt.

11B–7   Hale, Tell, and Hanson agree to liquidate their partnership on January 1, 1975. A condensed trial balance prior to the beginning of the liquidation process is shown below.

HALE, TELL, AND HANSON
Trial Balance
January 1, 1975

Cash	$ 20,000	
Other assets	80,000	
Liabilities		$ 10,000
Hale, capital		40,000
Tell, capital		40,000
Hanson, capital		10,000
	$100,000	$100,000

Profits and losses are shared by the partners equally. None of the partners had any personal assets. The realization and liquidation proceeded as follows:

1. The other assets were sold for $47,000.
2. The liabilities were paid.
3. The remaining cash was distributed to the partners.

Prepare a schedule showing the effects of the liquidation process on the partners' capital accounts and the amounts distributed to the partners upon liquidation.

The Corporation: Organization and Capital Stock

A CORPORATION is an artificial "legal" person that is both separate and distinct from its owners and, as such, is permitted to engage in any acts which could be performed by a natural person. It may hold property, enter into contracts, and engage in other activities not prohibited by law. The classic definition of a corporation was given by Chief Justice Marshall in 1819 as ". . . an artificial being, invisible, intangible, and existing only in contemplation of the law."

Although there are fewer businesses organized as corporations than as either sole proprietorships or partnerships, corporations are by far the dominant form of business organization in terms of both total assets and dollar value of output of goods and services. Because of the dominance of the corporate form of business organization and the widespread ownership interests in corporations, accounting for corporations is a very important topic.

CHARACTERISTICS OF THE CORPORATION

Because it is a separate legal entity, a corporation has several characteristics which differentiate it from both partnerships and sole proprietorships. The most important of these characteristics are described in the following paragraphs.

Separate Legal Existence. A corporation, unlike both sole proprietorships and partnerships, is a legal entity which is separate and distinct from its owners. Accordingly, a corporate entity may acquire and dispose of property, enter into contracts, and incur liabilities as an individual entity separate from its owners.

Transferable Units of Ownership. Ownership of a corporation is usually evidenced by shares of capital stock. These shares permit the subdivision of ownership into numerous units which may be readily transferred from one person to another without disrupting business operations and without prior approval of the other owners.

Continuity of Life. Status as a separate legal entity provides the corporation with a continuity of life. Unlike a partnership, the life or existence of a corporation is not affected by factors such as the death, incapacity, or withdrawal of an individual owner. A corporation may have a perpetual life or in some instances, its existence may be limited by the terms specified in its charter.

Limited Liability of Owners. As a separate legal entity, a corporation is legally liable for any debts which it incurs. Usually, the creditors of a corporation may not look to the personal property of the corporate stockholders for payment of any debts which are incurred by the corporation. Thus, the maximum loss which may be incurred by an individual stockholder is normally limited to the amount of his investment in the capital stock he owns. This limited liability feature is a primary advantage of the corporate form of business organization from the viewpoint of the owners. In addition, the absence of stockholder liability and the transferability of ownership usually increase the ability of a corporate entity to raise substantial capital by means of individual investments made by many owners. On the other hand, the limited liability feature may limit the ability of a corporation to obtain funds from creditors in those instances where solvency of the corporate entity may be questionable.

Separation of Ownership and Management. Although a corporation is owned by the individuals who hold its shares of capital stock, their control over the general management of the business is generally limited to their right to elect a board of directors. The board of directors, as representatives of individual owners or stockholders of the corporation, establishes corporate policies and appoints corporate officers who are responsible for the day-to-day management of the business and its operations. Officers of a corporation usually include a president, one or more vice presidents responsible for various functions within the business, a treasurer, a secretary, and a controller. The controller is the officer responsible for the accounting function of the business. A summary organization chart indicating the normal structure of a corporation is presented in Illustration 12–1 on page 296.

Corporate Taxation. As a separate legal entity, corporations are required to file and pay local, state, and federal income taxes on corporate earnings. In addition, when corporate earnings are distributed to shareholders as dividends, these distributions are included in the taxable income

Illustration 12–1

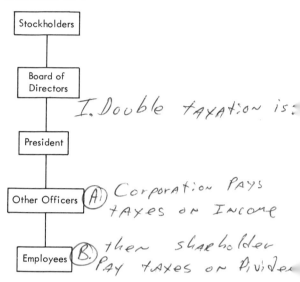

of individuals receiving the dividend. Thus, "double taxation" occurs because earnings of a corporation are taxed twice—initially as corporate income and subsequently as dividend income when distributed to stockholders.

Certain businesses may elect to operate as corporations without filing and paying corporate income taxes. In order to qualify for such an election, a corporation must meet certain requirements—for example, it must have only a single class of stock and ten or fewer stockholders. If this election is made, corporate income is taxed directly to the shareholders as it is earned by the corporation, just as would be the case if the business were organized as a partnership.

Government Regulation. Corporations are subject to numerous state and federal regulations and restrictions which are not imposed on either partnerships or sole proprietorships. This occurs primarily because corporations are separate legal entities and shareholders normally have limited liability for actions of the corporation.

FORMING A CORPORATION

A business corporation may be created by obtaining a charter from the state in which the business is to be incorporated. Although requirements for establishing a corporation vary, most states require a minimum of three natural persons to act as incorporators. An application for a corporate charter is usually made by filing articles of incorporation with the appropriate state official. Some of the more important information usually included in the articles of incorporation is:

1. Name of the corporation.
2. Location of its principal offices.
3. Nature of the business to be conducted by the corporation.
4. Identity and addresses of incorporators.
5. A detailed description of the capital stock authorized to be issued.
6. Identity of, and the amounts paid by, the original subscribers for the corporation's capital stock.
7. Names of the initial directors.

If the articles of incorporation are approved, the state issues a corporate charter which includes the general corporation laws of the state as well as any specific provisions of the articles of incorporation. The state usually charges a fee or organization tax for the privilege of incorporation.

Upon approval of the corporate charter, a corporation is authorized to begin its operations. Incorporators are required to hold a meeting in order to elect a board of directors and to adopt a set of bylaws which provide detailed operating regulations for the corporation. Directors of the corporation then elect appropriate corporate officers and authorize the issuance of capital stock certificates to the original stockholders.

Various expenditures such as those for state taxes and charter fees, legal costs, and other organizational costs are necessary in order to establish a corporation. These costs are normally accumulated in an intangible asset account referred to as organization costs. Since organization costs are expenditures which are necessary in order to provide for the creation and continued existence of a business, benefits obtained from these costs extend over the entire life of a corporation. Therefore, from a theoretical viewpoint, organization costs should be amortized over the life of the business. However, except when otherwise specified in the corporate charter, the life of a corporation is considered to be indefinite. Consequently, two different methods have evolved for accounting for organization costs. One is to simply retain organization costs as an intangible asset for an indefinite period of time without any amortization or charge to expense. The other alternative is to amortize these costs over a selected reasonable, but somewhat arbitrary, period of time. Although this alternative is certainly not justified in theory, it is usually acceptable in practice since organization costs are normally immaterial in amount and since this procedure is acceptable for income tax purposes. *Corporations Usually Ammortize Organizational Costs For Income Tax Purposes*

CAPITAL OF A CORPORATION

Owners' equity of a corporation is commonly referred to as stockholders' equity and is accounted for in separate classifications according to the source of capital. Two primary sources of equity capital are: (1) contributed capital—amounts invested directly by shareholders; and (2) earned capital—amounts which are provdied by profitable operations and retained in the business. A third major source of corporate capital, amounts obtained from creditors through borrowing, is discussed in Chapter 14.

Corporate capital provided by operations of the corporation is referred to as Retained Earnings. At the end of each period, any income or loss from operations of the corporation is transferred from the income summary account to retained earnings. The dividends account, which is used to record the dividends declared during the period, is also closed out to retained earnings during the closing process. Therefore, the balance in retained earnings at any point in time is equal to the total accumulated earnings of the business (net of any losses) less the total distributions which were paid to the stockholders in the form of dividends since the corporation's inception. If losses and dividends paid to stockholders exceed the cumulative earnings of the corporation, the resulting debit balance in retained earnings is referred to as a deficit. This deficit is deducted from invested capital in order to determine total stockholders' equity of the corporation.

NATURE OF CAPITAL STOCK

The investments made by stockholders in a corporation are represented by shares of ownership referred to as Capital Stock. Ownership of corporate stock is evidenced by a stock certificate. This certificate usually includes such information as the name of the corporation, rights of the shareholders, and the number of shares owned by each individual shareholder.

The maximum number of shares of stock *authorized* for issuance by the corporation is specified in the corporate charter. The number of shares *issued* refers to the total number of shares of stock which have been issued to stockholders since the formation of the corporation. Under certain circumstances, a corporation may reacquire shares of stock which were originally issued to its stockholders. Therefore, the remaining shares held by stockholders are referred to as *outstanding* shares. A current listing of the stockholders who own outstanding shares is maintained by the corporation's registrar or by the firm itself in a stockholders' ledger.

A corporation with a large number of shares outstanding which are traded regularly on an organized stock exchange must assign the function of transferring stocks and maintaining stock records to a stock transfer agent and a registrar. Banks or trust companies usually fulfill these functions for corporations. When a stockholder wishes to sell his stock, he endorses the stock certificate and forwards it to the transfer agent. The transfer agent cancels the certificate which was sold and prepares a new certificate which he sends to the registrar. The registrar records the stock transfer and issues a new stock certificate to the purchaser(s). Independent records maintained by the independent transfer agent and registrar provide additional controls which are intended to decrease the possibility of error or fraud in a corporation's ownership records.

RIGHTS OF STOCKHOLDERS *Common Stock*

Many corporations issue only a single class of stock. In this instance, each shareholder possesses identical ownership rights and privileges. For an individual stockholder, these rights are proportionate to the number of shares of stock owned. Among these basic rights are:

1 vote per share

1. The right to vote in stockholders' meetings. This includes the right to vote for directors and on decisions requiring stockholder approval as specified by the terms of the corporate charter. A stockholder has one vote for each share of stock that he owns. For example, if a stockholder owns 1,000 shares of stock, he is entitled to 1,000 votes. If a shareowner does not wish to attend a stockholders' meeting, he may assign his votes to a specified representative through a proxy statement.

2. The right to share in corporate earnings through dividends declared by the board of directors.

3. The right to maintain a proportionate interest in the ownership of the corporation whenever any additional shares of stock are issued by the corporation. This right, referred to as the preemptive right, provides that each stockholder may purchase a percentage of the number of new shares to be issued which is equal to his ownership percentage in the number of shares outstanding prior to the new issuance. To illustrate, assume that Aaron owns 100 (10 percent) of the 1,000 outstanding shares of stock of Matthews Co. If Matthews Co. decides to issue an additional 100 shares of stock, Aaron has a right to purchase 10 percent (100/1,000), or 10 of the new shares issued. Therefore, Aaron will be permitted to maintain his 10 percent interest (110/1,100) in the corporation. Thus, by exercising his preemptive right, a stockholder is able to maintain his relative interest or ownership in the corporation. However, a shareholder is not required to exercise his preemptive right; he may elect to do so at his option.

4. The right to a proportionate share in assets upon the liquidation of the corporation. Shareholders however, are entitled only to those assets which remain after all corporate creditors have been paid in full.

When a corporation issues only a single class of stock, its shares are referred to as common stock and the four basic rights described above apply to all shares issued and outstanding. In certain circumstances, a corporation may issue additional types of capital stock in order to satisfy management objectives and to appeal to investors who may have various investment objectives. These additional classes of stock usually grant certain preferential rights to the holders of these shares. Accordingly, such shares are usually referred to as preferred stock. Ordinarily, preferred stockholders either have no voting rights or only limited voting rights under certain conditions specified by the corporate charter. Preferred stock usually has one or more of the following preferences or privileges:

1. *Dividend preference.* Stock which is preferred as to dividends entitles its owner to receive a stated dividend *before* any distributions are made to owners of common stock. Dividends on preferred stock are normally limited to a fixed amount per share. However, this dividend preference does not assure the stockholder that he will receive a dividend. Thus, if the board of directors of a corporation chooses not to declare a dividend, neither common nor preferred shareholders will receive any distribution from the corporation.

2. *Cumulative preference.* Cumulative preferred stock provides that if all or part of the required dividend on preferred stock is not paid during a given year, the unpaid dividend accumulates and carries forward to succeeding years. The accumulated amount of unpaid dividends as well as current dividends must be paid before any dividends can be paid on common stock. Unpaid dividends on cumulative preferred stock are referred to as dividends in arrears. To illustrate, assume that a corporation has 10,000 shares of cumulative preferred stock outstanding and a $5 stated dividend per share was not paid in the preceding year. In the current year, no dividends may be paid on the common stock until preferred dividends of $50,000 ($5 × 10,000) from the preceding year and the dividend of $50,000 for the current year are paid. Dividends in arrears are not considered to be a liability of the corporation until they are declared by the board of directors. However, because this information is important to the users of financial statements, any dividends in arrears on preferred stock should be disclosed, usually by means of a footnote to the balance sheet.

Preferred stock not having cumulative rights is referred to as noncumulative. Dividends omitted in any one year on noncumulative preferred stock do not carry forward. Therefore, dividends may be paid on common stock if preferred stock dividends are paid for the current year. Since a dividend preference is usually one of the most important rights or features of preferred stock, noncumulative preferred stock is normally not considered to be a very desirable investment under most circumstances. Consequently, most preferred stock issues provide for cumulative dividends.

3. *Participating preference.* Preferred stock is usually entitled to receive a dividend of a specified amount each year. Preferred stock is nonparticipating when preferred stockholders receive only this amount regardless of the dividends paid to common stockholders. In some cases, however, certain types of preferred stock also provide for the possibility of dividends in excess of the normal amount. This preferred stock, referred to as participating, has the right to participate with common stockholders in dividends in excess of a specified amount paid to common shareholders.

The preferred stock contract must indicate the extent to which preferred shares will participate with common shares. Fully participating preferred stock is entitled to dividends at an amount which is equal to the excess of the common dividend over the regular amount for preferred. Partially participating preferred stock is entitled to participate with common stock, but it is limited to a maximum rate or amount. Issues of preferred stock normally do not include participation rights.

    4. *Liquidation preference.* Preferred stock is normally preferred as to assets upon liquidation of the corporation. That is, owners of such preferred stock are entitled to receive the stated liquidation value for their shares before any payments may be made to common stockholders.

    5. *Convertible preferred stock.* Preferred stock is convertible when it includes a privilege which allows stockholders to exchange their preferred shares for a specified number of common shares of the corporation at the shareholders' option. A conversion privilege allows the owner of preferred stock the option of obtaining common stock on which there is no dividend limitation in exchange for his preferred stock.

    6. *Callable preferred stock.* Preferred stock contracts frequently allow corporations to repurchase outstanding shares from preferred stockholders at a fixed price in excess of the issue price of the stock. When a corporation has this option, the preferred stock is referred to as callable.

PAR VALUE AND NO-PAR VALUE

    The par value of a share of capital stock is an arbitrary value established by the corporate charter. It is usually printed on the stock certificate and may be any amount decided upon by the corporation. The par value specified has no relationship whatsoever to the actual market value of the stock. Market value, which is the price at which a share of stock can be bought or sold, is dependent upon factors such as expected earnings and dividends, financial condition of the corporation, and general economic conditions. It is not unusual for a stock with a par value of $5 per share to be traded at a market value of $50, $100 or more.

    The primary significance of par value is that it is used in many states in order to establish the corporation's "legal capital." The concept of legal capital was used by state laws to protect corporate creditors from possible dishonest actions of stockholders or corporate directors. In the absence of such a provision, corporate assets could be distributed to stockholders prior to the final liquidation of a corporation. Since stockholders have no liability for corporate debts, creditors would be unable to obtain satisfaction of their claims. Therefore, the concept of legal capital limits the assets that may be distributed to stockholders prior to the liquidation of the corporation and the settlement of its debts. Consequently, dividends cannot be declared by a corporation if such payments would decrease the owners' equity to an amount which is below the specified minimum legal capital—that is, the par value of the outstanding shares or, in some instances, par value plus a certain additional amount. Most state laws also provide that if the amount invested by individual stockholders is less than the established par value of the stock purchased, the stockholders may be held liable to the corporation's creditors for any difference between the amount paid and par value in the event the corporation is unable to meet its debts.

Laws requiring that stock have a par value were originally intended to protect the creditors of a corporation by restricting the distribution of a portion of corporate capital. However, the existence of a par value for capital stock has also caused certain problems. In some instances, investors have confused an arbitrary par value with the actual value of the ownership interest in the corporation. Also, if the market value of the stock falls below the par value established by the corporate charter, a potential liability to the investor may prevent the sale of additional[1] shares of stock by the corporation unless or until the corporate charter is amended to change the par value of the stock. Consequently, some states have enacted legislation permitting the issuance of stock without par value, referred to as no-par stock. In these states, the legal capital of the corporation may be the total amount paid for the shares by the stockholders, or a stated value per share may be established by the board of directors.

ISSUANCE OF PAR VALUE STOCK

The primary significance of par value from an accounting viewpoint is that the capital stock account is credited with the par value of shares issued regardless of the amount received when the stock is sold. For example, if 1,000 shares of $10 par value common stock are sold at par value for cash, the entry would be as follows:

Cash	10,000	
Common Stock		10,000

When stock is sold for more than its par value, the amount received in excess of the par value is recorded as "additional paid-in capital." To illustrate, assume that 1,000 shares of $10 par value common stock were sold for $12 per share. The entry to record the issuance is as follows:

Cash	12,000	
Common Stock		10,000
Additional Paid-in Capital in Excess of Stated Value		2,000

The additional paid-in capital account is added to the capital stock account in reporting the total invested or contributed capital of the corporation.

---

[1] This liability applies only to the original issue of stock, not to stock purchased and then resold by investors.

Contributed capital of the corporation in the above example would be shown in the stockholders' equity section of the balance sheet as shown below:

STOCKHOLDERS' EQUITY:

Common Stock, $10 par value, 5,000 shares authorized, 1,000 shares issued and outstanding	$10,000
Additional paid-in capital on common stock	2,000
Total Contributed Capital	$12,000

If capital stock is issued for an amount less than its par value, the difference is charged or debited to a "discount on capital stock" account. This account would be shown as a deduction from the capital stock account in the balance sheet. Since selling stock at a discount is illegal in many states and usually represents a contingent liability to the creditors of the corporation in the remaining states, it is seldom encountered in practice. The par value of stock will normally be set at an amount which is less than its anticipated selling price, thus avoiding this problem.

obtract from total amount capital stock

ISSUANCE OF STOCK FOR NONCASH ASSETS

Sometimes a corporation may issue shares of its capital stock in exchange for assets such as land, buildings, or equipment. In such a case, the transaction may be recorded at the market value of the shares issued or at the market value of the assets acquired, whichever is a better indicator of market value. The market value of stock may be determined by reference to recent cash purchases and sales of the same class of stock by investors. Often, many shares of a large, publicly held corporation are traded daily through stock exchanges. Alternatively, if the market value of the shares issued cannot be determined, recent cash sales of similar assets or an independent appraisal of the asset may be used in order to record the transaction. Usually, the board of directors is given the responsibility by law for establishing a proper valuation for the issuance of stock for assets other than cash. To illustrate, assume that a corporation acquired land in exchange for five hundred shares of its $10 par value common stock. If the stock is traded on an established stock exchange and the current market price was $20, the transaction would be recorded as follows:

Land	10,000	
Common Stock		5,000
Additional Paid-in Capital		5,000

Cost of LAND
PAR value
Selling Price - PAR val

If there is no established market for the stock, the market value of the asset acquired may be used in recording the exchange. For example, if similar acreage had recently sold for $11,000, the entry to record the transaction would be:

Land	11,000	
Common Stock		5,000
Additional Paid-in Capital		6,000

ISSUANCE OF NO-PAR STOCK

At one time, all states required that stocks have a specified par value. However, to eliminate problems such as the liability for issuance discount and potential confusion over the meaning of par value, many states now permit the issuance of stock without par value.

The accounting entries which are necessary in order to record the issuance of no-par capital stock depend upon the specific laws of the state in which the shares are sold. Some states require that the entire issue price of no-par stock be regarded as legal capital. In these states, the capital account is credited for the entire amount received when the stock is issued. To illustrate, assume that a corporation issues 1,000 shares of its no-par common stock for $12 per share. This transaction would be recorded as follows:

Cash	12,000	
Common Stock		12,000

Other states allow the corporation to specify a stated value for no-par shares. When a stated value has been established, that amount is credited to Capital Stock and any excess is credited to Additional Paid-in Capital in Excess of Stated Value. For example, assume that the board of directors established a stated value of $10 per share for its stock. Issuance of 1,000 shares at a price of $12 would be recorded as follows:

Cash	12,000	
Common Stock		10,000
Additional Paid-in Capital		2,000

The additional paid-in capital in excess of stated value account is reported as a part of contributed capital in the stockholders' equity section of the balance sheet.

SUBSCRIPTIONS FOR CAPITAL STOCK

In some instances, a corporation may make an agreement with an investor to sell a number of shares of stock to him at a stipulated price. If the purchaser agrees to pay for the stock at some future date or with installment payments over a period of time, the sale of stock is referred to as a subscription. Subscriptions are an asset to the corporation since they represent cash or other assets to be received from the investor at some future date. Therefore, an account entitled subscriptions receivable is debited when subscriptions are accepted. Although shares are not actually issued until they are paid for, a corporation accepting stock subscriptions is committed to issue the shares upon receipt of the total specified purchase price. Accordingly, a common stock subscribed account is credited for the par value of the stock subscribed. The difference between the specified subscription price and par value is credited to additional paid-in capital (or discount). For example, assume that a corporation accepts subscriptions for 1,000 shares of its $10 par value common stock at a price of $18 per share. The subscription contract requires payment in two equal installments due in 60 and 90 days. This transaction would be recorded as follows:

Subscriptions Receivable.	18,000	
Common Stock Subscribed		10,000
Additional Paid-in Capital.		8,000

When subscribers make payments on their subscriptions, the amount collected by the corporation is credited to the subscriptions receivable account. For example, upon receipt of the first installment of the subscription illustrated above, the following entry would be made:

Cash	9,000	
Subscriptions Receivable		9,000

When the subscription price has been collected in full, shares of stock are issued to the investor by the corporation. For example, when the second installment is collected, stock certificates for 1,000 shares of stock will be issued. Collection of the installment payment and issuance of the shares would be recorded as follows:

Cash	9,000	
Subscriptions Receivable		9,000
Common Stock Subscribed	10,000	
Common Stock.		10,000

During the period in which subscriptions are outstanding, subscriptions receivable from investors are reported as an asset on the balance sheet and common stock subscribed is shown as a part of contributed capital in the stockholders' equity section of the balance sheet.

STOCKHOLDERS' EQUITY IN THE BALANCE SHEET

The stockholders' equity section of the balance sheet should report adequate information concerning each class of corporate stock outstanding.

If more than a single class of stock is issued, the nature, special rights, and dollar amounts outstanding should be shown for each. Presentation of stockholders' equity in the balance sheet might appear as follows:

STOCKHOLDERS' EQUITY:

6% preferred stock, $100 par value, 10,000 shares authorized,		
6,000 shares issued and outstanding		$ 600,000
Common stock, $10 par value, 100,000 shares authorized,		
50,000 shares issued and outstanding		500,000
Common stock subscribed, 1,000 shares		10,000
Additional paid-in capital:		
Common stock issued and subscribed	$130,000	
Preferred stock	60,000	190,000
Total Contributed Capital		$1,300,000
Retained earnings		450,000
Total Stockholders' Equity		$1,750,000

KEY DEFINITIONS

Additional paid-in capital Additional paid-in capital is the amount received on the issuance of capital stock in excess of its par or stated value.

Articles of incorporation Articles of incorporation are included in the application made to the state for a corporate charter and include information concerning the corporation.

Capital stock Capital stock is transferable shares of stock which evidence ownership in a corporation.

Charter A charter is a contract between the state and the corporation which includes the general corporation laws of the state and the specific provisions of the articles of incorporation.

Common stock Common stock is stock which has the basic rights of ownership and represents the residual ownership in the corporation.

Continuity of life Status as a separate legal entity gives the corporation a perpetual existence.

Contributed capital Contributed capital is capital invested directly by the shareholders of the corporation.

Controller The controller is an officer who is responsible for the accounting function of the business.

Convertible preferred stock Convertible preferred stock is stock which includes the privilege of allowing the shareholder to exchange preferred shares for a specified number of common shares at his option.

Corporation A corporation is an association of persons joined together for some common purpose, organized in accordance with state laws as a legal entity, separate and distinct from its owners.

Cumulative preferred stock Cumulative preferred stock is backed by a provision that if all or part of the specified dividend on preferred stock is not paid during a given year, the amount of the unpaid dividends accumulates and must be paid in a subsequent year before any dividends can be paid on common stock.

Earned capital   Earned capital includes amounts provided by profitable operations and retained by the business.

Incorporators   Incorporators are the persons who legally form a corporation.

Legal capital   Legal capital is a limit on the amount of assets that can be distributed to the stockholders of a corporation prior to liquidation and settlement of the corporate debts.

Limited liability   The creditors of the corporation have a claim against the assets of the corporation and not against the personal property of the stockholders.

No-par stock   No-par stock is stock without a par value.

Organization costs   Organization costs are the costs which are necessary to form the corporation.

Par value   Par value is an arbitrary value which is established in the corporate charter and printed on the stock certificate. It establishes the legal capital of the corporation in many states.

Participating preferred stock   Participating preferred stock is preferred stock which has the right to participate in some specified manner with common stockholders in dividends in excess of a stipulated amount paid to the common shareholders.

Preferred as to dividends   Stock which is preferred as to dividends is entitled to receive a stated dividend each year before any dividend is paid on the common stock.

Preferred stock   Preferred stock is a class of stock which has different rights from those associated with common stock.

Stock subscriptions   Stock subscriptions involve an agreement by the corporation to sell a certain number of shares at a specified price to an investor with the payment at some future date(s). Upon full payment, the purchaser gains control of the stock.

QUESTIONS

1. What are some of the main advantages of organizing a business as a corporation rather than as a sole proprietorship or partnership?

2. Describe the following characteristics of a corporation:

    a.   separate legal entity
    b.   limited liability
    c.   transferability of ownership interest
    d.   continuity of existence

3. Explain the meaning of the term "double taxation" as it applies to a corporation.

4. Explain what is meant by the number of shares of stock authorized, issued, and outstanding.

5. What are four basic rights of a stockholder?

6. Describe the following features which may be applied to an issuance of preferred stock:

a. cumulative
b. participating
c. preferred as to assets
d. callable
e. convertible

7. Explain the meaning of par value. Describe the accounting treatment of stock issued for more or less than par value.

8. Distinguish between par value and no-par stock.

9. What is the primary disadvantage of issuing stock for an amount less than par value?

10. What are organization costs? Describe two alternative accounting treatments for such costs.

11. Indicate the nature and balance sheet classification of the subscriptions receivable and common stock subscribed accounts.

12. What information regarding preferred stock should be disclosed in the balance sheet?

13. How should preferred dividends in arrears be reported in the balance sheet?

EXERCISES

12–1 Give the journal entries required to record each of the following stock transactions:

a. Issuance of 1,000 shares of $10 par value common stock at $14 per share.

b. Issuance of 100 shares of $100 par value preferred stock for a total of $12,000.

c. Issuance of 500 shares of no-par common stock for $20 per share.

d. Issuance of 2,000 shares of $10 par value common stock for land. Recent sales and purchases of the stock have been made at a price of $20 per share. The value of the land is not readily determinable.

12–2 Make the journal entries necessary to record the issuance of stock in each of the following independent cases.

a. One hundred shares of $25 par value stock are sold at par for cash.

b. Eighty shares of $15 par value stock are sold at $17 each for cash.

c. One thousand shares of no-par capital stock are issued at $14 per share.

d. Five hundred shares of no-par capital stock with a stated value of $10 per share are sold for $11 per share.

12–3 Jeffry Company was organized on March 1, 1975. The authorized capital was 20,000 shares of $50 par value, 6 percent, cumulative preferred stock and 50,000 shares of $10 par value common stock. At the date of organization, all the common stock was issued at $20 per share and 10,000 shares of the preferred stock were sold at par.

Prepare the stockholders' equity section of the balance sheet for Jeffry Co. on March 1, after the issuance of the stock.

12–4 Niblet Corporation was organized on January 1, 1974. On that date, the corporation issued 1,000 shares of $100 par value, 6 percent preferred stock and 20,000 shares of $10 par value common stock. During the first five years of its life, the corporation paid the following total dividends to its stockholders.

1974	$	0
1975		6,000
1976		20,000
1977		15,000
1978		18,000

Determine the total dividends paid to each class of stockholders assuming that the preferred stock is:

a. cumulative and nonparticipating.
b. noncumulative and nonparticipating.

12–5 Loggins Music Stores, Inc. accepted subscriptions for 250 shares of its no-par, $10 stated value capital stock on January 1, 1975, at a price of $13 per share. On March 1, the firm collected $1,625 as a partial payment on the subscriptions. Then, on April 1, the balance in the subscriptions account was paid and all the shares were issued. Prepare the journal entries necessary to record the above transactions on the books of Loggins Music Stores, Inc.

PROBLEMS

Series A

12A–1 The Fabian Co. is organized on January 1, 1975, with authorized stock of 30,000 shares of $5 par value common and 5,000 shares of $100 par value preferred. Give the entries required to record each of the following transactions:

1. Assets are accepted as payment for 10,000 shares of common stock. The assets are valued as follows: land, $50,000; buildings, $130,000; and equipment, $20,000.
2. The 5,000 preferred shares are sold at $105 per share.
3. Subscriptions are received for 5,000 shares of common stock at $25.
4. A payment of $50,000 is received on the subscribed stock.
5. Subscriptions receivable of $75,000 are collected and the stock is issued.
6. The remaining common stock is sold for $30 per share.

12A–2 1. Kanoch, Inc. issues 50 shares of $25 par value stock in exchange for land appraised at $1,500. The shares are not actively traded but a company official guesses that they are worth about $32 per share. Record the issuance of the stock on the books of Kanoch, Inc.

2. Red Rider Stables, Inc. acquired 100 acres of prime grazing land in exchange for 200 shares of no-par capital stock. It was found that a similar 100-acre tract had sold the previous year for $11,000. The company's stock has not been registered with a major exchange but the company's balance sheet reveals a book value of $50 per share. Record the issuance of the stock on the books of Red Rider Stables, Inc.

3. Monzingo Grocers, Inc., obtained a new store site in exchange for 400 shares of its $15 par value capital stock. The store site is in a recently developed area. Ten years ago wooded lots of similar size sold for $8,000. The latest New York Stock Exchange quotation for the stock was $30 per share. Record the issuance of the stock on the books of Monzingo Grocers, Inc.

12A–3 Jones Co. had the following stock outstanding from January 1, 1973, to December 31, 1978:

1. Common stock, $10 par value, 20,000 shares authorized and outstanding.
2. Preferred stock, $100 par value with a $6 stated dividend, 10,000 shares authorized, 5,000 shares issued and outstanding.

During that period, Jones Co. paid the following dividends:

1973	–0–
1974	$80,000
1975	–0–
1976	$30,000
1977	$70,000
1978	$20,000

Compute the amount of preferred dividends and common stock dividends in each year assuming that:

1. The preferred stock is noncumulative.
2. The preferred stock is cumulative.

12A–4 Smith Corporation was organized on January 1, 1975, with 100,000 shares of $10 par value common stock and 10,000 shares of $50 par value preferred stock authorized. During 1975, Smith Corporation had the following stock transactions:

January   1 Issued 5,000 shares of preferred stock for $60 per share.

January   1 Issued 5,000 shares of common stock for $60 per share.

October   1 Accepted subscriptions for 1,000 shares of common stock at a price of $16 per share. Payment is to be made in two equal installments payable in 60 and 120 days.

November 30   Collected the first installment on the subscribed stock but issued no stock at this time.

Required:

a.   Prepare the journal entries to record the stock transactions.
b.   Prepare the stockholders' equity section of the balance sheet for Smith Corporation as of December 31, 1975. (Assume that retained earnings are $64,000 on December 31, 1975.)

12A–5   Akens Co. was organized on January 1, 1972. A portion of the December 31, 1975, balance sheet of Akens Co. appeared as follows:

STOCKHOLDERS' EQUITY

6% preferred stock, $100 par value, 20,000 shares authorized		$ 500,000
Preferred stock subscribed		100,000
Common stock, $10 par value, 100,000 shares authorized		400,000
Common stock subscribed		50,000
Additional paid-in capital:		
On common stock issued	$200,000	
On common stock subscribed	50,000	
On preferred stock issued	25,000	
On preferrred stock subscribed	10,000	285,000
Retained earnings		330,000
Total Stockholders' Equity		$1,665,000

Required:

a.   How many shares of preferred stock are outstanding?
b.   How many shares of common stock are outstanding?
c.   How many shares of preferred stock are subscribed?
d.   How many shares of common stock are subscribed?
e.   What were the average issue prices of the common and the preferred shares outstanding?
f.   What were the average subscription prices of the common stock and the preferred stock?
g.   What is the total contributed capital of Akens Co.?

Everything   Except.   Ret   Earnings

Series B

12B–1   Wilson Co. was organized on January 1, 1975, with 100,000 shares of common stock authorized. On January 15, 1975, 50,000 shares of stock were issued for $60 per share. Give the journal entry required to record the issuance in each of the following cases:

a.   The stock has a $50 par value.
b.   The stock is no-par. The state in which the corporation is organized requires that stock have a par or stated value. The board of directors assigned a stated value of $10 per share.

    c. The stock has no par value. The state in which the corporation is organized requires that the entire amount received on stock issuances be included in legal capital.

12B–2   Thompson Co. issued 10,000 shares of common stock in exchange for a plot of land. Prepare the journal entry to record the transaction in each of the following cases:

    a. The stock has a par value of $10 and is currently selling at $25 per share on a stock exchange.

    b. The stock is no-par and is currently selling at $25 per share on a stock exchange.

    c. The stock has a par value of $10 and is not traded on a stock exchange. Recently, similar plots of land have sold for $30,000.

12B–3   Determine the amount of cash which Mark Schneider, who holds 100 shares of common stock and 200 shares of preferred stock in Darnell Manufacturing Company, would receive in the following situations.

Dividend information:

Dividends in 1975	$ 9,000
Dividends in 1976	21,000
Dividends in 1977	120,000

Stock information:

Preferred stock–$100 par, 6% cumulative, nonparticipating

Outstanding, 1975	3,000 shares
Outstanding, 1976	4,000 shares
Outstanding, 1977	5,000 shares

Common stock–par $100

Outstanding, 1975	2,000 shares
Outstanding, 1976	6,000 shares
Outstanding, 1977	10,000 shares

Cash to Schneider for:

1975–
1976–
1977–

12B–4   In examining the accounts of Longhorn Steel Company, you discover the following information pertaining to the stockholders' equity of the company at December 31, 1975.

    a. 3,000 shares of $100 par value preferred stock issued, 9,000 shares authorized.

    b. The preferred dividend requirement for the year was met by paying dividends of $18,000.

    c. 16,000 shares of $10 par value common stock issued and outstanding.

    d. 20,000 shares of $10 par value common stock authorized.

    e. 2,000 shares of common stock subscribed.

f. The average issue price of the common stock was $17.

g. The average issue price of the preferred stock was $106.

h. The average subscription price of the common stock was $19.

i. Retained earnings were $219,000.

Required:

Prepare the stockholders' equity section of Longhorn Steel Company's balance sheet at December 31, 1975.

12B–5 Baker Corporation was formed on January 1, 1975, with 10,000 shares of $5 par value common stock authorized. The following transactions occurred during the month of January:

January   2   Issued 2,000 shares for $22 a share.

          4   Paid corporate charter fees of $500.

     10   Accepted subscriptions for 1,000 shares at $25 per share. The subscribers made a down payment of 10% of the subscription price.

     25   Collected $10,000 on subscriptions receivable.

     27   Issued 2,000 shares at $30 a share.

Give the journal entries to record the above transactions and prepare the stockholders' equity section of Baker Corporation's balance sheet as of January 31, 1975.

13

The Corporation: Earnings and Dividends

THE STOCKHOLDERS' equity section of a corporation is divided into two major segments, contributed capital and retained earnings. Retained earnings represent accumulated earnings which were retained in the business. The retained earnings account is increased by the net income of the business and reduced by net losses and distributions to shareholders in the form of dividends. In the end-of-period closing entries, revenue and expense accounts are closed to the income summary account. When revenues exceed expenses, the credit balance which remains in the income summary account is equal to the firm's net income for the period. Conversely, a debit balance in the income summary account indicates a net loss for the accounting period. The balance in the income summary account is closed to retained earnings. Similarly, the debit balance in the dividends account is transferred or closed out as a reduction in retained earnings. This chapter considers the accounting for transactions affecting retained earnings and discusses various issues which are related to both corporate earnings and dividends.

NATURE OF EARNINGS

A primary purpose of reporting corporate earnings is to provide useful information to stockholders, potential investors, creditors, and other interested users of financial statements. The net income or loss of a corporation is determined in basically the same manner as that of a partnership or sole proprietorship.

314

There are several special problems which are related to the preparation of the income statement that have not been discussed previously. These include (1) accounting for transactions which are not related to the normal business activities and which occur infrequently; (2) accounting for discontinued operations; (3) prior period adjustments; (4) recording the effects of accounting changes; and (5) determination of earnings on a per share basis.

EXTRAORDINARY ITEMS

The net income of a corporation as reported in its income statement includes earnings from normal operations of the business as well as certain infrequently occurring transactions which are not related to the ordinary activities of the business. As a result of *Opinions No. 9* and *No. 30* of the Accounting Principles Board, transactions which occur infrequently and which do not result from the normal operations of the business, referred to as extraordinary items, are reported as a separate amount in the income statement.

In order to be classified as an extraordinary item in the income statement, an item must be both unusual in nature and not reasonably expected to recur in the foreseeable future. Determining the degree of abnormality and the probability of recurrence of a particular transaction should take into account the environment in which the business operates. In addition to these criteria, the effect of an extraordinary event should be classified separately only if it is considered to be material in amount in relation to income from normal operations. To illustrate, assume that in 1976 the Dolphin Company had income after taxes from normal operations of $100,000 and a $20,000 gain (net of taxes) which meets the criteria for classification as an extraordinary item. A simplified income statement for the Dolphin Company might appear as follows:

DOLPHIN CO.
Income Statement
For the Year Ended December 31, 1976

Net sales	$400,000
Cost of goods sold	100,000
Gross margin.	$300,000
Expenses	200,000
Income before extraordinary items	$100,000
Extraordinary gain, net of tax	20,000
Net Income	$120,000

Certain gains or losses should not be classified as extraordinary items, even if material in amount, because they could be expected to occur in the ordinary operations of the business. For example, a loss resulting from a write-down made to recognize a decline in the value of inventory due to obsolescence should not be reported as an extraordinary item. Such an item should be included in the computation of income before extraordinary items. Other examples of items that would not normally be considered extraordinary items regardless of their amount include write-offs of uncollectible receivables or gains or losses from fluctuations in foreign exchange rates.

DISCONTINUED OPERATIONS

The term discontinued operations refers to the operations of any subsidiary, division, or department of a business that has been or will be sold, abandoned, or otherwise disposed of. In APB Opinion No. 30, the Board concluded that the results of continuing normal operations should be reported separately from discontinued operations. Any gain or loss from the disposal of a segment of a business along with the results of operations of the segment should be reported in a separate section of the income statement. Accordingly, an income statement of a firm that has discontinued operations would appear as follows:

KINGSBERY COMPANY
Income Statement
For the Year Ended December 31, 1976

Sales		$10,000
Less: Cost of goods sold		4,000
Gross profit		$ 6,000
Operating expenses		4,000
Income from continuing operations before income taxes		$ 2,000
Provision for income taxes		800
Income from continuing operations		$ 1,200
Discontinued operations (Footnote):		
Income from operations of discontinued division (less taxes of $300)	$500	
Loss on disposal of division (less tax effect of $200)	(300)	200
Net Income		$ 1,400

PRIOR PERIOD ADJUSTMENTS

Certain gains or losses which represent material corrections of reported earnings of prior periods should be excluded from the income statement and shown as a direct adjustment of retained earnings. These corrections, which are referred to as prior period adjustments, are limited to those items which:

1. Can be specifically identified with business activities of a prior period, and
2. Are not attributable to economic events occurring subsequent to the date of the financial statement for the prior period, and
3. Are determined primarily by persons other than management, and
4. Were not susceptible to reasonable estimation prior to the final determination.[1]

Thus, prior period adjustments are limited to situations in which uncertainties at the time of a past event were such that a reasonable measurement of the transaction was not possible. For example, payment of a material amount during the current period in settlement of a lawsuit instituted against the firm during a prior period could meet the criteria for a prior period adjustment. Such a payment would be reported as a correction of retained earnings at the beginning of the current period. Corrections to retained earnings resulting from prior period adjustments are encountered very infrequently in practice.

ACCOUNTING CHANGES

Changes in accounting occur because of the uncertainty involved in the preparation of periodic financial reports. Subsequent to the preparation of financial statements, additional information may be obtained which necessitates an adjustment of the accounting records. Three types of changes may be involved: (1) a change in accounting principle; (2) a change in accounting estimate; and (3) a correction of an error of a prior period.[2] These three types of changes will be illustrated and discussed in the paragraphs that follow.

Change in Accounting Principle. A change in accounting principle results from the adoption of a generally accepted accounting principle which differs from the one that was previously used. An example would be a change from the sum-of-the-years'-digits method of depreciation to the straight-line method.

To illustrate, assume that a company acquired a truck on January 1, 1974, at a cost of $4,000. The useful life of the truck was estimated to be 4 years with a salvage value of $400. At the date of acquisition, the company decided to use the sum-of-the-years'-digits depreciation method. Further assume that the company decided to switch to the straight-line method at the end of 1976. At the time of the change in methods, the cumulative difference between the old and the new methods of depreciation

---

[1] *Opinions of the Accounting Principles Board, No. 9,* "Reporting the Results of Operations" (New York: American Institute of Certified Public Accountants, 1966), p. 23.

[2] A fourth type of accounting change, a change in reporting entity, is not applicable to this discussion.

must be determined. The amount of this difference would be computed as follows:

Year	Sum-of-the-Years' Digits	Straight-Line	Difference to December 31, 1975
1974	$1,440	$ 900	$540
1975	1,080	900	180
	$2,520	$1,800	$720

The $720 difference in depreciation between the two methods would be adjusted during 1976 as follows:

Accumulated Depreciation 720
    Depreciation Adjustment, Change in Accounting Principle   720

This entry reduces the balance in the accumulated depreciation account to what it would have been had the straight-line method been used from the time the asset was purchased. The depreciation adjustment would appear in the income statement as an extraordinary item. After the adjustment is made, the depreciation expense for 1976 and 1977 would be recorded at $900 per year based on the straight-line method.

The effect of this change on the current and prior years' income should be explained by a footnote to the financial statements. A change in accounting principle is appropriate only when it can be demonstrated that the new method provides more useful financial information.

Change in Accounting Estimate. Changes in the estimates used in accounting may occur as additional information regarding the original estimate is obtained. An example of such a change would be a change in the estimated salvage value or service list of an asset. The procedure used in adjusting for this change is to spread the remaining undepreciated cost of the asset over its remaining useful life. This procedure will allocate the remaining book value of the asset, less the new estimated salvage value, to expense over the revised estimated remaining useful life of the asset.

To illustrate, assume the company in the previous example decided in 1977 that while the straight-line method should be used, the useful life of the asset should have been six (rather than four) years and the salvage value should have been $100 (instead of $400). The amount of depreciation expense for 1977 would be computed as follows:

Original cost.	$4,000
Less: Accumulated depreciation to December 31, 1976	2,700
Book value at December 31, 1976	1,300
Less: Estimated salvage value	100
Amount to be depreciated.	$1,200
Divide by: Estimated remaining useful iife.	3 years
Depreciation per year	$ 400

At the end of 1977, 1978, and 1979, the following entry would be made to record the depreciation expense:

```
Depreciation Expense  . . . . . . . . . . . . . . . . . . . . . . . . . . . . .  400
     Accumulated Depreciation  . . . . . . . . . . . . . . . . . . . . . . . .        400
```

Errors. Accounting errors may result from mistakes in the application of accounting principles, oversights, misuse of facts, or mistakes in mathematics. To illustrate, assume that the truck acquired on January 1, 1974, had been incorrectly recorded as an expense rather than as an asset. This error was discovered on December 31, 1975, at which time it was decided that the asset should have been assigned an estimated useful life of four years and a $400 salvage value. The company uses the straight-line method of depreciation. The entry at December 31, 1975, to record the correction of the error would be:

```
Asset . . . . . . . . . . . . . . . . . . . . . . . . . . . . . . . . . . . . .  4,000
     Accumulated Depreciation  . . . . . . . . . . . . . . . . . . . . . .          900
     Prior Period Adjustment. . . . . . . . . . . . . . . . . . . . . . . .        3,100
```

This entry records the asset at its cost of $4,000, the accumulated depreciation of $900 that should have been recorded in 1974, and an adjustment of the prior year's earnings of $3,100 ($4,000 asset expenditure erroneously recorded as an expense less $900 depreciation expense which should have been recorded in 1974). The prior period adjustment would be a correction of retained earnings and would not appear in the income statement. Depreciation for 1975 would be recorded in the normal manner:

```
Depreciation Expense  . . . . . . . . . . . . . . . . . . . . . . . . . . . . .  900
     Accumulated Depreciation  . . . . . . . . . . . . . . . . . . . . . . . .        900
```

EARNINGS PER SHARE

An amount referred to as earnings per share is basically the net income of a company per share of common stock outstanding for a given period. Data on earnings per share of a corporation probably receive more attention than any other single item of financial information. Earnings per share ratios are included in annual reports issued by corporations and receive extensive coverage in the financial press and the investment services. Earnings per share is often considered to be an important indicator of the market price of common stock and, in some cases, an indication of expected dividends per share.

Because of the widespread attention given to earnings per share data, it was recognized that such information should be computed on a consistent and meaningful basis by all companies. Accordingly, *Opinion No. 15* of the Accounting Principles Board provided detailed procedures for the computation and presentation of earnings per share figures under different circumstances.[3] Further, the APB concluded that earnings per share data should be disclosed in income statements for all periods covered by the statement. If extraordinary items and gains or losses from discontinued operations are included in net income for the period, separate earnings per share figures would normally be provided for: (1) income from continuing operations; (2) discontinued operations; (3) extraordinary items; and (4) net income. This data is usually presented in the income statement following the net income figure.

The computation of earnings per share is relatively simple when the capital structure of the corporation includes only common stock. In this case, earnings per share of common stock is computed by dividing net income by the number of shares of common stock outstanding. To illustrate, assume that Dolphin Co., whose income statement appeared in the previous section of this chapter, had 40,000 shares of common stock outstanding during 1976. Its earnings per share information would be computed as follows:

$$\text{Ordinary Income} \dots \dots \quad \frac{\$100,000}{40,000} = \$2.50$$

$$\text{Extraordinary Gain} \dots \dots \quad \frac{\$\ 20,000}{40,000} = \quad .50$$

$$\text{Net Income} \dots \dots \dots \dots \quad \frac{\$120,000}{40,000} = \$3.00$$

When there are both common and preferred stock outstanding, the net income must be reduced by the preferred dividend requirements to determine the net income available to common stockholders. If the firm issues or acquires shares of stock during the period, the divisor in the calculation is the average number of shares outstanding during the year. In such circumstances, the earnings per share is computed as follows:

$$\text{Earnings Per Share} = \frac{\text{Net Income} - \text{Preferred Dividends}}{\text{Average Number of Common Shares Outstanding}}$$

The capital structures of many corporations include convertible securities, stock options, and other securities which may include rights that can be converted into shares of common stock at the option of the holder. A capital structure is considered to be complex when it includes securities and rights that could potentially decrease earnings per share by increasing the number of common shares outstanding. The existence of a complex

---

[3] *Opinions of the Accounting Principles Board, No. 15,* "Earnings Per Share" (New York: American Institute of Certified Public Accountants, 1969).

capital structure results in significant complications in computations of earnings per share data. Essentially, they involve the calculation of a hypothetical earnings per share figure which assumes conversion of certain securities into common stock. The details of these considerations, however, are beyond the scope of this text.

DIVIDENDS

Dividends are distributions made by a corporation to its shareholders. Such distributions are paid in proportion to the number of shares owned by each stockholder. Dividends may be in the form of cash, other assets, or shares of the corporation's own stock. Unless otherwise specified, a dividend represents a distribution of cash. Payment of dividends is provided by action of the board of directors. The board has complete control of the type, amount, and timing of any and all dividend payments. However, once dividends are declared, they become a legal liability of the corporation to its stockholders.

In most cases, dividends represent a distribution of accumulated corporate earnings. It is ordinarily illegal to declare dividends in excess of the balance in the retained earnings account. In other words, an ordinary dividend usually may not be paid from any amounts which were invested by stockholders. The existence of a credit balance in the retained earnings account, however, does not necessarily indicate that there is cash available for the payment of dividends. Retained earnings is unrelated to the balance in the cash account because funds obtained from the accumulated income of the business may have been used to increase noncash assets or to decrease liabilities. Thus, a corporation with a large retained earnings balance may be unable to distribute cash dividends to its stockholders. On the other hand, a corporation with a substantial amount of cash may decide to pay little or no dividends to its stockholders so that the cash may be retained and used for other corporate objectives.

Because dividends are important to investors and therefore have an effect on the market price of the stock, most corporations attempt to adhere to a well formulated or established dividend policy. Although the percentage of earnings paid out in dividends varies widely according to the objectives of the firm, most corporations usually attempt to maintain a stable or increasing record of dividend payments.

While ordinary dividends are usually limited to the amount of retained earnings, a corporation may pay a liquidating dividend in order to return to the stockholders a portion of their original investment. Such a dividend is normally paid in conjunction with a permanent reduction in the size of a business or, alternatively, upon liquidation of a firm. Accordingly, such distributions are recorded by reducing capital stock and additional paid-in capital accounts.

Important Dates Related to Dividends

There are three important dates related to dividends:

1. Date of declaration.
2. Date of record.
3. Date of payment.

On the date of declaration, the board of directors of a corporation formally establishes a liability of a specified amount to its stockholders. The dividend and related liability, dividends payable, are recorded at that time. If financial statements are prepared after dividends are declared but before they are paid, dividends payable are classified as a current liability in the balance sheet. Following the declaration date, the corporation prepares a list of the stockholders as of the date of record—these are the stockholders who are entitled to receive the dividends. No entry is required by the corporation on the record date.

A period of time is usually necessary between the record date and the date of payment to allow the corporation sufficient time to identify those stockholders who will receive dividends and to process the dividend checks. An entry is made on the date of payment to record the distribution of cash and to remove the liability for dividends payable.

Cash Dividends

Dividends are usually paid in cash. Such dividends result in a reduction of both the cash and retained earnings of a corporation. Dividends on common stock are usually stated as a specific amount per share, while preferred stock dividends may be stated at either a specific dollar amount or a percentage of the par value per share. For example, a dividend on $100 par value preferred stock might be specified as either $5 or as 5 percent of par value. In either case, dividends paid to each stockholder are in proportion to the number of shares owned.

To illustrate, assume that the Jet Co. has 10,000 shares of common stock and 5,000 shares of 6 percent, $100 par value preferred stock outstanding. Further assume that on December 15 the company declares the preferred dividend and a $5 per share dividend on common stock. The $30,000 preferred dividend ($.06 \times $100 \times 5,000 shares) and the $50,000 common dividend ($5 \times 10,000 shares) are payable on January 15 to its stockholders of record on December 20. The entries which are required to record the declaration of the dividend on December 15 and its payment on January 15 are as follows:

December 15	Preferred Dividends.	30,000	
	Common Dividends.	50,000	
	Dividends Payable		80,000
December 20	No Entry		
January 15	Dividends Payable.	80,000	
	Cash		80,000

The dividend accounts are closed to retained earnings during the normal year-end closing process. Assuming that the accounting period for the Jet Co. ends on December 31, the following entry would be made on that date:

December 31	Retained Earnings.	80,000	
	Preferred Dividends		30,000
	Common Dividends		50,000

In some instances, the corporation may debit retained earnings directly, rather than a dividend account. In these instances, a closing entry would not be required.

Stock Dividends

A distribution made to stockholders in the form of additional shares of a company's own stock is referred to as a stock dividend. Usually, such a distribution consists of additional common stock given to common stockholders. A stock dividend results in a proportionate increase in the number of shares owned by each stockholder. For example, a ten percent stock dividend entitles a stockholder to receive one additional share for each ten shares of stock he owns.

Since a stock dividend is paid on a pro rata basis, each stockholder retains the identical percentage interest in the firm after the dividend as he owned prior to the distribution. For example, assume that a stockholder owned 100 of 1,000 outstanding shares of a corporation. Thus, the stockholder owned 10 percent (100/1,000) of the corporation's outstanding stock. Further assume that the corporation declared a 5 percent stock dividend. The stockholder would receive 5 (.05 × 100) of the 50 (.05 × 1,000) additional shares of stock issued. Consequently, the stockholder's percentage interest in the corporation remains at 10 percent (105/1,050) after the stock dividend. A stockholder, however, may benefit from a stock dividend if there is less than a proportionate decrease in the market price of the stock associated with the distribution. In this case, the market value of the total shares owned by the stockholder would increase.

Unlike a cash dividend, a stock dividend does not result in a decrease in either the corporation's assets or its total stockholders' equity. If a stock dividend has no effect on either the assets or the equity of the corporation, or in the relative ownership interests of the shareholders, why do corporations distribute such dividends? A primary purpose of issuing stock dividends is to enable the corporation to give its stockholders some evidence of increased retained earnings without actually distributing cash. Thus, although a stock dividend does not affect corporate assets or increase the individual stockholder's relative interest in the corporation, it is perceived to be a distribution of earnings by many shareholders.

Another reason for distributing a stock dividend is to reduce the selling price of the corporation's stock. Because a stock dividend of a sizable amount increases the number of shares outstanding with no change in corporate assets, the market price of the stock normally decreases. A corporation may desire to reduce the market price of its stock so that it will be more readily marketable among investors.

Since a stock dividend increases the number of shares outstanding, many states require an associated increase in the legal capital of the corporation. Therefore, even though such a dividend has no effect on total stockholders' equity, an entry is required in order to transfer a portion of retained earnings to contributed capital if such capitalization is required by the state. This is referred to as "capitalizing" a part of retained earnings. Consequently, the retained earnings "capitalized" is no longer available for distribution to stockholders in the form of cash dividends.

In many states, the minimum amount which must be transferred from retained earnings to contributed capital is an amount equal to the par or stated value of the shares issued. In other states, there is no such requirement. However, because it is generally believed that most shareholders regard a stock dividend as something of value, the American Institute of CPAs has recommended that in certain circumstances an amount equal to the fair market value of the shares to be issued as a stock dividend should be capitalized. This reasoning was explained by the Committee on Accounting Procedure of the AICPA as follows:

> . . . many recipients of stock dividends look upon them as distributions of corporate earnings and usually in an amount equivalent to the fair value of the additional shares received. Furthermore, it is presumed that such views of recipients are materially strengthened in those instances, which are by far the most numerous, where the issuances are so small in comparison with the shares previously outstanding that they do not have any apparent effect upon the share market price and, consequently, the market value of the shares previously held remains substantially unchanged.[4]

The Committee further suggested that these circumstances exist with the issuance of a small stock dividend. A small stock dividend is defined as

---

[4] *Accounting Research Bulletin No. 43,* "Restatement and Revision of Accounting Research Bulletins" (New York: American Institute of Certified Public Accountants, 1953), Ch. 7, par. 10.

an increase of less than 20 percent to 25 percent of the number of shares previously outstanding.

To illustrate the entries for the issuance of a small stock dividend, assume that the stockholders' equity of a corporation on May 1 was as follows:

Common stock, $5 par value, 20,000 shares outstanding	$100,000
Additional paid-in capital	20,000
Total Contributed Capital	$120,000
Retained earnings	80,000
Total Stockholders' Equity	$200,000

Assume further that on May 2 the company declares a 10 percent stock dividend, or a dividend of 2,000 shares (.10 × 20,000), which is to be distributed on June 1. Assuming that the shares are selling in the market on the declaration date at a price of $20 per share, an amount equal to the fair value of the shares to be issued, or $40,000 (2,000 × $20), would be transferred from retained earnings to the appropriate contributed capital accounts. The capital stock account is credited for the par value of the shares issued and the remainder is added to additional paid-in capital. The following entries would be made to record the declaration and distribution of the stock dividend:

May 2	Retained Earnings	40,000	
	Stock Dividend Distributable		10,000
	Additional Paid-in Capital		30,000
June 1	Stock Dividend Distributable	10,000	
	Common Stock		10,000

If financial statements are prepared between the date of declaration and the date of distribution of a stock dividend, the stock dividend distributable account should be included in the stockholders' equity section of the balance sheet. It is not classified as a liability because the corporation has no obligation to distribute cash or any other asset.

As previously indicated, the distribution of a stock dividend has no effect on either the assets or the total stockholders' equity of a corporation. In the illustration above, the only effect on the corporation was a transfer of $40,000 from retained earnings to contributed capital. The stockholders' equity after payment of the stock dividend on June 1 would appear as follows:

Common stock, $5 par value, 22,000 shares outstanding	$110,000
Additional paid-in capital	50,000
Total Contributed Capital	$160,000
Retained earnings	40,000
Total Stockholders' Equity	$200,000

. The Committee on Accounting Procedure further indicated that stock dividends in excess of 20% to 25% would be expected to materially reduce the market value per share of stock. Accordingly, the Committee recommended that if capitalization is required by the state, such stock dividends should be recorded by capitalizing retained earnings only to the extent of the par or stated value of the shares issued. Under these circumstances, the entry to record the stock dividend would be a debit to retained earnings and a credit to capital stock for the par value of the shares issued. Again, there is no effect on the total stockholders' equity of the corporation.

STOCK SPLITS

A corporation may desire to reduce the selling price of its stock in order to facilitate purchases and sales of its shares by investors. Reducing the price of shares to a reasonable amount normally increases the number of investors who are willing to purchase a corporation's stock. This may be accomplished by increasing the number of shares outstanding and decreasing the par or stated value of the stock by a proportionate amount. This procedure is referred to as a stock split.

For example, assume that a corporation has 20,000 shares of $10 par value common stock outstanding with a current market price of $200 per share. The company might declare a two-for-one stock split in which each current stockholder receives two new shares with a $5 par value for each share of $10 par stock he owned prior to the split. This action would tend to cause the market price to decrease to approximately $100 per share because there would be twice as many shares outstanding after the split with no change in the value of the corporation.

A stock split is very similar to a large stock dividend—that is, there is a significant increase in the number of shares outstanding without a change in total stockholders' equity. A basic difference between the two types of distributions is the magnitude of the increase in the number of shares outstanding. Also, a stock split never requires any capitalization of retained earnings. Consequently, only a memorandum entry to the common stock account to indicate the change in par value and the new number of shares outstanding is required upon a stock split.

TREASURY STOCK

On occasion, a corporation may purchase shares of its own stock from its stockholders. If the corporation does not cancel these shares but instead holds the stock for later reissue, it is referred to as treasury stock. A corporation may desire to reacquire shares of its stock which have been previously issued in order to have stock available for employee stock purchase plans, for stock options, for bonuses, or for some other legitimate reason.

Unissued stock may not be used for these purposes because of the preemptive right of the existing stockholders. Purchases of treasury stock are limited to the amount of retained earnings if the corporation is to maintain its legal capital. This occurs because the purchase of treasury stock results in the distribution of cash to certain stockholders. If assets are distributed to stockholders in excess of the retained earnings, the corporation is returning a portion of the invested capital. Therefore, the purchase of treasury stock reduces the amount available for subsequent distributions to the stockholders.

Although the stock of another corporation is an asset of the firm which owns it, treasury stock is not an asset because a corporation cannot have an ownership interest in itself. Instead, the purchase of a corporation's own shares represents a return of capital to the selling shareholder and, thus, a reduction in the stockholders' equity of the corporation. Consequently, treasury stock is shown as a deduction in the stockholders' equity section of the balance sheet.

There are several different methods for recording treasury stock transactions. However, one approach, referred to as the cost method, is a method commonly used in practice for recording the acquisition of treasury stock. For this reason, the cost method will be discussed in the paragraphs which follow.

When a corporation acquires its own shares, treasury stock is debited for the cost of the shares purchased. Note that neither the par or stated value of the stock nor the amount originally received for the shares when they were issued is used to record the acquisition of treasury stock. If treasury shares are subsequently reissued, the difference between the cost of the shares and their selling price does not represent a gain or a loss to the corporation. Instead, the corporation has simply changed the amount of invested capital by acquiring and reissuing treasury shares. Consequently, any difference between the acquisition cost and the resale price of treasury stock is credited to paid-in capital if the selling price exceeds cost. If the shares are sold below cost, additional paid-in capital is reduced. If this account is not sufficient to absorb the excess of the cost over the selling price, any remainder may be charged or debited to retained earnings. To illustrate, assume that the stockholders' equity of a corporation appeared as follows on January 1:

Common stock, $10 par value, 10,000 shares authorized, issued, and outstanding	$100,000
Additional paid-in capital	20,000
Total Contributed Capital	$120,000
Retained earnings	30,000
Total Stockholders' Equity	$150,000

Further assume that the corporation purchased 300 of its outstanding

[handwritten margin note: Purchase of treasury stock]

shares on January 15 at a price of $20 per share. The following entry would be necessary to record the purchase:

```
Treasury Stock ................................  6,000
    Cash ....................................        6,000
```

To illustrate the reissuance of treasury stock, assume that the corporation subsequently sold 100 of the treasury shares on March 15 for $25 per share and another 100 shares on April 15 for $18 per share. The entries to record these transactions are as follows:

```
March 15   Cash ...............................  2,500
               Treasury Stock .....................        2,000
               Additional Paid-in Capital from Treasury
                   Stock Transactions. ...............        500
April 15   Cash ...............................  1,800
               Additional Paid-in Capital from Treasury
                   Stock Transactions .................        200
               Treasury Stock .....................        2,000
```

When the treasury shares were sold, the treasury stock account was credited for the acquisition cost and carrying value of the shares, or $20 per share. Further, note that the $200 excess of cost over the resale price in the April 15 sale was debited to an "additional paid-in capital from treasury stock transactions" account. In the absence of this account, the excess could be charged to other paid-in capital accounts or, if these are not sufficient, to retained earnings.

If a company holds treasury shares at the time financial statements are prepared, any balance in the treasury stock account should be shown as a deduction from total stockholders' equity. In addition, any restriction on the amount of retained earnings available for dividends should be disclosed. Additional paid-in capital from treasury stock transactions is reported in the contributed capital section of stockholders' equity. For example, the stockholders' equity of the corporation on April 15 would appear as follows:

[handwritten margin note: Retained Earning Source of money treasury stock.]

Common stock, $10 par value, 10,000 shares authorized and issued of which 100 shares are in the treasury.		$100,000
Additional paid-in capital:		
From stock issuances.	$20,000	
From treasury stock transactions.	300	20,300
Total Contributed Capital.		$120,300
Retained earnings (of which $2,000 is not available for dividends because of the purchase of treasury stock).		30,000
Total.		$150,300
Less: Treasury stock at cost (100 shares).		2,000
Total Stockholders' Equity		$148,300

[handwritten margin note: Recording of treasury stock]

For various reasons, stockholders may donate shares of stock to the corporation. Since there is no cost to the corporation, no entry is required for the receipt of the donated stock. When these shares are resold, the entire proceeds would be credited to the additional paid-in capital from treasury stock transactions account. An alternative treatment is to record donated treasury stock at its fair market value as of the date of donation with a corresponding credit to a donated capital account. If this procedure is followed, subsequent entries affecting treasury stock would be recorded in the same manner as if the treasury stock had been purchased.

RETAINED EARNINGS

Retained earnings is that portion of stockholders' equity which results from the total net earnings of the firm less any dividends paid to stockholders since its inception. Accumulated earnings include income from normal operations and discontinued operations, extraordinary gains or losses, and prior period adjustments. Thus, the following types of transactions all affect retained earnings, either directly or indirectly.

1. Transfer of the net income or loss for the period to retained earnings (including discontinued operations and extraordinary gains or losses).
2. Reduction in retained earnings for dividends declared during the period.
3. Increase or decrease in retained earnings for prior period adjustments.
4. Transfer from or to appropriation accounts.

The first three types of entries have been discussed previously. The appropriation of retained earnings is discussed below.

Appropriation of Retained Earnings

In general, the balance in the retained earnings account of a corporation is the amount which is legally available for dividend distribution to stockholders. However, in some cases the board of directors may restrict the amount of retained earnings that can be used to pay dividends. Such restrictions may be required either by law or by contract, or they may be made at the discretion of the board of directors. For example, retained earnings available for dividends are often legally limited by the cost of any treasury stock held by the company. In addition, contractual agreements with creditors or certain classes of stockholders may also impose limitations on the amount of retained earnings which is available for dividends. On the other hand, the board of directors may desire to voluntarily restrict dividends in order to provide for a future use of the assets represented by accumulated earnings. For example, a firm may wish to retain assets generated from profitable operations for future expansion of the business.

There are several methods which may be used for disclosing such restrictions on the amount of the retained earnings available for distribution to shareholders. The simplest and probably the most logical method is to indicate the amount and nature of the restriction by footnote or parenthetical disclosure in the financial statements. However, because many stockholders may not readily understand such disclosures, an alternative is to reclassify a portion of the retained earnings in order to indicate the amount of earnings which is unavailable for dividends. This reclassification, referred to as an appropriation, is accomplished by transferring the desired amount of retained earnings to an appropriation account.

To illustrate an appropriation of retained earnings, assume that the directors of a corporation with retained earnings of $300,000 decide that $100,000 of retained earnings should be restricted for future plant expansion. The following entry is necessary to record this appropriation:

Retained Earnings	100,000	
Appropriation for Plant Expansion.		100,000

This appropriation does not affect either the assets or liabilities of the corporation. The appropriation account is not an asset to be used for expansion nor does it guarantee that cash or other assets will actually be available for this purpose. Instead, it merely restricts the assets that may be distributed to shareholders. Further, the appropriation does not change the total retained earnings; it simply divides it into appropriated and unappropriated segments. The retained earnings of the corporation in the example would appear as follows after the appropriation was made:

Retained earnings:		
Appropriated for plant expansion	$100,000	
Unappropriated	200,000	
Total Retained Earnings	$300,000	

When the purpose for the appropriation ceases to exist, the amount of the appropriated retained earnings account should be transferred back to unappropriated retained earnings. Since an appropriation represents a segregation of retained earnings, no other entry may be made to this account. For example, assume that the corporation in the previous illustration completed the desired expansion of the business. The appropriation would be restored to unappropriated retained earnings by means of the following entry:

Appropriation for Plant Expansion	100,000	
Retained Earnings		100,000

In recent years, the formal appropriation of retained earnings has been recognized as potentially confusing or misleading to the users of financial statements. Consequently, there has been a trend to disclose both voluntary and required restriction of retained earnings in the notes accompanying the financial statements.

Statement of Retained Earnings

Normally, the periodic financial statements issued by a corporation include a statement of retained earnings as well as a balance sheet, income statement, and statement of changes in financial position. The retained earnings statement indicates all changes which have occurred in that account during the period. The format of the statement varies considerably, and sometimes the changes in retained earnings are included with income data in a combined statement of income and retained earnings. The general form of the statement is illustrated below.

REDSKINS COMPANY
Statement of Retained Earnings
For the Year Ended December 31, 1976

Balance at beginning of the year:		
As originally reported		$200,000
Prior period adjustment–settlement of a		
lawsuit applicable to 1975.		(50,000)
Restated balance		$150,000
Add: Net income for the year		90,000
		$240,000
Less: Cash dividends:		
$6 per share on preferred	$30,000	
$5 per share on common	50,000	(80,000)
Balance at end of the year		$160,000

A combined income statement and statement of retained earnings for Anheuser-Busch, Inc. for 1973 is presented in Illustration 2–10 on page 40.

BOOK VALUE PER SHARE OF COMMON STOCK

The book value of a share of stock is the amount of stockholders' equity which is applicable to a single share of stock. Since the stockholders' equity is equal to total assets minus total liabilities, book value also represents the net assets per share of stock. Data on book value per share of a corporation's common stock is often included in corporate annual reports and in the financial press.

If a corporation has only common stock outstanding, book value per share is computed by dividing total stockholders' equity by the number of shares outstanding. When a corporation has both preferred and common stock outstanding, the stockholders' equity must be divided between or among the various classes of stock. This allocation depends on the nature of the preferred stock. Generally, if preferred stock is nonparticipating, the equity allocated to the preferred shares is an amount equal to the liquidation or redemption value of the preferred stock plus any cumulative dividends in arrears. To illustrate, assume that a corporation has the following stockholders' equity:

5% cumulative preferred stock, $100 par value, 1,000 shares authorized and outstanding, (callable at $106)		$100,000
Common stock, $10 par value, 20,000 shares authorized, issued, and outstanding		200,000
Additional paid-in capital:		
On preferred stock	$40,000	
On common stock	10,000	50,000
Total Contributed Capital		$350,000
Retained earnings		56,000
Total Stockholders' Equity		$406,000

If there are no unpaid dividends on the preferred stock, equity equal to the call price or redemption value of the preferred stock ($106 per share) is allocated to the preferred shares, and the remainder applies to the common stock. Thus, the book value per share of common stock is computed as follows:

Total stockholders' equity	$406,000
Less: Amount allocated to preferred	106,000
Equity to common stock	$300,000

$$\text{Book value per share of common stock} = \frac{\$300,000}{20,000} = \$15$$

If there are unpaid preferred dividends, an additional amount equal to the arrearage is allocated to the preferred stock. For example, assume that the preferred stock mentioned in the previous illustration had one year of dividends in arrears. In that situation, the unpaid preferred dividends of $5,000 would also be allocated to the preferred stock, and the book value per share of common stock would be computed as follows:

Total stockholders' equity		$406,000
Less: Amount allocated to preferred:		
Redemption value	$106,000	
Dividends in arrears	5,000	111,000
Equity to common stock		$295,000

$$\text{Book value per share of common stock} = \frac{\$295,000}{20,000} = \$14.75$$

Because the market value of the assets may differ from book values based on generally accepted accounting principles, the book value per share does not indicate the amount that would be distributed to the owner of each share of stock if the assets of the corporation were sold and its liabilities were paid. That is, any gains or losses from the disposal of assets or the settlement of liabilities, and any expenses involved in the liquidation process, would affect the shareholders' equity. As noted above, book value per share is not necessarily equal to the market price of the stock. Although book value per share may have some effect on the market price, market price is much more likely to be influenced by factors such as current and expected future earnings, dividend prospects, and general economic conditions. Depending upon the specific circumstances, book value per share may be more or less than market price per share. Therefore, book value data should be used with extreme caution in making decisions concerning the value of a corporation's stock.

KEY DEFINITIONS

Appropriation of retained earnings An appropriation of retained earnings is the reclassification of a portion of retained earnings by transfer to an appropriation account.

Book value per share Book value per share is the amount of stockholders' equity (i.e., net assets) applicable to each share of common stock outstanding.

Capitalization of retained earnings The capitalization of retained earnings is an amount which is transferred from retained earnings to contributed capital at the time a stock dividend is declared.

Cash dividend A cash dividend is a distribution of cash to stockholders in the form of a dividend.

Change due to accounting errors Changes due to accounting errors may result from errors in the application of accounting principles, oversights, misuse of facts, or mistakes in mathematics.

Change in accounting estimate A change in accounting estimate occurs as additional information modifying an original estimate is obtained.

Change in accounting principle A change in accounting principle results from the adoption of a generally accepted accounting principle which differs from one that was previously used.

Date of declaration The date of declaration is the date on which the board of directors formally establishes a liability for a dividend of a specified amount to the stockholders.

Date of payment The date of payment of a dividend is the date on which the dividends are paid to the stockholders of record.

Date of record The date of record of a dividend is the date on which the corporation prepares a list of stockholders who are to receive the dividends.

Deficit A deficit is a debit balance in the retained earnings account.

Discontinued operations Discontinued operations refers to the operations of any subsidiary, division, or department of a business that has been, or will be sold, abandoned, or disposed of.

Dividends   Dividends are distributions which are made by a corporation to its shareholders.

Earnings per share   The earnings per share is the amount of net income per share of the common stock outstanding during a period.

Extraordinary item   An extraordinary item is a gain or loss which is both unusual in nature and not reasonably expected to recur in the foreseeable future. As a result of *Opinions No. 9* and *No. 30* of the Accounting Principles Board, these items are reported as separate amounts in the income statement.

Prior period adjustment   Prior period adjustments are items of gain or loss which represent material corrections of reported earnings of prior periods and are shown as a direct adjustment of retained earnings.

Retained earnings   Retained earnings represent the accumulated earnings of the corporation, increased by net income and reduced by net losses and distributions to shareholders.

Stock dividend   A stock dividend is a distribution of additional shares to the stockholders in proportion to their existing holdings.

Stock split   A stock split is a proportionate increase in the number of shares outstanding, usually intended to effect a decrease in the market value of the stock.

Treasury stock   Treasury stock consists of shares of stock which have been previously issued and are reacquired by the corporation but not formally retired.

QUESTIONS

1. Distinguish between an ordinary item and an extraordinary item on an income statement. How is an extraordinary item presented in the income statement?

2. What are the criteria for determining if an item is a prior period adjustment? Where is a prior period adjustment shown in the financial statements?

3. Define earnings per share of common stock. Where is this information shown in the financial statements?

4. What is the effect on earnings per share presentation when a company has extraordinary gains or losses?

5. Describe the nature of the following three dates related to dividends: (*a*) date of declaration, (*b*) date of record, and (*c*) date of payment. What is the accounting significance of each of these dates?

6. Distinguish between a cash dividend and a stock dividend.

7. Why does a corporation normally declare (*a*) a stock dividend and (*b*) a stock split?

8. Why is a portion of retained earnings capitalized upon the issuance of a stock dividend?

9. What is the difference between a stock dividend and a stock split? How does the accounting for a large stock dividend and a stock split differ?

10. For what purposes might a company purchase shares of its own stock?

11. What is treasury stock? How does it affect the ability of the corporation to pay dividends? How does it differ from authorized but unissued stock?

12. What is the effect on stockholders' equity when treasury stock is reissued for (a) more than the original cost, (b) less than its cost to the corporation?

13. What is the purpose of an appropriation of retained earnings? How does a company provide for and eliminate an appropriation of retained earnings?

14. What is the significance of the book value per share of common stock? Does the book value equal the amount of assets which would be distributed to each share of stock upon liquidation? Explain.

15. How is the book value per share of common stock computed when there is preferred stock outstanding?

EXERCISES

13-1   Assume that Ham Farm Supplies, Inc. had income after taxes from normal operations for 1974 of $200,000. Also, the firm had an extraordinary loss of $40,000 (net of tax). The firm had 25,000 shares of stock outstanding throughout 1974. Compute the earnings per share figures required by APB *Opinion No. 15*.

13-2   Make the journal entries necessary to record the declaration and payment of dividends in each of the following situations:

   a. Bruin Company has 8,000 shares of common stock and 3,000 shares of 7 percent, $100 par value preferred stock outstanding. On June 15 the company declares a preferred dividend and a $3.50 per share dividend on the common stock. The dividends are payable on July 15 to the stockholders of record on June 30.

   b. Wolfpack Company has 10,000 shares of $15 par value common stock outstanding. On May 1 the company declares a 10 percent stock dividend to be distributed on May 15. At the time, the market price of a share is $19.

13-3   On March 15, the board of directors of Gunsmith Corporation declared a cash dividend of $1 per share to the stockholders of record on March 20. The dividend is payable on April 1. The corporation had 10,000 shares of common stock outstanding. Prepare the journal entries required on the date of declaration, the date of record, and the payment date.

13-4   The Robinson Corporation was organized in 1970. The company was authorized to issue 5,000 shares of $50 par value common and 1,000 shares of $100 par value, cumulative preferred stock. All of the preferred and 4,000 shares of common were issued at par. The preferred was entitled to dividends of 6 percent before any dividends were paid to common. During the first 5 years of its existence, the corporation earned a total of $120,000 and paid dividends of 50 cents per share each year on common stock.

Required:

Prepare *in good form* the stockholders' equity section as of December 31, 1974.

13–5   Shown below is the stockholders' equity section of the balance sheet of Falcon Company at December 31, 1975.

Common stock, 10,000 shares issued and outstanding,	
$10 par value	$100,000
Additional paid-in capital	50,000
Retained earnings.	75,000
Total Stockholders' Equity	$225,000

On January 1, 1976 the company reacquired 500 shares of its stock at $15 per share.

Required:

a.   Prepare the entry to record the purchase of the stock.
b.   Give the entry to record the reissuance of the treasury stock at $18 per share.
c.   Prepare the entry to record the reissuance of the stock at $13 per share.

13–6   Arnold Company had a $100,000 balance in its retained earnings account on January 1, 1975. On January 2, 1975, by action of the board of directors, $25,000 of retained earnings was appropriated for future plant expansion. The plant expansion was completed on December 31, 1976, and the appropriation of retained earnings was released.

Required:

a.   Give the journal entry necessary to record the appropriation.
b.   Give the entry necessary to release the appropriation.

13–7   The stockholders' equity section of the balance sheet of Park Company on December 31, 1975, is shown below.

6% preferred stock, $100 par value (callable at $105) 5,000	
shares authorized, issued, and outstanding.	$ 500,000
Common stock, $5 par value, 60,000 shares, authorized	
and 50,000 shares issued and outstanding	250,000
Additional paid-in capital	400,000
Retained earnings.	75,000
Total Stockholders' Equity	$1,225,000

Required:

Compute the book value per share of common stock.

13–8   Williams Company purchased a machine for $22,000 on January 1, 1970. At the time, it was estimated to have a useful life of 10 years and a salvage value of $2,000. Depreciation was recorded for five years on the straight-line basis. During 1975, it was determined that the total estimated life of the machine should be 15 years with the same estimated salvage value. Prepare the entry to record the depreciation expense for 1975.

13–9 Walters Company purchased a machine for $15,000 on January 1, 1970. At that time, it was estimated to have a useful life of 5 years and no salvage value. Depreciation was recorded for 1970 and 1971 using the sum-of-the-years'-digits method. During 1972, the company decided to change to the straight-line method of depreciation.

Required:

a. Give the adjusting entry required to record the change in depreciation method.
b. Give the journal entry to record depreciation expense for 1972.

PROBLEMS

Series A

13A–1 Certain account balances of the Gobbler Company as of December 31, 1975, are shown below.

Sales	$1,000,000
Cost of goods sold	500,000
Gain on sale of Meat Packing Division (net of tax)	100,000
Loss from earthquake (net of tax)	50,000
Operating expenses	350,000
Cash dividends:	
Common stock	250,000
Preferred stock	100,000
Loss on lawsuit (net of tax)	100,000
Taxes on income from normal operations	75,000

The retained earnings balance on December 31, 1974, was $850,000. The sale of the Division should be treated as a discontinued operation and the loss on the lawsuit qualifies as a prior period adjustment.

Required:

a. Prepare an income statement for 1975.
b. Prepare a statement of retained earnings for the year ended December 31, 1975.

13A–2 The income statement for Bonko Company for the year ending December 31, 1975, is shown below.

BONKO COMPANY
Income Statement
For the Year Ended December 31, 1975

Sales	$200,000
Cost of goods sold	100,000
Gross profit	$100,000
Operating expenses	80,000
Income before extraordinary items	$ 20,000
Extraordinary gain (net of tax)	10,000
Net income	$ 30,000

Bonko Company had 60,000 shares of common stock outstanding during 1975. Compute earnings per share for 1975.

13A–3   By using the following code, indicate each transaction's effect on the respective columns.

+ = increases
− = decreases
0 = no effect
? = cannot be determined

The market value of the company's common stock exceeds par value.

	Common Stock	Retained Earnings	Stockholders' Equity	Book Value per Share of Common Stock
Company declared a cash dividend payable in the next fiscal year to persons holding shares of preferred stock.	0	0	0	0
Company received shares of its own common stock, donated by a wealthy shareholder.	0	0	−	0
Company purchased shares of its own common stock through a broker at the New York Stock Exchange.	0	0	−	0
Company declared and issued a stock dividend on the common stock.	+	−	0	0
A cash dividend was declared and paid.	0	−	−	−
Retained Earnings were appropriated for plant expansion.	0	0	0	0
Treasury shares of common stock were sold at an amount in excess of the purchase price to the corporation.	0	0	+	+

13A–4   The stockholders' equity section of the Buckeye Company appeared as follows on January 1:

Common stock, $15 par value, 20,000 shares authorized,
    issued, and outstanding $300,000
Additional paid-in capital   75,000
Total contributed capital $375,000
Retained earnings.   80,000
    Total Stockholders' Equity $455,000

On February 1, the company purchased 800 of its outstanding shares at $25 per share. On June 15, the company reissued 500 of these shares at $29 per share. Then, on July 15, the company resold the other 300 shares for $24 per share.

Required:

Prepare the journal entries necessary to record the above transactions on the books of the Buckeye Company. Also, prepare the stockholders' equity section of their balance sheet as of July 15.

13A–5   The stockholders' equity section of the X Corporation as of December 31, 1974 shows:

120,000 x3 = 360,000

6% preferred, cumulative capital stock,
    $100 par value, 50,000 shares authorized,
    20,000 shares issued and outstanding $2,000,000
Common stock, no par, $10 stated value,
    400,000 shares authorized, 260,000
    shares issued and outstanding   2,600,000
Additional paid-in capital:
    On preferred stock . . . . $ 80,000
    On common stock 1,560,000   1,640,000
Retained earnings.   1,200,000
    Total Stockholders' Equity $7,440,000

NOTE: Dividends on preferred stock are three years in arrears.

Required:

Compute the book value per share of the common stock at December 31, 1974.

13A–6   The Texan Co. had the following stockholders' equity on January 1, 1974.

Common stock, $5 par value, 100,000 shares authorized,
    50,000 shares issued and outstanding $250,000
Additional paid-in capital   150,000
    Total Contributed Capital. $400,000
Retained Earnings   100,000
    Total Stockholders' Equity $500,000

During 1974, the company had the following transactions related to the stockholders' equity:

January 20	Issued 5,000 shares of stock for $10 per share.
February 15	Purchased 3,000 shares of Texan Co. common stock for $11 per share.
May 10	Declared a $.20 per share cash dividend to the stockholders of record on May 15. The dividend is payable on June 1.
June 1	Paid the cash dividend.
June 15	Sold 1,000 shares of treasury stock for $13 per share.
August 15	Sold 1,000 shares of treasury stock for $10 per share.
September 10	Declared a 10 percent stock dividend for the stockholders of record on September 15 to be distributed on October 1. The market price of the stock was $11 per share on September 15.
October 1	Distributed the stock dividend.
November 1	The Board of Directors decided to appropriate $20,000 of retained earnings for future plant expansion.
December 31	Net income for the year was $35,000. The income summary and dividend accounts were closed to retained earnings

Required:

1. Give the necessary journal entries to record the transactions.
2. Prepare a statement of retained earnings at December 31, 1974.

13A–7   The stockholders' equity of the National Company at December 31, 1973, was as follows:

6% noncumulative preferred stock, $100 par value, call price per share $110, authorized 70,000 shares, issued 10,000 shares	$1,000,000
$5 noncumulative preferred stock, $100 par value, call price per share $105, authorized 100,000 shares, issued 5,000 shares.	500,000
Common stock, $50 par value, authorized 100,000 shares, issued 40,000 shares, of which 1,000 shares are held in the treasury.	2,000,000
Additional paid-in capital:	
On 6% preferred stock	100,000
On common stock	255,000
Total Contributed Capital.	$3,855,000
Retained earnings (of which $60,000, an amount equal to the cost of the treasury stock purchased, is unavailable for dividends)	1,500,000
	$5,355,000
Deduct: Cost of treasury stock (1000 shares)	60,000
Total Stockholders' Equity	$5,295,000

NOTE: Preferred dividends for 1972 and 1973 have not been paid.

During 1974, National Company had the following transactions affecting the stockholders' equity:

January 5	Sold 11,000 shares of the common stock at $55 per share.
February 1	Declared a 10 percent stock dividend on the common stock; the market value of the stock on that date was $60 per share.
February 28	Paid the stock dividend declared on February 1.
May 1	Purchased 500 shares of the common stock for the treasury at a cost of $65 per share.
May 5	Sold all of the treasury stock held for $70 per share.
May 9	Stockholders voted to reduce the par value of common stock to $25 per share and increase authorized shares to 200,000. The Company issued the additional shares to effect this stock split.
June 30	The Board of Directors declared a $1 per share dividend on common stock and the regular annual dividend on both classes of preferred stock. All dividends are payable on July 20 to shareholders of record as of July 10.

Required:

1. Prepare the necessary journal entries to record the preceding transactions.
2. Prepare the stockholders' equity section of the balance sheet at June 30, 1974.

Series B

13B–1 Selected account balances of the Aggie Company as of December 31, 1975, are listed below.

Sales	$1,600,000
Cost of goods sold	900,000
Loss on sale of a segment of a business (net of tax)	150,000
Loss from earthquake (net of tax)	100,000
Loss from lawsuit	50,000
Operating expenses	300,000
Cash dividends:	
Common stock	75,000
Preferred stock	50,000
Taxes on income from normal operations	200,000

The retained earnings balance on January 1, 1975 was $1,200,000. The earthquake loss qualifies an an extraordinary item.

Required:

a. Prepare an income statement for 1975.
b. Prepare a statement of retained earnings for 1975.

13B–2 The income statement for the Smith Co. as of December 31, 1975, appeared as follows:

SMITH CO.
Income Statement
For the Year Ended December 31, 1975

Sales	$1,000,000
Less: Cost of goods sold	600,000
Gross margin.	$ 400,000
Operating expenses	200,000
Income before extraordinary items.	$ 200,000
Extraordinary loss (net of tax)	(60,000)
Net income	$ 140,000

Compute the earnings per share for 1975 assuming that the company has only common stock and there were 100,000 shares outstanding during 1975.

13B–3   The stockholders' equity of Tarheel, Inc., appears as follows on their January 1, 1975, balance sheet.

Common stock, $5 par value, 19,000 shares outstanding	$ 95,000
Additional paid-in capital	35,000
Total Contributed Capital.	$130,000
Retained earnings.	60,000
Total Stockholders' Equity	$190,000

Make the journal entries necessary to record the transactions in the following independent cases:

a.   Tarheel, Inc., declares and distributes a 50 percent stock dividend on June 1 when its stock is selling at $35 per share.

b.   Tarheel, Inc., declares a 2-for-1 stock split on June 1 when the market price of its stock is $50 per share.

c.   Tarheel, Inc., declares and distributes a 5 percent stock dividend on June 1 when the market price of its stock is $10 per share.

13B–4   The Peterson Company was organized on January 1, 1970, with 10,000 shares of $10 par value common stock authorized, issued, and outstanding. Journalize the following transactions which took place in 1974:

January 1	The Corporation purchased 100 shares of its common stock for $15 a share.
February 1	The Corporation sold the 100 shares purchased on January 1 for a total price of $1,750.
March 1	Mrs. Moneybags, a stockholder, donated 100 shares of the X Corporation's common stock to the Corporation.
March 5	The Corporation sold the 100 donated shares for a total price of $2,500.
April 1	The Corporation purchased 100 shares of its own stock for $9 a share.

May 1 The Corporation sold the 100 shares purchased on April 1 for a total price of $500.

December 15 A $.50 per share dividend on common stock was declared, to be paid on January 15, 1975.

13B–5 Thurmond Company's stockholders' equity section of its balance sheet appeared as follows on January 1, 1974.

7% cumulative preferred stock, $100 par value, 2,000 shares authorized, issued, and outstanding (callable at 107)		$200,000
Common stock, $20 par value, 8,000 shares authorized, issued, and outstanding		160,000
Additional paid-in capital:		
Preferred stock	$25,000	
Common stock	30,000	55,000
Total Contributed Capital.		$415,000
Retained earnings.		70,000
Total Stockholders' Equity		$485,000

The preferred stock of Thurmond Company has two years of dividends in arrears.

Required:

Compute the book value per share of the common stock.

13B–6 Below is given the stockholders' equity section of the balance sheet of the Virginia Company as of December 31, 1975:

6% preferred stock, $100 par value, 1,000 shares authorized, 100 shares issued and outstanding, callable at $110	$10,000
Common stock, $5 par value, 20,000 shares authorized, 200 shares issued, 180 shares outstanding	1,000
Additional paid-in capital:	
On common stock	2,000
From treasury stock transactions.	100
From preferred stock	2,000
Retained earnings.	40,000
Treasury stock, 20 shares, at cost	(150)
Stockholders' Equity.	$54,950

Required: ·

a. Using the above stockholders' equity section, you are to prepare journal entries for each of the transactions which follow. Each transaction is to be treated as *independent* of all others *unless* otherwise noted.

1. Sold 10 shares of common at par.
2. Sold 10 shares of common at $7 per share.
3. Sold 10 shares of common at $4 per share.
4. Obtained subscriptions to 10 shares of common at a price of $8 per share.

5. Received cash and issued shares for the 10 shares subscribed to in (4) above.
6. Declared the annual dividend on the preferred stock and a $1 per share dividend on the common stock.
7. Date of record on the dividend in (6) above.
8. Paid the dividend in (6) above.
9. Declared a 10 percent stock dividend on the common stock; the fair market value of the common stock was $15 per share.
10. Date of record on the dividend declared in (9) above.
11. Distributed the dividend in (9) above.
12. Split the common stock 5 for 1 and changed the par value to $1 per share.
13. Sold the treasury shares for $150.
14. Sold the treasury shares for $200.
15. Sold the treasury shares for $30.

b. Calculate the book value per share of common stock from the stockholders' equity section shown above.

13B–7 The Jones Co. was organized on January 1, 1970, with 20,000 shares of $10 par value common stock and 5,000 shares of $100 par value, 6 percent preferred stock authorized. The balances in the stockholders' equity accounts on December 31, 1973, were as follows:

Preferred stock	$100,000
Common stock	120,000
Additional paid-in capital:	
On preferred stock	5,000
On common stock	60,000
Retained earnings.	$190,000

During 1974, the company had the following transactions that affected the stockholders' equity:

		Number	Amount
a.	Issuance of common stock.	5,000	$ 20 per share
b.	Purchase of its own shares of		
	common stock	4,000	$ 22 per share
c.	Reissuance of treasury stock.	1,000	$ 24 per share
d.	Issuance of preferred stock	1,000	$102 per share
e.	Payment of dividend on common stock		$ .50 per share
f.	Payment of dividend on preferred stock		$ 6 per share
g.	Appropriation of retained earnings for		
	future plant expansion		$100,000
h.	Net income for the year		$ 60,000
i.	Stock split on common stock with par		
	value reduced to $5 per share	2 for 1	

Prepare the stockholders' equity section of the balance sheet for Jones Co. on December 31, 1974.

14

Liabilities

LIABILITIES are obligations of a firm which arise from past transactions and which are to be discharged at a future date by payment of cash, transfer of other assets, or performance of a service. In an economic system such as ours, which is based so extensively on credit, almost all business concerns incur liabilities.

Creditors of a business have claims against the assets of the firm. Depending upon the nature of the particular liability, a claim may either be against specific assets or against assets in general. In any case, claims of creditors have priority over the claims of owners. Thus, in the event of the liquidation of a business, all debts must be satisfied before any payments are made to owners.

Amounts shown in the balance sheet as liabilities may be classified as either current or noncurrent liabilities. A proper distinction between current and noncurrent liabilities is essential because comparison of current assets with current liabilities is an important means of evaluating the short-run liquidity or debt-paying ability of the firm.

This chapter considers the problems related to the determination and presentation of both current liabilities and noncurrent, or long-term, liabilities.

CURRENT LIABILITIES

Current liabilities are those debts or obligations of a firm that must either be paid in cash or settled by providing goods or services within the operating cycle of the firm or one year, whichever is longer. Recall that the operating cycle of a business is the average period of time that elapses between purchase of an inventory item and conversion of the inventory into cash. This cycle includes the initial purchase of the inventory, the sale of the item on credit, and the collection of the receivable. The most common current liabilities include accounts payable, notes payable, and accrued liabilities.

Accounts Payable

The major source of accounts payable are debts to trade creditors for goods or services purchased on a credit basis by the business. Other accounts payable may consist of various debts such as advances from officers, employees, or stockholders, or refundable deposits which were made by customers. Accounts payable are normally classified in terms of their origin in the balance sheet.

An account payable does not usually involve the payment of interest, and there is no formal written promise to pay signed by debtor.

Notes Payable

A note payable is a *written* promise to pay a definite sum of money on demand or at some future date to the holder of the note. Notes payable may result from several different types of transactions. For example, a note may be used when money is borrowed from a bank to obtain an extension of the due date of an open account payable, or for the purchase of real estate, equipment, or other assets.

The date on which a note becomes due and payable is referred to as its maturity date. In addition to the principal amount, the borrower is usually required to pay interest over the term of the note. Interest that the borrower pays is an expense and is deducted in arriving at his net income for the period. Interest is normally expressed as an annual rate, regardless of the actual period of time the note will be outstanding. Interest on a note is computed as follows:

$$\text{Interest} = \text{Principal} \times \text{Rate} \times \text{Time}$$

Since many notes involve a period of less than a year, time is usually expressed in days. For purposes of simplifying interest calculations, it is usually assumed that a year has 360 days. For example, assume that Bennett Co. borrows $1,000 from its bank and signs a 90-day, 8 percent note. Interest on this note for the 90-day period would be computed as follows:

$$\$1,000 \times \frac{8}{100} \times \frac{90}{360} = \$20$$

Interest actually accrues continuously over the period that an interest-bearing note remains outstanding. Therefore, no interest expense is recorded at the time a note is issued. The journal entry on the books of Bennett Co. to record the bank loan is:

```
Cash ....................................... 1,000
      Notes Payable. ...............................        1,000
```

When a note is paid at its maturity, the borrower must pay both the principal amount of the note and the interest. The entry to record the payment of the note by Bennett Co. is as follows:

```
Notes Payable . .................................. 1,000
Interest Expense ................................    20
      Cash . .....................................        1,020
```

Discounted Notes. Another common method used by the lender to charge interest on a note is to deduct the interest (often referred to as a discount) from the principal amount at the time the note is issued. If this form of a note is used, the interest is deducted in advance rather than paid at maturity.

For example, assume that Stanga Co. borrows $1,000 on a 90-day note bearing an 8 percent rate of discount. Nominal interest on this note is the same as on the 8 percent interest-bearing note—only the time the interest is paid differs. The entry to record the note is:

```
Cash ....................................... 980
Discount on Notes Payable .........................  20
      Notes Payable. ...............................        1,000
```

Since interest accrues over time, the $20 which is shown as a discount on notes payable at the date the note is issued is not interest expense at that point in time. The actual net liability to the bank at the date of the loan is equal to the amount of cash received, or $980. Therefore, a balance sheet prepared at the time of the loan would include Discount on Notes Payable as a contra-liability deducted from Notes Payable as follows:

```
Notes payable ..................... $1,000
Less:  Discount on notes payable. ........    (20)
                                         $  980
```

When a note is paid at its maturity, two entries are required. The first entry records satisfaction of the liability, and the second entry reclassifies discount as interest expense. Entries for the Stanga Co. to record the payment are:

Discounted Note Paid At Maturity [handwritten annotation]

Notes Payable	1,000
Cash	1,000
Interest Expense	20
Discount on Notes Payable	20

Accrued Interest Expense

In the previous example, total interest expense applicable to the notes was recorded at the date payment was made. However, interest expense related to a note is actually accumulating or accruing continuously over the period the note is outstanding. Therefore, when a note is issued in one accounting period and is due and payable in a subsequent period, interest expense should be apportioned between the periods during which the note is outstanding. This allocation is accomplished by an end-of-period adjusting entry.

To illustrate, assume that Butkus Co. borrows $1,000 from its bank on December 1, 1976, on a 6 percent, two month note. Total interest on this note is $10 ($1,000 \times \frac{6}{100} \times \frac{60}{360}$). If the firm's accounting period ends on December 31, interest for one month ($5 = $1,000 \times \frac{6}{100} \times \frac{30}{360}$) has accrued on the note. The required adjusting entry on December 31 is therefore:

to Record Interest Expense As it Accrues [handwritten annotation]

Interest Expense	5
Accrued Interest Payable	5

When the note matures in the next accounting period and is paid, payment is recorded by the following entry:

Notes Payable	1,000
Accrued Interest Payable	5
Interest Expense	5
Cash	1,010

A different format is required for the adjusting entry for notes payable in which interest is deducted in advance (i.e., the note was issued at a "discount"). The difference between the amount borrowed and the amount due at maturity is classified as Discounts on Notes Payable at the date of issuance. If this type of note remains outstanding at the end of an accounting period, an adjusting entry is necessary to reclassify a portion of Discount on Notes Payable as interest expense. For example, assume that on November 1, 1976, Sayers Co. borrows $1,000 on a 3-month note with a 6 percent rate of discount. The entry on November 1 to record the loan of $985 [$1,000 − ($1,000 \times \frac{6}{100} \times \frac{3}{12})$] would be:

Cash	985
Discount on Notes Payable	15
Notes Payable	1,000

The following adjusting entry is necessary on December 31 in order to recognize interest expense of $10 ($1,000 × $^6\!/_{100}$ × $^2\!/_{12}$) for the months of November and December:

Interest Expense	10	
Discount on Notes Payable		10

When the note matures and is paid, the entry to record the payment is as follows:

Notes Payable	1,000	
Interest Expense	5	
Cash		1,000
Discount on Notes Payable		5

Thus, the total interest expense recognized on the note and recorded in the accounts is $15—$10 in 1976 and $5 in 1977. This allocation is necessary in order to properly determine net income by "matching" revenues and expenses.

LONG-TERM LIABILITIES

When a corporation desires to raise additional capital for long-term purposes, it has several alternatives. It may borrow funds by issuing a long-term mortgage note or by issuing bonds, or it may obtain funds by issuing additional stock to shareholders. Each source of funds has its particular advantages and disadvantages to the issuing corporation. A bondholder is a creditor of a corporation while a stockholder is an owner. As creditors, bondholders normally do not participate in the management of the firm. Therefore, by issuing bonds, a corporation does not spread or dilute control of management over a larger number of owners.

Mortgage Notes

A firm may borrow funds by the use of a long-term note, for example, in order to finance a major expenditure such as the purchase of fixed assets. This is accomplished by placing a mortgage or lien on its property. The note indicates the terms of the loan (maturity date, interest rate, etc.) and the mortgage is in fact a conditional conveyance of property to the creditor as security for the loan. If the terms of the loan are not met, the holder of the mortgage has the right to foreclose in order to satisfy his claims. The terms of the mortgage usually require the borrower to maintain and insure the mortgaged property, to pay interest on the note, and make payments on the principal of the debt.

Since a mortgage note is essentially a long-term note payable, the entries required for a mortgage are similar to those for notes payable discussed earlier in this chapter. Any unpaid principal of the mortgage is classified as a long-term liability in the balance sheet. However, any payments which will become due on the principal during the next accounting period should be reclassified and shown separately as a current liability.

Borrowing by means of a mortgage note usually involves only a single lender. If it is impossible to obtain the desired funds from a single lender, bonds may be issued to a group of investors. The issuance of bonds allows a large loan to be divided among many lenders. Since long-term borrowing by corporations is usually effected by the use of bonds, the remainder of this chapter considers the accounting for bonds.

BOND OBLIGATIONS

Bonds are issued as a means of borrowing money for long-term purposes. The desired funds are obtained by issuing a number of bonds with a certain denomination (usually $1,000). Normally, a corporation sells all of its bonds to an investment firm, referred to as an underwriter. The underwriter then resells the bonds to investors. For accounting purposes, only the amount received from the underwriter is relevant to the issuing firm. Individual bonds are sold to investors with a promise to pay a definite sum of money to the holder at a fixed future date and periodic interest payments at a stated rate throughout the life of the liability. Since bonds usually do not name individual lenders, they may be bought and sold by investors until their maturity.

When funds are borrowed by issuing bonds, interest payments and the timing of the repayment of the principal of the debt to bondholders are obligations which are fixed in amount and must be paid at specified dates regardless of the amount of income earned by the firm. If the rate of earnings on invested funds exceeds the interest rate on the bonds, it is usually to the owners' advantage for the firm to issue bonds. However, if the expected rate of earnings is less than the interest rate, it would not be to the advantage of the owners to borrow funds. Furthermore, interest payments must be made when due regardless of whether or not sufficient income is earned. If interest payments are not made, the bondholders may bring action in order to foreclose against the assets of the corporation in the settlement of their claims. Bondholders are creditors and their claims for interest and the repayment of principal have priority over the claims of owners. Therefore, the feasibility of obtaining funds by issuing bonds depends upon factors such as the expected rate of interest and the stability of the earnings of the firm.

Bond interest payments are a deductible expense in the computation of taxable income, while dividends paid to owners are not deductible for tax purposes. Because of the magnitude of corporate income taxes (up to 48 percent of net income), the effect of taxes is often an important factor in determining the source which will be used by the business to obtain its long-term funds.

Approval of the board of directors and stockholders of the corporation is normally required prior to issuance of bonds. In addition, the firm issuing bonds selects a trustee to represent the bondholders. The trustee acts to protect the bondholders' interests, and takes legal action if the pledged responsibilities of the corporation are not satisfied.

CLASSES OF BONDS

Bonds may be either secured by specific assets or unsecured. Unsecured bonds are referred to as debenture bonds. Debenture bonds have as "security" the general credit standing of the issuing corporation. Therefore, debenture bonds are usually issued successfully only by companies with a favorable financial position.

A secured bond gives the bondholder a prior claim against specific assets in the event that the issuing corporation is unable to make the required interest or principal payments as they become due. Secured bonds differ as to the type of assets pledged. Real estate mortgage bonds are secured by a mortgage on specific land or buildings. Equipment trust bonds are secured by mortgages on tangible personal property such as equipment. Collateral trust bonds are secured by stocks and bonds of other companies owned by the corporation issuing the bonds.

A bond issue that matures on a single date is referred to as a term bond. Bonds that mature on several different dates and are retired in installments over a period of time are called serial bonds. Bonds that may be retired before maturity at the option of the issuing corporation are referred to as callable bonds. Bonds which may be exchanged for a specified amount of stock at the option of the bondholder are termed convertible bonds.

Bonds may also differ as to the method of interest payment. Registered bonds require that the bondholders' names be registered with the issuing corporation. The corporation issuing bonds is required to maintain a record of the current owners and periodic interest payments are mailed directly to the registered owners. Other bonds, called coupon bonds, have interest coupons attached which call for the payment of the required amount of interest on specified dates. A bond coupon is similar to a note payable to the holder at the date specified on the coupon. At each interest date the appropriate coupon may be detached by the bondholder and presented at a bank for payment.

Despite the wide variety of bonds offered, it should be noted that the value of bonds to the investor depends to a significant degree on the financial condition and long-term earning prospects of the issuing corporation. While the various optional provisions that may be included in a bond issue may affect the issue price of the bonds, it would be difficult for a company in poor financial condition to issue bonds regardless of the provisions.

When a corporation issues bonds, it is obligated to pay the principal or face amount of the bonds at a specified maturity date and to make periodic interest payments as well. The interest rate specified on the bonds is referred to as the coupon rate. The interest rate which investors are willing to accept on a bond at the time of its issue depends upon factors such as the market evaluation of the quality of the bond issue as evidenced by the financial strength of the business, the firm's earnings prospects and the particular provisions of the bond issue. This rate is referred to as the market or effective interest rate. If the effective interest rate exceeds the coupon rate, the issue price of the bonds will fall below the face amount of the bonds. When the issue price is less than face value, the difference is referred to as a discount. For example, if Pearson Co. offers bonds with an interest rate of 7 percent when the market rate is 8 percent for similar bonds, the selling price of the bonds will be less than their face value. Since annual interest payments on each $1,000 of bonds will be $70 (.07 × $1,000), the issue price of the bonds will fall to the point where the interest received will yield an effective rate of 8 percent. Similarly, if the coupon rate exceeds the market interest rate for comparable bonds at the time of the issue, the price of the bonds will exceed the face amount. That is, the bonds will be issued at a premium. The bonds will sell at their face amount only when the coupon rate is exactly equal to the market rate.[1]

Bonds Issued at Face Value

If the coupon rate offered on bonds is identical to the market rate, the bonds will be issued at their face value. To illustrate, assume that Dascher Co. had authorization to issue $100,000 of 25-year, 6 percent debenture bonds on January 1, 1976, with interest payable semiannually on June 30 and December 31. If $50,000 of the bonds are issued at face value on January 1, 1976, the entry for the issuance would be:

```
Cash ...................................... 50,000
    Bonds Payable .................................     50,000
```

No journal entry is made for the authorization of the bonds. The balance sheet, however, should disclose all of the pertinent facts with respect to the bond issue. For example, a balance sheet for Dascher Co. on January 1, 1976, would include the following information:

> Long-term liabilities:
> 6% debenture bonds payable,
>   due on December 31, 2000 . . . . . . $50,000

---

[1] The procedures for computing the selling price for a bond are presented in the appendix to this chapter.

After the bonds are issued, Dascher Co. must make semiannual interest payments of $1,500 on each June 30 and December 31 that the bonds remain outstanding ($50,000 $\times$ %$_{100}$ $\times$ ½). The entry to record each payment would be as follows:

```
Interest Expense ............................... 1,500
    Cash ......................................        1,500
```

If the accounting period used by the firm ends between interest dates, an adjusting entry must be made to accrue the interest expense from the last interest date to the end of the period. For example, if the accounting period of Dascher Co. ended on September 30, the following adjusting entry would be necessary in order to record the accrued interest expense of $750 ($50,000 $\times$ %$_{100}$ $\times$ %$_{12}$) from June 30 to September 30.

```
Interest Expense ................................. 750
    Interest Payable. ...........................      750
```

Interest expense will be closed to the Income Summary account, and interest payable will remain as a liability until the next regular semiannual interest payment. The entry to record the interest payment on December 31 would be:

```
Interest Expense ................................. 750
Interest Payable ................................. 750
    Cash ......................................        1,500
```

Issuance between Interest Dates

Once authorized, bonds may be issued at any time. Bonds are often issued at a time between the interest dates. Since the corporation will pay the full semiannual interest on all bonds outstanding at an interest date, the bondholder is usually required to purchase the interest that has accrued from the previous interest date to the date of sale. This interest paid by the bondholder is returned as part of the first interest payment after issuance. To illustrate, assume that the Dascher Co. bonds from the previous example were issued at face value plus accrued interest on March 1, 1976. The issue price would be $50,000 plus two months' interest of $500 (50,000 $\times$ %$_{100}$ $\times$ %$_{12}$). The entry to record the issuance is:

```
Cash ........................................... 50,500
    Bonds Payable .............................        50,000
    Interest Payable ..........................          500
```

On the first semiannual interest payment date, June 30, which occurs four months after issuance, a full six months' interest ($1,500) will be paid. Of this amount, $500 is a return to the investor of accrued interest paid at the time of the purchase of the bonds and the remaining $1,000 represents the interest expense for the four months since the issuance. Therefore, the entry for the interest payment on June 30, 1976, would be as follows:

Interest Payable.	500	
Interest Expense	1,000	
Cash		1,500

Issuance of Bonds at a Discount

When the coupon rate on a bond issue is less than the prevailing market interest rate for similar bonds, the bonds will sell at a discount. For example, assume the prevailing market interest rate exceeds 6 percent when Dascher Co. offers $50,000 face value of 6 percent, 25-year debenture bonds. As a result, assume that the $50,000 of Dascher Co. bonds are issued at a price of $47,500 on January 1, 1976. The $2,500 excess of the face value over the issue price represents a discount. Normally bonds are carried in the accounts at face value with the discount recorded in a separate contra account. The issuance of the bonds would be recorded by the following entry:

Cash	47,500	
Discount on Bonds Payable	2,500	
Bonds Payable		50,000

Although the issuing corporation receives less than the face amount of the issue when bonds are sold at a discount, the entire face amount must be repaid at maturity. Therefore, the total cost of borrowing includes the discount as well as the interest payments. To illustrate, the total interest cost to Dascher Co. for the bonds issued at a discount is computed as follows:

Amount to be repaid at maturity	$50,000
Amount received at issuance.	47,500
Excess of cash to be paid over cash received (discount)	$ 2,500
Cash interest payments ($3,000 annually for 25 years).	75,000
Total Interest Cost	$77,500

The average yearly interest expense over the period until the maturity of the bonds is $3,100 ($77,500 ÷ 25). Therefore, in order to reflect the total interest cost of the bonds, bond discount should be allocated to expense over the 25-year life of the bonds as additional interest expense. The process of transferring a portion of bond discount to interest expense during each period is referred to as amortization. One common method of amortizing discount is to transfer or write off equal amounts at each interest payment date. This process is referred to as straight-line amortization.[2] In the illustration above, application of the straight-line method would yield amortization of $100 ($\frac{1}{25} \times$ $2,500) each year, or $50 on each semiannual interest date. The following entry would be made at each interest payment date.

```
Interest Expense ...............................  1,550
    Discount on Bonds Payable ....................         50
    Cash .........................................      1,500
```

[handwritten annotation: "Amort", "Interest over time"]

Because of the amortization of the discount, total interest expense recorded over the life of the bond issue will be equal to the cash interest payments plus the bond discount. Further, amortization reduces the balance in the Discount of Bonds Payable account to zero at the maturity date of the bonds.

Unamortized discount on bonds payable should be classified as a deduction from the related Bonds Payable account. To illustrate, the Dascher Co. bonds in the preceding example were issued at a discount of $2,500 on January 1, 1976. After two years, on December 31, 1977, a total of $200 ($2,500 $\times$ $\frac{2}{25}$) of the original discount would have been amortized, and the balance sheet would include the following amounts in the long-term liabilities section.

```
Long-term liabilities:
    6% debenture bonds payable, due on December 31, 2000. . . . . . .  $50,000
    Less:  Unamortized discount on bonds payable . . . . . . . . . . .    2,300   $47,700
```

If the accounting period of the firm falls between interest dates, amortization of bond discount must be included in the adjusting entry which is made for the accrual of interest expense. For example, if the accounting period of Dascher Co. ends on September 30, the following adjusting entry would be required in order to record the interest expense for the period from June 30 (the last regular interest payment date) to September 30.

```
Interest Expense ................................  775
    Discount on Bonds Payable .....................        25
    Interest Payable ..............................       750
```

The interest payable of $750 ($50,000 $\times$ $\frac{6}{100} \times \frac{3}{12}$) and the discount amortization of $25 ($\frac{1}{4} \times$ $100) is the interest expense for the three-month period since the last interest payment was made.

---

[2] The interest method of discount amortization is discussed in the appendix to this chapter.

Issuance of Bonds at a Premium

If the coupon rate on a bond issue exceeds the prevailing market interest rate for comparable bonds, the bonds will sell at an amount above their face value. The excess of the issue price over the face value is referred to as premium. For example, assume that $50,000 of Brenner Co. 25-year, 6 percent debenture bonds are issued on January 1, 1976, when the market rate is less than 6 percent. As a result, assume that the bonds are sold for $55,000. The entry to record the issuance of the bonds would be:

Cash	55,000	
Bonds Payable		50,000
Premium on Bonds Payable		5,000

When a premium is received on the issuance of bonds, the total cost of borrowing funds is equal to the cash interest payments made reduced by the amount of the premium. The total interest cost for Brenner Co. over the life of the bonds is calculated as follows:

Amount received at issuance.	$55,000
Amount to be repaid at maturity	50,000
Excess of cash received over cash paid (premium)	($ 5,000)
Cash interest payments ($3,000 × 25)	75,000
Total Interest Cost	$70,000

Like ADD.
Pd. in Capitol
Reduces the total Interest Cost.

The average yearly interest cost over the life of the bond issue is $2,800 ($70,000/25). Consequently, in order to reflect the actual interest cost of the bond issue, the premium should be periodically written-off or amortized as a reduction of the interest cost over the life of the issue. The procedures for the amortization of premium are similar to those used for bonds issued at a discount. In the Brenner Co. example, application of the straight-line method would result in premium amortization of $200 ($\frac{1}{25}$ × $5,000) each year, and, therefore, $100 on each semiannual interest date. The entry to record each semiannual interest payment and premium amortization would be as follows:

Interest Expense	1,400	
Premium on Bonds Payable	100	
Cash		1,500

The unamortized balance in the premium account would be reported as an addition to bonds payable on the balance sheet.

As indicated with respect to bond discount, if the firm's accounting period falls between interest payment dates, an adjusting entry is required in order to record the accrued interest expense and amortization of premium for the period since the last interest date.

Convertible Bonds

In certain circumstances, a company may issue bonds which are convertible at a specific rate into the common stock of the corporation at the option of the bondholder. This provision may be attached to a bond in order to enhance the marketability of the bond issue. The holder initially has the right of a creditor, but he may later convert to common stock and share in the earnings of the business.

The entries to record the issuance of convertible bonds are similar to those which were discussed previously. At the date of conversion, the carrying value of the bond (face value plus any premium or less any discount) is normally transferred to the stockholder equity accounts which are associated with the new shares of stock issued in the conversion. To illustrate, assume that a corporation had issued a $1,000, 10-year, convertible bond for $1,100 on January 1, 1972. The bond is convertible into 20 shares of $10 par value common stock at the option of the holder. Further assume that the holder converted the bond into common stock on December 31, 1976. At the time of the conversion, there is unamortized premium of $50. The entry to record the conversion would be as follows:

```
Bonds Payable. . . . . . . . . . . . . . . . . . . . . . . . . . . . . . . .   1,000
Premium . . . . . . . . . . . . . . . . . . . . . . . . . . . . . . . . . . . .      50
    Common Stock. . . . . . . . . . . . . . . . . . . . . . . . . . . . . .              200
    Additional Paid-in Capital. . . . . . . . . . . . . . . . . . . . . . .               850
```

RETIREMENT OF BONDS

Bonds may be retired by the issuing corporation at maturity or before the maturity date either by redeeming callable bonds or by repurchasing bonds in the open market. If bonds are retired at their maturity, any premium or discount will have been completely amortized and the entry to record the retirement of the bonds would be a debit to bonds payable and a credit to cash for an amount equal to the face or maturity value of the bonds.

Callable bonds may be redeemed at the option of the issuing corporation within a specified period and at a stated price referred to as the call price. The call price is usually an amount which is in excess of face value, with the excess referred to as call premium. In the absence of a call provision, the issuing corporation may retire its bonds by purchasing them in the open market at the prevailing market price.

If bonds are repurchased by the issuing corporation at a price less than their book value (i.e., maturity value less discount or plus premium), the corporation realizes a gain on the retirement of the bonds. The carrying value of the bonds is equal to the face value plus any unamortized premium or less any unamortized discount. Similarly, if the purchase price is greater than the carrying value, a loss is incurred on the retirement of the debt.

To illustrate a redemption prior to maturity, assume that the Carpenter Co. has a $50,000 bond issue outstanding with $2,000 of unamortized premium. Further assume that the corporation has the option of calling the bonds at 105 (i.e., 105 percent of the face value) and that the company exercises its call provision. The entry to record the redemption of the bonds for $52,500 ($50,000 × 1.05) would be as follows:

```
Bonds Payable. . . . . . . . . . . . . . . . . . . . . . . . . . . . . . .    50,000
Premium on Bonds Payable . . . . . . . . . . . . . . . . . . . . . .     2,000
Loss on Redemption . . . . . . . . . . . . . . . . . . . . . . . . . .       500
    Cash . . . . . . . . . . . . . . . . . . . . . . . . . . . . . . . . . .                52,500
```

If the bonds do not include a call provision, the corporation could purchase the bonds in the open market. For example, assume that Carpenter Co. purchased one fifth of the $50,000 face value bonds outstanding for $9,800. The carrying value of the bonds purchased is $10,400 (face value plus one fifth of the unamortized premium), while the purchase price is $9,800. Therefore, the company would realize a $600 gain on the retirement. The entry to record the retirement of the bonds would be as follows:

```
Bonds Payable. . . . . . . . . . . . . . . . . . . . . . . . . . . . . . .    10,000
Premium on Bonds Payable . . . . . . . . . . . . . . . . . . . . . .       400
    Gain on Retirement . . . . . . . . . . . . . . . . . . . . . . . . . .                 600
    Cash . . . . . . . . . . . . . . . . . . . . . . . . . . . . . . . . . .               9,800
```

BOND SINKING FUND

In order to offer additional security to the investor, a provision may be included in the bond indenture which requires the issuing corporation to set aside funds for repayment of the bond at maturity by periodic accumulations over the life of the issue. These funds may be accumulated by periodically depositing cash in a bond sinking fund. The cash deposited in the fund is usually invested in income producing assets. Therefore, the total deposits made by the issuing corporation over the life of the bond issue are normally less than the total maturity value of the bonds. At maturity, the securities in the fund are sold and the proceeds are used to retire the bonds.

Cash and securities in a sinking fund are not classified as current assets in the balance sheet since they are not available for the retirement of current liabilities. Instead, individual assets in the fund are normally shown as a single total under the caption of Investments. Similarly, earnings on the sinking fund assets are shown as a separate item in the income statement.

RESTRICTION ON DIVIDENDS   _or_   _Appropriation_

Another means of increasing the security of the bondholder is a provision whereby dividend payments by the issuing company will be restricted during the life of the bond issue. The actual restriction on dividends may vary. For example, a restriction may limit the payment of dividends during a given year to the excess of net income over the sinking fund requirements for the period. There are various methods for disclosing this restriction in the financial statements. Such a restriction could be shown by a footnote or parenthetically in the balance sheet. Alternatively, the restriction could be indicated by appropriating retained earnings each year. To illustrate, assume that the sinking fund requirement for the year is $20,000 and that net income is $35,000. If dividends are limited to the excess of net income over the sinking fund requirement, an appropriation of retained earnings could be made with the following entry:

```
Retained Earnings ...........................   20,000
     Appropriation for Bonded Debt .................        20,000
```

BALANCE SHEET PRESENTATION

The presentation of long-term liabilities in the balance sheet should disclose all information which is relevant to the debt including the maturity dates, interest rates, conversion privileges, etc. In addition, if a liability is secured by specific assets, or restricts the payment of dividends, such information should also be disclosed in the financial statements. To illustrate, the long-term liabilities section of the balance sheet might appear as follows:

```
Long-term liabilities:
 25-year, 8% mortgage bonds due on December 31, 1989 ......   $100,000
    Less:  Unamortized discount.....................      4,000   $ 96,000
 20-year, 6% debenture bonds, convertible into 15 shares of
    common stock, due on December 31, 1984.............   $ 50,000
    Add:  Unamortized premium.......................      1,000     51,000
       Total Long-term Liabilities .......................             $147,000
```

KEY DEFINITIONS

Accrued interest expense   Accrued interest expense is interest that has been incurred on a note payable but not paid.

Amortization of premium or discount   Amortization is the process of allocating a portion of the bond discount to increase interest expense, or of bond premium to decrease interest expense during each period of the life of the bond.

Bond   A bond is an issuance of debt used as a means of borrowing money for long-term purposes.

Bond discount   The discount is the amount by which the face value of a bond exceeds the issue price. A discount occurs when the coupon rate on the bonds is less than the market interest rate at the time the bonds are issued.

Bond premium   The premium is the amount by which the issue price of a bond exceeds the face value. A premium occurs when the coupon rate of interest on a bond is higher than the market interest rate at the time of issuance.

Bond sinking fund   A sinking fund is accumulated by the issuing corporation specifically for the repayment of bonds at maturity. A sinking fund may be created voluntarily or required by provisions of the bond issue.

Callable bonds   Callable bonds may be repurchased at the option of the issuing corporation within a specified period at a specified price.

Convertible bonds   Convertible bonds may be exchanged for a specified amount of capital stock at the option of the bondholder.

Coupon bonds   Coupon bonds have interest coupons attached which call for the payment of a specified amount of interest on the interest dates.

Coupon rate   The interest rate specified on the bond is the coupon rate. Periodic interest payments equal the coupon interest rate multiplied by the face amount of the bond.

Current liability   Current debts of a firm which must be paid within the operating cycle of the firm or one year, whichever is longer.

Debenture bonds   Debenture bonds are not secured by any specific assets of the corporation. Their security is dependent upon the general credit standing of the issuing corporation.

Discounted note   On discounted notes payable, the interest is deducted from the maturity value of the note at the time the note is issued.

Effective interest rate   The effective interest rate is the actual rate of interest that the issuing corporation pays on the bond as evidenced by the relationship between the periodic interest payment and the issue price of the bonds.

Liability   A liability is an obligation which arises from a past transaction and which is to be discharged at a future date by the transfer of assets or the performance of services.

Maturity value   Maturity value constitutes the amount that the holder of a note is entitled to receive at the due date. This amount includes the principal plus any accrued interest.

Mortgage   A mortgage is a conditional conveyance or transfer of property to a creditor as security for a loan.

Note payable   A note payable represents a written promise to pay a definite amount of money on demand or at some specified future date to the holder of the note.

Registered bonds   Registered bonds have the name of the owner registered with the issuing corporation. Periodic interest payments are mailed directly to the registered owner.

Retirement of bonds   Retiring bonds is the process of redeeming bonds or repurchasing bonds in the open market.

Secured bond   Secured bonds are secured by prior claim against specific assets of the business in the event that the issuing corporation is unable to make the required interest or principal payments.

Serial bonds   Serial bond issues are bonds which mature on several different dates.

Term bonds   A term bond is a bond issue that matures on a single date.

QUESTIONS

1. Distinguish between current and long-term liabilities.

2. Define each of the following terms related to the issue of bonds: (*a*) debenture, (*b*) secured, (*c*) callable, (*d*) convertible, (*e*) serial bonds.

3. How are interest payments made to the holders of (*a*) coupon bonds, and (*b*) registered bonds?

4. Smith Co. borrowed $5,000 from the bank and signed a 60-day, 6 percent note dated June 1. (1) What is the face amount of the note? (2) What is the amount of interest on the note? (3) What is the maturity value of the note?

5. How can bonds be sold when the market interest rate for comparable bonds is higher than the stated contract rate on the bond certificate?

6. How does a discount on the issuance of bonds affect the total cost of borrowing to the issuing corporation?

7. What is the effect of a premium on the interest expense of the company issuing bonds? Explain.

8. What is the effect of a discount on the interest expense of the company issuing bonds? Explain.

9. Give the journal entries required for the amortization of (*a*) Discount on Bonds Payable and (*b*) Premium on Bonds Payable.

10. How should Discount on Bonds Payable and Premium on Bonds Payable be classified and presented on the balance sheet?

11. If bonds are issued at a time between interest payment dates, why does the issuing company receive an amount of cash equal to the issue price of the bonds plus the accrued interest?

12. Describe the purpose of a bond sinking fund. How is it reported in the balance sheet?

13. Describe two means of reporting a restriction on dividends imposed by a bond issue.

EXERCISES

14–1   Determine the interest on each of the following notes.

	Face Amount	Interest Rate	Days to Maturity
a.	$1,000	6%	60
b.	$5,000	8%	90
c.	$4,000	4%	180
d.	$2,500	5%	36

14–2   On December 1, King Inc. issued a 90-day, 6 percent note for $3,000 to Miller Co. to replace an account payable. Give the journal entries necessary to record the following on the books of King Inc.

    a. Issuance of the note by King, Inc.
    b. Adjusting entry on December 31.
    c. Payment of the note at maturity.

14–3   Assume that Richardson Company borrows $1,500 on a 6-month note bearing a 9 percent rate of discount. Three months later the company closes its books. In the next accounting period, the note matures and is paid by Richardson Company. Prepare the necessary journal entries for Richardson Company related to this note.

14–4   Thompson Co. issues a 180-day, non-interest-bearing note for $10,000 to First National Bank on May 1. The bank discounts the note at 8 percent. Give the necessary journal entries for Thompson Co. to record the issuance of the note and the payment of the note at maturity.

14–5   Stengel Company has authorization to issue $200,000 of 10 year, 7 percent bonds on January 1, 1975, with semiannual interest payments on June 30 and December 31. Stengel Company issues $100,000 of the bonds on January 1 at face value. Another $100,000 of bonds are issued on August 1, 1975, at face value plus accrued interest. Assume Stengel Company's accounting period ends March 31.

Required:

Give the firm's journal entries with respect to the bonds for 1975.

14–6   Terry Tractors, Inc., has outstanding a $100,000 10-year bond issue which was sold on January 1, 1970, at a price of $110,000. The following liability, shown below, appeared on the balance sheet on December 31, 1974:

> Bonds payable. $100,000
> Premium 5,000 $105,000

Make the entry necessary to record the retirement of the bonds in each of the following two situations:

    a. The firm calls the bonds at 106 on January 1, 1975.
    b. Terry Tractors, Inc., purchases half of the outstanding bonds in the open market for $51,000 on January 1, 1975.

14–7   Boyer, Inc., issued 100, $1,000, 20-year convertible bonds at a price of $1,020 each on January 1, 1975. Each of the bonds is convertible into 20 shares of $20 par value common stock. On December 31, 1981, 50 of these bonds were converted into common stock. Make the journal entry necessary to record the conversion on the books of Boyer, Inc.

PROBLEMS

Series A

14A–1 Dixie Inc. had the following transactions with regard to notes payable during the year ended December 31, 1975.

September 1   Purchased merchandise from Silver Co. in the amount of $2,000. Signed a 60-day, 6 percent interest bearing note.

October 1   Borrowed $5,000 from the City Bank, signing a 120-day non-interest-bearing note with an 8 percent discount.

October 15   Purchased a machine at a cost of $10,000 from Olson Corp. Signed a 6 percent, two-month note in payment.

October 30   Paid the note to Silver Co.

December 14   Paid the interest on the note payable to Olson Corp. and issued a new 60-day, 6 percent note.

Required:

a. Prepare the necessary journal entries to record the above.

b. Give the necessary adjusting entries required at December 31.

14A–2 Kubek Company is authorized to issue $50,000 of 10-year, 8 percent bonds with semiannual interest payments on June 30 and December 31. Record the journal entries necessary on January 1 and June 30, 1975, on the books of Kubek Company in each of the following independent cases.

a. The bonds are issued at a price of $45,000 on January 1, 1975. Interest is paid on June 30 and December 31.

b. The bonds are issued at a price of $53,000 on January 1, 1975. Interest is paid on June 30 and December 31.

14A–3 Blue Co. issued $100,000 of 6 percent, 20-year debenture bonds with interest payable semiannually on June 30 and December 31 of each year. Blue Co.'s accounting period ends on December 31. Give the necessary journal entries to record the firm's transactions with respect to the bonds for 1975 in each of the following cases:

a. The bonds were issued for $102,000 on January 1, 1975.

b. The bonds were issued for $100,000 plus accrued interest on April 1, 1975.

c. The bonds were issued for $105,000 on January 1, 1975, and the firm's accounting period ends on September 30.

14A–4 Dean Co. issued $100,000 of 6 percent 20-year debenture bonds on January 1, 1973. Interest is payable semiannually on June 30 and

December 31. The following information is given on the bonds at December 31, 1973:

Carrying value of bonds $103,800
Interest expense for the year   5,800

a. Were the bonds issued at a premium or discount?
b. What was the amount of premium or discount on the issuance of the bonds?
c. How much of the discount or premium was amortized during the year?

14A–5   On January 1, 1974, the stockholders of Howard Company authorized the issuance of $8,000 (par value) of 3-year bonds paying interest (8 percent) semiannually on June 30 and December 31. The bonds were sold on April 1, 1974, for $8,330 plus accrued interest. On April 1, 1975, Howard Company retired half of the issue at 102 (plus accrued interest).

Required:

Prepare all general journal entries for:

1. Issuance of the bonds.
2. Interest payment on June 30, 1974.
3. Interest payment on December 31, 1974.
4. Retirement of portion of issue on April 1, 1975.
5. Interest payment on June 30, 1975.

14A–6   Dorey Co. issued $500,000 of 20-year 8 percent bonds on April 1, 1973, with interest payable on June 30 and December 31. The bonds were callable after January 1, 1980, at 105 percent of face value and mature on December 31, 1992. The fiscal year of the company ends on September 30. Give the necessary journal entries for the following transactions:

1973
April 1   Issued the bonds for $529,750 including accrued interest.
June 30   Paid interest.
September 30   Recorded adjusting entry for accrued interest.
December 31   Paid interest.
1980
January 1   Called the bonds.

Series B

14B–1   Selected transactions of Blanton Company during 1975 are listed below.

September 15   Purchased merchandise from DCB Company in the amount of $5,000. Signed a 90-day 8 percent interest-bearing note.

October 1	Purchased a $4,000 truck from Beal Ford. Signed a 9 percent 60-day note in payment.
November 1	Borrowed $10,000 from First National Bank, signing a six-month non-interest-bearing note with 10 percent discount.
November 30	Paid the interest on the note payable to Beal Ford and issued a new 60-day 9 percent note.
December 14	Paid the note to DCB Company.

Required:

a. Prepare the necessary journal entries to record the above transactions.

b. Prepare the necessary adjusting entries relating to the notes at December 31.

14B–2 Jason Company issued $100,000 of 6 percent, 10-year debenture bonds at face value plus accrued interest on April 1, 1974. Interest is payable semiannually on January 1 and July 1.

Prepare the journal entries necessary to record the issuance of the bonds and to record interest expense for the first interest date subsequent to issuance.

14B–3 Brown Co. issued $100,000 of 6 percent, 20-year debenture bonds on April 1, 1973, and received $99,130. The bonds were authorized on January 1, 1973. Interest is payable semiannually on June 30 and December 31 of each year. Brown Co.'s accounting period ends on December 31. Give the necessary journal entries to record the firm's transactions with respect to these bonds for 1973 and 1974.

14B–4 On October 1, 1974, the Badger Company issued $10,000 (face value) of 3 percent bonds which will mature on September 30, 1976. On December 31, 1974, the company's accountant made the following adjusting journal entry relative to the bonds (Badger Company's accounting period is the calendar year):

Interest Expense	90	
Interest Payable		75
Discount on Bonds Payable		15

Required:

Give the journal entry made to record the sale of the bonds on October 1, 1974. Assume that interest is payable annually on September 30.

14B–5 The following data related to long-term liabilities appeared on the books of Summer Co. on December 31, 1974:

Bonds payable—6 percent 20-year debenture bonds due on December 31, 1989, $100,000 authorized interest payable semiannually on June 30 and December 31	$100,000	
Discount on bonds payable	3,000	$97,000

On January 1, 1975, half of the bonds were purchased and retired at 102 percent of face value. Prepare the necessary journal entries to record the semiannual interest payment on December 31, 1974, and the retirement of $50,000 of bonds on January 1, 1975.

APPENDIX TO CHAPTER 14
INTEREST AND PRESENT VALUE CONCEPTS

The principles used in discounting cash flows due at certain future points in time by the use of compound interest concepts are discussed in this appendix. These concepts have a broad application in business decisions. For example, most business entities often make decisions to: (1) borrow funds in the current period in return for a promise to pay cash or other resources in future periods; and (2) invest resources at the current time with the expectation of receiving benefits at various future times. For both of these types of decisions, the timing of the various cash inflows and outflows has a significant effect on the desirability of the various possible investment and borrowing alternatives. Timing of the cash flows is important because of the following principle: *an amount of cash to be received in the future is not equivalent to the same amount of cash held at the present time.* This statement is true because money has a time value—it can be invested to earn a return (i.e., interest or dividends). For this reason, in both borrowing and investing decisions, consideration must be given to the time values of the various cash inflows and outflows.

In order to understand the implications of such decisions, the accountant must be able to determine the *present value* of future cash flows. Although there are a number of important applications of present value concepts in the financial accounting area, this appendix is limited to the application of these concepts to long-term liabilities.

INTEREST

Interest represents the amount received by the lender and paid by the borrower for the use of money for a given period of time. Thus, upon payment of a debt, interest is the excess of the cash repaid over the amount originally borrowed (referred to as the *principal*). Interest is normally stated as a rate for a one year period.

Simple interest is the amount of interest that is computed on the principal *only*, for a given period of time. Simple interest is computed as follows:

$$\text{Interest} = \text{Principal} \times \text{Rate} \times \text{Time}$$
$$\text{Interest} = P \times I \times T \tag{1}$$

To illustrate, interest on $1,000 for 6 months at an annual interest rate of 10 percent is:

$$\$50 = \$1,000 \times .10 \times \tfrac{6}{12}$$

Compound interest is interest that is computed for a period of time both on the principal and on the interest which has been earned but not paid. That is, interest is compounded when the interest earned in each period is added to the principal amount and both principal and interest earn interest in all subsequent periods. To illustrate, assume that $1,000 is deposited in a bank which pays interest at 10 percent annually. If the interest was withdrawn each year (simple interest), the depositor would collect $100 in interest each year (or $300 in interest over a three-year period):

$$\text{Interest per Year} = \$1,000 \times .10 \times 1 = \$100$$
$$\text{Total Interest for 3 Years} = \$100 \times 3 = \$300$$

However, if the interest at the end of each period is added to the principal sum (compound interest), the amount earned over the three-year period is computed as follows:

Original investment.................................... $1,000.00
Balance at the
End of Year: 1. $1,000.00 + (.10 × $1,000.00 × 1)   1,100.00
              2. $1,100.00 + (.10 × $1,100.00 × 1)   1,210.00
              3. $1,210.00 + (.10 × $1,210.00 × 1)   1,331.00

Compound interest for the three-year period is $331 ($1,331 − $1,000), the difference between the balance at the end of the three-year period and the original investment. This amount exceeds simple interest because interest was earned each year both on the principal and on the interest earned in previous years.

Since compounding occurs when interest is earned on previously accumulated interest, a formula can be developed for computing the compound amount at which the principal sum will increase over a given time period. To develop this formula, consider the compound interest on one dollar invested at an interest rate of I percent. The amount accumulated at the end of the first year would be [$1 + (1 \times I)] or (1 + I). If this amount is allowed to accumulate and earn interest for the second year, the amount accumulated is (1 + I)(1 + I) which is equal to (1 + I)^2. Similarly, the amount at the end of T periods is (1 + I)^T. Consequently, the amount (A) that a principal amount (P) will accumulate over a time period (T) at an interest rate (I) is expressed as:

$$A = P(1 + I)^T \tag{2}$$

Compound Interest For example, if $1,000 is invested for three years at 10 percent interest per year, the amount accumulated at the end of three years is computed as follows:

$$A = \$1,000(1 + .10)^3$$
$$A = \$1,000(1.331)$$
$$A = \$1,331$$

This computation of the sum for a single principal amount and the compound interest at a specified future time may be illustrated as follows:

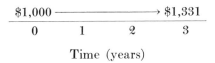

Time (years)

PRESENT VALUES OF A FUTURE SUM

The present value of a given amount at a specified future time is the sum that would have to be invested at the present time in order to equal that future value at a given rate of compound interest. For example, it was determined that $1,000 invested at 10 percent compound interest would accumulate to a total of $1,331 in three years. Therefore, $1,000 is the *present value* of $1,331 three years from the present time (given a 10 percent rate of interest). That is, if you could earn 10 percent on a bank deposit, you would be indifferent between receiving $1,000 now (which could be deposited to accumulate to $1,331 in three years) or $1,331 three years from now, all other factors being equal.

The present value of a future amount is determined by computing the amount that a principal sum will accumulate to over a specified period of time. Consequently, by dividing equation (2) by $(1 + I)^T$, ~~we obtain the formula for computing the present value of a future amount (A):~~

Present Value of Future Sum →

$$P = \frac{A}{(1 + I)^T} \tag{3}$$

For example, the present value of $1,331 three years from now would be computed as follows:

$$P = \frac{\$1,331}{(1 + .10)^3}$$

$$\frac{3200}{(1 + 12)^x} = 2,277.69E$$

$$P = \$1,000$$

Because of the number and variety of decisions which are based on the present value of future cash flows, tables have been developed from the formula which give the present value of $1 for various interest rates and for various periods of time. These values may be multiplied by any future amount to determine its present value. The factors for the present value of $1 are listed in Table 14A–1.

To illustrate the use of this table, let us compute the present value of $1,331 to be received three years from now at a compound interest rate of 10 percent. The value from the table for 3 years at 10 percent is .7513. This is the present value of $1. Accordingly, the present value of $1,331 is computed as 1,331 × .7513 = $999.80, (this amount is not exactly equal to $1,000 because of the rounding error in the present value factor included in the table). The computation of the present value of a simple payment due in the future may be illustrated as follows:

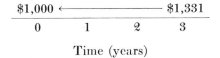

Time (years)

COMPOUND INTEREST AND PRESENT VALUE
ON A SERIES OF EQUAL PAYMENTS

Business decisions involving a series of cash flows to be paid or received periodically are more common than decisions involving the accumulation of a single principal sum. It is possible to determine the present value of a series of payments (or receipts) by computing the present value of each payment or receipt and adding these values to obtain the present value for the entire series. However, if all the payments are equal, formulas or tables may be used to compute the present value of a series of payments. Such a series of equal periodic payments is normally referred to as an *annuity*. If the payments are made at the end of each period, the annuity is referred to as an *ordinary annuity*.

The accumulated amount (future value) of an ordinary annuity is the sum of the periodic payments and the compound interest on these payments. For example, the future value of an annuity of $1,000 per year (at the end of each year) for three years at 10 percent interest could be determined as follows:

The initial payment accumulates at 10 percent for two years to $1,210
The second payment accumulates at 10 percent for one year to   1,100
The third payment is due at the end of the third year   1,000
Amount of an ordinary annuity of $1,000 for three years at 10 percent. $3,310

The computation of the future value of a series of payments may be expressed as follows:

$1,000 ——————————→ $1,210
        $1,000 ——————————→   1,100
                $1,000→   1,000
0   1   2   3 $3,310

Time (years)

The present value of an ordinary annuity is the amount which, if invested at the present time at a compound rate of interest, would provide for a series of equal withdrawals at the end of a certain number of periods. The present value of an ordinary annuity may be computed as the present values of each of the individual payments. For example, the present value of an ordinary annuity of $1,000 per year for three years at 10 percent could be computed as follows (see Table 14A–1):

Present value of $1,000 in one year. . . . . .9091 × 1,000 = $ 909.10
Present value of $1,000 in two years . . . . .8264 × 1,000 =   826.40
Present value of $1,000 in three years . . . . .7513 × 1,000 =   751.30

Present value of an annuity of $1,000 for
three periods at 10 percent $2,486.80

This computation indicates that if $2,486.80 is invested at an interest rate of 10 percent, it would be possible to withdraw $1,000 at the end of each year for three years.

The formula for the present value of an ordinary annuity of $R per period for T periods at I rate of interest may be stated:

$$P = R \left[\frac{1 - \dfrac{1}{(1 + I)^T}}{I} \right]$$

Table 14A–2 gives the present value of an ordinary annuity of $1 per period for various periods at varying rates of interest. By multiplying the appropriate value from the table by the dollar amount of the periodic payment, the present value of the payments may be calculated. For example, the present value of three annual cash payments of $1,000 made at the end of the next three years at a 10 percent interest rate would be computed as follows:

$$1,000 \times 2.4869 = \$2,486.90^1$$

This amount may be interpreted as the present cash payment which would be exactly equivalent to the three future installments of $1,000 if money earns 10 percent compounded annually. The computation of the present value of a series of future payments may be illustrated as follows:

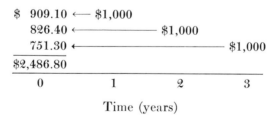

Time (years)

APPLICATION OF PRESENT VALUE CONCEPTS TO BONDS PAYABLE

A bond is a contract between an issuing company and the purchaser of the bond. There are two types of payments that a company will have

---

[1] Difference of $.10 due to rounding in tables.

~~to make to bondholders.~~ One payment is a lump-sum payment made at the end of the life of the bond, which is the return of the *face value* or *maturity value* of the bond. The other payment is for interest, which will be made at specific intervals in fixed amounts over the life of the bond. Interest is usually paid semiannually by the issuing company. Bond contracts will state the *coupon* or *nominal rate* of interest on an annual basis.

To calculate the selling price of a bond (the amount the firm will receive upon issuance of the bond), consider a company that has sold a $1,000 face value bond with a nominal rate of interest of 8 percent. The bond will mature in 5 years and the interest is payable June 30 and December 31 of each year. The company has made two promises to the purchaser of the bond:

Promise 1: To pay $1,000 at the end of 5 years.
Promise 2: To pay $40 semiannually for 5 years.

The price that any investor would pay for a bond would depend upon the *effective rate*[2] of interest on the date that the investor decided to buy the bond. The effective rate will be dependent upon many factors such as the prime interest rate in money markets, the risks involved in buying the bond of that specific company, and the provisions of the bond that may make it more attractive for investment purposes. In general, the effective rate will be determined by supply and demand in the bond market.

There are three possible general cases that illustrate the potential selling price of the bond. These three cases are dependent upon the earnings expectations of buyers of bonds in the market place. In the prior example, where the nominal rate is eight percent, the three possible cases are:

a.   The effective (market) rate of interest is equal to eight percent.
b.   The effective (market) rate of interest is below eight percent.
c.   The effective (market) rate of interest is greater than eight percent.

If the market is demanding an eight percent return on bonds of like kind, and the company enters the market with an eight percent coupon rate on its bond, the bond should sell at its face value of $1,000. The buyer is demanding eight percent and the seller is paying eight percent; therefore the bond would sell at *par*.

If the market is demanding a return that is less than eight percent and the company enters the market with an eight percent coupon rate on its bond, the company is paying a greater return than is demanded in the market. Therefore, the bond will sell for a price in excess of $1,000. This excess is referred to as a *premium*. The investors will buy the bond at a price greater than $1,000 because the coupon rate exceeds the rate demanded by the market.

---

[2] The effective rate is also referred to as the market rate or the yield.

If the market is demanding a return that is greater than eight percent and the company enters the market with an eight percent coupon rate on its bond, the company is paying less than the return demanded by the market. Therefore, the bond will sell for less than $1,000. The difference between $1,000 and the selling price will be a *discount* on the bond.

To calculate the selling price of the bond, assume that the market rate of interest was either eight percent, six percent, or ten percent. Note that the bond contract provides for a lump-sum payment at maturity and semiannual interest payments over the life of the bond. Thus, in order to find the current value, or selling price, of the bond, it is necessary to determine the present value of the lump-sum payment at maturity and the present value of the periodic interest payments (an ordinary annuity). Illustration 14A–1 presents the calculations which are necessary to determine the selling price of the $1,000 bond at the three market rates of interest assumed above.

Illustration 14A–1
Selling Price of a Bond with 8% Coupon Rate,
5-Year Life, and Semiannual Payments

	Present Value Factors for 10 Periods at 4% Semiannual Interest		
	Table 1	Table 2	Totals
8% Coupon, 8% Market *Bond Sells at Par*			
Promise #1 = $1,000–lump sum	.6756		= $ 675.60
Promise #2 = $40–annuity		8.1109	= 324.44
	Selling price (rounded)		= $1,000.00
8% Coupon, 6% Market *Bond Sells at Premium*			
Promise #1 = $1,000–lump sum	.7441		= $ 744.10
Promise #2 = $40–annuity		8.5302	= 341.21
	Selling price (rounded)		= $1,085.31
8% Coupon, 10% Market *Bond Sells at Discount*			
Promise #1 = $1,000–lump sum	.6139		= $ 613.90
Promise #2 = $40–annuity		7.7217	= 308.87
	Selling price (rounded)		= $ 922.77

Even though the selling price of the bond will vary according to the three different market rate assumptions, it is important to remember that the bond is a fixed contract that will pay a return of $40 to the bondholder semiannually and $1,000 at its maturity date. These amounts are paid regardless of the initial selling price of the bond.

ACCOUNTING FOR PREMIUM OR DISCOUNT ON BONDS— THE INTEREST METHOD

The following example will be used to illustrate the accounting treatment of a bond issue sold at a premium or discount using the interest method. Assume that on July 1, 1976, a company sold a $1,000,000 bond issue with a nominal interest rate of eight percent and a maturity date of July 1, 1981. Interest will be paid on June 30 and December 31. The company's fiscal year ends on December 31.

The calculations necessary in order to compute the initial selling price of the bond are the same as the calculations in Illustration 14A–1, except that the entire issue, $1,000,000, is under consideration. If the market rate of interest demanded is eight percent, the bonds will sell for $1,000,000. If the market rate of interest is six percent, the bonds will sell at a premium. The selling price will be $(1,000,000 \times .7441) + (40,000 \times 8.5302) = \$1,085,308$. If the market rate of interest demanded is ten percent, the bonds will sell at a discount. The selling price will be $(1,000,000 \times .6139) + (40,000 \times 7.7217) = \$922,768$.

The face value of the bonds is paid to bondholders at the maturity date regardless of the original price of the bonds. The premium or discount on a bond is paid or received, respectively, to adjust the interest that will be paid on the bond to the return on the investment demanded by the market (market rate of interest) given the type of bond and the risk involved as perceived by investors.

There are two acceptable methods for amortizing bond premium or discount. One technique for amortization, the straight-line method, was discussed in Chapter 14. A second technique, referred to as the interest method, has been suggested by the Accounting Principles Board.[3] This method of amortization results in recognizing a constant rate of interest on the bond liability over the life of the bond. The interest expense for each period is computed by multiplying a constant rate of interest by the beginning liability for that period. The interest method is described in this appendix.

Bonds Sold at a Premium

If the market rate of interest in the prior example is six percent, the bonds will sell at a premium of $85,308 ($1,085,308 — $1,000,000). The interest method will yield a different interest expense for each interest period. To determine the interest expense, the carrying value of the liability (face value plus unamortized premium or minus unamortized discount) is multiplied by the semiannual effective rate of interest. Thus, the interest expense will be a constant percentage (equal to the effective semiannual

---

[3] *APB Opinion No. 21* (New York, American Institute of Certified Public Accountants, 1972).

interest rate on the issuance of the bonds) of six percent per year or three percent on the outstanding liability at the beginning of each semiannual interest period. The following journal entries would be made in 1976 under the interest method:

```
June 30, 1976       Cash. . . . . . . . . . . . . . . . . 1,085,308
                      Bond Premium . . . . . . . .              85,308
                      Bonds Payable . . . . . . . . .        1,000,000
December 31, 1976   Interest Expense. . . . . . . . . .   32,559.24
                      Bond Premium. . . . . . . . . .        7,440.76
                      Cash . . . . . . . . . . . . . .                 40,000.00
                    (Interest Expense = $1,085,308.00 × .03 = $32,559.24)
```

At the end of 1976, the balance sheet presentation of the liability will include both the bonds payable and bond premium accounts. The bond premium account is rounded in the example.

```
Bonds payable  . . . . . . . . . . . . . .  $1,000,000
Add:  Bond premium . . . . . . . . . . .        77,867
        Total Bonds Payable . . . . . . . . . .   $1,077,867
```

When bonds are issued at a premium, use of the interest method will cause the *interest* expense to decrease over the life of the bond because both the premium account and the carrying value of the liability will decrease over the life of the bonds. The bond premium amortization will increase because the cash payment to bondholders remains constant and the interest expense decreases each period. The total interest expense and premium amortization schedule is given in Illustration 14A–2.

Illustration 14A–2
Interest Expense and Premium Amortization Schedule

Date	Debit to Interest Expense*	Debit to Bond Premium	Credit to Cash	Bond Premium Balance	Total Liability
July 1, 1976.	—	—	—	$85,308.00	$1,085,308.00
December 31, 1976.	$32,559.24	$ 7,440.76	$ 40,000	77,867.24	1,077,867.24
July 1, 1977.	32,336.02	7,663.98	40,000	70,203.26	1,070,203.26
December 31, 1977.	32,106.10	7,893.90	40,000	62,309.36	1,062,309.36
July 1, 1978.	31,869.28	8,130.72	40,000	54,178.64	1,054,178.64
December 31, 1978.	31,625.36	8,374.64	40,000	45,804.00	1,045,804.00
July 1, 1979.	31,374.12	8,625.88	40,000	37,178.12	1,037,178.12
December 31, 1979.	31,115.34	8,884.66	40,000	28,293.46	1,028,293.46
July 1, 1980.	30,848.80	9,151.20	40,000	19,142.26	1,019,142.26
December 31, 1980.	30,574.27	9,425.73	40,000	9,716.53	1,009,716.53
July 1, 1981.	30,291.47*	9,716.53	40,000	–0–	1,000,000.00
		$85,308.00	$400,000		

* To determine interest expense, the total liability at the beginning of the period was multiplied by the semiannual market interest rate of three percent. Any rounding errors are included in the July 1, 1981, debit to interest expense.

Bonds Sold at a Discount

If the market rate of interest demanded by investors is ten percent, the bonds in the prior example will sell at a discount because the face rate of interest is eight percent. The discount will be the difference between the maturity value of $1,000,000 and the selling price of $922,768, or $77,232.

The concepts underlying the *interest* method for bond discount are the same as those discussed in the prior section on bonds sold at a premium. The journal entries for 1976 for bonds sold at a discount are:

```
June 30, 1976      Cash. . . . . . . . . . . . . . . .    922,768
                   Bond Discount. . . . . . . . . .    77,232
                      Bonds Payable. . . . . . . .                1,000,000

December 31, 1976  Interest Expense. . . . . . . . .   46,138.40
                   Bond Discount . . . . . . .                     6,138.40
                   Cash . . . . . . . . . . . . .                 40,000.00
(Interest Expense = $922,768 × .05 = $46,138.40)
```

At the end of 1976, the balance sheet presentation of the liability will include both the bonds payable and the bond discount account. The bond discount is rounded in the example.

```
Bonds payable. . . . . . . . . . . . . . . . . .   $1,000,000
Less:  Bond discount. . . . . . . . . . . . . .        71,094

    Total Bonds Payable . . . . . . . . . . . .                   $928,906
```

In the case of bonds sold at a discount, using the interest method, interest expense increases over the life of the bond because discount decreases and the carrying value of the bonds increases. The total interest expense and discount amortization schedule is given in Illustration 14A–3.

Illustration 14A–3
Interest Expense and Discount Amortization Schedule

Date	Debit to Interest Expense*	Credit to Bond Discount	Credit to Cash	Bond Discount Balance	Total Liability
July 1, 1976.	—	—	—	$77,232.00	$ 922,768.00
December 31, 1976.	$46,138.40	$ 6,138.40	$ 40,000	71,093.60	928,906.40
July 1, 1977.	46,445.32	6,445.32	40,000	64,648.28	935,351.72
December 31, 1977.	46,767.59	6,767.59	40,000	57,880.69	942,119.31
July 1, 1978.	47,105.97	7,105.97	40,000	50,774.72	949,225.28
December 31, 1978.	47,461.26	7,461.26	40,000	43,313.46	956,686.54
July 1, 1979.	47,834.33	7,834.33	40,000	35,479.13	964,520.87
December 31, 1979.	48,226.04	8,226.04	40,000	27,253.09	972,746.91
July 1, 1980.	48,637.35	8,637.35	40,000	18,615.74	981,384.26
December 31, 1980.	49,069.21	9,069.21	40,000	9,546.53	990,453.47
July 1, 1981.	49,522.53*	9,546.53	40,000	–0–	1,000,000.00
	$77,232.00	$400,000			

* To determine interest expense, the total liability at the beginning of the period was multiplied by the semiannual market interest rate—in this case, five percent. Any rounding errors are included in the July 1, 1981, debit to interest expense.

Table 14A–1
Present Value of $1.00

Periods (n)	1%	1½%	2%	2½%	3%	3½%	4%	4½%	5%	6%	7%	8%	10%
1......	0.9901	0.9852	0.9804	0.9756	0.9709	0.9662	0.9615	0.9569	0.9524	0.9434	0.9346	0.9259	0.9091
2......	0.9803	0.9707	0.9612	0.9518	0.9426	0.9335	0.9246	0.9157	0.9070	0.8900	0.8734	0.8573	0.8264
3......	0.9706	0.9563	0.9423	0.9286	0.9151	0.9019	0.8890	0.8763	0.8638	0.8396	0.8163	0.7938	0.7513
4......	0.9610	0.9422	0.9238	0.9060	0.8885	0.8714	0.8548	0.8386	0.8227	0.7921	0.7629	0.7350	0.6830
5......	0.9515	0.9283	0.9057	0.8839	0.8626	0.8420	0.8219	0.8025	0.7835	0.7473	0.7130	0.6806	0.6209
6......	0.9420	0.9145	0.8880	0.8623	0.8375	0.8135	0.7903	0.7679	0.7462	0.7050	0.6663	0.6302	0.5645
7......	0.9327	0.9010	0.8706	0.8413	0.8131	0.7860	0.7599	0.7348	0.7107	0.6651	0.6227	0.5835	0.5132
8......	0.9235	0.8877	0.8535	0.8207	0.7894	0.7594	0.7307	0.7032	0.6768	0.6274	0.5820	0.5403	0.4665
9......	0.9143	0.8746	0.8368	0.8007	0.7664	0.7337	0.7026	0.6729	0.6446	0.5919	0.5439	0.5002	0.4241
10......	0.9053	0.8617	0.8203	0.7812	0.7441	0.7089	0.6756	0.6439	0.6139	0.5584	0.5083	0.4632	0.3855
11......	0.8963	0.8489	0.8043	0.7621	0.7224	0.6849	0.6496	0.6162	0.5847	0.5268	0.4751	0.4289	0.3505
12......	0.8874	0.8364	0.7885	0.7436	0.7014	0.6618	0.6246	0.5897	0.5568	0.4970	0.4440	0.3971	0.3186
13......	0.8787	0.8240	0.7730	0.7254	0.6810	0.6394	0.6006	0.5643	0.5303	0.4688	0.4150	0.3677	0.2897
14......	0.8700	0.8118	0.7579	0.7077	0.6611	0.6178	0.5775	0.5400	0.5051	0.4423	0.3878	0.3405	0.2633
15......	0.8613	0.7999	0.7430	0.6905	0.6419	0.5969	0.5553	0.5167	0.4810	0.4173	0.3624	0.3153	0.2394
16......	0.8528	0.7880	0.7284	0.6736	0.6232	0.5767	0.5339	0.4945	0.4581	0.3936	0.3387	0.2919	0.2176
17......	0.8444	0.7764	0.7142	0.6572	0.6050	0.5572	0.5134	0.4732	0.4363	0.3714	0.3166	0.2703	0.1978
18......	0.8360	0.7649	0.7002	0.6412	0.5874	0.5384	0.4936	0.4528	0.4155	0.3503	0.2959	0.2502	0.1799
19......	0.8277	0.7536	0.6864	0.6255	0.5703	0.5202	0.4746	0.4333	0.3957	0.3305	0.2765	0.2317	0.1635
20......	0.8195	0.7425	0.6730	0.6103	0.5537	0.5026	0.4564	0.4146	0.3769	0.3118	0.2584	0.2145	0.1486
21......	0.8114	0.7315	0.6598	0.5954	0.5375	0.4856	0.4388	0.3968	0.3589	0.2942	0.2415	0.1987	0.1351
22......	0.8034	0.7207	0.6468	0.5809	0.5219	0.4692	0.4220	0.3797	0.3418	0.2775	0.2257	0.1839	0.1228
23......	0.7954	0.7100	0.6342	0.5667	0.5067	0.4533	0.4057	0.3634	0.3256	0.2618	0.2109	0.1703	0.1117
24......	0.7876	0.6995	0.6217	0.5529	0.4919	0.4380	0.3901	0.3477	0.3101	0.2470	0.1971	0.1577	0.1015
25......	0.7798	0.6892	0.6095	0.5394	0.4776	0.4231	0.3751	0.3327	0.2953	0.2330	0.1842	0.1460	0.0923
26......	0.7720	0.6790	0.5976	0.5262	0.4637	0.4088	0.3607	0.3184	0.2812	0.2198	0.1722	0.1352	0.0839
27......	0.7644	0.6690	0.5859	0.5134	0.4502	0.3950	0.3468	0.3047	0.2678	0.2074	0.1609	0.1252	0.0763
28......	0.7568	0.6591	0.5744	0.5009	0.4371	0.3817	0.3335	0.2916	0.2551	0.1956	0.1504	0.1159	0.0693
29......	0.7493	0.6494	0.5631	0.4887	0.4243	0.3687	0.3207	0.2790	0.2429	0.1846	0.1406	0.1073	0.0630
30......	0.7419	0.6398	0.5521	0.4767	0.4120	0.3563	0.3083	0.2670	0.2314	0.1741	0.1314	0.0994	0.0573
40......	0.6717	0.5513	0.4529	0.3724	0.3066	0.2526	0.2083	0.1719	0.1420	0.0972	0.0668	0.0460	0.0221
50......	0.6080	0.4750	0.3715	0.2909	0.2281	0.1791	0.1407	0.1107	0.0872	0.0543	0.0339	0.0213	0.0085

Table 14A–1 (continued)
Present Value of $1.00

12%	14%	15%	16%	18%	20%	22%	24%	25%	26%	28%	30%	40%	50%
0.893	0.877	0.870	0.862	0.847	0.833	0.820	0.806	0.800	0.794	0.781	0.769	0.714	0.667
0.797	0.769	0.756	0.743	0.718	0.694	0.672	0.650	0.640	0.630	0.610	0.592	0.510	0.444
0.712	0.675	0.658	0.641	0.609	0.579	0.551	0.524	0.512	0.500	0.477	0.455	0.364	0.296
0.636	0.592	0.572	0.552	0.516	0.482	0.451	0.423	0.410	0.397	0.373	0.350	0.260	0.198
0.567	0.519	0.497	0.476	0.437	0.402	0.370	0.341	0.328	0.315	0.291	0.269	0.186	0.132
0.507	0.456	0.432	0.410	0.370	0.335	0.303	0.275	0.262	0.250	0.227	0.207	0.133	0.088
0.452	0.400	0.376	0.354	0.314	0.279	0.249	0.222	0.210	0.198	0.178	0.159	0.095	0.059
0.404	0.351	0.327	0.305	0.266	0.233	0.204	0.179	0.168	0.157	0.139	0.123	0.068	0.039
0.361	0.308	0.284	0.263	0.225	0.194	0.167	0.144	0.134	0.125	0.108	0.094	0.048	0.026
0.322	0.270	0.247	0.227	0.191	0.162	0.137	0.116	0.107	0.099	0.085	0.073	0.035	0.017
0.287	0.237	0.215	0.195	0.162	0.135	0.112	0.094	0.086	0.079	0.066	0.056	0.025	0.012
0.257	0.208	0.187	0.168	0.137	0.112	0.092	0.076	0.069	0.062	0.052	0.043	0.018	0.008
0.229	0.182	0.163	0.145	0.116	0.093	0.075	0.061	0.055	0.050	0.040	0.033	0.013	0.005
0.205	0.160	0.141	0.125	0.099	0.078	0.062	0.049	0.044	0.039	0.032	0.025	0.009	0.003
0.183	0.140	0.123	0.108	0.084	0.065	0.051	0.040	0.035	0.031	0.025	0.020	0.006	0.002
0.163	0.123	0.107	0.093	0.071	0.054	0.042	0.032	0.028	0.025	0.019	0.015	0.005	0.002
0.146	0.108	0.093	0.080	0.060	0.045	0.034	0.026	0.023	0.020	0.015	0.012	0.003	0.001
0.130	0.095	0.081	0.069	0.051	0.038	0.028	0.021	0.018	0.016	0.012	0.009	0.002	0.001
0.116	0.083	0.070	0.060	0.043	0.031	0.023	0.017	0.014	0.012	0.009	0.007	0.002	
0.104	0.073	0.061	0.051	0.037	0.026	0.019	0.014	0.012	0.010	0.007	0.005	0.001	
0.093	0.064	0.053	0.044	0.031	0.022	0.015	0.011	0.009	0.008	0.006	0.004	0.001	
0.083	0.056	0.046	0.038	0.026	0.018	0.013	0.009	0.007	0.006	0.004	0.003	0.001	
0.074	0.049	0.040	0.033	0.022	0.015	0.010	0.007	0.006	0.005	0.003	0.002		
0.066	0.043	0.035	0.028	0.019	0.013	0.008	0.006	0.005	0.004	0.003	0.002		
0.059	0.038	0.030	0.024	0.016	0.010	0.007	0.005	0.004	0.003	0.002	0.001		
0.053	0.033	0.026	0.021	0.014	0.009	0.006	0.004	0.003	0.002	0.002	0.001		
0.047	0.029	0.023	0.018	0.011	0.007	0.005	0.003	0.002	0.002	0.001	0.001		
0.042	0.026	0.020	0.016	0.010	0.006	0.004	0.002	0.002	0.002	0.001	0.001		
0.037	0.022	0.017	0.014	0.008	0.005	0.003	0.002	0.002	0.001	0.001	0.001		
0.033	0.020	0.015	0.012	0.007	0.004	0.003	0.002	0.001	0.001	0.001			
0.011	0.005	0.004	0.003	0.001	0.001								
0.003	0.001	0.001	0.001										

Table 14A-2

Present Value of Annuity of $1.00 per Period

Periods (n)	1%	1½%	2%	2½%	3%	3½%	4%	4½%	5%	6%	7%
1....	0.9901	0.9852	0.9804	0.9756	0.9709	0.9662	0.9615	0.9569	0.9524	0.9434	0.9346
2....	1.9704	1.9559	1.9416	1.9274	1.9135	1.8997	1.8861	1.8727	1.8594	1.8334	1.8080
3....	2.9410	2.9122	2.8839	2.8560	2.8286	2.8016	2.7751	2.7490	2.7232	2.6730	2.6243
4....	3.9020	3.8544	3.8077	3.7620	3.7171	3.6731	3.6299	3.5875	3.5460	3.4651	3.3872
5....	4.8534	4.7826	4.7135	4.6458	4.5797	4.5151	4.4518	4.3900	4.3295	4.2124	4.1002
6....	5.7955	5.6972	5.6014	5.5081	5.4172	5.3286	5.2421	5.1579	5.0757	4.9173	4.7665
7....	6.7282	6.5982	6.4720	6.3494	6.2303	6.1145	6.0021	5.8927	5.7864	5.5824	5.3893
8....	7.6517	7.4859	7.3255	7.1701	7.0197	6.8740	6.7327	6.5959	6.4632	6.2098	5.9713
9....	8.5660	8.3605	8.1622	7.9709	7.7861	7.6077	7.4353	7.2688	7.1078	6.8017	6.5152
10....	9.4713	9.2222	8.9826	8.7521	8.5302	8.3166	8.1109	7.9127	7.7217	7.3601	7.0236
11....	10.3676	10.0711	9.7868	9.5142	9.2526	9.0016	8.7605	8.5289	8.3064	7.8869	7.4987
12....	11.2551	10.9075	10.5753	10.2578	9.9540	9.6633	9.3851	9.1186	8.8633	8.3838	7.9427
13....	12.1337	11.7315	11.3484	10.9832	10.6350	10.3027	9.9856	9.6829	9.3936	8.8527	8.3577
14....	13.0037	12.5434	12.1062	11.6909	11.2961	10.9205	10.5631	10.2228	9.8986	9.2950	8.7455
15....	13.8651	13.3432	12.8493	12.3814	11.9379	11.5174	11.1184	10.7395	10.3797	9.7122	9.1079
16....	14.7179	14.1313	13.5777	13.0550	12.5611	12.0941	11.6523	11.2340	10.8378	10.1059	9.4466
17....	15.5623	14.9076	14.2919	13.7122	13.1661	12.6513	12.1657	11.7072	11.2741	10.4773	9.7632
18....	16.3983	15.6726	14.9920	14.3534	13.7535	13.1897	12.6593	12.1600	11.6896	10.8276	10.0591
19....	17.2260	16.4262	15.6785	14.9789	14.3238	13.7098	13.1339	12.5933	12.0853	11.1581	10.3356
20....	18.0456	17.1686	16.3514	15.5892	14.8775	14.2124	13.5903	13.0079	12.4622	11.4699	10.5940
21....	18.8570	17.9001	17.0112	16.1845	15.4150	14.6980	14.0292	13.4047	12.8212	11.7640	10.8355
22....	19.6604	18.6208	17.6580	16.7654	15.9369	15.1671	14.4511	13.7844	13.1630	12.0416	11.0612
23....	20.4558	19.3309	18.2922	17.3321	16.4436	15.6204	14.8568	14.1478	13.4886	12.3034	11.2722
24....	21.2434	20.0304	18.9139	17.8850	16.9355	16.0584	15.2470	14.4955	13.7986	12.5504	11.4693
25....	22.0232	20.7196	19.5235	18.4244	17.4131	16.4815	15.6221	14.8282	14.0939	12.7834	11.6536
26....	22.7952	21.3986	20.1210	18.9506	17.8768	16.8904	15.9828	15.1466	14.3752	13.0032	11.8258
27....	23.5596	22.0676	20.7069	19.4640	18.3270	17.2854	16.3296	15.4513	14.6430	13.2105	11.9867
28....	24.3164	22.7267	21.2813	19.9649	18.7641	17.6670	16.6631	15.7429	14.8981	13.4062	12.1371
29....	25.0658	23.3761	21.8444	20.4535	19.1885	18.0358	1o.9837	16.0219	15.1411	13.5907	12.2777
30....	25.8077	24.0158	22.3965	20.9303	19.6004	18.3920	17.2920	16.2889	15.3725	13.7648	12.4090
40....	32.8347	29.9158	27.3555	25.1028	23.1148	21.3551	19.7928	18.4016	17.1591	15.0463	13.3317
50....	39.1961	34.9997	31.4236	28.3623	25.7298	23.4556	21.4822	19.7620	18.2559	15.7619	13.8007

Table 14A–2 (continued)
Present Value of Annuity of $1.00 per Period

8%	10%	12%	14%	15%	16%	18%	20%	22%	24%	25%	26%	28%	30%	40%	50%
0.9259	0.9091	0.893	0.877	0.870	0.862	0.847	0.833	0.820	0.806	0.800	0.794	0.781	0.769	0.714	0.667
1.7833	1.7355	1.690	1.647	1.626	1.605	1.566	1.528	1.492	1.457	1.440	1.424	1.392	1.361	1.224	1.111
2.5771	2.4869	2.402	2.322	2.283	2.246	2.174	2.106	2.042	1.981	1.952	1.923	1.868	1.816	1.589	1.407
3.3121	3.1699	3.037	2.914	2.855	2.798	2.690	2.589	2.494	2.404	2.362	2.320	2.241	2.166	1.849	1.605
3.9927	3.7908	3.605	3.433	3.352	3.274	3.127	2.991	2.864	2.745	2.689	2.635	2.532	2.436	2.035	1.737
4.6229	4.3553	4.111	3.889	3.784	3.685	3.498	3.326	3.167	3.020	2.951	2.885	2.759	2.643	2.168	1.824
5.2064	4.8684	4.564	4.288	4.160	4.039	3.812	3.605	3.416	3.242	3.161	3.083	2.937	2.802	2.263	1.883
5.7466	5.3349	4.968	4.639	4.487	4.344	4.078	3.837	3.619	3.421	3.329	3.241	3.076	2.925	2.331	1.922
6.2469	5.7590	5.328	4.946	4.772	4.607	4.303	4.031	3.786	3.566	3.463	3.366	3.184	3.019	2.379	1.948
6.7101	6.1446	5.650	5.216	5.019	4.833	4.494	4.192	3.923	3.682	3.571	3.465	3.269	3.092	2.414	1.965
7.1390	6.4951	5.988	5.453	5.234	5.029	4.656	4.327	4.035	3.776	3.656	3.544	3.335	3.147	2.438	1.977
7.5361	6.8137	6.194	5.660	5.421	5.197	4.793	4.439	4.127	3.851	3.725	3.606	3.387	3.190	2.456	1.985
7.9038	7.1034	6.424	5.842	5.583	5.342	4.910	4.533	4.203	3.912	3.780	3.656	3.427	3.223	2.468	1.990
8.2442	7.3667	6.628	6.002	5.724	5.468	5.008	4.611	4.265	3.962	3.824	3.695	3.459	3.249	2.477	1.993
8.5595	7.6061	6.811	6.142	5.847	5.575	5.092	4.675	4.315	4.001	3.859	3.726	3.483	3.268	2.484	1.995
8.8514	7.8237	6.974	6.265	5.954	5.669	5.162	4.730	4.357	4.033	3.887	3.751	3.503	3.283	2.489	1.997
9.1216	8.0216	7.120	6.373	6.047	5.749	5.222	4.775	4.391	4.059	3.910	3.771	3.518	3.295	2.492	1.998
9.3719	8.2014	7.250	6.467	6.128	5.818	5.273	4.812	4.419	4.080	3.928	3.786	3.529	3.304	2.494	1.999
9.6036	8.3649	7.366	6.550	6.198	5.877	5.316	4.844	4.442	4.097	3.942	3.799	3.539	3.311	2.496	1.999
9.8181	8.5136	7.469	6.623	6.259	5.929	5.353	4.870	4.460	4.110	3.954	3.808	3.546	3.316	2.497	1.999
10.0168	8.6487	7.562	6.687	6.312	5.973	5.384	4.891	4.476	4.121	3.963	3.816	3.551	3.320	2.498	2.000
10.2007	8.7715	7.645	6.743	6.359	6.011	5.410	4.909	4.488	4.130	3.970	3.822	3.556	3.323	2.498	2.000
10.3711	8.8832	7.718	6.792	6.399	6.044	5.432	4.925	4.499	4.137	3.976	3.827	3.559	3.325	2.499	2.000
10.5288	8.9847	7.784	6.835	6.434	6.073	5.451	4.937	4.507	4.143	3.981	3.831	3.562	3.327	2.499	2.000
10.6748	9.0770	7.843	6.873	6.464	6.097	5.467	4.948	4.514	4.147	3.985	3.834	3.564	3.329	2.499	2.000
10.8100	9.1609	7.896	6.906	6.491	6.118	5.480	4.956	4.520	4.151	3.988	3.837	3.566	3.330	2.500	2.000
10.9352	9.2372	7.943	6.935	6.514	6.136	5.492	4.964	4.524	4.154	3.990	3.839	3.567	3.331	2.500	2.000
11.0511	9.3066	7.984	6.961	6.534	6.152	5.502	4.970	4.528	4.157	3.992	3.840	3.568	3.331	2.500	2.000
11.1584	9.3696	8.022	6.983	6.551	6.166	5.510	4.975	4.531	4.159	3.994	3.841	3.569	3.332	2.500	2.000
11.2578	9.4269	8.055	7.003	6.566	6.177	5.517	4.979	4.534	4.160	3.995	3.842	3.569	3.332	2.500	2.000
11.9246	9.7791	8.244	7.105	6.642	6.234	5.548	4.997	4.544	4.166	3.999	3.846	3.571	3.333	2.500	2.000
12.2335	9.9148	8.304	7.133	6.661	6.246	5.554	4.999	4.545	4.167	4.000	3.846	3.571	3.333	2.500	2.000

NOTE: To convert this table to values of an annuity in advance, take one less period and add 1.0000.

EXERCISES—APPENDIX

1. Determine the amount that $1,000 will accumulate to in three years at an 8 percent annual interest rate.

2. Determine the present value of $1,000 due in five years at each of the following interest rates:

    a. 6 percent
    b. 8 percent
    c. 10 percent

3. An investor wishes to have $5,000 available at the end of five years. State the amount of money that must be invested at the present time if the interest rate is:

    a. 6 percent
    b. 8 percent
    c. 12 percent

4. Determine the present value of an ordinary annuity for a period of five years with annual payments of $2,000, assuming that the interest rate is:

    a. 7 percent
    b. 10 percent
    c. 12 percent

5. What is the maximum amount you would be willing to pay at the present time in order to receive 10 annual payments of $1,000 beginning one year from now? The current interest rate is 10 percent.

6. Hays Company leases a building at an annual rental of $2,000 paid at the end of each year. The company has been given the alternative of paying the remaining 10 years of the lease in advance on January 1, 1975. Assuming an interest rate of 8 percent, what is the maximum amount that should be paid now for the advance rent?

7. Determine the selling price of the bonds in each of the following situations (assume that the bonds are dated and sold on the same date):

    a. A 10-year $1,000 face value bond with annual interest of 9 percent (payable annually) sold to yield 8 percent effective interest.
    b. A 10-year $1,000 face value bond with annual interest of 9 percent (payable annually) sold to yield 10 percent effective interest.
    c. A 10-year $1,000 face value bond with annual interest of 9 percent (payable annually) sold to yield 9 percent effective interest.

8. Nancy Company issued $10,000 of bonds payable on January 1, 1975, with an 8 percent coupon interest rate, payable annually on December 31. The bonds mature in 5 years and were sold at a 10 percent effective interest rate.

    a. Determine the selling price of the bonds.
    b. Prepare a schedule showing the amount of discount to be amortized

Required:

each year for the life of the bonds, assuming the interest method of amortization.

c. Give the journal entry to record the interest payment on December 31, 1975.

9. Joyce Company issued $10,000 of bond payable on January 1, 1975, with an 8 percent coupon interest rate payable annually on December 31. The bonds mature in 5 years and were sold at a 7 percent effective interest rate.

Required:

a. Determine the selling price of the bonds.
b. Prepare a schedule showing the premium to be amortized each year for the life of the bonds, assuming the interest method of amortization.
c. Give the journal entry to record the interest payment on December 31, 1975.

15

Long-Term Investments and Consolidated Financial Statements

CORPORATIONS frequently acquire the stocks and bonds of other corporations as investments. If the securities are readily marketable and if a firm intends to hold these securities for a relatively short period of time, the investments are normally classified as a current asset, marketable securities (see Chapter 7). On the other hand, investments in stocks and bonds which do not meet the criteria for marketable securities are classified as a noncurrent asset, long-term investments.

INVESTMENTS IN BONDS

Bonds may be purchased as a long-term investment and are accounted for at cost. The cost of a bond includes the quoted price of the bond plus brokerage commissions, transfer taxes, etc. When bonds are purchased between interest dates, the purchase price of the bonds usually includes payment for the interest which has accrued since the previous interest payment date. To illustrate, assume that on June 1, 1975, Edwards Co. purchases $10,000 face value of 12 percent bonds of the Bell Co. at 111½ plus accrued interest. The bonds pay interest on June 30 and December 31. The entry to record the purchase would be:

Investment in Bonds	11,150	
Bond Interest Receivable	500	
Cash		11,650

The debit to the Investment in Bonds account records the cost of the bond—the face value of $10,000 × 111.5 percent or $11,150. This indi-

382

cates that the bonds were purchased at a premium. Note that this premium is not recorded in a separate account, but instead is included as a part of the Investment in Bonds account. The debit to bond interest receivable records the fact that Edwards Co. purchased five months accrued interest along with the bonds ($10,000 $\times$ .12 $\times$ $\frac{5}{12}$ = $500). The credit to cash is for the total amount paid by Edwards.

Amortization of Premium

On June 30, 1975, Edwards Co. will receive its first interest payment which will be recorded as follows:

Cash	600	
Bond Interest Receivable		500
Investment in Bonds		10
Interest Income		90

This entry records the receipt of the $600 interest payment ($10,000 $\times$ .12 $\times$ $\frac{6}{12}$ = $600). Of this amount, $500 is the return of the accrued interest that was purchased when the bonds were acquired. Recall that the bonds were purchased at a premium of $1,150 ($11,150 purchase — $10,000 face value). This premium is amortized as a reduction of interest income over the life of the bonds (June 1, 1975 to December 31, 1984 = 115 months). The amortization is $10 per month ($1,150 ÷ 115 months). Since Edwards Co. had held the bonds for one month (June 1 to June 30) when the first interest payment was received, $10 of the purchase premium was amortized at that time. Note that the amortization is recorded by a credit to the bond investment account. The income for June is $90, one month's interest of $100 ($10,000 $\times$ .12 $\times$ $\frac{1}{12}$ = $100) minus $10 amortization of premium.

On December 31, 1975, Edwards Co. will receive its second interest payment of $600. The entry to record the receipt of this interest and the amortization of premium is:

Cash	600	
Investment in Bonds		60
Interest Income		540

Again, the debit to cash records the receipt of six months interest ($10,000 $\times$ .12 $\times$ $\frac{6}{12}$ = $600). The credit to the Bond Investment account is for six months amortization of premium ($1,150/115 months = $10 per month $\times$ 6 months = $60). The interest income is the receipt of $600 less the $60 amortization. The total interest income recognized over the life of the bonds will be equal to the total cash interest received minus the amount of the premium.

At December 31, 1975, the bond investment account would appear in the balance sheet as follows:

Investment in bonds $11,080

This represents the original cost of the bonds, $11,150 less $70 for seven months amortization of premium.[1] The investment in bonds account will decrease each period by the amount of the premium amortized and, therefore, at maturity will be equal to the face amount of the bonds.

Amortization of Discount

When bonds are purchased at less than their face value, the discount is not shown separately, but as a part of the investment in bonds account. Discount is amortized as an increase in the interest income earned over the life of the bonds. The interest income recognized on bonds that were acquired at a discount and held to maturity is equal to the total of the cash interest payments received plus the amount of the purchase discount. The carrying value of the investment will increase each period by the amount of the discount amortized and at maturity will equal the face amount of the bonds.

Sale of Bonds

If bonds are sold prior to maturity, accrued interest from the last interest payment date to the date of sale should be recorded. Any difference between this accrued interest plus the carrying value of the bond investment account and the net cash proceeds of the sale represents a gain or loss on the sale and is recorded as such. For example, assume that the bonds used in the above illustration were sold on January 1, 1976, for $12,000. The entry to record the sale would be as follows:

Cash 12,000
   Investment in Bonds 11,080
   Gain on the Sale of Bonds 920

Alternatively, had the selling price on January 1, 1976 been $11,000, the entry would have been:

Cash 11,000
Loss on Sale of Bonds 80
   Investment in Bonds 11,080

---

[1] Premium or discount on bonds held as long-term investments is amortized over the life of the bonds. If bonds are held as a temporary investment, no amortization is required.

INVESTMENTS IN STOCKS

Investments in stocks which are not held as temporary investments are classified as long-term assets. Such investments are recorded at their cost as of the date of acquisition. This cost includes the purchase price of the shares plus all brokerage fees, transfer costs, and excise taxes paid by the purchaser. Subsequent to acquisition, long-term investments are accounted for under one of the following methods: (1) *the cost method*—the investment is valued at the original or historical acquisition cost; or (2) *the equity method*—the investment is valued so as to reflect changes in the underlying net assets of the investee corporation.

The cost method is based on the fact that the two corporations are separate legal entities. Therefore, the carrying value of the investment included in the accounts of the investor remains at the original cost. Any changes in the underlying net assets of the investee corporation which may have occurred as a result of its operations are ignored under this method. The equity method, on the other hand, is intended to reflect the economic relationship which exists between the two companies. This method recognizes that an investment in stock which allows the investor company to exercise significant control or influence over the operations of the investee company should be accounted for in such a way that changes in the underlying net assets of the investee company are reflected in the accounts of the investor company. The procedures which are employed in accounting for each of these two methods are summarized below:

Cost Method. Under the cost method, the investment account is carried at the original cost of the investment. Any increases or decreases in the net assets of the investee company resulting from earnings or losses do not affect the investor company's investment account. Dividends received by the investor company are recorded as dividend income.

Equity Method. Under the equity method, the investment is initially recorded at its original cost. After acquisition, the investment account is adjusted for any increases or decreases in the net assets of the investee company which have occurred since the stock was acquired. Net income of the investee results in an increase in its net assets. Therefore, the investor company increases the carrying value of its investment and recognizes investment income to the extent of its share (determined by the percentage of the investee's stock owned by the investor company) of the net income of the investee. For example, assume that an investor firm owned 20 percent of the outstanding voting stock of an investee. If the investee reported earnings of $50,000, the investor would increase the carrying value of its investment by $10,000 and simultaneously recognize investment income of $10,000. Similarly, a net loss incurred by the investee company would result in a reduction of the investment account and the recognition of a loss on investments by the investor firm. Since dividends also reduce the net assets of the investee, any dividend distributions made to the investor are recorded by a decrease in the investment account balance. The effect of the equity method is to value the investment at the original cost plus the investor's share of the undistributed retained earnings (net income less dividends) of the investee company since its acquisition of the stock.

To illustrate the difference between the cost and the equity methods, assume that Stolle Company purchases 1,000 of the 5,000 outstanding shares of Most Company stock on January 1, 1976, at a cost of $10 per share. During 1976, Most Company reports net income of $20,000 and pays dividends of $10,000, and during 1977 Most Company reports a net loss of $5,000 and pays no dividends. The journal entries of Stolle Company under both methods are shown in Illustration 15–1.

These entries have the following effect on the financial statements of Stolle Company as of the end of 1977.

	Cost Method	Equity Method
Investment in Most Co.–December 31, 1977	$10,000	$11,000
Income Statement:		
1976	2,000	4,000
1977	0	(1,000)

Under the cost method, Stolle Company would report its investment in Most Company at December 31, 1977, at its original cost of $10,000. Under the equity method, the investment would be carried at $11,000. The $1,000 increase in the investment account under the equity method reflects Stolle Company's share (20 percent) of the $5,000 increase in the net assets of Most Company since the time the Most Company stock was acquired by Stolle.

Under the cost method, the investor recognizes income only to the extent of assets received from the investee (i.e., dividends). The equity method, on the other hand, recognizes income to the extent of the investor's share of the net income of the investee company, whether or not dividends were received.

The choice between the cost and equity methods was, for all practical purposes, optional prior to the issuance of *Opinion No. 18* of the Accounting Principles Board in 1971. However, the Board stated in this Opinion that the equity method should be used if the investment in stock enables the investor company to exercise significant influence over the operating and financial policies of an investee. The Board assumed that, in the absence of evidence to the contrary, ownership of 20 percent or more of the voting stock of an investee represented evidence of the ability of the investor company to exercise significant influence over the activities of the investee firm. Thus, the cost method would normally be used for an invest-

Illustration 15–1

Event	Cost Method	Equity Method

January 1, 1976 Acquisition of 1,000 shares of the common stock of Most Company	Investment in Most Co. 10,000
	  Cash 10,000
		Investment in Most Co. 10,000
		  Cash 10,000

December 31, 1976 Net income of $20,000 reported by Most Company	No Entry	Investment in Most Co. . . . . . . 4,000 Investment Income . . . . 4,000 To record Stolle Company's $4,000 share (20% × $20,000) of Most Co.'s net income.

June 30, 1976 Stolle Company received dividends of $2,000. (20% of $10,000 dividend paid by Most Co.)	Cash 2,000
	  Dividend Income 2,000
		Cash 2,000
		  Investment in Most Co. 2,000

December 31, 1977 Net loss of $5,000 reported by Most Co.	No Entry	Investment Loss. . . . . 1,000 Investment in Most Co. . . . . 1,000 To record Stolle Co.'s $1,000 share (20% × $5,000) of Most Co.'s $5,000 net loss.

ment of less than 20 percent of the voting common stock and the equity method would be used for an investment of 20 percent or more of the voting stock of an investee. Most investments in preferred stocks would also be accounted for by the cost method because preferred stock does not normally have voting rights.

CONSOLIDATED STATEMENTS

In many instances, investments in stock are made in order to secure ownership of a controlling interest in the voting stock of another company. A firm owning a majority of the voting stock of another company is usually referred to as a *parent company,* and the company whose stock is owned is often called the *subsidiary company.* A parent company and one or more of its related subsidiary companies are usually referred to as *affiliated companies.* Since a parent and its subsidiary are separate legal entities, separate financial statements are prepared for the stockholders and creditors of each company.

The relationship between a parent and its subsidiary is disclosed in the parent company's financial statements in the investment in stock account. However, parent company statements do not reflect the complete economic effect of the parent's ownership of the subsidiary. Therefore, it is often useful to prepare financial statements based on the financial position and operating results of the combined affiliated companies as if they were a single economic entity. The combined finanical statements of two or more affiliated companies are called *consolidated statements.* Consolidated statements provide the stockholders and creditors of the parent company with an overall view of the combined financial position and operating activities of the parent company and its subsidiaries.

Two basic criteria are used in deciding whether or not to prepare consolidated statements. The subsidiary company must be under the continuing control of the parent and the activities of the affiliated companies must be similar. There is no general agreement among accountants as to the percentage ownership which gives the parent company sufficient control to influence the activities of a subsidiary. In many cases, however, ownership of a majority of the voting stock of a subsidiary is considered to be adequate evidence of the ability to control a subsidiary for the purpose of deciding whether or not to prepare consolidated statements. If the operations of the parent and subsidiary companies are unrelated (for example, a bank owning a manufacturing concern), consolidated statements should not be prepared even if the parent owns a majority of the voting stock of the subsidiary. An evaluation of the relationship between the operations of the two firms is based primarily upon the nature of the business activities and the structure of their respective financial statements. For example, consolidated statements prepared for a retail firm that held a controlling interest in an insurance company would normally be of little value to the user of such statements.

From a legal standpoint, a subsidiary company is a separate entity. Accordingly, the subsidiary maintains its own accounting records and prepares separate financial statements. However, since the parent owns a majority of the voting stock of its subsidiary, the parent and subsidiary companies are a business entity under common control. Therefore, individual financial statements of the parent and subsidiary do not provide a comprehensive view of the financial position of the affiliated companies as a single economic unit. Consolidated financial statements, which ignore the legal distinction between the parent and its subsidiary, serve this purpose by reflecting the financial position and results of operations of the affiliated companies as a single economic entity.

Consolidated Balance Sheet at Date of Acquisition

In preparing a consolidated balance sheet, the accounts which are included in the individual parent and subsidiary company records are combined. In the process of this combination, however, certain adjustments must be made in order to avoid duplication or double-counting in determining the balances to be used. For example, the investment account of the parent company reflects its equity in the net assets of the subsidiary. Including both the parent company's investment account and the net assets of the subsidiary in a consolidated statement would result in double-counting the net assets of the subsidiary. Therefore, the parent's investment account should not be included in the consolidated statements. Since the stockholders' equity of the subsidiary is represented by the investment account, it should also be excluded from the consolidated financial statement. The investment of the parent company is referred to as the reciprocal of the stockholders' equity of the subsidiary. Therefore, these accounts and any other reciprocal accounts which may exist as a result of transactions between the parent and its subsidiaries must be eliminated in combining the accounts of the parent and subsidiary companies.

Preparation of consolidated statements is facilitated by the use of a worksheet. Entries included on the consolidations worksheet are made for the sole purpose of preparing consolidated financial statements. Consequently, consolidating adjustments and eliminations are not posted to the books of either the parent or its subsidiary.

Preparation of consolidated balance sheets under varying circumstances is illustrated by the following examples. First, let us consider the process of consolidating two balance sheets at the time a parent company initially acquired the stock of a subsidiary company.

Complete Ownership Acquired at Book Value. Assume that the parent company, P, acquired 100 percent of the common stock of a subsidiary company, S, at a price of $20,000 on December 31, 1976. Separate balance sheets of P Company and S Company immediately following the acquisition are presented in Illustration 15–2.

Illustration 15–2

P COMPANY AND S COMPANY
Balance Sheets
At December 31, 1976

	P Company	S Company
Cash	$ 10,000	$ 5,000
Accounts receivable	10,000	5,000
Fixed assets	60,000	20,000
Investment in S Company	20,000	–0–
Total Assets	$100,000	$30,000
Accounts payable	$ 10,000	$10,000
Capital stock	60,000	15,000
Retained earnings	30,000	5,000
Total Liabilities and Equities	$100,000	$30,000

P Company paid an amount equal to the stockholders' equity (common stock and retained earnings) of the subsidiary for 100 percent ownership of S. This indicates that the acquisitiion was made at the book value of the subsidiary's net assets. Since no transactions have occurred between the companies, the only adjustment required is to eliminate the investment account of the parent against the stockholders' equity accounts of the subsidiary, as shown in Illustration 15–3.

As previously indicated, the elimination entry is made on a worksheet which is used in order to facilitate the preparation of the consolidated balance sheet. No entries are made in the accounting records of either the parent or the subsidiary.

Complete Ownership Acquired at More than Net Asset Value. In most cases when the parent acquires stock in a subsidiary, the cost of the investment will differ from the recorded value of the net assets (assets — liabilities) of the subsidiary. From a consolidated standpoint, the purchase of subsidiary stock may be regarded as similar to the purchase of the subsidiary's net assets (i.e., its assets less liabilities). Consequently, subsidiary assets should be recorded at an amount equal to the price paid by the parent for its 100 percent interest in the subsidiary. To adjust the carrying values of subsidiary assets to reflect the price paid by the parent for the stock, information concerning the fair values of the subsidiary assets at the time of acquisition must be obtained.

The amount paid by the parent company for the subsidiary's stock may

Illustration 15–3

P COMPANY AND S COMPANY
Consolidation Worksheet
At December 31, 1976

| | | | Eliminations | | Con- |
	P Co.	S Co.	Dr.	Cr.	solidation
Cash	$ 10,000	$ 5,000			$ 15,000
Accounts receivable.	10,000	5,000			15,000
Fixed assets	60,000	20,000			80,000
Investment in S Company	20,000			$20,000 [(a)]	
Total Assets	$100,000	$30,000			$110,000
Accounts payable	$ 10,000	$10,000			$ 20,000
Capital stock.	60,000	15,000	$15,000 [(a)]		60,000
Retained earnings	30,000	5,000	5,000 [(a)]		30,000
Total Liabilities and Equity	$100,000	$30,000			$110,000

[a] Elimination of the investment account against book value of the subsidiary's stock.

differ from the net asset value of the subsidiary for two primary reasons. First, subsidiary assets may have a fair market value which differs from their recorded book value. This may occur because the accounting methods used for recording assets are normally not intended to reflect the fair value of the assets of the firm. Thus, if the parent company pays an amount which is in excess of book value, this excess may exist because the net assets of the subsidiary are undervalued (that is, the book value of the assets determined on the basis of proper accounting methods is less than their fair market value). Also, the excess may be due to the existence of unrecorded intangible assets of the subsidiary or from anticipated advantages which are expected because of the affiliation. If the assets of the subsidiary are undervalued, any specific tangible or intangible assets with fair market values in excess of recorded book values should be restated at fair market value in the consolidation worksheet. Thus, identifiable assets will be reported in the consolidated balance sheet at an amount equal to their fair market values at the date of acquisition. If the cost of the subsidiary stock still exceeds the amount assigned to the net assets of the subsidiary in the consolidation worksheet, this excess is assigned to an intangible asset, Goodwill or "Excess of Cost Over Book Value." Therefore, the total excess of the cost of the subsidiary stock over the book value of the subsidiary's net assets is included among consolidated assets—either as increases in the value of specific assets or alternatively as goodwill. Again, it is important to note that these adjustments are made only in the consolidation worksheet.

To illustrate, assume the same facts as in the previous illustration except that P Company acquired all of the stock of S Company at a cost of $25,000. Thus, the cost of investment ($25,000) exceeds the stockholders' equity of the subsidiary ($20,000) by $5,000. Apparently the management of P Company believes that the fair value of specific assets of S Company is greater than their recorded book value or that there are advantages of affiliation, such as future earnings prospects, which justify payment of $5,000 in excess of book value for S Company's net assets. In this illustration, assume that the excess of cost over book value existed because the fair market value of S Company's land exceeded its recorded book value by $5,000. Therefore, this excess would be assigned to land (which is summarized in fixed assets in this example) in the consolidation worksheet. The consolidation worksheet would be as shown in Illustration 15–4. The eliminating entries on the consolidation worksheet would be:

(a) Fixed Assets–S Company   5,000
        Investment in S Company   5,000
(b) Capital Stock–S Company   15,000
        Retained Earnings–S Company   5,000
            Investment in S Company   20,000

It is important to note that these entries would not appear in the accounts of either P Company or S Company. These are worksheet entries

Illustration 15–4

P COMPANY AND S COMPANY
Consolidation Worksheet
At December 31, 1976

	P Co.	S Co.	Eliminations Dr.	Eliminations Cr.	Consolidation
Cash	$ 5,000	$ 5,000			$ 10,000
Accounts receivable.	10,000	5,000			15,000
Fixed assets	60,000	20,000	$ 5,000 (a)		85,000
Investment in S Company	25,000			$ 5,000 (a) $ 20,000 (b)	
Total Assets	$100,000	$30,000			$110,000
Accounts payable	$ 10,000	$10,000			$ 20,000
Capital stock	60,000	15,000	15,000 (b)		60,000
Retained earnings	30,000	5,000	5,000 (b)		30,000
Total Liabilities and Equity	$100,000	$30,000			$110,000

a Adjustment for undervaluation of Subsidiary's assets.
b Elimination of the investment against the book value of the Subsidiary's stock.

that would be used to facilitate the consolidation of the financial reports of the parent and subsidiary company.

If the excess cannot be assigned to any specific assets (that is, the recorded book values of the subsidiary assets are equal to their fair values at acquisition), the $5,000 excess would have been reported in the consolidated balance sheet as Goodwill or "Excess of Cost Over Book Value." This is a new account which is introduced in the consolidated worksheet—it does not appear in the accounts of either P or S.

Complete Ownership Acquired for Less than Net Asset Value. If the cost of the stock acquired by the parent company is less than book value, a similar problem exists. When specific overvalued assets can be identified, the excess would be reflected on the balance sheet by reducing the value of specific assets of the subsidiary. Thus, subsidiary assets would be reported at their fair values in the consolidated balance sheet. When specific assets which are overvalued cannot be identified, the excess is used to reduce noncurrent assets. If the allocation reduces the noncurrent assets to zero, the remainder of the excess is credited to an account referred to as "Excess of Book Value of Subsidiary Interest Over Cost." This account is shown as a reduction of assets on the consolidated balance sheet. For example, assume P Company purchased 100 percent of the stock of S Company at a price of $18,000 on December 31, 1976. At that date the stockholders' equity of S Company was $20,000, consisting of $15,000 capital stock and $5,000 retained earnings. Eliminating entries on the consolidation worksheet would be as follows:

(a)	Investment in S Company	2,000	
	Specific Assets of S Company.		2,000
(b)	Capital Stock–S Company.	15,000	
	Retained Earnings–S Company	5,000	
	Investment in S Company (from P's books).		20,000

Less Than Complete Ownership. A parent company may obtain control of a subsidiary by acquiring less than 100 percent of the capital stock of the subsidiary. When a parent owns less than 100 percent of the stock, the remainder of the stock held by stockholders outside the affiliated companies is classified as a *minority interest* in the consolidated balance sheet. The existence of a minority interest does not affect the amount at which the assets and liabilities of the affiliated companies will ultimately appear on the consolidated balance sheet. However, only a portion of the equity in the net assets of the subsidiary company is owned by the parent since a portion of the owners' equity is held by minority stockholders. Equity held by minority stockholders, or minority interest, is a part of the stockholders' equity of the consolidated entity.

To illustrate, assume that P Company acquired only 90 percent of the capital stock of the subsidiary at a cost of $18,000. The remaining 10 percent of the subsidiary's stock represents the minority interest in S Company. The only change required in the elimination entries is that only 90 percent of the capital stock and retained earnings of S Company is eliminated. The remaining 10 percent of S Company stockholders' equity represents the minority interest in the subsidiary and is classified as such in the consolidated balance sheet. The consolidation worksheet used to prepare the consolidated balance sheet is shown in Illustration 15–5.

Illustration 15–5

P COMPANY AND S COMPANY
Consolidation Worksheet
At December 31, 1976

	P Co.	S Co.	Eliminations Dr.	Eliminations Cr.	Consolidation
Cash	$ 12,000	$ 5,000			$ 17,000
Accounts receivable.	10,000	5,000			15,000
Fixed assets	60,000	20,000			80,000
Investment in S Company	18,000			$18,000[a]	
Total Assets	$100,000	$30,000			$112,000
Accounts payable	$ 10,000	$10,000			$ 20,000
Capital stock	60,000	15,000	$ 1,500[b] 13,500[a]		60,000
Retained earnings	30,000	5,000	500[b] 4,500[a]		30,000
Minority interest	-0-	-0-		2,000[b]	2,000
Total Liabilities and Equity	$100,000	$30,000			$112,000

a Elimination of investment against 90 percent of the Subsidiary's stockholders' equity.
b Adjustment to reclassify 10 percent of the Subsidiary's stockholders' equity as minority interest.

The initial consolidation entry (a) eliminated 90 percent of the capital stock and retained earnings of S Company against the investment account of the parent. The remaining 10 percent of the stockholders' equity of S Company was then reclassified as a minority interest in entry (b).

It should be noted that, in this example, the parent company paid an amount which was equal to book value for its interest in the subsidiary. Therefore, the investment account was exactly equal to 90 percent of the stockholders' equity of S Company at acquisition. The existence of a minority interest, however, would not affect the procedures which are required when the investment is acquired at either more or less than book value. Any difference between the cost of the investment and the amount representing the parent company's interest in the stockholders' equity of the subsidiary increases consolidated assets if cost exceeds book value, and reduces consolidated assets if cost is less than book value.

Consolidated Balance Sheet after the Date of Acquisition

Net assets of a subsidiary change subsequent to the date of affiliation as a result of the difference between the net income earned and the dividends paid by the subsidiary since the date the parent acquired its interest in the subsidiary. If the parent company carries its investment using the equity method, the parent's share of such changes in the net assets of a subsidiary are reflected in the investment account. This occurs because the parent company increases the investment account and records investment income for its share of subsidiary earnings and reduces the investment account for any dividends which it receives from the subsidiary. Similarly, a loss incurred by the subsidiary is recorded by the parent as a decrease in the investment account and a corresponding decrease in the parent company's earnings. At any time subsequent to the date of affiliation, the change in the parent's investment account for each year must be equal to the parent company's share (that is, the parent company's percentage ownership of the voting stock of its subsidiary) of the change in the retained earnings of the subsidiary company. The eliminations which are required in order to prepare a consolidated balance sheet are basically the same as those which were required at the date of acquisition except that the amount eliminated from the investment account of the parent and the stockholders' equity of the subsidiary will change each year. Since the two entries which are made in the elimination of the parent's investment account against the stockholders' equity of the subsidiary will change by the same amount, the original difference between the cost of the investment and the book value of the subsidiary will be the same for each period.

To illustrate the procedures required for the preparation of a worksheet for a consolidated balance sheet, assume that P Company purchases 90 percent of the outstanding stock of S Company on December 31, 1976, at a price of $21,000. At that time, S Company had capital stock of $15,000 and retained earnings of $5,000. Therefore, the cost of the investment exceeded the book value of the subsidiary stock by $3,000 (the book value of the net assets purchased was 90% × $20,000 or $18,000). It was determined that this excess of cost over book value was attributed to the excess of the market value of land owned by the subsidiary over the book value of the land. Further, assume that the subsidiary company had net income of $20,000 and paid dividends totaling $10,000 during 1977. The effect of these transactions is to increase the retained earnings of the subsidiary by $10,000, from $5,000 to $15,000 (retained earnings on December 31, 1976, of $5,000 plus 1977 net income of $20,000 minus 1977

Illustration 15–6

P COMPANY AND S COMPANY
Consolidation Worksheet
At December 31, 1977

	P Co.	S Co.	Eliminations Dr.	Eliminations Cr.	Con- solidations
Cash	$ 10,000	$ 7,000			$ 17,000
Accounts receivable.	10,000	6,000			16,000
Fixed assets	70,000	20,000	$ 3,000(a)		93,000
Investment in S Company	30,000			$ 3,000(a) 27,000(b)	
Total Assets	$120,000	$33,000			$126,000
Accounts payable	$ 15,000	$ 3,000			$ 18,000
Capital stock.	60,000	15,000	{ 1,500(c) 13,500(b)		60,000
Retained earnings	45,000	15,000	{ 1,500(c) 13,500(b)		45,000
Minority interest				3,000(c)	3,000
Total Liabilities and Equity	$120,000	$33,000			$126,000

a Adjustment for undervaluaton of Subsidiary's assets.
b Elimination of investment against 90% of the Subsidiary's Stockholders' equity.
c Adjustment to reclassify 10% of the Subsidiary's stockholders' equity as minority interest.

Illustration 15–7

P COMPANY AND S COMPANY
Consolidated Balance Sheet
At December 31, 1977

Current assets:
Cash $17,000
Accounts receivable 16,000
    Total current assets . . . . $ 33,000
Fixed assets 93,000
    Total Assets. $126,000

Liabilities:
Accounts payable. . . . . $ 18,000
Minority interest in S Co. 3,000
Stockholders' equity:
Capital stock $60,000
Retained earnings. 45,000 $105,000
    Total Liabilities and Equities $126,000

dividends of $10,000). Similarly, net income and dividends paid by the subsidiary will cause a net increase of $9,000 in the parent company's investment account (90% of $20,000 net income minus 90% of the $10,000 dividends). The remaining 10 percent of the increase in the subsidiary's retained earnings represents an increase in the equity of the minority stockholders and would be classified as such. The worksheet (Illustration 15–6) for consolidation illustrates the procedures which are required in preparing a consolidated balance sheet (Illustration 15–7) one year after the date of acquisition of the subsidiary.

OTHER RECIPROCAL ACCOUNTS

In preparing a consolidated balance sheet, the investment account of the parent company must be eliminated against the stockholders' equity accounts of its subsidiary. If any transactions occurred between the parent and subsidiary companies, there might be additional reciprocal accounts which would also be eliminated in the consolidation worksheet in order to avoid the double counting of assets and liabilities.

One of the most common of these additional reciprocal accounts involves intercompany receivables and payables. If one affiliated company borrows from another, the debtor firm incurs a liability (payable) equal to an asset (receivable) of the creditor company. From a consolidated standpoint, the payable does not represent an amount owed to an entity outside the affiliated group, nor does the related asset represent a receivable from an outside group. Therefore, in the consolidation worksheet, both the reciprocal asset and liability should be eliminated.

To illustrate this point, assume that the parent company owes the subsidiary company $5,000 as of December 31, 1977. The following entry would be made on the consolidation worksheet in order to eliminate the reciprocal accounts:

Accounts Payable–P Company 5,000
    Accounts Receivable–S Company   5,000

POOLING OF INTEREST

In the discussion of consolidated statements included in the preceding section of this chapter, it was assumed that the parent company purchased the stock of the subsidiary with cash or other assets. The consolidated statements were prepared on the premise that the purchase of stock represented a purchase of the underlying net assets of the subsidiary. Therefore, in the consolidated statements, the cost of the acquisition was allocated to the individual assets of the subsidiary with any excess reported as "excess of cost over book value."

A subsidiary may also be acquired by the exchange of the parent's stock for the stock of the subsidiary. Under certain circumstances, this combination may be accounted for as a pooling of interests. Because the stockholders of the subsidiary become stockholders of the parent company, one group has not acquired the interests of the other. Rather, both have "pooled" their interests in a combined entity. A pooling of interests unites the ownership interests of two or more firms by the exchange of stock. A purchase transaction is not recognized because the combination is accomplished without disbursing the assets of either company. A key feature of a pooling is that the former ownership interests continue and the basis of accounting remains the same.

Since no purchase is recognized and basically the same ownership interests continue, there is no justification for revaluing assets in a pooling of interests. All assets and liabilities of the companies are carried forward to the consolidated statements at their recorded book value. The parent company records the acquisition by debiting the investment account for the par value of the stock issued. Since assets and liabilities are combined at their recorded amounts, there is no excess of cost over book value to be accounted for in the consolidated statements. In addition, retained earnings of the subsidiary at acquisition may be combined with the parent's retained earnings in determining consolidated retained earnings.

To illustrate, assume that P Company issued 1,000 shares of its $50 par value stock in exchange for all of the stock of S Company. Assume that S Company has 6,000 shares of $10 par value stock outstanding. The parent company records the acquisition at the par value of the stock issued as follows:

Investment in S Company	50,000	
Capital Stock		50,000

Under the pooling of interests method, the fair values of the subsidiary's assets are not considered to be relevant for purposes of consolidation. Therefore, the entry required on the worksheet eliminates the investment account of the parent company against the capital stock of the subsidiary. The consolidation worksheet at the date of acquisition is shown in Illustration 15–8. Since the par value of the stock issued by the parent ($50,000) is less than the par value of the shares acquired ($60,000), the difference was shown as an addition to capital in excess of par value in the consolidated balance sheet. If the par value of the stock issued exceeds the par value of the shares acquired, the difference may be charged or debited to capital in excess of par value. If capital in excess is insufficient to absorb the difference, the remainder may be charged against retained earnings.

Note that combining the parent and subsidiary retained earnings accounts is allowable under the pooling method. In the example, consolidated

Illustration 15–8

P COMPANY AND S COMPANY
Consolidation Worksheet
At January 1, 1977

	P Co.	S Co.	Eliminations Dr.	Eliminations Cr.	Con-solidations
Other assets	$250,000	$120,000			$370,000
Investment in S Co..	50,000	-0-		$50,000(a)	-0-
Total.	$300,000	$120,000			$370,000
Liabilities	$ 30,000	$ 20,000			$ 50,000
Capital stock—					
P Co. ($50 par value). . . .	150,000	-0-			150,000
S Co. ($10 par value). . . .	-0-	60,000	$60,000(a)		-0-
Capital in excess of					
par value	50,000	-0-		10,000(a)	60,000
Retained earnings.	70,000	40,000			110,000
Total.	$300,000	$120,000			$370,000

a Elimination of investment account against an equal amount of stockholders' equity.

retained earnings at acquisition ($110,000) was equal to the sum of the parent's and subsidiary's retained earnings balances. Consolidated retained earnings may be less than the sum of the retained earnings balances if the par value of the stock issued by the parent is more than the par value of the shares acquired and if there is insufficient capital in excess of par value to absorb this difference.

Prior to 1970, accountants often considered the purchase and pooling of interests method to be acceptable alternatives for accounting for any given business combination. The pooling of interests method was popular because in circumstances where the fair value of the subsidiary assets exceeds the recorded book values, the pooling treatment results in higher future net income and earnings per share to be reported than does the purchase method. In addition, pooling normally causes higher retained earnings than the purchase method. The Accounting Principles Board, however, attempted to resolve this problem by issuing *Opinion No. 16*. With respect to the purchase versus pooling issue, the Board concluded that ". . . the purchase method and the pooling of interests method are both acceptable in accounting for business combinations, although not as alternatives in accounting for the same business combinations." The Board specified the conditions under which each of the two methods is applicable to a business combination.[2]

---

[2] Discussion of the specific criteria for purchase vs. pooling is beyond the scope of this text.

USEFULNESS OF CONSOLIDATED STATEMENTS

In a situation where one corporation owns a majority of the voting stock of one or more other corporations, financial statements which are prepared for the separate legal corporate entities may not provide the most useful information to management, stockholders, and potential investors of the parent company. Instead, these users are interested in the financial position and results of operations of the combined entity, i.e., the parent company and all other companies under the control of the parent.

On the other hand, minority stockholders of a subsidiary company ordinarily have little use for consolidated financial statements. Since minority stockholders are primarily concerned with their ownership in the subsidiary company, separate financial statements of the subsidiary are usually more useful to them. Similarly, creditors of either the parent or a subsidiary are primarily concerned with their individual legal claims. Therefore, separate financial statements based on the individual entities concerned are of primary interest to these creditors.

APPENDIX TO CHAPTER 15
CONSOLIDATED INCOME STATEMENT

A consolidated income statement is prepared by combining the revenues and expenses of the parent and subsidiary companies. If the parent company owns 100 percent of the subsidiary stock and there have been no transactions between the parent and its subsidiary, consolidation is simply a combination of revenues and expenses resulting from the parent and subsidiary companies' operations. The only adjustment necessary is that which is required in order to eliminate the investment income of the parent company (the parent company's share of the subsidiary's net income). This amount must be eliminated in order to avoid duplication or double-counting of earnings in the consolidated income statement.

As in the case of the consolidated balance sheet, elimination of reciprocal accounts may be necessary in order to avoid duplication or double-counting of revenues and expenses resulting from transactions which have occurred between the parent and its subsidiary. For example, interest expense of one company and interest income of the other resulting from an intercompany loan are eliminated because they do not change the net assets of the total entity from a consolidated viewpoint.

MINORITY INTEREST

If the parent owns less than 100 percent of the subsidiary stock, an additional adjustment is required in the consolidated worksheet in order to allocate the net income of the subsidiary between the parent company and the minority stockholders of the subsidiary. This division of the consolidated income is based on the percentage of the subsidiary stock owned by the parent company and the minority stockholders.

To illustrate the consolidation procedure for the income statement, again assume that P Company purchased 90 percent of the stock of S Company on December 31, 1976. The 1977 income statement for P Company is presented in Illustration 15A–1. Also assume that the parent rents

Illustration 15A–1
P COMPANY AND S COMPANY
Income Statements
For the Year Ended December 31, 1977

	P Company	S Company
Revenues:		
Sales	$195,000	$100,000
Rent revenue . . . . :.	5,000	0
Investment income	18,000	0
Total Revenues	$218,000	$100,000
Expenses:		
Cost of goods sold	$150,000	$ 70,000
Other expenses	20,000	10,000
Total Expenses	$170,000	$ 80,000
Net Income	$ 48,000	$ 20,000

a building to its subsidiary at a rental of $5,000 per year. The procedures which are necessary in order to prepare a consolidated income statement are illustrated in the consolidated worksheet in Illustration 15A–2. It should be noted that the worksheet has a self balancing format. That is, the net income figures have been included along with the expenses so that revenues are equal to income plus expenses.

Elimination (a) removes the duplication or double-counting effect of the intercompany building rental. This entry has no effect on consolidated net income since it simply offsets rent revenue of P Company against an equal amount of rent expense of S Company. Elimination (b) cancels the investment income which P Company records as its share of the net income of S Company under the equity method. This entry corrects the double-counting of S Company's net income. Elimination (c) allocates 10 percent of S Company's net income to the minority stockholders of the subsidiary company.

The amounts in the consolidation column of the worksheet are used in order to prepare the consolidated income statement in Illustration 15A–3. Notice that the minority interest in net income is treated as a reduc-

Illustration 15A–2

P COMPANY AND S COMPANY
Consolidation Worksheet
At December 31, 1977

	P Co.	S Co.	Eliminations Dr.	Eliminations Cr.	Con- solidations
Sales	$195,000	$100,000			$295,000
Rent revenue	5,000	0	$ 5,000(a)		
Investment income	18,000	0	18,000(b)		
Total revenues.	$218,000	$100,000			$295,000
Cost of goods sold	$150,000	$ 70,000			$220,000
Other expenses	20,000	10,000		$ 5,000(a)	25,000
Net income–P Co.	48,000				48,000
Net income–S Co.		20,000		2,000(c) 18,000(b)	
Minority interest in net income.			2,000(c)		2,000
Total expenses and net income	$218,000	$100,000			$295,000

a Elimination of intercompany rent revenue and rent expense.
b Elimination of investment income against 90 percent of subsidiary net income.
c Adjustment to reclassify 10 percent of the subsidiary's net income as minority interest.

Illustration 15A–3

P COMPANY AND SUBSIDIARY
Consolidated Income Statement
For the Year 1977

Sales	$295,000
Cost of goods sold	220,000
Gross profit	$ 75,000
Other expenses	25,000
Combined net income	$ 50,000
Less minority interest in net income	2,000
Consolidated Net Income	$ 48,000

tion of net income of the consolidated entity to arrive at consolidated net income.

PROFIT ON INTERCOMPANY SALES

An additional problem occurs if the assets which were transferred in intercompany sales were sold at a price which differed from the cost to the selling affiliate. If these assets were not resold by the end of the period, the gain or loss on the sale between the affiliates must be eliminated in the consolidation process. To illustrate this point, assume that the following transactions take place between a parent company (P) and its subsidiary (S):

1. P purchases two ten-speed bicycles for $100.
2. P sells the two bicycles to S for $120 on account.
3. S sells one of the bicycles to an outsider for $80 in cash.

These entries would be recorded on the books of P and S as follows:

"P" Books			"S" Books		
1. Inventory 100			No Entry		
Cash		100			
2. Accounts Receivable 120			Inventories. 120		
Sales		120	Accounts Payable.		120
Cost of Goods Sold. 100					
Inventories		100			
3. No Entry			Cash 80		
			Sales		80
			Cost of Goods Sold 60		
			Inventories		60

As a result of these transactions, there is a receivable of $120 from S on P's books and a payable of $120 to P on S's books. Also, P's books show sales of $120 (to S) and a related cost of goods sold of $100, while S's books show the cost of the bicycle sold to the outsider as $60. The unsold bicycle is carried in S's inventory at a cost of $60.

The problem, in terms of preparing consolidated financial statements, is that the intercompany receivables and payables and the effects of the intercompany sales must be eliminated. Also, the cost of the bicycle remaining in S's inventory must be reduced from $60 to $50 (the cost to P) and the $10 profit on the "sale" of this bicycle by P to S must be eliminated from the net income of P Company. The worksheet entries required to accomplish these objectives are as follows:

Accounts Payable 120		
Accounts Receivable		120
Sales 120		
Cost of Goods Sold		120
Cost of Goods Sold 10		
Inventories		10

The first entry eliminates the intercompany receivables and payables. The second entry eliminates the intercompany sale and the related cost of goods sold, while the final entry corrects the cost of goods sold (and therefore net income) by eliminating the intercompany profit in the ending inventory.

KEY DEFINITIONS

Affiliated companies A parent company and one or more related subsidiary companies are said to be affiliated.

Consolidated statements Consolidated financial statements present the combined assets, equities, and results of operations of affiliated corporations.

Consolidation worksheet Consolidation working papers are used in the preparation of consolidated statements for two or more companies. The consolidating adjustments and eliminations are never posted to the books of the individual companies involved, only to the worksheet.

Cost method The cost method of accounting is used for an investment in the stock of another company in which the investment account is carried at the original cost and income is recognized when dividends are received.

Equity method The equity method of accounting is used for an investment in the stock of another company in which the investment account is adjusted for changes in the net assets of the investee, and income is recognized by the investor company as the investee earns profits or incurs losses.

Long-term investment in stock This involves the acquisition of stock of other corporations as long-term, income-producing investments. Such purchases are often made for the purpose of obtaining a controlling interest in a company or for some other continuing business advantage.

Minority interest Shares held by stockholders of a subsidiary company when the parent acquires less than 100 percent of the subsidiary stock are referred to as a minority interest.

Parent company A firm owning a majority of the voting stock of another company is called a parent company.

Pooling of interests Pooling of interests is a method used for recording a business acquisition where the assets and liabilities of the combining companies are combined at their existing book values.

Purchase The purchase method for recording a business acquisition is the use of the cost to the acquiring corporation in valuing the assets of the subsidiary.

Subsidiary company A subsidiary company is a firm which has a majority of its voting stock owned by a parent company.

QUESTIONS

1. Differentiate between long-term (permanent) and short-term (temporary) investments in stocks.
2. Explain the essential characteristics of the cost method.
3. Explain the essential characteristics of the equity method.
4. Under what circumstances would each of the following methods of accounting for long-term investment in stocks be used: (*a*) cost method? (*b*) equity method?
5. Define: (*a*) parent company (*b*) subsidiary company (*c*) affiliated companies.

6. Describe the two essential conditions for the preparation of consolidated financial statements.

7. A consolidated balance sheet prepared for a parent company that owns less than 100 percent of the common stock of the subsidiary shows an item called "minority interest." What is the nature of this balance sheet account, and where does it appear on the consolidated balance sheet?

8. How is the difference between the cost of the subsidiary stock and the book value of the stock at the date of acquisition reported on the consolidated balance sheet?

9. Explain why intercompany debts and receivables should be eliminated in preparing consolidated balance sheets.

10. Why is the investment account of the parent company eliminated in preparing a consolidated balance sheet?

11. What types of users of financial statements are primarily interested in consolidated financial statements?

12. If the parent owns less than 100 percent of the subsidiary stock, the consolidated income statement shows an item called "minority interest in subsidiary income." What does this item represent?

13. Where are the entries recorded for the eliminations that are made in the process of preparing consolidated statements?

EXERCISES

15–1   On January 1, 1975, Lang Company acquired 25 percent of the outstanding shares of stock of Brenner Company at a cost of $250,000. On that date, Brenner Company had common stock of $750,000 and retained earnings of $250,000. Brenner Company reported net income of $100,000 during 1975, and paid a cash dividend of $20,000. Make the necessary journal entries on Lang's books during 1975 using the equity method.

15–2   Assume that Lang Company (Exercise 15–1) acquired only 10 percent of the shares of Brenner Company at a cost of $100,000. Prepare the necessary journal entries on Lang's books during 1975 using the cost method.

15–3   On December 31, 1975, P Co. acquired a controlling interest in S Co. The balance sheets prior to acquisition were as follows:

	P Co.	S Co.
Current assets	$100,000	$ 50,000
Fixed assets (net)	300,000	70,000
	$400,000	$120,000
Liabilities	$ 40,000	$ 20,000
Common stock	300,000	80,000
Retained earnings	60,000	20,000
	$400,000	$120,000

Prepare a consolidation worksheet at the date of acquisition assuming that P Co. paid $100,000 cash for all the outstanding common stock of S Co.

15–4   Prepare a consolidation worksheet at the date of acquisition assuming that P Co. (of exercise 15–3) paid $90,000 cash for 90 percent of the outstanding common stock of S Co.

15–5   On December 31, 1975, the account balances of a parent and its subsidiary included the following amounts.

	Parent	Subsidiary
Notes receivable.	$ 10,000	$ 20,000
Notes payable	30,000	15,000
Sales	500,000	100,000
Purchases	300,000	70,000

All of the subsidiary sales were made to the parent company. All of the goods purchased from the subsidiary were sold by the parent company during the year. The parent company owed the subsidiary $10,000 as of December 31, 1975.

a.   What amounts of notes receivable and notes payable should be reported on the consolidated balance sheet?

b.   What amount of sales and purchases should be reported on the consolidated income statement?

15–6   Walton, Inc. is a 100 percent owned subsidiary of Portland Company. The following transactions occurred in 1975:

a.   Portland Company purchased two basketballs for $10.

b.   Portland Company sold the two basketballs to Walton, Inc. for $12 on account.

c.   Walton, Inc. sold one of the basketballs to an outsider for $8.

Required:

a.   Prepare journal entries on the books of Portland Company and Walton, Inc., to reflect the above information.

b.   Prepare the necessary elimination entries for consolidation.

15–7   Armor Company purchased a $1,000 face value, 5-year, 8 percent bond on April 1, 1975, for $1,020 including accrued interest. Interest on the bond is paid semiannually on June 30 and December 31. Prepare the journal entries required on the books of Armor Company on April 1, June 30, and December 31, 1975.

PROBLEMS

Series A

15A–1   Gorman Company purchased as a permanent investment $10,000 (face value) of 8 percent bonds on March 1, 1975, at $12,380 plus accrued interest. The bonds mature on December 31, 1994, and interest is payable semiannually on June 30 and December 31 of each year. Prepare the journal entries related to this investment which would be required on:

a. March 1, 1975;
b. June 30, 1975;
c. December 31, 1975;
d. December 31, 1994, assuming that the bonds were held until maturity.

15A–2 The ABC Co. acquired 1,000 shares of XYZ Co. on December 31, 1974, for $10.00 per share. XYZ Co. has 2,000 shares of stock outstanding. At the end of 1976, XYZ Co. reported net income of $20,000 and paid a cash dividend of $8,000. At the end of 1975, XYZ Co. reported a net loss of $6,000 and no dividends were declared.

Required:

a. Make the necessary journal entries to account for the investment on ABC's books using the cost method and determine the balance in the investment account on December 31, 1976.
b. Repeat *a*, assuming the equity method is used.

15A–3 The balance sheets of Stevens Corporation and Thomas Corporation reflected the following on December 31, 1975.

	Stevens Corp.	Thomas Corp.
Current assets	$100,000	$ 30,000
Other assets	500,000	100,000
Investment in Thomas	120,000	–0–
	$720,000	$130,000
Current liabilities	$100,000	$ 10,000
Common stock	500,000	100,000
Retained earnings.	120,000	20,000
	$720,000	$130,000

Stevens Corp. purchased 100 percent of the capital stock of Thomas Corp. on January 1, 1975, for $111,000. The stockholders' equity of Thomas Corp. on that date included common stock of $100,000 and retained earnings of $11,000.

Stevens Corp. had an account payable of $10,000 to Thomas Corp. at December 31, 1975.

Prepare the December 31, 1975, consolidated balance sheet.

15A–4 The balances presented below were taken from the books of the Burns Co. and its subsidiary, the Gentry Co., as of December 31, 1976. Burns Co. purchased 90 percent of the stock of Gentry Co. for $110,000 on December 31, 1975. At the date of acquisition, Gentry Co. had common stock of $100,000 and retained earnings of $10,000. The difference between cost and book value was attributed to land owned by Gentry Co. Burns Co. uses the equity method for accounting for its investment in Gentry Co.

	Burns Co.	Gentry Co.
Cash	$ 20,000	$ 20,000
Accounts receivable	40,000	20,000
Inventories	60,000	25,000
Land	80,000	25,000
Buildings and equipment (Net)	281,000	60,000
Investment in Gentry Co.	119,000	-0-
	$600,000	$150,000
Accounts payable	$120,000	$ 30,000
Capital stock	400,000	100,000
Retained earnings	80,000	20,000
	$600,000	$150,000

At the end of the year, Gentry Co. owed Burns Co. $10,000 on open account.

Required:

a. Prepare a worksheet for a consolidated balance sheet as of the end of 1976.
b. Prepare a consolidated balance sheet in good form for the two companies.

15A–5 Below are given the trial balances of Moore Company and its 90 percent owned subsidiary, Parker Company, as of December 31, 1975:

	Moore Company		Parker Company	
Cash	$ 31,000		$ 12,750	
Accounts receivable	24,000		12,400	
Advances to Parker Company	10,000			
Investment in Parker Company	76,500			
Inventory	26,000		28,100	
Other assets	80,840		50,000	
Accounts payable		$ 31,960		$ 8,250
Advances from Moore Company				10,000
Capital stock		200,000		60,000
Retained earnings		16,380		25,000
	$248,340	$248,340	$103,250	$103,250

Additional data:

The advances are non-interest bearing. At the time of acquisition Parker Company's equity section was as follows:

Capital stock	$60,000
Retained earnings	15,000

Required:

1. Elimination entries.
2. Consolidated balance sheet.

15A–6   On January 1, 1975, Ace Co. purchased a 90 percent interest in Deuce Co. Income statement data for 1975 are shown below:

	Ace Co.	Deuce Co.
Sales	$500,000	$ 88,000
Rental income.	-0-	12,000
Interest income	1,000	-0-
Investment income	9,000	-0-
Total Income	$510,000	$100,000
Cost of goods sold	$300,000	$ 55,000
Operating expenses (including rent)	180,000	30,000
Interest expense.	10,000	5,000
Total Expenses	$490,000	$ 90,000
Net Income	$ 20,000	$ 10,000

Intercompany items were as follows:

1. Deuce Co. rented a building to Ace Co. for $1,000 a month during 1975.
2. Deuce Co. paid Ace Co. $1,000 interest on intercompany notes during the year.
3. Ace Co. sold goods to Deuce Co. for $50,000 during the year. All the goods were resold by Deuce Co. to outsiders by the end of the year.

Required:

a. Prepare working papers for a consolidated income statement for 1975.
b. Did the parent company use the cost method or equity method for accounting for its investment in the subsidiary?
c. If you had not been told that Ace Co. owned 90 percent of Deuce Co., how could you have determined this fact from the income statement data?

Series B

15B–1   Hart Company purchased as a permanent investment $10,000 (face value) of 8 percent bonds on March 1, 1975, at $8,810 plus accrued interest. The bonds mature on December 31, 1994, and interest is payable semiannually on June 30 and December 31 of each year. Prepare the journal entries relating to this investment on:

a. March 1, 1975;
b. June 30, 1975;
c. December 31, 1975;
d. December 31, 1994 assuming that the bonds were held until maturity.

15B–2 Assume that Wooden Company purchased 3,000 of the 10,000 out-standing shares of Wicks Company on January 1, 1975, at a cost of $20 per share. On June 30, 1975, Wooden Company received dividends of $2,500 from Wicks Company. Wicks Company reported net income of $30,000 on December 31, 1975. On December 31, 1976, Wicks Company reported a loss of $7,000.

Required:

Record the above transactions on the books of the Wooden Company under both the cost and equity methods.

15B–3 JiJo Co. purchased 80 percent of the outstanding stock of Eli Co. for $175,000 on January 1, 1975. Balance sheet data for the two corporations immediately after the transaction are presented below.

	JiJo Co.	Eli Co.
Cash	$ 10,000	$ 5,000
Accounts receivable	30,000	15,000
Inventories	60,000	30,000
Fixed assets (net)	300,000	170,000
Investment in Eli Co.	175,000	–0–
	$575,000	$220,000
Accounts payable	$ 75,000	$ 20,000
Common stock	400,000	150,000
Retained earnings	100,000	50,000
	$575,000	$220,000

Assume that the difference between the cost of the investment and the book value of the subsidiary was attributed to advantages of affiliation.

Prepare a consolidated balance sheet for JiJo Co. and Eli Co. at January 1, 1975.

15B–4 Condensed balance sheet information of P Co. and S Co. at the end of 1975 is shown below:

	P Co.	S Co.
Current assets	$300,000	$ 50,000
Other assets	500,000	100,000
	$800,000	$150,000
Liabilities	$100,000	$ 30,000
Capital stock ($100 par value)	500,000	100,000
Retained earnings	200,000	20,000
	$800,000	$150,000

Each of the cases described below involves a situation in which P Co. acquires a controlling interest in the stock of S Co. on December 31, 1975. Prepare a consolidated balance sheet at the date of acquisition for each of the following cases:

a. P Co. purchased all of the outstanding shares of S Co. for $140,000. There was evidence that the buildings and equipment of S. Co. were worth more than their book value.

b. P Co. purchases all the outstanding shares of S Co. for $110,000.

c. P Co. purchases 80 percent of the outstanding shares of S Co. for $105,000. The management of P Co. paid more than book value because of anticipated advantages of affiliation.

15B–5   On January 1, 1975, the Strock Co. acquired 90 percent of the common stock of the Bristow Co. for $145,000. The stockholders' equity of Bristow Co. on that date was as follows:

Common stock	$120,000
Retained earnings	30,000
	$150,000

During 1975, the Bristow Co. earned $20,000 of net income and paid cash dividends of $12,000. The Strock Co. reported net income of $50,000 (including investment income) and paid dividends of $20,000. The Strock Co. uses the equity method for accounting for its investment in Bristow. The stockholders' equity of the Strock Co. on December 31, 1975, was as follows:

Common stock	$400,000
Retained earnings	180,000
	$580,000

Determine the amounts at which the following items would be shown in the December 31, 1975, consolidated statements.

a. Difference between cost and book value of subsidiary stock.
b. Consolidated net income.
c. Consolidated retained earnings.
d. Minority interest.

15B–6   Income statement data for 1975 for King Co. and its 100-percent-owned subsidiary, Queen Co., are shown below.

	King Co.	Queen Co.
Sales	$200,000	$100,000
Investment income	20,000	–0–
	$220,000	$100,000
Cost of goods sold	$100,000	$ 60,000
Operating expenses	80,000	20,000
	$180,000	$ 80,000
Net income	$ 40,000	$ 20,000

During 1975, Queen Co. sold all of its goods to King Co. An intercompany profit of $5,000 was recorded by Queen Co. on the sale of goods held in King Co.'s inventory at the end of 1975.

Prepare the worksheet to develop a consolidated income statement at the end of 1975.

16

Financial Statement Analysis

REASON FOR FINANCIAL STATEMENT ANALYSIS

The financial statements of a business enterprise are intended to provide much of the basic data used for decision-making and, in general, evaluation of performance by various groups such as current owners, potential investors, creditors, government agencies, and in some instances, competitors. Because general-purpose published financial statements are by their very nature issued for a wide variety of users, it is often necessary for particular user groups to extract the information in which they are particularly interested from the statements. For example, owners and potential investors are normally interested in the present earnings and future earnings prospects of a business. Similarly, short-term creditors are primarily concerned with the ability of a firm to meet its short-term obligations as they become due and payable. Consequently, a somewhat detailed analysis and interpretation of financial statements is usually required in order to obtain the information which may be relevant for the specific purposes of a particular user. In this chapter, several selected techniques which are useful in financial analysis will be described and discussed.

COMPARATIVE FINANCIAL STATEMENTS

In general, the usefulness of financial information is increased when it can be compared with related data. Comparison may be internal (i.e., within one firm) or external (i.e., with another firm). External comparisons may be difficult to make in practice since financial statements of firms may not be readily comparable because of the use of different generally acceptable accounting principles. However, some useful information may be obtained by comparison with industry averages, ratios, etc. (such as those compiled by *Moody's* and *Standard and Poor's*) or by direct comparison with the statements of another firm. Obviously, considerable caution must be exercised when making this type of analysis.

The financial statements of a particular firm are most useful when they can be compared with related data from within the current period, information from prior periods, or with budgets or forecasts. Comparative statements are useful in providing a standard which facilitates the analysis and interpretation of changes and trends which have occurred in elements of the financial statements. Generally, published annual reports of corporations provide comparative accounting statements from the previous period and often also include selected historical information for the firm for a longer period of time, such as ten years.

Assume that the income statement of a firm for the year ended December 31, 1977, disclosed net income of $100,000. This information, in and of itself, provides a user with only a single indicator of the absolute amount of income for the year. If an income statement for 1976, disclosing net income of $80,000, was also presented, 1977 net income would become much more meaningful information to the user. The 25 percent increase of 1977 income over that for 1976 indicates a significant improvement in performance that could not be determined from the 1977 statements alone.

BASIC ANALYTICAL PROCEDURES

Comparisons of financial statement data are frequently expressed as percentages or ratios. These comparisons may represent:

1. Percentage increases and decreases in an item in comparative financial statements;
2. Percentage relationships of individual components to an aggregate total in a single financial statement; or
3. Ratios of one amount to another in the financial statements.

Application of each of these three methods will be illustrated by the use of the comparative financial statements of Dolbey Company which follow. These comparative statements will also serve as a basis for the analysis presented in the remainder of this chapter.

Horizontal Analysis

Analysis of increases or decreases in a given financial statement item over two or more accounting periods is often referred to as horizontal analysis. Generally, this type of analysis discloses both the dollar and percentage changes for the corresponding items in comparative statements. An example of horizontal analysis is included in the comparative financial statements presented for Dolbey Company. These statements include data with regard to income, retained earnings, and financial position for a two-year period with the dollar and percentage changes for each item listed in the final two columns.

Illustration 16–1

DOLBEY COMPANY
Comparative Balance Sheet
December 31, 1977 and 1976

	1977		1976		Increase (Decrease)	
	Dollars	Per-cent of Total Assets	Dollars	Per-cent of Total Assets	Dollars	Per-cent
ASSETS						
Current assets:						
Cash	$ 80,000	5.0	$ 40,000	2.8	$ 40,000	100.0
Net accounts receivable	100,000	6.3	80,000	5.5	20,000	25.0
Inventories	200,000	12.5	160,000	11.1	40,000	25.0
Prepaid expenses	20,000	1.2	8,000	.6	12,000	150.0
Total Current Assets	$ 400,000	25.0	$ 288,000	20.0	$112,000	38.9
Land, buildings, and equipment (Net)	1,200,000	75.0	1,152,000	80.0	48,000	4.2
Total Assets	$1,600,000	100.0	$1,440,000	100.0	$160,000	11.1
LIABILITIES						
Current liabilities:						
Accounts payable	$ 200,000	12.5	$ 130,000	9.0	$ 70,000	53.8
Notes payable	100,000	6.3	60,000	4.2	40,000	66.7
Total Current Liabilities	$ 300,000	18.8	$ 190,000	13.2	$110,000	57.9
Bonds payable	200,000	12.5	200,000	13.9	–0–	–0–
Total Liabilities	$ 500,000	31.3	$ 390,000	27.1	$110,000	28.2
STOCKHOLDERS' EQUITY						
Common stock ($30 par)	$ 900,000	56.2	$ 900,000	62.5	–0–	–0–
Retained earnings	$ 200,000	12.5	$ 150,000	10.4	$ 50,000	33.3
Total Liabilities and Stockholders' Equity	$1,600,000	100.0	$1,440,000	100.0	$160,000	11.1

Interpretation of the increases or decreases in individual statement items cannot be completely evaluated without additional information. For example, the comparative balance sheet discloses an increase in inventory during 1977 of $40,000, to an amount 25 percent greater than in 1976. This increase may have been required in order to support a higher sales volume as net sales increased by a third during 1977. Alternatively, however, this

Illustration 16-2

DOLBEY COMPANY
Comparative Income Statement
For the Years Ended December 31, 1977 and 1976

	1977		1976		Increase (Decrease)	
	Dollars	Percent of Sales	Dollars	Percent of Sales	Dollars	Percent
Net sales	$2,000,000	100.0	$1,500,000	100.0	$500,000	33.3
Cost of goods sold	1,400,000	70.0	1,080,000	72.0	320,000	29.6
Gross profit on sales	$ 600,000	30.0	$ 420,000	28.0	$180,000	42.9
Operating expenses:						
Selling expenses.	$ 300,000	15.0	$ 240,000	16.0	$ 60,000	25.0
Administrative expenses	180,000	9.0	129,000	8.6	51,000	39.5
Total Operating Expenses . .	$ 480,000	24.0	$ 369,000	24.6	$111,000	30.1
Operating income	$ 120,000	6.0	$ 51,000	3.4	$ 69,000	135.3
Interest expense.	10,000	.5	9,000	.6	1,000	11.1
Income before income taxes. . .	$ 110,000	5.5	$ 42,000	2.8	$ 68,000	161.9
Income taxes	30,000	1.5	12,000	.8	18,000	150.0
Net Income	$ 80,000	4.0	$ 30,000	2.0	$ 50,000	166.7

DOLBEY COMPANY
Comparative Statement of Retained Earnings
For the Years Ended December 31, 1977 and 1976

	1977	1976	Increase (Decrease)	
			Dollars	Percent
Retained earnings, January 1	$150,000	$135,000	$15,000	11.1
Net income	80,000	30,000	50,000	166.7
	$230,000	$165,000	$65,000	39.4
Less: Dividends	30,000	15,000	15,000	100.0
Retained earnings, December 31	$200,000	$150,000	$50,000	33.3

Data from the 1975 statements: Total Assets (December 31, 1975) $1,160,000
Stockholders' Equity (December 31, 1975) $1,035,000
Net Receivables (December 31, 1975) . . . . $ 70,000
Inventory (December 31, 1975) . . . . $ 110,000

increase could have resulted from a buildup of an obsolete inventory item. Obviously, the point to be made here is that additional information is often useful and sometimes absolutely necessary for meaningful interpretation.

Percentage changes included in the statements for Dolbey Company were stated in terms of the data for two years. When a comparison is made between statements of two periods, the earlier statement is normally used as a base in computing percentage changes. For statements which include more than two years, there are two methods which may be used in selecting a base year. One alternative is to use the earliest year as a base. If this alternative is selected, each amount on all succeeding statements will be expressed as a percentage of the base year amount. Since this procedure results in a constant base, percentage changes for more than two years can be interpreted as trend values for individual components of the financial statements. A second alternative is to compare each statement with the statement which immediately precedes it. Adoption of this procedure results in a changing base that may make comparisons of percentage changes over a period of several years more difficult.

Vertical Analysis

The percentage relationship of an individual item or component of a single financial statement to an aggregate total in the same statement often discloses significant relationships. These relationships may be useful information for decision-making purposes. For example, in reporting income data, it may be useful to indicate the relationship between sales and other elements of the income statement for a period. This analysis of the elements included in the financial statements of a single period is often referred to as vertical analysis.

Vertical analysis is also illustrated in the financial statements presented for Dolbey Company. In the comparative balance sheet, the total assets balance and the total liabilities and stockholders' equity balance for each year are used as a base. Each item in the statement is then expressed as a percentage of this base. For example, the statements indicate that current assets increased from 20 percent of total assets in 1976 to 25 percent at the end of 1977. An analysis of the composition of the current asset balance provides additional details of the changes in various individual categories of current assets.

Vertical analysis may also be employed in presenting a comparative income statement. In the Dolbey Company illustration, each individual item is stated as a percent of net sales for the period.

Common-Size Statements

Horizontal and vertical analyses are frequently useful in disclosing certain relationships and trends in individual elements included in the financial statements. The analysis of these relationships may be facilitated by the use of common-size statements, i.e.,—statements in which all items are stated in terms of percentages or ratios. Common-size statements may be prepared in order to compare data from the current period with that from one or more past periods for a firm. These statements may also be used to compare data of two or more business firms for the same period or periods, subject to the limitations mentioned previously.

A common-size statement comparing income statement data for Dolbey Company with that of Nutt Company is presented in Illustration 16-3. The column for Dolbey Company is prepared by using the percentage

Illustration 16–3

DOLBEY COMPANY AND NUTT COMPANY
Condensed Common-Size Income Statement
For the Year Ended December 31, 1977

	Dolbey Company	Nutt Company
Net sales	100.0%	100.0%
Cost of goods sold	70.0	72.5
Gross profit on sales	30.0%	27.5%
Operating expenses:		
Selling expense	15.0	17.5
Administrative expense	9.0	7.5
Total Operating Expenses	24.0	25.0
Operating income	6.0%	2.5%
Interest expense	.5	1.0
Income before income taxes	5.5%	1.5%
Income taxes	1.5	.5
Net Income	4.0%	1.0%

figures that were included in the comparative income statement previously given. Net sales of each firm are set as a base of 100 percent and each individual item included in the statement is shown as a percentage of net sales. Consequently, use of this statement format provides a comparison of the relationships of the income statement items for the two firms regardless of the absolute dollar amount of sales and expenses of either company. It can be seen, for example, that Dolbey Company obtained $.04 of net income from each dollar of net sales, while Nutt Company netted only $.01 of net income from each sales dollar.

RATIO ANALYSIS

A ratio is an expression of the relationship of one numerical item to another. Significant interrelationships which may be present in financial statements are often identified and highlighted by the use of ratio analysis. A simple example of such a relationship would be the ratio of cash to current liabilities for Dolbey Company at the end of 1977. The ratio would be calculated or computed as follows:

$$\frac{\text{Ratio of Cash to}}{\text{Current Liabilities}} = \frac{\text{Cash}}{\text{Current Liabilities}}$$

$$.27 = \frac{\$\ 80,000}{\$300,000}$$

Ratios may be expressed in several different ways. Generally, ratios are stated in relation to a base of one. For example, for the ratio computed above, it could be stated that the ratio of cash to current liabilities is .27

to 1 (which is sometimes simply stated as .27 with the "to 1" omitted). In any case, a ratio is a method used to describe a relationship between two financial statement amounts. The meaningful use of ratio analysis requires that there be a logical relationship between the figures compared, and that this relationship be clearly understood by the user.

Comparison with Standards

The analytical procedures employed in computing percentage changes (horizontal analysis), component percentages (vertical analysis), and ratios convert financial statement items into a form which may be comparable to various standards. It is comparisons made among the relationships derived from the financial statements and selected standards that allow the user to draw meaningful conclusions concerning the firm. Among the most commonly used standards of comparison against which the position of a particular firm may be measured are the following:

1. Past performance of the firm.
2. Financial data of similar or competing firms.
3. Average performance of a number of firms in the industry.

A major deficiency of comparison with the past performance of the firm is that there is no indication of what *should* have occurred given the nature of the firm, the economy of the period, etc. For example, the fact that the net income of a firm increased by 3 percent from the previous year may initially appear to be favorable. However, if there is evidence that net income *should* have increased by 6 percent, the performance for the current year would be regarded as unfavorable.

The weakness of comparisons with past performance of the firm may be overcome somewhat by using the performance of a similar firm or firms or an industry average as an additional standard for comparison. A problem with this approach, however, is that it is often difficult to identify firms which are truly comparable, both because of the nature of the firms themselves and because of the use of alternative "generally accepted accounting principles." In spite of these limitations, a careful analysis of comparative performance, both internal and external, often provides meaningful input for use in decision-making.

ANALYSIS FOR COMMON STOCKHOLDERS

Common stockholders and potential investors purchase securities of a firm in an attempt to earn a return on their investment through increases in the market price of the stock and by dividends. Because each of these factors is influenced by net income, the analysis of financial statements made by, or on behalf of, an investor is focused primarily on the company's record of earnings. Certain of the more important relationships which are of interest to the stockholder-investor are discussed in the following sections of this chapter.

Rate of Return on Total Assets

The rate of return on total assets provides a measure of management's ability to earn a return on the firm's assets. The income figure used in this computation should be income before the deduction of interest expense, since interest is the return to creditors for the resources that they provide to the firm. Thus, the rate of return on total assets is computed by dividing net income plus interest expense by the average investment in assets during the year.

$$\text{Rate of Return on Assets} = \frac{\text{Net Income (after taxes)} + \text{Interest Expense}}{\text{Average Total Assets during the Year}}$$

Although assets are continually acquired and disposed of throughout a period, an average of asset balances at the beginning and end of the period is generally used for this calculation. The calculation for Dolbey Company would be as follows:

	1977	1976
Net income	$ 80,000	$ 30,000
Add interest expense	10,000	9,000
Net income before interest expense	$ 90,000	$ 39,000
Total assets		
Beginning of year	$1,440,000	$1,160,000
End of year	1,600,000	1,440,000
Total	$3,040,000	$2,600,000
Average total assets	$1,520,000	$1,300,000
Rate of return on assets	5.9%	3.0%

This ratio indicates that the earnings per dollar of assets invested have almost doubled in 1977. It appears that the management of Dolbey Company has increased its efficiency in the use of the firm's assets to generate income.

Rate of Return on Common Stockholders' Equity

The rate of return on common stockholders' equity is a measure of a firm's ability to earn a profit for its residual owners, the common stockholders. Because interest paid to creditors and dividends paid to preferred stockholders are normally fixed in amount, the return on common stockholders' equity may not be equal to the return on total assets. If management is able to earn a higher return on assets than the cost (i.e., interest expense) of assets contributed by the creditors, the excess benefits the owners. This is often referred to as using debt as favorable "leverage" in order to increase the owners' rate of return or as "trading on equity." Of course, if the cost of borrowing funds exceeds the return on assets, leverage will be unfavorable and will reduce the rate of return to the residual owners. The rate of return on common stockholders' equity is computed by dividing net income, less preferred dividends, by the average equity of the common stockholders.

$$\frac{\text{Rate of Return}}{\text{on Common}} = \frac{\text{Net Income (after taxes) } - \text{ Preferred Dividends}}{\text{Average Common Stockholders' Equity}}$$

Since Dolbey Company has no preferred stock, the rate of return on common stockholders' equity would be computed as follows:

	1977	1976
Net income	$ 80,000	$ 30,000
Common stockholders' equity:		
Beginning of the year	$1,050,000	$1,035,000
End of the year	1,100,000	1,050,000
Total	$2,150,000	$2,085,000
Average common stockholders' equity	$1,075,000	$1,042,500
Rate of return on common stockholders' equity	7.4%	2.9%

The rate of return on the common stockholders' equity is higher than the rate of return on assets for 1977 because the cost of funds contributed by creditors is less than the rate earned on assets. Thus the company is experiencing favorable "leverage," using borrowed funds to earn a return in excess of their cost.

Earnings per Share of Common Stock

Since the owners of a business invest in shares of stock, they are usually interested in an expression of earnings in terms of a per share amount. If a company has only a single class of common stock outstanding, the earnings per share figure is computed by dividing net income for the period by the average number of common shares outstanding.[1] If the firm has other securities outstanding which have certain characteristics similar to those of common stock (such as convertible bonds), the usefulness of earnings per share data is enhanced if these other securities are also considered in the computation of earnings per share. These securities are often

---

[1] The calculation of earnings per share was discussed in Chapter 13.

referred to as common stock equivalents. While a discussion of the inclusion of common stock equivalents in the computation of earnings per share is beyond the scope of this text, the basic principle involved is that earnings per share figures are calculated so as to indicate the effects of the conversion of these securities into common stock.

When there is both common and preferred stock outstanding, net income must be reduced by preferred dividend requirements in order to determine net income available to common stockholders.

$$\text{Earnings Per Share} = \frac{\text{Net Income} - \text{Preferred Dividends}}{\text{Average Number of Common Shares Outstanding}}$$

In the case of Dolbey Company, which has no preferred stock, the earnings per share of common stock would be calculated as follows:

	1977	1976
Net income	$80,000	$30,000
Number of common shares outstanding	30,000	30,000
Earnings per share of common stock	$ 2.67	$ 1.00

Earnings per share is a ratio frequently mentioned in the financial press in relation to the earnings performance of business firms. In addition, earnings per share data is reported on the income statement, and usually in various other sections of corporate annual reports. Although the concept of earnings per share has received a great deal of attention, particularly in recent years, it should be viewed with some caution. As a minimum, it should be recognized that all of the significant aspects of a firm's performance simply cannot be reduced to a single figure. This point cannot be overemphasized.

Price-Earnings Ratio on Common Stock

Each investor must allocate his limited resources among various investment opportunities which are available to him. For this reason the rate of earnings in relation to the current market price of his investment often provides a useful basis for comparing alternative investment opportunities. This ratio is commonly referred to as the price-earnings ratio. It is computed by dividing the current market price per share of common stock by earnings per share.

$$\text{Price-Earnings Ratio} = \frac{\text{Market Price per Share of Common Stock}}{\text{Earnings per Share}}$$

Assuming that the market price per common share of Dolbey Company at the end of 1977 was $24.00 and at the end of 1976 was $8.00, price-earnings ratios would be calculated as follows:

	1977	1976
Market price per share at the end of the year	$24.00	$8.00
Earnings per share.	2.67	1.00
Price-earnings ratio	9	8

The price-earnings ratio may be interpreted as the value that investors in the stock market place on every dollar of earnings for a particular firm. An investor may compare the price-earnings ratio of a firm to that of other companies in an attempt to estimate whether a firm's stock is overpriced or underpriced.

Debt-To-Equity Ratio

The debt-to-equity ratio measures the proportion of funds supplied to the firm by its stockholders as opposed to funds provided by creditors. It is computed by dividing total debt by stockholders' equity.

$$\text{Debt-to-Equity Ratio} = \frac{\text{Total Debt}}{\text{Stockholders' Equity}}$$

The debt-to-equity ratio provides a measure of the risk incurred by common stockholders. Since debt consists of fixed obligations, the larger the debt-to-equity ratio, the greater is the chance that a firm may face a situation in which it is unable to meet its obligations. At the same time, however, a high debt-to-equity ratio can increase the rate of return on stockholders' equity through the use of favorable financial leverage. This can occur because interest on debt is fixed in amount, regardless of the amount of earnings. Consequently there is no ideal debt-to-equity ratio. Rather, each investor must define a satisfactory debt-to-equity ratio based on his desired degree of risk.

For Dolbey Company, the debt-to-equity ratios are calculated as follows:

	1977	1976
Total debt	$ 500,000	$ 390,000
Stockholders' equity	$1,100,000	$1,050,000
Debt-to-equity ratio	45.5%	37.1%

ANALYSIS FOR LONG-TERM CREDITORS

Bondholders and other long-term creditors, like stockholders and investors, are also concerned with measures of the profitability of a business. In addition, however, long-term creditors are particularly interested in a firm's ability to meet its interest requirements as they become due and payable. A good indicator of a firm's ability to pay interest is the margin between income and interest payments. A common measure of this margin is the ratio of net income available for interest payments to annual interest expense. This ratio, which is referred to as the number of times interest earned, is computed by dividing net income before interest expense and income taxes by the interest requirement for the period. Income taxes are added back to net income because interest charges are an expense which is deducted in computing income taxes. Similarly, interest charges are added back to net income because the ratio provides a measure of the ability of the firm to pay fixed interest charges.

$$\frac{\text{Number of Times}}{\text{Interest Earned}} = \frac{\text{Net Income} + \text{Interest Expense} + \text{Income Taxes}}{\text{Interest Expense}}$$

The computation for Dolbey Company would be as follows:

	1977	1976
Net income	$ 80,000	$30,000
Add back:		
Income taxes	30,000	12,000
Interest expense	10,000	9,000
Amount available for interest requirements	$120,000	$51,000
Number of times interest earned	12.0	5.7

The increase in the ratio from 5.7 times in 1976 to 12.0 times in 1977 would appear to be favorable with respect to a long-term creditor of Dolbey Company.

ANALYSIS FOR SHORT-TERM CREDITORS

Short-term creditors are also concerned with the earnings prospects of a firm. Of primary importance to the short-term creditor, however, is a firm's ability to pay its current debt on a timely basis and to meet its current operating needs. This is often referred to as the current position of the firm.

The ability of a firm to pay its current debts as they fall due depends largely upon the relationship between its current assets and its current liabilities. The excess of a firm's current assets over its current liabilities is termed working capital. Adequate working capital enables a firm to meet its current needs and obligations on a timely basis. However, an analysis of the components of working capital and the flow of working capital is necessary in order to determine the adequacy of the working capital position of a specific firm.

Current Ratio

The absolute amount of working capital may be an inadequate measure of a firm's ability to meet its obligations. As an illustration, consider the following data for two companies:

	Reed Company	*Frazier Company*
Current assets	$20,000	$50,000
Current liabilities	10,000	40,000
Working capital	$10,000	$10,000

In this example, both companies have $10,000 of working capital. However, the current assets of Reed Company could be reduced by 50 percent and still be equal to the current liabilities, while the current assets of Frazier Company could only shrink by 20 percent and remain equal to current liabilities.

Another means of evaluating working capital is to evaluate the relationship between current assets and current liabilities. This ratio is referred to as the current ratio.

$$\text{Current Ratio} = \frac{\text{Current Assets}}{\text{Current Liabilities}}$$

The use of the current ratio for the example given would disclose a ratio of 2 to 1 for Reed Company and 1.25 to 1 for Frazier Company. This clearly indicates the stronger current position of Reed Company.

The current ratio for Dolbey Company is calculated as follows:

	1977	*1976*
Current assets	$400,000	$288,000
Current liabilities	300,000	190,000
Current ratio.	1.3	1.5

Although the working capital of Dolbey Company increased from $98,000 in 1976 to $100,000 in 1977, current assets per dollar of current liabilities declined from $1.50 to $1.30. This is an unfavorable trend from the viewpoint of short-term creditors because the margin of safety has declined.

A satisfactory current ratio for a particular firm depends, of course, upon the nature of its business. Although short-term creditors generally feel safer as the current ratio increases in amount, this may not be efficient from a business standpoint. For example, a firm with excess cash in relation to its current needs is inefficient since cash is a nonproductive asset. A good measure of the adequacy of a firm's current ratio is often a comparison with the current ratios of similar firms or industry averages.

Acid-Test or Quick Ratio

In analyzing the ability of a firm to meet its obligations, the distribution of current assets is also important. For example, a firm with a large proportion of cash to current assets is better able to meet its current debts than a firm with a larger proportion of inventories. This is because inventories usually require more time for conversion into cash than do other current assets. Assets with a longer conversion period are usually referred to as being less liquid. For this reason, a ratio which excludes the less liquid assets is often used as a supplement to the current ratio. The ratio of the highly current assets—cash, marketable securities, and receivables—to current liabilities is known as the acid-test or quick ratio.

$$\text{Acid-Test Ratio} = \frac{\text{Cash} + \text{Marketable Securities} + \text{Receivables}}{\text{Current Liabilities}}$$

Since Dolbey Company owns no marketable securities, its acid-test ratio would be calculated as follows:

	1977	1976
Cash	$ 80,000	$ 40,000
Net accounts receivables	100,000	80,000
Total	$180,000	$120,000
Current liabilities	$300,000	$190,000
Acid-test ratio	.60	.63

In evaluating the acid-test ratio, again the nature of the business must be considered. The .6 acid-test ratio for Dolbey Company in 1977 may indicate a serious problem as there may not be sufficient liquid assets to meet current liabilities as they become due.

Analysis of Accounts Receivable

It is obvious that the rate at which non-cash current assets may be converted into cash is an important determinant of the firm's ability to meet its current obligations. Because neither the current nor the acid-test ratio considers this movement in current assets, short-term creditors should use additional tests in considering the liquidation of two significant working capital items, receivables and inventories.

An approximation of the average time which is required by a firm in order to collect its receivables may be determined by first computing the turnover of accounts receivable. Receivables turnover is computed by dividing net credit sales by the average accounts receivable balance. Ideally, a monthly average of receivables should be used, but generally only the balances at the beginning and end of the year are available to the user of the financial statements.

$$\text{Accounts Receivable Turnover} = \frac{\text{Net Sales on Account}}{\text{Average Accounts Receivable}}$$

The accounts receivable turnover is an approximation of the number of times accounts receivable were converted into cash during the period. Therefore, the higher the turnover, the more liquid are the firm's receivables.

Accounts receivable turnover of Dolbey Company is computed below. Assume that all sales were made on a credit basis and that only the beginning and end of the year balances of receivables are available.

	1977	1976
Net sales on account	$2,000,000	$1,500,000
Net receivables:		
Beginning of year	$ 80,000	$ 70,000
End of year	100,000	80,000
Total	$ 180,000	$ 150,000
Average	$ 90,000	$ 75,000
Accounts receivable turnover per year	22.2 times	20.0 times

This increase in the receivables turnover for Dolbey Company during 1977 indicates that the average collection period for receivables has decreased. This could be a result of more successful collection practices or a change in credit policies, or a combination of both factors.

The receivables turnover may be used to determine the average collection period, which can be readily compared with the firm's credit terms. The average number of days to collect receivables is computed by dividing 365 days by the receivables turnover.

$$\frac{\text{Average Number of Days}}{\text{to Collect Receivables}} = \frac{365 \text{ Days}}{\text{Accounts Receivable Turnover}}$$

If the average number of days required to collect receivables significantly exceeds the credit terms of the firm, this would indicate that the credit department may be ineffective in its credit granting and collecting activities.

The average number of days to collect receivables is calculated for the Dolbey Company as follows:

	1977	1976
Receivables turnover	22.2 times	20.0 times
Average number of days to collect receivables.	16.4 days	18.3 days

Analysis of Inventories

A procedure similar to that used for evaluating receivables may be employed in evaluating the inventories of a firm. One indication of the liquidity of inventories is obtained by determining the relationship between the cost of goods sold and the average balance of inventories on hand during a period. Cost of goods sold is used because it represents the cost (rather than selling price) of goods that have been sold from the inventories during the period.

Inventory turnover is calculated by dividing cost of goods sold by the average inventory. Again, if possible, monthly figures should be used to determine average inventory. Usually, however, only the beginning and end of the year inventory balances are available.

$$\text{Inventory Turnover} = \frac{\text{Cost of Goods Sold}}{\text{Average Inventory}}$$

A low inventory turnover may indicate management inefficiency in that excess cash has been committed to the investment in inventory. Although inventories are necessary to meet the demands of a firm, there are advantages in maintaining the investment in inventory at the minimum level necessary to service customers, thus minimizing carrying costs, risks of loss or obsolescence, etc.

Assuming that only the beginning and ending inventories are available, the computation of inventory turnover for Dolbey Company is as follows:

	1977	1976
Cost of goods sold	$1,400,000	$1,080,000
Inventory:		
Beginning of the year.	$ 160,000	$ 110,000
End of the year	200,000	160,000
Total.	$ 360,000	$ 270,000
Average inventory	$ 180,000	$ 135,000
Inventory turnover	7.8 times	8 times

It appears that the trend of the inventory turnover for Dolbey Company is somewhat unfavorable, since inventories were turned over more slowly in 1977 than in 1976. Again, the analyst would want to obtain additional information before making a definitive judgment.

INTERPRETATION OF ANALYSES

The user must exercise considerable caution in the use of ratios in order to analyze the financial statements of a business enterprise. Some of the problems inherent in ratio analysis are summarized below:

1. Comparisons of items for different periods or for different companies may not be valid if different accounting practices have been used. For example, one firm may use straight-line depreciation and the Fifo inventory method while a similar company may use accelerated depreciation and Lifo for its inventories.
2. Financial statements represent only one source of financial information concerning a firm and its environment. Consequently, other information not disclosed in financial statements may have an impact on the evaluation of the statements.
3. Most financial statements are not adjusted either for changes in market values or in the general price level. This may seriously affect comparability between firms over time.

4. As ratio analysis has increased in popularity, there has sometimes been a tendency to develop ratios which have little or no significance. A meaningful ratio can be developed only from items which have a logical relationship.

All of the ratios and measurements developed in this chapter need not be used as input in a particular decision. In determining the financial strengths and weaknesses of a particular firm, relevant measurements need to be selected, developed, and interpreted in view of the conditions relating to the business.

KEY DEFINITIONS

Accounts receivable turnover   Accounts receivable turnover is an approximation of the number of times accounts receivable were converted into cash during the period. It is defined as net sales on account divided by average accounts receivable.

Acid-test ratio   This ratio is a measure of a firm's ability to pay its current liabilities as they come due with the more liquid current assets. It is usually the ratio of cash, marketable securities, and receivables to total current liabilities.

Average collection period   This is a measure of the average time required by a firm to collect a receivable. Collection period is computed by dividing 365 days by the receivables turnover.

Common-size statements   In common-size financial statements, all items are stated in terms of stated percentages or ratios.

Current ratio   This ratio measures a firm's ability to pay current liabilities as they come due. It is defined as the ratio of current assets to current liabilities.

Debt-to-equity ratio   Debt-to-equity measures the proportion of funds supplied by stockholders as opposed to the funds provided by creditors. It is computed by dividing total debt by total stockholders' equity.

Horizontal analysis   The analysis of the increase or decrease in a given financial statement item over two or more accounting periods.

Inventory turnover   Inventory turnover gives an indication of the liquidity of inventories. Its computation involves dividing cost of goods sold by the average inventory.

Number of times interest earned   This measure of a firm's ability to pay interest is computed by dividing net income before interest expense and income taxes by the interest expense.

Price-earnings ratio   The current market price of a share of stock divided by the earnings per share.

Rate of return on common stockholders' equity   This measure of the firm's ability to earn a profit for its common stockholders is computed by dividing net income after taxes and preferred dividends by the average common stockholders' equity.

Rate of return on total assets   This measure of the ability of the firm's management to earn a return on the assets without regard to variations in the method of financing is computed by dividing net income plus interest expense by the average investment in assets during the year.

Ratio analysis   The analysis of items in a financial statement expressing the relationship of one numerical item to another.

Vertical analysis   The percentage relationship between an individual item or a component of a single financial statement to an aggregate total in the statement.

QUESTIONS

1. How is financial statement analysis related to the needs of the various users of financial statements?

2. Distinguish between vertical analysis and horizontal analysis.

3. What are common-size statements?

4. How are each of the following computed?

  a. Rate of Return on Total Assets.
  b. Rate of Return on Common Stockholders' Equity.
  c. Earnings per Share of Common Stock.
  d. Price-Earnings Ratio on Common Stock.
  e. Debt-to-Equity Ratio.
  f. Number of Times Interest Earned.
  g. Current Ratio.
  h. Acid-Test Ratio.
  i. Accounts Receivable Turnover.
  j. Average Number of Days to Collect Receivables.
  k. Inventory Turnover.

5. Each of the ratios (in Question 4 above) are utilized by one user group more than others. Indicate whether each item is utilized most by (1) common shareholders (or investors), (2) long-term creditors, or (3) short-term creditors.

6. What are the most commonly used standards against which to measure the position of a particular firm? What are the weaknesses inherent in these standards?

7. Business corporations usually provide comparative statements in their annual reports. What is a comparative statement? How do they enhance the usefulness of financial information?

8. What will be the effect (increase, decrease, none) on the rate of return on assets of each of the following?

  a. Cash purchase of a new machine.
  b. Increase in the tax rate.
  c. Reduction of accounts payable.
  d. Cash sale of a fully depreciated machine.

9. What is indicated if the average number of days to collect receivables significantly exceeds the credit terms of the firm?

10. What are the principal limitations that should be considered in evaluating ratios?

11. When percentage changes are given in comparative statements for more than two years, there are two methods for selecting the base year. What are they?

12. Which of the methods in question 11 makes comparison of percentage changes over several years more difficult? Why?

EXERCISES

16–1 The acid-test ratio at the beginning of 1975 was 2 to 1 for the Gilly Company.

Required:

How would the following transactions affect the acid-test or quick ratio?

1. Collection of note receivable from Silly Co. The note was due in 1978.
2. Collection of accounts receivable.
3. Sales on account.
4. Purchase of inventory on account.
5. Payment of accounts payable.
6. Collection of an account receivable.
7. Cash purchase of common stock of ABC Co. as a temporary investment.
8. Purchase of a new machine on a credit basis, the purchase price payable in 6 months.

16–2 The following information has been extracted from the financial statements of Cozeb Corp.

Common stock, $5 par.	$ 5,000,000
Common stock, $10 par	5,000,000
Preferred stock, $100 par	10,000,000
Net income	3,000,000
Preferred dividends	1,000,000

Required:

Compute earnings per share assuming the number of shares outstanding did not change during the year.

16–3 The December 31, 1975 financial statements of Flunkart Company included the following data:

Cash	$ 60,000
Accounts receivable.	200,000
Marketable securities	100,000
Prepaid expenses	25,000
Accounts payable.	200,000
Notes payable (current)	85,000
Inventory	115,000
Bonds payable (due in 5 years)	300,000
Wages payable	15,000

Required:

1. What is the current ratio? Acid-test ratio? Working capital?
2. Comment on the significance of this current ratio.

16–4 Using the information given, complete the balance sheet below.

a. The "quick" ratio is 2:1.

b. Notes payable are long-term liabilities and are four times the dollar amount of the marketable securities.

c. Accounts receivable are $2,000 and are one half of the "quick" assets, one fourth of the current assets, and equal to plant and equipment.

d. Total stockholders' equity is equal to the working capital and contributed capital is twice the dollar amount of the net accumulation of earnings.

ASSETS		LIABILITIES AND STOCKHOLDERS' EQUITY	
Cash	_____	Accounts payable	_____
Marketable securities	_____	Notes payable	_____
Accounts receivable	_____		
Inventories	_____	Capital stock	_____
Plant and equipment	_____	Retained earnings	_____
	═══════		═══════

16–5 Consider the following information concerning the 1975 and 1976 operations of ABC Co.

	1975	1976
Sales	$800,000	$1,000,000
Purchases.	400,000	450,000
Beginning inventory.	80,000	90,000
Ending inventory	90,000	90,000
Selling expense	40,000	50,000
Administrative expenses	10,000	40,000
Income taxes	100,000	200,000

Required:

Prepare a comparative income statement for the years ending December 31, 1975 and 1976. Indicate the changes both in percentages and dollars.

16–6 Small Company is a manufacturer of widgets. Industrywide averages (expressed in percentages of sales) for the production and sale of widgets are as follows:

Sales	100%
Cost of goods sold	70%
Selling expenses	10%
Administrative expenses	7%

In order to compare its own performance with industrywide standards, the Small Company has computed the following percentages:

Sales 100%
Cost of goods sold 60%
Selling expenses 20%
Administrative expenses 15%

Required:

1. Comment on the performance of Small Company.
2. What are the problems relating to the use of industry wide standards as a basis for evaluating an individual company's performance?

16–7 The current ratio for Lap Co. on December 31, 1975 was 2 to 1 ($200,000 to $100,000). In 1976 the following transactions occurred.

a. Payment of accounts payable, $125,000.
b. Collection of accounts receivable, $50,000.
c. Sales of $200,000, ¾ of which was cash; cost of goods sold was $125,000.
d. Purchase of goods, all on credit, $150,000.
e. A loan for $100,000, due in 5 years.
f. Cash purchase of marketable securities, $10,000.

Required:

On the basis of the preceding information, compute the current ratio at December 31, 1976.

PROBLEMS

Series A

16A–1

JOE COMPANY AND BLOW COMPANY
Comparative Income Statement
For the Year Ending December 31, 1975

	Joe Co.	*Blow Co.*
Net sales	$500,000	$250,000
Cost of goods sold	350,000	150,000
Gross profit on sales	$150,000	$100,000
Operating expenses:		
Selling expense	$ 50,000	$ 10,000
Administrative expense	10,000	7,000
Total Operating Expenses	$ 60,000	$ 17,000
Operating income	$ 90,000	$ 83,000
Interest expense.	30,000	5,000
Income before income taxes.	$ 60,000	$ 78,000
Income taxes	20,000	25,000
Net Income	$ 40,000	$ 53,000

Required:

Using the above information, prepare a common-size statement comparing income data for Joe Company and Blow Company.

16A–2   The income statements for 1975 for Spahn Company and Sain Company are presented below.

SPAHN COMPANY
Income Statement
For the Year Ended December 31, 1975

Sales		$225,000
Cost of goods sold		140,000
Gross profit from sales		$ 85,000
Expenses:		
Selling expense	$18,000	
Administrative expense	20,000	
General expenses	15,000	
Total Expenses		53,000
Income from operations		$ 32,000
Interest expense		2,000
Income before taxes		$ 30,000
Income taxes		7,000
Net Income		$ 23,000

SAIN COMPANY
Income Statement
For the Year Ended December 31, 1975

Sales		$300,000
Cost of goods sold		195,000
Gross profit from sales		$105,000
Expenses:		
Selling expense	$15,000	
Administrative expense	30,000	
General expense.	21,000	
Total Expenses		66,000
Income from operations		$ 39,000
Interest expense		6,000
Income before taxes		$ 33,000
Income taxes		4,000
Net Income		$ 29,000

Required:

Prepare a common-size income statement comparing Spahn Company with Sain Company.

16A–3 The following information was taken from the financial statements of Maker Company on December 31, 1975.

Cash	$ 75,000
Accounts receivable	125,000
Inventory	100,000
Fixed assets (net)	500,000
	$800,000
Accounts payable	$100,000
Bond payable (due December 31, 1990)	300,000
Capital stock ($10 par)	300,000
Retained earnings	100,000
	$800,000
Net Income	$ 50,000

Required:

Compute the following:
1. Current ratio
2. Working capital
3. Acid-test ratio
4. Earnings per share
5. Debt-to-equity ratio

16A–4 Following is the condensed common-size income statement for Francis Co.

FRANCIS COMPANY
Condensed Common-Size Income Statement
For the Year Ended December 31, 1975

Net sales	100.0%
Cost of goods sold	68.0
Gross profit on sales	32.0%
Operating expenses:	
Selling expense	16.0%
Administrative expense	6.0
Total Operating Expense	22.0%
Operating income	10.0%
Interest expense	0.5
Income before income taxes	9.5%
Income taxes	2.0
Net Income	7.5%

Net sales for the period were $3,000,000.

Required:

Prepare the income statement for Francis Company.

16A–5   Your examination of the balance sheet for Reswarts Corp. on December 31, 1974, 1975, and 1976 reveals the following information:

	1974	1975	1976
Cash	$ 50,000	$ 75,000	$100,000
Accounts receivable (net)	150,000	100,000	150,000
Inventory.	175,000	200,000	225,000
Prepaid expenses	25,000	25,000	40,000
Land	45,000	45,000	45,000
Buildings (net).	170,000	155,000	200,000
Machinery and equipment (net).	70,000	60,000	50,000
Accounts payable.	120,000	140,000	130,000
Notes payable	50,000	40,000	50,000
Capital stock.	400,000	400,000	400,000
Retained earnings	115,000	80,000	230,000

Required:

Prepare comparative balance sheets for the three years using (1) the first year presented as a base and (2) the previous year as a base. Include both percentage and dollar changes.

16A–6   Given below are the balance sheets for Meyers, Inc., for 1975 and 1976.

MEYERS, INC.
Comparative Balance Sheet
December 31, 1975 and 1976

	1976	1975
ASSETS		
Current assets:		
Cash	$ 20,000	$ 17,000
Accounts receivable (net)	45,000	60,000
Supplies inventory	8,000	6,000
Prepaid expenses	7,000	5,000
Total Current Assets	$ 80,000	$ 88,000
Land	120,000	70,000
Buildings (net).	200,000	100,000
Total Assets	$400,000	$258,000
LIABILITIES		
Current liabilities:		
Accounts payable.	$ 10,000	$ 7,000
Taxes payable	9,000	3,000
Total Current Liabilities	$ 19,000	$ 10,000
Bonds payable.	115,000	70,000
Total Liabilities	$134,000	$ 80,000
STOCKHOLDERS' EQUITY		
Common stock ($5 par)	$ 50,000	$ 45,000
Additional paid-in capital	125,000	80,000
Retained earnings	91,000	53,000
Total Liabilities and Stockholders' Equity.	$400,000	$258,000

Required:

Prepare a horizontal and vertical analysis of the balance sheets of Meyers, Inc. for 1975 and 1976.

16A-7   Shown below are partially completed comparative financial statements of Neil Company.

Required:

1. Complete the statements.
2. Complete the following for 1975:
   a.   Rate of Return on Total Assets
   b.   Rate of Return on Common Stockholders' Equity
   c.   Earnings per Share of Common Stock
   d.   Debt-to-Equity Ratio
   e.   Number of Times Interest Earned
   f.   Working Capital
   g.   Current Ratio
   h.   Acid-Test Ratio
   i.   Inventory Turnover
   j.   Average Number of Days to Collect Receivables

NEIL COMPANY
Comparative Balance Sheet
December 31, 1975 and 1974

	1975		1974		Increase (Decrease)	
	Dollars	Percent of Total Assets	Dollars	Percent of Total Assets	Dollars	Percent
ASSETS						
Current assets:						
Cash	$ 55,000		$ 50,000			
Net accounts receivable	200,000		175,000			
Inventories.	300,000		225,000			
Prepaid expenses	45,000		50,000			
Total Current Assets	$ 600,000		$ 500,000			
Land, buildings, and equipment (net)	1,400,000		1,250,000			
Total Assets	$2,000,000		$1,750,000			
LIABILITIES						
Current Liabilities:						
Accounts payable.	$ 300,000		$ 350,000			
Notes payable	200,000		100,000			
Total Current Liabilities	$ 500,000		$ 450,000			
Bonds payable.	500,000		500,000			
Total Liabilities	$1,000,000		$ 950,000			
STOCKHOLDERS' EQUITY						
Common stock ($20 par)	$ 600,000		$ 600,000			
Retained earnings	400,000		200,000			
Total Liabilities and Stock- holders' Equity	$2,000,000		$1,750,000			

NEIL COMPANY
Comparative Income Statement
For Years Ended December 31, 1975 and 1974

	1975		1974		Increase (Decrease)	
	Dollars	Percent of Sales	Dollars	Percent of Sales	Dollars	Percent
Net sales	$3,000,000		$2,000,000			
Cost of goods sold	2,100,000		1,500,000			
Gross profit on sales	$ 900,000		$ 500,000			
Operating expenses:						
Selling expenses.	$ 400,000		$ 200,000			
Administrative expenses	100,000		50,000			
Total Operating Expenses	$ 500,000		$ 250,000			
Operating income	$ 400,000		$ 250,000			
Interest expense.	40,000		30,000			
Income before income taxes	$ 360,000		$ 220,000			
Income taxes	90,000		45,000			
Net Income	$ 270,000		$ 175,000			

NEIL COMPANY
Comparative Statement of Retained Earnings
For Years Ended December 31, 1975 and 1974

	1975	1974	Increase (Decrease)	
			Dollars	Percent
Retained earnings, January 1	$200,000	$ 75,000		
Net income	270,000	175,000		
	$470,000	$250,000		
Less: Dividends	70,000	50,000		
Retained earnings, December 31	$400,000	$200,000		

Series B

16B–1

BLUE COMPANY AND WHITE COMPANY
Comparative Income Statement
For the Year Ending December 31, 1975

	Blue Co.	White Co.
Net sales	$800,000	$100,000
Cost of goods sold	550,000	60,000
Gross profit on sales	$250,000	$ 40,000
Operating expenses:		
Selling expense	$120,000	$ 8,000
Administrative expense.	60,000	10,000
Total Operating Expenses	$180,000	$ 18,000
Operating income	$ 70,000	$ 22,000
Interest expense.	40,000	3,000
Income before income taxes.	$ 30,000	$ 19,000
Income taxes	15,000	9,500
Net Income	$ 15,000	$ 9,500

Required:

Using the above information, prepare a common-size statement comparing income data for Blue Company and White Company.

16B–2   The income statements for 1975 for Blair Company and Powell Company are presented below.

BLAIR COMPANY
Income Statement
For the Year Ended December 31, 1975

Sales		$400,000
Cost of goods sold		250,000
Gross profit from sales		$150,000
Expenses:		
Selling expense	$25,000	
Administrative expense	10,000	
General expenses	25,000	
Total Expenses		60,000
Income from operations		$ 90,000
Interest expense.		10,000
Income before taxes		$ 80,000
Income taxes		32,000
Net Income		$ 48,000

POWELL COMPANY
Income Statement
For the Year Ended December 31, 1975

Sales		$1,100,000
Cost of goods sold		760,000
Gross profit from sales		$ 340,000
Expenses:		
Selling expense	$140,000	
Administrative expense	100,000	
General expenses	20,000	
Total Expenses		260,000
Income from operations		$ 80,000
Interest expense		5,000
Income before taxes		$ 75,000
Income taxes		30,000
Net Income		$ 45,000

Required:

Prepare a common-size income statement comparing Blair Company with Powell Company.

16B–3   The following information was taken from the financial statements of Stone Company on December 31, 1975.

Cash	$ 20,000
Accounts receivable	40,000
Inventory	70,000
Fixed assets (net)	240,000
	$370,000
Accounts payable	$ 60,000
Bond payable (due December 31, 1990)	200,000
Capital stock ($10 par)	100,000
Retained earnings	10,000
	$370,000
Net Income	$ 20,000

Required:

Compute the following:
1.   Current Ratio
2.   Working Capital
3.   Acid-Test Ratio
4.   Earnings per Share
5.   Debt-to-Equity Ratio

16B–4   Following is the condensed common-size income statement for Rose Company.

ROSE COMPANY
Condensed Common-Size Income Statement
For the Year Ended December 31, 1975

Net sales	100.0%
Cost of goods sold	75.0%
Gross profit on sales	25.0%
Operating expenses:	
Selling expense	10.0%
Administrative expense	3.0%
Total Operating Expense	13.0%
Operating income	12.0%
Interest expense.	1.5%
Income before income taxes.	10.5%
Income taxes	4.0%
Net Income	6.5%

Net sales for the period were $2,200,000.

Required:

Prepare the income statement for Rose Company.

16B–5   Your examination of the balance sheet for Bench Corp. on December 31, 1974, 1975, and 1976 reveals the following information.

	1974	1975	1976
Cash	$ 60,000	$ 65,000	$ 90,000
Accounts receivable (net)	50,000	60,000	80,000
Inventory	80,000	100,000	125,000
Prepaid expenses	30,000	25,000	25,000
Land	75,000	90,000	35,000
Buildings (net).	195,000	200,000	215,000
Machinery and equipment (net).	60,000	70,000	90,000
Accounts payable	90,000	110,000	140,000
Notes payable	60,000	60,000	50,000
Capital stock.	350,000	350,000	350,000
Retained earnings	50,000	90,000	120,000

Required:

Prepare comparative balance sheets for the three-year period using (1) the first year presented as a base and (2) the previous year as a base. Include both the percentage and dollar changes.

16B–6   Given below are the balance sheets for Johnson, Inc. for 1975 and
1976.

JOHNSON, INC.
Comparative Balance Sheet
December 31, 1975 and 1976

	1975	1976
ASSETS		
Current assets:		
Cash	$ 10,000	$ 15,000
Accounts receivable (net)	90,000	100,000
Inventory	120,000	140,000
Prepaid expenses	10,000	5,000
Total Current Assets	$230,000	$260,000
Building (net)	300,000	335,000
Land	70,000	80,000
Total Assets	$600,000	$675,000
LIABILITIES		
Current liabilities:		
Accounts payable	$ 70,000	$ 60,000
Notes payable	10,000	15,000
Total Current Liabilities	$ 80,000	$ 75,000
Bonds payable	175,000	200,000
Total Liabilities	$255,000	$275,000
STOCKHOLDERS' EQUITY		
Common stock ($10 par)	$ 20,000	$ 22,000
Additional paid-in capital	200,000	220,000
Retained earnings	125,000	158,000
Total Liabilities and Stockholders' Equity . . .	$600,000	$675,000

Required:

Prepare a horizontal and vertical analysis of the balance sheets of
Johnson, Inc. for 1975 and 1976.

16B–7   The following are financial statements of ZYX Corporation for 1975.

ZYX CORPORATION
Balance Sheet
December 31, 1975

ASSETS

Current assets:
Cash	$100,000	
Accounts receivable (net)	200,000	
Prepaid expenses	50,000	
Inventory	110,000	
Total Current Assets		$460,000

Fixed assets:
Land	$ 50,000	
Machinery (net).	100,000	
Building (net)	250,000	
Total Fixed Assets		400,000
Total Assets		$860,000

LIABILITIES AND STOCKHOLDERS'
EQUITY

Accounts payable	$ 50,000
Wages payable	5,000
Interest payable	2,000
Bonds payable (due December 31, 1980) . . .	200,000
Capital stock ($2 par value)	400,000
Retained earnings	203,000
Total Liabilities and Stockholders' Equity. . .	$860,000

ZYX CORPORATION
Income Statement
For the Year Ended December 31, 1975

Sales (net)		$1,000,000
Cost of goods sold:		
Beginning inventory	$ 90,000	
Purchases	600,000	
Goods available for sale	$690,000	
Ending inventory	110,000	
Cost of goods sold		580,000
Gross Profit on Sales		$ 420,000
Operating expenses:		
Sales salaries expense	$ 75,000	
Depreciation expense.	20,000	
Insurance expense	5,000	
Interest expense	10,000	
Total Operating Expense		110,000
Income before taxes		$ 310,000
Income taxes		100,000
Net Income		$ 210,000

January 1, 1974 data:
Common shares outstanding 200,000

Required:

Compute the following:
1. Earnings per Share of Common Stock
2. Debt-to-Equity Ratio
3. Number of Times Interest Earned
4. Current Ratio
5. Acid-Test or Quick Ratio
6. Inventory Turnover

17

The Statement of Changes in Financial Position

THE RATIOS and percentages which were discussed in the previous chapter represent only a single approach to the process of evaluating the effectiveness of a company. Various liquidity ratios such as the current ratio, acid-test ratio, and turnover of receivables and inventories were suggested as measures of a firm's ability to liquidate its current obligations on a timely basis and to meet its current operating needs. Even if these ratios are used on a comparative basis, however, they may not provide an adequate indication of the flow of the various elements of working capital which takes place during the business cycle. For this reason, a statement which discloses the analysis of the funds flows of a firm is now required along with the balance sheet and income statement as a part of a firm's basic report "package." The Accounting Principles Board concluded that:

> . . . information concerning the financing and investing activities of a business enterprise and the changes in its financial position for a period is essential for financial statement users, particularly owners and creditors, in making economic decisions. When financial statements purporting to present both financial position (balance sheet) and results of operations (statement of income and retained earnings) are issued, a statement summarizing changes in financial position should also be presented as a basic financial statement for each period for which an income statement is presented.[1]

This statement, the statement of changes in financial position, is a significant measure of the effectiveness of the financing activities of a firm.

---

[1] "Reporting Changes in Financial Position" *Opinions of the Accounting Principles Board, No. 19* (American Institute of Certified Public Accountants, 1971), p. 373.

444

The analysis of funds flow is designed to provide answers to several questions of significance to the various users of financial statements such as the following:

If comparative income statements indicate an increase in net income as compared to the previous year, why did the current position deteriorate?

Where did the company obtain the funds used to finance its expansion?

If the company had a net loss for the previous year, where did it obtain the funds to pay dividends to the owners?

As indicated above, this analysis and the information that it provides is considered to be of sufficient importance that it is now included as a formal statement in the published annual reports of firms. The Accounting Principles Board in its *Opinion No. 19* made the funds-flow statement, which is now to be titled "Statement of Changes in Financial Position," a required part of annual reports. The objectives of this statement are to summarize the financing and investing activities of a firm and to disclose the changes in financial position that occurred during the period.

DEFINITION OF FUNDS

A problem that has frequently arisen in the past with regard to funds flow reporting is the lack of a uniform definition of the term "funds." This is of the utmost importance since the definition of "funds" determines both the nature and format of the funds statement.

In everyday usage, the term funds usually means cash. Therefore, it might appear that a statement of changes in financial position would provide a summary of the firm's cash receipts and disbursements for the period. Using this definition of funds, the statement is essentially an analysis of cash flow.

In financial reporting, the term "funds" has usually been defined as working capital, or the excess of current assets over current liabilities. According to this concept, the statement reports financing and investing activities as a summary of the sources and uses of working capital for the period. Thus, the purpose of the statement is to indicate the sources of working capital inflow into the firm and the uses which were made of working capital during the period.

In recognition of the need for flexibility in the reporting practices of different firms, APB *Opinion 19* allows "funds" to be defined as either cash or working capital. The following section of this chapter will focus on the working capital definition of funds.

SOURCES AND USES OF WORKING CAPITAL

The statement of changes in financial position is divided into two major segments: funds that the firm has obtained during the period (sources of funds), and the outflow of funds which has occurred (uses of funds). The "sources of funds" section summarizes all transactions of the business that caused an increase in its working capital. Working capital may be increased by the operating activities of the firm as well as by its financing and other activities. The "uses of funds" section of the statement summarizes all transactions that caused a decrease in working capital during the period. Of course, a transaction that affects current assets and/or current liabilities but does not increase or decrease working capital is neither a source nor a use of funds. For example, the repayment of a short-term loan with cash decreases both current assets and current liabilities by an equal amount, and therefore does not affect working capital.

Sources of Funds

Transactions that increase working capital are sources of funds. The primary sources of working capital for a firm include:

1.   Current operations (inflows from revenues less outflows for expenses).
2.   The sale of noncurrent assets.
3.   Borrowing from long-term lenders.
4.   The sale of capital stock.

Funds from Operations

Net income of a firm for a particular period has been defined as the excess of its revenues over its expenses. Revenues generally result in an increase in current assets. For example, sales usually cause an increase in either cash or accounts receivable. Similarly, most expenses require either that a current outlay of cash be made or that a current liability be incurred. Thus, the operations of a firm are a source of funds if the inflow of working capital from revenues exceeds the outflow of working capital for expenses during the period.

The reported net income of a firm, however, is not necessarily equal to the amount of funds provided. This is because not all expenses require a current expenditure or the incurrence of a liability. Certain types of expenses enter into the determination of net income but have no effect on working capital. For example, depreciation of fixed assets is an expense which reduces income but does not require an outlay of funds and therefore does not affect working capital. In order to determine working capital provided by operations, it is necessary to deduct from revenues only those expenses which required an expenditure of funds and therefore caused a decrease in working capital. A convenient way of determining working capital from operations is simply to add back to net income all those expenses which did not require an outlay of funds, i.e., working capital.

It is important to note that the adding back of expenses which did not require the use of working capital to net income is not a source of funds in and of itself, but instead is simply a means of determining the amount of working capital generated by operations. Other expenses which do not affect working capital include amortization of the cost of intangible assets and amortization of discount on bonds payable.

Certain items included in the income statement decrease expenses (thereby increasing income) without increasing working capital. For example, the amortization of premium on bonds payable causes interest expense to be less than the amount of the cash paid. Therefore, these items should be deducted from net income in computing the amount of working capital provided by operations.

To illustrate, assume that Martin Company had net income of $1,000 during 1977, determined as follows:

Illustration 17–1
MARTIN COMPANY
Income Statement
For the Year Ending December 31, 1977

Sales		$20,000
Cost of goods sold		10,000
Gross margin.		$10,000
Operating expenses:		
Salaries.	$6,000	
Rent	1,000	
Depreciation	2,000	9,000
Net Income		$ 1,000

In this example, Martin Company had an inflow of $20,000 of working capital from sales, and outflows of $10,000 for cost of goods sold, $6,000 for salaries, and $1,000 for rent. Since the $2,000 depreciation expense did not require an outlay of funds, the increase in working capital is equal to sales of $20,000 less $17,000 of expenses which did cause an outflow of working capital. In other words, a total of $3,000 of funds was provided by operations. Alternatively, funds generated by operations can also be obtained by adding the $2,000 depreciation expense to the $1,000 net income, for a total of $3,000.

A firm that experiences a net loss for the period may still generate working capital from its operations if the total expenses which did not require the use of working capital exceed the amount of the loss. Thus, a firm with a net loss of $10,000 which included depreciation of $15,000 among its expenses would generate working capital of $5,000 from its operations. If the loss exceeds such adjustments, the difference constitutes a use of working capital during the period.

Additional adjustments may be required in order to obtain working capital provided by operations if net income includes either nonoperating gains or losses. For example, if land that had an original cost of $1,000 is sold for $1,500 during the period, a $500 gain on the sale of land is included in net income for the period. Since the $1,500 received from the sale represents the total funds provided and is shown in the statement as a separate item, it would be double counting to also include the $500 gain as a part of working capital provided by operations. Thus, in order to determine the amount of working capital provided by operations, it is necessary to deduct any nonoperating gains and add back any nonoperating losses.

The computation of the working capital provided by operations may be summarized as follows:

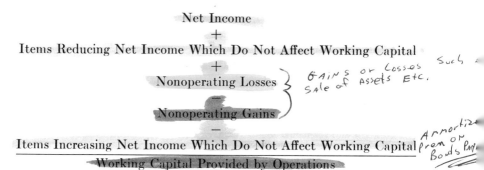

Net Income

+

Items Reducing Net Income Which Do Not Affect Working Capital

+

Nonoperating Losses } *GAINS or Losses Such a Sale of Assets Etc.*

−

Nonoperating Gains)

−

Items Increasing Net Income Which Do Not Affect Working Capital *Amortize Prem or Bonds Pay*

Working Capital Provided by Operations

Other Sources of Funds

The treatment of nonoperating sources of funds is fairly straightforward. Borrowing on long-term loans, for example, increases current assets without a corresponding increase in current liabilities, and therefore represents a source of funds. Similarly, the sale of additional capital stock or the sale of fixed assets results in a net inflow of current assets without an increase in current liabilities.

Uses of Funds

Transactions that decrease working capital are classified as uses of funds. Typical uses of working capital include:

1. Purchase of noncurrent assets.
2. Repayment of long-term debt.
3. Repurchase of capital stock.
4. Declaration of cash dividends.

Again, most uses of funds are fairly obvious. When noncurrent assets such as buildings, equipment, or land are purchased, a firm will usually make an outlay of cash, and/or increase its liabilities. In these instances, working capital is reduced and, thus, there is a use of funds. Similarly, the repayment of long-term debt such as a mortgage or bond, or the repurchase of outstanding capital stock, usually requires an outlay of funds.

The declaration of a cash dividend to be paid at a later date is also a use of funds. Working capital is reduced at the time the declaration is made because a current liability, dividends payable, is incurred and recorded at that time. The subsequent payment of the cash dividend does not affect working capital because cash, a current asset, and dividends payable, a current liability, are reduced by equal amounts.

DETERMINING SOURCES AND USES OF WORKING CAPITAL

The amounts of individual sources and uses of working capital necessary in order to prepare the statement of changes in financial position may be determined as follows:

1. Compute changes in current assets and current liability (working capital) accounts;
2. Compute changes in all the noncurrent accounts;
3. Analyze changes in the noncurrent accounts.

It is usually necessary to have comparative balance sheets for the beginning and end of the period and an income statement and retained earnings statement for the period available to determine sources and uses of working capital.

The following basic data will be used to illustrate the steps required for the preparation of a statement of changes in financial position.

Illustration 17–2

KRATON COMPANY
Income Statement
For the Year Ended December 31, 1977

Net sales		$1,000
Cost of goods sold		400
Gross margin.		$ 600
Operating expenses:		
Depreciation	$100	
Wage expense	100	
Other expenses	200	400
Net Income from Operations		$ 200
Gain on sale of land.		100
Net Income		$ 300

Illustration 17–2 (continued)

KRATON COMPANY
Retained Earnings Statement
For the Year Ended December 31, 1977

Retained earnings at beginning of year...............	$250
Add: Net income	300
	$550
Subtract: Dividends........................	100
Retained earnings at end of year	$450

KRATON COMPANY
Comparative Balance Sheet

	December 31		
ASSETS	1977	1976	Change
Cash	$ 250	$ 100	+150
Accounts receivable.....................	350	200	+150
Inventories............................	200	250	− 50
Building ....!.	600	400	+200
Accumulated depreciation–building	(200)	(100)	+100
Land	100	200	−100
Total Assets......................	$1,300	$1,050	

LIABILITIES AND STOCKHOLDERS' EQUITY

Accounts payable.......................	$ 300	$ 200	+100
Accrued wages payable....................	50	100	− 50
Bonds payable–long-term	100	200	−100
Capital stock..........................	400	300	+100
Retained earnings.......................	450	250	+200
Total Equities.....................	$1,300	$1,050	

Assume that the following additional information is available:

1. During the year, a building was purchased for $200 and land was purchased at a cost of $100.
2. Land with a cost of $200 was sold at a gain of $100.
3. All common stock was issued for cash.
4. A long-term bond was retired for $100.
5. A $100 dividend was paid during the year.

CHANGES IN WORKING CAPITAL

An increase in a current asset balance causes an increase in working capital. For example, if cash increases, current assets exceed current liabilities by a larger amount, other factors being equal. Similarly, a decrease in a current asset represents a reduction in working capital. An increase in a current liability, on the other hand, decreases working capital while a decrease in a current liability results in an increase in working capital. This is because current liabilities are deducted from current assets in determining working capital. Thus, the net change in working capital during the period can be easily computed by examining the changes in the current accounts in the comparative balance sheets.

The following illustration shows the changes in current assets, current liabilities, and working capital for Kraton Company from December 31, 1976, to December 31, 1977.

	December 31 1977	December 31 1976	Working Capital Increase	Working Capital Decrease
Current Assets:				
Cash	$250	$100	$150	—
Accounts receivable	350	200	150	—
Inventories	200	250	—	$ 50
Current Liabilities:				
Accounts payable	300	200	—	100
Accrued wages payable	50	100	50	—
			$350	$150
Increase in Working Capital				200
			$350	$350

(Handwritten annotations: CASH +, A/R +, INV. −, A/P +, W/P −, 200 ← + working capital)

In this situation the statement of changes in financial position will disclose sources of working capital exceeding uses by $200. The next step is to determine the nature of the various sources and uses of working capital. This is accomplished by analyzing all changes in the noncurrent accounts.

Changes in Noncurrent Accounts

Once the change in working capital has been determined, the next step is to compute the changes in all noncurrent accounts (noncurrent assets, [2] noncurrent liabilities, and [3] stockholders' equity). An analysis of these changes will indicate the sources and the uses of working capital during the period.

All changes in the noncurrent accounts of Kraton Company from December 31, 1976, to December 31, 1977, are summarized below.

	December 31 1977	December 31 1976	Increase	Decrease
Building	$600	$400	$200	
Accumulated depreciation— building	200	100	100	
Land	100	200		$100
Bonds payable—long-term	100	200		100
Capital stock	400	300	100	
Retained earnings	450	250	200	

(Handwritten annotations: Build. +, Depr. +, Sold Land −, Bought Bonds −, Issued Stock +, Made Money (RET. ERN.) + increase)

Once the amount of these changes has been determined, it is necessary to consider the effect that each change had on working capital. Each account must be considered in order to determine the cause of the change. If more than one transaction caused the change, the effect of each transaction must be analyzed separately.

Let us consider the changes in the noncurrent accounts of Kraton Company.

Building. The increase in the building account was the result of a single transaction in which a building was acquired at a cost of $200. The effect of this purchase on working capital was as follows:

> Use of Funds:
> Purchase of building $200

Land. The comparative balance sheet indicates that the land account decreased by $100 during 1977. This net decrease was a result of two transactions: one for the sale of land and another in which land was purchased. The source of funds from the sale of land is the total proceeds received from the sale. Thus, $300 of working capital was provided by the sale, the $200 book value of the land plus the $100 gain:

> Use of Funds:
> Purchase of land $100

As previously indicated, in order to avoid double counting, the $100 gain on the sale must be deducted from net income in the calculation of working capital provided by operations.

The cost of the land acquired during the year affected working capital as follows:

> Source of Funds:
> Sale of land $300

Accumulated Depreciation. The $100 increase in the Accumulated Depreciation—Building account resulted from recording depreciation expense for the year (see the income statement). The effect of depreciation on working capital will be considered in determining working capital provided by operations.

Bonds Payable. The next noncurrent item, bonds payable, decreased by $100 during the year. An analysis of the additional information provided indicates that this decrease resulted from the retirement of a bond at its face value. The effect on working capital is as follows:

> Use of Funds:
> Retirement of bonds payable $100

Capital Stock. The increase in the capital stock account resulted from the issuance of additional stock for $100 in cash during the year. This amount would be included in the statement as follows:

Source of Funds:
   Issuance of capital stock $100

Retained Earnings. An examination of the comparative balance sheets reveals that retained earnings increased by $200 during 1977. An analysis of the statement of retained earnings indicates that net income for 1977 was $300, and that dividends of $100 were declared and paid during the year. These two transactions account for the net change in retained earnings. The effect of the net income of the period on working capital is included in the calculation of working capital from operations described below. Declaration of the cash dividend affected working capital as follows:

Use of Funds:
   Cash dividend $100

WORKING CAPITAL PROVIDED BY OPERATIONS

As previously indicated, net income of Kraton Company is not equivalent to working capital from operations. One expense included in the income statement, depreciation, did not require either an outflow of current assets or an increase in a current liability. Therefore, it is necessary to add back depreciation expense of $100 to the net income of the period.

A second adjustment is required to eliminate the nonoperating gain on the sale of land from net income. The $100 gain was included in the proceeds from the sale of land as a separate source of working capital, and must be excluded from working capital provided by operations.

Thus, the working capital from operations is determined as follows:

Source of Funds:
   Operations:
      Net Income $300
      Add: Expense not requiring outlay of working
               capital during the period—depreciation 100
      Deduct: Nonoperating gain . . . . (100)
      Working Capital from Operations $300

It is only a coincidence that the working capital provided by operations is equal to the net income for the period.

FORM OF THE STATEMENT OF CHANGES
IN FINANCIAL POSITION

All information which is necessary to prepare the statement of changes in financial position has now been analyzed. The 1977 statement for the

Kraton Company prepared from this information is shown in Illustration 17–3.

Illustration 17–3
KRATON COMPANY
Statement of Changes in Financial Position
For the Year Ended December 31, 1977

Sources of Funds:

Operations:

Net income	$300	
Add: Depreciation	100	
Less: Gain on sale of land	(100)	
Working Capital Provided by Operations		$300
Sale of land	$300	
Sale of capital stock	100	400
Total Funds Provided		$700

Uses of Funds:

To acquire land	$100	
To acquire building	200	
To retire long-term bonds	100	
To pay dividends	100	500
Increase in Working Capital		$200

(handwritten margin notes: "From operation", "Income that other than operation")

The statement identifies and analyzes the sources and uses of working capital which resulted in the $200 net increase in working capital during 1977.

The statement of changes in financial position described above was simplified for purposes of illustration. Illustration 17–4 presents the actual statement of changes in financial position for Anheuser-Busch, Incorporated, for 1972 and 1973.

TRANSACTIONS NOT AFFECTING CURRENT ACCOUNTS

In the Kraton Company illustration, all financing and investing activities occurred through transactions that involved either a current asset or current liability account and a nonworking capital account. It is possible, however, to have transactions which affect only noncurrent accounts. For example, assume that $20,000 par value of capital stock is exchanged for a building with a fair market value of $20,000. Although this appears to be a significant financial transaction, it has no effect on the amount of working capital. Therefore, this exchange would be excluded from the statement of changes if a strict interpretation of the working capital definition of funds was used.

Because the strict application of working capital or cash definition of funds could omit the effect of certain significant transactions from the statement, APB *Opinion No. 19* broadens the concept underlying the

Illustration 17-4

ANHEUSER-BUSCH, INCORPORATED, AND SUBSIDIARIES

	1973	1972	
	(In Thousands)		
Financial resources were provided by:			
Operations —			
Income before extraordinary item	$ 65,577	$ 76,400	
Charges to income not involving working capital —			consolidated
Depreciation	41,059	38,970	
Deferred income taxes	12,825	7,353	
Deferred investment tax credit	2,855	94	statement
Other, net	359	691	
Working capital provided by operations	122,675	123,508	of changes in
Working capital provided by extraordinary item —			
Tax benefit of $4,006,000 less			financial position
expenses of $1,112,000	—	2,894	
Sale of common stock under stock option plans	264	1,808	
	122,939	128,210	
Financial resources were used for:			
Capital expenditures	91,801	84,217	
Investment properties	190	146	
Cash dividends paid	27,037	26,109	
Reduction in long-term debt	5,693	17,464	
Increased investment in unconsolidated subsidiaries,			
excluding transfers of land in the amounts of			
$134,000 and $2,640,000 respectively	5,579	1,218	
Other, net	1,108	1,988	
	131,408	131,142	
Decrease in working capital	$ (8,469)	$ (2,932)	
Increase (decrease) in current assets:			
Cash	$ (3,142)	$ (97)	
Marketable securities	(5,597)	14	
Accounts and notes receivable	9,906	4,381	
Inventories	8,643	(981)	
	9,810	3,317	analysis
Decrease (increase) in current liabilities:			of changes in
Accounts payable	(25,732)	(4,831)	
Accrued salaries and wages	(4,129)	(977)	working capital
Accrued taxes, other than income taxes	5,845	(1,133)	
Estimated federal and state income taxes	3,996	2,326	
Other current liabilities	1,741	(1,634)	
	(18,279)	(6,249)	
Decrease in working capital	$ (8,469)	$ (2,932)	

statement of changes in financial position to include financing and investing activities not directly affecting working capital. Under this concept, a significant transaction involving changes in noncurrent accounts must be reported as both a source and a use of funds. Of course, including this type of transaction does not affect the reported increase or decrease in working capital, but it does provide the user with a comprehensive view of the total inflow and outflow of all financial resources during the period. Among the most common of these nonworking capital transactions are:

1. The issuance of noncurrent debt or capital stock for noncurrent assets.
2. The issuance of capital stock to retire noncurrent debt.

To illustrate, again consider the case where a firm issued $20,000 par value of its capital stock for a building with a fair market value of $20,000. This transaction would have been recorded in the accounts as follows:

Building	20,000	
Capital Stock		20,000

Although this transaction did not affect working capital, it should be viewed as being comprised of two parts, the sale of stock for $20,000 and the purchase of a building for the same amount. Thus, it would be reported on the statement of changes in financial position as follows:

Source of Funds:
    Issuance of capital stock $20,000
Use of Funds:
    Purchase of building $20,000

CASH FLOW ANALYSIS

If funds are defined as cash, the statement of changes in financial position discloses individual sources and uses of cash. The analysis of cash flow is very similar to the analysis which was described for the working capital concept of funds. Additional adjustments, however, are necessary to convert the net income for the period to the amount of cash which was provided by operations.

Cash Flow from Operations

Several adjustments are required to convert a firm's net income to cash flow from operations. As illustrated previously, a nonfund expense, such as depreciation, is an allocation of a past cost and thus does not result in an outlay of cash during the current period. Therefore, nonfund expenses must be added back to net income in determining cash provided by operations. In addition, since income statement data are based on the accrual method of accounting, further adjustments are required to convert revenues and expenses to cash receipts and disbursements. The financial statements previously presented for Kraton Company will again be used as a basis for illustration.

Cash Received from Customers. Since many firms make sales on a credit basis, cash receipts depend on the collections from customers. If the accounts receivable balance increased during the period, credit sales must have exceeded collections from customers. Similarly, a decrease in accounts receivable during the year indicates that cash collected from customers exceeded net credit sales by the amount of the decrease in accounts receivable. Therefore, cash received from customers may be computed thus:

$$\text{Sales} \quad \begin{matrix} + \text{ Decrease in Accounts Receivables} \\ \text{or} \\ - \text{ Increase in Accounts Receivables} \end{matrix} \quad = \text{Cash Receipts From Sales}$$

The 1977 cash receipts from sales is computed as follows for Kraton Company:

Net sales	$1,000
Less: Increase in accounts receivable	150
Cash Receipts	$ 850

+ if Decrease occurs in A/R.

Cash Disbursements Associated with Cost of Goods Sold. The initial step in computing the cash disbursements associated with cost of goods sold is determining purchases for the period. Purchases will differ from cost of goods sold if the inventory balance increased or decreased during the year. If inventories decreased, then a part of the cost of goods sold came from the reduction of the beginning inventory and did not represent goods purchased during the year. Similarly, if inventories increased, purchases exceeded the cost of goods sold by the amount of the increase in the inventory balance.

$$\text{Cost of Goods Sold} \quad \begin{matrix} + \text{ Increase in Inventory} \\ \text{or} \\ - \text{ Decrease in Inventory} \end{matrix} \quad = \text{Purchases}$$

Since purchases are often made on a credit basis, purchases for a period may differ from cash disbursements if the accounts payable balance increased or decreased during the year. For example, if a firm increases its accounts payable,[2] it paid out less cash than the amount of its purchases for the period.

Thus, the procedure for computing cash disbursements for purchases is as follows:

$$\text{Purchases} \quad \begin{matrix} + \text{ Decrease in Accounts Payable} \\ \text{or} \\ - \text{ Increase in Accounts Payable} \end{matrix} \quad = \begin{matrix} \text{Cash Disbursements} \\ \text{for Purchases} \end{matrix}$$

To illustrate, Kraton Company's inventory decreased by $50 while its accounts payable increased by $100 during the year. Cash disbursements for purchases is computed as follows:

Cost of goods sold	$400
Less: Decrease in inventory	50
Purchases	$350
Less: Increase in accounts payable	100
Cash Disbursements for Purchases	$250

---

[2] In this example, it is assumed that all accounts payable were incurred for credit purchases.

Cash Disbursements for Expenses. Expenses incurred during the current period may differ from cash outlays because of changes in either prepaid expense or accrued liability balances.

If an accrued liability related to an expense increased during the year, then only a portion of the expense represented an expenditure of cash during the period. Thus, if an expense has a related accrued liability account, the cash disbursement associated with the expense may be determined as follows:

$$\text{Expense} \quad \genfrac{}{}{0pt}{}{+ \text{ Decrease in Accrued Liability}}{\genfrac{}{}{0pt}{}{\text{or}}{- \text{ Increase in Accrued Liability}}} = \genfrac{}{}{0pt}{}{\text{Cash Disbursement}}{\text{for Expenses}}$$

Similarly, if an expense has a related prepaid expense account, an increase in the prepaid account indicates that the cash outlay exceeded the amount of the expense. For example, assume that prepaid insurance was $500 on January 1 and $600 on December 31 and that insurance expense for the year was $200. The entry to record insurance expense would reduce the prepaid insurance account by $200 to a balance of $300. Therefore, an additional payment of $300 must have been made for insurance during the year.

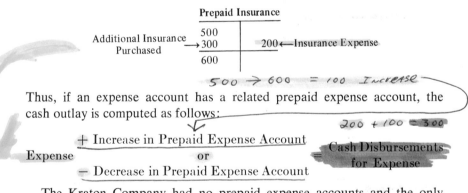

Prepaid Insurance

Additional Insurance Purchased → 500 / 300 / 600 | 200 ← Insurance Expense

500 → 600 = 100 Increase

Thus, if an expense account has a related prepaid expense account, the cash outlay is computed as follows:

200 + 100 = 300

$$\text{Expense} \quad \genfrac{}{}{0pt}{}{+ \text{ Increase in Prepaid Expense Account}}{\genfrac{}{}{0pt}{}{\text{or}}{- \text{ Decrease in Prepaid Expense Account}}} = \genfrac{}{}{0pt}{}{\text{Cash Disbursements}}{\text{for Expense}}$$

The Kraton Company had no prepaid expense accounts and the only accrued liability, wages payable, decreased by $50 during the year. Therefore, the only adjustment required is to determine the cash paid for wages during the year which is as follows:

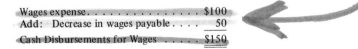

Wages expense.	$100
Add: Decrease in wages payable	50
Cash Disbursements for Wages	$150

Cash from Operations. Conversion of the net income of Kraton Company to cash provided by operations is shown below. It is derived from the computations which were made in the previous paragraphs.

Illustration 17–5

KRATON COMPANY

Conversion of Net Income to Cash Provided by Operations

For the Year Ended December 31, 1977

[handwritten: ADJUSTMENTS] *[handwritten: Restated Figures]*

	Income Statement	Add (Subtract)	Cash Receipts and (Disbursements)
Sales	$1000		
Less: Increase in receivables		–$(150) = →	$ 850
Cost of goods sold	400		
Less: Decrease in inventory		(50)	
Increase in accounts payable		–(100) = →	(250)
Gross Margin	$ 600		$ 600
Operating expenses:			
Depreciation	$ 100	– (100) = 0	
Wage expense	100		
Add: Decrease in wages payable		→ 50 = →	$(150)
Other expenses	200	+ – 0 = →	(200)
Net Income from Operations	$ 200		
Cash Provided by Operations			$ 250

[handwritten: 600 − 350 = 250]

Cash Used for Dividends

The computation of the cash used for dividends may also differ if there was a change in the dividends payable account from the beginning to the end of the year. For example, assume that dividends were declared on December 15, 1976, to be paid on January 15, 1977. The declaration of

Illustration 17–6

KRATON COMPANY

Cash Flow Statement

For the Year Ended December 31, 1977

Sources of Cash:			
Operations			
Net income			$300
Add: Depreciation expense	$100		
Decrease in inventory	50		
Increase in accounts payable	100	250	
		$550	
Less: Gain on sale of land	$100		
Increase in receivables	150		
Decrease in wages payable	50	300	
Cash Provided by Operations			$250
Sale of land			300
Sale of capital stock			100
			$650
Uses of Cash:			
To acquire land		$100	
To acquire building		200	
To retire long-term bonds		100	
To pay dividends		100	500
Increase in Cash			$150

[handwritten annotations: "Restated Income statement" next to the 250/$550 area; "Income outside of operations" bracketing Sale of land and Sale of capital stock]

Declaration of dividends would constitute a decrease in working capital during 1976 because a current liability, dividends payable, is increased. The use of cash, however, would occur during the following year when the dividends are actually paid.

CASH FLOW STATEMENT

Cash flow statements may vary considerably in both their format and terminology. Illustration 17–6 is comparable in form to the statement of changes in financial position, with funds defined as working capital (Illustration 17–3), which was prepared earlier in this chapter. The general format discloses the sources and uses of cash with the difference representing the increase or decrease in cash during the period. The statement of changes in financial position for the Kraton Company for 1977, with funds defined as cash, is shown below. This statement explains the $150 increase in the cash balance which occurred during 1977.

SUMMARY OF MECHANICS ON THE STATEMENT OF CHANGES IN FINANCIAL POSITION

The mechanics of the statement of changes in financial position may be summarized as follows:

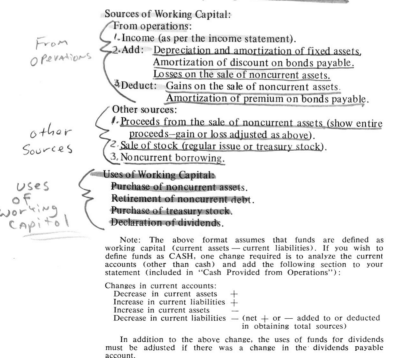

Statement of Changes in Financial Position

Sources of Working Capital:
From operations:
From Operations
1. Income (as per the income statement).
2. Add: Depreciation and amortization of fixed assets,
   Amortization of discount on bonds payable.
   Losses on the sale of noncurrent assets.
3. Deduct: Gains on the sale of noncurrent assets.
   Amortization of premium on bonds payable.

Other sources:
Other Sources
1. Proceeds from the sale of noncurrent assets (show entire proceeds–gain or loss adjusted as above).
2. Sale of stock (regular issue or treasury stock).
3. Noncurrent borrowing.

Uses of Working Capital:
Uses of Working Capital
Purchase of noncurrent assets.
Retirement of noncurrent debt.
Purchase of treasury stock.
Declaration of dividends.

Note: The above format assumes that funds are defined as working capital (current assets — current liabilities). If you wish to define funds as CASH, one change required is to analyze the current accounts (other than cash) and add the following section to your statement (included in "Cash Provided from Operations"):

Changes in current accounts:
Decrease in current assets   +
Increase in current liabilities   +
Increase in current assets   —
Decrease in current liabilities   — (net + or — added to or deducted in obtaining total sources)

In addition to the above change, the uses of funds for dividends must be adjusted if there was a change in the dividends payable account.

Comprehensive Illustration

The following example is used to illustrate the process of preparing a funds statement under both the working capital and cash concepts which have been discussed earlier in this chapter. Assume that the comparative balance sheet, income statement, and supplementary data for Lucas, Inc., is as follows:

Illustration 17–7

LUCAS, INC.
Comparative Balance Sheet
December 31, 1977 and 1976

ASSETS	1977	1976	Increase (Decrease)
Current Assets:			
Cash	$ 40,000	$ 35,000	$ 5,000
Accounts receivable	90,000	70,000	20,000
Inventories.	60,000	70,000	(10,000)
Prepaid expenses	20,000	15,000	5,000
Total Current Assets	$210,000	$190,000	$ 20,000
Noncurrent Assets:			
Land	$100,000	$ 50,000	$ 50,000
Buildings.	220,000	200,000	20,000
Accumulated depreciation–buildings	(60,000)	(50,000)	(10,000)
Equipment.	100,000	80,000	20,000
Accumulated depreciation–equipment	(20,000)	(10,000)	(10,000)
Patents.	50,000	60,000	(10,000)
Total Noncurrent Assets.	$390,000	$330,000	$ 60,000
Total Assets	$600,000	$520,000	$ 80,000
LIABILITIES AND STOCKHOLDERS' EQUITY			
Current Liabilities:			
Accounts payable.	$ 60,000	$ 50,000	$ 10,000
Notes payable.	20,000	30,000	(10,000)
Dividends payable	5,000	–0–	5,000
Accrued expenses.	35,000	30,000	5,000
Total Current Liabilities.	$120,000	$110,000	$ 10,000
Long-term liabilities:			
Bonds payable	$100,000	$150,000	$ (50,000)
Stockholders' Equity:			
Common stock ($100 par value)	$260,000	$200,000	$ 60,000
Additional paid-in capital	40,000	30,000	10,000
Retained earnings.	80,000	30,000	50,000
Total Stockholders' Equity	$380,000	$260,000	$120,000
Total Liabilities and Stockholders' Equity.	$600,000	$520,000	$ 80,000

Illustration 17–7 (continued)

LUCAS, INC.
Income Statement
For the Year Ended December 31, 1977

Sales		$1,500,000
Cost of goods sold		900,000
Gross margin		$ 600,000
Operating expenses:		
Depreciation and amortization expense	$ 40,000	
Selling and administrative expense	270,000	
Miscellaneous expense	175,000	
Total Operating Expenses		485,000
Net income from operations		$ 115,000
Other revenue and expense		
Add: Gain on sale of land		15,000
		$ 130,000
Less: Loss on sale of building	$10,000	
Interest expense	12,000	22,000
Net income before taxes		$ 108,000
Less: Income taxes		48,000
Net Income		$ 60,000

Supplementary data:

1. Cash dividends of $10,000 were declared during 1977.
2. Depreciation on buildings and equipment and amortization of patent costs during 1977 were as follows:

Buildings	$20,000
Equipment	10,000
Patents	10,000
Total	$40,000

3. Land valued at $80,000 was acquired in exchange for cash of $50,000 and common stock with a par value of $30,000.
4. A building with an original cost of $40,000 and accumulated depreciation of $10,000 was sold for $20,000.
5. A building was acquired for $60,000 cash.
6. Equipment was acquired for $20,000 cash.
7. Land with a cost of $30,000 was sold for $45,000.
8. Bonds payable of $50,000 were retired.
9. Common stock with $30,000 par value was sold for $40,000.

Preparation of Statement—Funds Defined as Working Capital

In this section, it is assumed that funds are defined as working capital. Details of the change in the working capital of Lucas, Inc., during 1977 are shown in Illustration 17–8.

Illustration 17–8

LUCAS, INC.

Statement of Changes in Working Capital

December 31, 1977 and 1976

	1977	1976	Working Capital Increase	Working Capital Decrease
Current Assets:				
Cash	$ 40,000	$ 35,000	$ 5,000	–
Accounts receivable	90,000	70,000	20,000	–
Inventories	60,000	70,000	–	$10,000
Prepaid expenses	20,000	15,000	5,000	–
Total Current Assets	$210,000	$190,000	–	–
Current Liabilities:				
Accounts payable.	$ 60,000	$ 50,000	–	10,000
Notes payable.	20,000	30,000	10,000	–
Dividends payable	5,000	–0–	–	5,000
Accrued expenses.	35,000	30,000	–	5,000
Total Current Liabilities.	$120,000	$110,000	–	–
Working capital	$ 90,000	$ 80,000	–	–
Increase in Working Capital				10,000
			$40,000	$40,000

To explain the $10,000 increase in working capital during 1977, it is necessary to analyze all changes in the noncurrent accounts shown in the comparative balance sheet. Of course, the effect of net income and dividends is included in the change in retained earnings for the year. Explanations of the individual sources and uses of working capital included in the Statement of Changes in Financial Position follow:

1. *Land.* The acquisition of land for $80,000 is reported as a use of funds. Under the all financial resources concept, the partial payment by issuance of $30,000 of common stock is reported as a source of funds. The sale of land for $45,000 is also reported as a source of funds, while the gain on the sale of $15,000 is deducted from net income in determining working capital provided by operations.

2. *Building.* The sale of a building for $20,000 is reported as a source of funds and the $10,000 loss on the sale is added back to net income in determining working capital provided by operations. The acquisition of a building for $60,000 is reported as a use of funds.

3. *Accumulated Depreciation—Building.* The increase in this account was $10,000. This increase consisted of depreciation expense of $20,000 recorded during the year less $10,000 of accumulated depreciation which was removed from the account when the building was sold.

4. *Equipment.* The acquisition of equipment at a cost of $20,000 represents a use of funds.

5. *Accumulated Depreciation—Equipment*. The $10,000 change in this account was caused by the depreciation expense for the year.
6. *Patents*. The $10,000 decrease in the patents account resulted from the amortization of the cost of the patents during the year.
7. *Bonds Payable*. The decrease in bonds payable of $50,000 is reported as a use of funds since bonds were retired.
8. *Common Stock*. The $60,000 increase in common stock was caused by two transactions. The $30,000 par value of stock which was issued for land was reported as a source of funds under the all financial resources concept. Additionally, the $30,000 par value common stock which was sold for $40,000 represented a source of funds.
9. *Additional Paid-in Capital*. The $10,000 increase in this account was caused by the sale of common stock mentioned above.
10. *Retained Earnings*. The net increase in retained earnings resulted from net income for the period of $60,000 less the $10,000 cash dividend declared. The dividend is reported as a use of funds. The working capital provided by operations is computed as follows:

Net income		$ 60,000
Add: Depreciation and amortization	$40,000	
Loss on sale of building	10,000	50,000
		$110,000
Less: Gain on sale of land.		15,000
Working capital provided by operations		$ 95,000

On the basis of the analysis of the noncurrent accounts, the statement shown on page 465 would be prepared.

This statement shows that of the total funds provided, less than half were generated by working capital provided by operations. Thus, the working capital provided by operations was sufficient to pay the dividends, but only a portion of the expansion in assets. The firm experienced an increase in working capital because it obtained $135,000 of funds from nonrecurring sources.

Preparation of Statement—Funds Defined as Cash

The procedures which are necessary to prepare a statement of changes in financial position using the cash concept of funds are similar to those described in the previous section of this chapter. Additional steps, however, are necessary in order to determine dividends in terms of cash and cash flow from operations. Cash applied to dividends during the period is determined by adjusting the reported dividends for the change in the Dividends Payable account during the period. The amount of cash applied

Illustration 17–9
LUCAS, INC.
Statement of Changes in Financial Position
For the Year Ended December 31, 1977

Working Capital Provided by:
  Operations:

Net income		$ 60,000	
Add: Expenses not requiring outlay of working capital during the current period:			
Depreciation and amortization	$40,000		
Loss on sale of buildings	10,000	50,000	
		$110,000	
Less: Gain on sale of land		15,000	
Working Capital Provided by Operations			$ 95,000
Sale of land		$ 45,000	
Sale of building		20,000	
Sale of common stock		40,000	
Common stock issued as part payment for land		30,000	135,000
			$230,000

Working Capital Applied to:
  Acquisition of:

Land	$80,000		
Building	60,000		
Equipment	20,000	$160,000	
Retirement of bonds		50,000	
Payment of dividends		10,000	220,000
Increase in Working Capital			$ 10,000

to dividends for Lucas, Inc. during 1977 is as follows:

Dividends	$10,000
Less: Increase in dividends payable	(5,000)
Cash applied to dividends	$ 5,000

over

Net income from operations was adjusted for nonfund expenses and nonrecurring gains and losses in determining the amount of working capital provided by operations. To determine cash provided by operations, net income must also be adjusted for changes in current assets (other than cash) and in current liabilities (other than dividends payable). These adjustments are necessary to convert the income statement data from the accrual to the cash basis and are reflected in the following statement (on page 466) of changes in financial position using the cash concept of funds.

CASh Method

Illustration 17–10

LUCAS, INC.

Statement of Changes in Financial Position

For the Year Ended December 31, 1977

Cash Provided by:			
Operations:			
Net income		$ 60,000	
Add:			
Depreciation and amortization	$40,000		
Loss on sale of building	10,000		
Decrease in inventories	10,000		
Increase in accounts payable	10,000		
Increase in accrued expenses	5,000	75,000	
		$135,000	
Deduct:			
Gain on sale of land	$15,000		
Increase in accounts receivable	20,000		
Increase in prepaid expenses	5,000		
Decrease in notes payable.	10,000	50,000	
Cash provided by operations			$ 85,000
Other sources:			
Sale of land		$ 45,000	
Sale of building.		20,000	
Sale of common stock		40,000	
Common stock issued as partial			
payment of land		30,000	135,000
			$220,000
Cash Applied to:			
Acquisition of:			
Land	$80,000		
Building	60,000		
Equipment	20,000	$160,000	
Retirement of bonds		50,000	
Payment of dividends		5,000	215,000
Increase in Cash			$ 5,000

KEY DEFINITIONS

All financial resources This concept modifies "funds" to include not only those transactions affecting cash or working capital, but also those transactions of significant amount that affect the financing and investing activities of the firm, even though they involve only noncurrent accounts.

Cash concept of funds This concept defines funds in terms of cash or near-cash, and utilizes the funds statement to point out changes in the cash flow of the firm.

Cash disbursement Any outflow of cash by the firm is a cash disbursement.

Cash flow Any transaction that increases or decreases the cash balance of the firm is a cash flow.

Cash flow statement A cash flow statement is a statement summarizing the cash flows of the firm. It normally discloses the beginning cash balance, sources of cash receipts, types of cash payments, and the ending cash balance.

Cash from operations The net of cash receipts and disbursements for a period resulting from the normal operating activities of the firm. It is determined by adjusting each item in the income statement to a cash basis.

Cash receipt Any transaction that increases the cash account of the firm is a cash receipt.

Funds According to APB Opinion 19, funds are either cash, near cash, or working capital.

Funds from operations The effect on funds caused by the normal operating activities of the firm.

Funds statement See "Statement of Changes in Financial Position."

Noncurrent account An account that is neither a current asset nor a current liability.

Sources of funds Sources of funds involve any transaction that has caused funds to flow into a firm, i.e., any transaction that has increased working capital or cash, depending upon the definition of funds.

Statement of changes in financial position A statement of changes in financial position is a statement summarizing the financing and investing activities of the firm and disclosing changes in financial position.

Uses of funds Any transaction that has caused funds to flow out of the firm, i.e., any transaction that has decreased working capital or cash.

Working capital Working capital is the excess of current assets over current liabilities.

Working capital concept of funds This concept defines funds in terms of working capital, and utilizes the funds statement to point out changes in the working capital of the firm.

Working capital provided by operations This is the net effect on working capital from the normal operations of the business.

QUESTIONS

1. What are the four primary sources of working capital? What are four typical uses of working capital?

2. What are the steps in determining the sources and uses of working capital?

3. Can a firm with a loss for a period still have a source of working capital from operations for the period? If so, how?

4. Explain why depreciation expense is added back into operating income when determining the funds from operations.

5. What are the objectives of the "Statement of Changes in Financial Position"?

6. What are the two main parts of a Statement of Changes in Financial Position?

7. Why does APB *Opinion 19* broaden the concept of funds to "all financial resources"?

8. How are the following amounts computed?

    a. cash receipts from sales
    b. purchases
    c. cash disbursements for purchases
    d. cash disbursements for expenses

9. Discuss the different connotations of the term "funds" and the resulting effects on the Statement of Changes in Financial Position.

10. What are two ways of computing working capital from operations?

11. How do nonoperating gains and losses affect the computation of working capital from operations?

12. Is the declaration of a cash dividend to be paid at a later date a use of funds? Why or why not? What about subsequent payment of the dividend?

EXERCISES

17–1   Consider the following income statement for Wills Company.

Sales		$1,000,000
Cost of goods sold		750,000
Gross margin		$ 250,000
Selling and administrative expenses		
Salary expense	$50,000	
Depreciation expense	25,000	
Administrative expense	25,000	100,000
Net Income		$ 150,000

175,000

Required:

Compute the working capital from operations.

17–2   Below is the income statement for Lopes Company for the year ending December 31, 1975.

LOPES COMPANY
Income Statement
For the Year Ended December 31, 1975

Sales (net)		$500,000
Cost of goods sold:		
Beginning inventory	$ 50,000	
Purchases	300,000	
Goods available for sale	$350,000	
Ending inventory	40,000	
Cost of goods sold		310,000
Gross margin.		$190,000
Expenses		
Wages	$35,000	
Depreciation	30,000	
Advertising	15,000	
Administrative	5,000	85,000
Income from operations		$105,000
Gain on sale of equipment		50,000
Net Income		$155,000

The following balances were derived from the balance sheet.

	December 31	
	1975	*1974*
Accounts receivable.	$100,000	$90,000
Accounts payable	30,000	50,000
Prepaid advertising expense	5,000	3,000
Wages payable	5,000	4,000

Required:

Prepare a schedule showing cash provided by operations.

17–3   Your examination of the financial statements of Russell Company reveals the following data.

	1975		1974	
Sales (net)		$100,000		$75,000
Cost of goods sold:				
Beginning inventory	$17,000		$12,000	
Purchases (net)	58,000		55,000	
Goods available	75,000		67,000	
Ending inventory	15,000		17,000	
Cost of goods sold		$60,000		$50,000
Accounts payable		20,000		25,000
Accounts receivable.		50,000		45,000

Required:

Compute the following for 1975:

a. Cash receipts from sales.

b. Cash disbursements for purchases.

17–4 Consider the following information for the period ending December 31, 1975, concerning the Cey Company.

a. Net income for 1975 was $250,000.

b. Depreciation expense on its buildings was $25,000. Accumulated depreciation on the buildings is $200,000.

c. Extraordinary (non-operating) gains and losses included a loss of $50,000 on an uninsured building destroyed by fire.

d. Dividends paid during the year in cash—$50,000.

Required:

Compute working capital from operations.

17–5 An outline of a statement of changes in financial position appears below. You may assume that the company operated at a profit for the year.

CRAWFORD COMPANY
Statement of Changes in Financial Position

Funds provided by:
Operations:
Net Income
    Add . . . .   (1)
    Deduct . . . .   (2)
    Other sources of funds. . . . .   (3)
Funds applied to:
    Uses of funds . . . .   (4)

Difference—change in working capital.

For each of the items listed below determine in which of the designated positions, if any, the item would appear. *If more than one position is appropriate, so indicate.*

Answer Choices:

(1) Position 1; (2) Position 2; (3) Position 3; (4) Position 4; (5) None of these.

Items:

1. Declaration of a cash dividend. . . . . ( )
2. Payment of cash dividend after above declaration . . . . ( )
3. Depreciation expense for the year . . . . ( )
4. Fully depreciated equipment written off the books . . . . ( )
5. Amortization of premium on long-term bonds payable . . . . ( )
6. Semiannual coupon *payments* on bonds mentioned in item #5 above . . ( )
7. Sale of common stock at a discount . . . . ( )
8. Purchase of treasury stock at a price above the original issue price . . . . ( )
9. Payment of wages accrued at the end of the prior year . . . . ( )
10. Sale of fixed assets at a loss . . . . ( )
11. Discounting the company's own 90-day note at a bank . . . . ( )
12. Sale of 10-year bonds at a discount. . . . . ( )
13. Three for one (3–1) split of the preferred stock. . . . . ( )
14. Sale of machinery at a price in excess of its book value . . . . ( )
15. Amortization of goodwill . . . . ( )

17–6 Wynn, Inc., hired you as an independent accountant to analyze the reasons for their unsatisfactory cash position. The company earned

$42,000 during the year (1975) but their cash balance is lower than ever. Your assistant prepared a worksheet providing you with the following information:

a. Additional capital stock was sold in 1975; the proceeds of the sale were $40,000.

b. Vacant land purchased in 1974 at a cost of $27,000 was sold in 1975 for $30,000.

c. A payment of $22,000 was made in 1975 on a long-term mortgage.

d. Equipment costing $89,000 was purchased during the year.

e. Included in the firm's expenses for 1975 were depreciation charges of $7,500.

f. The firm's Accounts Receivable increased by $4,000 and their Accounts Payable decreased by $4,500 during the year.

Required:

Prepare a Cash Flow Statement for the year ended December 31, 1975, which reflects the reasons for the firm's unsatisfactory cash position.

PROBLEMS

Series A

17A–1   The comparative balance sheet of Buckner Corp. is as follows:

BUCKNER CORPORATION
Comparative Balance Sheet
December 31, 1975 and 1976

ASSETS	1976	1975
Current assets:		
Cash	$ 50,000	$ 35,000
Accounts receivable	100,000	90,000
Inventory	60,000	65,000
Prepaid expenses	10,000	8,000
Total Current Assets	$220,000	$198,000
Fixed assets:		
Building and equipment (net).	$200,000	$220,000
Land	50,000	50,000
Total Assets	$470,000	$468,000
LIABILITIES AND STOCKHOLDERS' EQUITY		
Accounts payable.	$100,000	$ 80,000
Interest payable.	10,000	10,000
Notes payable (current)	50,000	40,000
Capital stock	200,000	200,000
Retained earnings.	110,000	138,000
Total Liabilities and Stockholders' Equity.	$470,000	$468,000

Required:

Prepare a schedule computing the change in working capital.

17A–2 Below is the income statement for the Rau Company for the year ended December 31, 1975.

RAU COMPANY
Income Statement
For the Year Ended December 31, 1975

Sales		$1,000,000
Cost of goods sold:		
Beginning inventory	$ 20,000	
Purchases	500,000	
Goods available for sale	$520,000	
Ending inventory	25,000	
Cost of goods sold		495,000
Gross margin.		$ 505,000
Operating expenses:		
Salaries.	$ 50,000	
Depreciation	20,000	
Bad debts	10,000	
Advertising	20,000	
Patent amortization	5,000	
Total operating expenses.		105,000
Operating income.		$ 400,000
Gain on sale of equipment		50,000
Net Income		$ 450,000

Required:

Prepare a schedule computing working capital from operations.

17A–3 Consider the following noncurrent account balances for Messerschmidt, Inc.

	December 31			
	1976	*1975*	*Increase*	*Decrease*
Buildings.	$800	$1,000		$200
Accumulated depreciation—				
building	175	150	$ 25	
Land	300	200	100	
Bonds payable—long-term	200	100	100	
Capital stock	200	300		100
Retained earnings.	300	150	150	

Working capital from 1976 operations: $100

Required:

Prepare a Statement of Changes in Financial Position for Messerschmidt, Inc., for the period ending December 31, 1976, assuming, where it is necessary, that the changes in the noncurrent account are the result of cash transactions. Funds are defined as working capital.

17A–4   Below is information pertinent to John Corp. for the period ending
December 31, 1975.

1. Sales, $50,000.
2. Cost of goods sold, $20,000.
3. Expenses, $10,000 (of which $2,000 was depreciation).
 4. Increase in accounts payable, $5,000. } *not Included since now-current Accounts are used only*
5. Increase in accounts receivable, $5,000.
6. Sold land which cost $500 for $1,000 cash.
7. Purchased a building for $10,000 cash and $10,000 par value
common stock.
8. Cash dividends paid, $5,000.
9. Retired bond payable of $500.

Required:

Prepare a Statement of Changes in Financial Position assuming
"funds" are defined as working capital.

17A–5   The condensed comparative balance sheet for Marshall Company is
presented below.

	December 31		
ASSETS	1976	1975	
Cash	$ 80,000	$ 65,000	$15,000
Accounts receivable (net)	100,000	90,000	10,000 since
Inventory	40,000	45,000	(5,000)
Prepaid expenses	12,000	10,000	2000
Fixed assets	173,000	150,000	23000 use
Accumulated depreciation–fixed assets	(35,000)	(30,000)	5000
Total Assets	$370,000	$330,000	$40,000
LIABILITIES AND STOCKHOLDERS' EQUITY			
Accounts payable	$ 80,000	$ 60,000	$20,000
Bonds payable	150,000	150,000	-0-
Capital stock	100,000	100,000	-0-
Retained earnings	40,000	20,000	20,000
Total Liabilities and Stockholders' Equity	$370,000	$330,000	$40,000

Supplemental data for 1976:

Net income . . . . . $20,000.
Depreciation expense . . . . . $5,000.
A building was purchased for $23,000 cash.

Required:

Prepare a statement of changes in financial position based on changes
in working capital.

17A–6) Following are financial statements for Brewer, Inc.:

HAnd   in !!

BREWER, INC.
Comparative Balance Sheet
December 31, 1976 and 1975

ASSETS	1976	1975	*Increase (Decrease)*
Current Assets:			
Cash	$ 5,000	$ 45,000	$(40,000)
Accounts receivable	100,000	75,000	25,000
Inventories	50,000	45,000	5,000
Prepaid expenses	30,000	35,000	(5,000)
Total Current Assets	$185,000	$200,000	$(15,000)
Noncurrent Assets:			
Land	$100,000	$ 75,000	$ 25,000
Buildings	200,000	175,000	25,000
Accumulated depreciation–buildings	(50,000)	(40,000)	(10,000)
Equipment	100,000	75,000	25,000
Accumulated depreciation–equipment	(35,000)	(15,000)	(20,000)
Patents	20,000	30,000	(10,000)
Total Noncurrent Assets	$335,000	$300,000	$ 35,000
Total Assets	$520,000	$500,000	$ 20,000
LIABILITIES AND STOCKHOLDERS' EQUITY			
Current Liabilities:			
Accounts payable	$ 50,000	$ 40,000	$ 10,000
Notes payable	25,000	25,000	0
Accrued expenses	40,000	35,000	5,000
Total Current Liabilities	$115,000	$100,000	$ 15,000
Long-term Liabilities:			
Bonds payable	$100,000	$140,000	$(40,000)
Stockholders' Equity:			
Common stock ($100 par value)	$230,000	$200,000	$ 30,000
Additional paid-in capital	40,000	30,000	10,000
Retained earnings	35,000	30,000	5,000
Total Stockholders' Equity	$305,000	$260,000	$ 45,000
Total Liabilities and Stockholders' Equity	$520,000	$500,000	$ 20,000

BREWER, INC.
Income Statement
For the Year Ended December 31, 1976

Sales		$2,000,000
Cost of goods sold		1,500,000
Gross margin		$ 500,000
Operating expenses:		
Depreciation and amortization expense	$ 50,000	
Selling and administrative expense	265,000	
Miscellaneous expense	170,000	
Total Operating Expenses		485,000
Net income from operations.		$ 15,000
Other revenue and expense		
Add: Gain on sale of building		20,000
		$ 35,000
Less: Loss on sale of land	$ 10,000	
Interest expense	15,000	25,000
Net income before income taxes		$ 10,000
Less: Income taxes		5,000
Net Income		$ 5,000

Supplementary data:

1. Depreciation and amortization of patents were as follows:

Buildings	$20,000
Equipment	20,000
Patents	10,000
Total	$50,000

GAIN over Book value
50-10=40
20 GAIN

2. A building which cost $50,000 and had accumulated depreciation of $10,000 was sold for $60,000.
3. Common stock with $30,000 par value was sold for $40,000.
4. Land with a cost of $25,000 was sold for $15,000. *Loss*
5. Land was purchased for $50,000.
6. Bonds of $40,000 were retired.
7. A building was purchased for $75,000.
8. Equipment was acquired for $25,000 cash.

Required:

Prepare statements of changes in financial position for Brewer, Inc. assuming:

a. Funds are defined as working capital.
b. Funds are defined as cash. *(Cash flow statement)*

Series B

17B–1   The comparative balance sheet of Yaeger Corp. is as follows:

YAEGER CORPORATION
Comparative Balance Sheet
December 31, 1976 and 1975

ASSETS	1975	1976
Current Assets:		
Cash	$ 60,000	$ 95,000
Accounts receivable	240,000	260,000
Inventory	350,000	382,000
Prepaid expenses	10,000	18,000
Total Current Assets	$ 660,000	$ 755,000
Fixed Assets:		
Building and equipment (net)	800,000	920,000
Land	50,000	50,000
Total Assets	$1,510,000	$1,725,000

LIABILITIES AND STOCKHOLDERS' EQUITY		
Accounts payable	$ 250,000	$ 280,000
Notes payable (current)	100,000	110,000
Wages payable	20,000	30,000
Capital stock	900,000	1,000,000
Retained earnings	240,000	305,000
Total Liabilities and Stockholders' Equity	$1,510,000	$1,725,000

Required:

Prepare a schedule computing the change in working capital.

17B–2   Below is the income statement for the Downing Company for the year
ended December 31, 1976.

DOWNING COMPANY
Income Statement
For the Year Ended December 31, 1976

Sales		$2,500,000
Cost of Goods Sold:		
Beginning inventory	$ 120,000	
Purchases	1,500,000	
Goods available for sale	$1,620,000	
Ending inventory	40,000	
Cost of Goods Sold		1,580,000
Gross Margin		$ 920,000
Operating Expenses:		
Salaries	$ 450,000	
Depreciation	120,000	
Bad debts expense	20,000	
Selling expenses	20,000	
Patent amortization	15,000	
Total Operating Expenses		625,000
Operating income		$ 295,000
Gain on sale of equipment		150,000
Net Income		$ 145,000

Required:

Prepare a schedule computing working capital from operations.

17B–3   Given below are the balance sheets for Zahn Company for 1974 and 1975.

ZAHN COMPANY
Comparative Balance Sheet
December 31, 1974 and 1975

	1974	1975
Cash	$ 100	$ 300
Accounts receivable	400	350
Inventories	300	500
Fixed assets	900	1,000
Less: Accumulated depreciation	(100)	(200)
	$1,600	$1,950
Accounts payable	$ 400	$ 600
Bonds payable (due in 1980)	400	200
Capital stock	500	700
Retained earnings	300	450
	$1,600	$1,950

Additional information:

The corporation paid a 10% stock dividend on January 2, 1975, when its capital stock was selling at par. Net income for 1975 was $200. During the year, the company sold a fixed asset with an original cost of $100 (and a book value of $25 at the date of sale) for $50. All other changes in the accounts are the results of transactions typically recorded in such accounts.

Required:

Prepare a statement of changes in financial position for Zahn Company (where funds are defined as working capital).

17B–4   Below are the balance sheets of the McMullen Company.

	December 31	
	1976	1975
Cash	$ 356	$ 168
Accounts receivable	600	480
Allowance for bad debts	(26)	(20)
Inventories	740	800
Buildings and equipment	840	720
Allowance for depreciation	(360)	(380)
Total Assets	$2,150	$1,768
Accounts payable	$ 440	$ 420
Long-term bonds	600	600
Discount on long-term bonds	(36)	(42)
Capital stock	714	540
Retained earnings	432	250
Total Equities	$2,150	$1,768

Additional information is as follows:

a. Income for 1976 was $436.
b. Dividends paid during 1976 included a stock dividend of $54.
c. During 1976, equipment costing $80 and having a net book value of $20 was sold for $8.

Required:

Prepare a statement of changes in financial position for the year 1976 (funds defined as working capital).

17B-5   From the following information prepare a statement showing in detail the sources and uses of working capital for 1975.

FERGUSON COMPANY
Trial Balances
(in thousands)

	December 31, 1975		*December 31, 1974*	
Account	*Debit*	*Credit*	*Debit*	*Credit*
Cash	$ 178		$ 84	
Accounts receivable.	300		240	
Allowance for bad debts		$ 13		$ 10
Merchandise inventory	370		400	
Building and equipment	420		360	
Allowance for depreciation		180		190
Accounts payable		220		210
Mortgage bonds		300		300
Unamortized bond discount	18		21	
Capital stock		357		270
Retained earnings.		125		90
Net sales		4,200		4,000
Cost of goods sold	2,300		2,100	
Salaries and wages	1,500		1,400	
Administrative expense	110		100	
Depreciation expense.	20		20	
Maintenance expense	10		10	
Interest expense.	16		15	
Bad debt expense	20		20	
Loss on equipment sales*	6		0	
Dividends paid†	127		300	
	$5,395	$5,395	$5,070	$5,070

* In 1975, equipment costing $40,000 and having a net book value of $10,000 was sold for $4,000.
† Dividends paid in 1975 include a stock dividend of $27,000.

17B-6   The 1976 financial statements for the Alston Company are shown on the following page.

ALSTON COMPANY
Income Statement
For the Year Ended December 31, 1976

Net sales		$50,000
Cost of goods sold		30,000
Gross margin		$20,000
Operating expenses:		
Depreciation	$2,000	
Wage expense	7,000	
Other expenses	1,000	10,000
Net income from operations.		$10,000
Gain on sale of land		5,000
Net Income		$15,000

ALSTON COMPANY
Retained Earnings Statement
For the Year Ended December 31, 1976

Retained earnings at beginning of year	$25,000
Add: Net income	15,000
	$40,000
Subtract: Dividends.	5,000
Retained earnings at end of year	$35,000

ALSTON COMPANY
Comparative Balance Sheets
At December 31

	1976	1975
Assets:		
Cash	$ 69,000	$ 60,000
Accounts receivable	25,000	20,000
Inventories	15,000	10,000
Building	100,000	100,000
Accumulated depreciation–building	(27,000)	(25,000)
Land	125,000	100,000
Total Assets.	$307,000	$265,000
Liabilities and Stockholders' Equity:		
Accounts payable.	$ 35,000	$ 15,000
Accrued wages payable	7,000	5,000
Bonds payable–long-term	130,000	120,000
Capital stock	100,000	100,000
Retained earnings.	35,000	25,000
Total Equities.	$307,000	$265,000

The following information is also available:

1. Land with a cost of $25,000 was sold for $30,000.
2. Additional land was purchased for $50,000.
3. A long-term bond was issued for $10,000.
4. $5,000 cash dividends were paid during the year.

Required:

Prepare a statement of changes in financial position for the Alston Company for the year ending December 31, 1976 based on the:

a. "Working capital" concept of funds.
b. "Cash" concept of funds.

18

Price-Level Changes

A BASIC assumption underlying conventional accounting practice is that the unit of measure, the dollar, is a stable common monetary denominator of the accounting process. The result of this assumption is that accounting systems record the inflows and outflows of historical, or original, dollars. Since the amounts represented in account balances are stated in terms of original dollar flows, the accounting system is valid only if the value of the dollar remains stable over time. If inflation or deflation occurs, the value of the dollar changes. As a result, dollars of different purchasing power are entered and combined in the same account (or accounts) over a period of time. Therefore, even though all accounts in the financial statements include "dollars" they do not represent dollars of equal purchasing power. Combining dollars of different purchasing power in the accounts affects both the balance sheet and the income statement. Assets purchased at different times are reported in the financial statements in terms of dollars at the date of purchase. Thus, the account balance for a particular asset group (e.g., machinery) represents an aggregate amount comprised of dollars of unequal purchasing power. The cost of these assets, stated in dollars of both current and prior years, are allocated to depreciation expense. This expense is deducted from revenues which are expressed in terms of dollars of relatively current purchasing power.

Adherence to the stable unit of measure assumption implies that changes in the purchasing power of the dollar are not significant. Obviously, the greater the fluctuation in purchasing power of the dollar over time, the less valid the stable monetary unit assumption and the resulting financial statements are.

In the United States, the rate of change in the purchasing power of the dollar was not considered particularly important until around 1940. With the steady increase in the level of prices both during and after World War II, however, there has been a growing concern with the limitations of financial statements based on the assumption of a stable monetary unit. As a result, numerous proposals have been made for the use of "price-level" accounting in order to take into consideration the effects of changes in the purchasing power of the dollar.

Although price-level accounting has received considerable attention from accountants in the United States during the past two decades, the profession has taken few definitive steps in the direction of financial reporting in terms of a stable monetary unit.[1] At the present time, the primary authoritative support for price-level accounting is provided by Statement No. 3, "Financial Statement Restated for General Price-Level Changes," issued by the Accounting Principles Board of the American Institute of Certified Public Accountants in 1969. In this pronouncement the APB suggested that statements adjusted for changes in the purchasing power of the dollar may be quite useful if presented as *supplements* to conventional historical-dollar financial statements. The Board also concluded, however, that general price-level information is not required for fair presentation of financial statements in conformity with generally accepted accounting principles. The means of providing price-level information and certain of the problems involved in this process are examined in this chapter.

MEASURE OF THE INSTABILITY OF THE DOLLAR

The change in the value or purchasing power of the dollar is measured by the changes over time in the amount of goods and services which a given quantity of money will buy. These movements in the price structure of goods and services as a whole are often referred to as shifts in the *general price level*. The purchasing power of the dollar is, of course, inversely related to the general level of prices. Thus, during periods of inflation, the general level of prices increases and the purchasing power of the dollar decreases. Similarly, a period of deflation results in a decrease in the general level of prices and a corresponding increase in the value of the dollar. Although the general level of prices cannot be measured in absolute terms, a relative measure of general price changes can be obtained by computing an index of the prices of a collection of goods and services during one period compared with the prices of these same goods and services during a selected base period. The price index of the base year is set equal to 100, and the prices of all other periods are stated as a percentage of this

---

[1] However, the Financial Accounting Standards Board is currently considering the issue. See "Proposed Statement of Financial Accounting Standards: Financial Reporting in Units of General Purchasing Power," December 31, 1974.

amount. For example, if the prices of all goods and services totaled $100,000 for the base period and $200,000 for a subsequent period, the price-level index would be 100 for the base period and 200 for the latter period. The ratio of the current index of prices to the index in the base period shows the percentage change in the prices of all goods and services which were included in the index. The change in the value of the dollar or the change in purchasing power is the reciprocal of the ratio of the price level index of two different periods. In the above example, the general price-level index increased from 100 in the base year to 200 in a later year. During this period prices have doubled while the purchasing power of the dollar has declined by one half.

Price-level index numbers may be used to convert dollars of one period into an equivalent number of dollars of purchasing power in another period. The conversion ratio is determined as follows:

$$\text{Conversion Ratio} = \frac{\text{Index of Current Year}}{\substack{\text{Index for the Year from Which You Are Adjust-}\\ \text{ing Purchasing Power.}}}$$

To illustrate the use of a price-level index, assume that Staubach obtained $100 in cash several years ago when the price-level index was 100, and held this cash during a period when the price-level index increased to 200. Therefore, in terms of the current purchasing power, Staubach would now need $200 to have the equivalent purchasing power he possessed when the cash was originally received. This amount of dollars of equivalent purchasing power was computed as follows:

$$\$100 \times \frac{200}{100} = \$200$$

Theoretically, the measurement of changes in the general price-level should be based upon the prices of all goods and services in the economy. As a practical matter, however, price indexes are usually based upon a sampling of selected commodities. Therefore, price-level indexes provide only an estimation of the extent of inflation or deflation during a given period. In the United States there are several published indexes that provide estimates of the change in the general level of prices. These index values differ because each index is computed on the basis of prices of a different group of goods and services. Although there is not complete agreement as to the index that should be used for accounting purposes, the Accounting Principles Board in its *Statement No. 3* recommended the use of the GNP implicit price deflator for restating financial data for general price-level changes. This index was selected because it attempts to measure the average price changes in all goods and services produced in the United States during a given year.

The extent of price changes in the United States as measured by the GNP implicit price deflator, prepared by the Office of Business Economics of the

United States Department of Commerce, is shown in the following table. In this index, the value for 1958, the base year, is equal to 100.

Year	GNP Implicit Price Deflator
1945	59.7
1950	80.2
1955	90.9
1958 (base year)	100.0
1960	103.3
1965	110.9
1970	134.9
1973	153.9

This shows that the general level of prices increased more than 20 percent from 1965 to 1970, and that the price level more than doubled in the period from 1945 to 1970. Similarly, it indicates that the purchasing power of the dollar is less than half as great in 1970 as it was in 1945.

EFFECTS OF GENERAL PRICE-LEVEL CHANGES

In determining the effects of general price-level changes, it is necessary to classify assets and liabilities as either monetary or nonmonetary items. Monetary items are assets and liabilities that are fixed in terms of dollars either by law or by contract and thereby do not change in terms of dollars when a change in the general price-level occurs. Monetary assets, which are in essence claims to a fixed quantity of dollars, include such items as cash, accounts receivable, and long-term investments in bonds. Monetary liabilities, which are obligations to pay a fixed amount of dollars, include debts such as accounts payable and notes payable. All other assets and liabilities which are not fixed in amount either by contract or law are referred to as nonmonetary items. The most common nonmonetary items include assets such as inventories, land, buildings, and equipment. Let us consider the effects of price-level changes on monetary items first.

Monetary Items

The number of dollars to be received (monetary asset) or paid out or expended (monetary liability) in the future remains fixed for a monetary item regardless of changes in the price level. Thus, if the amount of the monetary claims and obligations remains constant, a change in the purchasing power of the dollar results in general price-level gains or losses. For example, assume that Morton Company held $100,000 in cash (monetary asset) during a period when the price level increased from 100 to 150 (an increase of 50 percent in the price level). At the end of the period, Morton Company would need $150,000 (150/100 × $100,000) to maintain the same purchasing power at the end of the period that it held at the beginning of the period. That is, $150,000 would purchase the same amount of goods and services, in general, at the end of the period as could have been purchased for $100,000 at the beginning of the period. However, the cash available at the end of the period is the $100,000, and the result is a purchasing power loss of $50,000.

Holding a monetary liability during a period of changing prices has exactly the opposite effect. Suppose that Hill Company had borrowed $10,000 at the beginning of a year on a note which was due at year-end. If the price level increased by 50 percent during the year (i.e., the index increased from 100 to 150), the company would require $15,000 at the end of the year to repay the equivalent purchasing power of the $10,000 cash originally borrowed. However, since the $10,000 debt is fixed in amount, this amount is all that is required to satisfy the obligation and therefore Hill Company will have realized a purchasing power gain of $5,000 during the year. In other words, if you incur a liability during a period of increase in the price level you have a "gain" since you are repaying your debt in dollars that are "worth" less (i.e., have less purchasing power).

Based on the previous illustrations, it is apparent that during a period of increasing prices, a general price-level loss results from holding monetary assets and a general price-level gain results from holding monetary liabilities. Both are caused by the loss in the purchasing power of the dollar. On the other hand, during a period of decreasing prices, a general price-level gain results from holding monetary assets and a general price-level loss results from maintaining monetary liabilities, because of the increase in the purchasing power of the dollar.

Nonmonetary Items

Nonmonetary assets include those items the dollar price of which may fluctuate over time with changes in the general level of prices. Since the price of a nonmonetary asset may fluctuate with changes in the purchasing power of the dollar, there will be no gains or losses from changes in the general price level.

To illustrate the effect of a change in the general level of prices on a nonmonetary asset, assume that Garrison Company purchased land at the beginning of a year for $100,000. Garrison Company held the land during the year, and the price-level index increased from 100 at the beginning of the year to 110 at year-end. Land, a nonmonetary asset, can be restated for the change in price level since its acquisition. This restatement converts the cost of the land from original dollars to dollars of equivalent purchasing power at the end of the year. In this illustration the $100,000 acquisition cost of the land is equivalent to $110,000 ($100,000 × 110/100) in current dollars.

It should be noted that restatement of the original cost of a nonmonetary asset in terms of current dollars does not indicate either the current value or cost of that asset. Due to specific factors of supply and demand for a particular asset, the actual current value of the asset may be more or less than its original cost restated for price-level changes. Changing the unit of measurement does not really change the "amount" of the item. The restated amount simply indicates the amount of current dollars that are equivalent to original cost in terms of a stable monetary unit or purchasing power. This restatement of nonmonetary assets does not result in a price-level gain or loss, but adjusts the original costs of these items, regardless of the time of purchase, to equivalent dollars of current purchasing power.

PRICE-LEVEL ADJUSTED FINANCIAL STATEMENTS

Restating financial statements for changes in the general level of prices requires converting the "dollars" in unadjusted historical cost statements to current dollars of equivalent purchasing power. As previously indicated, this restatement requires that a distinction be made between monetary and nonmonetary items.

In a price-level adjusted balance sheet, each nonmonetary item should be converted into dollars of current purchasing power at the end of the current period. In restating these items, it is necessary to recognize the price-level change which has taken place since the time that *each* item was acquired. Since this conversion simply adjusts the original costs of these items to their current purchasing power equivalent, the restatement does not result in either a price-level gain or loss. Because monetary assets and liabilities are fixed in terms of dollars which will be received or paid, they are already stated in terms of their current purchasing power. Therefore, these items do not require any restatement in the balance sheet. Since these monetary claims and obligations remain constant while the purchasing power of the dollar fluctuates, a separate gain or loss on monetary items should be reported in the price-level adjusted income statement.

Many of the amounts which are reported in conventional income statements are not stated in terms of dollars of current purchasing power. For example, the annual depreciation charge is an allocation to expense of the original cost of fixed assets which were acquired at different times. Therefore, each income statement item should be converted to dollars of equivalent purchasing power at the end of the period. The converted revenues less the converted expenses is equal to the income before adjustment for general price-level gain or loss. This income amount plus or minus any gain or loss on monetary items equals the price-level adjusted net income for the period.

Illustration of Price-Level Adjusted Financial Statements

The following illustration indicates the basic procedures which are required for the restatement of financial statements in terms of dollars of uniform purchasing power. This illustration is based on the operations of

Typo Co., a company engaged in typing and copying services, for 1977. Typo Co. began its operation on January 1, 1973. The illustration assumes the following hypothetical general price-level index at the end of each year from 1972 through 1977 (1976 is the base year).

End of Year	Price Level
1972	60
1973	65
1974	70
1975	80
1976	100
1977	120

A conventional income statement reporting the results of operations for 1977 and conventional balance sheets indicating the financial position at the end of 1976 and 1977 are presented in Illustration 18–1.

Illustration 18–1

TYPO CO.
Income Statement
For the Year Ended December 31, 1977

Service revenues		$110,000
Operating expenses:		
Salaries and wages	$ 55,000	
Supplies expense	22,000	
Depreciation of equipment	10,000	
Depreciation of building	10,000	
Total Operating Expenses		97,000
Net Income		$ 13,000

TYPO CO.
Balance Sheets
December 31, 1976 and 1977

	December 31	
ASSETS	*1976*	*1977*
Cash	$ 5,000	$ 25,000
Accounts receivable	25,000	75,000
Equipment	120,000	120,000
Less: Accumulated depreciation	(10,000)	(20,000)
Building	250,000	250,000
Less: Accumulated depreciation	(40,000)	(50,000)
Total Assets	$350,000	$400,000
LIABILITIES		
Accounts payable	$ 13,000	$ 50,000
STOCKHOLDERS' EQUITY		
Capital stock	$275,000	$275,000
Retained earnings	62,000	75,000
Total Stockholders' Equity	$337,000	$350,000
Total Liabilities and Stockholders' Equity	$350,000	$400,000

The following additional information is assumed in the illustration:

1. The price level increased uniformly during each year. Therefore, the average index for a year is the average of the index values at the end of the current year and the end of the previous year. For example, the average index for 1977 is 110 or $\left(\dfrac{120 + 100}{2}\right)$.

2. It is assumed that the service revenues were earned uniformly or evenly throughout the year and that the wage and supplies expense were incurred evenly during the year.

3. The building was purchased on January 1, 1973, for $250,000. It has an estimated useful life of 25 years, and depreciation was recognized at $10,000 per year. Therefore, the accumulated depreciation balance is $50,000 and the book value of the building is $200,000 at the end of 1977.

4. The existing equipment was purchased on December 31, 1975, for $120,000. It has an estimated useful life of 12 years, and depreciation is recognized at $10,000 per year. Since the equipment is two years old, accumulated depreciation at the end of 1977 is $20,000 and the book value is $100,000.

5. The capital stock was issued at the date the firm was organized.

PREPARATION OF THE RESTATED INCOME STATEMENT

An income statement for the year ended December 31, 1977, restated for changes in the general level of prices, is shown in Illustration 18–2. Each item included in the conventional income statement was converted to dollars of equivalent purchasing power at the end of 1977.

Illustration 18–2

TYPO CO.
Income Statement Adjusted for Price-Level Changes
For the Year Ended December 31, 1977

	Conventional Income Statement	Conversion Ratio	Price-Level Adjusted Statement
Service revenues.	$110,000	120/110	$120,000
Operating expenses:			
Salaries and wages	55,000	120/110	60,000
Supplies expense	22,000	120/110	24,000
Depreciation–equipment	10,000	120/80	15,000
Depreciation–building	10,000	120/60	20,000
Total Expenses	$ 97,000		$119,000
Income before price-level loss	$ 13,000		$ 1,000
General price-level loss (see Illustration 18–3).			(6,400)
Net Loss After Price-level Loss			($ 5,400)

Normally firms earn revenues and incur expenses at various times during the year. Theoretically each amount of revenue earned and expense incurred during the year should be separately converted to end-of-year dollars. However, for practical purposes, it is usually assumed that revenues are earned and expenses incurred uniformly throughout the year. Therefore, the average price level for the period may be used in making the conversion.

Revenues

Since services are assumed to be performed evenly throughout the year, the service revenue balance is restated in terms of dollars of the average purchasing power for the year. In order to restate the service revenues in dollars of equivalent purchasing power at the end of the year, the balance is multiplied by the ratio of the end of 1977 index to the average index for the year $\dfrac{120 + 100}{2}$.

$$\$110,000 \times \frac{120}{110} = \$120,000$$

Expenses Which Affect Monetary Items

Wage expense and supplies expense were also assumed to have been incurred evenly throughout the year. Thus, these expenses are restated in terms of end-of-year dollars by multiplying them by the ratio of the end of 1977 index to the average index for the year.

$$\text{Wage Expense} \quad 55,000 \times \frac{120}{110} = \$60,000$$

$$\text{Supplies Expense} \quad 22,000 \times \frac{120}{110} = \$24,000$$

Allocated Expenses

Depreciation expense on the conventional income statement represents an allocation of the cost of a building acquired five years ago and the allocation of the cost of equipment acquired two years ago. Therefore, conventional depreciation is stated in terms of the purchasing power at the time of the acquisition of the assets. The restated amount can be calculated by adjusting the depreciation on a historical cost basis to 1977 dollars. To restate depreciation expense on equipment, the conventional amount is multiplied by the ratio of the index at the end of 1977 to the index at the time the equipment was acquired in 1975 (80). Similarly, the restated depreciation expense on the building is computed by multiplying the unadjusted depreciation expense by the ratio of the index at the end of 1977 to the index at the date of acquisition, January 1, 1973 (60). These calculations are as follows:

$$\text{Depreciation} - \text{Equipment} \quad \$10,000 \times \frac{120}{80} = \$15,000$$

$$\text{Depreciation} - \text{Building} \quad \$10,000 \times \frac{120}{60} = \$20,000$$

Monetary Gains and Losses

Restatement of revenue and expense items in the conventional income statement provides the income for the period before any adjustment for price-level gain or loss on monetary items. The net price-level loss of $6,400 included in Illustration 18–2 resulted because the loss in purchasing power from holding monetary assets exceeded the gain in purchasing power from holding monetary liabilities during a period of increasing prices. The price-level loss is computed by comparing the net monetary assets available to the firm during the year expressed in terms of end-of-year dollars with the actual net monetary items held at the end of the year. The restated net monetary items available to the firm during the year equal the monetary assets and liabilities at the beginning of the period (restated

Illustration 18–3
TYPO CO.
Computation of Price-Level Loss

	Balance on Conventional Statement	Conversion Factor	Restated Amount
Beginning net monetary assets 12/31/76:			
Cash	$ 5,000	120/100	$ 6,000
Accounts receivable	$ 25,000	120/100	30,000
Accounts payable	$ (13,000)	120/100	(15,600)
	$ 17,000	120/100	$ 20,400
Add: Increase in monetary items during the year:			
From sales	$110,000	120/110	$120,000
Less: Decrease in monetary items during the year:			
Salaries and wages	$ (55,000)	120/110	$ (60,000)
Supplies expense	(22,000)	120/110	(24,000)
Net monetary items available during the year in end-of-year purchasing power			$ 56,400
Ending net monetary assets 12/31/77:			
Cash	$ 25,000		
Accounts receivable	75,000		
Accounts payable	(50,000)		$ 50,000
General Price-Level Loss			$ (6,400)

to end-of-year dollars) plus increases in monetary items from revenues and decreases in monetary items from expenses during the year (again restated to end-of-year dollars). The depreciation expense is omitted from this computation because it represents an allocation of a cost incurred in a previous period and does not affect monetary items during the current year. Details of the computation of the $6,400 price-level loss are presented in Illustration 18–3.

PREPARATION OF THE RESTATED BALANCE SHEET

A balance sheet at December 31, 1977, restated for the general price-level change is presented in Illustration 18–4. Since monetary assets and

Illustration 18–4

TYPO CO.
Balance Sheet Adjusted for Price-Level Changes
December 31, 1977

ASSETS	Conventional Balance Sheet	Conversion Ratio	Price-Level Adjusted Statement
Cash	$ 25,000	NA	$ 25,000
Accounts receivable	75,000	NA	75,000
Equipment	120,000	120/80	180,000
Less: Accumulated depreciation	(20,000)	120/80	(30,000)
Building	250,000	120/60	500,000
Less: Accumulated depreciation	(50,000)	120/60	(100,000)
Total Assets	$400,000		$650,000
LIABILITIES			
Accounts payable	$ 50,000	NA	$ 50,000
STOCKHOLDERS' EQUITY			
Capital stock	$275,000	120/60	$550,000
Retained earnings	75,000		50,000
Total Stockholders' Equity	$350,000		$600,000
Total Liabilities and Stockholders' Equity	$400,000		$650,000

liabilities are fixed in amount, the balances for cash, accounts receivable, and accounts payable are the same in the price-level adjusted balance sheet as in the unadjusted balance sheet. The nonmonetary assets, equipment and buildings, are restated to end-of-year dollars by multiplying the conventional balances by the ratio of the current-year price index to the index at the time the assets were acquired. Similarly, capital stock is expressed in terms of original dollar investment at the date of organization of the firm. This amount is restated in terms of current dollars by multiplying the conventional balance by the ratio of the 1977 price index to the index at the date the stock was issued.

$$\text{Equipment} - \$100,000 \times \frac{120}{80} = \$150,000$$

$$\text{Building} - \$200,000 \times \frac{120}{60} = \$400,000$$

$$\text{Capital Stock} - \$275,000 \times \frac{120}{60} = \$550,000$$

The retained earnings balance of $50,000 in the price-level-adjusted balance sheet is equal to the restated assets less the restated liabilities and capital stock. This amount can also be determined by deducting the net loss from the price-level adjusted income statement from the price-level adjusted beginning retained earnings in terms of end-of-year dollars. The beginning retained earnings in end-of-year dollars can be computed by converting the December 31, 1976, balance sheet amounts to end-of-1977 dollars.

	December 31, 1976 Conventional Balance	Conversion Ratio	1977 Dollars
Cash	$ 5,000	120/100	$ 6,000
Accounts receivable	25,000	120/100	30,000
Equipment	120,000	120/80	180,000
Less: Accumulated depreciation	(10,000)	120/80	(15,000)
Buildings	250,000	120/60	500,000
Less: Accumulated depreciation	(40,000)	120/60	(80,000)
Accounts payable	(13,000)	120/100	(15,600)
Capital stock	(275,000)	120/60	(550,000)
Retained earnings at 12/31/76–the balancing amount	$ 62,000		$ 55,400

Note: Credit balances are indicated by parentheses.

Thus, the beginning and ending balances of retained earnings in the price-level adjusted balance sheet may be reconciled as follows:

Retained Earnings, January 1 (End-of-year Dollars)	$55,400
Net Loss After Price-Level Loss (Illustration 18–2)	(5,400)
Retained Earnings, December 31 (Illustration 18–4)	$50,000

CURRENT STATUS OF GENERAL PRICE-LEVEL ADJUSTED STATEMENTS

A basic argument for the presentation of price-level adjusted financial statements as a supplement to conventional financial statements is that the effects of changes in the purchasing power of the dollar are eliminated in the adjusted statements. Specifically, in the supplementary income statement, all revenues and expenses are stated in terms of dollars of common size or purchasing power. Similarly, all items in the supplementary balance sheet are expressed in terms of uniform or "common size" dollars. In addition, adjusted statements reveal gains or losses from holding monetary assets or owing monetary liabilities. Obviously, the greater the change in the purchasing power of the dollar over time, the greater is the potential benefit of the supplementary price-level adjusted statements.

Currently, however, there is not complete agreement as to the need for and the usefulness of price-level adjusted statements even as supplements to conventional financial statements. A major point of opposition is that the presentation of two different sets of financial statements for one period could result in considerable confusion to the users of financial statements. A second argument against the presentation of restated data is that since the general level of prices has increased only moderately during the past decade in the United States, the adjusted statements would not differ significantly from conventional statements. Recently, however, this argument has been less and less true. In any case, it should be remembered that the cumulative effect of inflation or deflation since the acquisition of assets by a firm affects the adjustment of fixed assets in the balance sheet and the related depreciation expense in the income statement. Thus, moderate inflation over a period of several years could result in significant differences between historical and adjusted financial statements.

The issue of price-level adjusted financial statements is currently unresolved. The Accounting Principles Board, in its *Statement No. 3* issued in 1969, concluded that supplementary statements ". . . present useful information not available from basic historical statements." However, the Board also stated that price-level information is not required for fair presentation of financial data in conformity with generally accepted accounting principles at this time. To date, very few firms have made an attempt to include price-level adjusted data in their annual reports.

KEY DEFINITIONS

Conversion ratio The ratio of the price index in the current year to the price index for the year from which purchasing power is adjusted. It is used to convert dollars from one period into an equivalent number of dollars in terms of purchasing power at another time.

Deflation Deflation is a general decrease in the average prices of goods and services over time; consequently, there is a corresponding increase in the purchasing power of the dollar.

General price level This is the average price of a collection of goods and services in the economy during one period compared with the prices of the same goods and services during a selected base period.

General price-level gain or loss   Gain or loss in general purchasing power from holding monetary assets and liabilities during a period of inflation or deflation.

General purchasing power of the dollar   This concept involves the ability of the dollar to buy goods and services in general.

GNP implicit price deflator   The GNP implicit price deflator is a measure of the general price level in the United States. It is recommended by APB *Statement No. 3* for use in preparing general price-level adjusted statements because it is usually regarded as the most comprehensive index compiled in the United States.

Inflation   Inflation is a general increase in the average prices of goods and services over time; consequently, there is a corresponding decrease in the purchasing power of the dollar.

Monetary assets   Monetary assets are cash or claims to a fixed number of dollars in the future.

Monetary items   Cash and other balance sheet accounts which represent a fixed number of dollars to be received or paid in the future are monetary items.

Monetary liabilities   Monetary liabilities are obligations of a fixed amount of dollars to be paid in the future; these include accounts payable, notes payable, and long-term debt.

Nonmonetary items   Nonmonetary items are those items which do not represent a fixed number of dollars to be received or paid in the future. These include inventories, plant and equipment, and stockholders' equity.

Price index   A price index is a relative measure of the general price-level over time. It is obtained by computing the ratio of the prices of a collection of goods and services during one period with the prices of the same goods during a selected base period.

Price-level adjusted financial statements   These are financial statements adjusted for changes in the general level of prices.

Purchasing power gain or loss   This is the same as general price-level gain or loss.

Restatement of nonmonetary items   The amounts of nonmonetary items are restated to dollars of current general purchasing power at the end of the period for which general price-level adjusted statements are prepared.

Stable unit of measure   The use of money as the unit of measure implies that the value of the dollar is constant over time and hence is a stable unit of measure.

QUESTIONS

1.   What is a price index? How is it derived?
2.   What is meant by general price-level adjusted financial statements? What are some of the arguments for price-level adjusted statements? Against them?
3.   Distinguish between monetary assets and nonmonetary assets.
4.   What general price index is recommended by the APB for price-level accounting purposes and why was it chosen?

5. What are the effects of holding monetary assets and liabilities in periods of inflation and deflation?

6. What is the stable-dollar assumption in the traditional accounting process? Why may comparisons of dollar amounts in conventional financial statements be misleading?

7. What is a conversion ratio? What is its use?

8. What are the effects of holding nonmonetary assets in periods of inflation or deflation?

9. Does the restatement of the original cost of a nonmonetary asset in terms of current dollars indicate the current value or cost of that asset?

10. To what extent must monetary assets be adjusted on a restated balance sheet?

11. What is the theoretically correct treatment for the conversion of expenses and revenues in price-level adjusted income statements? What is the practical treatment?

EXERCISES

18–1 In 1945 Shackleford Company received $400 which was placed in a safe and forgotten. Thirty years later, the cash was found by a company secretary and reported to the controller. Out of curiosity, the controller wishes to determine the cash needed at present in order to have the equivalent purchasing power the company possessed when the cash was originally received. Determine the amount, given each of the following sets of price indexes.

   a. 1945 = 50;   1975 = 125.
   b. 1945 = 75;   1975 = 125.
   c. 1945 = 120;   1975 = 80.

18–2 Determine the price level for 1971 through 1976 using 1973 as the base year, given the following information.

Year	Prices of a Market Basket of All Goods and Services
1971	$2,300
1972	2,400
1973	2,500
1974	2,750
1975	3,000
1976	3,125

18–3 The Walton Company purchased a machine at the beginning of 1974 when the price-level index was 150. The machine, which cost $20,000 and had no salvage value, was depreciated using the straight-line method over a period of 20 years. The company purchased a building on January 1, 1975, at a cost of $100,000 when the index was 200. The building had an expected life of 40 years and no salvage value, and was depreciated using the straight-line method. The depreciation expense for 1976 is $1,000 for the machine and $2,500 for the building. The price-level index at the end of 1976 is 250. What is the depreciation expense for 1976 restated for changes in the price level?

18–4   Data for 1976 and the two preceding years are given below.

	Sales	Price Index
1976	$500,000	200
1975	400,000	140
1974	300,000	100

Restate the sales for each year in terms of current-year dollars. What is revealed by a comparison of the restated amounts?

18–5   Brown Corp. purchased land in 1967 for $100,000. Adjust the asset to end-of-year prices for each year from 1968 to 1976. Assume the following price-level index.

Year	Index
1967	100
1968	110
1969	115
1970	125
1971	140
1972	150
1973	160
1974	180
1975	190
1976	200

18–6   The Patsy Company purchased equipment on January 1, 1973, for $20,000 when the price index was 80. The equipment has a 10-year life, no salvage value, and straight-line depreciation is used. The price index increased to 100 on December 31, 1973, 120 on December 31, 1974, and 180 on December 31, 1975. What was the adjusted depreciation expense for 1973, 1974, and 1975? Convert the historical machine account and accumulated depreciation balances at December 31, 1975, to 1975 dollars.

18–7   The Pun Co. purchased a machine on December 31, 1972, for $55,000 when the price-level index was 100. The machine had a salvage value of $5,000 and an estimated life of 20 years, and is to be depreciated using the straight-line method. Assume that the price-level index at the end of each of the subsequent five years was as follows:

Year	Index
1973	110
1974	120
1975	140
1976	130
1977	150

From the above information determine the values at which the depreciation expense and the building (net of depreciation) will be included in the price-level adjusted financial statements each year from 1973 to 1977.

PROBLEMS

Series A

18A–1   The price index increased from 100 to 120 during 1974 and from 120 to 140 during 1975. Shown below is a condensed income statement of Hanna Company for 1975.

HANNA COMPANY
Income Statement
For the Year Ended December 31, 1975

Revenues.		$100,000
Expenses:		
Wages	$40,000	
Supplies expense	15,000	
Miscellaneous expense	5,000	
Depreciation expense.	25,000	85,000
Net Income		$ 15,000

The depreciation expense was recorded on equipment purchased at the beginning of 1974. All other expenses were incurred evenly during the current year and revenues were earned evenly throughout the year. Adjust the company's income statement for price-level changes (assume that the general price-level loss from holding net monetary items was determined to be $2,400).

18A–2   State whether there has been a purchasing power gain, loss, or no change in each of the following situations (also state the amount of the gain or loss).

a.   Sum of $50,000 cash held over a period when the price level decreased from 125 to 75.

b.   Land purchased for $25,000 held over a period when the price level increased from 95 to 105.

c.   Account payable for $950 incurred when the price level was 120 and paid when the price level was 150.

d.   Bonds worth $200,000 issued when the price level was 100 and redeemed when the price level was 85.

e.   Purchase of $10,000 of inventory when the price level was 87, held until the price level was 103.

f.   Sale of $4,500 of goods on account when the price level was 95, and account receivable was collected when the price level was 110.

18A–3   The conventional financial statements for the FEE Corporation on December 31, 1975, are presented below.

FEE CORPORATION
Income Statement
For the Year Ended December 31, 1975

Service revenue		$220,000
Wage expense	$85,000	
General and administrative expense.	82,000	
Depreciation expense–building	15,000	
Depreciation expense–equipment	15,000	197,000
Net Income		$ 23,000

FEE CORPORATION
Balance Sheet
December 31, 1975

ASSETS

Cash	$ 40,000
Accounts receivable.	30,000
Prepaid expenses	15,000
Building (net of accumulated depreciation)	150,000
Equipment (net of accumulated depreciation).	54,000
Total Assets	$289,000

LIABILITIES AND SHAREHOLDERS' EQUITY

Accounts payable.	$ 50,000
Capital stock.	200,000
Retained earnings.	39,000
Total Liabilities and Shareholders' Equity.	$289,000

The equipment was purchased on December 31, 1972, and the building on December 31, 1970. All of the stock was issued on December 31, 1970. Assume that all revenues and expenses are earned and incurred evenly throughout the year and that the price-level changed at a constant rate each year. Prepare a price-level adjusted income statement and balance sheet for December 31, 1975 assuming the following price-level indexes at the end of each year:

Year	Index
1970	80
1971	95
1972	90
1973	95
1974	120
1975	100

Assume that the general purchasing power gain for the year was determined to be $20,000.

18A–4   Assume the following price-level indexes at the end of each year from 1971 through 1975:

Year	Index
1971	60
1972	80
1973	90
1974	100
1975	120

A conventional income statement for 1975 and a conventional balance sheet for 1974 and 1975 for the Comp Company are presented below.

COMP COMPANY
Income Statement
For the Year Ended December 31, 1975

Sales revenues		$280,000
Operating expenses:		
Wage expense	$140,000	
Miscellaneous expense	70,000	
Depreciation of equipment	25,000	
Depreciation of building	25,000	260,000
Net Income		$ 20,000

COMP COMPANY
Balance Sheet
December 31, 1974 and 1975

	December 31	
	1974	*1975*
ASSETS		
Cash	$ 10,000	$ 50,000
Accounts receivable	20,000	30,000
Equipment (net of accumulated depreciation)	125,000	100,000
Building (net of accumulated depreciation)	225,000	200,000
Total Assets	$380,000	$380,000
LIABILITIES		
Accounts payable	$ 20,000	–0–
STOCKHOLDERS' EQUITY		
Capital stock	$300,000	$300,000
Retained earnings	60,000	80,000
Total Stockholders' Equity	360,000	380,000
Total Liabilities and Stockholders' Equity	$380,000	$380,000

Assume that all revenues and expenses were earned and incurred evenly throughout each year and that the price level increased evenly in each year. The building was purchased on December 31, 1972, and the equipment on December 31, 1973. All stock was issued when the company was formed, at which time the index was 40. Prepare the 1975 income statement and balance sheet adjusted for price-level changes.

Series B

18B-1   The following information was derived from the December 31, 1975, balance sheet of Easy Company.

Cash	$ 20,000
Accounts receivable.	40,000
Equipment.	100,000
Building	150,000
Accounts payable	50,000
Capital stock.	200,000

The price-level index was 100 on December 31, 1975, and 120 on December 31, 1976. All capital stock was issued on December 31, 1974 when the index was 80. The equipment was purchased on December 31, 1975, and the building on December 31, 1974. The net loss on the price-level adjusted income statement for 1976 was $10,000. What is the price-level adjusted retained earnings at December 31, 1976?

18B-2   Assume that the price-level index is 100 at the end of 1975 and 200 at the end of 1976. The following balances existed at the beginning of 1976:

Cash	$200,000
Accounts receivable.	150,000
Accounts payable	100,000

During 1976 revenues of $180,000 were earned and expenses of $150,000 were incurred. The ending balances are:

Cash	$250,000
Accounts receivable.	175,000
Accounts payable	145,000

Compute the price-level gain or loss assuming revenues were earned and expenses incurred evenly throughout the period.

18B-3   The conventional balance sheet for Tab Co. for December 31, 1975, is presented below.

TAB COMPANY
Balance Sheet
December 31, 1975

ASSETS

Cash	$ 15,000
Accounts receivable.	30,000
Prepaid insurance	7,500
Building (net of accumulated depreciation)	150,000
Equipment (net of accumulated depreciation)	100,000
Total Assets	$302,500

LIABILITIES AND STOCKHOLDERS' EQUITY

Accounts payable	$ 30,000
Note payable	60,000
Capital stock.	140,000
Retained earnings	72,500
Total Liabilities and Stockholders' Equity.	$302,500

Assume that all capital stock was issued on December 31, 1971, that the building was purchased on December 31, 1972, and that the equipment was purchased on December 31, 1973. The following price-level index as of the end of each year is assumed.

Year	Price Level
1973	70
1974	80
1975	90
1976	100
1977	120
1978	140

Prepare a balance sheet adjusted for price-level changes.

18B–4   Shown below are the income statement for 1978 and comparative balance sheets for the years ended December 31, 1977 and 1978 for the Aaron Company.

AARON COMPANY
Income Statement
For the Year Ended December 31, 1978

Service revenues.		$156,000
Operating expenses:		
Salaries and wages	$ 65,000	
Supplies expense	39,000	
Depreciation of equipment	10,000	
Depreciation of building	12,000	
Total operating expenses		126,000
Net Income		$ 30,000

AARON COMPANY
Balance Sheets
December 31, 1977 and 1978

	1977	1978
Cash	$ 6,000	$ 30,000
Accounts receivable.	24,000	70,000
Equipment.	100,000	100,000
Less: Accumulated depreciation.	(10,000)	(20,000)
Building	240,000	240,000
Less: Accumulated depreciation.	(48,000)	(60,000)
Total Assets	$312,000	$360,000
Accounts payable	$ 12,000	$ 30,000
Capital stock.	$240,000	$240,000
Retained earnings	60,000	90,000
Total Stockholders' Equity	$300,000	$330,000
Total Equities	$312,000	$360,000

Aaron Company is engaged in typing and copying services. Aaron began its operation at the beginning of 1974. The problem assumes the following general price-level index at the end of each year from 1973 through 1978 (1976 is the base year).

Year	Index
1971	70
1972	75
1973	80
1974	95
1975	100

The following additional information is available:

1. The price level increased uniformly during each year.
2. It is assumed that the service revenues were earned evenly throughout the year and that the wage and supplies expense were incurred evenly during the year.
3. The building was purchased on January 1, 1974, for $240,000. It has an estimated useful life of 20 years and no salvage value.
4. The existing equipment was purchased on December 31, 1976, for $100,000. It has an estimated useful life of ten years and no salvage value.
5. The capital stock was issued at the date the firm was organized, December 1973.

Required:

Prepare a price-level adjusted balance sheet and income statement for 1978.

19

Income Tax
Considerations

INCOME taxes are periodic charges levied by federal, state, and city governments on the taxable income of both individuals and business corporations. Taxable income is a statutory concept, i.e., it is defined by law and is equal to gross income minus all allowable deductions. For businesses organized as corporations, income taxes are accounted for as an expense which is deducted in computing the net income for the period. The amount of taxes owed, but not paid, is a liability which is included in the balance sheet. Because income taxes normally represent a significant cost to a business enterprise, an awareness of the tax laws and how they are applied is essential to a complete understanding of accounting information.

Data which is required for the determination of income taxes is usually found in the accounting records. Taxable income, however, may not be the same as the income reported in the income statement even though both are determined from the identical set of accounting records. This difference often occurs because income tax regulations are not always the same as the basic concepts which are used for financial accounting purposes.

This chapter is devoted to a general discussion of the federal income tax and its implication for the financial reporting process of a business. Although many states and cities also impose income taxes, which may differ in application from the federal income tax, the tax liability to all governmental units is treated similarly in the accounting records. For this reason, the following discussion is limited to the federal income tax.

THE FEDERAL INCOME TAX

The present federal income tax originated in 1913 with the adoption of the Sixteenth Amendment to the Constitution. This amendment gave Congress the power to ". . . lay and collect all taxes on incomes from whatever sources derived, without apportionment among the several states, and without regard to any census or enumeration." Soon after the 16th amendment was adopted, Congress enacted the Revenue Act of 1913, which taxed all income. Since that time, Congress has passed numerous income tax statutes amending the various Revenue Acts so that there has been a continuous development of income tax law in the United States. In 1939 the Internal Revenue Code was enacted. This code was revised in 1954 and extensively amended and supplemented by both the Tax Reform Act of 1969 and the Revenue Act of 1971. Tax law is also supplemented by interpretations of the Internal Revenue Code by both the courts and the Treasury Department. The Treasury Department, operating through a branch known as the Internal Revenue Service, is charged with the enforcement and collection of income taxes.

The original purpose of the income tax was stated as simply to obtain revenues for the use of the federal government. The income tax on individuals under the 1913 Act consisted of a flat one percent tax on taxable income in excess of $4,000 for married persons plus a progressive surtax of one to seven percent on income in excess of $20,000. A progressive tax is one in which tax rates increase as taxable income increases.

Since 1916, however, both the objectives of the income tax and income tax rates have undergone a significant change. The purpose of the federal income tax today includes such diverse objectives as controlling inflation, influencing economic growth, decreasing unemployment, redistributing national income, and encouraging the growth of small businesses. All these purposes are in addition to the original objective of raising revenue to finance the operations of the government. Similarly, there has been a substantial upward trend in tax rates. Currently, for example, personal income tax rates on taxable income progress from a minimum of 14 percent to 70 percent on taxable income in excess of $100,000 ($200,000 for married individuals filing a joint return).

CLASSES OF TAXPAYERS

Income taxes are levied upon four major types of taxable entities: individuals, corporations, and estates and trusts. Business entities organized as sole proprietorships or partnerships are not taxable entities. Instead, their income is included in the gross income of the individual owner or owners, whether or not it is actually withdrawn from the business and distributed to these owners. A partnership, however, is required to prepare an information return which indicates the net income of the partnership and how this income was allocated to the partners. The individual partners then report these amounts in their own tax returns.

A corporation is treated as a separate entity for tax purposes and must pay taxes on its taxable income. In addition, individual corporate stockholders must include any dividends received from the corporation as a part of their taxable income. For this reason, it is often argued that the profits of a corporation are taxed twice—once to the corporation when the income is reported and again to its stockholders when dividends are distributed. Under limited circumstances, a corporation that meets certain qualifications may avoid this "double taxation" of corporate income by electing to be treated as a partnership for tax purposes; and the shareholders are taxed on undistributed income on a current basis.[1]

An estate is a separate legal entity which is created to take charge of the assets of a deceased person to pay the decedent's debts and distribute any remaining assets to the heirs. A trust is a legal entity which is created when a person by gift or devise transfers assets to a trustee for the benefit of designated persons. The tax rules that apply to estates and trusts are similar but will not be discussed in this chapter, as they are beyond the scope of this text.

INDIVIDUAL FEDERAL INCOME TAX

The cash basis of measuring taxable income is used by almost all individuals in preparing their tax returns. Generally, revenue is recognized upon the actual or constructive receipt of cash; and expenses are recognized as cash is expended.

Individual income tax rates depend on the status of the taxpayer. There are different tax rate schedules for married taxpayers who file a joint return, married individuals who file separate returns, unmarried taxpayers, and single taxpayers qualifying as a "head of a household." Generally, "head of household" status applies to certain unmarried or legally separated persons who maintain a residence for a relative or dependent. The tax rate schedule for married individuals filing a joint return is shown in Illustration 19–1.

The federal income tax for individuals is a progressive tax. A progressive tax is one in which each increment of taxable income is subject to a higher rate than the preceding increments of income. Such a tax is designed to accomplish certain of the objectives of the federal income tax which were mentioned previously. The current schedular individual income

---

[1] These entities are referred to as "Subchapter S Corporations." Among the qualifications for a Subchapter S Corporation are the following: (1) the corporation must have ten or fewer shareholders, and (2) the corporation must have only one class of stock issued or outstanding.

Illustration 19–1
Rate Table for Married Individuals
Filing Joint Returns
(effective for 1971 and following years)

Taxable Income		Tax Liability	
From	To	Amount	On Excess Over
$ 0	$ 1000	14%	
1000	2000	$ 140 plus 15%	— $ 1000
2000	3000	290 plus 16%	— 2000
3000	4000	450 plus 17%	— 3000
4000	8000	620 plus 19%	— 4000
8000	12000	1380 plus 22%	— 8000
12000	16000	2260 plus 25%	— 12000
16000	20000	3260 plus 28%	— 16000
20000	24000	4380 plus 32%	— 20000
24000	28000	5660 plus 36%	— 24000
28000	32000	7100 plus 39%	— 28000
32000	36000	8660 plus 42%	— 32000
36000	40000	10340 plus 45%	— 36000
40000	44000	12140 plus 48%	— 40000
44000	52000	14060 plus 50%	— 44000
52000	64000	18060 plus 53%	— 52000
64000	76000	24420 plus 55%	— 64000
76000	88000	31020 plus 58%	— 76000
88000	100000	37980 plus 60%	— 88000
100000	120000	45180 plus 62%	— 100000
120000	140000	57580 plus 64%	— 120000
140000	160000	70380 plus 66%	— 140000
160000	180000	83580 plus 68%	— 160000
180000	200000	97180 plus 69%	— 180000
200000	—	110980 plus 70%	— 200000

tax rates range from a minimum of 14 percent to a maximum of 70 percent. The tax is limited to a maximum marginal tax rate of 50 percent on earned income. Earned income includes such items as wages, salaries, and professional fees. However, the rate structures vary for different classes of taxpayers and these rates are frequently changed by Congress.

The amount of federal income tax that an individual must pay is computed by applying the appropriate tax rate to an amount defined by the Internal Revenue Code as taxable income. The computation of taxable income begins with "gross income." To arrive at taxable income, all deductions specifically allowed by law are subtracted from gross income. These deductions are divided into two principal categories: (1) deductions from gross income to determine adjusted gross income, and (2) deductions from adjusted gross income in arriving at taxable income. Deductions from gross income are generally business expenses. Deductions from adjusted gross income include certain nonbusiness expenses and personal exemptions.

Illustration 19–2
Process of Determining
Taxable Income For
Individuals

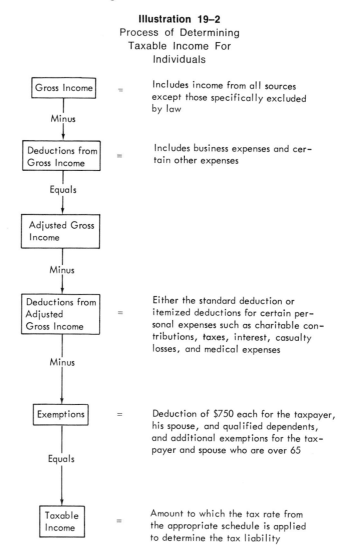

Gross Income = Includes income from all sources except those specifically excluded by law

Minus

Deductions from Gross Income = Includes business expenses and certain other expenses

Equals

Adjusted Gross Income

Minus

Deductions from Adjusted Gross Income = Either the standard deduction or itemized deductions for certain personal expenses such as charitable contributions, taxes, interest, casualty losses, and medical expenses

Minus

Exemptions = Deduction of $750 each for the taxpayer, his spouse, and qualified dependents, and additional exemptions for the taxpayer and spouse who are over 65

Equals

Taxable Income = Amount to which the tax rate from the appropriate schedule is applied to determine the tax liability

The procedures for determining taxable income are summarized in Illustration 19–2. A more detailed explanation of the items outlined in the determination of taxable income is given in the following paragraphs.

Gross Income.   Basically, gross income is defined as all income from whatever source derived, unless expressly excluded by law. This includes income from sources such as wages, dividends, interest, partnership income, rents, and numerous other items. Among the more important classes of income which are currently excludable from gross income by law are gifts, life insurance proceeds, social security benefits, inheritances (but not income from trusts and life estates), workmen's compensation, sick pay, and $100 of dividends from corporations ($200 on a joint return).

Deductions from Gross Income. The deductions from gross income are business expenses and other expenses connected with earning certain types of revenue. These include ordinary and necessary expenses incurred by the taxpayer in the operation of his unincorporated business or profession, certain business expenses of an employee, losses from the sale or exchange of property, expenses incurred in connection with earning rent or royalty income, net losses on the sale of capital assets (limited to $1,000), and one half of the excess of net long-term capital gains over capital losses.

Deductions from Adjusted Gross Income. All other expenses allowable by law are deducted from adjusted gross income in arriving at taxable income. These allowable deductions may be classified as personal expenses, referred to as itemized deductions, and personal exemptions.

Itemized deductions include such items as a limited amount of charitable contributions, interest payments, certain taxes paid by the taxpayer, a limited amount of medical expenses, casualty and theft losses in excess of $100, and certain other nonbusiness expenses. These nonbusiness expenses are the necessary expenses incurred in producing income or for the management of income-producing property. These include such items as legal fees relating to investments, dues to professional organizations, and expenses incurred for the preparation of tax returns. As an alternative to itemizing deductions, a taxpayer may elect to use a standard deduction. The standard deduction is currently 15 percent of adjusted gross income with a maximum of $2,000. There is also a low income allowance which affects taxpayers at low levels of income.

In addition to the itemized or standard deduction, each taxpayer is allowed a separate deduction for personal exemptions. An individual is entitled to a $750 exemption for himself and additional exemptions for each of his qualified dependents. Dependents usually include the taxpayer's wife (in a joint return), minor children, and other closely related relatives for whom the taxpayer provides more than half of the support. Additional exemptions are allowed if the taxpayer and/or his wife are over 65 years of age or blind.

Taxpayers are required to make payments on their estimated tax liability during the year. For employees, this is accomplished by the process whereby the employer withholds taxes from the employee's pay and forwards them directly to the government. Self-employed persons are required to make estimated tax payments in quarterly installments. In either instance, any difference between the amounts paid and the actual tax liability at the end of the year is settled when the tax return is filed.

Capital Gains and Losses. Gains and losses from the sale of certain property defined by the tax law as capital assets are given special treatment for income tax purposes. Capital assets most commonly held by taxpayers include stocks, bonds, personal residences, and land. To qualify for special tax treatment, capital gains or losses must be long-term. Long-term capital gains or losses result from the sale of capital assets held by the taxpayer for more than six months, and short-term gains or losses result from the sale of those held six months or less. Short-term capital gains do not qualify for special tax treatment and are taxed as ordinary income.

The special tax treatment applies to net long-term capital gains (long-term gains in excess of long-term losses) reduced by any net short-term capital losses.[2] Under the law, the tax on net long-term capital gains is the lesser of the amounts determined under two alternative computations. In the first computation, only one half of the amount of net long-term capital gains less any net short-term capital losses must be included in the adjusted gross income. This amount is a part of taxable income and is taxed at the ordinary rates. The alternative tax computation limits the total tax on long-term capital gains to 25 percent on gains of up to $50,000 and 35 percent on gains in excess of this amount. An excess of short-term capital gains over short-term capital losses is taxed as ordinary income.

To illustrate this somewhat complicated procedure, assume that during 1976 a taxpayer had the following capital gains and losses:

Long-term capital gains	$11,000
Long-term capital losses	2,000
Short-term capital gains	5,000
Short-term capital losses	6,000

In this case, the taxpayer has a net long-term capital gain of $9,000 ($11,000 — $2,000) and a net short-term capital loss of $1,000 ($6,000 — $5,000). As a result, one half of the excess of the net long-term gain over the net short-term loss, or $4,000 [($9,000 — $1,000) × ½], would be included in the taxpayer's adjusted income. If the taxpayer's marginal tax rate is 32 percent, the tax on the amount of gain included in taxable income would be computed as follows:

$$\$4,000 \times 32\% = \$1,280$$

In any case, the amount of the tax is limited to 25 percent of the total gain. Thus, if the taxpayer's marginal tax rate was 60 percent, the tax would be limited to $2,000—the smaller of one half the gain taxed as ordinary income ($4,000 × .60 = $2,400) or 25 percent of the total net gain ($8,000 × .25 = $2,000).

Computation of Individual Income Tax—An Illustration. The following example illustrates the computation of the income tax for an in-

---

[2] If total capital losses exceed capital gains, individual taxpayers may generally deduct up to $1,000 of capital losses in a year with any excess carried forward and treated as a capital loss in future years to be applied generally against capital gains.

dividual filing a joint return. The individual, who owns a drug store organized as a sole proprietorship, is married and has two minor children. The sources and amounts of gross income deductions and exemptions are presented below. In practice this information would be reported on standard income tax forms provided by the federal government.

Gross Income and Deductions from Gross Income

Sales			$100,000
Less:			
Cost of goods sold		$50,000	
Business expenses.		30,000	80,000
Net business income			$ 20,000
Interest on savings accounts			1,000
Rents received.		$ 5,000	
Less expenses		2,000	
Net rental income			3,000
Net long-term capital gain		$10,000	
Less: Long-term capital gain deduction		5,000	5,000
Adjusted Gross Income			$ 29,000
Itemized deductions:			
Charitable contributions.	$ 500		
Interest paid.	1,100		
Property taxes.	2,000		
Sales tax	100		
Casualty loss (in excess of $100)	300	$ 4,000	
Personal exemptions (4 × $750)		3,000	7,000
Taxable Income			$ 22,000
Income Tax (using rate table in Illustration 19-1):			
On $20,000	$4,380		
On excess ($2,000 × 32%)	640		
Total Tax			$ 5,020
Less: Tax credits			
Payments on estimated taxes			4,000
Amount Due			$ 1,020

CORPORATE INCOME TAX

A corporation is a taxable entity which is separate and distinct from its stockholders. In general, the taxable income of a corporation is computed by deducting its ordinary business expenses and special deductions from its gross income. Although a corporation is taxed in generally the same manner as individuals, there are several important differences:

1. The concepts of itemized deductions, standard deduction, and personal exemptions are not applicable to corporations.
2. Corporations may ordinarily deduct 85 percent of all dividends received on investments in stocks of other domestic corporations.

3. The deduction for charitable contributions is limited to five percent of taxable income (before charitable contributions and before the 85 percent dividend deduction) in any one year.
4. Corporations must include the entire excess of net long-term capital gains over short-term capital losses in taxable income. However, the tax is limited to a maximum of 30 percent of the gain.
5. An excess of capital losses over capital gains may not be deducted in the year of the loss. The net loss, however, may be used to offset capital gains of the preceding three years or the following five years.

The corporate tax rate also differs from the rate applied to individual taxpayers. A corporation pays a normal tax of 22 percent on all taxable income and a 26 percent surtax on all taxable income in excess of $25,000. For example, if a corporation has taxable income of $100,000, its tax would be computed as follows:

$$\begin{aligned}
\$100,000 \times .22 \dots\dots\dots &= \$22,000 \\
(\$100,000 - 25,000) \times .26 &= \underline{19,500} \\
\text{Income Tax} \dots\dots\dots\dots &\quad \underline{\underline{\$41,500}}
\end{aligned}$$

DIFFERENCES BETWEEN ACCOUNTING INCOME AND TAXABLE INCOME

The taxable income of a corporation often differs from the net income reported in its financial statements. Taxable income is determined by tax law while accounting income is based on generally accepted accounting principles. The rules and regulations comprising the income tax laws reflect the objectives of income taxation as well as administrative rulings which have been made to implement the law. Financial accounting, on the other hand, is concerned with the proper determination and matching of revenues and expenses in order to measure income.

Some differences between taxable income and accounting income occur because of special tax rules that differ from generally accepted accounting principles. Certain items of revenue are excluded by law from taxable income. For example, interest on state and municipal bonds is included in accounting income but not in taxable income. Similarly, certain expenses may not be treated as deductions for tax purposes. For example, goodwill is amortized as an expense for accounting purposes but it is not subject to amortization under current tax regulations. These items represent permanent differences between taxable and accounting income and are referred to as such.

Other differences between taxable income and accounting income are not permanent. These result from timing differences in the recognition of revenues and expenses. Timing differences occur because, in some instances, one method or procedure may be used for tax purposes and a different method or procedure for financial accounting purposes. The underlying reason that different methods are used is because of the differences in the objectives of accounting and taxation. The objective of financial accounting is a fair and accurate measurement of income and financial position, while the objective of a business in selecting tax methods is usually to minimize taxable income and postpone the payment of taxes. Although over a long enough period of time the timing differences should "wash out" so that total taxable income and total accounting income are the same, the difference during any one year may be significant. Two major examples of timing differences are as follows:

1. *Depreciation.* The tax laws allow the use of several depreciation methods. A firm may use an accelerated depreciation method such as double-declining balance or sum-of-the-years'-digits for tax purposes, and straight-line depreciation for purposes of financial accounting. The accelerated methods result in larger depreciation expense than the straight-line method in the earlier years of the life of an asset, and smaller depreciation charges in the later years. Thus, the use of the different methods results in lower taxable income than accounting income during the early years, but has the opposite effect in later years.

2. *Installment basis.* Businesses that sell merchandise on the installment basis may recognize revenue for financial accounting purposes at the time of sale but report the income for tax purposes as cash is actually received.

There are also several different methods of accounting for inventories (see Chapter 9). During periods of increasing prices, the last-in, first-out (Lifo) method results in higher costs and, thus, lower net income than the other acceptable inventory pricing methods. Consequently, with the general increase in prices in recent years, many firms have adopted the Lifo method for tax purposes. The use of Lifo for tax purposes, however, has not resulted in significant differences between taxable and accounting income because the tax law requires generally that a business must use this method for financial accounting if it is used for tax purposes.

Interperiod Tax Allocation

When one accounting method is used for tax purposes and a different method for financial accounting, revenues or expenses may be reported on the income statement and the tax return in different periods. Although the same total revenue and expenses (ignoring permanent differences) eventually are reported for both tax and financial accounting purposes, taxable income and accounting income during any one period may differ significantly. Therefore, as a result of timing differences, a part of the income tax liability during one period is caused by revenues and expenses reported during some other year for financial accounting purposes. Consequently, if income tax expense reported in the income statement is based on income taxes actually paid, there is a mismatching of revenues and expenses. That is, earnings may be included in the income statement of one period, and the related tax expense reported in a different period.

To illustrate this situation, assume that Ruth Company purchased a machine with an expected life of four years and no salvage value on January 1, 1976, for $100,000. The firm plans to use the straight-line depreciation method for financial accounting purposes and the sum-of-the-years'-digits method for tax purposes. Assume further that the income before taxes and depreciation remains constant at $100,000 for the years 1976 through 1979, and that the applicable tax rate is 50 percent (to simplify the illustration). Under these circumstances, the depreciation expense on the income statement will be $25,000 (100,000 ÷ 4) each year. The deduction for depreciation on the tax return, on the other hand, will be $40,000 in 1976 ($\frac{4}{10} \times \$100,000$), $30,000 in 1977 ($\frac{3}{10} \times \$100,000$), $20,000 in 1978 ($\frac{2}{10} \times \$100,000$), and $10,000 ($\frac{1}{10} \times \$100,000$) in 1979. The firm's taxable income and actual tax liability for the four-year period is as follows:

	1976	1977	1978	1979	Total
Income before depreciation and taxes	$100,000	$100,000	$100,000	$100,000	$400,000
Deduction for depreciation	40,000	30,000	20,000	10,000	100,000
Taxable income	$ 60,000	$ 70,000	$ 80,000	$ 90,000	$300,000
Income tax paid (50%)	$ 30,000	$ 35,000	$ 40,000	$ 45,000	$150,000

Using the income tax due the government for the year as the income tax expense on the income statement would result in the following determination of accounting income.

	1976	1977	1978	1979	Total
Income before depreciation and taxes	$100,000	$100,000	$100,000	$100,000	$400,000
Depreciation expense	25,000	25,000	25,000	25,000	100,000
Income before taxes	$ 75,000	$ 75,000	$ 75,000	$ 75,000	$300,000
Income tax expense	30,000	35,000	40,000	45,000	150,000
Net income	$ 45,000	$ 40,000	$ 35,000	$ 30,000	$150,000

It should be noted that even though Ruth Company had identical operating results during each year, the tax expense and the net income figures vary.

To correct this improper matching of revenues and expenses, tax expense in the income statement should be matched against the income reported therein, regardless of when the income will be included in taxable income and the tax actually paid. This procedure, known as interperiod tax allocation, relates the income tax expense for the period to accounting income rather than to taxable income. Thus, the tax expense reported on the income statement is equal to the tax rate applied to accounting income rather than the actual tax liability (tax rate × taxable income) for the period (after adjustments to reflect permanent differences have been made). If the timing differences cause the tax expense to exceed the taxes actually owed for the period, the excess represents a deferred credit—deferred income taxes. With regard to a particular timing difference, this deferred credit will eventually be eliminated in future periods when the tax liability exceeds the tax expense.

Using interperiod tax allocation, Ruth Company would report tax expense equal to the tax rate (50%) applied to the accounting income before taxes. The resulting income statements for the four-year period would be as follows:

	1976	1977	1978	1979	Total
Income before depreciation and taxes	$100,000	$100,000	$100,000	$100,000	$400,000
Depreciation expense.	25,000	25,000	25,000	25,000	100,000
Income before taxes	$ 75,000	$ 75,000	$ 75,000	$ 75,000	$300,000
Income tax expense	37,500	37,500	37,500	37,500	150,000
Net income	$ 37,500	$ 37,500	$ 37,500	$ 37,500	$150,000

Thus, under tax allocation procedures, the tax expense in the income statement of $37,500 in each year is logically related to the earnings before taxes of $75,000 (given a tax rate of 50 percent). Note that the tax expense over the four-year period is still $150,000, and the total tax liability is also $150,000. The entries to record the tax expense for the year are:

```
1976  Income Tax Expense. . . . . . . . . . . . . . . . . . . . . . .   37,500
           Income Taxes Payable. . . . . . . . . . . . . . . . . . .            30,000
           Deferred Tax . . . . . . . . . . . . . . . . . . . . . . .             7,500

1977  Income Tax Expense. . . . . . . . . . . . . . . . . . . . . . .   37,500
           Income Taxes Payable. . . . . . . . . . . . . . . . . . .            35,000
           Deferred Tax . . . . . . . . . . . . . . . . . . . . . . .             2,500

1978  Income Tax Expense. . . . . . . . . . . . . . . . . . . . . . .   37,500
      Deferred Tax . . . . . . . . . . . . . . . . . . . . . . . .    2,500
           Income Tax Payable . . . . . . . . . . . . . . . . . . .            40,000

1979  Income Tax Expense. . . . . . . . . . . . . . . . . . . . . . .   37,500
      Deferred Tax . . . . . . . . . . . . . . . . . . . . . . . .    7,500
           Income Tax Payable . . . . . . . . . . . . . . . . . . .            45,000
```

In this example, the difference between accounting income and taxable income was eliminated over the four-year period. Therefore, the deferred tax account has a zero balance at the end of the four years. In practice, the differences between accounting and taxable income may last for a considerable number of years or even indefinitely since the company is continually replacing its assets and seldom, if ever, would all assets be fully depreciated. The balance in the deferred tax account may, therefore, become a significant amount.

The situation can also occur where taxable income exceeds accounting income in earlier years. Under interperiod tax allocation, the excess of the tax liability over tax expense would be considered a prepayment of income taxes. The difference would be debited to an asset, deferred tax charges, representing income taxes paid on accounting income that will be recognized in a later period. For example, assume that Marion Company agrees to rent a portion of its office space to Dean Company on a one-time basis for 1976 and receives its annual rent of $3,600 for the year 1976 on December 31, 1975. None of this amount would be included in accounting income for 1975 since it will not be earned by Dean Company until 1976. For tax purposes, however, the entire amount would be included in taxable income for 1975 since prepaid rent is taxed as it is received rather than as it is earned. Assume that the income of Marion Company from all sources other than rentals was $10,000 for both 1975 and 1976. Its taxable income would be $13,600 (accounting income of $10,000 plus the $3,600 rent received) in 1975 and $10,000 in 1976. Further assume that the tax rate in both years was 50 percent. The entries to record the tax expense for 1975 and 1976 would be as follows:

1975	Tax Expense	5,000	
	Deferred Tax Charge	1,800	
	Income Taxes Payable		6,800
1976	Tax Expense	6,800	
	Deferred Tax Charge		1,800
	Income Taxes Payable		5,000

In this example, the difference between accounting income and taxable income due to the timing difference in recognizing the rental income was eliminated by the end of 1976.

In general, interperiod tax allocation for timing differences consists of charging income tax expense for an amount equal to accounting income $\times$ tax rate, crediting income tax payable for an amount equal to taxable income $\times$ tax rate, and debiting or crediting the difference to a deferred tax account. This "rule," of course, assumes that there are only timing and not permanent differences between accounting income and taxable income.

Allocation of Income Tax within a Period

According to Accounting Principles Board *Opinions No. 9* and *30*, the income statement should disclose separate income figures for: (1) income from continuing operations; (2) income from any segment or division of the business which has been, or is to be, discontinued or sold, referred to as discontinued operations; and (3) income from unusual, nonrecurring items, referred to as extraordinary items. Income from continuing operations, income or losses from discontinued operations, and extraordinary gains or losses may be included in taxable income and, hence, affect the tax liability for the period. For this reason, it is believed that allocation of the total amount of income taxes for the period among income from continuing operations, discontinued operations, and extraordinary gains or losses provides a more meaningful income statement.

This allocation, called intraperiod tax allocation, is accomplished by deducting from income from continuing operations taxes related to that amount, showing income or losses from discontinued operations and extraordinary gains and losses net of the tax applicable to the gain or income and less the related tax reduction due to losses.

To illustrate, assume that Cobb Company, which uses the same methods for tax purposes and for financial accounting purposes (so that there are no timing differences), determined its tax liability for 1976 as follows:

Revenues.	$100,000
Operating expenses	60,000
Operating income before taxes	$ 40,000
Income from discounted operations	20,000
Extraordinary gain	30,000
Taxable Income	$ 90,000

Further assume that the tax rate is 40 percent. The total tax liability would be $36,000 ($90,000 × 40%). Of this amount, $16,000 ($40,000 × 40%) is applicable to normal operating income, $8,000 ($20,000 × 40%) is due to discontinued operations and $12,000 ($30,000 × 40%) is applicable to the extraordinary gain. The following statement illustrates the intraperiod tax allocation.

COBB COMPANY
Income Statement
For the Year Ended December 31, 1976

Revenues.	$100,000
Operating expenses	60,000
Income from continuing operations before taxes	$ 40,000
Provisions for income taxes	16,000
Income from continuing operations	$ 24,000
Discontinued operations:	
Income from discontinued operations	
(less related taxes of $8,000)	12,000
	$ 36,000
Extraordinary items:	
Extraordinary gain (less related taxes of $12,000)	18,000
Net Income	$ 54,000

KEY DEFINITIONS

Accounting income   Accounting income is the amount of income determined using generally accepted accounting principles.

Adjusted gross income (for individuals)   Adjusted gross income is gross income less deductions for adjusted gross income.

Capital assets   Capital assets generally include all property except such items as trade receivables, inventories, copyrights or compositions in the hands of their creator, and government obligations issued on a discount basis and due within one year without interest. Real or depreciable property used in a trade or business may be treated as capital assets under certain circumstances.

Capital gain or loss   A capital gain or loss is a realized gain or loss incurred from the sale or exchange of a capital asset.

Deductions from adjusted gross income (for individuals)   Deductions from adjusted gross income are legally allowable deductions that may be classified as either itemized or standard deductions or personal exemptions.

Deductions from gross income (for individuals)   Deductions from gross income in computing adjusted gross income include business and other expenses connected with earning certain types of revenue. These include ordinary and necessary expenses incurred by the taxpayer in the operation of his business or profession and certain employee expenses.

Deferred taxes   Deferred tax is the cumulative difference between income tax expense and the income tax liability resulting from interperiod tax allocation.

Double taxation   The corporation is taxed on its reported income and stockholders are taxed upon the receipt of dividends from the corporation. This is sometimes referred to as double taxation.

Estate   An estate is a separate legal entity created to take charge of the assets of a deceased person, paying the decedent's debts and distributing the remaining assets to heirs.

Gross income   Gross income includes all income from whatever source derived unless expressly excluded by law.

Head of household   The title of head of household is a tax status that applies to certain unmarried or legally separated persons who maintain a residence for a relative or dependent.

Itemized deductions   Deductions for certain employee business expenses and for personal expenses and losses such as charitable contributions, taxes, interest, casualty losses, and medical expenses are referred to as itemized deductions.

Interperiod tax allocation   Interperiod tax allocation is a procedure used to apportion tax expense among periods so that the income tax expense reported for each period is in relation to the accounting income.

Intraperiod tax allocation   Intraperiod tax allocation is the allocation of the total amount of income tax expense for a period among income from normal operations, discontinued operations, extraordinary items, and prior period adjustments.

Long-term capital gains or losses   Long-term capital gains or losses are gains or losses which result from the sale or exchange of capital assets and certain productive assets of a business held by the taxpayer for more than six months. A special tax rate applies to net long-term capital gains.

Permanent difference   A permanent difference is a difference between taxable income and accounting income which occurs because of tax rules which differ from generally accepted accounting principles and which will not be offset by corresponding differences in future periods.

Personal exemptions   A personal exemption is a deduction of $750 from adjusted gross income for the taxpayer, his spouse, and qualified dependents. There are additional exemptions for the taxpayer and his spouse who are over 65 or blind.

Progressive tax   This is a tax in which the tax rates increase as taxable income increases.

Standard deduction   The standard deduction involves an alternative to itemized deductions equal to 15 percent of adjusted gross income with a maximum of $2,000 (for a joint return).

Taxable income   Taxable income is the amount to which the tax rate from the appropriate schedule is applied to determine the tax liability.

Timing differences   These are differences between taxable income and accounting income which occur because an item is included in taxable income in one period and in accounting income in a different period.

Trust   A trust is a legal entity which is created when a person transfers assets to a trustee for the benefit of designated persons.

QUESTIONS

1. Explain how the net earnings of the following types of business entities are taxed by the federal government: (*a*) sole proprietorships, (*b*) partnerships, and (*c*) corporations.

2. The earnings of a corporation are subject to a "double tax." Explain.

3. Certain factors may cause the income before taxes in the accounting records to differ from taxable income. These factors may be either permanent differences or timing differences. Explain.

4. Does a corporation electing partnership treatment for tax purposes (Subchapter S) pay federal income taxes? Discuss.

5. Define the following in relation to the determination of the income tax liability for an individual:

   a. Gross income.
   b. Adjusted gross income.
   c. Itemized deduction.
   d. Standard deduction.
   e. Personal exemptions.

6. What are the two income tax rates applied to the taxable income of corporations?

7. What are the four major classes of taxable entities?

8. What is the objective of using the interperiod tax allocation procedures?

9. Does it make any difference in computing income taxes whether a given deduction is for computing adjusted gross income or an itemized deduction? Explain.

10. For an individual taxpayer, it is better to have a net long-term capital gain than an equal amount of ordinary income, but it is better to have an ordinary loss instead of an equal amount of net capital losses. Explain.

11. What are some of the dfferences between the tax rules for corporations and those for individuals?

12. What are some of the objectives of the federal income tax?

13. What is the distinction between a long-term capital gain and a short-term capital gain?

EXERCISES

19–1 Indicate the income tax status of each of the items listed below. For each item, state whether it is (a) included in gross income, (b) a deduction from gross income to determine adjusted gross income (c) an itemized deduction, or (d) none of the above.

1. Property taxes paid on personal residence.
2. Interest paid on mortgage on personal residence.
3. Damages of $500 to personal residence from a storm.
4. Capital loss on the sale of stock.
5. Insurance on home.
6. Sales taxes.
7. Inheritance received upon death of a relative.
8. Interest received on municipal bonds.
9. Share of income from partnership.
10. Salary received as an employee.
11. Rental income.
12. Expenses incurred in earning rental income.
13. Contributions to church.

19–2 James and Martha Gentry, filing a joint return, are entitled to one personal exemption each and two additional exemptions for dependent children. James Gentry owns a business organized as a sole proprietorship. Additional information related to their income tax return is as follows:

Revenues.	$100,000
Cost of goods sold	60,000
Business expenses.	20,000
Life insurance proceeds (death of father)	10,000
Interest on city of Bowro Bonds	500
Rental income.	5,000
Allowable itemized deductions	1,800
Salary—Martha Gentry	6,000

Determine the following:

a. Adjusted gross income
b. Taxable income
c. Income tax liability (using rate schedule in chapter)

19–3 Don Looney had the following capital gains and losses in 1975.

Long-term losses	$ 3,000
Long-term gains	12,000
Short-term losses	8,000
Short-term gains	6,000

Determine the tax on Looney's capital gain assuming his marginal tax rate is 27 percent.

19–4 Studdard, Inc., purchased a new catalytic cracker on January 1, 1973, for $81,000. The machine has a four-year useful life and a salvage value of $1,000. For financial accounting purposes, the company uses straight-line depreciation while for tax purposes they use the sum-of-the-years'-digits method. Income before taxes and depreciation was $90,000 for 1973, $100,000 for 1974, $100,000 for 1975, and $110,000 for 1976. Assume a tax rate of 50 percent. Make the entries necessary to record the tax expense for 1973–1976.

PROBLEMS

Series A

19A–1 Jim Simmons and his wife are both 64 years old and own a dry cleaning store. His wife has been legally blind since she was in a car accident when she was 55. In reviewing the books of his dry cleaning store, Jim finds that it had revenues of $95,000 and expenses of $80,000. During the year, Jim rented a vacant lot to a friend at an annual rental of $3,000. Jim paid property taxes of $300 on the lot.

Jim and his wife have a $7,000 savings account and earned interest at six percent compounded annually on this amount. On July 30, Jim realized a $1,000 capital gain on stocks purchased January 1 and a $250 capital gain on other securities purchased June 1. In examining his personal records, Jim found that he had made charitable contributions of $275 and had paid interest on his mortgage of $300. Also, he had paid $300 of property taxes.

Required:

Compute Jim's taxable income for the year assuming he filed a joint return with his wife.

19A–2 In each of the following cases determine the amount of capital gains to be included in adjusted gross income or the amount of capital loss to be deducted for an individual taxpayer.

	A	B	C	D
Long-term capital gains.	$20,000	$20,000	$15,000	$15,000
Long-term capital losses	15,000	15,000	20,000	20,000
Short-term capital gains	4,000	6,000	4,000	6,000
Short-term capital losses	6,000	4,000	6,000	4,000

19A-3   Alvin (age 37) and Jeanne (age 35) Burns, who file a joint income tax return, have two dependent children. Alvin Burns owns a clothing store which is organized as a sole proprietorship and Jeanne Burns is a secretary in a local law office. The following information is available for preparation of their 1975 tax return:

Income:
Operations of clothing store:

Sales	$200,000
Cost of goods sold and expenses	180,000
Salary—Jeanne Burns.	6,000
Interest received:	
Savings account.	100
City of Blacksburg Bonds	200
Gain on sale of stock held two years	3,000
Loss on sale of stock held one year.	4,500
Proceeds of life insurance policy on death of an uncle	5,000
Rental income	1,200
Personal Expenses:	
Sales taxes.	300
Purchase of family car	2,500
Contributions to charities	500
Property taxes	600
Rental paid for summer cottage	1,200
Interest paid on mortgage	2,100
State income taxes	400
Storm damage to residence	1,100
Gasoline tax.	100
Grocery bills.	1,200
Other personal expenses.	3,000

Required:

Compute the tax liability for Alvin and Jeanne Burns. Use the tax table in the chapter.

19A-4   The records of the Noggle Company contain the following data for the year ended December 31, 1975:

Sales	$900,000
Cost of goods sold	600,000
Operating expenses.	200,000
Interest received on:	
State of Virginia Bonds	1,000
XYZ Corp. Bonds	2,000
Dividends received on ABC Co. stock (a domestic corp.)	10,000
Gain on sale of stock acquired on January 1, 1973	5,000
Loss on sale of stock acquired on November 30, 1975	1,000
Charitable contribution	500

The firm uses the same accounting methods for financial accounting and income tax purposes.

Required:

a. Compute taxable income for 1975.
b. Compute the tax liability for 1975 (assume the normal tax rate of 22 percent, surtax rate of 26 percent, and a 30 percent capital gains rate).

19A–5   The Hall Company uses accelerated depreciation for tax purposes and straight-line depreciation for its financial accounting records. Its taxable income and accounting income (before income taxes) for a four-year period are shown below:

	1973	1974	1975	1976
Taxable income....	$ 70,000	$100,000	$140,000	$210,000
Accounting income..	100,000	120,000	150,000	200,000

Assume that the corporate tax rate is 50 percent.

Required:

1. Compute the net income after taxes in the financial statement for Hall Company (a) assuming that interperiod tax allocation procedures are not used and (b) assuming the tax allocation procedure is used.
2. Determine the balance in the "Deferred Tax" account at the end of 1976 in 1(b) above.

19A–6   Bob Company began operations on January 1, 1976. At that time, it purchased a fixed asset for $300,000 which has an estimated useful life of 3 years and no salvage value. The management decided to adopt the sum-of-the-years'-digits method of depreciation for tax purposes and the straight-line method for the financial accounting records. Assume the following:

	1976	1977	1978
Revenues................	$500,000	$600,000	$700,000
Expenses (excluding depreciation and taxes)................	300,000	350,000	390,000
Income tax rate = 50%			

Required:

a. Compute the net income after taxes for each year assuming that interperiod tax allocation procedures are not used.
b. Compute net income after taxes for each year assuming that interperiod tax allocation procedures are used.

19A–7   The Brown Company had the following income during 1975.

Revenues.	$500,000
Expenses.	390,000
Operating income (before extraordinary items and income taxes).	110,000
Extraordinary items: Loss from natural disaster (fully deductible).	10,000

The tax rates applicable to corporate income are as follows:

Normal tax (on all ordinary taxable income) 22%
Surtax on taxable income over $25,000 . . . . 26%

Required:

a.   Compute the total tax liability of the Brown Company for 1975.
b.   Prepare an income statement for Brown Company using the intraperiod tax allocation procedure.

Series B

19B–1   Bob Barnett, who owns a grocery store, is married and has 3 dependent children. Compute the taxes payable given the following information.

Sales	$125,000
Cost of goods sold	60,000
Total operating expenses for store	35,000
Rental income.	5,000
Interest expense on house	2,000
Sales taxes paid	500
Personal property taxes paid	1,000
Net long-term capital gain	4,000
Net short-term capital loss.	2,000
Interest received on savings accounts.	500

19B–2   An individual taxpayer had the following capital gains and losses during 1975:

	Gains	*Losses*
Short term.	$ 6,000	$11,000
Long term	20,000	5,000

Required:

Compute the amount of income tax on the capital gains assuming that the taxpayer has a marginal tax rate of: (a) 32% and (b) 70%. Assume that the maximum tax on net long-term capital gains is 25%.

19B–3   Paul (age 37) and Paula (age 35) Anker, who file a joint income tax return, have three dependent children. Paul Anker owns a sporting goods store which is organized as a sole proprietorship, and Paula is a secretary for a local doctor. The following information is available for preparation of their 1976 tax return.

Income:
  Operations of sporting goods store:
    Sales $100,000
    Cost of goods sold and expenses 85,000
  Salary—Paula Anker 8,000
  Interest received:
    Savings account. 400
    City of Bryan Bonds 100
  Gain on sale of stock held four years. 4,000
  Loss on sale of stock held one year. 1,000
  Proceeds of life insurance policy on death of an aunt 5,000
  Rental income. 1,200
Personal expenses:
  Sales taxes 200
  Purchase of a summer cottage. 3,500
  Contributions to charities 800
  Property taxes. 900
  Vacation in Florida. 1,200
  Interest paid on mortgage 2,600
  State income taxes 900
  Storm damage to residence 1,100
  Gasoline tax. 100
  Grocery bills 2,200
  Other personal expenses 4,000

Required:

Compute the tax liability for Paul and Paula Anker. Use the tax table in the chapter.

19B–4   The records of the Vernon Company contain the following data for the year ended December 31, 1975.

Sales $600,000
Cost of goods sold 400,000
Operating expenses 100,000
Interest received on:
  State of Texas Bonds. 3,000
  Smith Corp. Bonds 3,000
Dividends received on Hammond Co. stock (a domestic corp.) 16,000
Gain on sale of stock acquired on August 31, 1975. 4,000
Loss on sale of stock acquired on November 31, 1973 2,000
Charitable contribution 500

The firm uses the same accounting methods for financial accounting and for income tax purposes.

Required:

a.   Compute taxable income for 1975.
b.   Compute the tax liability for 1975 (assume the normal tax rate of 22 percent, surtax rate of 26 percent, and a 30 percent capital gains rate.)

19B–5   The following information was included in the accounting records of the Zero Company over a three-year period:

	Accounting Income	Taxable Income
1976	$125,000	$150,000
1975	75,000	100,000
1974	100,000	50,000

In 1974 a $50,000 gain was recognized for financial accounting purposes but not for tax purposes. This gain was recognized for tax purposes in the amount of $25,000 per year in 1975 and 1976. All other revenues and expenses are the same in the financial accounting records and in the tax return in each of the three years.

Required:

1. Compute the income tax legally owed to the government in each year, assuming a 50 percent tax rate.
2. Prepare the journal entries to record the income tax expense in each of the three years using interperiod tax allocation.

19B–6   The following differences enter into the reconciliation of financial net income and taxable income of A.P. Baxter Corp. for the current year.

1. Tax depreciation exceeds book depreciation by $30,000.
2. Estimated warranty costs of $6,000 applicable to the current year's sales have not been paid. (Not deductible for tax purposes until paid.)
3. Percentage depletion deducted on the tax return exceeds cost depletion by $45,000.
4. Unearned rent revenue of $25,000 was deferred on the books but appropriately included in taxable income.
5. A book expense of $2,000 for life insurance premiums on officers' lives is not allowed as a deduction on the tax return (note: this is not a timing difference).
6. A $7,000 tax deduction resulted from expensing research and development costs for tax purposes while such costs were capitalized for financial reporting.
7. Gross profit of $80,000 was excluded from the taxable income because Baxter had appropriately elected the installment sale method for tax reporting while recognizing all gross profit from installment sales at the time of the sale for financial reporting.

Required:

Consider each reconciling item independently of all others and explain whether each item would enter into the calculation of income taxes to be allocated. For any which are included in the income tax allocation calculation, explain the effect of the item on the current year's income tax expense and how the amount would be reported on the balance sheet. (Tax allocation calculations are not required.)

Index